THE
SOCIOLOGY
OF
THE
FUTURE

The Sociology of the Future

Theory, Cases,
and Annotated Bibliography

Edited by
Wendell Bell
and James A. Mau
Yale University

RUSSELL SAGE FOUNDATION
NEW YORK

PUBLICATIONS OF RUSSELL SAGE FOUNDATION

Russell Sage Foundation was established in 1907 by Mrs. Russell Sage for the improvement of social and living conditions in the United States. In carrying out its purpose the Foundation conducts research under the direction of members of the staff or in close collaboration with other institutions, and supports programs designed to develop and demonstrate productive working relations between social scientists and other professional groups. As an integral part of its operations, the Foundation from time to time publishes books or pamphlets resulting from these activities. Publication under the imprint of the Foundation does not necessarily imply agreement by the Foundation, its Trustees, or its staff with the interpretations or conclusions of the authors.

To the memory of
ANDREW G. J. CAMACHO
West Indian educator and sociologist,
a man of the future who died before his time

CONTRIBUTORS

J. Victor Baldridge
Assistant Professor of Sociology
  and Education
Stanford University

Pauline B. Bart
Assistant Professor of Sociology
  in Psychiatry
The University of Illinois
  (Medical Center, Chicago)

Wendell Bell
Professor of Sociology
Yale University

Robert Boguslaw
Professor of Sociology
Washington University, St. Louis

Menno Boldt
Assistant Professor of Sociology
University of Lethbridge, Alberta,
  Canada

William R. Burch, Jr.
Associate Professor of Forestry
  and Sociology
Yale University

Kai T. Erikson
Professor of Sociology and
  Master of Trumbull College
Yale University

Scott Greer
Professor of Sociology
Northwestern University

Paul Hollander
Associate Professor of Sociology
University of Massachusetts
  (Amherst)
Associate, Russian Research
  Center
Harvard University

Bettina J. Huber
Lecturer
University of California,
  Santa Barbara

James A. Mau
Associate Professor of Sociology
Associate Dean of the Graduate
  School
Yale University

Ivar Oxall
Senior Lecturer in Sociology
Hull University, England

Henry Winthrop
Professor, Department of Inter-
  disciplinary Social Sciences
University of South Florida

CONTENTS

viii

FOREWORD

When I first heard of the project that resulted in this volume, and discussed it with Professors Bell and Mau, I knew that it was something I wanted to encourage. It has been encouraged by the Russell Sage Foundation, but it has also been encouraged by me as a colleague. Indeed, I used many of the editors' essential ideas for my own presidential address in 1966 to the American Sociological Association ("The Utility of Utopias") and persuaded Professor Bell to present a plenary session paper at the same convention on "The Future as the Cause of the Present."

It was only bad sociology that led us to think that we could not discuss social change, and particularly bad sociology that led us to think that history and the future had no connection with current plans. With this excellent collection of essays we are further forward.

The editors had a grand conception, based on deep knowledge and considerable field experience in the new nations of the Caribbean. The central idea was that new nations must invent a (possibly spurious) history and set future goals that will inform current decisions. Therefore, what is being discussed here is the invention of the past as well as the future. For to invent the future may require the invention of a past, often poorly recorded.

This book presents a set of essays, mainly arranged around the central theme of "images of the future." The editors explicate this theme in their introductory essay and show how it has informed a considerable amount of sociological literature, even though much of that literature has appeared to use static rather than dynamic models of social systems.

"Futurology" now commands considerable time and talent, and references to those efforts can be found throughout the volume and in an appendix. But the authors have spared us endless and tedious methodological discussions of modes of forecasting. Instead, they have attended to the uses of plans and of images of the future and the current consequences of envisioned future states. In this book we travel from the former sugar-and-slave islands of the British West Indies to New York University (another former colony of some imperial power?) and from the broadly theoretical to the specific without too many awkward sea-changes.

But the theme is constant and suffers no loss from application to a variety of settings. On the contrary. Did we not claim that sociology is a generalizing social science? Now we know once more that the claim is valid.

And did not some of us claim, with temerity or timidity, that sociology might be useful as well as merely informative and predictive? In an eloquent epilogue Professor Bell attends to the current crisis in the social sciences and in universities and in intellectual life generally. The critics and would-be destroyers of the Establishment dislike the future they foresee, and yet many are notably deficient in depicting and building a better one. They are willing, in the translated words of Omar Khayyám, to "grasp this sorry scheme of things entire and shatter it to bits," but not to "remold it nearer to the heart's desire."

This is patently not the best of all possible worlds, but it is the only one we have. Reason may not assure that world of a better future, or even of any future at all, but unreason will inevitably assure that it has none.

WILBERT E. MOORE

PREFACE

The purpose of this book took shape while the editors were struggling with another, earlier social research project. For a number of years we were engaged in a sociological study of change in the English-speaking Caribbean, focusing on the impact of the political transition from colony to independent nation-state. We found that some of the standard American sociological assumptions with which we arrived, especially those involving structural determinism, had not prepared us for this situation. Not only was there clearly considerable choice, but also most of the actors perceived this situation and acted accordingly. That is, social reality included a variety of *real* alternatives or possibilities for the future, and the participants knew it and spent a considerable amount of time and effort clarifying, evaluating, and choosing among those alternatives. Adjusting as best we could to this situation, we and our associates formulated "the decisions of nationhood" as a framework for a series of studies. We completed one study of images of the future, which we viewed as a key to understanding the deliberate choices and planned changes we saw taking place. But we remained dissatisfied with our original sociological orientation—the characteristic one of American sociology—and resolved to examine it in the light of our research experience. The result is this book on the sociology of the future.

Another feature of our earlier work on the new nations of the Caribbean merged with more recent clamorings on campuses in the United States and elsewhere to increase our resolve (and also, it should be added in the case of the latter, to delay the publication of this book, since both of us became involved in the campus dialogues, one as a Departmental Chairman and the other as an Assistant Dean of the Graduate School). That feature is "relevance." We regret the term; it is both overused and misused. But it may describe what we believed about our work in the Caribbean: by focusing our studies on the formation of the new states and aspiring nations, we asked questions of great moment, timely in the immediate situation and, if not timeless, certainly of great scope in a world where nation-states are an aspect of the social existence of all humankind. The "timeless" aspect may be far more important than the "timely," since many "relevant" books that have been focused solely on the timely—the present fads and fashions—have a way of becoming irrelevant with frightening speed.

To concerned students and colleagues alike, we suggest that the effort to study the future is itself an effort to be relevant to the socially important questions. It is relevant partly because the struggle to control the future frequently defines what is important now, and mostly because it is in the future to be that the ultimate judgment of what is important now will be made. The study of the future, as we try to show in this book, can bring one closer both to the struggle and to the emergent future itself. This route to relevance is appealing because one does not have to chase the coattails of current affairs—a futile exercise—and one does not have to leave one's profession to achieve it. All the tools of the social scientist can be brought to bear; and the trained professional can continue to function as a social scientist, not as another body marching in protest in the streets. It is more difficult than mere political action, and more constructive. The study of the future is nonetheless oriented toward a change in social theory, toward a redefinition of the role of the social scientist, and may well imply, if it does not simply become a tool of the establishment, a reorganization of society. But, as we try to show, there may be risks that many social scientists will not—or should not—want to take.

This book contains (1) a theory of social change based on the concept of image of the future; (2) some research strategies for studying the future; (3) a paradigm for the analysis of time perspectives and images of the future in social science literature, which is then applied by several of the authors in (4) an effort to tease out the implicit images of the future in studies that do not purport to be studies of the future; (5) some examples of images of the future in action; and, finally, (6) an annotated bibliography on social science studies of the future.

It differs in several ways from other books on the future. We do not deal extensively with technology, nor with those areas of economics and demography in which many forecasts have been made and which are now a part of standard procedures. Ample references to these can be found elsewhere. Rather we have tried to probe the less familiar areas. Also many other authors have stressed the importance of the military contributions to futuristics, and there is no denying their influence. (Planning weapons systems for a world fifteen or twenty years from now poses many of the technical problems involved in any kind of a study of the future.) Yet there exists a little-known social science literature quite apart from that produced as a result of the presumed military exigencies of the Cold War era; and we have stressed it, although not exclusively.

Unlike most books on the future, this one does not primarily try to describe what the future will be like. We do, however, make one major forecast. That forecast is: there will be a revolution in sociology in the 1970s with the development of social indicators, their use in monitoring

xii

social trends, and the involvement of thousands of sociologists as advisors to policy-makers and administrators in all major aspects of social life for the purposes of studying and shaping the future. We might also hope, but cannot safely predict, that some sociologists will orient their activities to the world views of non-Establishment groups, especially to emergent groups whose interests are not adequately served by presently existing political, economic, and social arrangements.

This book, then, is about a sociological revolution, already well underway, that is shifting the focus of sociology from the static study of the present and from the methodological dominance of prediction to the dynamic study of the future and to the methodological (and moral) dominance of control. We welcome such a revolution and the opportunities that it will bring—perhaps this book may even play a small part in accelerating it. But there will be disappointments and there are dangers, some of which we anticipate in the pages that follow. Perhaps the most important problems are: how self-consciously pluralistic value systems and commitments among the sociological revolutionaries themselves can be promoted and maintained as they take their places, as they certainly will, in the ranks of the new, yet-to-be-formed sociological establishment; and how sociology can, as it enters further into commitment, retain—even increase—its objective search for truth.

We are indebted to the Russell Sage Foundation for bringing the authors of this volume together in New York in April 1968, when most of the papers had already been written in draft form and were made available to all the contributors. We hope that our exchanges have enhanced the continuity of the different contributions. Also, the Foundation provided additional financial assistance to the editors to make possible the annotated bibliography.

We are deeply grateful to Wilbert E. Moore, who from the outset of this project gave us moral encouragement and intellectual direction. Furthermore, both he and his colleague, Eleanor Bernert Sheldon, gave us helpful advice as this book took shape.

Additionally, we wish to acknowledge the useful comments made by Professors Rodolfo Alvarez, George Huaco, and Harold D. Lasswell, and suggestions of the present or former Yale University graduate students who read much of the book in manuscript as part of a seminar in social change taught by Bell. We particularly wish to thank J. Victor Baldridge, Menno Boldt, Luis Fajardo, Jerry Gaston, Bettina J. Huber, and Roger E. Thomas. And we are grateful to Lorraine Estra, Joan Cianciolo, and Phyllis Swift for typing and proofreading the manuscript, and to Janet G. Turk for preparing the index. Of course, the authors take the sole responsibility for the final results.

We thank Appleton-Century-Crofts for permission to publish a revised version of Bell and Mau's "Images of the Future: Theory and Research Strategies" from J. C. McKinney and E. Tiryakian (eds.), *Theoretical Sociology*, 1970; and the American Sociological Association for permission to reprint Erikson's "Sociology and the Historical Perspective," from *The American Sociologist*, 5 (November 1970).

PART I

Images of the Future

"Change in the modern era," as Wilbert E. Moore (1967:161) has pointed out, is "characterized by two distinctive features: (1) Its magnitude has increased enormously. It is certainly more rapid in more places and more constant than ever before. (2) By any crude measurement, most contemporary social change is either deliberate or is the secondary consequence of deliberate change." Or, as Harold D. Lasswell (1966:161) has commented on the same facts, "mankind is passing from the *primacy* of the *past* to the *primacy of expectations of vast future change.*" In "Images of the Future: Theory and Research Strategies," Wendell Bell and James A. Mau briefly sketch a theory of social change in which they try to take account of these facts. As they state, it is only a brief sketch, crude and general. For the most part it contains standard sociological concepts, and many of its elaborations would do little more than to bring in additional terms that are in common use. It is designed, however, to serve the organizing and heuristic functions of a model by incorporating images of the future, decision-making, and a cybernetic orientation into the usual sociological net. Karl W. Deutsch (1963:ix) has suggested that "it might be profitable to look upon government somewhat less as a problem of power and somewhat more as a problem of steering" in which communication is of crucial importance. Bell and Mau suggest that it may be profitable to look upon society less as a problem of order and more as a problem of steering in which *images of the future* are of crucial importance. Their model stresses dynamism and change, the causal interaction of ideas—beliefs and values—and social structure, decisions, and the deliberate efforts of man to shape society.

The Bell and Mau theory makes one sensitive to the study of images of the future and to the possible relevance of social science research to the emerging future itself. Thus sensitized, one can deliberately set out to study images of the future, a course of action Bell and Mau recommend. But one can also achieve relevance to the future in other ways, some of which the authors suggest in a series of research strategies or directives.

In his preface to Karl Mannheim's *Ideology and Utopia*, Louis Wirth (1936:xv) stated:

> The distinctive character of social science discourse is to be sought in the fact that every assertion, no matter how objective it may be, has ramifications extending beyond the limits of science itself. Since every assertion of a "fact" about the social world touches the interests of some individual or group, one cannot even call attention to the existence of certain "facts" without courting the objections of those whose very *raison d'être* in society rests upon a divergent interpretation of the "factual" situation.

"True enough," say Bell and Mau, but they go beyond Wirth's view in their discussion of the implications of their orientation for the role of the social scientist. They see the social scientist as necessarily limiting or expanding future possibilities; shaping the beliefs about social reality that in turn enter into the steering of social action; supporting, carrying, or discrediting images of the future; being shaped by, and shaping, the social contexts of which they are part. The problems: the social scientist may limit more than he expands alternatives for the future; the danger is not so much the objections that may be courted but the myths of dominant groups that may be supported; the social scientist's commitments are unconscious; and the utility of social science may be appropriated by established and vested interests of society. The questions Bell and Mau raise are: "How conscious is the social scientist of his role as maker of the future?" and "Are there behaviors that will help the social scientist play this role better and more responsibly?"

It is understandable why such a theory, such research strategies, and such views about the role of the social scientist should be stated at this time. American sociology has been overly concerned with reliability, method, and social order and statics for some years. Today, social change is commanding attention; planned social change is the challenge; and social relevance is the demand, both from within and without the profession. Bell and Mau clearly call for a shift in the orientation of sociology, perhaps the creation of a new subdiscipline of futuristics. It is also clear that as scientists, they are committed to the "demand that theories or generalizations be evaluated in terms of their logical consistency and consonance with facts" (Merton, 1957:541), and that their views are consistent with many of the great traditions of sociology. For example, Frank E. Manuel (1962:6) says that Auguste Comte and the other "prophets of Paris"

> unveiled the future and in the same anxious breath tried to give it direction by persuading their contemporaries to adopt willingly and without bloodshed the course which they were inevitably destined to follow anyway. They were intoxicated with the future: they looked into what was about to be and they found it good. The past was a mere prologue and the present a spiritual and moral, even a physical, burden which at times was well nigh unendurable. They would destroy the present as fast as possible in order to usher in the longed-for future. . . .

Manuel points out that Condorcet was not only trying to foresee the future scientifically, he was trying "to tame it"; that Saint-Simon spent much of his time during his final years drawing up plans for the administrative organization of the future world; that Fourier's blueprints for the future included revolutionary reorganizations of love and work and the goal of self-fulfillment (and resulted in the well-known experiments of Brook Farm and the New Harmonies). For Comte, of course, the self-proclaimed *Foundateur de la religion universelle et Grand Prêtre de l'Humanité*, "the future was, after all, the whole purpose of his colossal labors—*savoir pour prévoir*" (Manuel, 1962:288). And Comte, who actually tried to create the future he predicted, "raised the specter of formlessness as the dread antiprogressist force, a French sociological tradition which culminated in Durkheim's conception of *anomie*" (Manuel, 1962:286). Marx and Engels, of course, founded a secular religion with a vision that has helped to shape the modern world and to give it many of its distinctive features. Thus, Bell and Mau do not suggest that the sociological traditions be discarded, but that there should be a return to some of those traditions that seem to have been forgotten by many in the mainstream of American sociology today.

The second chapter in Part I outlines "A Paradigm for the Analysis of Time Perspectives and Images of the Future." The authors—Bell and Mau joined by Bettina Huber and Menno Boldt—follow up one of the implications of the Bell and Mau essay and set the stage for several of the succeeding chapters of this book. Spengler (1926–28:130) said: "It is by the meaning that it intuitively attaches to time that one culture is differentiated from another." Bell et al. add that it is by the meaning that he attaches to time that one sociologist—or one group of sociologists—is differentiated from another. Just as all societies have a time orientation, so do all sociologists in their efforts to reconstruct the realities of social life. Frequently, the sociologist's time perspective does not derive from the nature of the social situation under investigation, but rather is brought into the situation as part of the sociologist's assumptions. Bell et al. argue that such time perspectives are linked to basic assumptions about the nature of man and society held by the investigator and serve to shape the specification and interpretation of data so as to promote certain images of the future, usually implicit, rather than others. They suggest a paradigm that may be used as a guide for the analysis of time perspectives and images of the future in social science literature. Examples of the use of the paradigm by Menno Boldt as applied in detail to MacIver Award winner John Porter's book, *The Vertical Mosaic*, and by Pauline B. Bart as applied to various schools of psychotherapy are included in Part III.

REFERENCES

Deutsch, Karl W.
    1963   The Nerves of Government: Models of Political Communication
           and Control. New York: Free Press.

Lasswell, Harold D.
  1966   "The changing image of human nature: the socio-cultural aspect, future-oriented man." American Journal of Psychoanalysis 26:157–166.
Manuel, Frank E.
  1962   The Prophets of Paris. Cambridge, Mass.: Harvard University Press.
Merton, Robert K.
  1957   Social Theory and Social Structure (revised and enlarged edition). Glencoe, Ill.: Free Press.
Moore, Wilbert E.
  1967   Order and Change: Essays in Comparative Sociology. New York: Wiley.
Spengler, Oswald
  1926–28 The Decline of the West. New York: Knopf, Vol. I. As quoted by Florence Rockwood Kluckhohn and Fred L. Strodtbeck et al., Variations in Value Orientations. Evanston, Ill.: Row, Peterson, 1961.
Wirth, Louis
  1936   "Preface." Pp. x–xxx in Karl Mannheim, Ideology and Utopia. New York: Harcourt, Brace & World, A Harvest Book.

Images of the Future: Theory and Research Strategies

WENDELL BELL AND JAMES A. MAU

In his presidential address to the American Sociological Association, Wilbert E. Moore (1966b:765) raised the following questions:

> Have we, in short, any obligation as social scientists to start taking account not only of the changeful quality of social life but also of the fact that some portion of that change is deliberate? And do we, still as social scientists, have anything positive to add to the fulfillment of human hopes for the future, or are we always fated to counsel the eager traveler that "you can't get there from here"?

Moore goes on to say that social scientists *do* have such an obligation and *do* have something positive to add to such fulfillment. In this chapter, we elaborate some of the implications of such a view—with which we heartily agree—for both social theory and the conduct of social research. Specifically, we (1) discuss the concept of "image of the future"; (2) briefly sketch a theory of social change based upon it; and (3) suggest a series of related directives for research strategy and for the role of the social scientist. Our purposes are—like Moore's—to bring the volitional aspects of social systems into the sociological net more fully and explicitly than is now being done under conventional social theory and to take account of the social scientist himself as an agent of social change. First, however, we discuss two basic assumptions. One assumption involves the sense in which the future can or cannot be thought of as real; the other deals with the increase in human mastery throughout history.

THE REALITY OF POSSIBILITIES FOR THE FUTURE

Time perspectives have varied considerably during the course of human history, and the immeasurable increase in the scale of modern man's conceptions of time has given new importance to the future and added meaning to the past and present. Modern man does not simply shrug off the past as mere history but views it more and more in terms of its meaning for the present and future. This view is not expressed by aphorisms such as "we learn from history" or "history repeats itself"; rather, it emphasizes that, through the interpretations and evaluations currently attached to the past, it has significance and reality in the present and in the future. "Since historical past is always part of the reality of the present, the past . . . will always have emergent aspects as long as history continues to be written" (Tiryakian, 1966:9).

The emergent future also has present meaning or, in a sense, "reality," with consequences shaped by man's thoughts and expectations about alternative futures. Following Heidegger, Tiryakian (1966:7) stated:

> . . . human existence stretches out into the future and into the past. The subject, understood phenomenologically, is not an entity contained in an absolute space but rather an existent whose being is a set of possibilities that became actualized in the present. The past and the future are therefore not separate entities, but are very much part of the present: the past is, existentially viewed, a *having-been* present, while the future is a *will-be* present, both being grounded in the phenomenal emergence of the here-and-now.

The significance of this temporal interplay lies in mankind's ability intentionally to deflect the direction of sociohistorical change. Modern man can alter his past as well as his future, although in different ways.[1] Nearly every generation of literate peoples has some who desire to shape the world to suit themselves by rewriting their history. Even if intentional falsification does not take place, facts can be mustered to support different interpretations. No one would deny this who has read Edmund Wilson or Alfred Cobban on the historians' conflicting versions of the French Revolution or who has compared the different scenarios that portray American history, or who has talked with twentieth-century elites of new nations as they decide their nations' histories.

This is not to say that there is no historical truth or that some versions of history are not better or more accurate than others. Rather, his-

---

[1] Here and elsewhere in this essay there are similarities to some of the views of George Herbert Mead. For example, see Strauss (1956).

tories are relative to the different frames of reference, selective perceptions, assumptions, concepts, and theories that are used to organize them. By recognizing this relativity, rather than denying it, and by making as much of the thought that went into the construction of the past as explicit as possible, one can view the conflicting versions of historical truth with some hope of discerning which seems most credible.

Although sociologists can see how this applies to history, they may have difficulty accepting that it is true also of sociology. The ways in which sociologists portray the present—sample surveys, questionnaires, interview schedules, data, and statistical analyses—are also relative. Different techniques may result in different versions of reality. In recent years, sociological "truths" have come, in turn, to influence the way people see themselves and their societies and, thus, have been consequential for the behavior that emerges from such conceptions. Sociologists, who have long recognized the relativity of values, are now confronting as well the relativity of their findings and interpretations. Although we cannot go beyond this point here, we believe trends can be detected in current thinking that may lead modern social scientists full circle, from value relativism to the belief that it is the good that is absolute and the truth that is relative.[2]

The future in some respects is as real as the past, since we know both in much the same way—through our conceptions of them. The future is in some sense as real as the present too, except for the momentary experience of the present in ways that transcend the organization of sense data into articulate and meaningful units for a given actor at a given time and place. (See Holzner, 1968). We must remember that we will never know most of what goes on in the present at other places and what we do presume to learn of it is gained through reconstruction of it by others. Our impressions are incomplete, even if such reconstructions are on-the-spot radio or television reports, since such reports are necessarily selected and edited, if by no more than a choice of the eyewitness interviewed or the camera angle. At a meeting of the American Physical Society, Harvard philosophy professor Hilary W. Putnam commented on the reality of the future. He contended that if one takes relativity seriously, then

---

[2] That "truth" is relative seems simple to demonstrate compared to the difficulty of showing that the "good" is absolute. We do not wish to press the latter point here, nor are we convinced that it is defensible, but we have in mind certain universal values that derive from the survival, health, and dignity of man. For example, Moore (1966b:771) in his presidential address cautiously suggests some common values and says that we have ". . . exaggerated the significance of cultural differences in human values, for many of these differences simply do not survive the extension of communication that makes the world a single system in important respects." Also see Moore (1966a). For three potential universal values, compare Cantril (1963).

what ". . . appears in the future to one observer is in the past for another. The future to us seems unreal . . . because we cannot remember it. But in the context of combined space and time the past and future are just as real as up and down" (*The New York Times*, 1966:10E). Although we don't go this far, the idea is provocative.

There is one important sense, however, in which the ontological status of the past, present, and the future differ. In a paper on "Applied Metaphysics: Truth and Passing Time," Robert S. Brumbaugh (1966: 649, 651) points out that:

> . . . there is a genuine ontological difference in the kind and the definiteness of being which past facts, present options, and future possibilities possess. Part of this difference can be summarized by the assertion that *there are no past possibilities, and there are no future facts*. It follows that we have created an unreal problem in our uncriticized assumption that the concepts of causation, truth, law, and determinism, which hold elegantly for the factual past domain, must also apply to the future. That past time is a fair sample of all time is a mistaken metaphysical assumption. . . . Determinism does hold for the past, but if we were not committed to notions of verifiability, truth, and fact which are all past-oriented, it would be evident from our own immediate experience that it does not necessarily follow that such determinism also holds for present or future.
> . . . there are cases—those, namely, of propositions with future time-references—in which the meaning is definite enough, but the truth is only fractional. A "choice now open" or a "possibility" has *some* ontological status; it is not a pure Parmenidean nonentity. It therefore also has *some*, though indefinite, correspondence with the propositions asserted about it. If our patterns of thought are to match the patterns of life, our logics must be modified to include indefinite "values." For example, a four valued scheme of 1, 0, $\neq 1$, and $\neq 0$ may be needed to distinguish the degrees of definiteness in the correspondence of assertion to reality. And, *in sharp distinction to nearly all antecedent formal systems*, those values are in some cases going to change with the relative dates of assertion and reference of the propositions. Otherwise, we perpetuate the illusion that there are future facts, that time is like space, that nothing is lost in translating a problem or decision that confronts us in the present into a language which allows no other modes of existence than the eternal and the past.

The future is real, then, to the extent to which present alternatives or possibilities for the future are real; and a purely deterministic model is inappropriate to deal with this reality because, until the future has become the present, some alternative possibilities may remain open. In addition, we suggest two related aspects in which the future is real. One is seen in the "design perspective" described by Robert Boguslaw in Part

IV: The future is prepared in the present and may be "known" through the actions—or inactions—and their effects that will bring it into being. Here a deterministic model has some utility as long as it is explicitly probabilistic. The second is that images of the future are real. They have existed in the past and exist in the present. They more or less orient human behavior and social action, according to our view, and, thus, give insight into what alternative futures are being prepared in the present. They themselves may constitute some of the alternative possibilities for the future. Brumbaugh's main point, however, is that there are no future facts. However real our conceptions of it, our actions that will produce it, and the certainty of its coming, the future is open. The *present possibilities* for the future are real.

THE RISE OF HUMAN MASTERY

The theory of social change discussed in this chapter rests, in part, upon the assumption that a major trend of history has been an increase in the mastery of man over his natural and social environment as well as a shift in his beliefs that this is so.[3] An implication is that explanations of social change are only more or less relevant to the events of particular epochs, depending upon how accurate the explanation is in assessing the degree of influence man himself may have, and thinks he has, in directing social change. For example, traditional ecological explanations may be of considerable relevance to the behavior of primitive man, since his chief struggle was with nature and since his life was shaped by that struggle. Primitive man may have been influenced by images of the future, but the content of his images did not allow him much freedom of choice among alternatives. Ends were seldom questioned and means were often invested with ritualistic significance. Possibly the gods could be persuaded to bring about a desired future event, but fatalism was widespread.

Likewise, explanations based on notions of economic determinism or technology, rather than ecology, had considerable relevance for industrializing men and societies of the seventeenth, eighteenth, and nineteenth centuries. Ends or goals were still largely unquestioned and fairly clearly defined, but means were increasingly free from religious dogma and were chosen according to criteria of efficiency and economy. Thus, then-current images of the future incorporated notions that permitted

---

[3] Our discussion of the rise of human mastery converges with the view of Lester F. Ward. Increase in human mastery or, as Ward defines it, civilization, is an increase in ". . . the utilization of the materials and forces of nature . . ." by man as the directive agent (Ward, 1914:468). It goes without saying that our usage of "mankind" and "man" includes both males and females.

choice of means, although the criteria were generally agreed upon, but allowed little choice of ends.

Today, traditional ecological and technological explanations are not sufficient to account for the behavior of an increasing number of people in advanced societies, because in such societies more and more men find that their chief struggle is with themselves and other men, not with nature or the lack of technology, and because both the ends and means of life have been increasingly freed for conscious choice. This freedom has been made possible for many people in advanced societies by their securing the essentials and amenities of life and by advances in philosophy and science, including social science, that have reduced people's dependence upon superstition and fatalistic conceptions of the future. Of course, this freedom to select both goals and ways of achieving them, which permits some individuals and groups to establish new norms and values for entire societies, occurs in a context of certain, limiting, agreed-upon principles of group survival, which are seldom extensively violated. Nonetheless, the latitude of decision is quite large. Large enough, for example, to bring new burdens of responsibility to modern man, especially the burden of knowing both that his life and environment may become, in important respects, what he will make of them *and* that he is not always certain just what he wants, or should want, to make of them. Thus, in the most advanced societies, traditional explanations of social phenomena must be supplemented with moral explanations. But the latter represent a new, secular morality, which is pragmatic and open to social choice and universal considerations.

John C. McKinney (1966:170–171) states a point of view similar to our own within the specific context of the difference between *Gemeinschaft* and *Gesellschaft* types of societies. His statement further clarifies the idea that theories of social change are relative to particular times and places:

> . . . It is now a standard view in the sociology of knowledge that different types of knowledge, as well as the techniques and motivations for extending knowledge, are bound up with particular forms of groups. *Gemeinschaft* types of society have a traditionally defined fund of knowledge handed down as conclusive and final, they are not concerned with discovering new ideas or extending their spheres of knowledge. Any effort to test the traditional knowledge, insofar as it implies doubt, is ruled out on moral grounds. In such a group the prevailing methods are ontological and dogmatic; its mode of thought is that of conceptual realism. In contrast, *Gesellschaft* types of organization institutionalize techniques for the attainment and codification of knowledge. In such a group the methods are primarily epistemological and critical; the mode of thought is nominalistic. Given such difference in structural types and modes of orientation, it

is clear that the problem of instigating change, of whatever purpose or form, must be perceived of in very different ways for the two contrasting types of systems. Moreover, there appears to be ample justification for saying that the instigation of any change will necessarily have to follow different procedures, adapted to two distinctly different social structures. The success of planning and execution of such change will in large part be determined by the extent to which it is appropriate to the system for which it is intended.

From the above, McKinney (1966:171) draws an implication for the conduct of social research in the modern world: "If sociology is to play a key role in contemporary social research, then the major inquiries must be made in a world where the patterns of the past are under increased pressure from a dynamic future." A reorientation of social research is in order, because the rise of human mastery is ushering in new dynamics of change, under which man is increasingly liberated from the bonds of the past and is increasingly able to transcend the limitations of the present. What is needed are new social theories and empirical inquiries that take this fact into account.

Most people today do not yet live under the liberating conditions that technologically advanced society makes possible. The poor and underdeveloped nations of the world, despite the positive future orientation of many of their people and especially of their modernizing leaders, contain masses of people who are at the mercy of natural forces or technological necessities. Some of them fatalistically perceive their destiny as being beyond their control. And we are well aware that even in advanced societies, some sections of the population do not have the liberating opportunities enjoyed by the majority, and that many people are victims as well as beneficiaries of modern technology. The pollution of air and water and the disfigurement of land are unwanted products of the application of technology, as is the economically marginal status of many groups in societies with advanced technical capacity. Yet the long-term trends are clear: human mastery over nature and the power of technology have increased in the past and can be expected to increase further in the future.

THE CONCEPT OF IMAGE OF THE FUTURE

The explanatory concept that we put forward as a key variable in a theory of social change is that of "image of the future." Here we rely on the prior work of Frederik L. Polak and Harold D. Lasswell.[4] In an effort

---

[4] Although we cite Polak and Lasswell extensively in this section and wish to acknowledge our debt to them, we have tried to state the concept of image of the future in a way that represents our use of it. We are less interested in exegesis than in creative synthesis.

aimed at "enlightening the past, orientating the present, and forecasting the future," Polak (1961), in a book analyzing the intellectual history of Europe, lays the foundation for a theory of social change based on images of the future.[5] Polak says that man lives simultaneously in three worlds with respect to time: past, present, and future. (There are, of course, with respect to space other worlds as well.) Actual past experiences of individuals and groups, perceptions and knowledge about the past of one's particular society and of the human past in general, both history and prehistory, shape what men and societies are in the present. They shape present forms, limitations, and possibilities; they shape fundamental fears and desires as well as conceptions of the good life; they influence the way people think about the future and what they are willing and able to do to alter or prepare for the actualities of the emerging future. In turn, the present conditions of everyday life, to which people adapt and which people more or less shape, affect perceptions and formulations of the past and can result in new and different meanings being attached to historical development. As one copes with present realities as well as with attitudes and beliefs about them, one's images of the future can change. Thereby, the present helps mold the future as well as the past. Furthermore, the emerging future itself shapes the past—the meanings that are attached to it *and* the "facts" of history themselves. For example, we know more about the past now, through archeological research, than ever before. The emerging future also affects the realities of the present as well as our perceptions and evaluations of them. New hopes and fears concerning the future can lead to new historical research as well as to the formulation of new interpretations of old realities. In fact, debates about which interpretations of history are correct are often debates arising from conflicting images of what is desired in the future. Just as an individual's future behavior is to some extent governed by his self-image of the kind of person *he has been, is,* and *hopes to be,* so also a nation's future course of development is, to some extent, controlled by the doctrines and dogmas of particular versions of the social and cultural history of that nation.

In the modern world, man is deliberately bent on "making himself" according to his own choosing, although, as Polak states, the liberation that comes with this orientation is matched by new responsibilities and uncertainties:

---

[5] It is perhaps inevitable that errors would crop up, as they do, in such a sweeping review as Polak (1961) undertakes. Some readers may be put off by this as well as by the fact that Polak occasionally becomes a bit mystical. It would be a shame, in our judgment, if these debilities were permitted to interfere with the useful message that Polak has for the modern sociologist.

In setting himself purposefully to control and alter the course of events man has been forced to deal with the concepts of value, means and ends, ideals and ideologies, as he has attempted to blueprint his own future. As long as the prophet-propitiator was acting only as a divine transmitter of messages from on high, man felt that he was accepting his ethics ready-made, with no alterations allowed. *In a later stage man staggers under the double load of not only having to construct his own future but having to create the values which will determine its design* (36–37, italics added).

For Polak the rise and fall of images of the future precede or accompany the rise and fall of cultures. History has been made what it is largely as a result of the ideas and ideals of man that have been congealed in the form of images of the future. The time that is yet to come rests importantly on the nature of the present images of the future. Thus, the vigor and potentialities of the society of tomorrow can be detected in the society of today.

Although Polak sees the transformation of man's orientation through history as involving a shift from fatalism to self-determination, he sees also that modern Western man, partly as a result of new burdens, is overcome by apathy and is increasingly likely to see life as meaningless. In Polak's view, the images of the future of Western culture are disintegrating, and the end result may be that it has no future. Polak sees a "fatal movement" in this direction, but he is optimistic about man's ability to intervene and reverse the undesirable trend, if only he will take the necessary steps to prevent it. Throughout his book Polak is clearly dedicated to positive idealism, constructive images, and to optimism; yet his own image of the future ironically contains an overriding negative and pessimistic element with respect to developments in the recent past and future projections. This combination of pessimistic prediction and an optimistic view of man's potential to intervene for the better is often phrased, as in Polak's book, as a veiled threat to act now or suffer the consequences. It is, of course, a "call to arms" to intellectuals, intended to deflect an undesirable course of events.

Today's images of the future need elaboration, refinement, and revision; the actual future is rolling over people and whole societies before they are prepared; the possibilities of a better life are not being fulfilled as adequately as they could be. Polak's distinctive contribution to this viewpoint is his effort to depict the social scientist qua scientist not only as an objective investigator but also as a creator and disseminator of images of the future:

> The concept *image of the future* is used in a double sense; as an object of research and as a statement of the problem. The social scientist is

answerable for the future, in that he is both the carrier and the creator of an image of the future, consciously or unconsciously. In this time of culture-crisis he ought to be made aware of his role in the creation of the future. In order to achieve this awareness he must also consider the image of the future as an object for research.

. . . The process of writing the history of the future through the study of the images of the future has its unique aspect in that the *writing* of history merges imperceptibly into the responsible act of *creating* history. One is reminded here of the concept of the personal equation—the influence of the observer on that which he observes. The formulation, as well as the act of describing the image of the future, may influence the future itself. *The social scientist (and this is part of his specific responsibility both towards social sciences and society) may discover ways to rewrite the history of the future* (57, italics added. See Jouvenel, 1963).[6]

Our purpose in citing Polak's work at some length is twofold: first, to call attention to the importance of images of the future in understanding social change; and, second, to emphasize the active role of social science in the process of social change.

Harold D. Lasswell, the American political scientist and pioneer advocate of the scientific approach to the study of political behavior, has in many of his works said much the same thing as Polak. Although Lasswell has been more cautious than Polak in stating that the scientist influences the future less as a scientist than as a citizen, he has gone well beyond Polak in working out some of the details of the methods of creating images of the future, which are similar to what Lasswell calls "developmental constructs," and in specifying the direction of particular trends of modern society.

Many features of Lasswell's developmental analysis,[7] the major tool of which is the developmental construct, are similar to Polak's concept of image of the future. A developmental construct expresses expectations about the future, contains explicit anticipations of the shape of things to come, and is related to the facts of past trends. Society is viewed as an interval on some continuum of social change, and the developmental construct delineates the end points of that continuum—"the from what and toward what of developmental sequences." Lasswell stresses the possibility of a shift in social science from description and prediction to

---

[6] Bertrand de Jouvenel (1963), in his introduction to the first volume of *Futuribles*, makes similar comments. He states that he and the group of authors in the *Futuribles* venture ". . . quite definitely take the view that what shall be depends upon our choices: it is precisely because the future depends upon our decisions and action, and these in turn upon our opinions regarding the future, that the latter so much need to be stated, weighed, and tested."

[7] An excellent summary of developmental analysis can be found in Eulau (1958).

control and the introduction of the manipulative standpoint into the contemplative. In formulating scientific questions as a search for courses of action leading to some goal or maximizing some value, he shows how scientists may self-consciously enlarge their role of influencing society in some desired direction, a role that, in our opinion, the scientist plays, whether or not he is conscious of it. Furthermore, Lasswell deals with the problems created for scientific analysis by the confounding nature of self-fulfilling or self-denying prophesies through which scientific predictions, as they become known, may themselves affect the very future predicted. In his developmental analysis, Lasswell attempts to make "a virtue of the fact—which gives social science in general a great deal of trouble—that a prediction, by becoming itself a factor in the definition of the situation, guarantees or prevents the emergence of anticipated results" (Eulau, 1958:240; cf. Miller, 1961).

Although Lasswell phrases his conceptions of the part to be played by social scientists in different terms from Polak, nonetheless he clearly urges the social scientist to make his work relevant to basic values and to the emerging future, particularly by using developmental constructs. These constructs serve the purpose of sensitizing the investigator to the relevance of his work for the future and especially for the conservation of values that he would desire to protect. Lasswell (1948:157) suggests that social science should include studies of "all factors that condition the survival of selected values."

Certainly, neither developmental constructs nor images of the future are dogmatic predictions, yet we see no reason why they cannot be used scientifically. That the study of the future can be scientific is not a new idea. Over fifty years ago, H. G. Wells (1913:36–37) proposed it in a lecture given at the Royal Institution in England:

> All applied mathematics resolves into computation to foretell things which otherwise can only be determined by trial. Even in so unscientific a field as economics there have been forecasts. And if I am right in saying that science aims at prophecy, and if the specialist in each science is in fact doing his best now to prophesy within the limits of his field, what is there to stand in the way of our building up this growing body of forecast into an ordered picture of the future that will be just as certain, just as strictly science, and perhaps just as detailed a picture that has been built up with the last hundred years of the geological past? Well, so far and until we bring the prophecy down to the affairs of man and his children, it is just as possible to carry induction forward as back; it is just as simple and sure to work out the changing orbit of the earth in the future until the tidal drag hauls one unchanging face at last toward the sun as it is to work back to its blazing and molten past.

Wells believed that the future, like the geological past, could be studied by induction; and he included the future of human affairs, although he thought that individual futures were beyond the scope of such investigation. With the subsequent explosive development of the social sciences, can we not reasonably expect an equal increase in capabilities to study the possibilities for personal and social futures?

Extrapolation of trends, such as in the demographic projection of time series, for example, is perhaps the most obvious scientific method for studying alternative futures. Others include the specification of dynamic processes of cause and effect, which may affect the future and go well beyond simple projection of time series. "If, then" statements can be made based upon knowledge of causal relationships, the implications of which are carried into the future: what are the probabilities of different possibilities for the future under specified conditions? Quite directly, individual and collective images of the future can be measured just like other beliefs and attitudes, and these can be tested against subsequent developments as they occur. The researcher may himself construct images of the future—for example, of some social group, an institution, or an entire nation—by any number of heuristic devices from the negation of selected aspects of the present to the hypothetical occurrence of alternative syntheses of different existing social forms. He could then estimate the probabilities of such images being fulfilled, according to whatever evidence his ingenuity would lead him to specify, and evaluate the desirability of such images against sample surveys of the values of relevant populations. Finally, to the extent to which the study of images of the future could be linked to social engineering, which seems increasingly feasible, quasi experiments could be performed testing various hypotheses about the future and especially the role of deliberate action in shaping it.

The relation of images of the future to action that is designed to bring about a particular future is the most significant fact in relation to the theory of social change to be proposed. Trying to look at the world through the eyes of new national leaders as they set about making the decisions of nationhood, we arrived in our earlier studies at the importance of images of the future. Thus, we have tried to incorporate the study of the future into our own empirical research.[8] Lasswell also apparently arrived at his notion of the developmental construct through his concern with decision-makers, and he connects a future orientation

---

[8] See Bell (1964), Bell and Oxaal (1964), Bell (1967), and Mau (1968). Also, the same orientation is more or less present in the recent work of two of our colleagues who participated with us in the Caribbean research; see Moskos (1967) and Oxaal (1968).

with decision-making, as the following comments on his work by Heinz
Eulau (1958:230–231) make clear:

> . . . a decision is an act, or a series of acts, involving the simultaneous
> manipulation of facts, values, and above all expectations. The decision-
> maker cannot do without expectations about the future—expectations re-
> lating, for instance, to the probability of a long or short war, rising or
> falling national income, the stability or instability of foreign governments.
> Being explicit about one's expectations necessitates their assessment in
> terms of values, goals, or objectives, on the one hand, and in terms of
> whatever factual knowledge may be available, on the other hand.
> . . . decision-making is predominantly future-oriented. It is, Lasswell
> points out, "forward-looking, formulating alternative courses of action ex-
> tending into the future, and selecting among the alternatives by expecta-
> tions of how things will turn out."
> . . . a theory of the political process or, at least, a conceptual schema
> that has decision-making behavior as its empirical referent is predicated on
> the availability of constructs which are descriptive of the emerging future.
> Such constructs presumably make possible "the planned observation of
> the emerging future [which] is one of the tasks of science."[9]

A THEORY OF SOCIAL CHANGE

The outlines of a theory of social change based on the assumptions
we have discussed are illustrated in the diagram on page 21. Social
change is explained within what we have called a "cybernetic-decisional
model," which treats the entire process as a feedback cycle resulting in a
spiral of progressive interaction between information and action. Motivated individuals, acting as individuals or members of groups, their images of the future, and their resultant behaviors are the key elements
that keep the system moving and bring a future into being in the present.
The behavior is viewed as largely the result of decisions (or in some cases
decisions not to decide), which are essentially choices among alternative
futures. Hence the use of "decisional" in the label. Images of the future
are of critical importance in influencing which of the alternative futures
becomes present reality.

Although our view of the nature of society—and of the sociological
enterprise—differs from what has been the dominant view in American
sociology, it is quite similar to the dialectical sociology of French sociolo-

---

[9] On this specific point, cf. Jouvenel (1965). In general, the idea of image of the
future has been elaborated by Kenneth E. Boulding (1956, 1965). We regret that, because of lack of space, we have been unable to discuss his work here. We refer the
reader in particular to *The Image: Knowledge in Life and Society* and *The Meaning
of the Twentieth Century: The Great Transition.*

gist Georges Gurvitch, whose work has been neglected in the United States. Gurvitch places emphasis upon the spontaneous as well as the organized aspects of social life. He sees society *en marche*. He sees determinism as interactive with human liberty, and he gives the ontological priority to freedom. He stresses the fluid, "the ever-changing, precarious equilibria of each of his totalities and their incessant processes of structuration, destructuration and restructuration" (Bosserman, 1968:iv). Social reality is, in Gurvitch's terms:

> . . . constantly moving, tension-filled, fluctuating, renewing, threatened by revolutions, in short characterized by a dynamic quality which St. Simon has called *société en acte*. . . . Dialectical sociology opens up a view of society as a whole in all its effervescent and vividly dynamic aspects. Underneath the crust of tradition and organization reside the well-springs of revolutions, of rapid change, the irrational roots of behaviour, the creative acts and attitudes. Together they provide the excitement and challenge to social science research, which in turn holds the clues to man's future (Bosserman, 1968:227, 303).

Although inadequately shown in the diagram, this is the conception of society—society as process—that we are trying to convey.

We further stress initiative, novelty, spontaneity, self-modification, creativity, goal-seeking, and self-determination by thinking of social change as a complex cybernetic system. Karl W. Deutsch (1963) has already constructed a detailed model of the polity as a system of communication and control, and we refer the reader to his important work for an elaboration of the cybernetic model. Here we are interested only in the orientation, and its implications for a conception of social change based upon images of the future. Deutsch (1963:245) says:

> . . . every autonomous system tends to act out the future implicit in the distributions of its memories and in the configurations of its communication channels; and insofar as its behavior leads it to acquire new memories and to change some of its internal communication patterns by learning, it will remake itself and its future to a limited extent at every such step. If the system has consciousness, if it monitors its own behavior, and derives and remembers images of itself that it applies to its own actions, then it may well also derive and use images projecting its behavior into the future. It will thus use goal images and entertain explicitly formulated aspirations.

The unit of analysis to which the model may be applied can be a single individual choosing a career, a family selecting a neighborhood, decision-makers of a business firm selecting an office site, national leaders formulating their country's foreign alliances, or a supranational group deciding who should be admitted to membership. Thus, in applying the model, the analyst must first specify the relevant unit and identify the appropriate context that should be identified with the other elements in the model. Of course, one may use the model simultaneously on different levels of abstraction with the added analysis of critical intersections, such as, on the one hand, the case of a university selecting its new students for admission and, on the other, a number of individual university applicants deciding where they will apply for admission.

Since we have already discussed indirectly most of what is in the diagram and why it is there, we will here explain only briefly its contents. We must, however, define our terms. Crucial to this theory of social change is the concept of belief, which we define as any ". . . given proposition about any aspect of the universe which is accepted as true . . ." (McKinney, 1966:181).

> . . . The significance of beliefs is not dependent upon the intrinsic, objective truth of the particular proposition. Of course, beliefs vary in accordance with the norms or standards against which they are tested. There are false beliefs (contrary to demonstrable evidence), true beliefs (in accord with empirical evidence), and beliefs that are methodologically untestable (unverifiable in form). A particular belief may be based on accumulated factual evidence or upon prejudice, intuition, superficial appearances, or faith. Accordingly, there can be empirical beliefs and nonempirical beliefs. The nature of its derivation need not affect the potency of the belief itself. People may act just as energetically and determinedly on the basis of unverified or unverifiable beliefs as upon the basis of empirically sound beliefs. . . . In brief, beliefs are formulations of what we think about the universe, its objects, and their relations. A belief system is a kind of cognitive mapping of the situation (McKinney, 1966:181).

We distinguish three kinds of beliefs in the cybernetic-decisional theory of social change: beliefs about the past, the present, and causation.

Beliefs about the past. Every individual and group has a history. Beliefs about that history limit the range of alternative images of the future and make it more probable that a particular one, rather than others, will be dominant. This is the "memory" of a cybernetic system.

Beliefs about the present. Individuals and groups have not only histories but also present existences. It is elementary to say that what individuals and groups think of themselves and what significant others believe to be true of them are important determinants of images of the future. Furthermore, formulations about the "facts" of the present define the maps of social reality that people use to make their way in the world. We include here not only beliefs about specific details of the present as perceived and understood by the actors but also definitions of the situa-

CYBERNETIC-DECISIONAL MODEL
OF SOCIAL CHANGE

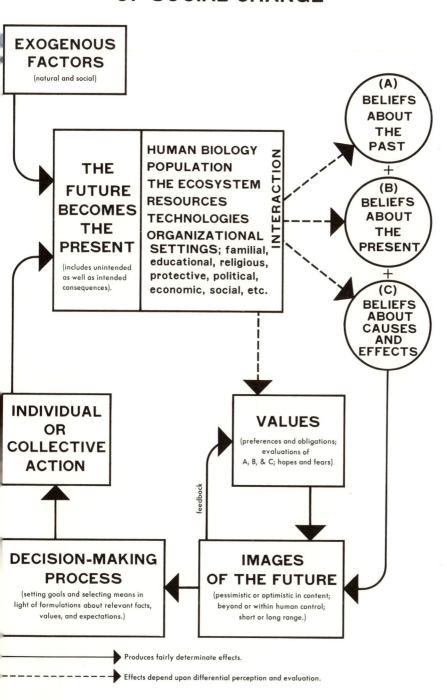

tion and, at the highest level of abstraction, basic views about the nature of man and the world.

Beliefs about causes and effects. The construction of an image of the future depends in part on the formulations about causes and effects held by the person or shared by the group doing the constructing. At one level, what people believe about the way the world works can contribute to making it work that way (for example, a widespread belief that bribes are offered and accepted by government officials may promote both offers and acceptances); and at another level it contributes, no matter how inaccurate the belief, toward directing human energies in one particular direction rather than in another. At the most general level, what people believe about social causation can lead them to adopt images of the future that are more or less fatalistic.

Values. Combined with beliefs about the past, present, and causation in shaping images of the future are the values that are held by individuals either for themselves, someone else, or some social group. We include here basic values, whether primarily preferred choices or felt obligations. These provide a frame of reference for evaluating the past, present, and presumed causes and effects and, in conjunction with such beliefs, for defining hopes and fears. Values also constitute a set of criteria for defining desirable and undesirable images of the future and provide a basis for the evaluation of the costs and complex interactions between alternative images of the future in different spheres of activity. As Lasswell (1966:157) says, "The accent put on future events gives new prominence to preferred events, to value goals, since the possibility is perceived that some act of selection may influence the sequence of future occurrences."

When one deals with persons as separate individuals as the units of analysis, the empirical problem is to determine the beliefs and values of particular individuals and how they enter into each individual's images of the future, decisions, and actions. When one deals with collectivities as the units of analysis, there are the additional empirical problems of the distribution of beliefs and values within the collectivity, the degree and intensity of conflict involved, and the relative influence and power of persons holding particular beliefs and values. These factors, of course, would influence the various outcomes. Each element in the diagram then may take on a complex structure that in its own right invites investigation.

The fact that beliefs and values are shaped by various constraining and socializing factors is shown in the accompanying diagram by the four arrows leading from the present to the various beliefs and values. Since Durkheim, sociologists generally have taken society as prior in time to the individual, and in the Western world—especially in the United States—most sociological effort in the past five decades has been devoted to the study of the shaping of individuals and their behaviors by the "natural" (e.g., studies in human ecology) and especially the social environments. Recent sociological inquiry has tended to focus on the structural determinants of social man and his behavior. We do not suggest that such studies be discontinued in favor of our proposal. That would not correct a fault but simply lead to another. Rather, we suggest that the other side of the coin has been neglected in recent times. The study of society as becoming—its structuration, destructuration, and restructuration, and specifically the role of man in the process—is no less a sociological question than studies of society's constraints on man or of the change that takes place as a result of impersonal forces. Thus, although in our model we take account of the influence of society on man, we emphasize in the cybernetic-decisional theory of social change that man, individually and collectively, comes to take some action that results in altering natural and social arrangements, and that "future events may be affected by subjective events that refer in advance to the possibility that the future events will take place" (Lasswell, 1966:157). (Cf. Bendix and Berger, 1959; and Etzioni, 1967.)

Images of the future. The definition of images of the future should be as spare as possible, other things one might say about them being taken not as intrinsic aspects of the definition itself but as extrinsic to it. Apart from its definition itself, a useful concept should also have many implications, a requirement met by the concept of image of the future. As a working definition, we propose: An image of the future is an expectation about the state of things to come at some future time. We may think most usefully of such expectations as a range of differentially probable possibilities rather than as a single point on a continuum.

Images of the future may vary in many ways. For example, they are specific to different aspects of reality and pertinent to different levels of abstraction. They may be about one's personal monetary success, a national military crisis, changing relations between different races, or the future of mankind as a whole. They may concern the immediate future or some time far off; and they may be about some particular location or some other place on this earth or elsewhere. They may be widely shared by many social groups or differentially held by different groups and in conflict; they may be considered desirable or undesirable; and they may promote either apathy or hyperactivity. They may serve different group interests, be simple or complex, more or less realizable, more or less believable and persuasive, more or less certain to become the present, more or less different from the past and present, consciously or unconsciously created, more or less intentionally manipulated, strongly or weakly held, and more or less influential in orienting behavior. They may be either old or new, sacred or secular. They may vary according to the conditions under which they arise. In understanding behavior, the proximity of the images is of great significance—whether they are long-range, and therefore of possible sustained importance in directing behavior, or short-range. Of considerable interest is the extent to which an image of the future negates some aspect of the present with the potential for its destruction.

Following Polak, we suggest two additional aspects of images of the future: (1) the pessimism or optimism of its content—that is, whether the future state of affairs according to the image is evaluated as worse or better than the present; and (2) the assumption contained in the image concerning the factors that will influence the actual future, whether they are beyond human control or directly (e.g., man himself) or indirectly (e.g., prayer to the gods) within it. Critical differences in human behavior are hypothesized to result from images that are basically pessimistic compared to those that are optimistic and from images that put man in the image as a causal factor compared to those that do not.

Decision-making process. It is beyond the scope of this chapter to discuss the details of the decision-making process itself, nor is there need to do so, since it has been the subject of considerable social inquiry in its own right (see Edwards and Tversky, 1967).

We assume that, before action takes place, some decision occurs resulting in a choice among alternative futures. This decision involves the specification of particular goals and the selection of means in the light of beliefs about the past, present, and causation and about values as they have become congealed in images of the future. This process varies in its deliberateness, consciousness, and rationality. The model may be applied even when the decision-making process is truncated, since the contents of the relevant beliefs, values, and images of the future explain in part how much conscious decision-making is likely to take place. The model, as an attempt to explain the liberated role of man as an agent of social change, however, is most efficacious when decision-making is most explicit. The trend toward human mastery leads us to hypothesize that the long-term trends characteristic of modernization result in increases of rationality and consciousness and, therefore, in deliberate planning of political, economic, social, and cultural change. For, by definition, planning ". . . is essentially the attempt to resolve the problems of the future by assessment of future consequences, as implicated in the activities and events of the present and our experience of the past" (McKinney, 1966: 176). To the extent to which such planning orientations become widespread, as they tend to do among people in advanced societies, they lead to the adoption of similar procedures at the microscopic level as ordinary individuals make their way through time and space in their own daily lives.

Individual or collective action. As a result of the decision-making process, some action takes place; it may be individual or collective depending on the unit under consideration and relevant context of applicability. Inaction is considered one alternative of possible actions with its own consequences for the future. Individual behavior or collective action of organizations or whole societies is consequential for the future. The ways in which images of the future cause social action are, of course, complex. An individual actor or social group may be trying to prevent something from occurring as well as trying to make something happen. An unstated image of the future that is the basis of action may be intended to negate stated images of the future. Meanings attached to behavior by the actors involved are of great importance in finding the link between images of the future, decision-making, and action.[10]

The future. Finally, there is the future as it emerges from individual and collective actions. Certainly, there may be—and usually are—variations between the images of the future and the future as it becomes the present with considerable discrepancy between the two and many unintended consequences in the latter. One need not necessarily search for causal factors outside the system we have described. Rather, the struggle to control the future with the accompanying negotiations, compromises, wins, and losses may introduce—in fact almost certainly does introduce—differences between the image and the actuality. The variety of images of the future governing any one aspect of life may be in conflict; but, even with unanimity about images of the future, beliefs about the past, present, and social causation may lead to action that is only more or less effective in achieving the intended results. For such beliefs may be inaccurate in ways that debilitate or misdirect social action.

Additional allowances must be made for various factors exogenous to the model that can and do help shape the emerging future as it is transformed into the present and past. Thus, such a natural phenomenon as an earthquake or tidal wave may unpredictably alter the future location or shape of a city quite apart from the collective action taken to locate it at a particular place and with a given internal structure. An outbreak of hoof-and-mouth disease may make a shambles of the future envisioned for the end of a five-year agricultural development plan. Social factors also may

---

[10] Thus, the interesting developments in ethnomethodology are of great significance in our view (see Garfinkel, 1967, and Garfinkel and Sacks, 1970).

be exogenous, depending on the specification of the units of analysis. For example, in studying the move of a Jewish family in the United States from the central city to the suburbs, one may discover that the family's efforts to escape the Jewish ghetto for a primarily gentile neighborhood are thwarted by the simultaneous decisions of other Jews to move to the same neighborhood. The residential choices of all but the Jewish family being studied may be exogenous to the explanatory scheme as applied to that family, although they can be studied in their own right by redefining the criteria of application of the model. To cite another example, the efforts of the emergent leaders of a new state to create national unity, expressed in new national symbols, may be undermined by the leaders of primordial groups within the country who cling to power by asserting the authority of tradition.

As the future emerges, more or less as planned but usually with unexpected features, it becomes the present and then the past. As aspects of the future (present or past), we show specifically in the diagram human biology, population, the ecosystem, resources, technologies, and organizational settings or institutions including familial, educational, religious, protective, political, economic, and social. In addition to these major institutions, others, of course, could be listed. These "social structures," if we can subsume them together under this term, are shaped within certain constraints by the relevant expectation structures of the actors and groups as they behave.

With the exploitation of the discovery that growth and heredity are controlled by deoxyribonucleic acid, human biology may soon be more subject to manipulation than it is now. Population has been affected less by wars than by the reduction of famine and international control of disease. Each of the latter involved technologies, to be sure, but they also involved revolutionary alterations in belief systems (including scientific knowledge) and implementation of the universal value of human life and survival. They involved, too, other actions of men such as those that result from the decisions of individuals to achieve their ideals of a particular number of children and a certain style of family life.[11]

Man is the chief disturber of ecological balance in the world, often as an unintended consequence of actions to achieve images of the future that are not related to ecology, but increasingly as a result of planned intervention in the ecological system (usually to correct past damage by human action). Obviously, resources are used up by man, and deliberate conservation may be increasingly necessary, but the relations between

---

[11] For a theory of population processes based upon decision theory, see Beshers (1967).

resources, beliefs, and images of the future are more subtle. In developed countries it is no longer resources that limit decisions, but in a fundamental sense it is the decisions that make the resources, at least if any appreciable length of time is included in one's conception beyond the immediate present. David M. Potter (1965:85) comments on the relativity of resources as follows:

> . . . it is, perhaps, necessary only to remember that the American Indians possessed, but benefited little from, the fertile soil which formed an unprecedented source of wealth for the colonists; that the colonists gained little more than the grinding of their grain from the water power which made magnates of the early industrialists; that the early industrialists set little store by the deposits of petroleum and ore which served as a basis for the fortunes of the post-Civil War period; that the industrial captains of the late nineteenth century had no conception of the values that lay latent in water power for generating electricity, which would be developed by the enterprisers of the twentieth century; and that these early twentieth-century enterprisers were as little able to capitalize the values of uranium as the Indians had been five centuries earlier. The social value of natural resources depends entirely upon the aptitude of society for using them.

That technologies and organizational settings or social institutions are created by man is too obvious to belabor here. Yet it is a major premise of this chapter that modern sociologists have so reified each that they have neglected the study of the processes involved in social development and change resulting from the actions of men themselves, especially actions that are directed toward planned change. Such reification has been the result of several factors, not the least of which is the fact that sociologists often deal with such overprocessed reality in the form of census statistics, IBM cards, computer printouts, and mathematical models that it is understandable if man himself somehow slips through their fingers. Also, while most sociologists are socially distant from the centers of power where the role of decision-making is most obvious, they are, at the same time, remote from the intimate details of the daily lives of average persons and fail to see how a model of change based upon images of the future may be applied on the little stage as well.

As the future becomes the present, an opportunity occurs to assess the adequacy of beliefs about the past, present, and social causation, and the desirability of goals and their relevance to basic values. Old images of the future and beliefs may be revised. In this way, a cycle is closed, but an element of feedback is introduced that keeps the system dynamic. Information is processed and changes occur. At every stage, between every element in the model, it is assumed that there is room for innovation and creativity.

The arrows in the diagram indicate both a time sequence and a flow of causality that results in maintaining or changing the various elements in the model. Present structures (human biology, population, etc.) shape beliefs about the past, present, and social causation and the nature of social values, although how they do it depends in part on the different meanings attached to the present as a result of different definitions of the situation. Beliefs and values help shape images of the future, which, in turn, interact with values to order images on a scale of preferences. The result leads to certain decisional outcomes and social action. Such action, along with exogenous factors, produces change by helping to shape the future along particular lines. The emerging future becomes the present that is perceived and given meaning; the cycle begins again, an unending spiral of the creation of society—sometimes in its old forms, but in the modern world usually in changed forms.

The entire model is a feedback loop. We have indicated additionally in the diagram one feedback subloop, since we hypothesize that the reciprocal effects between values and images of the future are of particular importance. Although additional feedback subloops could be shown, we have not done so, since we intend the arrows presumed to produce fairly determinate results not only to show direction of causality but also to indicate neglected questions for sociological research. For example, how do beliefs and values shape images of the future? How do images of the future enter into the decision-making process and shape individual and collective behavior?

SOME DIRECTIVES FOR THE SCIENTIFIC STUDY OF THE FUTURE

It seems clear that the use of scientific research for socially important purposes is increasing, regardless of the "pure" or "applied" intentions of the researcher. To the extent that this is true, what are the implications for the conduct of social research and for professional responsibilities? Must the social scientist be concerned with the action implications of his work? Should he be explicitly action-oriented? Some find the idea that they are playing such a role, consciously or not, totally disagreeable. Most of us have been educated to believe, if not in the naive notion of a value-free social science, at least in detachment, objectivity, and unbiased remoteness *as scientists* from the political and social controversies of the day. Some social scientists have seen the myth of scientific "purity" as a protective cover under which social science could be developed and free inquiry maintained without interference from powerful political and economic interests in the society. Most social scientists believe in it as devoutly as in any religious dogma; but if the assumptions and hypotheses we have presented here are correct, then some effort should be made to elucidate the contribution of social science to the shape of the future and to restudy the professional responsibilities of the social scientist as maker of the future.

Because decision-making requires thinking about the future, there has been more research on the future by agencies of decision-making bodies serving both public and private groups than by academic researchers. Such groups are oriented toward the future through a concern with policy. Although many academics have talked about the future or tried to predict it like oracles, they have not usually tried to study it. It is our view that social scientific images of the future surely will promote individual and collective actions that are designed to produce the future. Unless social scientists are willing to accept what may be intolerable consequences, the creation and dissemination of such images should not be left to the paid agents of special interests (whether of governmental organizations or private corporations); nor should they be left to the scientific "purists" among the social scientific fraternity who mistakenly claim that they are only after the facts and who deny that they are playing any role in shaping the future through their research and teaching beyond discovering and spreading the "truth."

What may be needed is a reorganization of the focus of the discipline of sociology itself so that the future becomes a standard concern for at least some group of sociologists. Even the lone academic investigator might responsibly make his work a significant contribution to the emerging future. Our contention is that it is more or less of a contribution whether the researcher believes it or not, but its relevance to the future can be enhanced and can be made explicit. Some sociologists have made similar observations in the past, and may agree with this view now. What has been neglected is strategy. How can those social scientists who wish to do so make their work as scientists more relevant to the future?

As answers to this question, we have formulated a set of directives, which, if followed in the conduct of social inquiry, may increase the relevance of social science to the future. We regard these directives as hypotheses and, therefore, as tentative and subject to revision and elaboration. Their sources are to be found in our own studies of new national decision-makers, in the literature on the study of the future (see the annotated bibliography in the Appendix), and in the cybernetic-decisional theory of social change.

1. The directive of dynamic orientation. To increase a study's relevance for the future, the study should have a dynamic orientation. Society should not be viewed as a static system existing only in the present.

Rather, past, present, and future should be seen as interpenetrating each other, and society should be viewed as moving *from* something *to* something else. A dynamic orientation leads the researcher to think in terms of what Lasswell calls "developmental constructs" where the time dimension is "built-in" and "trend-thinking" is required.[12] Although longitudinal data are not necessary, they are helpful. Mainly, the point of view and interpretation of the researcher are critical.

2. **The directive of uncertainty.** To increase a study's relevance for the future, the assumptions on which the study is based should include the notion that social reality is more or less uncertain. Reality should be viewed as problematic in at least two ways: first, it is problematic in the sheer knowing of it; second, and most relevant in the present context, reality is problematic in that it is contingent upon the actions men take. Although the emphasis should be on the probabilities of different outcomes for the emergent future, consideration should also be given to the problematics of the present and past, both of which are merely complexes of sense data organized with respect to some prior frame of reference.

Since our methods of attaching exact probabilities to different versions of social truth are so imprecise, the researcher may, at the conclusion of his work, report only one version of the past, present, and future, perhaps the most probable or the most significant; but as he carries out his investigation he may find it useful to create different versions, including (perhaps especially) unlikely or even currently outlandish ones, and examining their credibility. In this way, the scientist plays a role in creating new and different images of the future as well as in testing or finding means for implementing current images. In so doing, he himself, through the images he creates and clarifies, may become a causal factor in determining individual or collective action and, as such, the results of his work are among the contingencies upon which the emerging future depends.[13]

3. **The directive of self-awareness.** In order to increase a study's relevance for the future, the social scientist should recognize that his efforts are somehow, and to some degree, affecting the future. Researchers should be aware of the possible effects of their results in changing images of the future, and this awareness should be an explicit part of the inquiry. This requires that thought be given to the question of just what effect given results may have, and it requires such thought whether or not the inquiry was *intended* to have any effect or to be relevant to the future.

---

[12] Murphy (1961) advocates a similar future orientation and, to some extent, illustrates this and other directives.

[13] Several illustrations of the latter point are to be found in Jacques Freymond (1965).

4. The directive of value relevance. This issue has long been the subject of debate, and there still exist clear lines of disagreement that are sure to interfere with communication. Nonetheless, we suggest that to increase a study's relevance for the future the study should be oriented toward some basic values within a society. Special attention should be given to the possible existence of universal or common human values. The more value-relevant a study, the greater the chance that it will bear on the future, since the direction and tempo of change are geared to the basic values that are discovered, clarified, distributed, and created. Through social scientific research the sociologist can contribute to the discovery, clarification, and distribution of values. By combining different values on higher levels of abstraction he may even create new ones.

5. The directive of value-structure inconsistency. The study of those phenomena constituting areas of inconsistency or discrepancy between values (that define how society and people *should be* with respect to some particular social relationship) and social structure (that reveals how society and people *actually are*) should be of particular relevance to the emerging future. Assuming that there is tension in such situations that invites resolution through alteration of either the value or the structure, one may expect some change. Examples of such studies may be found in Myrdal's *An American Dilemma* and the Kinsey Report. In the former, the value of equality was set against the structure of inequality of the black American;[14] in the latter, values in the form of moral codes of sexual behavior were set against actual sexual behavior. The two authors differed in their suggested resolutions of the inconsistencies, and subsequent social change seems to have taken different courses. In the case of the black American, the structure is being altered to conform more closely to the value. In the case of sexual behavior, the moral codes appear to be eroding and conforming more to actual sexual practices.

Wilbert E. Moore (1963:20) states this general point as follows:

> Usually the inconsistency between the ideal and the actual is tension-producing and hospitable to change. Overt violation of prevalent practices must somehow be dealt with, for evil genuinely challenges the persistence of morally supported standards. Widespread recognition that human performance falls short of perfection may lead to the acceptance of more "realistic" standards, but this development is itself a significant change. Generally, however, ideals are somewhat more likely to be exalted than downgraded, and endure as a perennial challenge to imperfections.

---

[14] Myrdal at one point formulates the conflict as one between two different valuations rather than between a value and a structure. Since structures usually are supported by some value or values, there is validity in his view. However, we think that, given the history and importance of the value of equality in redesigning structures of inequality, a more accurate representation is the one we make between value and structure.

The inconsistency between the ideal and the actual is, of course, a well-known source of inspiration for utopian writers. It was the method of the most famous of utopian tracts that remains one of the few books of the Age of the Renaissance directly concerned with politics that is still widely read. J. H. Hexter (1967) says that what Thomas More

> seems to have contemplated was the contrast of the biblical Christian way of life that the humanists in his circle of friends held forth as the standard for man's imitation with the actual ways of life he had seen about him—from the low life that as deputy sheriff he had observed weekly for several years in the London sheriff's court all the way to the very high life that he occasionally encountered because of his friendships with men in the inner circle of the court of Henry VIII. The confrontation of a going society with biblical Christianity always has latent explosive possibilities, and in More's case these were realized when it led him to ask himself what the temporal conditions for a true Christian commonwealth actually were. Before he had quite finished writing what he intended to write about what a Christian commonwealth ought to be, he was offered a high position at the English court on terms both honorable and financially attractive. The comparison thus abruptly forced on his attention between the conditions necessary for a true Christian commonwealth and the conditions which actually prevailed in the putatively Christian commonwealth ruled by his native prince, Henry VIII, magnified the explosive force of his confrontation of the world as it was with the world as scripture said it should be. The result was a book, *Utopia*, that was both extraordinary and extravagant.

Related directives may be generated by seeking out discrepancies or conflicts not just between the actual and the ideal or between structure and value, but between structure and structure and between value and value. For example, in Part II Henry Winthrop discusses the utility of paying attention to current discrepancies between science and technology on the one hand and traditional group assumptions on the other. In general, one set of institutions of a society may be contradictory to others or one set of values in conflict with others. If there are areas of social life where such conflicting elements of institutions or values impinge on each other, these are prime possibilities for social change and for studying the emerging future.

   6. The directive of the pull of the future. To increase a study's relevance for the future, the researcher should be explicitly aware of the assumption that different possibilities for the future may be primarily manifested in the present by images of the future. Thus, images of the future relevant to any subject of social inquiry invite investigation. The actual future is to some extent a consequence of the images of the future that are present within a society, although not necessarily the most popular images. The most probable possibilities don't always occur; the less probable sometimes do. Among the questions that can be asked under this directive are: What images of the future are most commonly held? Do different socioeconomic, racial or ethnic, and age groups hold different images of the future? How do the elite differ from the masses in their images? How do images of the future function for the individual? What factors account for the strength of some images of the future and the weaknesses of others in affecting the future? Who are the creators of the significant images of the future and what explains the varied content of the images they create? What explains the rise and fall of dominant images of the future?

Arthur L. Stinchcombe in his book *Rebellion in a High School* found that differential images of the future among high school students helped to explain whether or not the students became rebels. He says that the "... future, not the past, explains adolescent rebellion, contrary to the hypothesis that deviant attitudes are the result of distinctively rebel biographies ... we hold that deviant values or crippling of the ego are traceable to differences in the futures of adolescents." His argument is that adolescents whose images of their own occupational future are such that they expect to become members of the manual working class in the next labor market cohort see no clear relation between what they are doing in school and their future status. Thus, their current performance loses meaning, and current self-restraint is perceived as irrelevant to the achievement of long-run goals. The student "... reacts negatively to a conformity that offers nothing concrete. He claims autonomy from adults because their authority does not promise him a satisfactory future" (Stinchcombe, 1964:6). Stinchcombe's study is an excellent illustration of how the future may cause the present, of some of the questions that may be asked about the pull of the future, and of the way conventional sociological explanations may be revised as a result of investigating the effects of the pull of the future.

7. The directive of the substitution of space for time. This directive is intended to alert the researcher to the possibility that the past or present of some particular place at one time may serve as a model of the future of some other place. Moore (1967:76) refers to this as the "replication of historic sequences," and sees the definite possibility of some repetition in developing areas "despite the social speedup that a common world experience affords." Thus, differentiation in space may serve as a heuristic device for differentiation in time. If one can determine that the flow of diffusion is from place x to place y, then one may be able to study the future of place y by studying the past and present of place x. In the same way that one might predict the weather in Chicago tomorrow by knowing the weather in Omaha today, one might predict the future internal structure of metropolitan Omaha by knowing how metropolitan Dallas or Los Angeles has grown and differentiated in the past decade. As another example, we might ask if we can learn anything about the future of Vietnam by studying the past and present of Korea. Clearly, no simple equating of one place with another will reveal any exact prophecy, but as a technique of analysis and projection the substitution of space for time offers many unexplored possibilities for the researcher of the future. Of course, assumptions and inferences will have to be made and borne out, as is always the case, if knowledge is going to be the result. If this directive is followed, comparative studies may take on a new significance in that they may acquire developmental and futuristic implications.

8. **The directive of manipulative priority.** To increase a study's relevance for the future, explanatory theories should be formulated to maximize the use of concepts that are within—or that are likely to be brought within—the power of men to control. Inevitable, natural, or impersonal forces as causes should be eschewed in favor of human behavioral or ideational variables. Explanations presented only in terms of broad processes, such as urbanization and industrialization, should be specified to include the actions, and ideas and ideals behind them, that men and groups have taken or might take to control their own individual and collective destinies. This may mean that the easy and handy explanation may have to be by-passed in the search for the manipulable variables that explain at least as much of the variance. One example of how the search for manipulative variables can be facilitated has been suggested by Robin M. Williams, Jr. (1953:81), in a discussion of the contribution of action-experience in intergroup relations to social research. He notes that:

> Above all, observation of social action aimed at alteration or stabilization of intergroup relations can increase our sensitivity to the degree and kind of *accessibility to manipulation* characterizing the major causal factors in the situation, and can provide preliminary indications as to the magnitude of effects that may be anticipated.

Williams suggests further that analysis of ". . . attempts to induce or retard social change can direct research attention to factors that are crucial, from the standpoint of social importance, but not seen in that perspective so long as a purely detached research orientation prevails" (1953:81). We agree with him that good theory should serve this purpose, but frequently it has not.

The implications of a shift in emphasis from description to control, of course, go beyond epistemology. They include, on the one hand, a different conception of man in society. The focus on control carries with it a conception of man as having integrity, dignity, and personal worth; or, perhaps more accurately, a conception that *permits* actors to have integrity, dignity, and personal worth. Deutsch (1963:131–132) gives these usually vague concepts operational meaning within his cybernetic model of the polity largely by linking them to the "unimpaired functioning of the *facilities* that carry the processes of self-determination." He defines them as "respect for every man's right to learn at his own speed and with his own inner equipment, in an unbroken sequence of autonomous acts of learning, in which his own unique stored past and his own acquired preferences at every single step have at least some share in the outcome."

On the other hand, focusing on control or self-determination rather than prediction permits a separation of the knowing activity from an implicit valuation. McWilliams (1966:100–101) puts it as follows:

> The most urgent necessity of contemporary life lies in breaking down the connection, established by early modern theorists, between *prediction* and *control*. We do not need to know how history is going in order to know how or for what purpose we might seek to control it. Prediction becomes relevant only as a second order question: once we know what sort of controls we desire, prediction may be essential to establishing them. The two questions, however, form a hierarchy and not a unity: the ethical question, implicit in the idea of control, ranks higher in the order of priorities. Unless the two are separated, we run the peril which modern theorists always ran: that of allowing prediction to command control, of allowing "what works" to determine what is right, of asserting with Hegel that *Weltgeschichte* is *Weltgericht*.

We believe, then, that *effective control* should be the prime criterion of knowledge rather than *accurate prediction* or *precise description*. Each of the latter can exist without the former. The idea of control or self-determination invites the creation of knowledge for shaping the social realities of the emerging future toward valued ends. Social scientists can then "forecast the future" not so much by projecting factors beyond man's control but rather by participating in the process of deciding what the future should be and finding the means for making it come about that way.

9. The directive of importing the future into the present. To increase a study's relevance to the future, it should be linked to efforts to import the future into the present. ". . . [O]ne of the most powerful ways of achieving social change is to imagine in vivid detail a desirable and achievable future, and then *build* a part of that future in the present—rather than merely pleading for it to be built" (Waskow, 1969:78). For the social scientist, of course, the additional obligation is to design whatever part of the future that he tries to build in such a manner that he can test hypotheses, or if it is an exploratory study, at least learn what effect particular variables may have. This is, in a sense, an effort to approximate the experimental model through designing and monitoring social action for change.

An example—the sit-ins of the civil rights movement—may help illustrate the sort of thing we have in mind. If the sit-ins had been planned *and* studied by a social scientist, one can think of them as a deliberate and conscious method. Waskow (1969:79–80) describes what the civil rights movement said:

> Our desirable-achievable future is that we want to be able to eat in integrated restaurants. We will not petition legislatures to require integration, we will not petition the owners of the restaurants to integrate, *we will simply create the future.* That is, *we* will integrate the restaurants, and it will rest upon those who have the power of law and the power of ownership in their hands, to decide how to respond to that creation. So we will build *now* what it is we want to exist in the future, and society will have to react to that. It will have to let us build it, or it will have to punish us for building it. If it punishes us for building it, we believe we can build support around that vision of the future, and can, therefore, mobilize people into action to achieve that future.

If we add to this a design of action that includes experimental controls and variables (different types of restaurants, different types of persons as sit-ins in different numbers, a longitudinal approach, etc.), the readiness of the present for the future—this particular future—can be determined along with an assessment of effective means of achieving it.

Clearly, there are dilemmas for the social scientist who ventures so boldly into deliberate social change, although not all efforts to import the future into the present are as controversial as were the sit-ins. One must confront the question of the rights of human research subjects, the restaurant owners as well as the persons sitting-in, and the possible negative consequences of the disorder that one may produce. As Waskow (1969:80) says, it is "disorder because it obeys the 'law and order' of some more or less distant future, and is therefore likely to be 'unlawful' or 'disorderly' by the standards of the present." Disorder may be creative, however, in helping to produce social change in some desired direction.

10. The directive of making "possidictions." Finally, we suggest that the relevance of a study for the future may be increased by making what Waskow calls "possidictions":

Just as this kind of future-building looks for the possible rather than either a replica of the present or an impossible though desirable future (impossible within the given time span) so it is an examination of the seriously *possible* rather than the most likely. Instead of being a prediction—that is, the author's best judgment as to what present trends are likely to produce—it is what might be called a *possidiction*—that is, the author's projection of how certain seeds of change that exist already might be made to flourish, given certain kinds of political action. The possidiction describes worlds that are, say 30% likely—as against either worlds that are only 1% likely or those that are 60% likely. There is a serious chance they can be brought into being, but it will take a lot of doing. And the possidiction acts as an incitement to the necessary action (Waskow, 1969:83).

The directive of making possidictions is a logical conclusion to much that we have said about social change and images of the future in the preceding pages. The directive explicitly takes into account the search for the real possibilities for the future that may exist in the present. One place, of course, that the researcher may look for possidictions—for the seeds of the future in the present—is not with those sections of the population "who are utterly out of power and see no hope of ever gaining it; not those who presently hold it; but those who can seriously imagine that they might be able to change the way the society operates" (Waskow, 1969:83). Although we agree that such "emergent" groups are particularly important, we would exclude neither the powerful nor dispossessed groups because the former can lead genuine change too and the latter may have latent capacities for change if only their interests are articulated.[15]

SOME DIRECTIVES FOR SOCIOLOGISTS AS MAKERS OF THE FUTURE

Implicit in this discussion are two directives that define the role of the social scientist as maker of the future. *The first is the directive of social responsibility.* In the course of scientific investigation sociologists and other social scientists, as makers of the future, should take responsible action about the effects their results may have. There is, perhaps, little that we can add here to this much discussed and long-debated issue. On the one hand, there are the well-known relations to social values of the processes of selection of a problem for study, dissemination of results, and recommendations for policy. On the other hand, there is the

---

[15] For a list of twelve ways to predict social trends, see Beckwith (1967). Beckwith's list overlaps considerably with our ten directives.

equally well-known conflict between being simply a "tool" of some client, or even of "truth" in the abstract, and being an active judge of the purposes for which knowledge should or should not be used. Despite all that has been written about it, the latter course remains largely uncharted, but we know of the experience of the atomic scientists and of the impersonal bureaucratic behavior of the Nazi functionaries: sticking one's head in the sand is not a satisfactory solution.

We suggest four neglected directions for future concern that involve the directive of social responsibility. First, the effects of social science knowledge on policy formation and action should receive greater attention as a subject of investigation itself.[16] A sociology of social science could tell us to what degree and in what way social science does in fact affect the future. Without knowing this and without testing our hypotheses about it in some rigorous way, there is nothing to judge about the effects of social science on the future.

Second, there are a few guidelines leading to the specification of common or universal values. Most people can now agree upon such values as human life, health, security, affection, and level of living. Other candidates for inclusion are emergent and generally derive from the values of human dignity and individual self-fulfillment. Given the fact that ends as well as means are increasingly open to choice and manipulation, then one must acknowledge that they are open also to be influenced by, among other things, social science. What are the dimensions of the good life? Is there an emergent set of universal or common values? What is the dynamic mechanism that tends to make certain values universal? Are there neglected social goals that should be pursued in the place of those that are being pursued? If so, in what way are their implications for social life superior to the goals they might replace? What might be accepted as convincing evidence that some values are better than others? In trying to answer such questions, the social scientist not only studies values in the usual way, but also consciously enters into the creation and appraisal of values.

Third, one strategy that may face the social science community as it becomes increasingly responsible for the future is the choice between monopoly or sharing of enlightenment. The level of control or the timing of release of certain information may itself importantly affect the future. The present tendency among sociologists to avoid facing this question

---

[16] Rainwater and Yancey's (1967) social science and public policy report on *The Negro Family: The Case for National Action* by Daniel Patrick Moynihan deserves to be mentioned as a good example of one approach to evaluation of the effectiveness of policy-relevant social science findings. The controversy over the report is documented in their book.

squarely by repeating the litany of a free and open dissemination of information is understandable. It is a difficult question. One can envisage a situation in which the sociologist might behave just as public health officials do today when, fearing to cause panic and widespread disorganization, they decide to withhold certain information about the spread of a dread disease in a city. Our concern here is: should the individual social researcher of the future be left to confront such choices without guidance and institutional support from his professional group?

Fourth, the recruitment of social scientists may have significant effects on the nature of social scientific findings. Most of us would agree that the social backgrounds and social contexts within which social scientists work affect their selection of problems, style of research, and interpretation of findings. What strategies should be followed in recruiting social scientists so that their numbers contain a representative sampling of world experience? Persons of different nationalities, social classes, races, and religions, for example, should be represented in the profession. Such persons, we assume, would carry into their professional careers many of their previous experiences and identifications with consequences for the direction and form of new formulations about social reality. Whom do we select to become social scientists in order to decrease the probability that the blind parochialisms of any one section of world experience will dominate the process of the production of new social scientific knowledge? We are not suggesting that only those who experience a phenomenon are qualified to study it, that, for example, only blacks can study blacks or that only military elites can study military elites. Rather, our point is that important sociological questions deserve to be seen from a number of different perspectives simultaneously. It may be by the conflict in competing views that truth is served.

A second directive may be stated as follows: *the researcher should strive to give as much consideration to the formulation of positive idealistic images of the future as to negative and cynical ones.* The construction of desirable self-fulfilling propositions should be as much the strategy of the scientific architect of the future as the picturing of deleterious trends combined with the faint, and usually unanalyzed, hope that somebody may intervene and prevent them from continuing.[17] We raise the question: until we know more about the effects of images of the future, is it not dangerous to create negative, pessimistic, or cynical images? Counter-utopias may, as Moore (1966b:772) says, ". . . dampen and redirect trends of change." But mightn't they sometimes become self-ful-

---

[17] For some of the blunders of *negative* forecasting, see Gamarra's (1967) *Erroneous Predictions and Negative Comments Concerning Exploration, Territorial Expansion, Scientific and Technological Development.*

filling? We are neither calling for the sort of optimism that Mills (1961) termed "sunshine moralism," nor are we suggesting that the researcher should not be skeptical and realistic; rather, we suggest that the social scientist should search reality to the point where he can reveal some solutions for the problems he sees and can counter negativism with positive solutions equally founded upon social facts. The stubborn researcher who refuses to accept lightly an emergent conclusion of his research because it contains a pessimistic image of the future should perhaps drive himself on to additional data, other frames of reference, or new concepts that reveal reality more completely than before while also creating not complacency but rational hope and purposive action.

Positive idealism concerns the future. What we suggest is the opposite of glossing over present inadequacies. An attack on present practices in the automobile industry that produce cars that are "unsafe at any speed" may contain a devastating critique of the present and at the same time contain idealistic images of the possibilities for the future. The inadequacies can be corrected. Our point is that the future is open, the possibilities for it are real. Until the future becomes present, it is not strictly known: *there are no future facts.*

This directive should be followed by social scientists without giving up their critical function as intellectuals and without becoming toadies to the Establishment. We are simply saying that hypercritical negativism can become as much of an obstacle to progress as can unwarranted optimism. The tough combination of realistic observation with idealistic creativity that transcends the boundaries of the present into the real possibilities for the future may help us tell Moore's "eager traveler" how he can get there from here. Thus, can sociologists combat those who would condemn the future to the limitations of the present and, like the *philosophes* of the Enlightenment, help to change the world through their reinterpretations of it.

In conclusion, we stress that we do not intend to say anything antiscientific in this essay. Quite the contrary, the theory of change and the directives should be put to work within the scientific framework. The canons of science with respect to data specification, collection, analysis, and interpretation must be met. Falsification must be avoided. The facts, such as they are, must be faced; the truth, relative though it may be, is itself to be valued. However, we wish to stress what every scientist knows: the practice of science includes speculation, and the scientific method is based to an important degree on the use of creative imagination. In the study of the future there is a need to cultivate both speculation and creative imagination.

REFERENCES

Beckwith, Burnham P.
1967   The Next Five Hundred Years. Jericho, N.Y.: Exposition-University Book.
Bell, Wendell
1964   Jamaican Leaders: Political Attitudes in a New Nation. Berkeley and Los Angeles: University of California Press.
Bell, Wendell (ed.)
1967   The Democratic Revolution in the West Indies: Studies in Nationalism, Leadership, and the Belief in Progress. Cambridge, Mass.: Schenkman.
Bell, Wendell, and Ivar Oxaal
1964   Decisions of Nationhood: Political and Social Development in the British Caribbean. Denver, Colorado: Social Science Foundation, University of Denver.
Bendix, Reinhard, and Bennett Berger
1959   "Images of society and problems of concept formation in sociology." Pp. 92–118 in Llewellyn Gross (ed.), Symposium on Sociological Theory. Evanston, Ill.: Row, Peterson.
Beshers, James M.
1967   Population Processes in Social Systems. New York: Free Press.
Bosserman, Phillip
1968   Dialectical Sociology: An Analysis of the Sociology of Georges Gurvitch. Boston: Porter Sargent.
Boulding, Kenneth E.
1965   The Meaning of the Twentieth Century: The Great Transition. New York: Harper & Row.
1956   The Image: Knowledge in Life and Society. Ann Arbor: The University of Michigan Press.
Brumbaugh, Robert S.
1966   "Applied metaphysics: truth and passing time." Review of Metaphysics 19 (June):647–666.
Cantril, Hadley
1963   "A study of aspirations." Scientific American 208 (February): 42ff.
Deutsch, Karl W.
1963   The Nerves of Government: Models of Political Communication and Control. New York: Free Press.
Edwards, Ward, and Amos Tversky (eds.)
1967   Decision Making: Selected Readings. Harmondsworth, Middlesex, England: Penguin Books.
Etzioni, Amitai
1967   "Toward a theory of societal guidance." American Journal of Sociology 73 (September):173–187

Eulau, Heinz
    1958   "H. D. Lasswell's developmental analysis." Western Political
            Quarterly 11 (June):229–242.
Freymond, Jacques
    1965   "Introduction—forecasting and Europe." Pp. xiii–xxx in Bertrand
            de Jouvenel (ed.), Futuribles: Studies in Conjecture II. Geneva:
            Droz.
Gamarra, Nancy T.
    1967   Erroneous Predictions and Negative Comments Concerning Ex-
            ploration, Territorial Expansion, Scientific and Technological De-
            velopment. Cited in The Futurist 2 (August 1968):120–121.
Garfinkel, Harold
    1967   Studies in Ethnomethodology. Englewood Cliffs, N.J.: Prentice-
            Hall.
Garfinkel, Harold, and Harvey Sacks
    1970   "On formal structures of practical actions." Pp. 337–366 in J. C.
            McKinney and E. A. Tiryakian (eds.), Theoretical Sociology.
            New York: Appleton-Century-Crofts.
Hexter, J. H.
    1967   "Claude de Seyssel and normal politics in the Age of Machia-
            velli." Pp. 389–415 in Charles S. Singleton (ed.), Art, Science and
            History in the Renaissance. Baltimore: Johns Hopkins Press.
Holzner, Burkart
    1968   Reality Construction in Society. Cambridge, Mass.: Schenkman.
Jouvenel, Bertrand de
    1965   Futuribles: Studies in Conjecture II. Geneva: Droz.
    1963   Futuribles: Studies in Conjecture I. Geneva: Droz.
Lasswell, Harold D.
    1966   "The changing image of human nature: the socio-cultural aspect,
            future-oriented man." American Journal of Psychoanalysis 26
            (no. 2):157–166.
    1948   The Analysis of Political Behavior: An Empirical Approach. Lon-
            don: Routledge & Kegan Paul.
McKinney, John C.
    1966   Constructive Typology and Social Theory. New York: Appleton-
            Century-Crofts.
McWilliams, Wilson C.
    1966   "On time and history." Yale Review 56 (Autumn):91–103.
Mannheim, Karl
    1936   Ideology and Utopia. New York: Harcourt, Brace & World, A
            Harvest Book.
Mau, James A.
    1968   Social Change and Images of the Future: A Study of the Pursuit
            of Progress in Jamaica. Cambridge, Mass.: Schenkman.

Miller, Cecil
1961   "The self-fulfilling prophecy: a reappraisal." Ethics 72 (October):46–51.
Mills, C. Wright
1961   The Sociological Imagination. New York: Grove Press.
Moore, Wilbert E.
1967   Order and Change: Essays in Comparative Sociology. New York: Wiley.
1966a   "Global sociology: the world as a singular system." American Journal of Sociology 71 (March):475–482.
1966b   "The utility of utopias." American Sociological Review 31 (December):765–772.
1963   Social Change, Englewood Cliffs, N.J.: Prentice-Hall.
Moskos, Charles C., Jr.
1967   The Sociology of Political Independence: A Study of Nationalist Attitudes Among West Indian Leaders. Cambridge, Mass.: Schenkman.
Murphy, Gardner
1961   Human Potentialities. New York: Basic Books.
The New York Times
1966   (January 30):10E.
Oxaal, Ivar
1968   Black Intellectuals Come to Power: The Rise of Creole Nationalism in Trinidad and Tobago. Cambridge, Mass.: Schenkman.
Polak, Frederik L.
1961   The Image of the Future: Enlightening the Past, Orientating the Present, Forecasting the Future, Vols. I and II. New York: Oceana.
Potter, David M.
1965   People of Plenty: Economic Abundance and the American Character. Chicago: The University of Chicago Press, Phoenix Books.
Rainwater, Lee, and William L. Yancey
1967   The Moynihan Report and the Politics of Controversy. Cambridge, Mass.: MIT Press.
Stinchcombe, Arthur L.
1964   Rebellion in a High School. Chicago: Quadrangle Books.
Strauss, Anselm
1956   The Social Psychology of George Herbert Mead. Chicago: The University of Chicago Press.
Tiryakian, Edward A.
1966   "Sociohistorical phenomena: the seen, the unseen, the foreseeable." Paper prepared for a joint session of the American Studies Association and the American Historical Association (December).

Ward, Lester F.
  1914   Pure Sociology: A Treatise on the Origin and Spontaneous Development of Society. London: MacMillan.
Waskow, Arthur I.
  1969   "Looking forward: 1999." Pp. 78–98 in Robert Jungk and Johan Galtung (eds.), Mankind 2000. Oslo: Universitets-forlaget.
Wells, H. G.
  1913   The Discovery of the Future. New York: B. W. Huebsch.
Williams, Robin M., Jr.
  1953   "Application of research to practice in intergroup relations." American Sociological Review 18 (February):78–83.

A Paradigm for the Analysis of Time Perspectives and Images of the Future

WENDELL BELL, JAMES A. MAU,
BETTINA J. HUBER, AND MENNO BOLDT

Paradigms may serve a variety of functions, from simply bringing assumptions into the open to promoting cumulative theoretic interpretation. They may be no more pretentious than an outline, or they may constitute a systematic theory in which every concept is logically related to others in the system. In between, a paradigm may be viewed as "a device for instituting systematic description," (Gross, 1959:78). Their general purpose is to provide a fieldglass not a blinder, a tentative tool not an absolute formula (Merton, 1957:16). In this chapter we offer a paradigm of the "in-between" type as a tentative tool for the analysis of time perspectives and images of the future in social science literature.

In this book, the authors describe the utility and the ways of studying society as process, as a sequence of past, present and future, and they give some concrete examples. In the preceding chapter Bell and Mau hypothesized that time perspectives, especially images of the future, help shape both action and the future as it comes into existence. All societies, of course, have time orientations. They all must deal with the problem of time and have their conceptions of past, present, and future. For example, Kluckhohn and Strodtbeck (1961) single out five problems that are both crucial and common to all human groups. Among them is the temporal focus of human life—time orientation (see Moore, 1963b). Where societies "differ is in the preferential ordering of the alternatives (rank-order emphases), and a very great deal can be told about the particular society or part of a society being studied and much can be predicted about the direction of change within it if one knows what the rank-order emphasis is" (Kluckhohn and Strodtbeck, 1961:14). We add that all social scientists have their conceptions of time and their images of the future, that such conceptions and images are more or less implicitly imbedded in social scientists' constructions of social reality, and that much can be learned about the message of any particular social scientist by making his time perspectives and images of the future explicit. Several of the contributors to this volume touch on this point in their contributions, and Menno Boldt and Pauline B. Bart devote their entire essays to applications of parts of our paradigm. Thus, for us, the study of the future importantly includes the analysis of time perspectives and images of the future in social science literature itself, as it also includes such studies in the natural and physical sciences, religion and philosophy, and art, literature, drama, films, journalism, and television.

Time orientations are linked to other basic orientations, although possibly in different ways for different groups, and are important parts of total world views. Thus, basic conceptions of man and society are interwoven with time perspectives and images of the future as part of the same matrix. We assume that all intellectuals—artists, scientists, and priests—are involved in creating or popularizing different views of the world, varying constructions of time and the nature of man and society. Although today politics may be most obviously replacing religion as the source of those images of the world that are most powerful in shaping the future, science is of increasing importance and, for images of the social world, social science is growing in influence. Thus, the analysis of time perspectives and images of the future in social science is in part an effort to understand some of the basic orientations and key constructions of social reality that are profoundly part of world views that shape the direction and tempo of change in society. This is taken into account in the paradigm.

The definition of time can become appallingly complex. With St. Augustine, one might say, "What then is time? If no one asks me, I know; if I want to explain it to a questioner, I do not know" (Priestley, 1968; 146). Yet he went on and developed a theory of time based upon experience, memory, and expectation:

> What happens, happens *now*, he argued; that is, it is always an experience, idea, or thing which is "present." Nevertheless, we can construct a meaningful temporal series accounting for past and future in terms of memory and expectation. By "past" we then mean the present memory experience of a thing past; by "future," the present expectation of anticipation of a future thing (Meyerhoff, 1960:8).

Clearly, time as experience is in part subjective and "differs radically from the regular, uniform, quantitative units characteristic of an objective metric" (Meyerhoff, 1960:13).

Following Moore (1963a:23), we additionally think of time as necessarily tied to change. He says that "Without time, then there is no change. Without change, however, there is no sense of time." Time, then, is "experienced as a duration between significant events" (Holzner, 1968:81). Some changes occur in repetitive cycles of varying lengths that constitute the basic rhythms of society. They may be based on hours (e.g., traffic peaks in a large city), days (e.g., sleep), weeks (e.g., Sunday churchgoing), months (e.g, paying the rent), or years (e.g., Christmas dinner). Such recurring events act as landmarks in structuring time. Other changes are nonrepetitive and may be irreversible, the ultimate changes being life and death. Change alone, however, does not give us time. It is rather the relationship between change and nonchange, "some things moving and others apparently keeping still. . . . With this relation between what is changing and what is not changing, or between changes that are fast and those that are slower, the problem of Time is bound up" (Priestley, 1968:41).

With this brief introduction, we turn to the paradigm itself. Although it focuses on time perspectives and images of the future, it deals, necessarily as we have seen, with questions of basic assumptions and presuppositions as well and with questions of perspectives on change.[1]

I. HOW DOES THE AUTHOR USE THE CONCEPT OF TIME?

This is the basic query in the paradigm. It is designed to determine the author's temporal orientation in the particular work or works under consideration. (A) Does the author have a static or dynamic orientation? Does he treat time as (1) a single point separate from other times or (2) as "an interval on some continuum of change" (i.e., polity, economy, and society as in a state of becoming)? (B) Does he deal with past, present, and future (1) as independent of each other or (2) as interpenetrating each other? And (C) does he think of time as revealing trends in political, economic, or social development that can be extrapolated into the future?

II. WHAT ARE THE AUTHOR'S BASIC ASSUMPTIONS ABOUT HUMAN NATURE?

The aspect of human nature of particular relevance here is presumed rigidity or capacity for change. Its importance rests on the assumption

---

[1] For example, see Berger and Luckmann (1966), Holzner (1968), Merton (1957, especially Chapters 12 and 13), and Mannheim (1936).

that conceptions of political, economic, and social change and images of the future are influenced and constrained by a researcher's or theorist's notions about the malleability of human nature. Also, the sort of man who is put into the political, economic, and social system by a social scientist has implications for the kinds of alternative futures that are deemed possible. Thus, we ask (A) is man viewed as being basically good, neutral, or evil? And what are the relevant dimensions of good and evil contained in the author's assumptions? (B) What are the limits of political, economic, and social change imposed by the presumed nature of man? How do assumptions about the flexibility of human nature influence an author's concepts and theories? Specifically, does the author view man's possibilities for development as being (1) rigidly fixed or limited, (2) capable of slow evolution and change, or (3) widely flexible and constantly being modified? If human nature is not viewed as being rigidly fixed, then is man conceived (a) as "making himself" or (b) as the product of impersonal forces beyond his control? And if man's nature is viewed as in flux (or not changing except in relation to a changing environment), is it "moving" toward (c) improvement or (d) deterioration, according to the author's reconstruction of social reality?

III. WHAT ARE THE AUTHOR'S BASIC ASSUMPTIONS ABOUT THE NATURE OF POLITY, ECONOMY, AND SOCIETY?

Again, rigidity or capacity for change is the specific facet of the author's assumptions about the nature of polity, economy, and society that concerns us. Images of the future in an author's work, we assume, will be related to his basic assumptions about the nature of structures, organizations, and institutions. We begin by asking (A) whether the author views polity, economy, and society as being essentially good, neutral, or bad. And, we ask, what does the author mean by these terms?

(B) What are the limitations of change imposed by the author's assumptions and preconceptions about the nature of polity, economy, and society? How do assumptions about the potential of these structures for change and how do positive or negative evaluations of them relate to the social scientific concepts and theories applied by the author? (1) Are polity, economy, and society viewed as essentially stable systems that tend toward the maintenance of equilibrium, or (2) are they viewed as dynamic systems constantly changing? If they are conceived as constantly changing, then (a) is that change viewed as a slow process of evolution or (b) is change viewed as rapid, revolutionary, or cataclysmic?

(C) Does the author assume that polity, economy, and society have potential for progressive change with respect to (1) the mastery of material resources and the development of technical capacities, and (2) the mobilization of human resources and the modification of values, norms, and institutions?

Or (D) does the author assume that they are moving generally in a deleterious direction and that they are unlikely to experience progressive changes with respect to (1) material resources and technology and (2) social and cultural elements? We ask in (C) and (D) whether the author views the contemporary state of affairs in polity, economy, and society as satisfactory or unsatisfactory for the general population or some specified subpopulations, and whether he sees structures as capable of being changed and as likely to change in a more desirable direction.

IV. WHAT ARE THE AUTHOR'S BASIC ASSUMPTIONS ABOUT CAUSE AND EFFECT?

An author's view of social reality, including the assumptions we have discussed concerning the nature of man and society, the nature of change, and his temporal orientations, is intricately involved with basic notions about cause and effect. We must, therefore, ask several questions concerning the author's assumptions that are interrelated and possibly overlapping. At the most general level we inquire: (A) does the author assume or imply that some kinds of phenomena or that some parts of social reality are supernaturally determined? (We doubt that we will find affirmative answers to this question in social science.) Or (B) does he view the patterns and dynamics of social reality as explainable by other than supernatural causes? Among the "natural" causes, (1) does the author use a model of social reality that has primarily deterministic explanations of political, economic, and social events, or (2) does he treat social phenomena as primarily uncertain and problematic? We suggest the examination of writings for dogmatic and unconditional propositions, and for conditional and probabilistic propositions, the latter characteristically reflecting the scientific perspective of explanations of phenomena as uncertain and problematic. Additionally, we ask (3) whether the author gives primacy to single-factor explanations of social events, and, if so, to what factor? Or (4) does he utilize multiple factors in constructing a causal system, and, if so, what are they? We ask further, does he attribute primary causal weight to (i) sociological, (ii) psychological, (iii) technological, (iv) physical environmental factors, or (v) some combination of these different levels of analysis and explanation?

Our particular interests lead us to pursue further assumptions regarding cause and effect as they relate to temporal sequences, the role of ideas, and the manipulability of social events. Specifically, in terms of

(C) the author's temporal orientation, we ask (1) does the author give logical standing only to past social facts and congeries of historical events as causes of the present and of the future? (See I above.) Or (2) does the author view both reconstructions of the past and the future as uncertain and problematic in their causal relation to the present? That is, does the author ascribe any explanatory importance to the present in the analysis of reconstructions of the past, to the possibilities for the future in the explanation of present events and regularities, and to images of the future as important in understanding images of the past?

(D) Concerning the role of ideas in providing adequate causal explanations of social reality, we ask (1) whether the author views ideas as having independent causal power (through orienting human behavior) in systems of social action. (2) Does he assume that ideas and social action are interdependent and that both are causally necessary to understand social reality? Or (3) does he view ideas primarily as "ideology" devised to justify and preserve existing social events and circumstances?

(E) The final query regarding the nature of assumptions about cause and effect is focused on the manipulability of the social world. The assumption that man shapes society and the belief in the value relevance and social responsibility of science leads to an attempt to discover causes and to offer explanations of social events that are phrased in terms of variables that are accessible to human control and manipulation. We ask (1) does the explanation of social phenomena offered by an author include variables that are manipulable or can be brought within the realm of man's control? Or (2) does he offer "inevitable forces," "uncontrollable factors," and "structural constraints" as causes of the human condition? In general, does the author go beyond prediction and description toward the ideas of control and self-determination as the criteria and desirable goals of knowledge?

V. WHAT ARE THE AUTHOR'S VALUES AND PURPOSES?

The questions raised above about the manipulability of the social world and man's causal role in social change point to the importance of a scholar's purposes in his work and ultimately to his values. We assume that goal and value commitments may affect an author's work, and that knowing what they are helps in understanding and evaluating his research. Thus, we are led to inquire about his values and the intended consequences, if any, of his research and theoretical writing. We begin by asking (A) what role an author's values play in his scientific work? (1) Does he promote certain values consciously and explicitly in his writing, or (2) does he unintentionally and implicitly reveal them?

In either case, (3) what justifications, if any, does the author give for his commitment to particular values? And (4) is there a hierarchy of values that is (a) openly proposed, or (b) implicitly apparent in the author's work?

We also include the obvious query concerning the impact of an author's values upon the credibility and reliability of his work. Most generally, (5) do the author's value commitments have apparent consequences for his perception of social reality? Specifically, how do they affect (a) his purposes, both scientific and other; (b) his theoretical framework; (c) his methods of collecting and analyzing evidence; (d) the logic of interpretation and his judgment where alternative interpretations might be possible; and (e) his willingness to speculate about the broader implications of his work? Certainly, these few questions cannot exhaust the possible implications and potential consequences of a scholar's values for his intellectual productions. Rather they are intended to point to some of the now commonplace arguments concerning the importance of an author's values in his work, and the folly of denying their intrusion.

A scholar's value commitments and their consequences for his work, of course, may be convergent with his purposes. Therefore, we ask (B) does he expect his work to have any effect? Is he aware that his scholarly conclusions and interpretations may affect the future course of social action? And, if so, (1) does this awareness affect his scientific work (such as the phrasing of his conclusions), and (2) does it promote a willingness to make explicit and to develop the extrascientific implications of his work?

VI. DOES THE AUTHOR PRESENT AN IMAGE OF THE FUTURE?

In each of the foregoing sections of the paradigm we have posed questions that should serve largely as examples of lines of inquiry to be further developed and expanded. Because of our explicit and specific interest in analyzing the role of images of the future in social change, we give here a more detailed treatment of images of the future than can be culled and collated from the foregoing sections of the paradigm. The basic query that introduces the section inquires if the author presents an image of the future. The fact is that in much, if not most, social science writing the images of the future are implicit and frequently unintended, multiple, inconsistent, and contradictory. But, as we have reasoned, they are nevertheless potentially significant for the possibilities for the future and should therefore be explicitly and intentionally clarified, as far as possible. Thus, if we presumed a bit more, the initial question of this section would be "What is the image of the future presented by the author?" And is it explicitly stated and developed in its implications or not? From this point we can go on to analyze more significant questions about the content of the images and the means and likelihood of their achievement as viewed by the author.

(A) What is the content of the image of the future presented by the author? (1) What is the author's focus of concern or unit of analysis in his image of the future? (a) Is the image of a particular sociogeographic unit such as a supranational region, a nation, a city, or a particular community, and if so, is it (i) specific to a certain region, nation, city, neighborhood, and no other? Or (ii) is it intended to project the future of all similar cities, or all advanced countries, or all neighborhoods?

Rather than dealing with a unit of analysis that is geographically located, (b) does the image focus on a particular institution or some set of institutions? Because the focus of the image of the future may be as general and as varied as any subject of sociological interest, it may deal, for example, with such institutions as the family, the economy, the polity, the military, or the church. Thus, we ask (i) is the projected future specific in orientation, e.g., does it apply to a certain religious denomination, a certain occupational group, a certain government, a certain military organization, or (ii) is the image general in orientation, e.g., does it apply to all religious institutions, to all occupations in the economy, to all governments, or to all military organizations? And (iii) does the image concentrate on material or technological aspects such as changes in communication, transportation, automation, and generally in the utilization of material resources? Or (iv) does the projected future deal primarily with changes in people, values, norms, the organization of social institutions and roles, and other social and cultural elements in the institutions under examination?

In addition to the unit of analysis that an author uses in his image of the future, another aspect of the image's content is (2) the nature of the projected future. (a) How does the author evaluate his image of the future? (i) Does the author present a utopian future, a desired state of affairs in contrast to the present, or (ii) does he elaborate an undesirable future in the form of a warning or a negative utopia? In either case, (b) what are the goals that are projected into the future? What are the goals to be achieved in the utopia? What values will be served by heeding the alarm and avoiding the negative utopia portrayed by the author? (c) What is the nature of the change that is anticipated? (d) Who will benefit from the change? (i) The population at large? Or (ii) some special group? More generally, (e) how is the projected future different from the present, and (f) are the goals contained in the image of the future consistent with existing social values?

It should be apparent that the content of images of the future either explicitly or implicitly presented by social scientific writers could be as varied as the interests and values of the different individuals involved. Almost any facet of the polity, economy, and society, in any of its past, present, or *possible* future forms, might be taken by a writer as the basis for his image of the future, as his utopia or its opposite.

(B) Does the author specify, or even speculate about, the means by which his image of the future might be fulfilled (or, in the case of a negative utopia, avoided by human intervention)? Does the author view the causes of social change and the emergent future (1) predominantly as factors that are beyond the control of man such as fate, chance, and the supernatural; (2) as natural environmental and ecological forces, which though comprehensible, may be currently difficult to manipulate; (3) as structural, institutional, or organizational factors largely beyond the control of man; or (4) as factors that are within the scope of man's control? If the latter, does the author expect that his image of the future will be achieved by the change-producing action of (a) individual great men or elites; or (b) by the collective action of many men, including ordinary citizens, organized to achieve the goals inherent in the image of the future? (i) Is the social basis of the collective action specified as government, social class, movements of political, economic, and social reform etc., or (ii) is the action thought to be the outcome of some vague and unspecified processes or components of society? Still with reference to the means of achieving the image of the future presented by an author, we ask (5) are the means proposed or advocated by the author consistent with and legitimized by existing social values or (b) has the author been innovative and perhaps utopian at the level of values, of ends rather than means?

VII. WHAT MIGHT BE THE CONSEQUENCES FOR THE FUTURE IF THE AUTHOR'S THESIS WERE ACCEPTED AND USED AS A BASIS FOR ACTION?

(A) Is it possible or probable that the author's image of the future could be achieved? From the standpoint of the most widely accepted and relevant current values, (1) would the author's image of the future be acceptable, and (2) would the means necessary to fulfill the image, if available, also be acceptable?

(B) Can the author's data or supporting evidence be differently interpreted to allow another conclusion and a different image of the future? If so, then (1) what would that different future be like? (2) Is that future more or less likely than the one proposed by the author? And (3) is that different future more desirable according to (a) the standards the author himself has presented, (b) the standards current in society, or (c) some other specifiable set of standards?

The purpose of this paradigm is to provide a tool for the analysis of social science literature that emphasizes and explicates the complex network of related assumptions that are relevant in examining time perspectives and images of the future. An analysis of time perspectives and images of the future in social science is especially needed at this time both because of the increased and explicit efforts being devoted to studies of the future and to the search for methods and interpretive devices to carry out such studies adequately (witness the sampling of items in the annotated bibliography) and because of the current crises over the role and relevance of social science itself. In sociology, for example, the latter is caused by, among other things, an unfortunate—and perhaps unnecessary—split between those striving to create an empirically oriented, value-free science and those striving to make sociology more engaged with the tasks of curing the social problems of the day. The scientific study of the future may bridge the gap by showing how one does social change by doing social science.

REFERENCES

Berger, Peter L., and Thomas Luckmann
    1966   The Social Construction of Reality. Garden City, N.Y.: Doubleday.
Gross, Llewellyn (ed.)
    1959   Symposium on Sociological Theory. Evanston, Ill.: Row, Peterson.
Holzner, Burkart
    1968   Reality Construction in Society. Cambridge, Mass.: Schenkman.
Kluckhohn, Florence Rockwood, and Fred L. Strodtbeck with the assistance of John M. Roberts et al.
    1961   Variations in Value Orientations. Evanston, Ill.: Row, Peterson.
Mannheim, Karl
    1936   Ideology and Utopia. New York: Harcourt, Brace & World, A Harvest Book.
Merton, Robert K.
    1957   Social Theory and Social Structure (revised and enlarged edition). Glencoe, Ill.: Free Press.

Meyerhoff, Hans
    1960   Time in Literature. Berkeley and Los Angeles: University of California Press.
Moore, Wilbert E.
    1963a   Social Change. Englewood Cliffs, N.J.: Prentice-Hall.
    1963b   Man, Time, and Society. New York: Wiley.
Priestley, J. B.
    1968   Man and Time. New York: Dell, A Laurel Edition.

PART II

Constructing the Past and Making the Future

The two chapters constituting Part II each contribute a distinctive, though mutually reinforcing, view of time perspectives. The first, by Kai T. Erikson, dealing with the historical perspective, may at first seem a strange contribution to a book on the sociology of the future. Yet any doubts about its relevance are quickly dispelled. Past, present, and future are interconnected; social change and the dynamic orientation are concerns of historians; and some of the methodological questions that historians ask are directly applicable to the nature of social inquiry required by the study of the future.

Erikson begins by saying that the two formal and obvious distinctions dividing sociology from history—the generalizing and the present orientations of sociologists—are not compelling differences on the operational level. Rather, there are a number of other, less visible barriers between the two disciplines. These include the hidden costs for sociology of focusing so exclusively on the social order: important and relevant variables are thereby "screened out." For example, of considerable relevance to our critique of much modern sociology is that the ". . . social man who appears in many of our reports . . . yields his autonomy rather easily to the demands of the social environment" and that restraints on thinking about time may be imbedded in the sociological language itself. Here, of course, is a problem that we hope to address by stressing such concepts as cybernetics, decision-making, and images of the future as part of a theory of social change.

Historians relate to their data differently from sociologists, and may offer a beneficial model for the sociologist interested in "bringing time back in" sociological theory and method. Erikson says that the historical researcher "loses his anchor in the present" and becomes skeptical, both about the evidence itself and his relationship to it. Working with historical materials ". . . requires an approach to data tempered by a kind of skepticism and uncertainty—an awareness of self, perhaps—which seems to come naturally to many experienced historians but fits uneasily among the other professional reflexes of most sociologists." This is certainly true also of the requirements for studying images of the future, including—perhaps especially—the implicit images of the future in social science literature. One is led to the skepticism of the historian and to the orientation of the sociologist of knowledge. How do data come to be what they are? What assumptions about nature, man, and society shape them? And what are the consequences for the future contained in research findings and interpretations? Furthermore, having traveled halfway along this particular intellectual journey, one finds it difficult not to stay until the end of the line: an awareness, skepticism, and uncertainty, as several of our contributors try to show, should be standard tools in any kind of social research or theorizing.

We wish to stress two of Erikson's main points, because they are also among the major themes of this book: it is neither humanly nor technically possible to eliminate the researcher from his data and his results. Nor is it desirable to do so. In a field where the ". . . energies of those sociologists concerned with method have been largely spent in an attempt to neutralize whatever qualities of insight and sympathy an investigator brings to his work . . . ," we regard these views as revolutionary. It is the burden of a considerable part of this book to demonstrate that such views are correct, whether one is studying the past, present, or future. We do not hold with the view that the truth of a statement is in doubt when its social origins or consequences are discovered. The only test is an empirical measure of objectivity. Yet ". . . any research finding is a datum about the investigator as well as a datum about the subject at hand." Looking at social research this way, we may become aware of the extrascientific factors shaping social science and the uses made of it. This should raise questions about alternative starting points, frames of reference, interpretations, relevant data, and the personal and social interests being served. The risk, we suppose, is that with such awareness villainy may replace naïveté. Yet the risk is worth taking, because enlightenment seldom destroys good faith and because social science could be enriched by new and more intricate hypotheses.

Man constructs conceptions of the past in the stories he tells about it, and he also constructs conceptions of the future. Henry Winthrop discusses utopia-construction and future-forecasting in the second chapter in Part II. His particular interest includes the impact of science and technology on the possibilities for the future. Further, he specifies some issues for a social philosophy for an age of science.

Early utopia-construction, he points out, tended to be holistic, static (existing outside history), enervating, dull for the inhabitants of the utopia, and often implicitly authoritarian and explicitly totalitarian. Such holistic descriptions have been superseded by specific studies, which, although permitting more verified detail than holistic studies with respect to some particularities, tend to be fragmented, uncoordinated, and uninformed by the interaction effects of other changes that may occur. Choosing a small, comfortable, and manageable problem, future-forecasters do what too many American sociologists have typically done in the recent past; they end with isolated results, in this case predictions, which may be quite wrong.

The importance of history—of a dynamic, longitudinal perspective —is reaffirmed by Winthrop in his discussion of the "backward look." Here he proposes some critical, retrospective studies of the traditional assumptions underlying current beliefs and behavior to see if current developments in science and technology have made them irrelevant or false. It is to be hoped that such studies could be used to help change behavior that rests upon outmoded assumptions. Moreover, he says that this approach can be turned into the "forward look" by being directed toward the study of emerging developments in science and technology and their implications for traditional assumptions and current institutional practices.

Finally, Winthrop raises some issues that should concern studies of the future in an age of science and technology. The list is long and many of the issues complex. In our judgment, budding futurists will benefit from following his directions, because he has identified many of the key questions and decisions that face members of any group or society that have accepted the emergent possibilities for shaping the future. His issues succinctly illustrate how thinking about the future is embedded in a matrix of values, and he argues "that the greatest return in social welfare from future-forecasting would be to gear such forecasting to a notion of the good life—in short, social philosophy." As mankind acquires the knowledge, the power, and the will to act, the future will be created by deliberate and conscious design. Then alternative futures must be evaluated and chosen. But how do we know what to choose except by recourse to our values, which themselves are subject to change? Some values Winthrop takes for granted—such as those that lead to the elimination of alienation or wars; others he treats as problematic. They are open for invention—such as the kind of human nature future man should have. In any case, the clarification, discovery, invention, and distribution of values are essential aspects of the proper study of the future.

Sociology and the Historical Perspective

KAI T. ERIKSON

The relationship between sociology and history has interested scholars from both disciplines for a long time. By now a considerable library of materials is available on the subject, ranging from involved philosophical essays on the nature of the borderline separating the two fields to ceremonial addresses of various kinds urging a greater volume of traffic across that line. Literature from the sociological side of the border, at least, has been almost unanimous in its insistence that sociologists should devote more attention to history—so much so that the argument would appear to have lost much of its urgency for simple lack of opposition. Nevertheless, sociology in the United States continues to lack historical focus. One can cite the works of men like Bellah, Bendix, Lipset, Merton, Moore, Nesbit, Smelser, Swanson, and Tilly to demonstrate that sociology sometimes reflects a strong sense of history; but these distinguished names only serve to suggest by contrast that most of what passes for sociological research in this country is not informed by much in the way of a historical perspective.

I should perhaps begin by explaining that I once spent a period of several years working with historical records, even though I was involved in a project that seemed eminently "sociological" to me at the time. Like others before and since I went into that experience fully convinced that the study of history and the study of social life are logically different forms of scholarship. I emerged from the experience, however, in a more confused frame of mind. On the one hand, it seemed obvious that the

MacIver Lecture, presented at the annual meetings of the Southern Sociological Society, Atlanta, Georgia, 1968.

traditional distinctions we usually draw between history and sociology do not pose any real barriers to the actual conduct of social research, whatever merit they may have in abstract principle. On the other hand, I thought there must be a number of other obstacles and inhibitions lying elsewhere in the structure of the field that make it difficult for a sociologist to deal comfortably with historical data, and this is the line of thought I hope to pursue in this chapter.

FORMAL DISTINCTIONS

The sociologist who elects to use historical records in his work is likely to approach the assignment with some misgiving. For one thing, if he has been recruited into the profession in the usual manner and has been exposed to the usual kind of professional training, he does not know very much about history. Beyond that he carries with him as part of his intellectual equipment a set of distinctions that confirm the separate identity of sociology by differentiating it from other fields like history; and yet it is not at all clear to him how these distinctions are supposed to orient his research.

The most familiar of these distinctions, of course, is that historians are interested in something called "the past" and sociologists in something called "the present." As a practical matter, this simply means that students in each of the two fields customarily address themselves to different locales in time—a point of no importance here. As a methodological matter, however, the distinction is somewhat more complicated. Generally speaking, historians depend upon the passage of years to inform them what moments in the past have influenced the course of future events and are, for that reason, "historic"; and to that extent, at least, historians can be said to rely on fate to determine not only what data shall filter down to them but what portion of the past shall engage their attention. Sociologists, on the other hand, are apt to be more suspicious of fate. They are generally encouraged by the logic of their method to generate their own information, extracting it from the contemporary social setting themselves because they hope to reach *behind* the historical appearance of things and have no reason to suppose that the information they require will be deposited in the ordinary run of historical records. In theory, then, historians should find it easier to make sense of data that have been seasoned by the effects of time, and sociologists should find it easier to make sense of data over which they can exercise some immediate measure of control.

This distinction, if it ever meant anything, is almost surely losing force, partly because it is no longer so clear that historians and sociologists rely upon different sources of information. Historians are beginning to generate their own data by procedures developed in the social sciences; and sociologists, in turn, are frequently deriving their material from documents of precisely the sort employed by historians. The whole character of historical data has changed anyway because sociologists are currently in the business of data gathering; sociological reports are now sent to the archives for storage along with state papers and official records, and there they have simply become a new species of historical document. In general, it is difficult to see how a reasonable line can be drawn between the two fields on that score alone.

Yet the feeling persists within both disciplines that the kinds of intellectual orientation necessary for studying the past are somehow different from those necessary for studying the present, and one must look for the sources of that feeling in the professional climates of the two fields themselves. The past has generally been studied in an atmosphere of scarcity: the traditional task of the historian has been to sift through a finite supply of data as thoroughly and as carefully as he can, and the working arrangements he has devised for that purpose—the quiet reserve of his workshops, the vigor of his arguments over seemingly small matters of texture and detail—can be both unfamiliar and a little intimidating to the sociologist. The present, however, is generally studied in an atmosphere of abundance: the traditional job of the sociologist is to take rough and approximate samplings of the data as they splash around him in an endless flow, and the working arrangements he has fashioned for that purpose—the abstractness of his vocabulary, the impersonality of his procedures, the spare geometry of his charts and tables—can be strange and sometimes offensive to the historian. Carl Bridenbaugh, the distinguished American historian, was once horrified when a sociologist asked him: "What is *your* method of sampling?" The question may have been shrewder than Bridenbaugh recognized, but the notion that one can examine a problem responsibly by selecting a tiny fraction of the available evidence lies far outside what more traditional historians would define as proper scholarship. Sampling is the strategy of persons who work with vast universes of data; it is a strategy of plenty.

As a result of these differences in atmosphere, students often overestimate the degree to which the working arrangements of the other field are governed by some hidden method of approach, some implicit logic not readily apparent to outsiders. For what it is worth, I can report that I drifted through the beginning stages of the study mentioned earlier thinking that there must be ways to "do" history that I could learn if I only consulted the right scholar or read the right book; and now, several years later, I frequently encounter students of history looking for inside hints on how to "do" sociology, as if some manageable recipe were involved. Students often hesitate to move across the border between the two fields, then, because they mistake the professional postures they confront on the other side for a formidable and exclusive set of methods.

A second and more telling distinction between the two fields is an old and honored tradition that sociologists should concern themselves with the more *general* properties of social experience, the everyday patterns of activity that appear again and again in the life of the social order, while historians should concern themselves with those *specific* moments in the flow of time that have influenced the character of an age or tempered the course of the future. According to this academic division of labor, the sociologist's assignment is to look for regularities and correspondences in the conduct of men in the hope of discovering general "laws." The historian's assignment, in turn, is to look for the unique and distinctive in the conduct of men in the hope of capturing as accurately as possible what actually happened in the past. Sociology is nomothetic, history idiographic.

This distinction makes a good deal of sense in the abstract, but it is sometimes difficult to know what to do with it in any given case. On the one hand, it seems perfectly reasonable that some events in the past (decisive elections, for example) should attract the attention of historians because they literally "made" history, while other events (say the voting activities of housewives in Omaha) should attract the attention of sociologists precisely because they are undistinguished acts, representative acts, passing instances of some more inclusive social pattern. On the other hand, it is also important to recognize that human actions themselves are neither generic nor specific. Every event has properties that can be subsumed under a more general heading: if this were not so, we would be unable to identify the event in the first place. Yet every event is also peculiar to *some* historical sequence, whether it be the life history of one of those housewives in Omaha, the emergence of Western civilization, or a sweep of time as broad in scale as the evolution of the human species. This division of labor, then, fails because it obscures the extent to which each of the two fields employs the perspective attributed to the other. Historians generalize all the time, as numbers of them have pointed out; and sociologists are always dealing with particularities, no matter how energetically they cut and trim the data to fit the abstract logic of their procedures.

Whenever a sociologist looks carefully at a human scene, he is actually observing a unique moment in historical time as well as an instance of some broader regularity; and thus the social landscape he surveys does not differ in any appreciable way from the landscape viewed by the historian. Why is it, then, that sociologists and historians usually produce works that are so distinct from one another in style and content? One reason, presumably, is that each attends to different features of the common landscape and reports on different activities taking place within it. A sociologist is more likely to note the structure of the scene than the character of its leading actors, he is more likely to be interested in the activities of civil society than in the actions of governments, and, in general, he is more likely to be concerned with some underlying pattern in the events he is studying than with the moments of crisis: the sudden shifts of fortune, the contests among commanding adversaries, the ironies of fate, and all the other human dramas around which the conventional historical narrative is organized.

Still, this is not the only reason accounts written by historians are so easy to distinguish from those written by sociologists. Even the barest analysis of sociological prose would probably confirm the suspicion held by many critics both inside and outside the profession that the abstract quality of sociological work is conveyed as much by the prevailing conventions of sociological reporting as by the contents of the reports themselves. Take titles, for example: sociology must be one of the few scholarly fields where a study of hospital rates in Massachusetts could be called *Psychosis and Civilization* or where a study of young men and women in industrial England could be called *Youth and the Social Order*. Or take prefaces: it is a standard practice in sociological reporting to introduce a set of findings by simply naming the academic species to which it hopefully belongs, whether or not any further connections are drawn between the two ("the following is intended as a contribution to the sociology of . . ."). Or the presentation of data: even where an author is careful to note that his evidence on delinquency comes from a working-class section of Scranton during the third and fourth months of a steel strike, the next person to mention that evidence may very well treat it as a "finding" about delinquency everywhere, a standard item in "the literature."

Other usages, too, have the sometimes inadvertent effect of wrapping sociological merchandise into nomothetic packages. In the interests of protecting the anonymity of their informants, for example, sociologists frequently omit from their published reports exactly the kind of identifying information that would place the study in its proper historical context. When one invents names like "Western Hospital" or "Southern City" for his research sites and then is purposefully vague about persons and dates and locations, he is introducing a note of generality and abstractness into the finished product that does not accurately reflect the substance of the findings themselves. The presumption, of course—sometimes stated, more often not—is that the site in question is somehow representative of other locales and other times; yet the researcher does not ordinarily know whether this is so. If he simply states or implies that the scene he has studied is "typical" and then deals only with those features that make it appear so, he is making it almost impossible for the reader to arrive at his own reasoned conclusion. The problem for the responsible investigator, then, is twofold. He cannot distinguish the regular pattern from the unique happening unless he is careful to study both, in which case his research procedures are necessarily similar to those of the historian. And if he hopes to show the reader how he made that discrimination, he must include a good deal of local color and "historical" detail in his report.

These, then, are two of the formal boundaries dividing sociology from history—the notion that sociologists are anchored to the present by the special logic of their methods and the notion that sociologists have a particular investment in the more general contours of social life. I would say, to repeat, that these distinctions do not in themselves represent a very compelling difference between the two fields at the operational level; but I would also say that they sometimes serve to mask a network of other barriers that lie below the visible surface and help keep the sociologist confined within his own academic preserve. These barriers have not been declared in philosophical essays on the nature of knowledge: they are built into what we might call the "professional reflexes" of the sociologist—those habits of mind and temper that become the hidden products of a sociological apprenticeship and constitute the normative climate of the discipline. We have noted two or three of these implicit barriers. It is time now to consider several others by backing away from the subject for a moment and returning to it along a different line of approach.

PROFESSIONAL REFLEXES

Sociology, in common with several of the social sciences, claims the entire range of human experience as its proper subject matter and thus does not observe very many jurisdictional limits in its search for relevant data. Therefore, the niche occupied by sociology in the structure of academic life is sometimes difficult to portray. When a sociologist is asked to describe his profession, he is likely to say in terms that sound a little vague to students in neighboring fields that sociology is a "perspective" rather than a subject matter, an "approach" rather than an inventory of known facts. What he means by this, normally, is that sociologists do not have a natural territory in the world of human phenomena and can only be distinguished from students in other fields by the *way* they pursue data—by the way their senses are conditioned, the way their imaginations are tuned, the way their minds are disciplined.

To think sociologically, then, is not simply a matter of rehearsing certain theories or developing certain skills: it is a matter of learning new devices for sorting out the various details that crowd one's consciousness and of learning new ways to determine what impressions in the world of human experience are worth one's attention. When a sociologist studies a conversation between two people, for instance, he is presumably trained to note the patterning of the relationship rather than the contributions of the individual participants—the words and gestures that are drawn from a common cultural vocabulary rather than those that suggest personal idiosyncracies. He is trained to look at the *space between* the interacting pair rather than at the spaces they occupy as separate persons, to visualize the two as a single social unit rather than as discrete objects in space that happen to intersect for a passing moment. He sees the actors as reflections of one or another abstract position in the social order—as occupants of statuses, players of roles, representatives of class interests or ethnic traditions.

This (or something like it) is what sociologists normally have in mind when they talk about their perspective or approach. When we say that groups of scholars share a common discipline, we are suggesting, among other things, that they turn their attention to the same universe of detail and try to screen out from their line of vision all other details that might interfere with that concentration. It is the essence of all specialization, presumably, that students will deliberately limit the number of variables they take into account for the explicit purpose of sharpening their focus on those they accept as their proper concern; in that respect, at least, the disciplined eye is one that sees both more and less than the untutored eye.

The difficulty here is that members of a discipline do not always recognize the price they have paid to achieve this clarity of focus, and they sometimes act as if the variables they have screened out in an attempt to improve their concentration have conveniently disappeared in the meantime. In the case of sociology, it might be argued that our ability to appreciate the effects of general social forces on human conduct has often been purchased at the cost of reducing our awareness of *personality processes:* the social man who appears in many of our reports, at any rate, is a creature who does not seem to be governed in any important way by unconscious impulses and who yields his autonomy rather easily to the demands of the social environment. Or, again, it might be argued that our ability to appreciate the influence of culture on human conduct has been purchased at the cost of dulling our sensitivity to *biological processes:* indeed, it is taken for granted in many sociological circles that serious discussions about the effect of genetic factors on behavior are not only scientifically unsound but politically suspicious.

These professional screens have played an important part in the emergence of sociology and will continue to do so as long as we remember what they are. But there is another screen in common use which probably serves to impair rather than improve the quality of sociological vision: the ability sociologists have developed to perceive relationships between persons and events and institutions that coexist in time by muting their sense of time altogether. I do not mean to suggest that sociologists are less aware of the passage of years than other men, or that dour theorists from Columbia and Harvard have somehow managed to force time out of our imagery in the interests of promoting a structural-functional view of the universe, as some commentators have implied. I mean, rather, that it has been one of the professional reflexes of the sociologist (in the United States, at least) more or less to freeze time in order to get a more leisurely look at the patterns of relationship obtaining at a given moment. In this sense, sociologists are often poorly equipped to handle historical data, not simply because they are unresponsive to the persisting pleas that they learn to think more historically, but because the conceptual language of the field and the standards of relevance that are built into its models do not always lend themselves conveniently to that purpose.

It follows, then, that one of the more important hidden barriers dividing the two fields is a matter of conceptualization and terminology. As a general rule, sociologists and historians tend to invest their energies differently when they look at *connections between* the variables they study, sociologists spending more time on relationships that are essentially *lateral* in time and historians on relationships that are essentially *sequential.* This insight may seem something less than profound, but sociologists who work with historical data in a sustained way often discover that a large part of the vocabulary they have been trained to use when portraying the connection between social objects makes sense principally when those objects coexist. Sociologists who incline toward a structural-functional vision of social life have a vocabulary at their disposal—interaction, exchange, balance, equilibrium, function, consensus, and the like—that does not translate easily into narrative figures. Sociologists who lean toward a somewhat less symmetrical view of social life approach historical data with much the same disadvantage; terms such as coercion, conflict, tension, ambivalence, antagonism, and dissensus, like terms featured in the language of structural-functionalism, deal almost entirely with objects present at the same moment in time. I do not mean to imply that the schools of thought in which these vocabularies have developed are themselves frozen in timelessness, for some of our richest work on "institutionalization," say, or "socialization"—two areas of study that depend very much on a sense of time—have come out of the same conceptual frameworks. But it is probably fair to point out that the everyday vocabularies of sociology are very largely geared to lateral connections in social life.

The various formulations one finds in American sociology under the heading of "social change" may be a case in point, for the very *idea* of change can sometimes sound awkward when expressed in conventional sociological prose. Many of our standard descriptions of change—check any current text—draw attention to successive stages in the development of a given institution or structure, almost as if the only way we can introduce the element of time into our calculations is to visualize several different stages of equilibrium or several different states of conflict stacked one on top of the other like so many building blocks. A historian, on the other hand, is more inclined simply to take for granted the fact that change takes place in the life of the social order—that people mature, that institutions age, that generations replace one another, that one event gives way to another in a relentless sweep of time. His language deals with continuities, ours with discrete shifts in the arrangements of society. His language is tuned to growth and decline as genetic processes built into the very nature of social order; ours is tuned to the linkages among social objects that happen to fit together in the same temporal frame.

Another of the hidden barriers between sociology and history, closely related to the first, is that each field entertains a somewhat different set of notions as to what constitutes a plausible "explanation." To *explain* a fact, of course, means to *account for it*—to align it with other facts in such a way that the appearance of this one seems logical, reasonable, perhaps even inevitable. In general, historians are likely to feel that a given outcome is explained if they can relate a credible story about the sequence of events that led up to it or the motives that impelled it, while sociologists are likely to feel that an outcome is explained if they can trace its connection to other institutions and forces in the surrounding environment. I do not want to get into this enormously complex problem at any length, but I do want to note one of its less visible consequences for styles of academic work—namely, that historians and sociologists tend to fall back to different methodological shelters whenever their data prove thin and inconclusive. When a historian is unsure of his data, he is invited by the conventions of his trade to fill in the missing information with a fairly deliberate exercise of sympathy and intuition, on the theory that the facts of the case are forever lost and that, in any case, the imagination of a disciplined professional mind is itself a research tool of no mean power. It is surely no accident that history is the one social science recognizing a muse. When a sociologist is unsure of *his* data, however, he is under a certain constraint from the conventions of his trade to withdraw to a more secure and sometimes more trivial ground where his position can be defended and his conclusions substantiated. The records of history cannot always be counted on to furnish information of the sort a sociologist thinks he requires to explain his findings, and this realization often quickens his retreat from the awkward past to the more accommodating present.

The most subtle and yet most compelling of the hidden barriers dividing the two fields, however, is that scholars who deal with the historical past usually visualize their own relationship to the data they study in a different way from scholars who deal with the social present. I shall devote a moment to this subject because I suspect it relates importantly to the kinds of collaboration we can reasonably expect in the future between sociology and history.

Sociologists often proceed as if they have experienced the data they use in their studies at first hand: after all, they can reach out and touch the walls of the institutions they are interested in, speak to people they are trying to understand, observe the social scenes they are writing about, and consult the records of their own era. Because we have prominent examples of field work to cite, we may forget that working sociologists are often just as remote from their sources of information as are historians, since their data are so often gathered for them by intermediaries of one sort or another: student assistants, institutional surveys, official agencies, and so on. Nevertheless, sociologists are often inclined to take a certain methodological comfort from the illusion that they remain close to their data, and as a result they are sometimes rather vague and unreflective about the kinds of concern that belong in the realm of epistemology when they are actually engaged in research. Whatever we teach in courses on the "sociology of knowledge," we generally approach data with the idea that the world is pretty much as it seems and that the evidence we happen to obtain about the world is a fair enough representation of reality.

When an investigator turns to historical data, however, and loses his anchor in the present, he is in a more precarious position—if only because he cannot sustain any further illusion of sensory contact with the human experience he is studying. Because his evidence is second-hand and his subject matter remote, he is more or less forced to be more thoughtful about the evidence at his disposal and more skeptical about his relationship to it. To begin with, he is fated to work with documents of uncertain ancestry and must ask several questions about the material even before he examines it. Why were these particular scraps of information recorded? Who wrote them down and why? How accurate an observer was the writer? How well did he represent the mood and spirit of his age? This is only the beginning of the problem, for the one quality all these documents have in common is their survival; and even though a researcher has complete faith in the authenticity and reliability of the documents, he must wonder by what law or accident they came to be preserved. They are not the random remains of a dead age, like the debris found at an archeological site. Every generation of men that has lived meantime has served for a period as custodian of those records, and thus the surviving library of materials is in many ways a record of all the intervening years as well.

To use the example with which I am most familiar, a large number of documents are available to the student of seventeenth-century New England, rich in texture and broad in coverage; but one cannot spend more than a few hours in their company without wondering whose history they record. Not only were they originally composed by men with a vested interest in the events they were reporting, but they have been passed along to us by a succession of other men, each of whom has taken a turn sifting, rearranging, and even rewriting those materials. The surviving records, then, register not only what impressed John Winthrop in the early years of settlement, but what Cotton Mather regarded as worth remembering in the second half of the seventeenth century, what Thomas Hutchinson considered "historic" in the eighteenth century, and what whole generations of chroniclers and antiquarians decided to place on the shelves in the nineteenth century. The attitudes as well as the fingerprints of many men are attached to this (or any) set of documents. The problem does not end here, for any investigator who learns in this demanding school how one generation of persons can influence the work of another will sooner or later begin to wonder how he, in his own turn, is liable to influence the work of students yet to come.

In short, working with historical materials requires an approach to data tempered by a kind of skepticism and uncertainty—an awareness of self, perhaps—that comes naturally to many experienced historians but fits uneasily among the professional reflexes of many sociologists. Historians are aware that their own minds are the spheres in which the past comes alive again and that the data of their researches are converted into "histories" by a process involving personal qualities of insight, sympathy, and imagination. I do not mean by this that every journeyman historian stays awake at night worrying about the degree to which his personal susceptibilities intrude upon the larger character of his work, but rather that it is generally understood throughout the discipline that written history is bound to reflect the talent and temper of the mind that produced it. When a historian reviews the available data and draws new conclusions from them, for instance, the work he publishes is likely to be called an "interpretation"—suggesting both that the intellectual posture of the author is an important feature of his work and that the work itself is apt to be replaced in time by another interpretation. Should someone conclude that historians are subject to all the private subjectivities and social biases that flesh is heir to, the historian can reasonably respond that this is not always a handicap. If he is an interpreter of history *for* his generation, he may find it helpful to share the perspectives *of* his generation; if as a scholar he relies upon some measure of insight and intuition to breathe life back into pasts that are forever dead and gone, he may find it fully appropriate to employ the arts of the dramatist as well as the skills of the scientist. This argument, at least as it appears in some of the more idealistic discussions of historical method, sometimes trails off into a form of mysticism that most sociologists and many historians find uncongenial, but the main point is widely accepted throughout the profession.

It is probably unnecessary to add here that considerations of this sort have not figured prominently in sociological discussions of method. The energies of those sociologists concerned with method have been largely spent in an attempt to neutralize whatever qualities of insight and sympathy an investigator brings to his work—and this on the basis of two very questionable assumptions: the first, that proper scientific procedure requires one to systematically reduce one's own influence on the data; the second, that it is humanly and technically possible to do so. We shall return to these two assumptions in a moment.

HISTORY AND METHOD

It has become more important to take a careful look at the boundary dividing sociology and history because the traffic across that line has been increasing over the past several years. Historians have moved across the border in search of new techniques to help them handle the large masses of data that are increasingly being recognized as their main concern and in search of new conceptualizations to help them order the past in more "social" terms. Sociologists have moved across the border primarily because they are interested in the rich caches of data located in the historians' archives. The rapid pace of change in the modern world, among other things, has encouraged sociologists to view the present *as* history, and they are beginning to search in the records of the past for older parallels to the processes of industrialization and urbanization and revolution they see in the world around them. In a sense, then, what sociologists have tried to gain from their commerce with history has been additional information that can be analyzed by standard sociological methods and used in the service of standard sociological hypotheses.

The final paragraphs of this chapter will suggest, however, that sociologists might profit from a different form of commerce with history —one in which they consider the degree to which *historical methods* can help in the analysis of *sociological data*. Perhaps "methods" is not the proper term: some historians bristle at the suggestion that their work is governed by anything so strict and binding as a method, and many sociologists are only too ready to endorse that judgment. Still, scholars who study the past in a systematic way can be said to share a certain cast of mind, a certain set of professional reflexes, and I would like to propose that these qualities can broaden and inform the scope of sociological inquiry.

One way in which sociologists might profit from paying closer attention to the historical method is to acquire a sharper sense of the relationship between social events over time. In order to appreciate how the institutions we study are molded by the passage of years, we probably need to learn how to think in narrative terms, to develop a feeling for the temporal nature of social forces; and the only way we are likely to attain these skills is to become more "historical" ourselves.

C. Wright Mills, among others, has insisted that the sociologist is really a contemporary historian. Whether he is studying a school district or analyzing election returns or observing the activities of a religious sect or conducting experiments with laboratory groups, the sociologist is observing the history of his own age as well as looking for broader indicators of regularity and law. Unless he becomes aware of this, he runs the risk of losing not only his historical but his *sociological* command of the social scenes he is studying. For one thing, a setting that appears to reflect general social properties may later prove to have been but an instance of some wider arc of change. As one looks back on some of the truly remarkable studies coming out of American sociology a generation or more ago, for example, they sometimes seem a little antiquated and (to use a curious but meaningful expression) *dated*. This is not because the methods or the vocabulary employed in those works have become obsolete, but because it is clearer to us than it was to the original writers that their works reflect the age in which they were produced—an age of immigration, an age of prohibition, an age of depression and collapse. These studies offer particular insights into the history of places like urban Chicago and rural North Carolina as well as general insights into the anatomy of society; and yet it is not at all evident that the sociologists who did those projects were aware of the difference—or, indeed, that investigators on the scene are themselves *ever* aware of the difference. It is easy to imagine that a number of contemporary classics now honored as monuments to the craft will seem equally dated, equally anchored in time and place once another generation has passed. If so, it will demonstrate again that the greatest difficulty we face in determining whether a given set of findings should be counted as "generic" or "specific" is that, like most of the other data of history, their actual contours become apparent only at a distance.

This problem becomes even more complicated when we consider that sociologists continually change the history of the settings they study by the very act of paying attention to them. However representative and typical an institution may appear at first, it takes on a special character simply because an investigator has introduced himself into it; and the investigator is liable to misunderstand the information he obtains unless he sees *himself* as a unique historical event in the life of the institution and remains aware that the report he writes may change the structure he is viewing. In both of these senses, then, the sociologist is something of a participant historian whether the title appeals to him or not, and it seems reasonable to suggest that he can best understand his data if he accepts both roles.

A second way in which sociologists might profit from paying attention to the historical "method" is to take a somewhat closer look at the relationship between an observer and his data. As suggested earlier, sociologists often seem to derive a certain comfort from the illusion that their evidence is close at hand and that their procedures are largely automatic. There are living populations of subjects to draw upon, tables of significance values to consult, and elaborate hardware to employ in the processing of data; and on the whole we are not especially troubled by the degree to which our own posture as social beings intrudes upon our results. Yet sooner or later the data we use have to be sifted through the soft tissues of a human mind; and when this occurs, the matter of how these tissues operate and how they relate to the rest of the social order becomes an important technical concern rather than an artistic whim. This is an issue to which historians (or philosophers of history, at any rate) have devoted a good deal of attention, but it has provoked little systematic thought in sociology.

It is probably fair to observe that sociologists who worry about this matter are regarded by their fellows as "soft" and humanistic, while those who do not—who think that their use of standard measures and mechanical procedures protects them from subjective bias—are regarded as "hard" and scientific. Yet this contrast is very likely a misreading of the scientific ethos. If a theoretical physicist were to listen in on a professional conversation about sociology and history, he might conclude that a skeptical historian in the tradition of Croce or Collingwood is in many ways more scientific than is his positivistic colleague in history or his neighbor in sociology—not because his standards of investigation are more precise or his conclusions more amenable to verification, but because his approach to data allows for a margin of indeterminacy and uncertainty and takes for granted that the subjective condition of the observer is an objective fact about the research setting itself. Our physicist might very well want to give the historian credit for understanding something that sociologists sometimes overlook—that any research finding is a datum about the investigator as well as a datum about the subject at hand.

This brings us back to the subject of *discipline*. Whatever else the term may mean, a discipline is a set of ideas shared among a community of scholars as to what constitutes a proper order of evidence, a proper method of investigation, a proper standard of criticism. These notions, presumably, do not have any special authority beyond the fact that they happen to make sense to the men who hold them, and to this extent a discipline must be understood as a normative order, a system of belief, a cultural product.

One of the important functions of a discipline is to represent standards of performance against which scholars can evaluate their own research, a process that often goes under the heading of "developing objectivity" or "being scientific." In many respects this way of phrasing the issue can be highly misleading. Any individual in a research setting brings with him from the different corners of his mind a potential for distortion and bias—inclinations that are related to his own private life and experience, his social class position and ethnic background, and so on. When we talk about making someone "more objective," we are generally talking about submerging his private subjectivities into the subjectivities of a larger collectivity—shifting the moral center of gravity, as it were, from a private individual to a wider group.

For example, it is standard procedure in several of the social sciences to rely on a panel of judges whenever a researcher's impartiality is called into question, and then to be reassured when those judges agree. What happens, of course, is that the biases of one researcher have been washed away by the biases of several judges—experts, perhaps, and shrewd observers, but representatives of the same general sector of the moral order from which the researcher himself has ordinarily come. When the grayest elders of a tribe testify that polyandry is a law of nature, we call it culture; when the leading spokesmen of a religious movement insist that some article of creed is based on revelation, we call it ideology; but when five or six sociologists agree that the behavior of a subject falls into a particular category, we call it science. This can put the sociologist in a curious position: while he may be the first to argue that the things "everyone knows" are often a result of cultural conditioning, he is sometimes slow to realize that professional agreement on a method of procedure or a set of findings may amount to the same thing.

A discipline, then, reflects the best sense a community of scholars can make of the way they work and the best rules they can fashion for handling the data they view as their responsibility. That there may be room in these arrangements for bias of one sort or another should go without saying: the problem for a mature profession is to arrange its affairs as reasonably as it can *knowing this to be the case*. And this can prove to be a highly sensitive matter because a discipline—like any human group—is always struggling against the tendency of some of its members to settle for a seemingly simple and lasting solution to the ambiguity of its position. On the one hand, there is the very real danger that a discipline will dissolve into a kind of mindless antinomianism where everyone does his own thing and listens only to the sounds of his own voice. On the other hand, there is the equally real danger that a discipline will harden into a brittle orthodoxy where ritual rules and formulae long outlast the logic responsible for their invention.

Historians have been struggling with both of these inclinations for a number of years, but to one sociologist looking in from the outside (and perhaps with an outsider's readiness to idealize) it would seem that the academic atmosphere in which history is studied often reflects an easier balance between the two. At his best, a person who works with historical documents comes to accept as a working principle the fact that the eyes with which he sees have all the defects of the age in which he lives, and that other eyes will see things differently as a matter of course; yet at the same time he accepts the conventional lore of his discipline as a provisional source of wisdom, a base from which to operate. He manages to resist the attractive notion that every man is his own historian, responsible only to his own convictions and impulses; and he manages to resist the equally attractive notion that history is a discipline governed by natural laws of inquiry.

Sociology in the United States has generally leaned in the more positivistic of those directions, developing a form of scientism that no longer seems to resemble the natural science models from which it derived. There have been unmistakable signs in recent years, however, of a swing in the opposite direction—toward a species of radical skepticism in which persons distrust their own intelligence and all the established apparatus of sociology for fear of the various class and racial and ideological biases that might be hidden within them. We may hope that historical experience and historical consciousness can help us to find a responsible stance somewhere between the two extremes.

Utopia Construction and Future Forecasting: Problems, Limitations, and Relevance

HENRY WINTHROP

THE HOLISTIC STRAIN IN UTOPIAN WRITING: ADVANTAGES AND DEFICIENCIES

Utopias characteristically have emphasized new visions of social order, whether their creators lived before or during the Great Age of Science, which for purposes of convenience only we can regard as beginning with the twentieth century. An emphasis on social order is almost by definition the raison d'être of the utopian dream. This emphasis can be seen in such disparate utopias as those of More (1935) and Bellamy (1967), separated by approximately 372 years, or those of Wells (1967) and Skinner (1948), separated, approximately, by only 44 years. I am referring only to utopias, taken as serious projections of desired, novel social possibilities and ideals—of new worlds that their fabricators have knit entire—and not to those satires of the dreams of reason that have come to be called "dystopias" or "antiutopias."

In almost all utopias—with the possible exception of Skinner's *Walden Two*, which explicitly stresses the desirability of involuntary manipulation of people by the laws of operant conditioning rather than a Socratic call for the examined life—the element of rationality is overemphasized. Their populations respond to issues and problems—if, indeed, they have any problems at all—chiefly through reason and sometimes through reason alone. Their standardized, daily routines have been completely "rationalized" in the managerial sense of this term. Intelligence is worshipped and planning is a virtue. The conditions of life and any novel problems that may arise are almost all handled abstractly, impersonally, and by aggregative types of decision-making that leave little or no room for human feeling, idiosyncrasy, unique identity, tragedy associated with what Goffman (1965) has called spoiled identity, psychological pluralism or the frustrations associated with nonconformity. In some utopias, in fact, the intransigent, the unpliable, the discontented, the imaginative, and the dissenters are either liquidated or exiled.

Utopias also tend to be static, in the sense that they are unwittingly made to exist outside history, enervating in the sense that they are grandiose, sensory-deprivation chambers, and dull in the sense that major novelty and revolutionary change are often banished from the lives of the inhabitants. Even worse, most utopian visions blithely celebrate the loss of human freedom—a dispiriting condition to which the author blinds his readers and which he usually conceals from himself by the use of laudatory description and an honorific terminology. In this respect the artificer of utopias is hoist by his own semantic petard. The utopian thinker often seems to be completely unaware of what Unamuno (1954) has called "the tragic sense of life." And all too often the constructors of utopias are frequently so alienated from Nature that they see an urban hell as a social paradise. They envision a megalopolis that has been joyfully separated forever from forest, field, and stream, from murmuring brooks and bursting buds, from majestic mountains and breathtaking landscapes, from the scent of flowers and a sense of communion with creatures in their natural habitats.

That these are fair characterizations of most utopias can be seen by scanning brief descriptions of some of the foremost utopias that have been formulated historically. Excerpts and descriptions of these utopias have been given by Negley and Patrick (1962). The justice of the preceding indictments may also be noted from the themes expressed in various utopias, which were examined in a relatively recent issue of *Daedalus*.[1]

From Plato to H. G. Wells, almost every utopian thinker has been preoccupied with a vision of a more perfect social order and the need for drastic innovation in the institutional structures of the West. Not many utopians show any sense of *Realpolitik*, with the exception of a few figures like Sir Thomas More, who have had some direct political experience. Many of the dreams of reason are visions of societies which all men of good will could welcome with unreserved enthusiasm. But then, too,

---

[1] The title of the issue was *Utopia*, edited by Graubard (1965).

the dreams are often really dystopian nightmares. Hindsight enables the modern student of imaginary utopias to see the degree to which utopian thinkers, lacking direct experience of political life, would usher in communal hells that we of a later age would unhesitatingly recognize as totalitarian societies. In the name of such noble considerations as our common humanity, our social sentiments, the religious impulse, and a widespread desire for justice, mercy, and a more perfect social order, utopian thinkers have welcomed and projected social visions of human formicaries and apiaries as desirable forms of society. World political, social, and economic centralization is worshipped; and a variety of constraining institutions and decision-making structures are often envisaged to take the place of our present sorry scheme of things entire.

A new set of administrative samurai is assumed to run everything, people everywhere gladly consenting. This top-notch echelon for running the world is variously referred to as the Central Committee, The Well-Doers, The World Controllers—or some similar impressive cognomen—and, of course, in the antiutopian satires these visions have spawned, the leadership at the top may be referred to as The Big Brothers or by some other tongue-in-cheek label. In the writings of H. G. Wells (1967), particularly in *A Modern Utopia*, the characteristics of the functional elite anticipated for a planetary, social order come clearly into view. The members of this elite are, of course, chosen from the educated, from the professional classes, and from those trained in the technical and social expertise that will be required for a complex, social order. It is easy to imagine many utopian thinkers loudly rejoicing over the use of our modern Planning-Programming-Budgeting System (PPBS) and the advantages of cost-benefit ratio analysis. It is somewhat harder to imagine them concerned with indicators of the quality of life, such as those promulgated in the thinking of Bauer (1966) and Gross (1967) and their associates.

Let us return, however, to the characteristics of the utopian samurai. They are sometimes assumed to be the only legitimate voters or decision-makers. They have submitted themselves to a rigorous course of training and have proved themselves competent for the lordliest of functions—the management of men—by having passed some very difficult and searching examinations. They are also thought of as austere, indulging neither in drinking, smoking, gambling, nor what Veblen (1953) would have called conspicuous consumption and conspicuous display. Although Wells, for instance, thought of his philosopher-kings as individuals who would never take drugs, perhaps if he were living today, he would concede that the burden of decision-making in the face of our current social complexity might justify at least the use of tranquilizers.

Whether he would have gone along with some of the modern claims—often from reputable sources—that the use of psychedelic drugs might help to generate some good ideas in keeping with the responsibility for designing and administering the welfare functions of the state is uncertain. It is even more uncertain—considering his pronounced cerebral emphasis—whether Wells would have conceded that psychedelic drugs might promote more feeling for the invisible subject populations and therefore, perhaps, less alienation from them.[2]

Decision-makers in utopias are also expected to keep physically fit. They are often expected to keep alert—through reading, research, meditation, philosophical discussion, formal study, or devotion to intellectually taxing problems that lie outside their social expertise. All these regimens are intended, in a sense, as "alertness courses" to keep utopian controllers awake on the job. Occasionally the fabricator of a utopia believes that if members of its elite are too preoccupied with sex, they may lose the disinterested, clear-minded attitude required to carry out their enormous responsibilities. As a result, some utopias demand celibacy, others chastity but not celibacy, and others a regulation, usually by indirection, of the sexual functions in marriage. This regulation is somewhat similar to the scheduling of relations between husbands and wives that was required in the Chinese Commune. Some utopias provide a retreat for the controllers—an area for meditation, rest, review, and stock-taking.

Many traditional, utopian thinkers frequently take pains to describe the intellectual functions of controllers. This theme is, in fact, sometimes the central idea in a description of a utopia. Here again note that these functions are aggregative and are exercised upon human beings far removed from the sight, contact, or knowledge of the decision-makers. It is difficult to find a utopia in which it is possible for the decision-makers to have existential feelings for the people they serve and for the day-to-day vicissitudes of their subjects' existence. Upon close analysis, we find most utopias are in part implicitly authoritarian and many are, in fact, explicitly totalitarian. If we combine the mental traits of the controllers with the described techniques of control, we find that these techniques are frequently expected to be in principle quantitative and highly structured. Utopian writers rarely work out these techniques of control in detail, but their general pattern and intent and their highly structured nature are clear enough. Although projected in generalities, it is clear that the administrative prerogatives of utopian elites frequently enable them

---

[2] The potentialities of drugs for producing social benefits as well as social liabilities have been emphasized by many writers. In this connection, see Miller (1961: 92–109) for a balanced essay.

to control in spirit every aspect of the individual's life. They are formulated in precisely the spirit that made Dostoyevsky (1961) despair and
that he described in his *Notes From Underground:*

> . . . But men love abstract reasoning and neat systematization so much
> that they think nothing of distorting the truth, closing their eyes and ears
> to contrary evidence to preserve their logical constructions. . . . (107–108)
>
> Nevertheless, there's no doubt in your mind that he (man) will learn
> as soon as he's rid of certain bad old habits and when common sense and
> science have completely reeducated human nature and directed it along the
> proper channels. You seem certain that man himself will give up erring
> *of his own free will* and will stop opposing his will to his interests. You
> say, moreover, that science itself will teach man (although I say it's a lux-
> ury) that he has neither will nor whim—never had, as a matter of fact—
> that he is something like a piano key or an organ stop; that, on the other
> hand, there are natural laws in the universe, and whatever happens to him
> happens outside his will, as it were, by itself, in accordance with the laws
> and man will no longer be responsible for his acts. Life will be really easy
> for him then. All human acts will be listed in something like logarithm
> tables, say up to the number 108,000, and transferred to a timetable. Or,
> better still, catalogues will appear, designed to help us in the way our dic-
> tionaries and encyclopedias do. They will carry detailed calculations and
> exact forecasts of everything to come, so that no adventure and no action
> will remain possible in this world (108–109).
>
> Then—it is still you talking—new economic relations will arise, rela-
> tions ready-made and calculated in advance with mathematical precision,
> so that all possible questions instantaneously disappear because they re-
> ceive all the possible answers. Then the utopian palace of crystal will be
> erected; then . . . well, then, those will be the days of bliss. . . . (109)
>
> Now, human nature is just the opposite. It acts as an entity, using
> everything it has, conscious and unconscious, and even if it deceives us,
> it lives. I suspect, ladies and gentlemen, that you're looking at me with
> pity, wondering how I can fail to understand that an enlightened, cultured
> man, such as the man of the future, could not deliberately wish to harm
> himself. It's sheer mathematics to you. I agree, it is mathematics. But let
> me repeat to you for the hundredth time that there is one instance when a
> man can wish upon himself, in full awareness, something harmful, stupid,
> and even completely idiotic. He will do it in order to *establish his right* to
> wish for the most idiotic things and not to be obliged to have only sensible
> wishes. But what if a quite absurd whim, my friends, turns out to be the
> most advantageous thing on earth for us, as sometimes happens? Spe-
> cifically, it may be more advantageous to us than any other advantages,
> even when it most obviously harms us and goes against all the sensible
> conclusions of our reason about our interest—because, whatever else, it
> leaves us our most important, most treasured possession: our individual-
> ity. (112–113)

It should not be thought that the utopian spirit with respect to descriptions of the intellectual functions—rather than the characteristics —of rulers of a world-order, is to be found only among intellectuals, philosophers, the literati, and occasionally the projections of some natural scientists or of those who lean heavily upon the advances in modern science and technology, even though they themselves may not be natural scientists. We find the utopian quantitative bias even in the writings of some well-known sociologists, although in such cases it is cryptic rather than explicit. Thus Dodd (1947)—although in no sense authoritarian in outlook—has nevertheless set forth in mathematical form in his book, *Systematic Social Science*,[3] a collection of techniques dealing with various aspects of social control and planning, which could easily be one form in which the expertise of planetary, utopian administrators might be expressed. The abuse of such techniques and the prospect of their being used in a highly alienated fashion, lacking in imagination, sympathy, and moral concern for the plight of real individuals, would obviously bear out Dostoyevsky's fears.

It would be quite possible, in discussing the social patterns revealed by classical utopian writing, to show the various expressions of abstract social order these reflect. We have here touched briefly upon only a few of these aspects, but many more could be cited. The depiction, however, of complete and packaged utopias—totalistic in the classical sense—has dwindled in our time. Here and there we find conspicuous exceptions, like Zamyatin's *We* (1924), Capek's *R.U.R.*[4] (1961), Huxley's[5] *Brave New World* (1932), or his more recent *Island* (1962). But most of these works of the human imagination really depict surrealistic nightmares. Even if they do tend to describe complete but abstract social orders, they

---

[3] There are two chapters in this work to which my comments are relevant. These are Chapter 13, "Group Tensions," pp. 394–434, which deals with social control, and Chapter 18, "Planned Societies," pp. 602–634, which deals quite obviously with the nature of planning. From past acquaintance and correspondence with Professor Dodd, I can attest to his democratic values. What I am trying to stress here is only that the quantitative paraphernalia of social control and planning worked out by Dodd could lend itself to totalitarian use and abuse in the hands of members of an administrative elite possessing an authoritarian character structure.

[4] *R.U.R.* is an abbreviation for the firm Rossum's Universal Robots, which in Capek's play mass-produces millions of human beings to do the many chores required in this world. Capek's work centers around the theme of how the robots acquire the baggage of conscience, psyche, and soul, and then revolt against their masters. Capek's intent was an early equivalent in literary form of what Ellul (1964) means when he declares that technology has its own imperatives.

[5] In this connection see also Huxley's *Brave New World Revisited* (1958). This volume is not a depiction of a packaged utopia, but it should be read as a postscript to *Brave New World*. In this second volume Huxley is concerned with indicating how far the West has moved in the direction of some of the grimmer features of dystopia since the publication of the earlier volume.

are really antiutopias. In fact, in comparison with the true horrors of Stalin's Russia, Hitler's Germany, the Soviet slave-labor camps, and the Nazi death-camps most efforts at complete descriptions of abstract, social order seem merely tongue-in-cheek satires. The centralism of authoritarian, mass societies is now deeply feared and hated; and one result is the modern tendency to equate utopian thinking with the loss of human freedom and many other precious values. The price of this attitude is, of course, abstention from utopian preoccupations.

Thoughtless technicians and planners are blind to the despotisms inherent in large-scale social and political organization and support forward tendencies toward the type of dystopia that is now so much satirized. Intellectuals inveigh bitterly against authoritarian centralism and in recent years have promoted decentralization in its various forms, overlooking the fact that there can be undesirable forms of decentralization as well as of centralization. Thoughtful scientists and technologists who display social concern constitute a halfway house; they are unsympathetic toward totalitarian tendencies but at the same time, they preserve the banner of value-free research. They engage in research efforts to forecast, on as sound a basis as possible, either coming developments in science and technology or the possible social consequences of individual inventions. Some students of the future attempt to do a little of both.

But as a result, current work on studies of the future—occupying some of our best minds, impressed by the significance of the social impact of science and technology—has tended to sound the death knell to serious efforts at utopian versions of social order. The literati do not have the scientific information to do a creditable and a credible job. The scientists and technologists prefer the more prosaic, more fragmentary, and more prudent preoccupation with the effects of specific discoveries and inventions. And so, the utopian daemon makes its thrust today—covertly, to be sure—within the new field of studies of the future. We have escaped the traps of utopian, intellectual holism only to walk into a new labyrinth engendered by uncoordinated, piecemeal prediction. Let us turn, then, to this new set of difficulties.

STUDIES OF THE FUTURE: LIMITATIONS AND NEEDS

The impact of social complexity and the knowledge explosion. As we have noted, by and large contemporary projections tend to be piecemeal rather than global in nature. Utopian description has been superseded by studies of the future in every imaginable direction. But even if thinkers today wished to distill a utopian vision out of the alembic of modern science and technology, most would hesitate, and for some very sound reasons. First, the social systems and subsystems that science and technology are generating in our time are too complex to be understood well by anybody. Second, as a result of the knowledge explosion, so many new scientific and technical developments are occurring with smaller and smaller time lags in application, that everybody's knowledge is becoming increasingly fragmentary.

Consider the first of these barriers. The complexity of our modern social systems and many of their subsystems is beyond imagination. Even in so limited a subsystem as that of economics, some of the econometric models required for even a first approximation to economic realities tax man's powers of analysis to a staggering degree. It is not so much that the mathematics involved is highly advanced (which it frequently is not), but that the properties of the physical analogues and control systems upon which they are sometimes based may require much information if they are to be properly understood and considerable ingenuity in an engineering sense, if they are to be broadly heuristic. This, for instance, can be seen in the work of Tustin (1953). Occasionally these economic subsystems are a strain upon attention because they require such a variety of new mathematical techniques. The breadth of that mathematical spectrum can be roughly gauged from the work of Baumol (1961).

Yet the universe of discourse of economics is only a subsystem at best. When the focus of our attention is the macrosystem of our physical environment or our sociopolitical macrosystem, the situation becomes much more complicated. W. L. Rogers (1967:260) has put it succinctly:

> It is amazing and somewhat frightening to consider the rate at which our environment is increasing in complexity. By adding two states to our union, the number of political interfaces on the state level has increased almost 2,500-fold. By adding one new cabinet post to the existing ten, the number of departmental interfaces has increased by eleven-fold, not by 10 per cent. In all areas one can see that each component added to the political or physical environment increases its complexity factorially and not linearly, and correlation and control of this proliferation of components require greater and greater analytical skills as well as much more rapid evaluation techniques.

In the face of such increasing social complexity, the likelihood that a contemporary thinker will be able to construct a utopia based upon modern science, technology, and social invention begins to dwindle toward the vanishing point. In such cases future-forecasters may feel that they are much better off doing precisely what has always been done typically in research; that is, they will choose a small, comfortable, and manageable problem.

Consider the second of these barriers—the time lags in the application of new discoveries. The shorter these time lags are, the less likely
they are to come to the attention of someone who tries to prevision completely a future state—one in which the total system described will be
scientifically and technologically up to date. The less likely the possibility
that important new developments can be known and incorporated into
the work of a forecaster trying to prevision a utopia based upon science,
the more likely is that utopia to be out of kilter for having missed a technological development that may come into widespread use.

Thus Baker (1965) has shown that the time lags in the application of
new discoveries are constantly dwindling.[6] The time lag for the electric
motor was approximately sixty-six years (1821–1886); for the vacuum
tube, approximately thirty-four years (1882–1915); for radio broadcasting, approximately thirty-six years (1887–1922); for X-ray tubes, approximately nineteen years (1895–1913); for the nuclear reactor, approximately eleven years (1932–1942); for radar, approximately six years
(1935–1940); for the atomic bomb, approximately eight years (1938–
1945); for the transistor, approximately four years (1948–1951); for the
solar battery, approximately three years (1953–1955); and for stereo-
specific rubbers and plastics, approximately three years (1955–1958).
Only eighteen months elapsed between the discovery of coherent light
and the ability to make practical use of it, and the same interval of time
was required to develop the super-conducting solenoid magnet. These
magnets can create magnetic fields thousands of time more powerful
than those previously produced by magnets of other types and of the
same size. Such development is so important that Baker points out that
if we ever succeed in controlling nuclear fusion or certain applications
of magnetohydrodynamics—both of which could revolutionize the power
industry—it will probably be done by means of the super-conducting
solenoid magnet.

The accelerated pace of technological development, as described by
Baker, is clearly yielding a world of smaller and smaller time lags between discovery and application. In such a world a utopian writer could
err considerably. In the judgment of history, he could be criticized for
having missed the mark. If he had projected a vision of the future at a
specified date not too distant from the time of writing, that utopia
could be considerably different from the actual world at the actual date
at which the writer had cast his utopia. And, of course, the evolution of
the actual world might have depended upon important scientific and
technological developments that had never come to his attention, because

---

[6] The paper in question appears as a chapter in a book edited for the Columbia
University Seminar On Technology And Social Change. Baker is Executive Vice-
President of Bell Laboratories.

of the dwindling time lags between their discovery and application. Many such developments, of course, would have taken place after the fabricator of a utopia had finished his work, precisely because of these dwindling time lags. The more he had missed of the forms of things unknown, the greater could one expect the future gap to be between his utopia and the real world.

It is quite true, of course, that these diminishing time lags are a result of the large-scale Research and Development functions of modern corporate enterprise and of federally financed crash programs. But the point is that future-forecasters may in fact be quite sensible in not constructing complete utopian, social orders, rooted in man's scientific and inventive ingenuity, when their knowledge of the state of the arts must necessarily be very incomplete. Utopian projections are likely to be obsolescent even before they are completed.

In the face of inescapable ignorance and burdensome complexity, it is professionally risky to try one's hand at a global utopia based upon modern science and technology. Short-term specialized forecasts in specialized contexts are the rule (and by short-term I mean the period between the present and 2000 A.D.). Such forecasts reduce the margin of uncertainty and error and can do less damage to one's reputation.

Yet in spite of the paucity of utopian projections of the short-term variety, nevertheless, there have been some attempts at nonutopian, large-scale forecasts, notably in the work of some of the contributors to the volumes of the Commission on the Year 2000,[7] particularly in Volumes II and II-A by Kahn and his associates. Such forecasts take a large panorama over a short period, but do not try to furnish a utopian vision of the good life, molded nearer to the heart's desire of the forecaster. Almost all the first ten chapters of this volume are examples of nonutopian, large-scale forecasts, as the titles themselves indicate: Postindustrial Society in the Standard World; International Politics in the Standard World; Some Canonical Variations from the Standard World; Some Possibilities for Nuclear Wars; Other Twenty-First Century Nightmares; and The International System in the Very Long Run. In addition to nonutopian, large-scale forecasts of the future, there have also been some examples in the field of future-forecasting, of quasi-utopian scenarios, based upon science and technology. These scenarios risk disjointed descriptions of large-scale, abstract order, but they have been projected so far into the future that their fabricators run little risk of

---

[7] The prime examples of this venturesome activity are the volumes by Kahn, Pfaff, and Wiener (1966) and Kahn and Wiener (1967). A few of the papers in the remaining volumes are similarly bold in approach. A highly abbreviated version of the material by Kahn and his co-workers also appears in a paper by Kahn (1967) in *Daedalus*.

being proven wrong for some time to come. This is particularly true, for instance, of the work of Thomson (1955), Darwin (1952), and Bacon (1959) and of some of the projections of Arthur C. Clarke (1963), particularly for the period 2000–2100 in a by now famous table.

Interaction of new developments and their effects. There are, of course, other reasons—besides the knowledge explosion and the growing complexity of our social systems—that explain why utopias do not arise out of the projections of our future-forecasters. First, the main purpose behind the current rash of studies of the future is to assess, as accurately and as reasonably as possible, scientific and technological developments that seem reasonably achievable in the near future, in the light of current scientific knowledge and the state of the technological arts. Second, most predictions are temporally linear in relation to current and anticipated developments, that is, the forecaster seeks imaginatively to prevision possible social and technological consequences that may arise in time out of those scientific and technological developments with which he is familiar and with which he concerns himself. We see this to some extent in the work of Prehoda (1967) and MacBride (1967), to name two of the more representative and recent volumes in the field of studies of the future. But in work of this type there is, of course, little or no effort to provide a coordinated picture, which would evaluate the tendencies of some of these developments to reinforce or hamper one another's anticipated social effects. This coordinated picture is obviously essential to a rational, scientific utopia, but difficult in a world as complex as our own. To effect such a coordinated picture requires intellectual teamwork, because the complexity is usually beyond the capacity of a single man. But utopias are the product of individual vision rather than intellectual togetherness.

Third, to construct a utopia the writer must prefer some set of goals or alternatives over all other possible sets. In short, he must be value-biased and willing to explore which technologies will support these goals, in what way, and through what exploitative instrumentalities. Furthermore, the utopian writer has to justify in moral terms his particular choice of goals. The future-forecaster usually seeks to avoid value-biases of this sort. Only by avoiding them can he preserve the professional image of value-neutrality and the public expectation that he avoid what Caldwell (1968) calls *biopolitics*.[8] As a result of these considerations, most

---

[8] Caldwell (1968:424) defines biopolitics as follows: " 'Biopolitics,' then, though it certainly does not designate a science, is a useful piece of shorthand to suggest political effects to reconcile biological facts and popular values—notably ethical values —in the formation of public policies. It affords a selective focus on a portion of the larger issue of the relationship of science to technology."

of the work in the new field of studies of the future is completely different from global utopian writing and efforts to project improvements in the condition of man.

As we have noted, most projections of future scientific and technological developments lack two things: one is the frequent failure to develop techniques for assessing the possible social effects of each predicted scientific and technological development; and the other is the absence of reliable methodologies for determining the probable relationships among all such effects. These two defects produce an unexplored and uninvestigated inconsistency when an entire set of inventions or discoveries are predicted by forecasters, whether they act alone or as members of a team. It is these lacks I had in mind when, at the close of the previous section, I noted that future-forecasters had escaped the trap of utopian holistic thinking with respect to abstract social order, only to run into the ambiguities and difficulties created by uncoordinated, piecemeal predictions.

The considerations neglected in short-term forecasts, then, where a host of future scientific and technological possibilities are previsioned, flow from the failure to consider the consistency of sets of forecasts. For clarity, I shall present the argument in somewhat abstract form. Consider a ledger of forecasts in which the following inventions have been predicted: $I_1, I_2, I_3, \ldots I_n$, in which I_n is the nth invention (scientific, technical, or institutional) that has been predicted. Since every invention or development will have both social and technical effects, if we designate the kth effect of the rth invention or development, as E^r_k, then the state of the system of effects envisioned by the ledger, L, can be represented as follows:

$$I_1 \longrightarrow E^1_1, E^1_2, \ldots E^1_r$$
$$I_2 \longrightarrow E^2_1, E^2_2, \ldots E^2_j$$
$$\cdot \quad \cdot \quad \cdot \quad \cdot \quad \cdot \quad \cdot \quad \cdot \quad \cdot \quad \cdot$$
$$I_n \longrightarrow E^n_1, E^n_2, \ldots E^n_m$$

where the arrow is to be read as "yields."

The ledger schema I have symbolized in abstract form assumes, of course, that one or more fairly reliable methodologies have been developed to assess the probable social and technical effects of a given invention for a known social context, an established development of the sciences, and a known state of the technological arts. Such methodologies, as I have emphasized, have not as yet actually been evolved.[9] The schema

---

[9] Those methodologies that have been developed and used to date, in the field of future-forecasting, have been brought together by Jantsch (1967).

is constructed on the assumption that such methodologies can in fact be developed and must of necessity be forthcoming.

The first thing to notice about this ledger schema is that some of the E's from various I's can discourage the development of still other I's forecast by the ledger, if some effects put in an appearance earlier than those inventions that are expected to produce the second batch of effects. Thus, it would make no sense to forecast increased longevity, health, and biological vigor, due to inventions or developments, I_s, I_t, and I_u, and then to forecast one or more other inventions, I_a, I_b, I_c, which are bound to have the effect of increasing air pollution, water pollution, nutritionally poor food products, and a host of other effects that can reasonably be assumed will collectively reduce the life expectancy.

The second feature to notice is that if all of the E's from each given I have been reasonably estimated, certain inconsistencies are bound to result. The effect, E^k_r, may make it senseless to consider the effect, E^q_p, for if E^k_r, is an anticipated, rising standard of living in underdeveloped countries—a standard of living gradually approximating that of the West, either currently or in the near future—and if E^q_p is the expectation that essential resources, R_1, R_2, . . . R_L, will be rapidly depleted from those same countries, then at $t = t'$, the critically based time of the ledger schema, these joint effects may become incompatible or, at least, highly improbable. By this I mean that a future-forecaster cannot reasonably expect country A, to experience a rising standard of living (E^k_r) from I_k, at time t_1, if country A's proven resources, R_x, R_y, and R_z, will have been considerably depleted because of I_q which became commercially available at time t_2, and t_2 is earlier than t_1. This is clearly true if we assume an economic world in which the terms of trade—as at present—determine the ability to purchase or manufacture inventions like I_k. In such a world, country A will simply not be able to earn the hard currency to purchase or make I_k, if it has insufficient amounts of R_x, R_y, and R_z to export.

A third feature of this schema involves the accuracy of the time forecast. If the schema predicts that all the I's will have put in an appearance no later than $t = 2000$ A.D., and if some of the expected effects flowing from a given set of I's, all of which appeared between 1975–1985, are reasonable anticipations from these I's, then we face the following possibility. Some of these anticipated effects can be expected to reinforce some of the anticipated effects that will stem from a set of I's, that are expected to appear sometime after 1985. In that case some of the effects expected to be socially observable by 2000 A.D., may appear considerably earlier than that year. Or we may face the antithetical situation, in which the earlier set of effects can be expected to inhibit the action of some anticipated later ones (from later inventions), giving rise to the opposite error, namely, that effects expected by 2000 A.D. may never occur at all or occur negligibly. Furthermore, early effects may have reinforcing or inhibitory action not upon other later anticipated effects but rather upon other later expected inventions and developments. In this case the ledger schema could prove historically to be in error in two different senses. First, if the effects are reinforcing, some inventions may occur far earlier than expected. Second, if the effects are inhibitory, some of the inventions postulated in the ledger may never occur at all. The first type of error is temporal, the second, substantive.

There are still other errors in ledger forecasts. The relation between some pairs of expected effects is *unilateral;* that is, one effect occurring earlier in time can be expected to reinforce or even produce a second effect, but not vice versa if their temporal order is reversed. A ledger schema is not of much value when we have no idea which pairs of effects are unilateral. This, in turn, would demand a good estimate of the temporal order in which we can expect effects to occur. Some effects may have proven to be reciprocally related, that is, they may prove to be mutually reinforcing or mutually inhibitory. These would be examples, of course, of positive feedback. Some pairs of effects would be related in the sense that an increase in one dampens the growth of the other and a decrease in the first enhances the growth of the second. These would be examples of negative feedback relationships. Some effects are variable in nature and some are of a one-time nature. The first type of effect can conceivably be controlled by factors exogenous to the social system in which the *I*'s are playing out their consequences. The second type of effect, however, is controllable only with great difficulty. For instance, a one-time effect could be a decision to locate a new and large city for the administration of a world government, constructed at a great cost in time and money. In that case, the prospect of a relocation for almost any reason—except possibly a widespread disaster like an earthquake—would be practically nil. The value of a ledger schema is thus curtailed when we do not or cannot separate out those effects that are variable and controllable from those of the type that are not.

One of the most crucial deficiencies of a ledger forecast will occur if we fail to try to predict the social effects of all the *I*'s. In that case we face a real problem, since some effects are desirable and some are not. If we do not know which undesirable effects are to be expected, we will be in no position to block them off exogenously, and they might usher in a fund of misery more than offsetting all the expected beneficial effects. But perhaps the most ludicrous aspect of a ledger of *I* predictions involves what I choose to call *technological irrelevance.* Let me explain what I mean.

Suppose that we can describe the state of the social system, *S*, at

$t = t'$. Let us now suppose that a future-forecaster has predicted I_j at $t \leq t'$ but has also predicted I_k at $t = t'' > t'$. But because the effects of the technology available to S at time, t', require time to work themselves out, the state of the system, S, at t'' may be such that I_k would be totally irrelevant to it and could in no sense be incorporated in S at t''. If we assume no price advantages for either I_j or I_k and the ability to meet any amount of demand for either, then technological irrelevance can occur.

For instance, suppose a forecaster predicts the development of new synthetics (I_j) at $t = t'$ and suppose that his ledger-schema also forecasts an unusual demand for the raw material export products of several underdeveloped economies, because of an agrobiological invention (I_k) that will rapidly multiply yields per acre. Then, if the industrial end-uses of I_j are largely the same as those obtained from underdeveloped economies, by virtue of I_k—and remembering that I_k was predicted for t''—the latter forecast is somewhat absurd. I_k has no *technological relevance* for the system, S, at t'', since it will not be absorbable into the system, S, already employing I_j for the same end-uses.

Many of the considerations stressed in the preceding paragraphs are simply ignored by a number of scholars who work on studies of the future. To the extent that the effects of inventions and developments upon the system, S, are not worked out, to that extent many ledger projections may prove to be worthless and, in other cases, highly questionable. What seems to me to be absolutely necessary is that in all studies of the future, I-E ledger systems should be constructed. By doing so, the practical relevance of the forecasts and the possibility of their future social utilization, will thereby be increased.

Predicting events versus predicting trends. There have been few checks on scientific and technological forecasting since this type of effort came into its own following World War II. Too little time has elapsed to do scientific soothsaying any justice. Occasionally, however, a forecaster makes some short-term predictions that are susceptible to confirmation or falsification. One such series, for instance, was made by Ithiel de Sola Pool (1967:931–933) and several of these have already been disconfirmed—all within the period 1965–1968.[10] Among these are the following: (1) Major fighting in Vietnam will peter out about 1967; (2) Lyndon Johnson will have been re-elected President of the United States in 1968; and (3) Negro voting in 1968 will have come up to white levels, except in five states. If mistakes of this sort can occur in forecasting only three years ahead, it would seem that longer-range forecasts

---

[10] De Sola Pool forecast for the following periods: 1965–1970, 1970–2000, and 2000–2015, A.D.

should be subject to even greater error. Much depends on whether the forecast is of a specific event like examples (1) and (2) or of a trend, like example (3). It may be argued, of course, that the risk of error in forecasting may prove to be less for long-term trends than short-term specific events. Historians, I imagine, would champion this claim.

However, future-forecasters still share one tendency with many of the utopian thinkers and that is—when dealing with aspects of social life, institutions, and processes—to think in abstract terms. I am not here referring to the complete description of whole, but drastically reconstructed, societies, so as to give free rein to the penchant for creating utopian dreams. I am referring, instead, to global and statistical generalities, even though these are not necessarily related to one another by the forecaster, through some imputed pattern. Since future-forecasting must be largely made in aggregative terms and with deference to trends, the necessity of being abstract is inescapable because this type of abstracting is an intrinsic and inescapable feature of trend-forecasting and of aggregative analysis. Thus forecasts of substantial and important aspects of social order will of necessity be abstract. This is a prime necessity, for instance, in intersectoral analysis in economics. I do not want to be misunderstood here. I well recognize that predictions of concrete events, scientific discoveries, and the prediction of future, commercial applications of contemporary science and technology, are held in many quarters to be the chief pièces de résistance of future-forecasting. But some of that forecasting *must* be made in terms of trends and aggregative analysis and, by definition, such forecasts will involve projections of abstract aspects of large-scale, social order. Projections of this type are frequently indispensable. But—although indispensable and inescapable—nevertheless, it still remains true that much that was repugnant in abstract utopian projections of complete societies may also be found to be repugnant in the future-forecasting of trends. This is because the information we seek through trends and aggregative analysis, will, as always, overlook the plight of the flesh-and-blood individual. Is there much of a choice between the alienation from one's fellow man that results from the utopian, panoramic view and the alienation that results from the quantitatively shored-up trend line or curve or the standardized treatment of the individual that results from aggregative analysis?

Likewise, much of the moral criticism that was leveled against aspects of total, abstract, social order in utopian thinking may prove to be equally cogent when hurled against future-forecasts of novel social processes and institutional innovations. Both these types of forecasts can also be abstract in nature, even though they are made on a smaller-than-utopian scale. It is not, of course, the forecasters who are being put morally on the spot, so to speak. The forecasters may not even like what they foresee. If it is an undesirable condition that is forecasted, in what way does the moral posture come into the picture? It is only when (1) there are people who welcome the condition uncritically and do nothing to stop it exogenously and (2) when there are people who do not welcome the undesirable condition but argue that nothing can be done about it—that history is just wound up that way—who are morally blamable.

The backward look. The fragmentary projections of future-forecasters, as we have said, tend to be value-free. If, then, men do what they can to make these projections come true, there is often no telling what type of social transformations they may usher into being. This will be particularly true when men make little effort to assess the social effects of new developments. One has a feeling, however, that such indifference to the effects of science and technology will result in an exacerbation of the worst features of mass society—bureaucracy, alienation, anomie, authoritarianism, dehumanization, depersonalization, dishonest forms of egalitarianism, and so on. Thus it can be argued that the greatest return in social welfare from future-forecasting would be to gear such forecasting to a notion of the good life—in short, social philosophy. Notions of the good life can vary, of course. I strongly suspect, however, that most millennial dreams (and a good many short-term ones, in addition) could achieve consensus on many goals. This type of partnership—between social philosophy and forecasts concerning the anticipated developments that can shore up the goals of men—has not as yet, however, been tried very seriously.

What has been tried, however, is not the forward look but the backward look. That is, much of our present behavior is based upon assumptions that sprang up before the Great Age Of Science and that were regarded as self-evident for a long time. But science and technology have given the lie to many of these assumptions and made others highly questionable. It is a valuable project and exercise to see how many of our workaday assumptions have been rendered invalid by science and technology.

The backward look is able to indicate how both current and anticipated developments in science and technology tend to render invalid or obsolescent many of the assumptions of traditional group behavior in some specified context. The value of the backward look is that if some examples of current social behavior rest on assumptions now clearly irrelevant or patently false, there is an outside chance that men may drop them and cease those forms of group, pathological behavior that rest on such outmoded assumptions. The task, in making use of science and technology for the backward look, is always to show that either (1) *current* science and technology make certain traditional group assumptions archaic and dysfunctional, or (2) that *anticipated* developments in science and technology will make such assumptions unusable. The use of studies of the future for taking the backward look can, therefore, be quite valuable. For this reason more studies of this critically retrospective type should be pursued by scholars specializing in the social, cultural, intellectual, educational, economic, and political impacts created by current and emerging developments in science and technology.

The forward look. The backward look possesses two inherent virtues. First, it serves to indicate how developments in science and technology have already partially or completely invalidated historical assumptions in the area of learning and how they have rendered either absurd or irrelevant some of the national and international practices of our time. This type of scholarly concern is, I think, in line with the prescription of Professors Bell and Mau, when they state that—although studies of the future should emphasize emerging tableaus—"consideration should also be given to the problematics of the present and past, both of which are merely complexes of sense data organized with respect to some prior frame of reference." Second, this type of concern can also be transformed into what might also be called "the forward look." By this I mean that studies of the future can also be directed to predicting which of our traditional assumptions and current institutional practices—particularly in the social sciences, law, and business administration—can be expected to become obsolescent and dysfunctional in the near future, as a result of emerging developments in science and technology. Studies of this type then become double-barreled forecasts, for they not only try to substantiate the predictions they make of new developments in science and technology but they also entail the scholarly and social obligation of making clear those forms of contemporary group and institutional behavior that can be expected to have little or no survival-value in the decades that lie ahead. Predicting in this sense serves a most useful social function and, at the same time, serves as a testing ground for the quality of scholarship and methodology in studies of the future.

One type of forward look involves a task that is mandatory, I think, for scholars in the area of studies of the future. The task depends upon the recognition that those areas of the globe that have always been regarded as uninhabitable by men and economically worthless are now actually or potentially open for human settlement, are economically quite valuable, and may be, in many instances, far richer than even some of the well-settled and well-endowed areas of the globe. Man's adaptation of nature tends to be a neglected area in the emerging discipline of studies of the future. At the same time the conception of settlement possibilities, that is, our concepts of what can become positions on the community spectrum, in terms of physical viability, is considerably enlarged. These geographical prospects, therefore, become at the same time an enlargement of the working area for studies of the future.

TOWARD A SOCIAL PHILOSOPHY
FOR STUDIES OF THE FUTURE

It must be admitted that current fears that our much-vaunted progress in science and technology could lead to the dystopias and antiutopias of contemporary literature are not unreasonable. Certainly the dystopian end results with which we have all become familiar in the literature could become a reality if scientific and technological advances are allowed to drift toward any social results, as long as they create foci of profit for private enterprises, groups, and institutions. Ellul's (1964) fears that technology may contain its own imperatives are perfectly sound, unless men act as exogenous agents upon the system of applied science and technology, to direct it toward social goals and purposes on which consensus has been reached.

What we therefore need is a rough tableau of a first approximation to a social philosophy for an age of science and technology. Although I am well aware of the risks of dealing with the question of which social values and goals are most worthwhile for a scientific humanism, I feel that my efforts will be useful to those who are interested in the study of the future. Essentially my first approximation to such a tableau is an effort to state either those large-scale problems to whose solution science and technology (and I subsume under this pair of terms all the *methods* of science) can be expected to make a contribution or an effort to state those broad problems, issues, and questions that will still have to be dealt with in some way, in any of the rosy scientific futures that are being projected in our time.

A Tableau of Issues for the Construction of a Social Philosophy
for an Age of Science and Technology

Economic Issues

1. How can we learn to distinguish between worthless consumer commodities and economic wealth in personal and social needs, so that science and technology (hereafter referred to as S & T) can be bent toward the production of wealth only?

2. Can "managed demand" for the new products created by S & T be exercised so as to avoid the waste of natural resources?

3. Can we develop a new quantitative economics—*cybermetrics*, the chrematistics for the affluence created by the S & T of a cybernating society?

4. How can we prevent the corporate control of S & T in the transition period toward the postindustrial society?

5. How shall public resources of staggering value—such as the shale oil deposits in Colorado, Utah, and Wyoming—be protected from private control?

6. How can S & T contribute to the liquidation of poverty in partnership with social and economic inventions?

7. How can S & T, together with social inventions, help to create a just reallocation of terrestrial planetary resources? Of the resources of the oceans and the seas? Of the Arctic and Antarctic?

8. In what ways can the methods of science, combined with projections of future populations and data on proven world resources, be used to determine the number of generations that can be expected to enjoy a specified standard of living?

9. If, as certain writers like Theobald (1968) and McHale (1968) seem to think, a cybernated society is now possible, in what ways can S & T and social invention bring about the economic program envisaged in the by now well-known *Manifesto of the Ad Hoc Committee on the Triple Revolution?*

10. What type of welfare planning is most appropriate for a cybernating society, which intends to distribute affluence rather than compete for it?

11. In what ways can agricultural and export-import practices become rational and equitable, so that one can end situations such as the ability of advanced nations to manipulate entire economies of undeveloped countries, particularly economically monolithic, one-crop economies?

12. In what ways can the pathologies of American agriculture be ended—such as the situation in which plantation owners and corporate farmers in the South are paid thousands of dollars not to produce, while sharecroppers nearby do not receive enough to survive?

13. How can waste produced by industrial practices and irrational consumption be eliminated in a scientific society that seeks to exhibit moral concern for posterity and to husband resources?

14. How can the housing needs of the citizens of technologically advanced countries be met, as long as the distribution of income remains uneven?

15. How can the regressive tax structures of advanced countries, like that of the United States, be changed? These are the tax structures that ease up on corporations through various types of exemption but corral large amounts of the income of the middle class and workers, in order to pay for wars, define research, explore space, and so on?

16. In what ways can scientific method be married to an egalitarian ethic, so that a substitute for the profit motive can be found that will move us just as effectively toward affluence and economic security as does the present system of competition?

17. What scientific (as contrasted with ethical) reasons can be adduced for moving toward an egalitarian distribution of wealth; what are the practical

means for accomplishing this objective; and what would be the advantages and disadvantages it would bring in its wake?

18. How can our social fabric be reconstructed so that there is a useful economic niche for both the young and the old? At present, the young are reduced to innocuous desuetude by the schools acting as babysitters, while the retired are thrown on the scrap heap, some as young as the forties. We are economically permissive only in the middle range of age.

Social Issues

1. How can a garrison state be avoided? The militarization of our urban police and their coalition with military units, in order to quell riots, is regarded by some social critics as an early portent of an authoritarian trend.

2. How can national, pathological forms of bureaucracy and overcentralization be liquidated in the face of the management tasks facing all governments in our complex world? By the same token, how can the international system be stabilized by appropriate, international managerial controls that do not act as millstones on national development?

3. How can man end wars once and for all, regardless of their ostensible causes? If these causes are inherent in human nature, how can aggressive energies be deflected into socially useful purposes on an international scale in order to create an international public sector?

4. The number of different types of community that can be constructed by men is potentially quite large. By historical accident, however, the community spectrum has been quite limited. How can a wider band of this spectrum be realized in a world increasingly subject to homogenization? How can science, technology, scientific method, and ethics be brought to bear upon the problem of designing more possibilities on this community spectrum? What are the types of community that can generate the most social welfare at minimum input costs (community cost-benefit ratios)? The types of input to which we refer are resources, time, money, and talent.

5. What types of community can best promote the great Greek educational ideal of *paideia*? This is the ideal that demanded that men not only develop their own potentialities to the full but also move toward self-conscious social and community responsibility.

6. What can be done to make the world less Hobbesian in nature? What curbs and safeguards can be developed to reduce the exploitation of man by man?

7. What is the proper use of political power in an age of affluence ushered into being by a cybernated society? What can the powerful gain in a society which assures income, security, health, education, and every other type of social welfare, with little variation in the amounts of these goods from person to person?

8. How shall a complex society, dominated by the union of science, technology, and social altruism, decide who shall control and manage it as an organism? What shall the qualifications of such controllers be? How often shall con-

trollers be rotated? What would be the motivations to achieve power status in the cybernated society?

9. What are man's most valid social needs? Can we achieve consensus as to what needs are universal for all cultures that rest upon the foundations of science and technology? Is any budget of needs—apart from organic needs—subject only to conditioning and manipulation or are there psychic needs that are stable over time? Social needs? Aesthetic needs?

10. How shall we distribute social rewards and punishments, to whom, why, upon what occasion, and for what purposes? What kinds of rewards are socially available in an affluent society—other than psychic rewards of prestige and rewards of special opportunity?

11. How can all forms of alienation be eliminated from mass society? In particular, how can we reduce or eliminate alienation from self, one's fellowman, the opposite sex, work, society, Nature, and what some philosophers have called the Mystery of Being?

12. How shall we eliminate race prejudice? Class differentiation for status, snobbery, selfishness, and a separatism that seeks a false sense of personal identity?

13. How shall we deal with the conflict between the generations? We are now facing a generational gap of those raised in the industrial society of our time and those first beginning to glimpse the possibilities of the post-industrial society.

14. How can we get rid of the spiritual social pathologies of mass society? We here contrast the spiritual pathologies with the behavioral and institutional ones: crime, prostitution, alcoholism, poverty, racism, and so on. These latter are the standard concerns of social welfare and social reforms. The spiritual pathologies have been named and are widely known. They include, among others, bureaucracy, alienation, anomie, depersonalization, dehumanization, homogenization, and *acedia,* or spiritual sloth. These malaises are not caused by large-scale science and technology but they have surely been reinforced by them—as well as by the large-scale institutions that mediate their impact on the social organism. In addition, these are the malaises that most utopias neglect and that most dystopias satirize.

15. How can we measure the increasing *social complexity* of modern life and relate the effects of such increasing complexity to the present distribution of human intelligence? In short, is there a danger that the complexity of our society may act as an information overload for the average man? He is expected to understand his society and to express his consent to suggested alternatives for manipulating it, in order to effect given ends.

16. How shall we measure the quality of life in our socitey? Have thinkers like Bauer (1966) and Gross (1967) made the right start in this direction? How shall we improve it? Does democracy entail the necessity of a quality-spectrum that goes from the bestial (appreciation of bullfights and other sadistic delights) to the sublime? Or must we insist that spiritual taste, social sensitivity, and intelligent discrimination are social obligations?

17. When will scientists—particularly natural scientists—abandon the

impossible rhetoric that science must be value-free and neutral? Scientists and technologists are the primary makers of the future. It is precisely for this reason that it is clearly their obligation to keep separate the notion that scientific inquiry must not be surcharged with sentiment from the notion that the results of science must not be linked to special pleading on behalf of our common humanity. As Robert Lynd (1939) put it in his perceptive book, *Knowledge For What?*, the use of the findings of science to serve mankind's evolutionary and social needs is one of its two basic raisons d'être. The other is the satisfaction of the intellectual lust to pattern experience in one or another reliable form. It is acceptable professional rhetoric, of course, to restrict science to the latter aim and to eschew the former purpose. But under such rhetoric many modern scientists are refusing to face up to their social obligations as men and as citizens. Dr. A as a scientist has every right to keep his professional endeavors unsullied by ideology, partisanship, sentiment, or moral concern. But as a man and a citizen, it is his duty and social obligation to borrow what he knows from the realm of science and use it in the interest of improving the human condition—doubly so when it has a particular bearing on important issues. He should unquestionably bind himself to fulfill the second half of the great Greek ideal of *paideia*, namely, to leave his society a little better off for his efforts than it was when he entered it. Instead, however, of assuming this obligation, many natural scientists are trying to escape it. This moral paralysis was strongly reaffirmed recently by the 24,000 members of the American Physical Society, who voted to keep the organization free of "political issues." Hentoff (1968:57) bitterly comments on their posture:

> . . . They call themselves "value-free" scientists, like the man who invented napalm and assures us he has no feeling of responsibility or concern for the way it has been used. In actuality they are respectable agents of death—both literally and figuratively.

Only when the scientific fraternity can reverse itself on this attitude of being morally neutral can we expect that science and technology may play a bigger and a more pertinent role in the social issues of our time.

Cultural, Moral, Educational, and Scientific Issues

1. What can be done to increase substantially the average fund of human intelligence? In this complex world the intellectual capacity of the average human being has to be raised considerably in order to render the process of socio-economic adjustment both authentic and meaningful. Inasmuch as concerted efforts to improve human intelligence, from the standpoint of recently won knowledge in genetics, brain chemistry, and other biological approaches, will be both remote and morally unacceptable for a long time to come, what can be done by means of formal education, the possibilities of television as envisaged by McLuhan (1966), prenatal control and trait selectivity, better techniques of child-rearing, and more definite community concern for the personal interrelationships of other people, hopefully crystallized in the form of clear-cut, innovative social structures? One thing is certain. Most studies of the future will

be vitiated if public understanding of projections proves to be woefully inadequate and their social acceptability practically nil. Yet unless the distribution of
human intelligence is substantially bettered, studies of the future will degenerate into interesting exercises concerning possibilities only. To translate some of
the projections that have been, and will be made, into social realities, the distribution of human intelligence must be considerably improved.

2. If human nature is infinitely pliable—if, in fact, several human natures
are possible—how shall we determine the best set of traits to work for in man's
makeup, if we want both socially acceptable traits that result in individual distinction and man's social impulses to be developed to the fullest? What do we
want to be the biological-genetic characteristics of specified human groups, al-
lowing for a desirable continuum of variation within such groups? What do we
want the socially desirable psychological repertoires to be? What educational
means can be found to ensure voluntary social acceptance of these ends—
where the educational means are morally humane and honest? Should not
the various possibilities for change, engendered by advances in such areas as
genetics, brain chemistry, the laws of learning in psychology, be brought officially to public attention?

3. How shall we eliminate the grossly alienated types of education, which
now characterize learning at all levels of society? To what ends should education be revamped for an age of science, technology, human welfare, and expected leisure? What is the redefinition of liberation for the human spirit in
such an age? Leonard (1968) has painted a picture of a world in which education is the central activity and has ceased to be alienated—a world in which
every useful educational finding and device is exploited. Should his tableau be
the educational model and benchmark for our time?

4. How shall the compass of human love be spread? By this I mean how
can we reduce the traditional stress by men on their egocentric concerns and
amplify their preoccupation with the life space, needs, and ways of life of other
men—both those within their own culture and those who live in different cultures? Cultural and social provincialism are dangerous traits in a complex society. At the same time they are certainly antithetic to the scientific humanism
that is needed for any coming era in which science and technology are to play
central roles in the improvement of the human condition. More than ever, what
Allport (1960) calls ego-extension—which includes the capacity to identify with
and appreciate other cultures, persons, and ideals—is a needed virtue. By
what means can the compass of love and concern be increased? Will the rise
of nationalism and the defensiveness of modern cultures make the needed increase in ego-extension virtually an impossible expectation?

5. Although physical courage can be found in abundance, intellectual and
moral courage are rare. What institutional innovations can restore the status of
these virtues in Western civilization? How can they be made relevant in the
type of future—cybernated and rationalized—toward which we seem to be
moving?

6. In an age of science and technology and "hard culture" in general, what
will be the roles of literature and the arts? Will "soft culture"—depending, as

it does, upon the unstructured, the autonomous, the unregulated, the behaviorally innovative, the unique pattern of behavior—seem idiosyncratic, abnormal, and irrelevant to a society that is increasingly being bureaucratized, rationalized, and homogenized? What in fact can we expect to be the major themes and frustrations of personal life, in an affluent, smooth-running, and logico-empirical future? Will the broad social panorama be dystopian in nature—resembling the lackluster utopias described by Hillegas (1967)? Will philosophy tomorrow have any of its traditional speculative and normative roles, apart from such areas as linguistic analysis, philosophy of science, logic and scientific method, and the other more rigorous philosophical disciplines? If philosophy is to possess its famous role in which the unexamined life is not worth living, what part will it play in the smooth-running, well-regulated, scientifically tempered world which is the promise of the more distant future?

7. What will the mass culture of the future be like? Will it be excitement, stimulation, novelty, fornication, and distraction, as it is now? Will it be the opiates of the crowd, such as Wolfe described (1965, 1968)? Or will it be soma and psychedelic drugs and organized leisure-time activities, such as have been suggested in a variety of antiutopias? Will taste and subtlety rise in the arts? Will the individual nuance and the subjective continue to receive treatment in belles-lettres? Will the culture of a future age of science and technology be sensate, as Sorokin (1946) described contemporary, mass culture? Will it be even more sensate than it is now? Or will there be a renaissance of high culture that will constitute a pinnacle of aesthetic experience for men?

These, then, constitute a small but, I think, representative sample of some of the issues with which studies of the future must become involved. The issues mentioned merely serve to highlight the call for a social philosophy for an age of science and technology—a social philosophy that must be wedded to studies of the future. The future—and this cannot be emphasized enough—is embedded in a matrix of values.

I come then to the end of my task. I have tried to stress in this chapter a few of those aspects in the study of the future that, I feel, are being insufficiently emphasized. The important point, however, is that the study of the future should take these or similar areas into account. If the themes I have dealt with here are judged to widen our perspectives on the study of the future, then my purpose shall have been served.

REFERENCES

Allport, Gordon W.
   1960   Becoming: Basic Considerations for a Psychology of Personality. New Haven: Yale University Press.

Bacon, Allen
1959   Man's Next Billion Years: On Our Conquest of the Universe. New York: Exposition Press.
Baker, William O.
1965   "The dynamism of science and technology." Pp. 82–107 in Eli Ginsberg (ed.), Technology and Social Change. New York: Columbia University Press.
Bauer, Raymond A. (ed.)
1966   Social Indicators. Cambridge, Mass.: MIT Press.
Baumol, William J.
1961   Economic Theory and Operations Analysis. Englewood Cliffs, N.J.: Prentice-Hall.
Bellamy, Edward
1967   Looking Backward. Cambridge, Mass.: Belknap Press of Harvard University Press.
Caldwell, Lynton K.
1968   "Biopolitics: science, ethics, and public policy." Pp. 423–435 in William R. Nelson (ed.), The Politics of Science: Readings in Science, Technology, and Government. New York: Oxford University Press.
Capek, Karel
1961.   R.U.R. Pp. 1–104 in Joseph and Karel Capek, R.U.R. and The Insect Play. New York: Oxford University Press.
Clarke, Arthur C.
1963   Profiles of the Future: An Inquiry Into the Limits of the Possible. New York: Harper & Row.
Darwin, Sir Charles Galton
1952   The Next Million Years. London: Rupert Hart-Davis.
Dodd, Stuart Carter
1947   Systematic Social Science: A Dimensional Sociology. Beirut, Lebanon: American University of Beirut.
Dostoyevsky, Fyodor
1961   Notes From Underground. White Nights. The Dream of a Ridiculous Man and selections from The House of the Dead. New York: Signet Classics.
Ellul, Jacques
1964   The Technological Society. New York: Knopf.
Goffman, Erving
1965   Stigma: Notes on the Management of Spoiled Identity. Englewood Cliffs, N.J.: Prentice-Hall.
Graubard, Stephen R. (ed.)
1965   "Utopia." Daedalus 94 (Spring):271–525.
Gross, Bertram M. (ed.)
1967   Social Goals and Indicators for American Society. 2 vols. Annals of the American Academy of Political and Social Science 371 (May):1–291 and 373 (September):1–313.

Hentoff, Nat
    1968   "On revolutionary professionalism." Evergreen Review 12 (October):55–57.
Hillegas, Mark R.
    1967   The Future as Nightmare: H. G. Wells and the Anti-Utopians. New York: Oxford University Press.
Huxley, Aldous
    1932   Brave New World. New York: Harper & Row.
    1958   Brave New World Revisited. New York: Harper & Row.
    1962   Island. New York: Harper & Row.
Jantsch, Erich
    1967   Technological Forecasting in Perspective. Paris: Organization for Economic Cooperation and Development.
Kahn, Herman, William Pfaff, and Anthony J. Wiener (eds.)
    1966   The Next Thirty-Three Years: A Framework For Speculation. Vol. II-A. Croton-on-Hudson, N.Y.: Hudson Institute.
Kahn, Herman, and Anthony J. Wiener (eds.)
    1967   The Next Thirty-Three Years: A Framework For Speculation. Vol. II. Croton-on-Hudson, N.Y.: Hudson Institute.
Leonard, George B.
    1968   Education and Ecstasy. New York: Delacorte Press.
Lynd, Robert S.
    1939   Knowledge For What? The Place of Social Science in American Culture. Princeton, N.J.: Princeton University Press.
MacBride, Robert O.
    1967   The Automated State: Computer Systems as a New Force in Society. Philadelphia: Chilton.
McHale, John
    1968   "A global view." Pp. 195–216 in Robert Theobald (ed.), Social Policies for America in the Seventies: Nine Divergent Views. Garden City, N.Y.: Doubleday.
McLuhan, Marshall.
    1966   Understanding Media: The Extensions of Man. New York: McGraw-Hill.
Miller, James G.
    1961   "The individual response to drugs." Pp. 92–109 in Seymour M. Farber and Roger H. L. Wilson (eds.), Man and Civilization: Control of the Mind. New York: McGraw-Hill.
More, Sir Thomas
    1935   Utopia. New York: Heritage Press.
Negley, Glenn, and Max J. Patrick (eds.)
    1962   The Quest For Utopia: An Anthology of Imaginary Societies. Garden City, N.Y.: Doubleday.
Prehoda, Robert W.
    1967   Designing the Future: The Role of Technological Forecasting. Philadelphia: Chilton.

Rogers, W. L.
   1967   "Aerospace systems technology and the creation of environ-
            ment." Pp. 260–268 in William R. Ewald, Jr. (ed.), Environment
            For Man: The Next Fifty Years. Bloomington: Indiana Univer-
            sity Press.
Skinner, Burrhus F.
   1948   Walden Two. New York: Macmillan.
Sola Pool, Ithiel de
   1967   "The international system in the next half century." Daedalus
            96 (Summer):930–935.
Sorokin, Pitirim A.
   1946   The Crisis of Our Age. New York: Dutton.
Theobald, Robert
   1968   "Policy Formation For New Goals." Pp. 149–169 in Robert
            Theobald (ed.), Social Policies for America in the Seventies:
            Nine Divergent Views. Garden City, N.Y.: Doubleday.
Thomson, Sir George
   1955   The Foreseeable Future. Cambridge, England: Cambridge Uni-
            versity Press.
Tustin, Arnold
   1953   The Mechanism of Economic Systems: An Approach to the
            Problem of Economic Stabilization from the Point of View of
            Control-System Engineering. Cambridge, Mass.: Harvard Uni-
            versity Press.
Unamuno, Miguel de
   1954   The Tragic Sense of Life. New York: Dover Publications.
Veblen, Thorstein
   1953   The Theory of the Leisure Class: An Economic Study of Institu-
            tions. New York: Mentor Books.
Wells, Herbert G.
   1967   A Modern Utopia. Lincoln: University of Nebraska Press.
Wolfe, Tom
   1965   The Kandy*Kolored Tangerine*Flake Streamline Baby. New
            York: Farrar, Straus & Giroux.
   1968   The Pump House Gang. New York: Farrar, Straus & Giroux.
Zamyatin, Evgenii
   1924   We. New York: Dutton.

PART III

Some Images of the Future in Sociology and Psychoanalysis

In "The Myth of a Value-Free Psychotherapy," Pauline Bart applies our paradigm for the analysis of time perspectives and images of the future given in Part I to various schools of thought in psychotherapy. She shows that the different schools have different images of man, different concepts of society, and different time foci. Images of the future, especially images of the ideal future of the patient, also differ markedly. The traditional psychodynamic image of the future contains the implied assumption that the future will consist of more of the same. Based on an economy of abundance, the existential-self-actualizing school sees a future in which people will be able to realize their potential in a society that is more expressive and less instrumental than today's society. Rationality is stressed by the behavior modification school, rationality oriented toward the elimination of psychological discomfort among individuals. And, predictably, Soviet psychiatry aims for the reduction of schizophrenia in a (presumably) classless society in which there are no social problems.

Unlike the other essays in Part III, Bart's chapter deals with an applied science. Thus, there is a deliberate relevance in the materials with which she is working not found in many subfields of social science. Psychotherapists try to help their patients cope with the tensions and significant experiences that occur in their daily lives. Yet how the clinician reacts and what he tries to change vary from the essentially conservative role of the therapists who look only inside the individual for the intrapsychic factors and who focus their treatment on adjusting or conforming the individual to society to the more radical role of those who look to the society itself in an effort to help the patient manipulate his social world so that the problems that distress him in his environment can be removed through social change. Although few, if any, psychotherapists go so far as to teach their patients to be revolutionaries, the implications of some theories would lead us to conclude that some patients may never be made "well" until important economic and social changes have taken place —or have been engineered—in the larger society. The black Martiniquais, Frantz Fanon, after being educated in France and while treating mentally ill patients in Algeria, reached this conclusion. He prescribed the "cleansing" medication of violence as a cure for psychological oppressions suffered by colonial peoples, claiming that this remedy would give such "patients" their freedom.

Although most of Bart's discussion is devoted to the work and ideas of practicing therapists, she briefly discusses the ideologies and utopias of three major social psychiatric groups in which sociologists played major roles. A. B. Hollingshead, Jerome K. Myers, and others of the New Haven team focused on social class and mental illness; the Stirling County studies focused on stability and adjustment; and the Midtown

Manhattan Studies focused on poverty. The results and recommendations of these works have aided the effort to change some of the emphases in the treatment of patients: the poor are somewhat less harshly treated; institutionalized care in some places is shifting from a primarily custodial to a treatment orientation; programs of mental health education, still too few, are helping to change attitudes toward the mentally ill in the larger society; and community mental health centers are delivering their services in community settings.

Bart shows how larger social changes have altered the structure of knowledge in psychotherapy (Freud's Victorian father-analyst gives way to the unassertive or disappearing therapist as society is democratized; abundance makes possible existential psychiatry focused on man's higher needs) and, in so doing, illustrates how circular our knowledge is: we find the reality we seek and what we seek is an unconscious reflection of the reality we think we experience.

William R. Burch, Jr. also is interested in the fact that we find the reality we seek and that we seek that which we think we experience. He describes the images of future leisure of three different groups: (1) classical utopian writings represented by More and Bellamy, whom he calls the "moral crusaders"; (2) modern business, whose images he characterizes by "commercial utopianism"; and, (3) today's intelligentsia, who display what he calls "literati Arcadianism." He shows their different directions of hope or despair, and, more importantly, argues that "because these groups are caught in vocabularies of illusion their symbology only accidentally connects with the many images in a socially diverse society."

He next turns to the "socially diverse society" itself; and in analyses of both social stratification and the life cycle in relation to leisure, he illustrates existing and, as he sees them, emergent patterns of future leisure in different segments of the population. Although the details are of use in their own right as a contribution to the sociology of the future, the major point is the way in which diversity—and conflict—can be included in the construction of images of the future: by linking differential images to basic forms of social differentiation, to the differential life experiences, social needs, opportunities, and obligations of different groups.

Finally, he identifies an emergent aspect of images of future leisure. Within the "troubled diversity" of the present and the different demands and images to which it gives rise, he nonetheless sees a search for a kind of unity through style, through the empathic, universally understood "poetry in one's action." One possibility for images of future leisure is that they will be built, as Burch says, from "the voices of diversity seeking their time of communion."

If the "voices of diversity are seeking their time of communion," it is not evident in the image of Canadian society given in John Porter's book, *The Vertical Mosaic*. Menno Boldt, using our paradigm, analyzes this study of socioeconomic and ethnic diversity, which offers little encouragement for optimism. Porter sees Canada's future prospects as including increasing powerlessness for the average Canadian in the political process; increasing domination of the society by a shrinking circle of elites who are committed to perpetuating their privileged position; an alienated life of mechanism, subordination, depersonalization, and conformity at the hands of the bureaucratic dictatorship; an increasing number of Canadians whose occupational skills will be obsolete and who will have little hope that their families will have the opportunity for upward social mobility; and a growing French-Canadian nationalism that will deprive the average Canadian of the sense of identity and self-fulfillment that can come from identifying with a nation-state that commands the loyalty of all its citizens.

Here clearly is a negative, pessimistic image of the future imbedded in a book reporting the results of sociological research. Boldt, also a Canadian, claims that Porter has failed to see viable alternative futures that are both less pessimistic and compatible with his own data. Porter falls prey, according to Boldt, to self-defeating prophecies and ignores his own demand for "creative politics," by displaying the not uncommon tendency to think of existing social structures as insurmountable and to give insufficient attention to the influence of images of the future and the actions of men as significant causes of change.

Unlike many sociologists, Porter, of course, is not exclusively preoccupied with the present and explicitly "deals both with past trends and future projections of phenomena that are basic in Canadian society." He is also aware of a need of a charter myth and a national image of the future; he expresses his regret that Canada appears to him to lack a worthy image of its future that is distinctively its own. And he is aware, further, that his study may have some effect in altering the very facts about which he is reporting "insofar as a competent critique of contemporary conditions influences the thinking of decision-makers." But could Porter have reached different and less pessimistic conclusions from the same data? Boldt says "yes." Boldt argues that Porter's data are consistent with possibilities for change that would shatter the vertical mosaic and eliminate the major psychological and social barriers to upward mobility.

Through his work, Porter held up a mirror to Canadian society. What he saw, however, was not simply what was there. His purposes and orientations were also reflected back to him, and so too was his sociology itself. Paul Hollander, in the final chapter in Part III, is interested in sociology as a mirror to society and he sees sociology itself as "a reflection of societal self-consciousness, of the surfacing of doubt, of uncertainty and the purposeful search for its alleviation." How, he asks, have American and Soviet sociology reflected the societies in which they exist?

Sociologists in both societies "have amassed much uncomplimentary information on problems" that plague each society. American sociologists particularly have made a ". . . detailed and rich catalogue" of virtually all serious problems of America today, often using the device of value-structure inconsistency to create such a catalogue of when the "ideal and actual, theory and practice do not mesh." Positive idealism, however, has not generally characterized sociological work. Instead sociologists have been content to list the failures of society, rather than to suggest remedies for them.

In contrasting orientations toward the future among American and Soviet sociologists, Hollander concludes that there is more of an effort in the Soviet Union, consistent with Marxist-Leninist philosophy, than in the United States for self-conscious and deliberate prediction and control. Yet he rightly points out that American sociologists have been forced to do some thinking about the future, as have Soviet sociologists too, simply because of the rapid social change that has occurred in each society. Thus, some sociologists studying the present often cannot avoid thinking about the future. (Our own experience studying the transition to nationhood in the English-speaking Caribbean in the late 1950s and 1960s may be taken as an example.) Additionally, he reminds us that prediction itself leads even the most scientific of sociologists to a concern with the future if they are theoretically ambitious; and he identifies the trend, visible in both countries, toward an increasing number of sociologists interested in social engineering and planning, both of which require a future orientation.

Finally, Hollander observes that American sociology may be becoming more ideological and politicized while Soviet sociology may be moving toward greater detachment. In fact, he sees the new era of American sociology not so much threatened by the safely trivial, the narrowly empirical, or the overly abstract and theoretical, but by "the ideological engulfment" of sociology by the significant issues of society. He sees such engulfment as more of a problem to American sociology than to Soviet sociology, since in the United States it will come from within the person himself, from intense personal commitments, thus will be more difficult to evade and combat than if it were obvious, crude, and contained in the orthodoxies and doctrines of dominant social institutions.

We share his fear and add our voices to his warning. Ideology *instead* of sociology brings an end to enlightenment. We have in this book, however, argued that detachment is no answer. In fact, it can, if it continues to dominate the thinking of the sociological leadership, hasten the emergence of the very politicized sociology it supposedly prevents; the "new sociology" would be in the hands of the presently disaffected and alienated sociologists. We see a possible solution in the combination of relevance and science in the study of the future.

The Myth of a
Value-Free Psychotherapy

PAULINE B. BART

Two psychiatric concepts—depression and fantasy—are related to one's image of the future. Depression can be considered a stage in which the individual has no hope that conditions will be better in times to come. Indeed, in a study of middle-aged women hospitalized for mental illness (Bart, 1967), I found that *impending* role loss was as closely associated with depression as present role loss. On the other hand, an optimistic image of the future may be considered a fantasy. Frank (1965) has addressed himself to the patient's view of the future; he conceives one of the functions of psychotherapy as enhancement of the patient's positive expectations. The title of a paper in which he summarized research supporting this position was "The Role of Hope in Psychotherapy."

Dynamically oriented psychotherapists deal with the reconstructed past of the individual and have a (usually implicit) goal or image of the future for their patients. What past is reconstructed depends partly on the theoretical orientation of the therapist. A Freudian past is full of repressed sexuality and an unsuccessful resolution of the Oedipal conflict. A Jungian past is replete with archetypes, the anima, and the animus. An Adlerian past focuses on feelings of inferiority.

Images of the patient's future also differ among therapists. They would like patients to become "mature," but what therapists consider maturity depends partly on their ideology and orientation. Lerner's (1968: 96–97) "Index of maturity . . . is the capacity for conformity with the broad sanctions of society, and loyalty to one's country and one's way of life. . . ." Freud wanted his patients to be able to work and to love and to make choices unencumbered by unconscious determinants. He wished to increase the scope of his patients' individual freedom, knowing that such freedom would still be limited as the price to be paid for civilization.

Thus, images of the future are relevant to psychotherapy, since a Freudian or analytically oriented psychotherapist would attempt to explore the unconscious of the patient and, by giving him insight concerning his past, would try to make his future different from his present. However, this approach to the future, limiting one's concern to the future of each individual patient, ignores the possibility of social change, and thus opts for the position that the future will be very much like the present or, to be more specific, like the past of Vienna. If psychotherapists take this stance, no changes in techniques, perhaps more appropriate to a changing world, are necessary. A more extreme position, but a common one, assumes that the therapist deals only with man's intrapsychic state, and thus today's society, much less tomorrow's, is irrelevant.

Different psychotherapeutic orientations—traditional-psychodynamic, existential self-actualizing, and behavior-modifying—have different images of man, time focuses, and concepts of society, cause and effect, and social change. Because of such differences, their images of the future and the implications of the therapy they practice for the future differ. These differences reflect different values, hence the major conclusion of this chapter: value-free psychotherapy is a myth.

AMERICAN PSYCHIATRY: FROM MORAL MANAGEMENT TO THE CLASSLESS CLINIC

Changes in the treatment of mental patients historically reflect changes in society. Before the great wave of immigration in the nineteenth century, mental hospitals had a therapeutic program called "humane care" or moral treatment. Cure was effected through interaction with the psychiatrist, and the atmosphere was what now might be termed a "therapeutic community." For example, the psychiatrist and the patient in that era ate their meals together.[1] (See Foucault, 1967, for a discussion of this type of treatment in Europe.)

This program was abandoned for the "warehousing" of inmates in asylums usually located far from urban areas. The only treatment given was somatic, and many patients received merely custodial care. This

---

[1] In my field observations in several mental hospitals I noticed a direct relationship between the eating arrangements and the social class differential between staff and patients. In the upper-class hospital staff and patients ate together; in the lower-middle-class hospital, while the same dining room was used, the staff ate at a raised platform at one end of the room; however, in the state hospital there were separate dining rooms.

hange in orientation and care occurred concomitantly with the influx
f immigrants into mental hospitals. The custodial ideology has now
een abandoned—at least verbally—and the "humane" therapeutic com-
nunity concept is once again in the ascendancy. One wonders if the
riginal change in policy did not result from the existence of a large
umber of patients different in ethnicity and social class from the psychi-
trists—patients to whom the psychiatrists might have felt they could
ot comfortably "relate."

Folta and Schatzman (1968) suggest that the minimal care given
nental patients in the past century reflected the ideology of Social Dar-
vinism current at that time. The decline of that ideology and its replace-
nent with the concepts of the New Deal and the Great Society—ideolo-
ies that insist that no groups be "written off"—are consistent with the
hanges in treatment of mental patients, particularly the current emphasis
n treatment in the community. The growing importance in the treatment
rograms of social workers and psychologists, many of whom where
hildren of immigrants, led to milieu therapy in the hospitals. Their in-
luence sensitized the population to problems of emotional disturbance
nd created a large clientele for psychotherapeutic services. Folta and
chatzman predict the growth of an eclectic, pragmatic, public urban
sychiatry, serving the varied urban populace, focusing on the client's
resent problem and its social determinants. In such a program even the
vell-documented social class differentiations found in clinics will disap-
ear, since they are "uneconomical and ineffective."

PSYCHOTHERAPEUTIC PESSIMISM: FREUD

To understand the traditional quietist nature of psychiatry and its
ulture-bound character, one must examine some factors that influenced
reud's thought and his image of man and society. Freud has been ad-
nirably placed in a sociological and historical context by Reiff, Riesman,
nd Marcuse. Reiff (1959:xiii, 4–5) sees Freud as a moralist, ". . . the
irst out-patient of the hospital culture in which we live. . . . Once again,
istory has produced a type specially adapted to endure his own period:
he trained egoist, the private man, who turns away from the arenas of
ublic failure to reexamine himself and his own emotions." Freudian
sychology supports this privatization since it interprets "politics, reli-
ion, and culture in terms of the inner life of the individual and his im-
nediate family experiences." This legitimation of the privatization of the
elf and the definition of radicalism as an expression of individual neu-
osis are ideological positions still affecting psychotherapy—an approach
call psychotherapeutic quietism. Riesman (1954:202) sees Freud as the

Summary: Application of the Paradigm to Psychotherapy

| | Psychotherapeutic Orientations | | | |
	Traditional Psychodynamic	Existential Self-Actualizing	Behavior Modification	Soviet Psychiatry
Major theoretician(s)	Freud	Maslow, Carl Rogers	Skinner.	Marx, Pavlov
Concept of human nature	*Hobbesian.* Existence of strong biological drives. Change in personality and behavior possible only through *insight* obtained in psychotherapy.	*Rousseauian.* Change possible through "real" communication, acceptance by others, development of noncognitive, nonverbal skills and sense modalities.	*Tabula rasa.* Behavior change possible through changed patterns of reinforcement.	A function of the relations of production. Pavlov's view was a *tabula rasa,* Marx's view was Rousseauian.[a]
Time focus (in psychotherapy)	Past	Present	Present	Present
Concept of society	Relatively unchangeable, in equilibrium, although it is possible for the area of rationality to be increased through insight.	Progressing	Changeable through the application of reason (*Walden Two*)	Progressing through the dialectic of History to the classless society.
Concept of cause and effect	Generally deterministic	Antideterminism (part of the existential ideology)	Deterministic	Deterministic

Values and purposes of the authors	Where id was, there shall be ego, i.e., increasing area of individual's conscious control of his behavior.	Self-actualization, humanistic values. High value placed on nonrational skills, body awareness, sensitivity to nature, aesthetic pleasures.	Elimination of symptoms thus increasing the patient's comfort. General value on rationality.	To make "good" Soviet citizens.
Images of the future	No overt image. The implied assumption about the future is that it will consist of more of the same.	The future will consist of an economy of abundance, with the Protestant Ethic no longer appropriate. People will be able to actualize themselves (realize their potential), society will be more expressive in contrast to today's instrumental orientation.	The future will consist of a more rational society, resulting in less individual discomfort.	The classless society. There should be no social problems.
Consequences for the future	If the focus continues to be on intrapsychic processes, then part of the "creative elite" will become "trained egoists" lacking concern for institutional problems. Such behavior would have deleterious consequences for the society.	If their world view gains more general acceptance, the society will become more expressive. Should the Rousseauian image of man[b] function as a self-fulfilling prophecy, then in fact the good society may be upon us.	Increased technology of behavior modification, or mind control—to use a pejorative term—may lead to a greater use of these techniques. While on the one hand such a technology can lead to decreasing individual discomfort, in its worst form it can lead to a Brave New World.	Possible reduction of schizophrenia.

[a] Soviet psychologists now posit a spontaneity in the human psyche, potentialities for certain aptitudes and abilities, and a predisposition towards certain types of temperament. These can account for the continuation of "social problems" in a socialist state.

[b] It should be pointed out that a Rousseauian image of man, should it not function as a self-fulfilling prophecy, may have deleterious consequences for the future, since law makers may not build controls for individual liberty into their proposed legislation. In contrast, the framers of the Constitution, men with Hobbesian views of human nature, built checks and balances in which was preserved individual liberty.

bearer of the Protestant Ethic, who makes the "Ascetic rationalist dichotomy between work and play." Freud's therapeutic techniques were
shaped by his cultural and class outlook. Since Freud's patients and
friends were upper-middle-class, he assumed that individualistic mobility
motives were natural. His concept of work as the "inescapable and tragic
necessity" and his position on ". . . man's natural laziness and the futility
of socialism" can be understood as products of a century dominated by
scarcity economics and Malthusian fears (Riesman, 1954:176, 184).

Marcuse (1962:224), on the other hand, considers Freud's metaphysical theories radical, but his psychotherapy conservative. Although
Freud knew that the "sickness of the individual is ultimately caused and
sustained by the sickness of his civilization, psychoanalytic therapy aims
at curing the individual so that he can continue to function as part of a
sick civilization "without surrendering to it altogether."

Although in *The Future of an Illusion* (1934), Freud has hope for
increasing rationality among men, his pessimism is shown in the conclusion of *Civilization and Its Discontents* (1961:92):

> I can offer them [my fellow men] no consolation. . . . The fateful ques-
> tion for the human species seems to me to be whether and to what extent
> their cultural development will succeed in mastering the disturbance of
> their communal life by the human instinct of aggression and self-destruc-
> tion. . . . Men have gained control over the forces of nature to such an
> extent that with their help they would have no difficulty in exterminating
> one another to the last man. They know this, and hence comes a large
> part of their current unrest, their unhappiness, and their mood of anxiety.
> And is it not to be expected that the other of the two "Heavenly Pow-
> ers," eternal Eros, will make an effort to assert himself in the struggle with
> his equally immortal adversary (Thanatos). But who can foresee with what
> success and with what result?

Although Freud was pessimistic about social change and viewed
civilization as "essentially antagonistic to happiness" and therapy as a
"course in resignation," Marcuse considers the unconscious the "drive
for integral gratification, which is absence of want and repression." Marcuse's (1962) reading of Freud is such that he can envision a society without "surplus repression" (137) where there will no longer be the necessity
for societal domination and individual alienation, a state "derived from
the prevalent social organization of labor" (128).

As shown in the summary of the application of the Bell et al. paradigm to psychotherapy, Freud's conception of human nature was Hobbesian; the time focus in psychoanalysis was on the past, and he conceived of society as relatively unchangeable because of man's instincts
and the necessity of controlling them for "civilization" to endure. An

xample of the difficulty of social change in his theoretical framework is hown by his view of women. He had a traditional view of women's role ecause he considered her situation rooted in her biology ("Anatomy is Destiny"). Thus no change was possible. His thought was generally deterministic, although the individual could increase the scope of his freedom through insight, freeing himself from actions determined by his unconscious. One can see both the romantic (Reiff, 1959) and the rational Hughes, 1961) strains in his thought. He was generally pessimistic bout the possibility of social change, and his focus on the intrapsychic ed to the quietist nature of much psychotherapy today.

PSYCHOTHERAPEUTIC QUIETISM:
T'S WHAT'S INSIDE THAT COUNTS

The theoretical groundwork for psychotherapeutic quietism was laid down by Freud and explicated in Reiff's analysis. Certainly, if all problems and responses to problems spring from individuals' intrapsychic processes, then the society can be ignored save as "superstructure." Social change, should it indeed be necessary at all, would have to be a function of individual change. Such individual change would occur because of the individual's awareness of the unconscious determinants of his behavior. However, if, for example, the radical "learns" that his desire to restructure society and overthrow its leaders is but a displacement of his desire to restructure his childhood family constellation and overthrow his father, then the implication is that he should abandon his revolutionary activity, since it is but a symptom of his neurosis. Lest one think such an analysis is overdrawn, Anna Freud (1968) recently interpreted the protest movement among today's youth as not so much a result of real interest in solving social ills but a mask for concealing personal inadequacies. She considered introspective therapy and psychoanalysis to be exactly what he students need. The genetic fallacy states that the origin of an idea has no bearing upon its validity, yet in the real world, when the origin is denigrated, the idea is at least partially discredited. Thus, the intrapsychic approach can lead to a psychotherapy of adjustment—one not frequently advocated nowadays, but still occasionally voiced—as will be shown.

Not only do some psychiatrists see their role as adjusting the individual to society or to the needs of the group, but the psychiatric equivalent of original sin, "immaturity," can be invoked to discredit radical political activity. For example, Lerner (1968:96) states:

> In an organization such as the armed forces, the allegiance and loyalty of the psychiatrist to the organization must transcend consideration of the individual. If any organization—or, for that matter, society—is to endure,

those persons who are in a position to affect the integrity and efficiency of the organization or of society must make a clear choice between the best interests of the individual and the best interests of society.

. . . When the psychiatrist is concerned with evaluating an individual from the point of view of that person's loyalty to his country and its way of life, the psychiatrist must make a decision so that his natural and customary concern for the individual is subordinated to his own personal obligation never under any circumstances to permit the best interests of his country and its way of life to be jeopardized. This calls for not merely honoring his oath and obligation, but utilizing psychiatric principles which foster maturity of the personality. The index of maturity of the personality is the capacity for conformity with the broad sanctions of society and loyalty to one's country and one's way of life. . . .

Rejection of the Father and/or the Mother figure closely parallels rejection of our country as an object of our concern and respect. We see symptoms of "disloyalty" or "rejection" in the person who develops patterns of behavior which are disturbing to his parents, his family, his community, or his culture. This hostility or disloyalty is a common *symptom complex* in psychiatric practice. . . . [emphasis added]

Disloyalty of whatever nature is associated with
1) Emotional disturbance or psychiatric illness
2) Opportunistic attempts to achieve status, notoriety and power
3) The illusion that such activities will ameliorate personal, social, and economic status.

If concern with social problems or structural deficiencies in the society is merely a projection of one's inner dynamics, such dialogues as the following may take place. A therapist dealt with "a Negro patient's complaints about race relations in a partially segregated hospital by telling the patient that he must ask why he, among all the other Negroes present, chose this particular moment to express this feeling, and what this could mean about him as a person, apart from the state of race relations in the hospital at the time" (Goffman, 1961:377). Such a psychologistic approach was built into a research project at the UCLA Neuropsychiatric Institute. Each psychiatric resident had to fill out several precoded forms dealing with sociological and psychological characteristics of the patient. One such item dealt with the patient's attitude about his present illness. While the first possible answer was *"recognizes* emotional problems as the main cause," the next alternatives were *"attributes* illness mainly to external stress," *"attributes* illness mainly to physical cause," and "unaware of any illness" [emphases added].

London (1964:9, 10) notes that this rhetoric of lack of concern with the external world may in fact be limited under certain circumstances. He reports an analyst's saying, " 'When I am working in the privacy of the analytic session, I don't care if the world is coming down around my patient's ears on the outside.' He does not stipulate, incidentally, whether his attitude would be the same if the financial world of the patient were collapsing, indicating that he would no longer be able to be paid, or if the patient were, on the outside 'acting out' in a fashion which interfered with the analysis." Also, London (1969:41) observes that therapists can be irresponsible if they insist on totally denying responsibility for social change they may foster. They may become "insidious and potentially destructive" because the "potential of mental health experts for social engineering is quite large, though few of them are publicly concerned about it." This lack of concern with values and with society, of course, does not mean a value neutrality, because the failure to take a position, in itself, is a position indicating values.

Psychotherapists function nowadays as priests did in the Middle Ages, and Seeley (1953) states that the mental health movement is vying for the vacuum caused by the passing of the church. What are the values and images of the future, implicit or otherwise, expounded by this movement? I have already noted the implicit conservative values of the "it's what's inside that counts" ideology. Value-laden psychotherapy is possible because the imprecision of psychiatric theory, especially the ambiguity concerning "normality," permits the psychiatrist's moral preferences to be enunciated "in the disguise of scientific descriptions of fact" (Szasz, 1961:105). Such ambiguity has resulted in the mental health movement being in effect the Protestant Ethic writ large (Davis, 1938: 580). At a Symposium on Preventive and Social Psychiatry sponsored by the Walter Reed Army Institute of Research (1957:445), an army psychiatrist said supervisors in industry can promote the mental health of workers:

> . . . by insisting that they perform adequately on the job. Any time a supervisor shows any preference or allows a worker to perform inadequately, he's doing both the group and the individual a great disfavor. [Note the alleged identity of interests between the two.] The next psychiatrist "quite agreed" with him. "I think it is part of the task of the mental hospital to establish this attitude inside the hospital as well."

The mental hospital as factory is a rather interesting model. Lest one think such an approach is dated, let me quote from the health book used by California elementary school children today, which mouths the same platitudes under the guise of "what is mental health?" (Byrd et al., 1967: 9–16). This book says a person with good mental health can handle disappointments as well as success, making "a good adjustment or adapting himself to the demands made upon him by his environment."

The children are told that they have good mental health if they are truth-ful, loyal, cooperative, friendly, and think positively instead of negatively. They are advised to "smile at people" and practice a "positive attitude" toward their parents and brothers or sisters. They should work off their frustration through "physical activity or physical work."

Parsons (1951:301) considered the process of psychotherapy:

> . . . the case in our society where those fundamental elements of the proc-esses of social control have been most explicitly brought to light. For cer-tain purposes it can serve as a prototype of the mechanisms of social con-trol.

And Laing (1965:12), the English existential psychiatrist, eloquently de-clares:

> Psychiatry could be, and some psychiatrists are, on the side of transcend-ance, of genuine freedom, and of true human growth. But psychiatry can so easily be a technique of brainwashing, of inducing behavior that is ad-justed, by (preferably) non-injurious torture. In the best places where straitjackets are abolished, doors are unlocked, leucotomies largely fore-gone, these can be replaced by more subtle lobotomies and tranquilizers that place the bars of Bedlam and the locked doors *inside* the patient.

That psychotherapy is a form of social control and that sanity is "a trick of agreement" (Ginsberg, 1961:13), has long been noted by poets and novelists. Though they may not be the unacknowledged legislators of the world, they do "see with the eyes of the angels" (Williams, 1956:8). Emily Dickinson, who would be considered extremely "impaired" on any mental health rating scale, wrote in the last century (1890:435):

> Much madness is divinest sense
> To a discerning eye;
> Much sense the starkest madness.
> 'Tis the majority in this, as all, prevails.
> Assent, and you are sane;
> Demur,—you're straightway dangerous
> and handled with a chain.

William Burroughs' (1959) fictional psychiatrist, Dr. Benway, is the controller and advisor to the antiutopia Freeland Republic. He is a manip-ulator and coordinator of symbol systems and an expert in all phases of interrogation, brainwashing, and control. Kesey's (1962) depiction of a psychiatric ward reads like a dramatization of all the organizational analyses of mental hospitals. Though Big Nurse is the agent of social control, the patients are manipulated into cooperating in the destruction of their selves. Big Nurse interprets any act of self-assertion as pathology, and the ward psychiatrist is generally unable to perform his therapeutic function (see Goffman, 1961; Caudill, 1958; Dunham and Weinberg, 1960; Belknap, 1956, for sociological and anthropological analyses coming to similar conclusions).

Psychotherapy as social control bodes ill for an increase of human freedom and dignity in the future. In the Soviet Union individuals protesting political conditions have been confined in mental hospitals, since they were, of course, "sick." The cases of Ezra Pound, General Edwin Walker, and Governor Earl Long of Louisiana show that this approach is not limited to other countries. In the latter two cases, the attempts to have individuals who took deviant political stances committed for psychiatric care failed. Long's case showed that there are no objective criteria enabling us to distinguish between paranoid schizophrenia (his diagnosis) and the normal behavior of a Southern governor. General Walker, who led the opposition to integration at Old Miss, considered his behavior appropriate for a patriotic American and a general of the U.S. Army. The government preferred to label him insane rather than admit that there are high-ranking members of the armed forces who think and act this way. The government called Ezra Pound insane; thus, he could be shut up—in both senses—in St. Elizabeth's Hospital. Thus, although the government was not placed in the awkward position of trying a major poet for treason, Pound could no longer publicly make pro-Fascist statements.

Attempting to discredit an opponent by labeling him sick rather than bad or incorrect has spread to the halls of Congress and to the Oakland police force. In response to reports linking cigarette smoking to lung cancer, the FTC sought to curb cigarette advertising. It was reported in *The New York Times* (1964:12) that Rep. Cooley of North Carolina, a tobacco-growing state, said, "I think someone in the FTC must be emotionally disturbed." More recently, the chief of the Oakland police stated on television that people who support the Black Panthers and the Peace and Freedom party were "sick."

Invoking psychiatric vocabularies to discredit behavior and attitudes with which one disagrees not only has the latent function of enabling one to ignore the issues that are raised in the argument, but makes unnecessary a search for structural factors conducive to such behavior and attitudes. Each time there has been a multiple murder or an assassination, the individual has been defined as "some nut"; and, since the behavior of mentally ill individuals is believed by most people to be unpredictable, then no safeguards or structural changes are presumed necessary. For example, according to the testimony of the clinical psychologist at the trial of Sirhan Sirhan, Robert Kennedy was assassinated because:

> Sirhan's prime problem [became] . . . a conflict between instinctual demands for his father's death and the realization through his conscious that killing his father is not socially acceptable.
> The only real solution is to look for a compromise. He does. He finds a symbolic replica of his father in the form of Kennedy, kills him and also regains the relationship that stands between him and his most precious possession—his mother's love (*San Francisco Chronicle*, 1969).

Sirhan's father was fifty-five. Kennedy's image was always considered "boyish" rather than fatherly. King Abdullah of Jordan was assassinated because of the fear that he was too friendly to Israel. It would seem that a cultural explanation would be more parsimonious. Certainly, if the only way to prevent political assassination is to produce a world in which no one hated his father, then a solution would be impossible. Such wide invocation of psychiatric vocabularies of explanation has an "elective affinity" with psychotherapeutic quietism; the implications for the future are similar.

PSYCHOTHERAPEUTIC ACTIVISM:
YES, VIRGINIA, THERE IS A SOCIAL STRUCTURE

Since 1963, when I wrote a paper criticizing psychiatry for the "it's what's inside that counts" ideology, changes have occurred in the orientation of the field. The psychiatrists discussed as "psychotherapeutic activists" exemplify these changes; they consider psychiatry a tool to build the good society. Federal and state financing has led to the burgeoning of community mental health clinics, and community psychiatry has become so popular that in some circles it is being decried as a fad (see Dunham, 1965; Manis, 1968). The 1967 research report of the American Psychiatric Association was called *Poverty and Mental Health* (Greenblatt and Sharaf, 1967), and the most recent compendium on psychoanalysis (Marmor, 1968) devotes one of its four sections to culture and society. Even in the clinical section, one chapter deals with social factors in the discussion of the treatment of low socioeconomic groups. When such changes in a field parallel social developments, this lends support to the central hypothesis of the sociology of knowledge—that existential factors condition thought. Traditional psychotherapy, with its one-to-one relationship between the therapist and patient reflected the "inner-directed man," whereas current trends—the discovery of the social structure and its impact on the individual, and the growth of group therapy—are more appropriate to today's "other-directed" man.

Duhl (1963:73) believes that the psychiatrist "must play a role in controlling the environment which man has created." He considers the ecological model more appropriate to our era than the linear causal model; thus man is to be studied *in* society. Disease is a socially defined condition. He decries the post-World War II trend of psychiatrists committing themselves to "office therapeutics with little recognition of the possibility of working with environmental factors," and he notes that with the advent of research funds, programs, and training, as well as with increasing public awareness, a "major revolution has occurred" (Duhl, 1963:65). Increasing interest has been shown in the biological and the sociopsychological aspects of mental illness. Such concern has led to a focus on the processes of the family, the hospital, and the community as they relate to mental health and illness.

Where poverty has been discovered by the psychotherapists, the basic image of man has changed from passive client to active participant and planner in matters affecting his destiny. Duhl (1967) says that the time has passed when professionals define how services are given. When the poor in one community were polled concerning their needs, their priorities were markedly different from those of "the helping professions." One community member said that, while they might be viewed as a hard-core community with multiproblem people living in it, "We see you as being hard core social workers. You're insulting with your belief that you have everything to give me. You forget that I not only know how to take, but I can give, too" (Geiger, 1967:61).

The "activist" psychiatrists are aware of the intimate interaction between the social systems and personal system; they assume that in order to change the behavior of individuals, the institutions must be changed. For example, Peck et al. (1967) consider it their obligation as community psychiatrists to promote neighborhood service centers and become involved in voter registration, code enforcement in housing, and the organization of rent strikes.

In order to overcome "the customary professional constraints ordinarily required of those who work in the health field"—which have little meaning for the disadvantaged—techniques must be revamped. Storefront satellites, psychiatry not limited to a fifty-minute hour, home visits, the use of indigenous workers to mediate between the professionals and the community: these are some of the techniques suggested (Rome, 1967; see Reiff and Riessman, 1965, for a discussion of the use of indigenous workers in the mental health field).

A focus on environmental change, particularly when working in poverty areas, is vital because:

> . . . there is reason to believe . . . that much of the disproportion in the reported demographic and epidemiologic characteristics of mental illness is

attributable to the direct and indirect effect of economics. . . . economic factors exercise prepotent influence in the provocation of symptoms, the mode of expression of symptoms, as well as the selection of the appropriate remedial measures (Rome, 1967:175).

Although this concern with the economics of social problems is well grounded in empirical studies (e.g., Langner and Michael, 1963, found that money can cushion the effects of stress), psychiatrists formerly underestimated its importance. For example, I found that the psychiatric residents at the UCLA Neuropsychiatric Institute, when given a choice of eight major areas of external precipitating stress for their patients, chose "financial problem" least frequently; even "Acute traumatic incident not classified elsewhere" was checked more often (Bart, 1962). Now, however, some psychiatrists at that hospital are researching the effects of poverty on mental illness.

Race, as well as poverty, is now seen as a relevant variable. Contrast the following remarks with the earlier statement in which the therapist gave an intrapsychic interpretation to a patient's complaints about segregation at St. Elizabeth's. According to Christmas (1966:164), ". . . situational and environmental factors play a large part in the emotional problems of Negro patients and their families." Because of the complex interrelationship between the individual psychic process and the sociocultural factors, therapy groups composed of many people having similar experiences are suggested, rather than individual treatment. The goal of this therapy is to enable the individual to function as a responsible actor rather than a powerless victim.

Coles considers these changes in psychiatric orientation and in models of patient-therapist interaction to be a reflection of world and national events and the changing social order (where problems of race and poverty are more salient). For example, he points out that Kenneth Clark set up a clinic in Harlem in the 1940s to work with delinquent and neurotic children, but the nature of his involvement has changed; now he is concerned with the effects of living in Harlem "not only as they are *reflected* in childhood pathology, but as they *generate* the social pathology" (Coles, 1967:29, emphases added).[2]

Because the humanistic and democratic values of these activist psychiatrists are apparent, it is possible to infer their image of the future. They see, or would like to see, a world without racism and poverty, a world where the decision-making process is democratized so that indi-

---

[2] We should not assume a one-to-one relationship between changes in psychiatric rhetoric and changes in psychotherapeutic practice. According to Spray (1968), psychiatrists working in community mental health clinics state that they use traditional psychotherapeutic techniques.

viduals have some control over their own destiny. Their view is that only in such a society is it possible for those now in "the other America" not to contribute disproportionately to the ranks of the mentally ill; the social institutions themselves will have to be changed for these values to be realized. These activists consider it their function as psychiatrists to act as midwives bringing about the birth of this good society.

PSYCHOTHERAPEUTIC POPULISM: PSYCHOTHERAPY AS A FORM OF RECREATION AND A SOCIAL MOVEMENT

Lift Your Burdens

If you cannot afford a Psychiatrist or a Psychologist, write box 2392 Santa Fe Springs, Cal. 90670, enclosing a self addressed stamped envelope with three dollars for a reply: From MARI-ASHIN (Los Angeles Free Press, 1967).

Psychotherapeutic populism. The therapeutic process is becoming more democratic. Reiff (1959) noted that the standard relationship between the analyst and the analysand replicated the relationship between the Victorian father and his wife or daughter. In keeping with the "strain toward consistency" in society, as the family structure became more democratic, so also did the interaction between the therapist and his patient. We have seen in the previous section how some psychiatrists work with community members to define what the community considers problems. I have pointed out that their image of man is that of the active decision-maker rather than the passive client. As will be shown later, in the "encounter groups" democratic ideology defines the relationship between therapist and patient, for, as Stoller (1969:42) says, "It is important that the approach of one human being to another predominate over the roles of professional to client." Moreover, he considers "mutuality inherent in marathon group therapy" and facilitates this mutuality by having sessions in his home with his wife as a participant.

From this democratization of the psychotherapeutic process it is a simple step to considering the presence of a professional in the "helping professions" unnecessary, if not harmful—a position I term "psychotherapeutic populism."[3] The latter position is taken by Yablonsky (1967: 370) when he attributes part of the success of Synanon to the "patient's reversing roles with the therapist." He says further (1967:368)

---

[3] Another example of this diffusion of democracy can be found in the New Left's commitment to participatory democracy, again a reflection of the populist tradition in the United States.

that Synanon's position "that some of its 'patients' can become therapists seems to draw fire from many professional quarters." The Diggers Creative Society in Los Angeles is another example of this populism. Each Monday night Richard Pine leads a "pre-acid seminar" where the participants, most of whom seem to be "post-acid," discuss their hang-ups and present their experiences.

The Diggers Creative Society, a hippie group, consider it their function to care for individuals on "bad trips," since, according to an informant, "The worst thing to do with a person like that is to take him to a doctor or a hospital" (a position consistent with that presented by Becker, 1967). Thus, in both the case of Synanon and of The Diggers, the absence of academically trained therapists is not a makeshift arrangement caused by shortages of funds, but part of a set of beliefs that such a system is better for the individual. Although both Synanon and The Diggers believe in therapeutic populism, ideologies concerning leadership in other areas differ. The internal structure of Synanon is hierarchical and authoritarian; and Chuck Dederich, the founder, is a charismatic leader. On the other hand, the hippies usually denigrate leadership. Thus, one of the participants in the seminar who was "coming down" from a trip refused to lead a group at a be-in in Griffith Park, saying "Nobody is a leader for anyone else. Everyone is his own leader. Everyone must help himself. I have my bag and they have theirs."

More recent examples of psychotherapeutic populism are the women's liberation consciousness-raising small groups. During the first few meetings the women tell their life stories and their pasts are reconstructed so that what they considered private problems, stemming from their own inadequacies, are redefined as public issues stemming from women's situation in society. They learn that other women have undergone similar experiences because of institutionalized sexism. This knowledge is therapeutic. Furthermore, because of the ideology of sisterhood, subsequent support is given to the group members whenever they need it. I think of women's liberation as an extended family without the history of atrocities that characterizes many relationships with one's biological extended family.

Psychotherapy as recreation. Here may be found the gift for the man who has everything:

> Wife and I wish to start a bicycle club. (Psychotherapy included if wish) $1. a month membership. Lic. psychologist (Los Angeles Free Press, 1968).

> *Big Sur Mendocino High Sierras Weekend Mountain Encounter*
> With a naturalist and an encounter group leader $35 per person—$45 per couple—food and lodging included. . . .

Sponsored by the Institute for the Development of Human Potential [an officially recognized Student Organization, but not an integral part of the University of California] (poster on bulletin boards at The University of California, Berkeley, 1969).

Not only is "participatory democracy" being applied to the psycho-therapeutic process, but psychotherapy or "games" are now considered a form of recreation for the man who has everything. According to Szasz (1961), when people have a surplus of money, they expect to be happy and they use their money to seek happiness. Therefore, the social function of therapy must be compared not only with religion, but also with alcohol, tobacco, and recreation. Thus, Endore (1967:9) refers to the Synanon games, which are similar to group therapy sessions, as "the human sport," the game "to make you grow up." The new, more flexible self-image that results occurs "by nothing more than a willingness to play an exciting game and have a good time while doing so." Endore and Frankie Lago, a long-time Synanon resident (former "dope fiend" and thief who was the main speaker at the orientation held every Sunday for people considering joining the Synanon club and the "games") deny that the games are therapy. However, Yablonsky (1967:viii) in the preface to his book on Synanon calls the Synanons (as they were then termed) "a new kind of group therapy, an effective approach to racial integration, a different way of being religious, a new method of attack therapy, an exciting fresh approach to the cultural arts and philosophy."[4]

Lago considered the "games" "adult education." He continued, "dope fiends" are "afflicted with character disorders" and should be residents of Synanon, but the 1,000 nonresident players might be people who have had success in their lives and "now want to get plugged into something else." Yablonsky (1967:vi) said that the Synanon Clubs "are comprised of hundreds of people who never had serious emotional problems but seem to *enjoy the thrill* of personal discovery the Games seem to produce" (emphasis added).

Hard-core hippies, such as The Diggers, consider drugs recreational and therapeutic. Drugs are a method of gaining enlightenment about oneself and the cosmos. Since insight can be achieved through drugs such as pot, hashish, and LSD, do-it-yourself psychotherapy is possible.[5]

---

[4] For one semester I participated in the "square" Synanons (those that include addicts and people who have never been addicts, or "squares") as part of a course I took from Yablonsky. It seemed like group therapy to me except that all the supportive statements were omitted and the rule of confidentiality was not applied.

[5] See the June 1968 issue of the *Journal of Health and Social Behavior* for articles on recreational drug use. Fred Davis' article, "Heads and Freaks," discussed the "heads' " use of drugs for self-improvement.

Some of the older hippies, such as Richard Pine, disapprove of using drugs only for kicks, rather than for self-awareness.

Psychotherapy as a social movement. Synanon and The Diggers (and other hard-core hippies), as well as some of the encounter groups to be discussed below are social movements, complete with "true believers." Yablonsky (1967:v) states:

> A part of Synanon's character that has become more articulate is its significance as a social movement. The organization has steadily moved beyond the limited work of treating drug addiction and crime. The function of Synanon as a vehicle for constructive personal and social change has become clearer as the theory and method is increasingly utilized by people who were never addicts, criminals, or had any history of serious character disorder in their past.

Synanon has mushroomed since its inception in an armory in Santa Monica. There are Synanon houses on the East and West coasts (four in California), in Reno, in Detroit, and Chicago. Synanon Industries own several gas stations. Residents' children now can go to a Synanon school. Synanon is not simply a "cure" for addicts but a full-blown social movement.

A striking example of therapy both as recreation and as social movement can be found in the booklet describing Kairos, the mental health spa in San Diego, where self-actualizing encounter therapy takes place. Not only can individuals join the Kairos Club, but they can give gift certificates of from $25 to $100 "for that person whom you know is open and really right for such an experience. . . . It provides the perfect Christmas gift from one or more friends or relatives." Can you imagine giving—or receiving—a gift certificate for a psychoanalysis?

If, in fact, as at The Diggers and Synanon, professional therapists are not necessary, but increasing self-knowledge should be a human goal, then the image of the future these groups hold becomes clear. The non-speed-freak hippies would like to "turn on" the whole world in order to have a better society where "no one studies war no more." Although the "drugless trip" has achieved a certain status, it is still common to believe that the war in Vietnam could have been ended if only someone had turned on Lyndon Johnson.[6] Hippie communes exist in the West Coast cities, but a number of "free men" are moving to rural areas to set up psychedelic kibbutzim. They believe that if everyone were free to "do his thing" a better world would result. It seems to me that "doing your

---

[6] The belief in drugs as a means of causing social change was a major difference between the hippies and the New Left in the late 1960s. By 1971, the Yippie branch was pro-drug (pro-youth culture), while the Maoist wing was anti-drug.

thing" is a twentieth-century version of Adam Smith's "invisible hand."[7] The section of the paradigm dealing with the existential self-actualizing therapies is also applicable to the hippies.

In sum, their image of the future consists of tribes living communally, probably in rural areas, in residences replete with American and East Indian decorations, with love given and accepted freely without the usual taboos and restrictions, with drugs available for the expansion of consciousness, and ultimately, as in Marx's vision, with the state withering away.

We leave the hippies cultivating their pot garden and turn to Synanon. Its adherents envisage the world as an enormous Synanon. Everyone plays the "games" and thus becomes mature. Unlike the hippies, Synanon is opposed to drugs—any drugs. People do not need chemicals of any sort to achieve a sense of well-being. Their image of man is more Hobbesian, so that a system of authority will continue to exist. Like the hippies, they feel free to experiment with time. Recently the residents at Synanon changed their time arrangements so that they worked a stretch of twelve-hour days, then participated in marathon group therapy, and finally had a period of free time (the cubic time schedule). Presumably, such experimentation would continue in the future; since, although they believe in the work ethic, they do not limit themselves to conventional work arrangements.

THE NEW THERAPIES

I have been discussing changes in psychiatric conceptions of man and of the treatment process in order to show that some psychiatrists are becoming aware of the interrelationship of social structure and the individual. The most striking changes in psychotherapy, however, have come from psychologists rather than psychiatrists. It is important to note that Freud was opposed to limiting analysis to medical men. And Reiff (1966:28) considers the elimination of lay analysts probably the most critical defeat suffered by psychoanalysis, and one for which the American analysts were largely responsible. The view in the United States that only M.D.'s are qualified to receive training enabling them to become analysts seems to be patently ideological, since it makes entry into the field extremely difficult for all those who do not have the financial resources to pay for the medical schooling itself, as well as the train-

---

[7] In his *Wealth of Nations,* Adam Smith developed the laws of the market where "the invisible hand" enabled each man by following his "private interests and passions" to arrive at what "is most agreeable to the interest of the whole society."

ing analysis most psychiatrists consider necessary. As a result, psychiatrists either come from upper- or upper-middle-class backgrounds, or have been successful in their desire for upward mobility. Their background may be one reason for the image of man—private man—held until recently by most psychiatrists. For people who are "making it" in society, societal factors are not perceived as being very important. On the other hand, psychologists have had for many years a running battle with medical men for their right to treat clients. Their lower status is reflected in lower fees. The radical changes in psychotherapy have come from psychologists, perhaps because of their lesser commitment to classic Freudian models and to the psychiatric profession, but more importantly, because of their differing education. Psychologists are more likely to have been exposed to other behavioral and social sciences, and thus they would be more aware of sociocultural variables. In addition, behavior-modification therapy, one of the new trends, is a natural outgrowth of the learning theory they are taught.

In this section I will discuss two psychotherapeutic approaches, each used mainly by psychologists, and each based on a completely different set of assumptions about man, and thus having different images of, and implications for, the future.

Man the self-actualizer: good-bye Mr. Weber. Because the "basic encounter" therapists I will discuss in this section work within an existential *Weltanschauung,* I will begin by presenting a work written by an existential psychiatrist, a work especially relevant to this book, since it deals with what Bell and Mau term "the future as a cause of the present." Existential psychiatry differs from traditional psychiatry in its antideterministic stance and in its rejection of two assumptions sometimes held in nonexistential psychiatry: (1) that man should be adjusted to society, and (2) that man may be reduced to a bundle of biological urges.

> It (existential psychiatry) conceives of the individual choosing and making his world rather than adjusting to it or succumbing to it. This view holds that the world is part of the existing human being, that he is part of it, and that he makes his world (Mendel, 1964:26, 27).

The future, rather than being merely the natural consequence of the past, is "recognized as a vital and strongly influential aspect of human existence in the present moment" (Mendel, 1964:27). The here and now is emphasized, since the patient needs experience rather than interpretation, for "learning and change occur only through activity" (Mendel, 1964:27).

Existential psychotherapy has for some time been popular in Europe, but has been taken up only recently in this country. The most popular current offshoot is "encounter therapy" or "encounter groups."[8] Many encounter therapists, predominantly psychologists,[9] call themselves humanistic psychologists, and as such have their own association and journal. (See Bugental, 1967, for a representative collection of their works.)

If Freud's thinking reflected nineteenth-century mechanistic physics, then it is not surprising that concomitantly with the discovery of the principle of indeterminacy in twentieth-century physics, a discovery that resulted in physicists perceiving that the objective was related to the subjective, psychology should once again focus on the more subjective aspects of the individual and a "humanistic psychology" should emerge. (It is also interesting to note that a similar trend has taken place in sociology with the existence of a "humanistic underground," to use Bernard Rosenberg's term.) I noted in the discussion of Freud that his psychology was a reflection of a society built upon the axioms of an economics of scarcity. With economics no longer the dismal science of the nineteenth century, with abundance possible, a new psychology was needed to reflect the increase of leisure time (at least for some segments of the population) and the decrease in the importance of the work ethic. Energy formerly required for mere survival could now be devoted to improving the quality of life through increased awareness both of oneself and of one's surroundings. Bugental (1967:345–346), a humanistic psychologist and adviser to the Esalen Institute, says that we are in the early stages of "another major evolution in man's perception of himself and thus the whole nature of human experience," due to the availability of this energy. He considers behavioristic psychology with its view of man as "nothing but a complex of muscle twitches" and its disposal of concepts such as "soul," "will," "mind," "consciousness" and "self" inappropriate to present and future conditions although appropriate in the past.

This new psychological vocabulary, rather than emphasizing regularity, uniformity, and predictability will highlight "the unique, the creative, the individual, and the artistic." More attention should be paid to man's internal subjective experiences, and it should be recognized that the supposed "law of causality" is

> simply a useful heuristic aid. . . . Some of man's behavior flows from *reason* and not from *cause*. The difference is revolutionary. Let this difference

---

[8] Some therapists, such as Rogers (1967), differentiate between group therapy, which is for people who have problems, and encounter groups, which are for everyone. Since this distinction is, however, rarely made in practice, because "sick" people are thought to benefit by encounter groups, I will use the terms interchangeably.

[9] I analyzed the Fall 1967 catalogues of Esalen and Kairos and found the following occupational characteristics of seminar and workshop leaders: thirty Ph.D. psychologists, twelve Ph.D.'s in other fields, nine M.D.'s, and forty-two others such as ministers, artists, and dancers.

be accepted and developed, and the torch is lit which will burn away the whole of the mechanomorphic picture of man and illuminate the human enterprise to entirely new levels of realization (Bugental, 1967:347).

Consequently, there will be a potential for improving social institutions so that they will be more suited to man's evolving needs.

Perls, a founder of Gestalt therapy (a therapy using body movement, similar ideologically to encounter therapy) and permanent resident psychologist at Esalen, agrees with Bugental that the traditional concepts of linear causation are no longer appropriate. In a fund-raising speech for the new Topanga Human Development Center, an Esalen-Kairos type of workshop located in a Los Angeles canyon, he stated that his approach was processual. In contrast to psychoanalytic thinking, he focuses on "the now and the how" rather than on "the wild goose chase of the past" (Topanga Human Development Center, 1967).

The goal of encounter therapy, in contrast to behavior modification therapy, is not the elimination of discomforting symptoms. Indeed, one need not have any symptoms at all. It is the therapy for the man who has everything. As Wesley (1967) states, this therapy is for "anyone who has come to recognize a vague dissatisfaction in his life arising from the lack of expressive spontaneity, love and joy." Rogers says, "Encounter groups are for those who are functioning normally but want to improve their capacity for living within their own sets of relationships" (1967:717).

The theory of human nature held by encounter therapists is Rousseauian, and the assumption is made that the potential for growth present in each individual will develop through the permissive and accepting climate of an encounter group. As a result of this experience, people will be able to fulfill their potentialities.

I have attempted to show the elective affinity between the decline of the Protestant Ethic, the rise of a leisure-oriented society, and self-actualization therapy. The relationship between time and the growth of industrial society has been frequently noted. Thus it is consistent with the decline in the work ethic that changed attitudes toward time should also be evidenced. Earlier, I mentioned the "cubic schedule" at Synanon. Marathon group therapy, used at Esalen, Kairos, and by many encounter therapists, "represents a challenge to conventional arrangements of time in that its basic characteristic is that of the continuous session ranging over one or more days. Regularly scheduled meetings of one or two hours duration, stretching out over many months or even years have been customary. The implications of the two basic approaches to people literally imply different views of men" (Stoller, 1968:42).

Traditional psychotherapists have criticized the marathons. In keeping with the nineteenth-century ideology out of which psychoanalysis developed, they believe that long periods of arduous work are necessary for any benefit to occur. They find it difficult to accept the claim that people may change as a result of participating in a thirty-hour, two-day period of therapy.

Not only are the traditional concepts of causation and determinism challenged and attitudes toward work and time changed, but conventional attitudes toward sex are also contested. In contrast to the Freudian conceptualization of genitality in which homosexual relationships are considered fixations, sexual activity not culminating in genital intercourse is considered polymorphous perverse, and promiscuity is considered immature, among some self-actualizing groups relatively free sex is considered part of the growth process. Thus Kairos offers a seminar entitled "Enjoying the Non-Permanent Relationship," the purpose of which seems to be to teach women to enjoy casual sex, since these nonpermanent interactions "constitute the majority of man-woman relationships." At Esalen, mixed nude bathing at the hot springs is part of the schedule; and although it is not required, it is expected.

Most encounter therapists and their followers spend some time at Kairos and at Esalen, a mental health spa located at Big Sur, on the California coast south of San Francisco and once the haunt of artists and writers such as Henry Miller and Robinson Jeffers (see Murphy, 1967, for a more detailed presentation of the program). Humanistic psychologists such as Maslow lead seminars there. But musicians, dancers, craftsmen, and specialists in Zen and Yoga are also present so that those attending can realize their full potential through body awareness, music, baking, ceramics, graphics, leatherwork, metal sculpture, photography, and textiles.

The importance of relating to nature, the anti-intellectualism, the emphasis on Eastern philosophy, techniques and music, and the Rousseauian image of man are found both among the hippies[10] and the self-actualizers. In addition, they are like American Romantics such as Emerson (1837:3) who said: "Why should we grope among the dry bones of the past or put the living generation into masquerade out of faded wardrobe? The sun shines today also." Both groups do not feel the past is relevant to their present experience.

As a participant-observer at a "Basic Encounter Group" that at-

---

[10] The use of the term "hippie" does not imply that they are a homogeneous group. There are, however, some common beliefs and behavior patterns distinguishing them from "straight" society.

tempted to recreate the Esalen atmosphere, I noted the following differences between this group and conventional group therapy:

1. A nonverbal therapist, a dancer, was present whose function was to increase the group members' body awareness.
2. The meeting neither started nor ended on time. In conventional therapy, lateness is interpreted as resistance, an approach to time consistent with the requirements of an expanding industrial economy.
3. The relationship between the therapists and the group was relatively egalitarian.
4. Part of the encounter was devoted to nonverbal communication between dyads, which in two instances resulted in what can most parsimoniously be called "making out."

This group emphasized various sense modalities not previously highly valued in our society, geared as it was to production rather than consumption. The permissive attitude toward sex, the emphasis on body awareness, the democratization of the therapeutic process, all are associated with similar trends in other areas of our society and assume a future very different from the past.

The values of these therapists are freedom, spontaneity, intimacy, and creativity. Their idea of the freedom man needs to grow is not simply Freud's goal of replacing id with ego, but rather freedom to express feelings, to become close to people with less fear of interdependence and intimacy, freedom to express oneself through nonverbal as well as verbal means, through movement and art and nature. The structure of society, with its emphasis on role-appropriate behavior in interaction, is considered a barrier to full humanness.[11] Thus, individuals are encouraged not to become "victimized by the social rigging in which his life moves . . . (which) chokes off the expansion of his life-self intimacy" (Kairos, 1967). Continuing on this theme, another Kairos seminar suggests that "people grow through developing trust, openness, realization and interdependence," so that the goal of this seminar is "growth toward a life that is more personal, intimate, self-determined, and role-free" (emphasis added). Often at Esalen individuals do not state their occupations in order to discourage interaction based upon roles.

An example of such an approach to changing institutions, and one that shows a Rogerian method of bringing about a society more suited for today's world, is the Educational Innovation Project of Carl Rogers

---

[11] This attempt to get through the presentation of self is also advocated by Synanon and the hippies. Synanon games propose to enable people to get away from the type of game playing that constitutes most of human interaction. The Diggers and other hippie groups believe that "tripping" enables a person to get to his "pure being" and away from his presented self.

and the staff of the Western Behavioral Sciences Institute working with the personnel and students of the Immaculate Heart Schools[12] (Rogers, 1967). The purpose of Rogers' (1967:717) "plan for self-directed change in an educational system" is to enable educational institutions to develop flexible and adaptive individuals who will be comfortable with rapid social change. "Basic encounter" groups with a maximum of freedom for personal expression, exploration of feelings, and communication are "one of the most effective means yet discovered for facilitation of constructive learning, growth, and change—in individuals or in the organizations they compose. . . ." (Rogers, 1967:718). The whole system must participate for change to be effective. Otherwise the changed individual either becomes frustrated or returns to his previous method of interaction because of group pressure. Rogers believes that whole systems can be changed in a relatively short period of time.

Rogers, in a symposium with Skinner on control of human behavior, has set down his values and beliefs concerning the role psychology should play in the increasing possibility of such control. He suggests that the type of therapy he advocates will result in greater maturity, variability, flexibility, openness to experience, increased self-responsibility, and self-direction. He values

> man as a process of becoming, as a process of achieving worth and dignity through the development of his potentialities; the individual human being as a self-actualizing process, moving on to more challenging and enriching experiences, the process by which the individual creatively adapts to an ever-new and changing world; the process by which knowledge transcends itself. . . . (Rogers and Skinner, 1956:1063).

Thus, he attempts to learn if science can

> aid in the discovery of new modes of richly rewarding living, more meaningful and satisfying modes of interpersonal relationships. Can science inform us on ways of releasing the creative capacity of individuals. . . . In short, can science discover the methods by which man can most readily become a continually developing and self-transcending process, in his behavior, his thinking, his knowledge? (Rogers and Skinner, 1956:1063).

He believes that the therapy that he and his followers practice express such values and produce a client who is "self-directing, less rigid, more

---

[12] The sisters of the Immaculate Heart of Mary direct and teach in the college, secondary, and primary schools involved in this experiment. Their innovations brought them into conflict with Cardinal MacIntyre of Los Angeles, a conflict that was finally mediated by the Vatican. One issue that disturbed some more conservative Catholics was the encounter therapy which these Catholics considered a means of breaking down traditional morality.

open to the evidence of his senses, better organized and integrated, more similar to the ideal which he (the client) has chosen for himself" (Rogers and Skinner, 1956:1063).

There are two limitations of this type of therapy. The development of each individual's full potentialities is possible only where there is an economic surplus. Maslow (1962) pointed out in his work on need hierarchies that self-actualization could occur only after other needs, such as the needs for safety, for food, and for shelter, were met. Thus those portions of our society still poorly housed, fed, clothed, and subject to the capricious behavior of police cannot afford the luxury of self-actualization (nor can most of the world). Stoller told me that when he applied the encounter techniques to welfare mothers and to drug addict prisoners, their structural situations made it impossible for the benefits they believed they obtained to be carried over into their daily life. Moreover, the goals of encounter therapy, which stress expressivity, would be most useful for individuals having had traditional WASP socialization emphasizing the virtues of stoicism and restraint. Other ethnic and class groups, white and nonwhite, whose significant others do not discourage expression of emotion and "acting out," would perhaps be better served by other modes of therapy.

Man, "the two legged white rat or larger computer:"[13] behavior modification therapy

> small, battery powered reliable conditioning
> apparatus for human subjects . . .
> Shock Box (variable intensity) $35
> Blinky Box (random order light stimuli) $25
> Tinkle Bell (moisture sensitive signal
>   for control of bedwetting) $25
> . . .
> Humanitas Systems, Orange City, Fla.
> (advertised in *Psychology Today,* December 1967)

Behavior modification therapy is the antithesis of the self-actualizing therapy. It is deterministic rather than indeterministic, is based on different theoretical groundwork, holds different views of human nature and of how society can and should be changed, and thus has a different image of the future (see paradigm). It reflects tendencies toward rationalization (in the Weberian, not Freudian, sense), dehumanization, and scientism in our society.

Although there are certain aspects of social control in every psychotherapeutic situation, whatever the rhetoric, and although Synanon self-consciously uses their "games" for social control of "dope fiends" there,

---

[13] Phrase taken from Bugental (1967:345).

in general most of the trends discussed have veered away from the social control model presented previously. Behavior modification therapy, however, seems most adequately conceptualized as a continuation of the tradition of therapy as social control. The therapist controls the situation.

The image of man these therapists use is derived from the behavior of animals. Their position is unique because they derive from the branch of psychology known as learning theory (London, personal communication). Because the basic theoretical work from which these programs derive was done on animals, these therapies are based on present observable behavior, rather than on unconscious factors or past events. Such therapies are designed to remove the symptoms causing the discomfort without "tampering with 'selves and souls' or even 'personalities.'" (London, 1964:37). Many behavior modification therapists believe that "the difficulties which bring people to therapy reflect learnings of fundamental behaviors which are at least as easily observed in lower animals as in people," and thus can be cured by mechanical procedures (London, 1964:77). They try to change the system of reinforcements so that the symptom they want to "extinguish" is no longer "reinforced" (rewarded). According to Kanfer and Phillips (1966), for this therapy to be effective, the patient must have a specific problem such as a phobia, rather than more general problems such as feelings of worthlessness, personal inadequacies, or chronic generalized anxiety. Mowrer (1963:579) considers behavior therapy the "method of choice" because "the way to *feel better* is to *be better* in the ethical and interpersonal sense of the term," but his position is different from those behavior modification therapists "who assume that all that is wrong with neurotics is that they have some unrealistic fears which need to be extinguished or counter-conditioned."

These therapists disagree with the Freudians who believe that insight will lead to changed behavior. They would be more likely to agree that changed behavior (which they would produce by manipulating reinforcements) would lead to insight. They are also opposed to the humanistic, nonscientific (according to their standards) approach of the encounter therapists, which they consider sentimental and muddleheaded. Thus, their papers have starkly mechanistic titles such as "The Therapist as a Social Reinforcement Machine" (Krasner, 1961; reported in London, 1964:239) and "The Psychiatric Nurse as Behavioral Engineer" (Ayllon and Michael, 1959). Some techniques they use seem more akin to Dr. Benway (Burroughs' character) than to Dr. Kildare. Thus, in the Ayllon and Michael study, the nurse changed the behavior of a patient who insisted on being fed but who wanted to be neat. The nurse deliberately dribbled food on the patient when she fed her. The patient eventually fed herself, but she "unexpectedly" relapsed after a four-week improvement in self-feeding.

No reasonable explanation is suggested by a study of her daily records; but, after she had been spoonfed several meals in a row, the rumor developed that someone had informed the patient that the food spilling was not accidental. In any event the failure to feed herself lasted only about 5 days (Ayllon and Michael, 1959:331).

Another example, this one unsuccessful, dealt with the attempt to eliminate violent behavior. This behavior had reached such proportions that "at the least suspicious move on her part the nurses would put her in the seclusion room." Since one of the nonviolent behaviors she exhibited was sitting, lying, squatting, or kneeling on the floor, it was decided to strengthen this class of responses since it "would control the violence and at the same time permit the emotional behavior of other patients and nurses toward her to extinguish" (Ayllon and Michael, 1959:329). She was to be socially "reinforced" by the nurses for a period of four weeks when she approached them while she was on the floor. During the four-week period her approaches to nurses increased and her attacks on other patients decreased. Then, the plan for the next four weeks was to discontinue reinforcing being on the floor "once the patient-nurse interaction appeared somewhat normal. Presumably this would have further increased the probability of approach to the nurses." However, "during the four weeks of extinction, the frequency of being on the floor returned to the pretreatment level," the attacks on patients and nurses increased, and the nurses started restraining the patient once more" (Ayllon and Michael, 1959:329).

> The patient's failure to make the transition from being on the floor to approaching the nurses suggests that the latter response was poorly chosen. It was relatively incompatible with being on the floor. This meant that a previously reinforced response would have to be extinguished before the transition was possible, and this, too, was poor strategy with a violent patient (Ayllon and Michael, 1959:329).

Perhaps the reader can think of alternative reasons for the failure of this experiment. Ayllon and Michael believe patients' behavioral problems result from events "occurring in the patients' immediate or historical environment. They are not manifestations of mental disorder" (Ayllon and Michael, 1959:323). [I do not understand their dichotomy.]

An attempt is made to discover and manipulate variables to modify the behavioral problem. Since the nurses are the major agents of social control and treatment in the hospital, a program is set up for the patient based on a rigid schedule of observation and the nurses are trained not to reinforce behavior they wish changed by giving attention or sympathy, but rather to reinforce desired behavior.

The logical extension of the model of man depicted in this section can be found in Colby's (1966) work—psychotherapy by computer. If the important part of therapy is not the relationship with the therapist, if, as described above, a nurse can be "programmed" to modify behavior, then why not make use of the new technology available and help solve the shortage of therapists? Colby (1966:151) considers the therapist

> an information processor and decision maker with a set of decision rules which are closely linked to short-range and long-range goals. With time he builds up a cognitive model of the patient; carries on thought operations on the model, using first and second order inferences in a partially specialized language; and finally decides on a communication to offer to the patient in natural language . . . guided by rough empiric rules telling him what is appropriate to say and not to say in certain contexts.

The person (as yet patients are not being used in the studies) types statements on a teletype and the program types answers substituting appropriate words in the responses for those found in the input sentences. For example:

PERSON: My mother dislikes me.
PROGRAM: Why do you feel your mother dislikes you? (Colby, 1966:148–149).

The program should identify and keep statistical track of important topics for the formulation of future responses.

Efficiency is obviously a value of these researchers, as it is noted the therapist is "much more efficient" since he can work with many more patients. Several psychologists with whom I have spoken think the programs are good; and their image of the future is to give all the chronic patients, who at this time receive no therapy, the opportunity of conversing with a tape. But in view of Rioch's (1963) success in training housewives in a brief period of time who are just as effective therapists as professionals with standard training one wonders why so little attention is being focused on this alternative possibility? Choosing a computer program over a housewife-therapist certainly is a reflection of values.

The workers in this area admit that they do not know how effective computer therapy will be. The program cannot handle sarcasm, shouting, or changes in feeling tone, and still arouses some antagonism, which is assumed to be due to defects in the program rather than to the process. An example of such hostility is the following:

PERSON: I hate you, you stupid machine.
PROGRAM: What don't you like about me?
PERSON: You have no feelings.
PROGRAM: How do you mean? (Colby, 1966:150).

It would be unfair to assume that the behavioral modification therapists are monsters—men with no feelings who wish to produce a generation of robots, men who have turned their back on the humanistic tradition in Western civilization to become mad scientists in the laboratory. It is obvious, for example, that B. F. Skinner, on whose work much of the application of learning theory is based, is a man of good will, a man who would like to apply what he has found out about how pigeons learn, to create a world[14]

> in which there is food, clothing and shelter for all, where everyone chooses his own work and works on the average only 4 hours a day where music and the arts flourish, where personal relationships develop under the most favorable circumstances, where education prepares every child for the social and intellectual life which lies before him, where—in short—people are truly happy, secure, productive, creative, and forwardlooking (Rogers and Skinner, 1956:1059).

In the above quote, Skinner is referring to his image of the future which he presented in his utopian novel, *Walden Two* (1962). The book has been severely criticized for its *Brave New World* aspects, the lack of real freedom, but Skinner believes: "All men control and are controlled. The question of government in the broadest possible sense is not how freedom is to be preserved, but what kinds of control are to be used and to what ends" (Rogers and Skinner, 1956:1060).

Like the behavioral modification therapists, and in contrast to the existential self-actualizing therapists, Skinner is a determinist. He does not believe that people behave in certain ways because of any innate goodness or evil but because they are reinforced for doing so:

> The resulting behavior may have far-reaching consequences for the survival of the pattern to which it conforms. And whether we like it or not, survival is the ultimate criterion (Rogers and Skinner, 1956:1065).

In his symposium with Carl Rogers he points out that there is no evidence "that a client ever becomes truly *self* directing."

> . . . The therapeutic situation is only a small part of the world of the client. From the therapist's point of view it may appear to be possible to relinquish control. But control passes, not to a "self," but to forces in other parts of the client's world. This solution of the therapist's problem of power cannot be our solution, for we must consider all the forces acting upon the individual (Rogers and Skinner, 1956:1065).

---

[14] Skinner appeared in September 1967 on a panel of five speakers at an Esalen-sponsored discussion in San Francisco, "The Scope of Human Potential."

Therefore, in *Walden Two* Skinner (1962:296–297) designs a total environment, or, as some might say, dictatorship, a total institution. Frazier, the designer in the novel, sees no conflict between dictatorship and freedom, since people are trained, through positive reinforcements, to "want to do precisely the things which are best for themselves and for the community. Their behavior is determined, yet they're free."

Frazier's (and Skinner's?) goal is the control of human behavior, not for exploitation of others, nor for his own benefit, nor for the benefit of some elite, but so that everyone may share in the advantages of the new technology of control:

> "What remains to be done?" he said, his eyes flashing. "Well, what do you say to the design of personalities? Would that interest you? The control of temperament? Give me the specification, and I'll give you the man! What do you say to the control of motivation, building the interests which will make men most productive and most successful? Does that seem to you fantastic? Yet some of the techniques are available, and more can be worked out experimentally. Think of the possibilities! A society in which there is no failure, no boredom, no duplication of effort!" (Skinner, 1962:292)

People marry young at Walden Two, but if the Manager of Marriages thinks there "is any great discrepancy in intellectual ability or temperament, they are advised against marrying. The marriage is at least postponed, and that usually means it's abandoned" (135). A "series of adversities" is *designed* to develop the greatest possible self-control in children (115). The approach is always pragmatic; every principle is experimentally tested. Thus, "History is honored at Walden Two only as entertainment" (115). In sum:

> Political action was of no use in building a better world, and men of good will had better turn to other measures as soon as possible. Any group of people could secure economic self-sufficiency with the help of modern technology, and the psychological problems of group living could be solved with available principles of "behavioral engineering" (Skinner, 1962:14).

SOVIET PSYCHOTHERAPY: A TEST OF THE SOCIOLOGY OF KNOWLEDGE

It is the central tenet of the sociology of knowledge that existential factors condition social thought. For, according to Marx (1904:11–12), "It is not the consciousness of men that determines their existence, but on the contrary, their existence determines their consciousness." Therefore, I have been attempting to relate sociocultural factors to the development of various psychotherapeutic ideologies and utopias. But if, in fact, societal factors condition men's thought, not only should there be differences in psychotherapy through *time*, but there should be cross-cultural differences as well. Szasz (1961:54) noted that while Karl Marx was the "social therapist" for the impoverished masses brought together in the process of industrialization, "The basic value of the individual—as opposed to the interests of the masses or the nation—was emphasized, especially by the upper classes. The professions, medicine foremost among them, espoused the ethical value of individualism." Thus, forms of behavior that might be labeled "mental illness" in different national settings may be quite different. Comparing the United States with the Soviet Union, Szasz (1961:296) says that differences

> arise from and reflect characteristic features of the social matrix of the therapeutic situation. They point to covert preferences of individualistic or collectivistic ethics and their attendant notions concerning the duties and privileges of citizen and state in regard to each other.

If we think of degree of socialism as one variable and of emphasis on the importance of sociological factors and of the community as another, we see that there is a positive relationship between the two, when examining the psychiatry in the United States, Great Britain, and the Soviet Union. In the United States it was only when the federal and state governments started funding community mental health centers and financing the training of social or community psychiatrists, in short, only since there was money in poverty, that community psychiatry and what I termed "psychotherapeutic activism" has burgeoned.[15]

In Great Britain since the National Health Act (1946), with the added impetus of the Mental Health Act (1959), community mental health services have been greatly developed. According to Skottowe 1966:363–364):

> Aldrich has pointed out that British and American psychiatry had followed the same pattern up to 1939 but have diverged since the War. Whereas the main British developments have been in social psychiatry

---

[15] The major funding of social psychiatric research and community mental health centers occurred in 1963 (for buildings) and 1965 (for staffing the buildings) after President John F. Kennedy's message to Congress calling for such legislation. The NIMH was set up in 1946 in response to the great number of psychoneurotic exemptions, breakdowns, and discharges during World War II; and in 1955 the Mental Health Study Act was passed, establishing the Joint Commission on Mental Illness and Health. Their policy recommendations emphasized the importance of the community, both in the etiology and the cure of mental illness (Felix, 1967). But it was not until the 1960s that psychiatric training included training in social psychiatry and that the psychiatrists became aware of the importance of sociological factors. Each year until 1968 financial support for NIMH has increased.

with particular reference to psychotic patients in hospitals, the main American developments have been in dynamic psychiatry with reference to ambulant neurotic patients. He tends to ascribe this . . . to the National Health Service. This has boosted mental hospital psychiatry . . . because it has brought mental hospital men out of their shells and has imposed on them the broader experiences to be found in outpatient departments, general hospitals, community work, and domiciliary consultations.

Many observers (Field, 1960; Wortis, 1950; Zifferstein, 1966; Babuan, 1966) have noted the emphasis in Soviet psychiatry on environmental manipulation, or in plain words, on making the patients' real world more comfortable. In addition to different conceptualizations of the relationship between the individual and society in the United States and the USSR, perhaps the "it's what's inside that counts" ideology is so much a part of American psychotherapy because the therapist does not have the resources available to manipulate the environment of his private patients. Thus he must limit himself to focusing on the patient's internal world. This limitation is then transformed into the ideology that all that matters is internal.[16]

In the Soviet Union heavy emphasis is placed on the physiological basis of mental illness (Pavlovian theory), which is compatible with their philosophical materialism, and on environmental manipulation, which is compatible with their theory concerning the dependence of the individual on his society. Both Wortis (1950) and Field (1960) agree that Freudian or psychologistic explanations for mental illness are considered "undialectical" or "idealist" in the Soviet Union.

Also, the problem of relating the psychology of man to his mode of existence in the Soviet Union becomes one of the main concerns of psychiatry. For this reason the most serious charges have been leveled against psychologists who seek to change people's minds without changing their activity and experience; and, conversely the greatest emphasis is placed on work therapy or on other forms of activity that serve to change people's minds (Wortis, 1950:6).

Field (1960:292) speaks of the somatic or physiological therapies (neurology and psychiatry are not two separate disciplines), psychological therapies, and the sociological therapies:

The sociological therapies are based on the Soviet theoretical conception of the importance of the milieu for mental health and mental illness and

---

[16] An American psychiatrist I know said that even the psychiatric social workers don't want to work with the patient's environment. They prefer to do dynamic therapy with their clients. Thus on occasion *he* would attempt to get jobs for and introduce girls to his schizophrenic male patients. His colleagues derisively called him a social worker.

the assumption that the care of the mentally ill is not only the responsibility of the psychiatrist, but also of others. . . . Health, and particularly mental health, is much too important to be left exclusively to physicians. The idea is very strong that in many instances the patient may be treated more effectively through a change in his environment: transferring him to a different job, encouraging treatment at home or in the community in familiar surroundings and with people who care for the patient . . . , having the psychiatrist or a visiting nurse see the patient on his home ground if necessary. . . . I have already touched on the importance which attaches to work therapy; this type of treatment finds additional ideological reinforcement in dialectical materialism which holds that the consciousness of the individual is a reflection of the objective world, is formed by the process of social labor, and appears early during human activity.

In a more recent article Zifferstein (1966:367) refers to "The Soviet Psychiatrists' Concept of Society as a Therapeutic Community." He contrasts the occupational therapy in the United States, where patients make sandals, stuffed animals, and ceramics with the work therapy in the Soviet Union, where patients make "real products" and are paid for their efforts. The therapy is directive and supportive. For example, a doctor thought that a patient with the capacity to be an engineer was unchallenged by the factory work he was doing, and this contributed to his mental illness. The doctor, therefore, prescribed that the patient be enrolled in an engineering institute and paid his full salary during the entire period of his schooling. Not only is it "the doctors' role to rearrange his [the patient's] life so that he has a better schedule of work, sleep, recreation, etc." (Wortis, 1950:84), but each community clinic has an office of social assistance which "examines the working and living conditions of the patients and undertakes measures for improvement" (Field, 1960:289). The emphasis on work in Soviet psychiatry as described by all the authors is in keeping with Marxian thought because Marx emphasized the importance of meaningful work in man's fulfilling his species nature. Needless to say, however, the use of patients' labor in a society suffering from a labor shortage may have other than therapeutic motivations.

In sum, problems of human happiness in Soviet psychiatry are not basically considered to be psychiatric questions. Soviet psychiatry can best be understood if it is related to its three basic sources of influences: (1) its social setting in a broad framework of public health services; (2) its conformity with the general principle of dialectical materialism; and (3) the teachings of Pavlov (Wortis, 1950). In the United States, where at least in the formal value system the individual is "master of his fate" and "captain of his soul," and where the psychiatrist, with the exception of those in the community health centers and the activist psychiatrists, does not have the power to manipulate the environment, the focus of therapy is on the individual and what he can do to change. In the Soviet Union, where individual behavior is considered a result of the social structural arrangements and where psychiatrists have the power to manipulate the patients' environments, the focus is on the physical treatment (consonant with philosophical materialism—the official ideology) and on changing the environment. Thus in both societies, the perceptions of the causes of, and the treatment for mental illness are related to the ideologies of the respective countries.

Soviet psychiatrists claim "that their type of society which has a clear-cut, well-defined goal and a collectivistic orientation in its culture, leads to a lesser degree of mental illness than a capitalistic society with its antagonistic classes, its violent competition, its irresponsible individualism, and its multiplicity of goals" (Field, 1960:292). Therefore, they believe that social problems such as juvenile delinquency and alcoholism should have withered away, and they are chagrined at their continued existence. But they do not consider psychotherapy the way to treat such problems. If the statistics presented by Field (1960) are valid, however, they have halved their rate of schizophrenia from 1940 to 1956, and thus we might expect that the rate would continue to decline, all other things being equal.

For the future, if an economic surplus becomes a fact of life of Soviet society, then perhaps matters of individual happiness will become a matter of concern. Although they might even become concerned with self-actualization, Soviet psychiatrists would find behavior modification therapy more consistent with their Pavlovian tradition. The use of psychotherapy by computer would not be incompatible with the "rational" and "directive" psychotherapy used and with the high value on technology in the Soviet Union. If the relationship with the therapist is not considered the essence of the treatment, were the proper programs available, the computer could well take over.

There is another more ominous possibility. The need for social control combined with distaste for traditional methods of terror may increase the use of mental hospitals as repositories for political troublemakers. Already several intellectuals who have written in opposition to the regime have been defined as mentally ill and "sentenced" to mental hospitals.

CONCLUSION

London (1969) notes that mental health experts working privately can be irresponsible if they insist on totally denying responsibility for the social changes they foster. Their role can become "insidious and potentially destructive." Such a destructive role is brilliantly described by Ken iston (1968) in a satirical image of the future, "How Community Mental Health Stamped Out the Riots (1968–78)." In his "projection," a psychiatric vocabulary is used to explain all forms of protest (much as Lerne did in the citation earlier in this chapter). Thus "the aggressive alienation syndrome" is "used to characterize the psychosocial disturbance of a large percentage of inner-city dwellers" (1968:21). Ronald Reagan, chairman of the Task Force on Civil Disorders, recommends that "massive federal intervention via the Community Health Centers, be the major instrument in action against violence" (Keniston, 1968:22). This violence since it is a product of personal and social pathology, requires treatment rather than punishment. Local citizens become "pathology detectors." Sociologists work on "interdisciplinary teams" with social workers, psychiatrists, and police, the latter providing the most important insights for the Mobile Treatment Team. General Westmoreland is appointed secretary for International Mental Health (formerly the Department of Defense). Congress passes the "Remote Therapy Center Act," which sets up 247 "psychologically healthy" communities "for the permanent recompensation of deep-rooted personality disorders" (Keniston, 1968:23).

Keniston further notes the relationship between what I termed the psychological quietism, or the "it's what's inside that counts" bias inherent in Freudian thought, and the developments he is "predicting." In this brave new ward it is found that concern with "objectivist" issues such as housing, sanitation, legal rights, and jobs leads to the patient's relapsing into violence; thus programs seeking to ameliorate these environmental factors are wrong, not only because they merely treat symptoms rather than the underlying personality pathology, but because they "undermined the mental health of those exposed to these programs" (23). Therefore, objectivism becomes "a prime symptom of individual and community dysfunction" (23) for which therapy must be instituted swiftly and effectively. College students, intellectuals, and certain foreign countries become targets for the "total mental health" program because they show such "objectivist" pathology.

Perhaps Keniston hopes, by making us aware of the social control implications of a mental health rhetoric widely applied, that his image of the future will function as a self-denying rather than a self-fulfilling prophecy.

Unlike Keniston, other academics and therapists who are concerned with the social control aspects of therapy, and particularly of hospitalization, do not have an explicit image of the future. It is clear, however that they would prefer a decrease in "total institutions" and an increase in the civil liberties of the patients or potential patients. Thus, they should approve trends toward day-treatment centers, night-treatment centers, and out-patient care using drugs as a substitute for hospitalization (see Pasamanick et al., 1967, for a study showing the superiority of such a program for schizophrenics over both hospitalization and non-hospitalization with placebos). Their rejection of the medical model may cause them to wince at terms such as "treatment" and items such as drugs. But because of the concern with "labeling" as a cause of deviance, any program diminishing hospitalization should meet with their approval, although ultimately they seem to prefer the development of a society with an increased tolerance for nonconforming behavior.

In general, the implications for the future seen by other writers sensitive to the problem focus on nonmedical significance of psychiatric and psychological thought. Bensman and Vidich (1957:57) believe that "the impact of psychoanalysis will ultimately be greater as a form of social awareness" and sensibility, than as a form of treatment for individual problems. Lindner (1957), like the therapists concerned with self-actualization, stresses the possibility of the development of new potentialities and capacities, such as telepathy.

Reiff (1966) extends his 1959 thesis concerning the rise of psychological man, calling what is happening today and presumably tomorrow "The Triumph of the Therapeutic." Reiff's concern is: "How are we to be saved?" He (1966:5) believes literature, sociology, and psychiatry converge, since their ultimate interest "turns on the question whether our culture can be so reconstructed that faith—some compelling symbolic self-integrating communal purpose—need no longer superintend the organization of personality." The decline of the work ethic is important since we are now learning "how not to pay the high personal costs of social organization," whereas "previously total social cooperation was necessary in order to survive hard reality in a world characterized by scarcity." The present trend toward "release" may be extended and permanent, since "an infinity of created needs can now be satisfied" easily (1966:239). Reiff is opposed to the new intellectuals because of their renunciation of the constraints of civilization and their worship of the self, disguised as the religion of art. They have an aversion to culture, and he considers their goal, the sense of well-being and impulse release, "the unreligion of the age" (1966:10). This revolution is unlike others in that it is not being fought in the name of a new communal order, but rather for

a permanent disestablishment of any deeply internalized moral demands. . . . For the culturally conservative image of the ascetic, enemy of his own needs, there has been substituted the image of the needy person, permanently engaged in the task of achieving a gorgeous variety of satisfactions (1966:239–241).

He believes, further, that we need "compassionate communities" rather than the "trained egoists" of this therapeutic age. Given his commitment to a certain kind of culture and civilization, I do not believe he would consider the hippie communes such compassionate communities but rather a further example of self-indulgence and self-worship. He (1966: 27) thinks we must find the moral equivalent of the Protestant Ethic because "the rules of health indicate activity."

Reiff continues, saying that although modern therapists may consider themselves social scientists and "the language of science is not revelatory," therapists today "must use a language of faith":

> A language of faith may be controlling or releasing, interdictory or counter-interdictory. It contributes vitally to what Mannheim called "collective definitions," not mere hypotheses or replaceable theories, but rather a "source of collective habits and actions" (1966:235).

Since most therapists seem to be men of good will and humanitarian outlook, they would envision a future in which psychotherapy would be available for all who need it. But social psychiatric studies have shown that the greatest need for such is among the lower socioeconomic status groups, and it is precisely these groups that do not receive it. One problem is that psychotherapists do not know effective, sound methods of psychotherapy for such groups. But even if they can reach and "relate" to poor people with problems, "overwhelming socioeconomic stresses" make such help ineffective (Redlich, 1967:66–67).[17] Redlich suggests that if techniques are developed for these strata, the techniques will probably involve group methods and nonverbal approaches. Tompkins (1966:2) agrees that:

> The future of psychiatry will be determined in large measure by the extent we commit ourselves to joining with the rest of the health and welfare services in meeting these demands thrust upon us by socioeconomic and political forces in a changing world.

Although believing that psychotherapy must continue as a part of medicine (for an opposing view, see Hollingshead and Redlich, 1958:377), Tompkins notes the value of cooperation with other groups and thinks

---

[17] A psychotherapist I know who works with lower-class and working-class people, because psychotherapy is included in their union health plan, tells me: "If I were really doing my job, I'd teach my lower-class depressed patients to become revolutionaries."

that the importance of private doctors making arrangements with private patients will diminish.

Greenblatt et al. (1967) suggest several ways to train psychiatrists to treat lower-class patients: (1) such patients should be accepted at teaching hospitals;[18] (2) psychiatric residents could live as participant observers in the homes of impoverished schizophrenic patients, because "It may be that a tour of residence in the home . . . would teach the psychiatric trainee far more than many hours of office practice with the same patient" (p. 156); (3) training residents so they are mobile and go where the need is, to the patient's home if necessary, and flexible so they can delegate responsibility to other therapeutic team members. Were these programs widely instituted, it is hoped that residents no longer would be trained to be what Paul Hoch termed "cream puff psychiatrists" (quoted by Greenblatt et al., 1967:151), men and women who are content to live out their professional lives dedicated to the welfare of a "thin layer of well heeled patients at the top of the economic heap." But even if such techniques are developed and effective in reducing psychic pain, ". . . as long as analytically-oriented individual therapy is regarded as *the* prestigious treatment, new modes will be implicitly declassé measures for declassé people (1967:152).

Most of this chapter has been devoted to the work and ideas of practicing therapists, as befits the title. However, because Bell and Mau believe that sociologists themselves are among the agents of social change, I will briefly discuss the ideologies and utopias of three major social psychiatric studies in which sociologists played major parts: the New Haven studies, the Stirling County studies in Nova Scotia, and the Midtown studies in Manhattan.

The New Haven team (Hollingshead and Redlich, 1958; Myers and Roberts, 1959) dealt explicitly with changes they advocated so that psychotherapy should not be the privilege of the rich and the shock box the medicine of the poor. (To paraphrase Anatole France, the society in its infinite majesty permits both the rich and the poor to pay $35 an hour,

---

[18] Training or university hospitals accept patients who they feel will be of use in teaching the psychiatric residents. Since some psychiatrists consider lower-class people unable to benefit from psychotherapy, and since the residents are being trained to do psychotherapy, such patients may not be admitted. Moreover, lower-class patients usually do not apply to university psychiatric hospitals. Some hospitals, such as the UCLA Neuropsychiatric Institute, require that patients come in voluntarily. Since many lower-class patients are court-committed, this practice excludes them. Thus, it was not surprising that in my research using five hospitals in the Los Angeles area, the UCLA Neuropsychiatric Institute patients ranked second in socioeconomic status, only the patients at an expensive nonsubsidized private hospital ranking higher.

four times a week to a psychoanalyst.) As Hollingshead and Redlich (1958:377) jokingly put it, ". . . what America needs is a 'good five dollar psychotherapist.' " Their projected program includes new treatment methods to develop effective and shorter methods of psychotherapy and professional training to train nonmedical "counsellors" or "psychothera-pists" for the multitudes who cannot afford what people in Los Angeles call "couch canyon" (the few blocks in Beverly Hills where most analysts have their offices). In addition, they believe that public mental hospitals must change so that in the future "the present institution with its back wards of paupers and unwanted people should disappear when emphasis on the care of institutionalized mentally ill persons is shifted from com-mitment to treatment" (1958:379). Their third suggestion is for mental health education, so that people would be taught "the proper use of psy-chiatry" (p. 380). These men, a sociologist and a psychiatrist, have been agents of social change. Their findings, together with the availability of federal funds, stimulated the development and growth of some of the new techniques and approaches I have presented in this paper.

The Stirling County studies (Leighton, 1959; Hughes et al., 1960 and Leighton et al. 1963) have as their model of man what I call *homo equilibriensus*, a man who must have stability to maintain his mental health. They found French-Canadian women the group with the best mental health. Thus, their design for the future would include a consen-sus-making machine, a stable social system with little mobility and shared values, with dissent not tolerated and adjustment rather than freedom the key.

The implication for the future of the Midtown Studies (Srole et al. 1962); Langner and Michael, 1963) would be a massive attempt to re-duce poverty so that the normal stresses of living, such as death of par-ents and physical illness, would not weigh more heavily on the poor than on the rich. Their criteria of normality, however, include not only fulfillment of role responsibilities, but finding satisfaction in one's role as an individual in relation to family, social, and civic life, the establishment and maintenance of a home, loving and giving, a mate and children, and so on, as well as the obligation to find and sustain a satisfying job. Not only are the former criteria based on middle-class ideals, but the latter seems increasingly difficult, given the increasing bureaucratization and rationalization of work.

If, on the basis of the New Haven and Midtown studies, because of their inclusion of poverty in the etiological scheme, and, because of the general growth of sensitivity to environmental factors such as race and poverty, psychotherapeutic *practice* as well as rhetoric changes on a significant scale, the structurally deterministic model presented earlier in this paper should be modified as follows:

Changed Existential Factors→ Changed Ideologies and Utopias→ Changed
Existential Factors

One indication of such a change in practice is the plan of the University of California Medical Center's psychiatric teaching hospital, Langley Porter, to function as a community mental health center serving the neighborhood in which it is located, and another is in several programs at Yale and the Connecticut Mental Health Center in New Haven, which are based in the community.

In sum, in this chapter I have attempted to show some of the existential conditioners of psychiatric thinking and of various psychotherapeutic postures; and I have noted some of the possible implications of the assumptions made regarding the nature of man and of his relationship to society. When no explicit image of the future was presented, I tried to draw out the implicit images of the future and consequences of these images. As long as intrapsychic factors were considered the "real causes" of mental illness, psychiatry played an essentially conservative role in the society. One can consider the changes in psychotherapy a reflection of similar trends in other segments of society. They are:

1. Apparent democratization of interpersonal relationships resulting not only in a democratization of the therapy sessions but in the advent of psychotherapeutic populism.
2. The presence of an economic surplus, so that many segments of our society are affluent and the work ethic is no longer a necessity.
3. The growing demand for psychotherapy, so that nonmedical personnel, psychiatric social workers, and clinical psychologists are becoming psychotherapists in ever-increasing numbers.
4. The greater awareness of the problems resulting from poverty, racism, and sexism.

The first three trends, combined with the growing popularization of a psychiatric vocabulary of motives, result in the increasing number of therapy groups.

One can take the "vulgar Marxist" cynical point of view and attribute psychiatrists' growing concern with environmental factors to the money in poverty. Nonetheless, psychiatric thinking *is* changing. The new therapies discussed are based on diametrically opposite views of man and of the future. It was noted that the concern with self-actualization seemed appropriate only in an economy of abundance.

Perhaps an ideological analysis will do for psychotherapy what

Freud hoped a psychoanalysis would do for the individual; by making explicit the hidden assumptions and implications of different types of psychotherapy, where id was there shall be ego.

REFERENCES

Ayllon, Teodoro, and Jack Michael
    1959   "The psychiatric nurse as a behavioral engineer." Journal of the Experimental Analysis of Behavior 2:323–334.
Babuan, E. A.
    1966   "Legal rights of mental patients in the U.S.S.R." British Journal of Social Psychiatry 1 (Winter):22–28.
Bart, Pauline
    1962   "Mobility and mental illness: a review and ideological analysis of the literature." Unpublished paper.
    1967   Depression in Middle Aged Women: Some Sociocultural Factors. Unpublished dissertation, University of California at Los Angeles. Ann Arbor, Michigan: University Microfilms.
Becker, Howard
    1967   "History, culture and subjective experience: an exploration of the social bases of drug-induced experiences." Journal of Health and Social Behavior 8 (September): 163–176.
Belknap, Ivan
    1956   Human Problems of a State Mental Hospital. New York: McGraw-Hill.
Bensman, Joseph, and Arthur J. Vidich
    1957   "The future of community life: a case study and reflections." Pp. 57–84 in Psychoanalysis and the Future. New York: National Psychological Association for Psychoanalysis.
Bugental, James T. F.
    1967   "Epilogue and prologue." Pp. 345–348 in James Bugental (ed.), Challenges of Humanistic Psychology. New York: McGraw-Hill.
Burroughs, William.
    1959   Naked Lunch. New York: Grove Press.
Byrd, Oliver E., et al.
    1967   Health (6). Sacramento: California State Department of Education.
Caudill, William A.
    1958   The Psychiatric Hospital as a Small Society. Cambridge, Mass.: Published for the Commonwealth Fund by Harvard University Press.
Christmas, June Jackson
    1966   "Group therapy with the disadvantaged." Pp. 163–171 in Jules H.

Masserman (ed.), Current Psychiatric Therapies (6). New York: Grune and Stratton.

Colby, Kenneth, et al.
1966   "A computer method of psychotherapy: a preliminary communication." Journal of Nervous and Mental Disease 142:148–152.

Coles, Robert
1967   "Discussion of Mr. Saul D. Alinsky's paper." Pp. 29–31 in Milton Greenblatt et al. (eds.), Poverty and Mental Health. Washington: Psychiatric Research Report #21 of the American Psychiatric Association.

Davis, Fred, with Laura Munoz
1968   "Heads and freaks: patterns and meanings of drug use among Hippies." Journal of Health and Social Behavior 9 (June):156–164.

Davis, Kingsley
1938   "Mental hygiene and the class structure." *Psychiatry* 1:55–65; reprinted in Arnold M. Rose (ed.), Mental Health and Mental Disorder. New York: W. W. Norton, 1955, pp. 578–598.

Dickinson, Emily
1890   Complete Works, Thomas Johnson (ed.). Boston: Little, Brown.

Duhl, Leonard
1963   "The changing face of mental health." Pp. 59–75 in Leonard Duhl (ed.), The Urban Condition. New York: Basic Books.
1967   "What mental health services are needed for the poor?" Pp. 72–78 in Milton Greenblatt, et al. (eds.), Poverty and Mental Health. Washington: Psychiatric Research Report #21 of the American Psychiatric Association.

Dunham, H. Warren
1965   "Community psychiatry: the newest therapeutic bandwagon." Archives of General Psychiatry 12 (March):303–313.

Dunham, H. Warren, and S. Kirson Weinberg
1960   The Culture of the State Mental Hospital. Detroit: Wayne State University Press.

Emerson, Ralph Waldo
1950   "Nature." P. 3 in The Complete Essays and Other Writings, Brooks Atkinson (ed.). New York: Modern Library.

Endore, Guy
1967   The Human Sport. Santa Monica, California: Synanon Foundation.

Felix, Robert H.
1967   Mental Illness: Prospects and Progress. New York: Columbia University Press.

Field, Mark
1960   "Approaches to mental illness in soviet society." Social Problems 7:277–297.

Folta, Jeannette R., and Leonard Schatzman
  1968   "Trends in public urban psychiatry in the United States."
          Social Problems 16 (Summer):60–72.
Foucault, Michel
  1967   Madness and Civilization. New York: New American Library.
Frank, Jerome
  1965   "The role of hope in psychotherapy." International Journal of
          Social Psychiatry 5 (May): 383–395.
Freud, Anna
  1968   Annual Freud Lecture at the New York Psychoanalytic Institute.
          Reported in Newsweek, April 4, 1968.
Freud, Sigmund
  1934   The Future of an Illusion, W. D. Robson-Scott (trans.). London:
          Hogarth Press and the Institute of Psychoanalysis.
  1961   Civilization and its Discontents, James Strachey (ed.). New
          York: Norton.
Geiger, H. Jack
  1967   "Of the poor, by the poor, or for the poor: the mental health
          implications of social control of poverty programs." Pp. 55–65 in
          Milton Greenblatt et al. (eds.), Poverty and Mental Health.
          Washington: Psychiatric Research Report #21 of the American
          Psychiatric Association.
Ginsberg, Alan
  1961   Kaddish and Other Poems. San Francisco: City Lights Books.
Goffman, Erving
  1961   Asylums, Garden City, N.Y.: Anchor Books.
Greenblatt, Milton, and Myron R. Sharaf
  1967   "Poverty and mental health: implications for training." Pp. 151–
          159 in Milton Greenblatt et al. (eds.), Poverty and Mental
          Health. Washington: Psychiatric Research Report #21 of the
          American Psychiatric Association.
Hollingshead, August B., and Fredrick C. Redlich
  1958   Social Class and Mental Illness: A Study. New York: Wiley.
Hughes, Charles Campbell, et al.
  1960   People of Cove and Woodlot. New York: Basic Books.
Hughes, H. Stuart
  1961   Consciousness and Society. New York: Vintage.
Kairos
  1967–   Kairos. Esalen Institute. San Francisco, California (pamphlet).
  1968
Kanfer, Frederick H., and Jeanne S. Phillips
  1966   "Review of the area of behavior therapy." Archives of General
          Psychiatry 15 (August):114–127.
Keniston, Kenneth
  1968   "How community mental health stamped out the riots (1968–
          78)." Trans-Action 5 (July–August):21–29.

Kesey, Ken
  1962   One Flew Over the Cuckoo's Nest. New York: Viking.
Laing, R. D.
  1965   The Divided Self. Middlesex, England: Penguin.
Langner, Thomas S., and Stanley T. Michael
  1963   Life Stress and Mental Health. New York: Free Press of Glencoe.
Leighton, Alexander Hamilton
  1959   My Name is Legion. New York: Basic Books.
Leighton, Dorothea C., et al.
  1963   The Character of Danger. New York: Basic Books.
Lerner, Thomas
  1968   "The psychiatrist's dilemma." Journal of the American Geriatrics
          Society. 16:94–98.
Lindner, Robert
  1957   "Psychoanalysis—2001 A.D." Pp. 143–144 in Psychoanalysis
          and the Future. New York: National Psychological Association
          for Psychoanalysis.
London, Perry
  1964   The Modes and Morals of Psychotherapy. New York: Holt, Rine-
          hart, and Winston.
  1969   "Morale and mental health." In Robert Edgerton and Stanley
          Plog (eds.), Changing Perspectives in Mental Illness. New York:
          Holt, Rinehart, and Winston.
Manis, Jerome
  1968   "The sociology of knowledge and community mental health re-
          search." Social Problems 15 (Spring):488–502.
Marcuse, Herbert
  1962   Eros and Civilization. New York: Vintage Books.
Marmor, Judd
  1968   Modern Psychoanalysis: New Directions and Perspectives. New
          York: Basic Books.
Marx, Karl
  1904   A Contribution to the Critique of Political Economy. Chicago:
          C. H. Kerr.
Maslow, Abraham
  1962   Towards a Psychology of Being. Princeton, N.J.: Van Nostrand.
Mendel, Werner M.
  1964   "Introduction to existential psychiatry." Psychiatry Digest 25
          (November):24–34.
Mowrer, O. A.
  1963   "Payment or Repayment? The Problem of Private Practice."
          American Psychologist 18:577–580.
Murphy, M.
  1967   "Esalen: Where It's At." Psychology Today 1 (December): 34–42.
Myers, Jerome K., and Bertram H. Roberts
  1959   Family and Class Dynamics in Mental Illness. New York: Wiley.

The New York Times
    1964   January 20:12.
Parsons, Talcott
    1951   The Social System. Glencoe, Ill.: Free Press.
Pasamanick, Benjamin, et al.
    1967   Schizophrenics in the Community. New York: Appleton-Century-Crofts.
Peck, Harris B., et al.
    1967   "Community action programs and the comprehensive mental health center." Pp. 103–121 in Milton Greenblatt et al. (eds.), Poverty and Mental Health. Washington: Psychiatric Research Report #21 of the American Psychiatric Association.
Redlich, F. C.
    1967   "Discussion of Dr. H. Jack Greiger's paper." Pp. 66–67 in Milton Greenblatt et al. (eds.), Poverty and Mental Health. Washington: Psychiatric Research Report #21 of the American Psychiatric Association.
Reiff, Phillip
    1959   Freud: The Mind of the Moralist. New York: Viking.
    1966   The Triumph of the Therapeutic. New York: Harper & Row.
Reiff, Robert, and Frank Riessman
    1965   "The indigenous nonprofessional: a strategy of change in community action and community mental health programs." Community Mental Health Journal, entire issue.
Riesman, David
    1954   Themes of work and play in Freud's thought." Pp. 174–205 in Selected Essays from Individualism Reconsidered. Garden City, N.Y.: Doubleday.
Rioch, Margaret J., et al.
    1963   "NIMH pilot study in training mental health counselors." American Journal of Orthopsychiatry 33:678–689.
Rogers, Carl R.
    1967   "A plan for self-directed change in an educational system." Educational Leadership 24 (May):717–731.
Rogers, Carl R., and B. F. Skinner
    1956   "Some issues concerning the control of human behavior." Science 124 (November): 1057–1066.
Rome, Howard P.
    1967   "Poverty and mental health: a synopsis." Pp. 172–175 in Milton Greenblatt et al. (eds.), Poverty and Mental Health. Washington: Psychiatric Research Report #21 of the American Psychiatric Association.
San Francisco Chronicle
    1969   March 13:15.
Seeley, John
    1953   "Social values, the mental health movement, and mental health."

Annals of the American Academy of Political and Social Science 286 (March):15–24.

Skinner, B. F.
1962   Walden Two. New York: Macmillan.

Skottowe, Ian
1966   "Trends and issues in British psychiatry." Pp. 360–366 in Jules Masserman (ed.), Current Psychiatric Therapies (6). New York: Grune and Stratton.

Spray, Lee
1968   Personal Communication.

Srole, Leo, et al.
1962   Mental Health in the Metropolis. New York: McGraw-Hill.

Stoller, Fred
1968   "Marathon group therapy." Pp. 42–95 in G. M. Gazda (ed.), Innovations in Group Psychotherapy. Springfield, Ill.: Charles C. Thomas.
1969   Personal communication.

Szasz, Thomas
1961   The Myth of Mental Illness. New York: Hoeber-Harper.

Tompkins, Harvey J.
1966   "The future of psychiatry." Pp. 1–7 in Jules Masserman (ed.), Current Psychiatric Therapies (6). New York: Grune and Stratton.

Topanga Human Development Center
1967   Privately printed brochure.

Walter Reed Army Institute of Research and the National Research Council.
1957   "Summary and discussion of papers on social psychiatry in the community." Pp. 445–459 in Symposium on Preventive and Social Psychiatry. Washington, D.C.

Wesley, S. M.
1967   "Experiential (experience) therapy: a way in, a way out." Privately printed brochure.

Western Behavioral Sciences Institute
1968   "Educational innovation project." Interim Report of the Western Behavioral Sciences Institute of La Jolla, California (April).

Williams, William Carlos
1956   "Introduction." Pp. 7–8 in Alan Ginsberg, Howl and Other Poems. San Francisco: City Lights Books.

Wortis, Joseph
1950   Soviet Psychiatry. Baltimore: Williams and Williams.

Yablonsky, Lewis
1967   Synanon: The Tunnel Back. Baltimore: Penguin Books.

Zifferstein, Isidore
1966   "The Soviet psychiatrist's concept of society as a therapeutic community." Pp. 367–374 in Jules Masserman (ed.), Current Psychiatric Therapies (6). New York: Grune and Stratton.

Images of Future Leisure: Continuities in Changing Expectations

WILLIAM R. BURCH, JR.

LEISURE AS A SOCIAL PROBLEM

Images of future leisure seem to be distorted reflections from our mirrors of the past. In the past leisure was an elusive dream of man, while the enlightened modern has made leisure standard fare in our literary cafeteria of despair. Dennis Gabor (1964) ominously tells us that along with nuclear destruction and overpopulation, leisure is a major threat to civilization. And he is supported by a host of books and articles that warn—Leisure in America—Blessing or Curse?, "Crises in Outdoor Recreation," Work and Leisure, A Contemporary Social Problem; The Challenge of Leisure (Charlesworth et al., 1964; Clawson, 1959; Smigel (ed.)., 1963; Brightbill, 1960). Meanwhile numerous committees, bulky statistical reports, and government bureaus have officially translated the promise of leisure into a problem. Exploring the relevance of leisure's social problem image may equal the utility of scientific surveys that rigorously discover that driving for pleasure and television viewing are major leisure activities in wealthy democracies.

Only when one realizes that ours is a civilization that measures its supremacy by a multiplying index of social problems can he begin to apprehend its genius and its future. To be sure, social problems have been the eternal companion of mankind. But only modern man and, perhaps, especially American man, has made the invention and articulation of social problems a full-time industry. The intellectual community has been the chief engine in this industry. The intellectual's pure world of ideas is inevitably in contrast to the crusty world of men; therefore, it is natural that intellectuals should consistently discover sharp breaks between social myths and social reality. And it is equally natural that their discovery should compel them to confront the comfortable with the discomforts facing less visible others. This tension between personal life and public problems seems intimately joined in leisure. For in leisure our very comfort becomes the challenge not to remain comfortable. The individual who enjoys his "choosing time"[1] may resent the experts who forevermore seem to be converting his "better life" into a social problem. Yet it is very likely that without the past invention of social problems our standard everyman's image of a better life would not exist.

Until modern times, few worried about the poor; few worried about improving mental health or about the rights and happiness of laborers, women and children, slaves and criminals. Until modern times, no one wondered about educating large numbers of children, let alone expanding universities to accommodate all classes and social groupings. Poor race relations seldom troubled the French, Dutch, and British powers during the era of mercantilism; troops, and Gatling guns, not Parliamentary debates and foreign aid, solved any problems. Of the illnesses and diseases that struck the characters in Shakespeare's plays, few trouble persons in an industrialized society. In the sixteenth century so many other things were killing people that heart disease, cancer, and traffic fatalities were hardly worth mentioning. Modern industrial man is probably the most problem-blessed in all history. For, encouraged by a sense of control over nature, he has joined the survival problems of the past to the style of life problems of the present.

In the case of leisure, the facts that excite our critics are familiar. There has been a dramatic decline in the gross number of hours worked —in 1840 around 75 per week; in 1968, 35 to 40. Also, increasing numbers of people are living longer, starting work at a much later age and ending it much earlier; automation will make large numbers of workers redundant. Most modern ills are laid to leisure, not work—sexual aberrations, alcoholism, addictions, juvenile delinquency, riots, neuroses, and the boredom of the "tepee-telly" syndrome. Apparently we still believe that the devil finds work for idle hands. And yet we are told that our society unduly emphasizes consumption, youthfulness, and fun as its central life goals.

---

[1] I view leisure as that aspect of life that, in contrast with labor or work, permits one to have a relatively greater range of activity options. This does not mean that leisure is free of normative constraints, but rather that less formal, less bureaucratic constraints operate. Leisure as "choosing time" suggests that discretion is the better part of one's constraints. Also, it is a general enough definition to include play, recreation, and diversion as well as artistic production.

COMMERCIAL UTOPIANISM

Why is there so much shrillness over leisure? Unlike other social problems, leisure is not a subject in which intellectuals are simply articulating the discomfort of the inarticulate. Instead, they are responding to their own discomfort as their traditional prerogatives seem threatened by barbarians either of the masses or of the power elites. Certainly the antinomy between idleness filled by the devil and fun filled by consumer goods is reflected in the competing rhetorics of the corporate enterprisers who celebrate the new leisure and the intelligentsia who condemn it. The enterpriser's clearest voice seems to be found in the *Time-Life-Playboy* "gee whiz" school of journalism. Their image of man is a gloriously mindless seeker of eternal diversion whose private life must be turned into public display. The chief problem in this promised commercial utopia seems to be encouraging people to adopt a "potlatch" mentality. In the hip prose of *Time* (1964:55), it is all quite wonderful:

> Of all the shifts in spending, none has been more dramatic than the increase for leisure. Of personal loans in New York City banks this summer, 21% are being taken out for travel; on the West Coast, tourists to the Orient have doubled in two years. Across the U.S. the housewife ranks second after the businessman as a passport applicant. Those who stay home spend on second homes, pleasure boats and swimming pools; in California 3% of all boat owners earn less than $5,000. In addition, 25% of all families now own two cars—and the latest trend is to a third. "There is only so much steak one can eat without getting indigestion," says Boston Banker Richard Chapman. "So it seems only logical that the three-car family and the second television is merely the next step."

> Seeking a way to describe the shifting patterns of the consumer, the Philadelphia Federal Reserve Bank recently decided that he has gone through three spending tiers and is now in the midst of a fourth. The bank called it the "life-enriching stratum." The average consumer would probably be content just to say that things are very good indeed.

An endless round of hedonism never culminating in enjoyment seems an odd moral center for the land of the free and the home of the brave. The corporate enterpriser should not be denied his stake in an ever-expanding economy producing more and more things of dubious human need. But he cannot nor should he be forgiven his moral assumption that man's highest aim is an erotic conjunction with the latest Detroit fantasy.

LITERATI ARCADIANISM

Unhappily, the intellectuals offer an equally dim alternative. Their challenge to commercial utopia seems to be a retreat into literary Arcadia. Vance Packard writes books by formula condemning modern society because it is organized by formula. With his forays into the world of status seekers and hidden persuaders, Packard offers by implication and contrast the small town or village where elites and the lesser classes had meaningful leisure and work. Packard, like others sharing his vision, fails to note that the little society's alleged virtues, as well as metropolitan virtues, extract their price. The village virtues are bought at the cost of prejudice, hostility to strangers and new ideas, and a grinding conservatism and petty intolerance that lock the villager in a narrow round of suspicion, superstition, and persecution. One suspects that "creative" leisure is not likely to emerge in such bucolic settings.

In a slightly different vein good scouts like Charles Brightbill and other "healthy outdoor play" writers would have us all exercising at the YMCA or climbing trees reveling in the joys of nature. No wonder the manchild in Harlem merely sneers. A park or playground is a pleasant amenity but no substitute for a dignified level of living.

On a more sophisticated level are Hannah Arendt and Sebastian de Grazia. These two, like many others, take an option on the aristocratic perspective. They advocated the rise of the masses; but now that the masses have arisen, they are worried about the deterioration of taste. As Arendt (1959:114–115) argues:

> The hope that inspired Marx and the best men of the various workers' movements—that free time eventually will emancipate men from necessity and make the *animal laborans* productive—rests on the illusion of a mechanistic philosophy which assumes that labor power, like any other energy, can never be lost, so that if it is not spent and exhausted in the drudgery of life, it will automatically nourish other, "higher," activities. The guiding model of this hope in Marx was doubtless the Athens of Pericles which, in the future, with the help of the vastly increased productivity of human labor, would need no slaves to sustain itself but would become a reality for all. A hundred years after Marx we know the fallacy of this reasoning; the spare time of the *animal laborans* is never spent in anything but consumption, and the more time left to him, the greedier and more craving his appetites. That these appetites become more sophisticated, so that the consumption is no longer restricted to the necessities but, on the contrary, mainly concentrates on the superfluities of life, does not change the character of this society, but harbors the grave danger that eventually no object of the world will be safe from consumption and annihilation through consumption.

Arendt's feminine tough-mindedness is balanced by de Grazia's male romanticism. For de Grazia the world has been on an ever downward spiral from the pinnacle of excellence in taste and leisure established by Periclean Greece. For our times de Grazia (1964:359) sees leisure as possible for only a minority of thinkers, artists, and musicians who ". . . find their happiness in what they do, who can't do anything else, their daemon won't let them."

It may be helpful to take de Grazia at his word and see how very small is this minority of Americans who have and will have "leisure." Of the experienced civilian labor force in 1960, those in the artistic occupations furnished only 0.67 percent of the total labor force (Gendell and Zetterberg, 1964:85). And of this small percentage many of the architects, art teachers, magazine authors, dancing teachers, photographers and "entertainers not elsewhere classified" would not meet de Grazia's high standards. According to de Grazia's scheme, the masses, more than 99 percent of the labor force, are eternally confined to amusing themselves in the trivia of modern life. It is interesting to note that there were about three times more Americans in artistic occupations in 1960 than there were citizens living in Periclean Athens, excluding the 100,000 slaves (Wallbank and Taylor, 1960:109).

Perhaps the Athenian image of leisure is neither prophecy nor model for our present and future. It may not even be real for the past. As Muller (1959:103–104) reminds us:

> . . . actually the Greeks were one of the most restless, immoderate peoples in history. They were as impulsive volatile, turbulent, and generally unplatonic as the modern Greeks. . . . Athens itself was the home of the smart, acquisitive businessman, the prototype of the modern Greek. Whitehead once remarked that the type of modern man who would feel most at home in ancient Greece is the average professional heavyweight boxer; but even an American businessman, for all he would miss in Periclean Athens, would have got along better there than the ordinary classical scholar. Athens rose when it took to trade and industry, while Sparta remained agrarian; its brilliant cultural enterprise rested on its enterprising business life, notably its invention of the practice of banking.

The Greeks, for all their marvelous accomplishments, seem to have been, as Kenneth Boulding (1963:156) notes, "an insufferably superstitious and quarrelsome bunch of slavers with an undeservably good press." And such would seem to be poor material for building an image for future leisure.

Further, is it really a "demon" that drives creative users of leisure? Biographies of the famous, and my observations of professional writers and artists, suggest that the demands of rent, food, or a nagging spouse are often the real motivations that force the creator to face the horror of blank paper or canvas. Who is to say that the operator of a D8 cat moving huge piles of earth is not deeply happy in what he does? Who is to say that the janitor polishing the floor finds no depth of meaning in using his mind, body, and machine to make what was dull now sparkle? Wasn't it a famous theoretical physicist who wished he had been a plumber instead? Indeed, our social critics are curious sorts; they are passionately devoted to the dignity of man, yet scorn him at close range.

Whenever confronting arguments similar to de Grazia's, one has the uneasy feeling of watching Plato's shadows in a cave. We must assume that a long dead society actually functioned the way its philosophy says it should have functioned. We must then assume that a set of selective anecdotes depict the realities of modern society, and American society in particular. I am certain that de Grazia would scoff at the American tourist who says he knows Europe after visiting fourteen continental capitals in seven days. Yet de Grazia writes about American society as if he started from New York City, moved west on the Pennsylvania turnpike, and many freeways later arrived in Los Angeles to proclaim the decadence of American civilization. There is a strong sense that he missed some important segments of the American nation.

Perhaps our images of "mass society" are too much based upon a surfeit of information that makes illusion seem more substantial than reality. Each day across the public eye flickers the summation of public sin extracted from the nation and the world; yet, concentrated in the living room, it seems that implacable destruction and sin lurk at every corner. Fiction, commercial, and reality are so blurred that death in play, death in war, and the ubiquitous cigarette pleasure all become part real and part fiction. As if human life could persist without "poor taste," sin, death, ugliness, and body odor!

Such confusions of fiction and reality seem as relevant to the social critic as to the man who is frightened by the crime summed on his television picture rather than eased by the peace outside his picture window. The person who shunpikes the standard American criticism may find that beneath the skin of freeway, urban sprawl, and gas station, there is something quite diverse and muscular, groping for new purpose. He may even conclude that American ugliness is but skin deep, with the inner beauty waiting for critical exposure and direction.

I have spent so much time on literati Arcadian images of leisure because it seems to be the most pervasive alternative to commercial utopianism. De Grazia and Arendt share their images with some of the most important intellectuals of our time—Dos Passos, Jean Paul Sartre, T. S. Eliot, Aldous Huxley, Ortega y Gasset, and others. All are devoted humanists concerned with the fate of man, yet underlying their rhetoric is the strong thread of class bias. Near the end of his book de Grazia "saves" leisure by effectively disposing of mass welfare, substituting aristocracy for democracy, and junking equality for the liberty of a meritocracy. His solutions may ring true for those equally aristocratically inclined, yet they provide a hopeless and ineffective alternative image to the very real threat of commercial utopianism turning everything into "consumption and annihilation through consumption."

THE CLASS BIAS IN IMAGES OF THE FUTURE

A rhetoric that fully understands its class bias might begin to work within the tensions between art and democracy. As Simmel noted, democracy tends to quantify decisions without regard to quality; and quality is of most concern to the artist. Simmel (1950:295–296) argues:

> The problem of the relation between personal and mere positional superiority branches out into two important sociological forms. In view of the actual differences in the qualities of men—differences eliminable only in a utopia—certainly, "dominion by the best" is that constitution which most precisely and suitably expresses the inner and ideal relation among men in an external relation. This, perhaps, is the deepest reason why artists are so often aristocratically inclined. For, the attitude of the artist is based upon the assumption that the inner significance of things adequately reveals itself in their appearance, if only this appearance is seen correctly and completely. The separation of the world from its value, of appearance from its significance, is *the* anti-artistic disposition. This is so in spite of the fact that the artist must, of course, transfer the *immediately* given so that it yields its true, supercontingent form—which, however, is at the same time the text of its spiritual or metaphysical meaning. Thus, the psychological and historical connection between the aristocratic and artistic conceptions of life may, at least in part, be based on the fact that only an aristocratic order equips the inner value relations among men with a visible form, with their aesthetic symbol, so to speak.

Recognition of this class bias might clarify that the intellectuals' glorious images of the common man were never realistic, and that the deception was in the images rather than the newly visible masses. As Kenneth Clark (1961:82) argues, art is created by and for a minority. He says:

> Here we reach the crux of the problem: the nature of the elite. It was my first conclusion that art cannot exist without one, my second that the elite must inspire confidence in the majority. During the last hundred years values in art have been established by a minority so small and so cut off from the sources of life, that it cannot be called an elite in my sense of the word. Let us call it a priesthood, and add that in preserving its mysteries from the profanation of all conquering materialism, it has made

them rather too mysterious. There is something admirable in all forms of bigotry, but I do not believe that we can return to a healthy relationship between art and society over so narrow a bridge. On the contrary, I believe that our hope lies in an expanding elite, an elite drawn from every class, and with varying degrees of education, but united in a belief that non-material values can be discovered in visible things.

Clark seems to suggest that the artists' retreat from public life is as defeating as total embracement of materialism. Neither commercial utopianism nor literati Arcadianism seem likely to furnish us the ability to ask radical questions and to propose radical solutions for our emerging history. Both assume that history marches inevitably beyond the control of men. The utopian assumes "progress" is inevitable, while the Arcadian is equally certain that eternal decline is our certain fate.[2] In a more innocent era it was felt that men and only men decide the shape of their history. Perhaps a look at their images will help us to recapture their vision.

MORAL CRUSADERS FROM THE PAST

After twentieth-century despair the early sixteenth-century images of moral optimism guiding the future are refreshing. In the Utopia viewed by Sir Thomas More each man "did his thing," but not in aimless drift as play was infused with discipline and an ethos of craftsmanship. More (1900:56–57) looked hopefully to a world where each man toiled but six hours a day with the rest of the time free for creating a self.

> The chiefe and almooste the onelye offyce of the Syphograuntes is, to see and take hede, that no manne sit idle: but that everye one applye hys owne craft with earnest diligence. And yet for all that, not to be wearied from earlie in the morninge, to late in the eveninge, with continuall worke, like labouringe and toylinge beastes. For this is worse than the miserable and wretched condition of bondemen. Whiche nevertheles is almooste everye where the lyfe of workemen and artificers, saving in Utopia. For they dividynge the daye and the nyghte into xxiiii. juste

---

[2] Obviously, since these groups keep attempting to persuade us as to the rightness of their faith, they are not as fatalistic in intent as I portray them. However, the very nature of their rhetoric is deterministic—if we follow a few simple steps then the future will inevitably be a bright cornucopia of goods and happiness, or if we don't slow down equality or block that freeway, the future will be dismal and we shall never reach Arcadia. Neither of these directives account for human adaptability and diversity, nor do they note the means by which we can secure some options and reject others, nor do they provide goals that seem within the reality context of individuals not sharing their faith.

houres, appointe and assigne onelye sixe of those houres to woorke, . . . All the voide time, that is betwene the houres of worke, slepe, and meate, that they be suffered to bestowe, every man as liketh best him selfe. Not to thintent that they should mispend this time in riote or slouthfulnes: but beynge then licensed from the laboure of their own occupations, to bestow the time well and thriftelye upon some other science, as shall please them. For it is a soempne custome there, to have lectures daylye early in the morning, where to be presente they onely be constrained that be namelye chosen and appoynted to learninge. Howbeit a greate multitude of every sort of people, both men and women go to heare lectures, some one and some an other, as everye mans nature is inclined. Yet, this notwithstanding, if any man had rather bestowe this time upon his owne occupation, (as it chaunceth in manye, whose mindes rise not in the contemplation of any science liberall) he is not letted, nor prohibited, but it also praysed and commended, as profitable to the common wealthe.

Three centuries after More, Edward Bellamy looked back from the year 2000 to 1897 and found that industrialization had furnished the means for men to save themselves. In Bellamy's future society, all men have dignified work and play regardless of their occupation. Money has been replaced by the universal credit card. The "telephone" (or FM radio or stereo phonograph?) symbolized for Bellamy the wonder of the new society, which had so reorganized itself that its technology was harnessed in the service of man's spirit. The "telephone" permitted one to turn a dial at any time of the day or night and have music, sermons, and lectures to fit his mood. As he says in referring to the nineteenth century, "If we could have devised an arrangement for providing everybody with music in their homes, perfect in quality, unlimited in quantity, suited to every mood, and beginning and ceasing at will, we should have considered the limit of human felicity already attained and ceased to strive for further improvements" (Bellamy, 1960:87).

Yet Bellamy's new society forces a morality more stringent than More's, but every bit as limiting of social diversity. Both writers are strong moralizers for their religious and upper-class values. Yet the mass of men, being imperfect, could not long endure such a joyless and highly principled social world.

Thus we have three images of a leisured future, each of them based upon distinctive class rhetorics. The literati reflect an Arcadian attempt to save aristocratic symbols of leisure. Their traditional monopoly of taste and feeling seems challenged by the machine, mass literacy, science, commercialism, equalitarianism, and rising levels of living for the masses. They retire to sectarian corners. Business reflects a utopian faith in the liberal-capitalist symbols of leisure. However, as the fictions of individualism, free enterprise, and progress depart farther and farther from reality, mass consumption becomes the "invisible hand" for preserving old ideologies. Caught in their own web of fate, commercial leaders enter the crowd to find out where to lead. More and Bellamy provide an optimistic attempt to save moral symbols. Their moral attitude is important but the specific standards of a theocracy stifle the imagination. Though each image significantly contributes to our expectations of the future none of them seems fully relevant for understanding patterns of the future.

DIVERSITY AND IMAGES OF THE FUTURE

The image of business, the intelligentsia, and moral crusaders give us directions of despair or hope. But because these groups are caught in vocabularies of illusion, their symbolism only accidentally coincides with the many images in a socially diverse society. Images of leisure can generate problems, but whose problems are they? Involuntary leisure for the poor may be played out in extended familism and religion or in action on the street and addictive psychoses. Voluntary leisure for the elite may be played out in the arts or in the privacy of neuroses. Scheduled leisure for the middle mass may be spent in "do-it-yourself" work, conspicuous consumption, or a vague sense of boredom. And these tendencies will be cross-cut with divergencies associated with life cycle, regional, residential, and reference group variations.

There is no one particular image of leisure but many images, which may share some points of similarity along with their central divergence. Gans' (1967) lower-middle-class Levittowners do not share the same images of the media, conformity, or suburban life as do their upper-class urban critics. Harrington's (1963) 50 million American poor (25 percent of the population) do not share the same images as the Levittowners. And the poor have no single image. The aged poor and the deprived youth, the poor Afro-Americans and the poor whites, the poor southerners and the poor midwesterners, the urban poor and the rural poor—all have varying images of present and future. The involuntary leisure of many industrial workers, the involuntary seasonal leisure of agricultural workers, the summer leisure of youth, the involuntary retirement of forty-year-old linotype operators, the inactivity of the sick, the lame, and the bored all project different images from the leisure pictured by those who write books about society's crises in leisure. Until we begin to think in social change concepts, which mix both improved and detrimental consequences for different population segments, we will not begin to understand the human dimensions of the future. A new freeway opens opportunities for many just as surely as it closes forever alternative opportunities for many others. And opportunity is not simply linear

with class—the construction and maintenance workers are as happy
with the new freeway as the middle-class white-collar commuters; and
the displaced working class are as unhappy as the middle-class ecologists,
though in the end we may all gain or suffer. In the next section I hope to
identify some ways in which we can include diversity in our images of
future leisure.

SOCIAL STRATIFICATION AND LEISURE

Leisure images are self-images and therefore tied to class and status.
When the stratification system is expanded by satellite and media organization to include the world, then elites can compose whole societies and
their life styles may serve as models for subordinates or as foci for revolution. The narrowing fan of income in industrial societies (Kuznets,
1962:31) is matched by the extending stretch between them and the third
world. But the gadgets and symbols of the elite filter down to the poor
who, as always, misunderstand the symbolism—the necktie worn by the
Peruvian Indian, books as talismans to be carried not read, wool blankets
in Polynesia. One suspects that leisure for many elites in recently decol-
onized nations is similar to the black bourgeoisie described by Frazier
(1962:168–169):

> For a large section of the black bourgeoisie, their activities as members of
> "society" are their most serious or often their only serious preoccupation.
> Their preoccupation with "society" has its roots in the traditions of the
> Negro community in the United States. . . . in their position of house serv-
> ants during slavery, Negroes acquired from their white masters notions of
> what constituted "social" life or "society." After emancipation they con-
> tinued in the role of personal servants, and therefore saw the white man
> only in his home or when he was engaged in recreation. They never saw
> the white man at work in the shop or factory and when he engaged in the
> serious matter of business. As a consequence they devoted much time and
> much of their meager resources in attempting to carry on a form of "so-
> cial" life similar to the whites'. For many Negroes, it appears that "social"
> life became identified with the condition of freedom. "Social" life among
> the masses of Negroes was a free and spontaneous expression of their de-
> sire to escape from the restraints of work and routine. But for those who
> set themselves apart as Negro "society," "social" life became a more
> formalized activity. Among the Negro elite as well as among the masses,
> "social" life acquired a significance that it did not have among white
> Americans.

Old elites may see such behavior as a slightly flattering though
ludicrous pronouncement of their superiority. Comfortable with their
"natural" understanding of their goods and standards of taste, the elite

may remain convinced that the "natives" cannot handle leisure except in somewhat barbaric form. Yet as Americans should know by now, such emulation is but a thin facade for self-hate and eventual explosion.

Leisure, then, can have both stabilizing and radical consequences depending upon the relevant groups who are exposed. As symbols of social hierarchy, the central tendency of leisure production is to stabilize values even though commercial and other social structures may radically change. Hierarchy is always part of organized groups; therefore, its symbolic representations in art, music, and literature have a timeless quality that links generations and stretches across civilizations. Modern concert-goers are more likely to be immersed in eighteenth- or nineteenth-century classical music than twentieth-century modern. As Herberg and others (Herberg, 1960; Yinger, 1963; Lenski, 1963; Aldous and Hill, 1963) have demonstrated, religion is another leisure activity that produces a set of values that link generations and form a basis of identity. Further, many specific play activities are links to archaic patterns—such as hunting, fishing, and camping. As I have reported elsewhere, some forms of adult play extend a net of values over three or more generations (Burch, 1967).

Yet, as in education, exposure to leisure values can have dramatic consequences. The same sort of education that served good upper-class British boys as confirmation of their traditional values when applied to the "natives" made them marginal to both tribal and Western conditions. For those so exposed the consequences were radical. Future leisure may have the same mixture of stability and change in postindustrial society. A whole new mass of internal natives are becoming visible to the upper-middle-class "taste makers" and culture contact is likely to have the same confused communication that characterized nineteenth-century anthropologists and missionaries. The natives may accept the alien items but adapt them to their traditional values.

Diaries and autobiographies such as those of Samuel Pepys or Frank Harris indicate that from the sixteenth century through the nineteenth century and including the present, styles of leisure have been little altered by temporal conditions within a given class culture. Both Pepys and Harris represented new bourgeoisie who mixed traditional low status values with their attempts to emulate elite values. They flirted with women, gambled, gossiped, cultivated wine and food, learned foreign languages, moralized about the upper and lower classes, toured the countryside, and prided themselves on their clever party conversation. In general, they sought the usual signs of status that would indicate that they had arrived at a satisfactory social position.

Such attempts at announcement and validation of newly won standards of living seem little different from the response of the new middle mass. What is different is the masses' relatively rapid and recent growth in size and thus their increased visibility to elites. It is highly questionable whether the masses of men have ever found their major source of satisfaction in work. As Weber (1958:167–169) notes: "The feudal and monarchial forces protected the pleasure seekers against the rising middle-class morality and the anti-authoritarian ascetic conventicles. . . . Impulsive enjoyment of life, which leads away both from work in a calling and from religion, was the enemy of rational asceticism in the form of seigneurial sports, or the enjoyment of the dance-hall or the public house of the common man."

In the future 35 to 40 percent of American families will probably continue to experience improved levels of living. It seems certain they will continue to hold rather strongly to their working and lower-middle-class culture. Their leisure may seem materialistic, family-centered, and bland, not because it is new, but because it represents real consistency and continuity in style of life. The shape of this life style is already fairly well drawn.

Richard Hoggart (1963:33), in his study of the British working class, suggests that "the more we look at working-class life, the more we try to reach the core of working-class attitudes, the more surely does it appear that the core is a sense of the personal, the concrete, the local: it is embodied in the idea of, first the family and, second, the neighborhood."

S. M. Miller and Frank Riessman (1961) have summarized a variety of studies on the working-class subculture, which seem to substantiate Hoggart. They suggest that the working class has manufactured from their conditions of existence a successfully adaptive pattern of life. The working-class life style reflects values that are traditional, "old-fashioned," religious, and patriarchal. The working-class person likes structure and order, is family-centered, has a negative attitude toward leaders, and is often stubborn when confronting change. He is concerned with stability and security and believes strongly in an "eye for an eye" psychology. He finds considerable excitement in new possessions. He is person-centered; that is, he relates to people rather than roles. He has a strong touch of pragmatism and anti-intellectualism, as well as an exaggerated though vague respect for the learned.

These working-class values seem to persist even when there is collective improvement in levels of living. The most significant change seems to be in the criteria used for personal evaluation. Young and Willmott (1965:162–163) report that in urban working-class districts an individual is viewed as a whole person with a multiplicity of statuses. However, when he moves to lower-middle-class housing, "he has something much more nearly approaching one status because something much more nearly approaching one criterion is used: his possessions." Yet an increase in possessions does not mean a significant change in leisure values. Bennett Berger's study of an American working-class suburb indicates little or no change in leisure behavior though living standards had improved (Berger, 1960:59–87).

Small-town lower-middle-class culture also seems to have a high degree of persistence. A 1935 study of married young men and women, 15 to 29 years of age, living in Tompkins County, New York, found that their most frequent leisure-time activities were of the "indoor passive type," such as reading and listening to the radio. "Outing activities" and "household activities" were next in importance. The home was the major center for leisure activity. A later study of unmarried youth in the same area found that their leisure activities were similar to the young marrieds. Though both groups of these rural-small-town people said reading was their most important activity, this reading was primarily newspapers and magazines. As the author says, "a chief problem with regard to magazines is the character of those read; many are trashy" (Anderson, 1937:36). And of the few who read books, they "read fiction almost exclusively." These people now comfortably settled before the television set in their suburban homes may have simply substituted a higher form of video entertainment for their past lower forms of literary entertainment.

Thirty-two years seems to have made little impact upon this culture. Gans (1967:418) in his study of Levittowners reports that:

> If left to themselves, lower middle class people do what they have always done: put their energies into home and family, seeking to make life as comfortable as possible, and supporting, broadening, and varying it with friends, neighbors, church, and a voluntary association. Because this way of life is much like that of the small-town society or the urban neighborhood in which they grew up, they are able to maintain their optimistic belief that Judeo-Christian morality is a reliable guide to behavior. . . .
>
> If "blandness" is the word for this quality, it stems from the transition in which the lower middle class finds itself between the familial life of the working class and the cosmopolitanism of the upper middle class. In viewing their homes as the center of life, Levittowners are still using a societal model that fit the rural America of self-sufficient farmers and the feudal Europe of self-isolating extended families.

Gans (1967:267–268) reports that though the move to the suburbs changed leisure time and activity, the changes in leisure style were minimal. Of those changes there was a tendency toward more sociability, more work around the house, and more organizational participation. Such changes suggest that "pleasure seeking" has become more "constructive," with "fixing the home," gardening and family pleasures such as boating and camping replacing the public-house and gambling. Certainly the shifting of concern from family to the suburban community represents a step toward fitting private troubles to wider issues of the nation and the world.

Some anthropologists tell us we should respect the integrity of the "natives' " culture, that their plan of life has a value and dignity equal to any other. However, Margaret Mead (1956:443–445) argues that these preservationist attempts are merely a polite means of exclusion. She says:

> How often has our Western attempt to preserve native dress, old customs, different styles of architecture, to respect native laws and customs, been only a thin disguise over an unwillingness to admit a people, newly entering into our way of life, to a full participation of the culture which we claim to value so highly? . . .
>
> Once this is recognized, it is possible for us to scrutinize with newly opened eyes each situation in the world where people of a different sex or race, the opportunities which are offered them, to become "like" the members of another class or race or culture. Many different kinds of failure and refusal become intelligible—of girls to learn physics, or bright-eyed little African children who learn so quickly as small children and turn apathetic and disinterested at puberty, of new immigrants in model housing developments who don't "appreciate" their excellent plumbing, of the contrast between the adjustment of Negro boys and their sisters when both are asked to meet the middle-class standards of a high school in a small Pennsylvania town, of the restlessness and refusal of regular employment by modern Maoris in New Zealand or by American Indian immigrants to the big cities. The situation in which children are taught by individuals whose full status—as men, or members of an excluding race, or nuns, or persons free to travel—they cannot hope to attain makes the goals held up to the pupils seem not to be the wonderful opportunities which they are so often represented to be. So bright girls strangely have no "ambition," and children of discriminated against minorities turn "dull" at adolescence, not because of intrinsic incapacity, but because the desire to learn is blocked by the knowledge that part of the pattern to which they aspire will be denied them.

Unlike Gans, Mead does not permit us to take as benign a view about continuing the images of working-class and lower-middle-class culture. The challenge is to open wider cultural issues but on the terms of the newly emerging groups. There are several models for such a future. Hoggart's attempt to dignify the morality and standards of conduct in a working-class culture free from commercialism is one such model. So are Gilbert Seldes' (1956) and Reuel Denney's (1957) solid attempts to furnish critical standards for the popular arts. Tom Wolfe's (1965) critical vocabularies for appreciating Las Vegas sign art and California auto culture represent a serious means for extracting morality from the aimless public symbols of postindustrial society. Each of these attempts to develop standards implies that critical distinctions and a way of ordering perceptions must be erected at the level where one finds people. Similar tendencies are found in the hobbyists and their organized groups, which develop a craft ethic that guides the performer to seek excellence, whether it be gem polishing or water skiing. A critical vocabulary enforces standards of good and bad, and once one accepts such distinctions he is close to extracting a morality not unlike that found in "higher" standards of art and leisure.

Thus one major expectation of future leisure is that the middle mass will continue old values but with improving levels of living and, perhaps, new standards of performance. The second expectation will note that the grave predictions of miniscule annual hours of work are not likely to occur. Prophets of an automated world of ease simply have not looked very closely at the American beginnings of a postindustrial society. They have somehow missed the people in the cities, failed to smell the air and drink of the no longer shining waters. The task of servicing a society with such an environment is not likely to require fewer man hours.

The patterns Walter Buckingham (1962:47) notes for our present seem likely to occur in our future:

> Since 1870, productivity in the U.S. has more than quadrupled. The same input now produces over four times as much value in goods and services. Yet employment increased over six times—from 10 million to over 65 million—during this period. It can also be shown that most of the jobs held by workers in the U.S. today would not exist if it were not for advanced technology.

There is little question that unless society develops a means of retiming technological changes in factory and clerical occupations, many persons will pay high personal costs for long-run social gains. There seems little doubt, however, that many new jobs will emerge. Creative scientific research is no more amenable to total automation than barbering. Nor are executives, transportation engineers, rocketry experts, teachers, students, policemen, social workers, soldiers, janitors, and other service workers not yet invented, likely to be replaced, though their efficiency may be improved, by automated equipment.

With greater population concentrations there will be greater complexity of regulations and laws, which in turn increase the risk of lawbreaking. Even if better models of control for present problems are developed, it is very likely that the new complexities and new problems will outrun old solutions. Coupled with population increase and concentration the increasing levels of sophistication and education will reflect greater sensitivity to identifying and treating mental illness and other problems. Professionals with an occupational stake in the deviant and the defective will pressure society to recognize the need for extensive professional care. Thus it is very likely that our institutionalized population of the mentally and physically ill and the criminally convicted could be considerably larger than the present less than 1 percent of the total population. The increase in institutionalized populations will be matched by proportional increases for probationary and preventive work on the outside. The professionals, custodians, technical, administrative, service workers, and suppliers will continue to work long hours to meet the needs of this growing industry.

The growth of a professional, technical, and managerial class is not simply a linear projection of their presently large proportional growth but reflects what will be the new industries of a predominantly tertiary economy. The growth of this class will also reflect continuing pressures by occupations such as morticians, town planners, foresters, and recreation directors to improve professional status.

These occupational changes have important consequences for leisure because the workers in these occupations voluntarily have the least off-work time, yet seem to have the most enriched and perhaps dignified leisure. In a national sample Wilensky found that professionals and administrators, men who control their own time, are working longer, not shorter, work weeks. Wilensky (1963:113) comments:

> . . . With economic growth the upper strata have probably lost leisure. Professionals, executives, officials, and proprietors have long workweeks, year-round employment. Their longer vacations and shorter worklives (delayed entry and often earlier retirement) do not offset this edge in working hours. Although life-time leisure decreases with increased status, the picture is one of bunched, predictable leisure for elites whose worklives are shorter; and intermittent, unpredictable, unstable leisure for the masses, whose worklives are longer.

Our expectations of a large professional and service class with control over the rhythms of their work suggest that a significant proportion of the labor force will have shorter worklives with concentrated, predictable leisure. Also, it is very likely that the growth in the educational industry will have large numbers of professionals who find ". . . the separation of work from the rest of their lives is virtually impossible even if it is thought desirable. Their work *is* their life; their vocation is their avocation" (Gerstl, 1961:48). And persons in occupations so driven by the work ethic are prime recruits as appreciators and creators in the "higher" levels of taste.

Of course, countervailing forces may seek to routinize and bureaucratize professional and service workers so that their work patterns more closely approximate present clerical routines. Strong professional guilds, however, would seem to be some guarantee against such a tendency. And such pressure should continue the attractiveness of the New Class. As Galbraith (1958:267) suggests:

> Some of the attractiveness of membership in the New Class, to be sure, derives from a vicarious feeling of superiority—another manifestation of class attitudes. However, membership in the class unquestionably has other and more important rewards. Exemption from manual toil; escape from boredom and confining and severe routine; the chance to spend one's life in clean and physically comfortable surroundings; and some opportunity for applying one's thoughts to the day's work, are regarded as unimportant only by those who take them completely for granted. For these reasons it has been possible to expand the New Class greatly without visibly reducing its attractiveness.

The "New Class" professionals, as service workers and the middle mass, are expanding strata which represent crucial elements in the emerging stratification pattern. Men will continue to build their future leisure style upon past expectations and, as I have argued, these are linked to occupational and class expectations. Leisure patterns in postindustrial society will be traditional but may seem quite new as traditional occupations expand to introduce new persons to timeless values and rhythms. Standard measures of income, occupation, cosmopolite and local, highbrow and lowbrow will remain relevant but seem transformed under the new conditions of existence. Without becoming involved in theoretical niceties, the extensive literature on social stratification suggests an outline of that future.[3]

There will be more persons who are given leisure for their productions—artists, critics, liberal arts professors, High Church clergymen, surgeons, research workers in medicine and social science—who will be joined by a scattering of staff admen, "liberal" politicians, and little-

---

[3] I have attempted to be faithful to the findings from most of the standard stratification studies. However, I have been most dependent upon the works of C. Wright Mills as modified by somewhat more reliable statistical data. My dependence upon Russell Lynes, Hugh Duncan, and Kenneth Burke should be apparent.

magazine writers. Located in the higher towers of metropolitan life, they will continue to form a coherent class of cosmopolitan tastemakers. They will continue to favor theories of social decay. Their occupational structures will emphasize inner-directed, Protestant ethic values toward work; and their leisure will be of a creative sort indistinguishable from the values found in their work. Though they may not often be found in the corridors of power they will represent a strong enough force to have their standards of taste reflected in policy—whether it be preservation of wilderness or state support of the arts. They will continue to be appalled by the barbaric opulence, taste, and power of the metropolitan corporate elites.

On the other hand, the corporate achievers will also be an expanding elite stratum, though of considerably larger size than cosmopolite tastemakers. This elite would embrace such occupations as corporation executives, high military officers and government administrators (except social services); they will be joined by technicians such as engineers, corporate lawyers, and line admen with a scattering of new oil, war, and electronic wealth. These groups will continue to view work as a social game. They will continue to favor theories of social progress that best reflect the patterns of their careers. They will continue to rate sociability and quantifiable individual productions higher than quality considerations. They are likely to continue favoring "active" leisure, which mixes work and play in the manner of the executive luncheon or golf match. They will also reflect "useful" interest in the arts and "pressure cooker" humanities courses. Though they will continue to control administrative and technical power, they may find that the tastemakers have sufficiently mobilized strength to compel the machinery to follow many of their "woolly, idealistic" policies.

Cosmopolite tastemakers will have their counterparts at the local level in the old guard social pathologists (Mills, 1943). These will be persons who reflect inner-directed, rural nostalgic values. Though they may work in the city, their hearts and minds are in the small homogeneous towns. Their occupations are solidly middle class and professional with much importance on the local level—rural sociologists, extension agents, foresters, social workers, school teachers, small-town professors, editors and writers such as Vance Packard. Their leisure would tend toward healthy outdoor activities, community improvement organizations, and little theater. They will attempt to translate and adapt some of the less extreme cosmopolite taste standards to their localities.

They will be matched by the local achievers who reflect many of the corporate values. They will be the small-town businessmen, small urban shopkeepers, decentralized corporate and government administrators, and others who have enough stake in the locality to emphasize "booster-sm." They will continue to fear creeping "isms" which emanate from the metropolitan area, being happier with the fundamentalism of a Barry Goldwater or a George Wallace. Whatever remaining source of Populism here is in the United States these persons will support and lead such movements. They too will emphasize outdoor activities but with most emphasis upon trophy collecting such as hunting rather than the more esthetic expressions of the social pathologists. They will participate in community improvement organizations but those of "right thinking" groups such as Kiwanis or Rotary rather than artistic groups. Both groups of locals will experience proportional declines.

The next stratum is the largest and will continue to grow. The middle mass who represent foremen, craftsmen, and skilled workers with relatively good pay plus the greatly increasing number of lower white-collar, clerical, and service workers. C. Wright Mills has described them, but Herbert Gans seems to have come the closest to understanding them.

Below the middle mass there will be a shrinking proportion of urban and rural proletariat. At the present and in the future these will be people who remain in the society but are set apart by isolating occupations or extremely variable incomes. They would be longshoremen, miners, fisherman, loggers, janitors, junkmen, some agricultural workers, and so forth. They will continue to view the world in highly personalized terms, spend a good deal of their off-work time with occupational equals, and often have a good deal of involuntary leisure. They will continue to be a fit subject of pastoral interest by urban cosmopolites when they romanticize the working class.

Outside the main social system may be some 15 to 25 percent of the population. These will be the rural and urban dispossessed—the aged, nonwhite, illiterate, unemployable youth, migratory and tenant farm workers. They will continue to be the other America, which Harrington described as poor relative to the larger society. Whatever the criteria of placement, leisure will be a cruel joke to the dispossessed. Though the proportion of the population in this category may decline from present levels, they seem unlikely to disappear. Exhortation to personal bootstrap pulling has long been the reward given in plenty to the poor by the wealthy. This was so even when the poor were in a majority; when they are in the minority it may simply mean there are more to tell fewer the same old story. The poor must discover personal enterprise and diligence while the majority righteously search within themselves to find similar attributes that will explain why they deserve the rewards historical fate has awarded them.

Perhaps another 5 to 8 percent of the population will build worlds

of retreat on the fringes of the main social discourse. Given present pat
terns there may be four distinguishable groups: (1) Those of *faith*, suc
as the Amish, Mennonites, and other specialized religious groups. An
ethnic enclaves such as some Mormon and Basque populations i
Northern Utah and Southern Idaho and reservation-bound Indians. (2
Those who specialize in *kicks*. The noninstitutionalized addicts of variou
sorts, the varieties of cultists—"hippie" or otherwise—in search o
"meaning." (3) Those who are *dislocated*. Those in job transit; the pre
maturely retired and technologically redundant; the roving, nonaddicte
homeless men. (4) The *institutionalized*. The physically and mentall
disabled and incarcerated criminals. Of these four groups, the fring
riders of faith and kicks may develop alternative lines of leisure for th
host society, while the latter two may see their enforced leisure as a fina
statement of social failure.

THE LIFE CYCLE AND LEISURE

Leisure is not only linked to the stratification patterns but is inter
woven by life cycle demands. Running through the whole social chain o
life, leisure follows the special permutations of the individual's life cycl
and the cycles of his family (Burch, 1966; Ryder, 1965).

To be sure, there will be cultural and temporal variations in the na
ture of life cycle restrictions. Nevertheless, within a given culture-tim
period the changes of life cycle and family life cycle will have fairly uni
versal consequences for all persons experiencing the same flow of time
Life cycle factors remain constant and do not permit images of the futur
to escape their continuing demands. Children will continue to socializ
themselves in play, adolescents will discover the rules of the game, youth
will actively court life, adults will validate their social status, and th
aged will resocialize themselves in leisure. These patterns will continu
to set the parameters of possibility.

Further, the middle-aged shapers of twenty-first-century leisur
are presently entering or soon will be entering the schools. The school a
society's major means of guaranteeing expectations tends to conserv
values. Certainly for many of the entering inmates the school ex
perience will have radical consequences in moving them away from th
ways of their fathers. But for the great mass the school will continue t
reaffirm old values on both the trivial and significant levels. The purita
ethic may no longer be relevant in the factory and for the consumer, bu
it is gaining, and may continue to gain, strength in the post-sputnik
schools where work has become an end in itself.

The age cohort presently entering school is probably the first whos

ork and work ethic in school is in major contrast to the world about
nem. Yet their work is still considered "play" in the sense of diversion.
t no point does the adult world permit the development of a morality
ppropriate to either their work or their play. Emphasis is upon drift
cheduled by the inevitable turn of age; over the age grades the student
narks his way, with ultimate purpose always being vague and externally
efined. He must continue in school to get a "good job." However, the
onnection between school and the world of work is tenuous at best, for
he simple reason that adults do not know what kinds of work will be
vailable and what kinds of training will be needed. Yet such mysteries
nd confusions must be treated as nonexistent. The experience of voca-
ional education suggests that the time lag in tooling up human beings is
natched by a rapidity in technological innovation, which seems to pro-
uce only graduates with trained incapacities (Douglas, 1921).

In this concern for ever-rising educational attainment the lessons
f World War II are conveniently forgotten. In a very short period un-
mployable, illiterate Southern men and "helpless" women were manag-
ng highly skilled occupations. The treatment of knowledge as a means
ather than an end in itself, and the function of the educational system
s a social sorter cannot but leave the inmates with less interest in the
ontent than the form.

The adolescent is told he is a child because he plays while others
vork. He must be serious in his recreation for this will prevent him from
he aimlessness and sin that trouble his elders. He must constantly pre-
are for long-run purposeful behavior by following purposeless ritual
ecause "even gas station attendants need a degree." So the student is
obbed of dignity and a necessary occupation is robbed of its dignity.
Vhen school is so serious and important, it is hard to see how work
ould be more so. The articles of adult faith may not seem self-evident to
dolescents; and like other subordinate minorities, many may fail to
hare the "faith" of their betters.

Though full-blooded hedonism may be the advertisers' dream im-
ge of California youthways, it is not likely to be the central goal of the
uture Californian or other adult products of the schools. There is a
endency to confuse the loss of respect for property with a loss of respect
or work. Only those with memories of the Great Depression would so
neatly confuse work and property as parts of the same coin. Today's
ntering university student cannot consider the dignity of property very
eriously, because there has been so much and it has come relatively
asily. But after twelve years of being tested, tracked, sorted, competed
vith, threatened, bribed, and retested in the scramble for academic
osition, he has a far better appreciation of the spirit and meaning of the

work ethic than his parents ever had. Yet as he nears the end of his academic career there may be an awareness that the payoff will not be in the ideal symbols he has used to motivate himself along the academic path rather the payoff will simply be more of the property he has already learned to devalue. In this case, the main function of leisure will be to serve as the means for converting property into forms more appropriate to academic styles of excellence.

In the United States, the passing of the issues and people associated with the Johnson and Nixon administrations may clearly mark when one generation's rhetoric comes to an end. For over 40 years the ideas of the Great Depression and World War II have combined and recombined until they have so mesmerized both leaders and followers that they have failed to notice that the majority of the population has little experience of the war and even less experience with the depression. The passing of clichés and the emergence of new ones always produce uncertainty but it is an uncertainty that seems to be universal whether the society is capitalist, communist, or newly emerging.

A TIME OF STYLE

The emphasis of new clichés would seem to be upon a style of poetry in one's action which involves self but is displayed for the grace and edification of others. Style is always more concerned with its own platitudes, with the form of conduct, rather than the content of action. As such, style may furnish forms of ingratiation that permit both diversity and communion by placing emphasis upon things money cannot buy. Though emphasis upon style can easily swing into totalitarian forms of play, it can as easily serve to link diverse individuals in democratic republics.

It is very likely there will be a developing esthetic of public demonstrations and riots for these events offer stylistic opportunities for playing with politics, developing a sense of communion, and treating property with the appropriate contempt. Without discounting the real anger grievances, and pain of present riots and public demonstrations, one can note the strong elements of playfulness with sacred symbols and an emerging art form. Such events challenge not simply the abuses of the social system but its very uses as they radically search for social communion.[4] There is a sense of boundedness, in terms of territory and time which contains a spirit of merging and mingling, of breaking out of pri

---

[4] See the description of early-phase and middle-phase rioting in *National Advisory Commission Report* (1968). Norman Mailer (1968) gives one of the best descriptions of public demonstrations.

ate lives into the midst of one's own, while all about one is the loud joy hat heralds the junking of restraints carried by an improbable system.

Minorities of the poor, the black, and the youth coming with differ-nt demands and different images of leisure may be developing an art orm that deprivatizes play by opening it to great public arenas and col-ective celebrations that radically re-alter, yet reaffirm, the symbols of au-hority. In embryo the new forms may represent North American fiestas of feeling which cleanse the many strains in the tight-lipped, privatized, ational Anglo-Saxon world. They may even suggest the stylistic beauty of Latin fiestas described by Octavio Paz (1961:50–52):

> The fiesta is by nature sacred, literally or figuratively, and above all it is the advent of the unusual. It is governed by its own special rules, that set it apart from other days, and it has a logic, an ethic and even an economy that are often in conflict with everyday norms. It all occurs in an en-chanted world: time is transformed to a mythical past or a total present; space, the scene of the fiesta, is turned into a gaily decorated world of its own; and the persons taking part cast off all human or social rank and become, for the moment, living images. . . .

> Anything is permitted: the customary hierarchies vanish, along with all social, sex, caste, and trade distinctions. Men disguise themselves as women, gentlemen as slaves, the poor as the rich. The army, the clergy, and the law are ridiculed. . . .

> Therefore the fiesta is not only an excess, a ritual squandering of the goods painfully accumulated during the rest of the year; it is also a re-volt, a sudden immersion in the formless, in pure being. By means of the fiesta society frees itself from the norms it has established. It ridicules its gods, its principles, and its laws: it denies its own self. . . .

> The group emerges purified and strengthened from this plunge into chaos. It has immersed itself in its own origins, in the womb from which it came. To express it in another way, the fiesta denies society as an organic system of differentiated forms and principles, but affirms it as a source of creative energy. It is a true "re-creation," the opposite of the "recreation" characterizing modern vacations, which do not entail any rites or cere-monies whatever and are as individualistic and sterile as the world that invented them.

Imbued with festive styles and goals, public demonstrations point the way to the Goodmans' (1960:125–153) city of efficient consumption. Yet they go further for they explode outside the packaging of the media and become a celebration of democracy, with far greater participation and joy than the smoke-filled shows of political conventions. These fiestas will emphasize the attributes most central and unique in North

American life—political democracy. After all, it should be evident b
now that there is nothing unique about a people who consume all that i
set before them.

We have glimpsed the beauty in organized public celebrations b
sharing the inauguration and funeral of John F. Kennedy. One joyousl
reaffirmed the prevailing system of authority, the other sadly reaffirme
the continuity in these symbols of authority. Though critics claim Ken
nedy added little to the accomplishments of the Presidency but style, thi
was the essence of his hope. For twice in his term of office American
moved from the localisms of football and baseball rituals to genuin
national celebrations of politics. His was the first administration to elab
orately stage the glory and dignity of American life, for his was the firs
to have both the sensitivity and the media to tribalize a great society.

A time of style need not deny the validity of content in social actior
A people well aware of their troubled diversity may equally need sen
sitivity of form to appropriately fit momentous action. Hopefully, ou
images of future leisure will continue to be built from the voices o
diversity seeking their time of communion.

REFERENCES

Aldous, Joan, and Reuben Hill
    1963   Family continuities through socialization over three generation
           Los Angeles: paper presented to American Sociological Associa
           tion Meeting (August 28).

Anderson, W. A.
    1936– Rural Youth: Activities, Interests, and Problems. Ithaca, N.Y.
    1937   Cornell University Agricultural Experiment Station. Bulletin
           649 and 661.

Arendt, Hannah
    1959   The Human Condition. Garden City, N.Y.: Doubleday.

Bellamy, Edward
    1960   Looking Backward: 2000–1887. New York: New America
           Library.

Berger, Bennett M.
    1960   Working-Class Suburb: A Study of Auto Workers in Suburbia
           Los Angeles and Berkeley: University of California Press.

Boulding, Kenneth
    1963   "Two recent studies of modern society." Scientific American 20
           (January):156.

Brightbill, Charles K.
    1960   The Challenge of Leisure. Englewood Cliffs, N.J.: Prentice-Hall.

Buckingham, Walter
  1962   "The great employment controversy." Automation. Charles C.
           Killingsworth (ed.). The Annals of The American Academy of
           Political and Social Science 340 (March):46–59.
Burch, William R., Jr.
  1966   "Wilderness—the life cycle and forest recreation choice." Journal
           of Forestry 64 (September):606–610.
  1967   "Camping." Pp. 562–573 in Ralph Slovenko and James A.
           Knight (eds.). Motivations in Play, Games and Sports. Spring-
           field, Ill.: Charles C. Thomas.
Charlesworth, James C. (ed.)
  1964   Leisure in America: Blessing or Curse? Philadelphia: American
           Academy of Political and Social Science (April).
Clark, Kenneth
  1961   "Art and society." Harper's Magazine 223 (August):82
Clawson, Marion
  1959   "The crises in outdoor recreation." Resources for the Future re-
           print number 13, from American Forests (March and April).
de Grazia, Sebastian
  1964   Of Time, Work, and Leisure. Garden City, N.Y.: Doubleday.
Denney, Reuel
  1957   The Astonished Muse. Chicago: University of Chicago Press.
Douglas, Paul
  1921   American Apprenticeship and Industrial Education. New York:
           Columbia University Studies.
Frazier, E. Franklin
  1962   Black Bourgeoisie. New York: Collier Books.
Gabor, Denis
  1964   Inventing the Future. New York: Alfred A. Knopf.
Galbraith, J. K.
  1958   The Affluent Society. New York: New American Library.
Gans, Herbert J.
  1967   The Levittowners. New York: Pantheon Books.
Gendell, Murray, and Hans L. Zetterberg (eds.)
  1964   A Sociological Almanac for the United States, second ed. New
           York: Charles Scribner's Sons.
Gerstl, Joel E.
  1961   "Determinants of occupational community in high status occupa-
           tions." The Sociological Quarterly 2 (January):48.
Goodman, Paul, and Percival Goodman
  1960   Communitas. New York: Vintage Books.
Harrington, Michael
  1963   The Other America. Baltimore: Penguin Books.
Herberg, Will
  1960   Protestant, Catholic and Jew. Garden City, N.Y.: Anchor Books.

Hoggart, Richard
    1963   The Uses of Literacy. London: Penguin Books.
Kuznets, Simon
    1962   "Income distribution and changes in consumption" The Chang
            ing American Population. New York: Institute of Life Insurance.
Lenski, Gerhard
    1963   The Religious Factor. Garden City, N.Y.: Anchor Books.
Mailer, Norman
    1968   "The steps of the Pentagon." Harper's Magazine 236 (March)
            47–142.
Mead, Margaret
    1956   New Lives for Old, Cultural Transformation—1928–1953. Lon
            don: Victor Bollancz, Ltd.
Miller, S. M., and Frank Riessman
    1961   "The working-class subculture: a new view." Social Problems
            (Summer):86–97.
Mills, C. Wright
    1943   "The professional ideology of social pathologists." American
            Journal of Sociology 49 (September):165–180.
More, Sir Thomas
    1900   Utopia. London: S. M. Dent and Sons.
Muller, Herbert J.
    1959   The Uses of the Past. New York: Mentor Books.
National Advisory Commission
    1968   Report on Civil Disorders. Washington, D.C.: Government Print
            ing Office.
Paz, Octavio
    1961   The Labyrinth of Solitude. Lysander Kemp (trans.). New York
            Grove Press.
Ryder, Norman B.
    1965   "The cohort as a concept in the study of social change." Ameri
            can Sociological Review 30 (December):843–861.
Seldes, Gilbert
    1956   The Public Arts. New York: Simon and Schuster.
Simmel, Georg
    1950   The Sociology of Georg Simmel. Kurt H. Wolff (trans.). Glencoe
            Ill.: Free Press.
Smigel, Erwin O. (ed.)
    1963   Work and Leisure. New Haven, Conn.: College and University
            Press.
Time
    1964   (August 7):55.
Wallbank, T. Walter, and Alastair M. Taylor
    1960   Civilization Past and Present, fourth ed. Chicago: Scott-Fores
            man.

Weber, Max
  1958   The Protestant Ethic and the Spirit of Capitalism. Talcott Parsons
          (trans.). New York: Charles Scribner's Sons.
Wilensky, Harold
  1963   "The Uneven distribution of leisure: the impact of economic
          growth on 'free time'." Pp. 107–145 in Erwin O. Smigel (ed.),
          Work and Leisure. New Haven, Conn.: College and University
          Press.
Wolfe, Tom
  1965   The Kandy*Kolored Tangerine*Flake Streamline Baby. New
          York: Farrar, Straus & Giroux.
Yinger, J. Milton
  1963   Sociology Looks at Religion. New York: Macmillan.
Young, Michael, and Peter Willmott
  1965   Family and Kinship in East London. London: Penguin Books.

Images of Canada's Future in John Porter's *The Vertical Mosaic*

MENNO BOLDT

The purpose of this chapter is to analyze the time perspectives contained in a contemporary sociological work, the dimensions and impact of which are generally considered to be of major proportions. John Porter won the MacIver Award in 1966 "for his comprehensive analysis of stratification in Canadian society, and his contribution to macrosociology." At the time, the MacIver Award was the only award of its kind given by the American Sociological Association and was bestowed upon "the author of a publication which contributed in an outstanding degree to the progress of sociology during the two preceding years." Porter's award-winning book was *The Vertical Mosaic* (1965). There is no question about the quality of this book—it is first-rate; and my purpose here is in no sense to be construed as an effort to detract from the high honor that it has received. Quite the contrary: it has been selected for study precisely because of its excellence.

Because it is an exceptionally good example of the sociological enterprise, Porter's book escapes many of the obvious criticisms that may be legitimately applied to much of contemporary sociology. It is free from arid scientism, triviality, and an exclusive preoccupation with the present. Porter's study of social class and power in Canada was done in the explicit context of value relevance, the primary value being equality; and it deals both with past trends and future projections of phenomena that are basic in Canadian society.

Yet applying our paradigm for the analysis of time perspectives to *The Vertical Mosaic,* one is forced to conclude that the book gives a misleading picture of the present state and future possibilities of the Canadian power structure and system of social stratification.[1] Here in one of the best sociological studies, one finds implicit judgments that blind the author to viable futures that are compatible with his data, a concentration on negative criticism instead of solutions, a censure of politics and politicians that shifts responsibility for the perceived inadequacies of society entirely away from other image-makers—including social scientists, an assertion that the masses are powerless to shape the emerging future, and a suggestion favoring the infusion of ideology into areas of political and economic life that many specialists believe are better off without it.

In the following pages, I elaborate on these and other assertions about the reconstruction of realities in Canadian society in *The Vertical Mosaic*. My purpose here is epistemological only in the broadest sense; but my hope is that, as a result of my analysis, we may learn something about doing social research as well as John Porter has done. Furthermore, since scientists have no compunctions about standing on "the shoulders of giants," perhaps we may learn more.

PORTER'S CONCEPTION OF CANADIAN SOCIETY

The Vertical Mosaic provides a complex portrait of class and power structures in Canadian society with special highlights on social mobility, ethnicity, income, and educational opportunities. In his analysis, Porter utilizes the concept of a "family of power," a constellation of elite groups that ". . . compromise with and encroach upon one another in an interplay which is always moving toward a balance" (206). The elite systems that constitute this family of power include the corporate, the political, the bureaucratic, the trade union, and the ideological, the latter including the educational and religious institutions as well as the mass media. Each of these elite systems, as Porter sees it, participates significantly, but not equally, in the decision-making process, the corporate and bureaucratic elites playing a preponderant role.[2]

Porter finds a great deal of overlap and interaction among the elites who participate in many small groups of interlocking memberships. They belong to the same clubs and their names appear together again and again on the boards of hospitals, universities, philanthropies, and cultural or-

---

[1] See "A Paradigm for the Analysis of Time Perspectives and Images of the Future," pp. 45–55 in this volume.

[2] Porter makes substantial use of C. Wright Mills' (1959) theory of a power elite, but he does not assume the confraternity of power among the elite systems that Mills does.

ganizations. These cross-memberships are ". . . not unlike a web of kinship and lineage which provides cohesion to primitive life. . . ." (304).
Continued high social position from generation to generation, similarity
in social background, and frequency of social contact all lead to a sharing
of viewpoints, attitudes, and values. This social homogeneity and interlocking membership structure within the elite systems, together with
the pervasiveness of their influence he proposes, have resulted in the
identification of corporate capitalism with the "common good."

Essential to an understanding of Canadian society is its division into
English- and French-Canadian ethnic communities. In Porter's words,
Canada is ". . . an adaptation of its British and French charter groups,
rather than one of a new breed in a new nation" (558). He characterizes
the English-Canadians as a group *seeking* a cultural identity and the
French-Canadians as a group concerned about *protecting* theirs. The
ease with which English-Canadians can borrow ideas from the United
States and Great Britain has resulted, according to Porter, in an underdeveloped capacity to originate new ideas. The French-Canadians, on the
other hand, having been thrown on their own resources, have produced a
distinctive and flourishing culture. The consequent emphasis on cultural
differentiation has produced dual loyalties, which constitute an obstacle
to the development of a unified national identity.

The Vertical Mosaic constitutes a moralistic indictment of Canadians. Porter infers that there are serious flaws in the character of the average Canadian because his orientation is materialistic and not ideological.
That is, he seeks to satisfy his appetite for American-style consumer
goods even at the expense of the nation's economic and political autonomy. As supportive evidence, Porter points out that Canadians generally
have been reluctant to invest in their own country, and at the same time
they are eager to sell control in domestic companies to foreign buyers
when the monetary inducement is sufficient. The "ordinary Canadian"
emerges from the pages of this book as a politically impotent and sub-
missive figure who permits himself to be manipulated by a handful of
men at the top and who considers rule by the few an acceptable state of
affairs.

Porter presents evidence of substantial inequality in the distribution
of incomes and in educational and occupational opportunities in Canada.
His study reveals that the top 1 percent of Canadian income recipients
receive 40 percent of all income from dividends, while at the bottom of
the ladder 37 percent of all income recipients received less than $2,000
per year. A similar inequity exists in the opportunity for a university
education: the proportion of students drawn from the highest occupational class attending university is approximately twenty-eight times

greater than that of the lowest occupational class. Upward mobility is also less than would be expected in an open society, as shown by his finding that over 85 percent of the economic elite come from middle-or-higher-class families and that during the past generation upward mobility has been decreasing.

Porter believes that Canadians generally are undisturbed by the inequalities in their society, which, to him, is a paradox in a society that claims to espouse the value of equal opportunity. He finds the explanation for this paradox in the Canadians' false conceptions of their society: their identification with the United States is so strong that they have come to believe that the legendary equalitarian tendencies of American society are also present in their own society. A part of this myth that Canadians believe about themselves is that they live in a society of "middle level classlessness," that there are no impediments to upward mobility, that preuniversity education is free, and that a university education is within the financial means of anyone who seriously wants it.

Using the methods of social research, Porter addresses himself to the consequences of this disjunction between the beliefs Canadians hold about their society and actual social realities as he finds them. He concludes that Canadians have adopted only the material aspects of the American image and not the equalitarian aspects, and that the "reality world" should be reorganized in order to bring it into closer conformity to the values Canadians hold.[3]

Although Canadians have the economic, technological, and social resources necessary to achieve a more equitable distribution of life opportunities, according to Porter, they have failed to channel their resources toward achieving that end. Focusing specifically on the educational system as an agent of change, he finds that education in both quality and quantity is a social class privilege. Failure on the part of the educational system to provide all Canadians with equal opportunities for mobility, he asserts, has contributed to the high correspondence between social class and ethnicity. The British charter group is overrepresented in the upper social classes, in higher education, and in the professions; all other ethnic groups (with the exception of Jews) are underrepresented in these categories. An important consequence of recruiting elites primarily from the ranks of the "WASP establishment," he suggests, is that traditionalism and conservatism predominate in Canadian politics, and at a time when Canada is in desperate need of creative social programs.

---

[3] It is interesting to note the close correspondence between Porter's conception of Canadian society and Myrdal's (*An American Dilemma*) conception of American society, on the issue of disjunction between societal values and social reality.

TRENDS IN CONTEMPORARY CANADIAN SOCIETY

Porter specifies a number of trends in contemporary Canadian society, some of which he views as being under the control of man. Others,
however, he views as being beyond man's control to influence. Using
Polak's (1961) terminology introduced by Bell and Mau in the first chapter, we must conclude that Porter combines influence optimism with influence pessimism, depending upon what particular trend he is considering. With respect to the content—or in Polak's term, the essence—of
Porter's image of Canada's future, it is generally pessimistic. A descrip-
tive presentation of several of the major trends that one finds in Porter's
book will serve to illustrate these generalizations; a critical analysis will
be reserved for the final section of this chapter.

The dimensional law of political forms. This law is derived from
an analogy to Galileo's assumption that there is a maximum size to any
construction if it is not to collapse from its own weight. Applied to political process, the dimensional law of political forms holds that with increasing population any individual citizen's active part in government
diminishes and he becomes increasingly subject to policies formulated
beyond his control. This has been a commonly held image of the future
as far as government is concerned—that the more populous the state, the
smaller the degree of effective popular participation. Porter subscribes to
this "law," and he assumes that, as far as Canadian society is concerned, minority rule is a perfectly acceptable and legitimate form of
power. His recommendations do not include any proposal to democratize
the process of government; in fact, the inference is that it cannot be
done: "It is this quality of bigness throughout present day institutions
which defies the effort of finding mechanisms to make for greater social
participation in institutional life. . . ." (359). He points out that even
pressure groups that have been organized specifically to give the ordinary
man an effective voice against the political oligarchies themselves become oligarchies. The latter assertion, of course, echoes Michels' "Iron
Law."

Porter's proposal for improving this situation is to democratize
education so that all may have an equal opportunity to achieve the top
levels of power. "If power and decision making must always rest with
elite groups, there can at least be open recruitment from all classes into
the elites" (558). Here he is advancing a modified utilitarian philosophy
based on the assumption that if relevant conditions are held constant for
all, then the most capable and most motivated will reach the top, and in
this way a more progressive elite ought to emerge. He makes no suggestion that the power structure should be changed in a revolutionary man-

ner; he does not argue with the principle of government by the few. He has chosen, instead, to challenge the criteria by which the few are selected. In Polak's terminology, Porter projects an attitude of influence pessimism and essence neutrality with respect to the trend toward decreased social participation by Canadians in institutional life.

The growth of rationalized bureaucracy. Porter takes the Weberian position that society is moving inexorably toward increased rationalization. He sees bureaucratic management as inevitable in public administration, large capital enterprises, political organizations, labor unions, religious and educational institutions, and in the mass media. This trend is the product of two irreversible and inescapable processes: increasing scale of organization, and increasing division of labor. Having discovered this "law" in history, Porter, like Weber, uses it to conceptualize the future, but for Porter this yields a very pessimistic image of the future. He identifies the process of bureaucratization with apathy, mechanism, subordination, and depersonalization. Furthermore, ". . . the increasing bureaucratization of the economic system through the development of national corporations leads to an increasingly closed system of stratification. . . ." (283). In his view bureaucracies exercise a pervasive influence; problems become defined as the bureaucracies see them, and they are solved as the bureaucracies recommend that they should be solved. As the bureaucracies grow and drain away independent experts, those organizations with the most expertise make the key decisions because of their influence and ability to sell their ideas.

Like Weber, Porter identifies two societies—Western democratic and totalitarian—and he assumes that the differences between them will disappear when the dominant social force in each becomes what Weber terms a dictatorship of the bureaucracy. "As industrial systems develop, the distinction between the two becomes thin because they all become characterized by oligarchy in organization, widespread apathy and a compulsion to conformity. . . ." (209). Having said this, Porter proceeds to differentiate between the two systems on the basis of coordination among elite groups. In the totalitarian system common party membership unites the elites; in Western democratic societies there are pressures that bring elites together and at the same time force them apart.

Porter's idea of the bureaucratic trend is a clear unilinear construction of the historic process in which there is no place for man to play a role in deflecting or turning back the trend. The justification for the trend analysis is that it is rationally grounded—it improves efficiency, hence it has legitimacy in the secular scheme of Canadian values. Using Polak's typology, we can best describe Porter's position on this trend as influence pessimism and essence pessimism.

Power relationships. Porter identifies two simultaneous, but seemingly opposite, trends in the relationship of the elite systems to each other. One trend is toward intensified coordination, which has come about as a result of competition with other societies; that is, Canadian elites, according to Porter, have cooperated and compromised to develop a set of ground rules designed to serve their common interests in the context of extra-Canadian relations. Facilitating this trend is the social homogeneity of the elites and their shared commitment to the ideology of corporate capitalism. The second trend is toward separation of the elite systems and is a result of functional specialization. Specialization of knowledge, in Porter's view, creates barriers to free interchange of key persons; and it also acts to limit encroachment of one elite system upon another, because each is incapable of performing the work of the other. This historical trend toward increased separation among elites results in distinct career systems and distinctive professional norms. The consequences of this trend for the restructuring of the social class system are not specified in *The Vertical Mosaic*.

A third trend identified by Porter in regard to power relationships is the concentration of power in fewer and fewer hands *within* each of the elite systems. His data on the cross-memberships to be found on the chief corporate boards provide convincing evidence that the circle of corporate elites, through an increasing number of interlocking directorates, is being drawn closer, while the financial empire they command is growing larger through consolidation, merger, and takeover (233,234). This trend has been justified by the corporate elites by a mythology that stresses "hugeness as a good" because it contributes to economic efficiency and, consequently, cheaper consumer products (242).

The bureaucratic apparatus plays a key role in facilitating this trend toward increased concentration of power within the elite systems since, through holding companies, a larger financial empire can be controlled by a smaller elite. The strategies of the holding company are simple: ". . . they are to acquire minority control by buying enough shares to outvote any other likely combination of shareholders, and thus to elect (their own) directors to the boards. . . ." (256). Employing this strategy a quartet of Canadian elites with an $18 million investment have gained control of six companies with assets totaling $900 million. Such concentration of corporate power has disposed the other elite systems to strive for a corresponding concentration of power in their own structure.

A fourth trend in power relationships is identified by Porter as the ascendancy of the corporate and bureaucratic elites over the other members of the family of power. As Porter sees it, the drift toward a rationalized bureaucracy is producing a power imbalance between the elite systems that is the product of unequal competition for the skills of experts. The labor and political elites, because they are not able to offer a stable career pattern, are at a clear disadvantage in this competition. The corporate and bureaucratic systems draw away the best talents from labor and politics through direct hirings or consulting arrangements. Even the bureaucratic elites are at a disadvantage vis-à-vis the corporate elites in the competition for experts. In an environment where knowledge results in power it is apparent that the elite system that can attract the most expertise will exercise the greatest power, and a "snowball" effect follows. In this competition the expert has limited freedom over the dispensation of his services, because he is dependent on the corporate and bureaucratic elites for the necessary facilities and resources to carry on his work.[4]

A fifth and final trend in power relationships discussed in *The Vertical Mosaic* is the entrenchment of the elite systems. Porter quotes Michels on this point: "Every human power seeks to enlarge its prerogatives. He who has acquired power will almost always endeavor to consolidate it and to extend it. . . ." (208). Porter identifies a number of factors at work that entrench the establishment in its power position, including the aforementioned trends toward a rationalized bureaucracy and concentration of power within the elite systems. No less important, he suggests, is the understandable reluctance on the part of those with a vested interest to change the rules by which they have done so well. Government intervention in the economy, for example, that does not alter the essential character of corporate ownership is supported by labor elites who are "respectable" radicals, meaning that they seek improved welfare legislation and better guarantees for their own operations, but who are extremely reluctant to propose basic changes in the system that has brought them success. Even the ideological elites are enlisted, according to Porter, in the cause of preserving the established order:

> Modern holders of power can control some of the psychological factors which are the foundations of legitimacy. The ideas . . . through which the mental processes of subjects can be controlled by those in power . . . with modern mass media of communication have become enormous weapons. . . . (227)

Porter does not consider the five trends regarding power relationships as inevitable. For example, to halt the decline in rivalry for expertise

---

[4] We have here yet another trend: increasingly, the scientist becomes dependent on bureaucracies for funding and equipping, for which he pays by forfeiting his property rights to the knowledge he produces. Therefore, development of new knowledge, and its application, is coming increasingly under control of bureaucratic organizations.

between elite systems and the resultant concentration of power in the hands of the corporate and bureaucratic elites, he proposes the democratization of the educational system, with the object of expanding the supply of experts and increasing social mobility. Presumably, this change would improve the competitive position of the political and labor elites in the rivalry for experts thereby diffusing power. He suggests, however, that this change is unlikely to happen because the very power resources that could produce change are being used instead to manipulate the system in such a way as to entrench the existing order. Porter is thus optimistic about the possibility of intervention, but pessimistic about man's determination to intervene.

French-Canadian nationalism. Porter believes that industrialization is widening the social class gap between the French- and English-Canadians, and he cites Weber's thesis concerning the relationship between the Protestant ethic and capitalism as a tentative explanation for this trend (99). Porter provides data showing that the French-Canadians have not developed the educational institutions nor the ethos necessary for training for industrial employment. At age 16, for example, only half as many Catholic boys as Protestant boys are in school relative to their respective populations (169). One of the effects of this inequity is that ". . . the proportion of British in each class generally increases from the lowest to the highest, whereas the reverse is true for the French. . . ."(90).

Porter writes that ". . . strong ethnic loyalties and strong religious loyalties can reinforce each other as adaptations to depressed economic status. . . ." (100), and he defines emergent nationalism as evidence that this has occurred in Quebec. The high correspondence between class and ethnicity on one hand, and religion and ethnicity on the other, has resulted in class conflict being translated into and reinforcing religio-ethnic nationalism. Intellectuals who could give leadership to the working class are, instead, leading the ethnic nationalist movement. The burden of cultural subordination having become more "real" for them than economic subordination, such leaders, it would appear, have internalized the equalitarian values one normally finds in those who lead the proletarian cause.

The historical isolation of French-Canadians from the rest of Canada and North America, largely due to language, cultural, and religious differences, has given rise to a separate elite system. This separate system is manifested in a strong provincial government, autonomous French-Canadian labor unions, and newspapers, universities, and a church all of which articulate the French-Canadian viewpoint. The French elites are jealous of their prerogatives and loyal to their cultural traditions.

The drive toward greater autonomy in Quebec, Porter asserts, is moving Canada toward a loose federal arrangement, resulting in the

emasculation of the central government.[5] Furthermore, the lack of sufficient national cultural integration "... prevents the emergence of social
power as an expression of the creative energies of Canadian society"
(383). In the face of rising provincial autonomy, federal politics is becoming more timid and conservative when, in Porter's opinion, the opposite
trend is needed for growth and social progress. Porter does not consider French-Canadian autonomy as a desirable future outcome. Instead,
he prefers a strong united Canada; and, in order to achieve this end, he
recommends reducing the dependence of class differences on ethnic differences by narrowing the educational gap, removing thereby the class
basis for dual loyalties. Although Canadians have the resources to
change this trend, according to Porter, they have not shown themselves
willing to apply their resources toward making the necessary adjustments.

Urbanization and industrialization. Porter portrays the trends toward urbanization and industrialization as, among other things, a transition from " 'John Canuck,' a character like a virtuous boy scout, very
likely standing amidst the pines by a lonely lake, holding a saw in one
hand and an axe in the other ..." to a "... character 'U No Who,' a
harrassed and bewildered white collar worker ... overtaxed to the point
of having to clothe himself in a barrel. ..." (134). Clearly, Porter is pessimistic about the essence of these trends toward urbanization and industrialization.

An important concomitant of these trends is a change in Canadian
class structure brought about by a "... complex division of labor,
gradations of skill, greater differentials in rewards and a more hierarchical structure of authority. ..." (145). Concurrently, the small entrepre-
neur is vanishing, and skilled blue- and white-collar workers are being
upgraded. Reduction of opportunities for unskilled laborers means that
the occupational stratum that might accommodate the off-farm migrant
is shrinking. In terms of Porter's conception of Canadian society as a
hierarchy of occupational compartments, entry into which is determined
by the level of the individual's educational qualifications, the off-farm
migrant enters the bottom compartment, from which he has small hope
of escaping.

These trends toward urbanization and industrialization are seen by
Porter as producing a depressed occupational status for a growing num-

---

[5] The corporate elite have also had a hand in this trend. When federal legislation
encroaches on the workings of the economic system, the vested interests have challenged federal jurisdiction in the courts. The outcome of such actions has been a series of judicial decisions that have impaired the central government's power to act,
while at the same time strengthening provincial jurisdictions.

ber of Canadians with redundant skills and insufficient education, yet neither industry nor government has shown itself willing to make the necessary expenditure to retrain these people. Here again we see Porter expressing himself with that familiar compound of influence optimism and essence pessimism.

Ideological and economic dependence on the United States. Porter believes that preoccupation with national unity has created an ideological vacuum in Canadian politics: "The dialogue is between unity and discord, rather than progressive and conservative forces. . . ." (369). Party politicians try to maintain unity by designing programs to appeal to particularized interest groups in the country. Competition for the support of these groups results in political policies and programs that generally seek to satisfy popular demands for contemporary American consumption styles rather than idealized goals embodying a purpose greater than the sum of the interests of the discrete groups. The emphasis on contemporary American consumption styles is not a chance phenomenon, since American magazines contribute substantially to the Canadian system of values and the Canadian world view. Such magazines apply themselves assiduously to the task of describing and promoting the American middle-class consumption model, glossing over other images. The uniformity of the images they create endows them with the appearance of reality. Porter attributes this uniformity of images to the fact that the writers, journalists, editors, and other image-creators are a relatively small and closely linked group, with similar social backgrounds and with similar contexts of work under strong corporate control.

American influence in Canada is not restricted to the ideological sphere, since Porter detects a clear trend toward increasing foreign, especially American, ownership and control in Canada. Viewing this trend as part of an international movement of Western capitalism, he presents convincing data that foreign ownership of Canadian manufacturing, mining, and oil industries has reached significant proportions and is still increasing (276–273). The same is true of Canadian unionism; in 1961, 80 percent of organized Canadian labor was subject to some degree of international control (323).

The nationalities of those who run the economic system apparently make little difference in corporate norms and executive behavior: "It is as difficult to tell the borderline at which a corporate executive ceases to be an American and becomes a Canadian, as it is to tell the borderline between being tipsy and being drunk. . . ." (273). The point is that both are committed to the same philosophy of corporate capitalism. National sentiment and national interest are, according to Porter, becoming subordinated to ". . . the historical and inexorable norms of capitalist enterprise. . . ." (269).

What sort of future will this trend toward ideological and economic dependence on the United States produce? Porter foresees the growth of an external elite that increasingly will be making important decisions concerning Canada's welfare from *outside* the country, leaving Canadians with a diminishing initiative for achieving social goals.

The solution to this problem, according to Porter, requires a willingness to sacrifice material well-being for more worthy social objectives such as economic and political autonomy. To achieve this end, Porter would have Canadian politics polarized along the progressive-conservative dimension so that idealized goals can emerge from the resultant dialogue. He fails to detail how Canadian society is to achieve this polarization, however, and generally seems pessimistic that it will occur. Here again his position on man's influence is that intervention is possible but unlikely.

ORIENTATION TOWARD TIME AND ASSUMPTIONS ABOUT SOCIAL CHANGE

Although he bases his study on recent and contemporary data and emphasizes contemporary power structures, Porter's time orientation is not restricted to the contemporary scene. His book is in part a study of decision-making processes, thus it necessarily contains a dynamic orientation toward time and an awareness that present actions have consequences for the future. In fact, contemporary potentialities for future development constitute an important theme of his book. For example, he gives a detailed discussion of educational, technological, economic, political, and related institutions, assesses the manner in which Canadians are deploying their institutional resources, and specifies the consequences for the future of Canadian society. As we have seen in the trends we have discussed, Porter's image of Canada's future does not encourage optimism. Projection of these trends provides us with the following image of the average Canadian's future prospects. The operation of the dimensional law of political forms will reduce his participation in the major decision-making processes to that of a helpless bystander. The inevitable growth of rationalized bureaucracy dooms him to a life of apathy, mechanism, subordination, depersonalization, and conformity, without any hope of escape from the pervasive influence of bureaucratic dictatorship. The evolving power relationships will permanently subject him to a highly coordinated family of power, dominated by a shrinking circle of corporate elites who are committed to perpetuating their privileged position. The growth of French-Canadian nationalism will deny him the sense of self-fulfillment that comes from identifying with a progressive Canadian government that commands the loyalty of all its citizens. The trends toward urbanization and industrialization will put his job skill in increasing jeopardy of obsolescence and, if his skill should become redundant, or if, like the off-farm migrant, he is without a skill, he will join a growing pool of fellow-Canadians who have no hope that they or their children will rise to a higher rung in the occupational hierarchy. Finally, the growth of foreign economic control condemns him to citizenship in a country that is without worthy social goals, that is manipulated by external powers, and that is, at best, a poor imitation of its neighbor.

In most of the trends he presents Porter assumes a causal relationship moving from the past, through the present, to the future. However, the idea of the "pull of the future" is also implied in his work. For example, it is evident in the following quotation that he harbors regret over the fact that Canada lacks a worthy image of the future:

> Canada has no resounding charter myth proclaiming a utopia against which periodically, progress can be measured. At the most, national goals and dominant values seem to be expressed in geographical terms, such as from "sea to sea" rather than in social terms, such as "all men are created equal" or "liberty, fraternity, and equality." In the United States there is a utopian image which slowly over time bends intractable social patterns in the direction of equality, but a Canadian counterpart of this image is difficult to find (366).

And again: "Canada lacks clearly articulated major goals and values stemming from some charter instrument which emphasized progress and equality. . . ." (368).

Implicit in these statements, and in the book generally, is the assumption that the lack of a utopian image of the future has had a profound effect on contemporary Canadian society, and that a utopian image of the future existing in the present is needed to help bring about a better future.

CONTROL OF THE FUTURE

Some of Porter's trends have a problematic quality; others have a deterministic quality. We find, for example, that in the trend toward a rationalized bureaucracy he links past, present, and future by irrevocable laws, while in the trend toward French-Canadian nationalism he assumes that man plays a meliorative role in linking past, present, and future. When he is deterministic, Porter reflects Cantril's dictum, "Certainty is the root of despair"—that is, he projects an extremely pessimistic image of the future. Where past, present, and future are not linked together by laws, Porter assumes that the democratic political system has the potential power to mobilize Canada's resources toward goals held by the majority. But he adds that such mobilization requires commitment to a unifying ideology and that Canadians are too secular in their values to want to make the material sacrifice required to alter the contemporary trends.

He ascribes to the political elites the power to generate the necessary ideological commitment. That is, by articulating positive, utopian conceptions of the future, politicians in Porter's view could mobilize Canadian society to strive for worthy goals. Unfortunately, as he has stressed, politicians are victims of the power structure in which they operate. They are restrained from acting creatively by their subordination to a conservative system of countervailing elites and by further limitations inherent in a system of brokerage politics. He also tells us that political elites are often mere extensions of corporate power promoting the image of middle-class consumption, that they have unstable career patterns placing them at a disadvantage in the rivalry for expertise, and that they do not have access to the expertise of the ideological elites. For example, mass media are controlled by the corporate elites; university-trained experts are drained away by the bureaucratic and corporate elites; and the churches are committed to the ideology of corporate capitalism.

Given these circumstances, one must conclude that the present Canadian political elite system is ill-equipped to perform the task of creating a charter myth that could lead Canadian society out of the secular wilderness and onto the path of ideological righteousness. To move onto such a path requires a political system that can elicit sacrifices from the electorate while continuing to command their support. This is not easily achieved. Social gratification, that is, the achievement of worthy social goals, is not identical with personal gratification. Even when the commitment to society is a strong one (and Porter tells us the Canadians' commitment is not strong), there is a problem of adequately motivating individuals to make sacrifices for collective goals. In effect, Porter seems to be asking the political elites to exercise power—power in the sense of imposing sanctions and encouraging sentiments to produce conformity to future-referring values. In Canada it is the corporate elites who possess the power to bring about social changes in the desired direction, but they are oppositely motivated; and their total resources are committed to the continuance of the trends over which they exercise control. Any meliorative action on the part of the corporate elites, then, is unlikely to produce the kind of future that Porter desires. A revision of social goals will require a rearrangement of the power hierarchy, because effective social goals are those that are desirable from the standpoint of the powerful. If Canadian political elites are to elicit sacrifices from their supporters, then they must acquire more power in the decision-making process and more control over the ideological resources of the country. They must wrest control over these resources from the other elite systems, particularly from the corporate elites. This course of action could well lead to what Apter (1964) terms a "political religion," and, by inference, to a totalitarian state. Those among us who have some reservations about greatly expanding the political prerogative in the economic sphere are not likely to greet Porter's blueprint for social progress with unrestrained enthusiasm.

PORTER'S SENSE OF SOCIAL RESPONSIBILITY AND SELF-AWARENESS

Porter would like to see the elimination of the social and psychological barriers that prevent persons of lower social class origin from obtaining a higher education. He wants the removal of the "class-ethnic" impediment to upward mobility. He prefers to see national loyalty substituted for ethnic loyalties. He prefers more autonomy for Canada in the fields of politics, finance, and labor. He desires an indigenous ideology. He favors a stronger central government. He advocates training programs for workers who are unemployed because they lack needed skills. He champions a more equitable distribution of goods and services. He seeks limits on the concentration of power in the hands of a single elite system. He seeks ideological polarization of politics. He favors a more socially heterogeneous power-elite. He desires a reorganization of the "reality world" through social action and change to remove its inadequacies and to bring it into line with the values held by a majority of Canadians.

To achieve these objectives he proposes "creative politics," "democratization of education," and greater "structural and behavioral assimilation." Creative politics is ". . . politics which has the capacity to change the social structure in the direction of some major goals or social values . . ." (369). Structural assimilation refers to ". . . the process by which ethnic groups have become distributed in the institutional structure of the receiving society, and in particular have assumed roles in civic life . . ." (72). Behavioral assimilation refers ". . . to the extent to which the minority group has absorbed the cultural patterns of the 'host' society and even perhaps had an effect on it . . ." (72).

Despite the positive tone of his objectives and his proposals for achieving them, Porter leaves unanswered the question of why Canadians should expend the effort necessary to establish a Canadian identity. Who would benefit? Nationalism is not a prerequisite to social progress, and in fact it may obstruct social progress when it leads to a preoccupation with unifying symbolism rather than to corrective action on critical but poten-tially divisive social issues.

According to Porter's thesis, the United States offers most of the things Canadians want, and in many respects represents something that Canadians think they are, would like to be, or ought to be. Then why should Canadians resist gradual assimilation into the American political, economic, and social systems? Some political commentators ascribe a positive role to Canada as a mediator in world conflicts—a view that rep-resents at least some justification for retaining autonomy—but Porter gives no justification at all. He might have legitimized an autonomous Canadian society along some positive dimensions; he might have speci-fied the potential resources that Canadians possess for achieving progres-sive nationhood; and he might have given Canadians reasons to believe that their resources could be put to work by themselves to achieve that goal. In such a context he might well have discussed the shortcomings and weaknesses in Canadian society. Indeed, it would be naive to pretend they don't exist; but, at least, Canadians would have another position to champion. It would not have left them motivationally bankrupt.

Porter points out that in Canadian society an intellectual is one who sells his knowledge in a marketplace composed of bureaucratic institu-tions, not one who leads causes (343). Following Porter's logic, however, one would judge that the social scientist is less limited by the structural factors that we have discussed, thus freer than the politician to bend so-cial patterns in the direction of worthy social goals. That is, the more sta-ble career pattern open to the social scientist attracts more competent per-sons; and, since the social scientist, unlike the politician, need not be merely an extension of the corporate elite, he enjoys greater freedom to seek social change. Perhaps Porter is expecting too much from politicians and too little from other image-makers like himself. A social scientist, through the positive images of the future that he projects and that mem-bers of society internalize, can make a contribution to a commitment to progressive social goals. Conversely, a social scientist who contents him-self with condemning the masses to their present limitations, or as Porter tends, dooms society to the outcomes that contemporary trends seem to suggest may, through the dynamic of the self-fulfilling prophecy, be has-tening the very end he is trying to avert. Furthermore, the social scientist who is committed to the tactic of "contingent doom," that is, one who de-votes his time and energy to articulating a message of imminent catas-trophe unless a specific type of intervention is exercised, may be less ef-fective than one who articulates images that will lead the masses to want to exercise the self-control necessary to produce a dynamic new nation. It is in this regard that Porter does not seem to exhibit a sense of awareness of the potentialities of such a study as *The Vertical Mosaic* for influencing the future of Canadian society.

We may speculate about the possible consequences of Porter's book for Canadian society, as it becomes part of a new generation's view of Canada. First, we should look at his audience. Accepting Porter's thesis, we assume that his readers will be the elites of Canadian society, that is, the small minority of the population who enter university and proceed from there to the top of the occupational hierarchy. Unfortunately, not all university students will read *The Vertical Mosaic*, but as winner of a MacIver Award, there is a good likelihood that it will become required reading in sociology and political science courses at many Canadian universities. Registration in these courses is relatively heavy, and one may reasonably assume that many future decision-makers will be exposed to this book.

Second, we might ask: what influence will this book have on its readers? We have already speculated on this to some degree by suggesting that a negative image of the future is unlikely to achieve positive results, both because it may become self-fulfilling and because it shifts the exploration and analysis away from the means and ends of alternative futures that are desirable. To go a step further, Porter's description of the elites suggests that they enjoy a number of privileges that they must surrender if the lower classes are to enjoy more privileges. This type of zero-sum conceptualization is of doubtful validity, and it is demonstrably false to assume that the lot of the poor can be improved only at the expense of the better off. To communicate such a message to the Canadian elite, then, would appear to be self-defeating for, as Porter has stressed, self-sacrifice and self-control tend to be scarce attributes among Canadians. It is unlikely that a reading of *The Vertical Mosaic* will dispose the prospective elites to give up their privileges. A more likely outcome may be a move by the elites to secure their position more firmly with the end result that the pessimistic expectations expressed in the trends that Porter delineates, rather than the positive objectives he has in mind, will be realized.

It can be safely assumed that Porter is aware that his study will be a causal factor in the developing future insofar as a competent critique of contemporary conditions influences the thinking of decision-makers. He has failed, however, to take into full account the second order of causality, that is, that the images of the future he communicates *also* have a causal effect on the emerging future. Instead of giving us "hoped-for self-fulfilling prophecies," he has given us "hoped-for self-denying prophecies" (Bell and Mau, 1970). Perhaps he hoped to achieve his goals by needling Canadians to action; but given the inert society he describes, one wonders if better results might have been expected had he communicated a positive image of the future. The point to be made relative to Porter's objectives is that social scientists as well as politicians are free to practice "creative politics" and that both share a responsibility for doing so.

THE PROBLEMATICAL NATURE OF PORTER'S IMAGES OF THE FUTURE

Porter has not given sufficient consideration to alternative constructions of the future, especially in view of the data with which he is working. A few brief examples should serve to illustrate this point. First, Porter assumes a certain relationship between size and democracy, which leads him to predict a diminishing role for the average citizen as the size of the population increases. However, it is not at all certain how size affects the amount of social participation in a democratic institution. Social participation in institutional life is not unidimensional; and while the *form* and *pattern* of participation may change with size, it is problematical whether *amount* or *intensity* of participation is a function of size. If one rejects Porter's deterministic assumptions about the relationship between size of population and social participation, then his pessimistic image of the average citizen's future falls apart. The way is then opened to using Porter's data in the explication and exploration of a variety of alternative outcomes.

For another example in which Porter's data might support an alternative construction of the future, consider the trend toward secularization. Secularization also implies greater dependence on scientific thought and technology, which will lead to the modification of traditional institutions and social formations. The effect of the secularization of society can be logically expected to lead to changing statuses as a result of changing productive forces, which in turn may produce a new ideology, and a future different from the one postulated by Porter. Even corporate capitalism, pervasive and invincible though it may appear in Porter's analysis, can survive only as long as it delivers the goods economically and efficiently. If one accepts the history of feudalism as instructive, then the apparent permanence that contemporary trends give to corporate capitalism must be reconsidered, and the data evaluated for alternative constructions of the future.

As a final example of an alternative image of the future from Porter's data, let us look at the trends toward French-Canadian nationalism and increased American influence. Porter's evaluation of these two trends, when considered together, suggests that he is operating with a very distinct bias—that of a fairly conventional, if not old-fashioned, socialist with strong nationalist tendencies. There is evidence in his praise of Canadian nationalism (he favors a reduction of the America presence), and in his condemnation of Quebec nationalism. The future of unity or diversity along ethnic lines in Canada is problematic, as is the future of Canadian-American relations; but it is doubtful that Porter's pessimism about Canada's future, if these issues are not resolved in favor of a strong autonomous central government, is justified. Creative solutions that resolve the conflict of goals in a way that permits compromise are needed; and there is no necessary conflict between the lofty social goals that Porter has in mind and a loose Canadian confederation in an interdependent relationship with the United States. For example, French-Canadians may have a more realistic chance of achieving greater political, economic, and social equality in an independent Quebec than as a minority group within a federal political structure. Indeed, Canadian history provides the French-Canadian nationalists with abundant evidence for their argument that a minority group can never hope for first-class citizenship without first sacrificing cultural integrity. Clearly a dogmatic position on nationalism is an obstacle to a consideration of more progressive alternatives.

Failure to take into account the problematic nature of the future limits one's ability to see beyond the anticipated outcome. For example, until recently many believed that society was inexorably moving toward an assembly-line era, in which occupations would become increasingly simple and routine. We know today that automation is eliminating many of the simple assembly-line tasks, and that the new wave of occupations requires more education and training than those it replaced. Yet, on the basis of what was known prior to World War II about the division of labor and mass production, increased routinization of occupations was a reasonable expectation. This type of error has been referred to by Bell and Mau under their "directive of uncertainty": social reality has not been viewed as problematic in the knowing of it, nor problematic in its contingency on man's actions. Some of Porter's trends are subject to this criticism.

The pessimism expressed in Porter's trends reflects a tendency to think of the contemporary power structure as insurmountable and to give insufficient weight to the influence of images of the future and the actions of men—particularly from among those people not now occupying the seats of power—as agents of change. Although Porter recognizes deliberate change, he emphasizes the prevention of changes not desired by the elite systems. Another side of this issue is that change will be brought about by the masses who are dissatisfied with the small amount of respect, prestige, and material rewards they receive. Porter quotes C. W.

Mills' assessment of the masses: "As a group they do not threaten any-one, as individuals they do not practice an independent way of life" (27). Yet the fact remains that within the framework of the democratic system the masses have the prerogative to organize and elect a political party that may increase the public sector of the economy, thereby changing the balance of power. Their leaders may now be preparing themselves for the task in the anonymity of out-of-the-way corners of the society. It would not violate Porter's data to say that the mass of ordinary men con-stitute another center of power in the system of countervailing power. Their potential to act against the established leadership has modified the trends in the past, and will do so in the future. Porter might have included this element in his formula. If he had, he could have depicted a future system equally consistent with past trends but more comfortably open. He could have justified giving equal time to a positive image of the future.

REFERENCES

Apter, David E.
  1964   "Political religion in the new nations." Institute of Industrial Re-lations and Institute of International Studies, University of Cali-fornia, Reprint 233.
Bell, Wendell, and James A. Mau
  1970   "Images of the future: theory and research strategies." Pp. 205–234 in John C. McKinney and Edward A. Tiryakian (eds.), Theo-retical Sociology: Perspectives and Developments. New York: Appleton-Century-Crofts.
Mills, C Wright
  1959   The Power Elite. New York: Oxford University Press.
Myrdal, Gunnar
  1962   An American Dilemma: The Negro Problem and Modern Democ-racy. New York: Harper & Row.
Polak, Frederik L.
  1961   The Image of the Future: Enlightening the Past, Orientating the Present, Forecasting the Future, Vols. I and II. New York: Oceana.
Porter, John
  1965   The Vertical Mosaic: An Analysis of Social Class and Power in Canada. Toronto: University of Toronto Press.

In the Mirrors of Sociology: Images of American and Soviet Society

PAUL HOLLANDER

SOCIOLOGY AND SOCIETY

Sociology holds a mirror to society. At times it may be a distorting mirror in which selected aspects of social existence shrink or expand; it may often reflect the unimportant. It may tell the beholder that it is "the most beautiful of all" or confront him with a collection of hideous, previously unnoticed features. Sociology can lavishly praise a particular society or delightedly wallow in its defects. Even its severest critics will grant that it does hold up a mirror, no worse and possibly better than those provided by other forms of analysis. Perhaps every society produces the kind of sociology it deserves. Despite its occasional claims to a scientific status, sociology can no more escape the imprint of society in which it is embedded than any other form of intellectual activity.

If sociology were true to its original hopes and persisting claims, it could provide the most reliable, accurate, and comprehensive information of the societies it describes and dissects. After more than a century, sociology is still a "young" discipline and may yet fulfill these hopes and promises. Even if it does not, if nothing else, it has collected mountains of data of varying significance. Future historians for the first time in history may turn to sociology for evidence and data in an effort to comprehend some societies of the twentieth century. Sifting through the innumerable volumes of sociological literature with a view to assembling a coherent picture of modern societies will be a novel, exciting, and gigantic undertaking that will require large teams of scholars, a formidable quantity of punch cards, patience, and curiosity.

At present the United States and the Soviet Union have produced the biggest bulk of sociological writings about themselves. Probably it is not accidental that the two greatest industrial powers have also taken the lead in this realm of production. Sociology needs trained people,[1] who emerge from systems of education as elaborate and well organized as the systems of industrial production. But probably some more intangible forces that prompt the spread of sociology are also at work. Sociology is a reflection of societal self-consciousness, of the surfacing of doubt, of uncertainty and the purposeful search for its alleviation. Sociology is also a product of rapid social change, of the collapse of "eternal verities," of the end of the belief in the immutability of social institutions and established social practices; in short, a product of secularization. Its emergence in Western Europe,[2] at any rate, signaled the end of an era when things were taken for granted in the social environment. Finally, sociology is also a product of a more optimistic problem-consciousness, of the belief that if understood properly, the ills of social and human existence can be remedied.

At the same time, it would be an error to treat the presence of sociology in various societies as an indication that they are similar, just as it would be doubtful to consider all societies fundamentally similar because they produced other shared fields of inquiry and learning. Deflating as it might be to our professional self-conception, the impact of sociology on society is a good deal smaller than that of society on sociology. Though it is flattering to believe that the society we live in is reeling under the impact of our discoveries, or that we represent a powerful intellectual force that visibly contributes to the shaping or reshaping of our social environments, the accomplishments and effects of sociology are more modest.

Sociology and society can relate to one another in various ways. Although it is true that certain types of sociological pursuits presuppose a high degree of intellectual and spiritual freedom (Inkeles, 1964:117),

---

[1] Not necessarily trained in sociology, though. At the time of writing, the Soviet Union still had not a single sociologist trained in sociology and certified as such. As a Soviet sociologist noted: ". . . there is not a single scholar with a diploma in sociology in our country today. There is no such specialty in our system of higher education" (Yadov, 1968:8). Soviet sociologists are self-trained, and while most of them have degrees in economics, history, philosophy, or law, some are journalists.

[2] As we will see later, its emergence in the USSR is related to somewhat different circumstances, which also included the desire for a fresh look at the social world and a cautious and implicit questioning of its sacred doctrines, Marxism-Leninism in this case.

sociology has shown—because of the wide variety of its modes and targets of inquiry—a great capacity to adapt to different social settings. Sociology may be a barely tolerated eccentric pursuit of the few, a powerful establishment in the good graces of the rulers of society, a group of embittered critics on the margins of society, or a discipline devoted to improving the efficiency of the existing social order[3] or to finding clues to its decay and destruction. Probably it has been all these things at different times in different societies and sometimes concurrently. It is a pursuit, a set of activities that can assume many guises. Yet, at least in its *potentialities*, sociology is unlike most other fields of learning. Its methods, findings, and propositions *can be* more "subversive" and explosive than those of other disciplines, history and political science included.[4] By focusing on the contemporary world, by claiming access to all types of information about society, by raising questions that are difficult and sometimes unpleasant to answer, or that have no answers derived from the prevailing values of a given society, by asserting its autonomy and independence of vested interests and of the status quo—sociology *can be* dangerous for any social order. But, of course, it may not claim such access, assert such independence, and raise such questions.

Though there is a great diversity of the images held by American sociologists of their society, a few major patterns may be discerned. This diversity reflects with reasonable accuracy the pluralism of the surrounding society, in which some forces and factions carry more weight than others. At least until very recently one among the dominant (and according to some *the* dominant) theoretical orientation in American sociology has focused on the "integration of social systems" (Parsons, 1968:xi). Associated with this orientation are the problems of social order, the

---

[3] A charge that, interestingly enough, has been made against both American and Soviet sociologists. Thus C. Wright Mills said that many American sociologists ". . . readily assume the political perspective of their bureaucratic clients and chieftains . . . they serve to increase the efficiency and reputation—and to that extent, the prevalence—of bureaucratic forms of domination in modern society" (Mills, 1959:101). A Soviet sociologist similarly noted that applied social research is "conducted on orders from local organizations and institutions" deploring this trend more on professional than ideological-philosophical grounds (Yadov, 1968:7). Indeed the assessments of the relationship between sociology and the various organizations and institutions of society depend on the researcher's basic assumptions about the nature of the social order in question. If he supports it he will not object to applied research that promotes their efficiency. "It is very noteworthy and hopeful [said a leading Soviet authority in sociology] that various organizations—the State Planning Committee, the ministries committees and press organs—have increasingly taken *the role of interested clients* seeking to utilize the sociologists' conclusions and recommendations" (Rumyantsev, 1968:8, emphasis added).

[4] It is of interest to note here that these two kindred disciplines, at least in the United States, have shown an increasing fascination with sociological methods, concepts, and questions. To the extent that this trend continues there will be a growing similarity between the social consequences of their findings.

questions of how society hangs together, how it manages (successfully) to reconcile divergent interests, how it handles tension, and how it ultimately resolves conflict. Many critics of this approach charged that, with or without ideological intent, it postulates an unreal harmony in society, that it ignores conflict—or takes an unduly optimistic view of its solubility—and that by implication it supports the powers to be, the status quo (for example, Gouldner, 1968). Curiously enough, Soviet sociology, avowedly based on Marxism (that is, on a conflict theory of society), could be accused with more justification of overemphasizing harmony and integration in Soviet society and ignoring its conflicts and tensions. Indeed, Soviet sociology today appears to take note of conflict only outside Soviet society. While the basic freedom from conflicts is a cornerstone of the sociological analysis of Soviet society, transitory, veiled conflicts of lesser significance are acknowledged, though not necessarily labeled as conflicts.[5] We will in the following pages discuss these and other features of Soviet sociology in greater detail.

Though there is a bias among many American sociologists toward a perspective of harmony and integration, under the impact of the social and political trends and events of the last few years, fewer and fewer would consider American society well-ordered, smoothly functioning, and problem-free. At the same time optimistic neoevolutionary ideas still have a strong hold on American sociologists (Tilly, 1969:24). Even while aware of its current problems and tensions, many consider their society the most advanced, most industrial, most urban, most mobile, most complex, and hence the most modern of all societies, the shape of things to come all over the world.[6] Such conceptions are usually implicit in the cult of modernity to which American sociologists are prone and in the notion that attachment to traditions hinders progress, innovation, and desirable change.[7] Above all, most American sociologists, not unlike most Americans, have a distinct reverence for change, often unexamined in its content and consequences. The very words "change," "changing," "dynamic," "growing," "expanding," "forward-moving" spell approval and admiration for the American sensibilities.

---

[5] For instance, the latent conflict between town and country, or between the demands of the consumer and the nature of the economy.

[6] Yet few sociologists would openly assert that it is superior to other contemporary societies or that it is the embodiment of social justice. Still fewer would claim that it is the best of all societies history has ever known. By contrast, such a view of their society is frequently expressed by Soviet sociologists. Just as the norms of intellectual and professional conduct in America proscribe assertions of patriotic sentiment, in the Soviet Union the norms of society at large compel their public expression on the part of intellectuals as well as other strata of society.

[7] This is somewhat paradoxical in light of the fact that sociology, according to some writers, originated in a strong conservative tradition (see Nisbet, 1968:73–89).

At the other end of the spectrum are those American sociologists who view the present and future of American society with foreboding, its major institutions with distaste, if not outright hostility, and who conceive of their principal professional obligation as the exposure of the flaws, defects, contradictions, or horrors (as the case may be) that are endemic to it. Whether their estimates of American society are based on the orthodox Marxist vantage point or not, they see no hope for this society, or at any rate such is the impression one gains from their writing and speeches.[8] Among those who hold the most negative conceptions of the nature of American society we find two forms of underlying pessimism. There are those, for example, Mills (1959), Marcuse (1964), Barrington Moore (1958), and their followers, who find it difficult to conceive of a decent social order within the framework of contemporary, highly industrialized societies, whatever their political institutions. They tend to believe that their political institutions have become increasingly similar, being controlled by ruthless, bureaucratic elites of some kind or another. Others may find the present and future of *capitalistic* industrial societies especially bleak and reserve their support and optimism for some communist societies, which, they believe, grapple more successfully with the problems of industrialization, or will manage somehow to preserve their peasant-revolutionary purity, simplicity, and authenticity.

In contrast to the diverse viewpoints and images of American society found in American sociological writings, there is a far greater degree of unanimity and uniformity in Soviet sociology concerning the nature of Soviet society and its fundamental characteristics. American sociologists are not much less bewildered than the American man on the street as to the direction in which American society is going.[9] By contrast, Soviet sociologists adhere to the spirit of compulsory optimism and

---

[8] Occasionally this attitude becomes almost paranoid. At a recent Annual Meeting of the American Sociological Association a young sociologist declared:

> . . . the Secretary of HEW is a military officer in the domestic front of the war against the people. . . . The department of which the man is head is more accurately described as the agency which watches over the inequitable distribution of preventable diseases, over the funding of domestic propaganda and indoctrination, over the preservation of a cheap and docile labor force. . . . This assembly here tonight . . . is a conclave of high and low priests, scribes, intellectual valets, and their innocent victims, engaged in the mutual affirmation of falsehood. . . . The profession [of sociology] is an outgrowth of 19th-century European traditionalism and conservatism, wedded to 20th-century American corporation liberalism. . . . The professional eyes of the sociologist are on the down people, and the professional palm of the sociologist is stretched toward the up people. . . . [He is] an Uncle Tom not only for this government and ruling class but for any. . . . (Gouldner, 1968:247).

[9] It is, however, fair to point out that many of them did sound warnings about the intensification of racial conflict (see Tumin, 1968:118–119).

good cheer that characterizes all Soviet public statements concerning the present and future of Soviet society. If there are a number of questions and unresolved problems that might cast doubt on such a stance, we see no evidence of them. Soviet sociologists are not showing any gloom or sense of foreboding (evinced by many of their American counterparts) on account of the problems that are said to be endemic to most modern, urban, industrial, and secular societies. The familiar visions of standardized, homogenized mass society do not haunt them, perhaps because the homogenization of attitudes and values—whether a reality or not— is, in a sense, a cherished goal of the rulers in Soviet society. Nor is it feared that the loss of certainties, confusion, and doubt that attends to the deepening impact of secularization will be a significant problem of the future, although some Soviet authorities have periodically voiced concern with the ideological upbringing of the younger generation that resembles the Western misgivings about the loss of tradition and the behavioral constraints maintained by them. Soviet sociologists are not assigned the task of keeping watch over the ideological steadfastness of the younger generations; and if such concerns occasionally find their way into their research (e.g., Grushin and Chikin, 1962), the emerging picture is reassuring enough for the ruling elites. Certainly Soviet sociologists have not forecast any difficulties with regard to the value commitments of future generations.

The concern of American sociologists with the future of their society is quite evident. It has two sources and two forms, which sometimes overlap. One source is the present. Those concerned with the present state of American society have similar reservations about its future. The acute awareness of the problems besetting American society predisposes to concern over its future development. In particular, the seemingly uncontrollable and certainly uncontrolled nature of rapid change is a matter of justified concern and not only for sociologists. Though the dynamic nature of American society has tended to be a source of pride for many, more and more have become aware of the dangers that are associated with the disruptive changes in many areas of life.

The second source of concern with the future is more theoretically based and closely tied to the persisting desire of sociologists to become truly scientific and thus capable of predicting social change. The sociologist professionally interested in the future of his society tends to be motivated by a theoretical ambitiousness. Trying to visualize what the future might bring is a tempting task; and even if he cannot make any scientific predictions, he can at least make educated guesses extrapolating from what he sees in the present. Moreover, the sociological concern with the future is often also closely allied with a benevolent social-engineering impulse, with the desire to plan ahead intelligently, and to forestall some of the malfunctioning of the social organization of which the present (and past) provide ample evidence.

The sources of the Soviet sociological concern with the future are in part similar to the American. The social-engineering impulse is much stronger than in the American case, since it is linked, in a more self-conscious and deliberate manner, to the needs of the Soviet social system as defined by its political elites (Rumyantsev, 1968). Furthermore, a built-in pressure toward prediction in Soviet sociology results from its Marxist-Leninist philosophical inspiration. In this case, the desire to predict is inseparable from the desire to control, rather than being merely an expression of theory-building aspirations. The dreaded tendencies toward spontaneity in the social and political sphere, first abhorred by Lenin, can best be combatted by the predictive control of the future. Prediction in Soviet sociology is a by-product of overall planning. In addition, the predictive tasks of sociology have increased because the present period, defined as one of transition to communist society, is characterized by growing "complexities" of social life, very often the unintended consequences of Soviet planning and policy decision.

REFLECTING SOCIAL PROBLEMS

The typical problems of American sociology arise from the immediate necessities of every day life. They assume the form of convergent planning and concerted action aiming at overcoming the difficulties threatening the progress of collective work (Mannheim, 1932:4).

A question raised with increasing insistence is whether every enterprise should have a chief sociologist and chief psychologist, in addition to its chief engineer, chief technologist and chief economist (Aleksandrov, 1968:12).

Despite their different ideological and political environments, both American and Soviet sociology offer much data for the future historian interested in the problems and conflicts of the two societies in the 1960s. Despite all the charges and criticisms that have been and can justifiably be made of the discipline and its practitioners in both societies, sociologists have amassed much uncomplimentary information on social problems and the many instances when ideal and actual, theory and practice do not mesh. It is perhaps natural that two societies that set themselves quasi-utopian goals should have many social problems, since social problems are largely matters of definition and perception (see Merton and Nisbet, 1966:5a, and Becker, 1966:4-7). The more unwilling people are to accept the defects and shortcomings of their life and society the more situations and behaviors will be labeled as problematic, that is, undesirable but subject to change. The greater the impatience with the imperfections of the social order and the more ardent the belief in the perfectibility of man, society, and social relations, the more social problems will be discovered and catalogued by social scientists.

Thus the choice of social problems dealt with by the sociologists depends not only on the relative freedom of the researchers to explore and expose them. More basic are the operative social definitions of what constitute social problems. Here we come to a surprising degree of agreement between American and Soviet definitions, originating no doubt in the pursuit of societal efficiency in both countries. Most of the situations and behaviors defined as social problems in American society and investigated on this assumption by American sociologists are defined in the same manner in the Soviet Union. Theft, robbery, physical violence (other than that indulged in by the political authorities), juvenile delinquency, dropping out of school, misuse of leisure, family instability, rural depopulation, urban overcrowding, isolation of the old, alcoholism, destruction of the natural environment (especially air and water pollution), bad housing conditions—all these are viewed as social problems in both societies. Sociologists are, to varying degrees, analyzing and revealing them.

It is probably fair to say that a large proportion of social problems in both American and Soviet society originate in the gap between aspirations and achievements, lofty ideals and pedestrian or cynical practices, inspiring words and uninspired deeds. Paradoxically, every conscious attempt to create a "good society" increases the sensitivity and intolerance toward the defects of social existence producing the well-documented state of relative deprivation. The other major source of social problems in both societies is the proverbial unintended consequences of various social arrangements, policies, and measures. Sociology in both countries bears witness to them.

The catalogue of social problems provided by American sociologists is far more detailed and thorough than that being assembled by their Soviet colleagues. For one thing, American sociologists had a head start over their Soviet counterparts; not only were there no sociological investigations in the Soviet Union before the late 1950s (except for the short-lived period of the 1920s) but social problems—at any rate as defined in the West—were not among the highest priorities even after the revival of sociology in the USSR. From the beginning Soviet sociological investigations have been hampered by the ideological constraints and the attendant ambivalence toward social problems. On the one hand, Soviet sociology owes its existence to the implicit recognition that there are problems in Soviet society; on the other, it cannot substantially depart from the official myth of basic perfection of Soviet institutions. Social problems had to be analyzed without calling into question the major values, institutions, and policies of Soviet society, without casting doubt on the fundamental soundness of the structure of society as a whole, without making too many or too significant connections between its allegedly advanced and healthy nature and the undesirable phenomena in question. Soviet sociologists have thus been handicapped from the beginning in thoroughly exploring certain facets of their society. Their revelation and analysis of social problems had to go hand in hand with the affirmation that Soviet society is the most advanced and the best of all societies hitherto extant, and that its problems are somehow unrelated to its principal characteristics. In particular, social problems had to be depoliticized, deprived of political meaning and connections.

American sociologists have been free of such restraints; and despite the influence of structural-functional theory (or research grants from governmental agencies or corporate foundations), many have addressed themselves to the study of social problems. In any event, a large proportion of sociologists do not subscribe to this theory, or not to an extent that would diminish their interest in or divert their attention from social problems. Furthermore, it could be argued that the structural-functional theory actually lends itself to a thorough analysis of social problems, since by its very nature it draws attention to the interrelationship between different social phenomena and institutions: the problematic and the unproblematic. Indeed, since Merton's first writings, it has become almost axiomatic that the "good" and "bad," the desirable and undesirable aspects of social life are tied together. Nevertheless, it is possible to distinguish between two approaches to social problems in American sociology. One treats them as disturbances or "disequilibria" of the social system and considers their solution both possible and desirable without a drastic overhaul of the entire institutional structure. At the same time in this perspective some social problems are seen as more or less endemic to social life, in a sense natural, like the collisions of conflicting human desires within the same personality. At any rate, in a large-scale, complex society the complete eradication of social problems—rather than the elimination of some at the expense of creating others—does not appear feasible, and a problem-free society is just as unattainable as perfect harmony in social relations and universal contentment.

The other approach to social problems in American sociology is more a by-product or derivative of social criticism. Social problems are analyzed with a view to accumulating evidence—part of an overall debunking enterprise—to show the corruptness, bankruptcy, or crisis of society as a whole by documenting specific manifestations and instances of its failures. The major topics of this school tend to be poverty, racial injustice, the malfunctioning of social institutions such as the community, the po-

lice, welfare agencies, hospitals, mental institutions, old-age homes, prisons, and others.

The two approaches can be and often are combined, but they part
company in the interpretations of data. For those motivated primarily
by the impulse of social criticism the failures of American society are
viewed as peculiarly American and corrigible only by the fundamental
transformation of society. For the structural-functionalists less concerned with a critique of society, the problems are more universal and
many of them corrigible without envisioning a total change of the social
order.

The two, often overlapping, approaches provide a detailed and rich
catalogue of—if not remedy to—virtually all serious problems of American society today. Criminal violence, racial conflict and discrimination,
poverty, unemployment, juvenile delinquency, the disruptive consequences of excessive geographical mobility, family instability, urban decay, the varieties of escapist behavior, the problems of the old and sick,
the inadequacies of public welfare, the stagnation (or too rapid change) of
small communities, the conflict of generations, the defects of the school
system, hospitals, prisons, and mental institutions—all these and others
have attracted the attention of American sociologists and have been duly
chronicled.[10]

The inventory of social problems emerging from the writings of Soviet sociologists is far less complete, though it has been in the process of
lengthening. Nevertheless, we do not know whether or not the social
problems in Soviet society have grown over the past decade (in comparison with the 1930s, 1940s and 1950s). It would seem that during the most
rigidly totalitarian periods of Soviet society, much of what we conventionally label as social problems were dormant or suppressed, despite the
rapid and disruptive strides of industrialization. Perhaps social disorganization was contained by the totalitarian pressures of the political framework, providing social integration of sorts, and a temporary substitute
for those types of informal mechanisms of social control which are said
to reside in the traditional, or at least enduring, forms of social groupings and communities. This is, however, guesswork, since we have no
data with which to compare the extent of various social problems during
the past and the previous decades. Until the late 1950s Soviet sources

---

[10] This is not to say that there are no neglected issues. For example, the inequalities of women, the problems of and resistance to the control of firearms (and the relationship between their easy availability and violence), the effects of commercial
advertising, the authoritarianism of sections of middle- and upper-middle-class youth
on the campuses—these are among the social problems of American society in the
1960s that received hardly any attention before 1968.

barely gave a hint of their existence, conforming to the official model of improbable perfection and harmony prevailing in Soviet social relations. Today, however, the admission and description of many social problems is compatible with the claim of the basic soundness of Soviet society. Not infrequently within the same piece of writing, the assertion of such claims is belied by the empirical findings presented. The flaws of Soviet society are made to appear as if they were somehow incidental to the nature of the institutional foundations. Another favorite device of cushioning the impact of "negative" research findings is to contrast them with the corresponding defects in capitalist societies, which, it is alleged, are far more grave and reprehensible. This trend, however, appears to be declining; and often Soviet sociologists reveal the problems of their society without ideological apologies and doubletalk.[11]

The future historian perusing the writings of Soviet sociologists of our times will have unmistakable evidence that work and its efficiency occupied the central place in the roster of social problems. Shortcomings of productivity, labor organization, turnover, work satisfaction, social relations within the plant—these topics are preeminent among the publications of Soviet sociologists. These are not the topics conventionally included in the catalogue of social problems of Western and particularly American sociologists, though they are studied in other contexts—those of industrial sociology and the sociology of complex organizations. Nor is the survival of religion (as opposed to its decline) a social problem in Western societies. Indeed, the approaches to religion among the sociologists of the two countries provide the most striking and spectacular illustration of the crucial importance of perception and definition in the realm of social problems, and of their relationship to the dominant values of society. In the Soviet Union, because of the roots of the official value system in orthodox Marxism, religion is defined as a highly undesirable phenomenon; its institutional existence is severely curtailed and its practice discouraged. Consequently, the persistence of religious attitudes is viewed as a serious social problem; and the regime has been engaged, since its very beginning, in an intense effort to eradicate it. With the emergence of sociology, its help was also enlisted in the struggle against religion, and it was noted that "Data obtained about the age, sex, and education of believers can help atheist propagandists . . ." (Yevdokimov, 1968:18). In this as in other instances, sociology is regarded as an instrument that can assist in the accomplishment of the ideological-political ob-

---

[11] According to an American student of Soviet sociology, that discipline reached a turning point in 1964, which signaled a new era of greater candor and concern with empirical facts rather than with ideological propositions concerning the nature of Soviet society (Simirenko, 1968).

jectives of the regime, and this goal is stated openly, without shyness or reluctance (see also CDSP, 1968). Still we do not get a precise idea from Soviet sociology of the magnitude of the "problem," namely the extent and intensity of religious beliefs of various sorts in the Soviet Union. What we do know is that to the degree that these beliefs have survived (or revived), they irritate the guardians of the official value system who would like to place atheistic propaganda on a "scientific" basis. For this purpose, they have enlisted the help of sociology, at any rate as an information-gathering agency.

We are also beginning to learn from Soviet sociology about crime and juvenile delinquency, though other social scientists, notably legal experts, have been doing most of the work in this field. The instability of the family is also beginning to capture the attention of our Soviet colleagues, though here again only a handful are working on these problems. Questions of escapism, and particularly alcoholism, are also among the emerging concerns of Soviet sociology, often linked to the study of free time and its misuse. The use of time in general is a prime concern of Soviet sociology. Here as in other areas of sociological interest, the underlying motives have to do with efficiency. How do people spend their working and nonworking hours? How does their leisure affect their work? What are the differences in the patterns of time use between urban and rural residents, men and women, skilled and unskilled workers? How can the waste of time be reduced or diminished? Many interesting data have been collected in the so-called time-budget studies showing the inequalities in access to free time among various groups, of the time wasted in trivial if necessary activities (e.g., shopping, housework, going to work), and the need and demand for more leisure and more and better amenities for its use (Grushin, 1967).

Thus, despite the tight grip of the political environment and ideological taboos, Soviet sociologists do sketch a portrait of many Soviet social problems. Admonishing writers who continue to adhere to the overly rosy-colored pictures of Soviet reality, a Soviet journalist-sociologist provides an example of some of the less cheerful aspects of Soviet life today:

> The elimination of the difference between mental and physical labor is not proceeding as rapidly as we would wish. . . . The general mechanic or lathe operator whose work was genuinely creative, is seldom encountered at machine-building plants today. He has been replaced by the operator of a semi-automatic machine that performs a few operations over and over again all day long. The number of conveyor lines, with the extreme forms of division of labor . . . is increasing. For young people, especially those with a secondary education, these forms of labor are oppressive. This is

a factor in labor turnover and even in population migration. . . . Demo-graphic studies have shown that despite the considerable funds and efforts invested in moving people from labor-surplus areas eastward, Siberia and the Urals have been losing population steadily. . . . An average of three out of four city dwellers who go to the virgin lands leave within the first year. Only 10% of the workers recruited for construction in Irkutsk Province settle there permanently. . . . Some of the money now allocated for recruit-ing and resettling workers would be better spent on the construction of good housing and child-care institutions. . . . Physical labor is disdained. . . . Studies conducted among school age children of both workers and of-fice employees show that they hope to work in white collar jobs. Some 80% of the students in general-education secondary schools plan to acquire higher education. Only about 30% are admitted to higher schools. Those not admitted are completely unprepared, by attitude and skills, to join the labor force. The required labor training studies, while time consuming, sel-dom give the students anything useful. . . . The *Komsomolskaya pravda* Public Opinion Institute has discovered that an impressive number of young people have no cultural interests at all. . . . There are millions of people with very limited cultural requirements and still more limited ability to satisfy such requirements . . . . The USSR has 1,631,000 engineers. The The USA has 725,000. How is it that we have a million more engineers than America, while our industrial output is 65% of America's? While our quality is not always up to world standards, and we hold a far smaller number of patents on inventions? . . . Labor is not well enough organized . . . . (Kantorovich, 1968:19).

Another recent article discussed the plight of women, a social prob-lem in its own right despite (or because?) of their greater equality of op-portunity in the Soviet occupational and educational realm than the American.

Only 23% of the country's preschool children attend nursery school or kindergarten. Economists have estimated that public services lift only 5% of the burden from the women's shoulders. Only 2% of the wash is done in laundries. Only three laundries in all of Moscow offer diaper service. There are no home child-care services, no one to take the children outside to play (Kuznetsova, 1968:19).

What is especially interesting to note is that many problems of So-viet society, and their origins, are very similar to those in the United States. In the USSR as in the United States, people with little or limited education want good jobs but cannot find them; they also want more higher education than is available. They remain, despite extended public education in both countries, an easily identifiable stratum of the popula-tion. When their leisure increases, so do their "leisure problems," which many attempt to solve by stepping up the consumption of alcohol in the

Soviet Union (in the United States there are more varied mechanisms with which to meet the crisis). Soviet juvenile delinquents are more likely to come from broken or incomplete families than from complete and stable ones; more of them attend trade (or vocational) schools than the regular high school (Minkovsky, 1966). Soviet social mobility has slowed down; "the intelligentsia is reproducing itself" (Kantorovich, 1966). Rural life would still outrage Marx, and it certainly does compel the young to flee in droves if they can (Shinokova and Yanov, 1966). Inadequate housing is among the sources of marital instability (Kharchev, 1964). Although these and many other problems are discussed in Soviet sociology and sociological journalism, some still are not mentioned, nor have all of them their counterparts in American life.

In fact many problems in Soviet society do not find expression in Soviet sociology (see also Hollander, 1965). To take a few: what are the effects of crowded housing conditions and limited privacy on the upbringing and personality of children? What are the prevailing standards of sexual behavior and morality among different social strata? What type of housing would Soviet people prefer (i.e., apartments, individual housing units, or "communal palaces" or "palace communes"[12])? What kind of social, political, and cultural conditions made the Stalinist terror possible? How did the Soviet system train and recruit the Soviet equivalents of Eichmann, who manned the immense coercive apparatus under Stalin? How did Soviet people react to the cult of personality (i.e., Stalin's)? Did they accept the official superman image of him? Was he a genuine father figure? Did this cult create an immunity to another one or a predisposition toward it? What are the aftereffects of coercive experience on millions of Soviet people who were condemned to labor camps, jails, or exile? How successfully have former concentration camp inmates been reintegrated into society? What are the prevailing popular attitudes toward dissent and especially the minority of dissenting intellectuals? What proportion of the population disbelieves the official propaganda and what parts of it (i.e., the statements about domestic social reality, foreign countries, and the approach of communism)? What are the popular conceptions of the nature of communist society? What are the processes of selection to high political position? What is the social background of various Soviet elites? What is the extent of ethnic prejudice and especially anti-Semitism in different segments and ethnic groups of the population? Can

---

[12] A famous Soviet economist-sociologist, Academician Strumilin, proposed a decade ago the setting up of these new forms of housing and communities, which would combine the place of residence, work, recreation and child-rearing—the latter largely taken out of the hands of parents. His proposal provoked much controversy and no sign of implementation so far (Strumilin, 1961).

people conceive of alternatives to the present political-institutional system? What are the popular attitudes toward Soviet foreign policy?

Soviet sociology is the least informative of the actual or potential political conflicts in Soviet society, indeed of Soviet political life in general. The answers are not hard to find. The political order of Soviet society is the least subject to questioning, probing, exploration or detached analysis. It is a firmly established order that invites neither change nor reform nor public inquiry into its merits or deficiencies. Unlike the economy, the efficiency of the political order is not expected to be improved by sociological fact-finding.

If there are strikes, demonstrations, or any form of political unrest in the Soviet Union (and not much is visible), the State Security Police and not social scientists will investigate its causes and ramifications. Dissenters are jailed or exiled rather than interviewed or studied. In a country where literally everybody votes (over 99 percent of those eligible) and where the votes are all cast for the same ticket (over 99 percent) the study of voting patterns holds little excitement. Participation in other political activities—such as attending meetings, rallies, political seminars, etc.—is, once more, a quasi-compulsory ritual. Although it would be interesting to know how Soviet people conceive of such activities, this question again is not the kind Soviet sociologists are encouraged to ask. Nor is the Soviet power elite, as one might expect, a fitting subject of sociological curiosity. Fascinating as it would be to delve into the structure of the Communist Party, its decision-making processes, criteria for advancement, social-psychological characteristics of members and functionaries, the critical skills and qualifications required for full-time party work, the social mobility of party members (versus matched groups of nonparty people), the entire part played by the party in Soviet stratification—these are all topics that are too sensitive for probing. They remain unilluminated by the insights and information sociology could provide.

REFLECTING THE INNER MAN

> . . . We expect our "national purpose" to be clear and simple, something that gives direction to the lives of nearly two hundred million people and yet can be bought in a paperback at the corner drugstore for a dollar. . . . We expect anything and everything. We expect the contradictory and the impossible . . . compact cars which are spacious; luxurious cars which are economical . . . to eat and stay thin . . . to be constantly on the move and ever more neighbourly, to go to "church of our choice" and yet feel its guiding power over us . . . . (Boorstin, 1964:4).

> As for the problems of the formation of the new man, our party has . . . elaborated and applied a system of scientific views—the teachings of com-

munist upbringing. . . . Thus have been forged the remarkable fighters for the people's cause, men of pure heart, daring thought, unbending will . . . a new man grew up on our land: the conscious and active builder of communism, a confirmed collectivist with a communist psychology, which the old world never knew (Frantsev and Filonovich, 1965:78–79).

The future historian may find it the most difficult to establish with the help of sociology what Americans and Soviet people of the 1960s believed in, what were their conceptions of the meaning of life, of their ultimate ends and innermost motives for partaking in competitive and routinized social existence. We cannot be too harsh on sociologists for not providing a rich and persuasive store of information on this subject. It is difficult to find out what people truly believe in, what values they genuinely embrace, and how they see the relationship between these values and their everyday life.

For some time American sociologists considered more or less axiomatic the functioning of certain values as cornerstones of American life and aspirations. Equality of opportunity, achievement, success, education, material abundance and comforts, freedom from government pressures and harrassment, belief in god, the perfectibility of human life and social relations, an optimistic attitude toward change—these have been some of the major values of American society as seen by historians, anthropologists, and sociologists (see, for example, Merton, 1957; Lipset, 1963; Parsons, 1962; Mead, 1965; DuBois, 1955). The past decades brought a degree of questioning and uncertainty about the persistence of these values, the firmness with which they are held, and the extent of their sway over the behavior of Americans.

For those who lived through them, the 1960s in America had all the hallmarks of crisis. Against a background of assassinations, slum riots, campus violence, escapist subcultures, an unpopular war, an apparent wave of crime, and sudden awareness of poverty, it is not unreasonable to believe that spiritual uncertainty has been growing; that this has been a time of doubt, questioning, and of beliefs discarded or hysterically embraced. Although no great sociological research effort is required to understand the restlessness of the American Negro, the problems of belief and disbelief of white society are more complex and less well understood. Sociology has not made a great contribution to understanding the spiritual malaise of our times in America, the rich assortment of alienations and anomies and their varied manifestations, the state of the inner man.

Religion has continued its pathetic floundering in an effort to become "relevant."[13] Of course, the story of secularization of religion in America

---

[13] "Relevance" and the quest for it are among the most interesting phenomena of the 1960s. The term and its new associations and connotations have so far not stimulated the curiosity of the sociologists of knowledge. The term seems to have acquired

had been told before (e.g. Herberg, 1955). But the present convulsions of the American denominations, their efforts to be "with it," to find a place somewhere between pop art and social work betray the same confused value orientation that is conveyed by individual behavior. American sociology does tell us something about these developments and crises in organized religion, but not much about the residue of religious beliefs left in the minds of Americans. Are most Americans aware of the loss of religious values? Do they miss them? Is there any longing for the traditional certainties deriving earlier from such religious values? What are the major substitutes for religious values and convictions?

As indicated earlier, Soviet sociology has begun to grapple with the issue of religion, though its role has been fairly limited so far. It has not raised or probed seriously the broader issues of belief and value commitment, for example, the part played by Marxism-Leninism in the personal value system of Soviet citizens, its adequacy or inadequacy in answering the most bothersome questions of human existence. Above all, we learn equally little from American and Soviet sociology about the societal handling of death and the ways in which people of various social backgrounds and level of education confront or evade its approach.

IDEOLOGICAL COMMITMENT AND DETACHMENT: OPPOSITE TRENDS

In analyzing the omissions and blank spots as well as the areas of emphasis of sociological inquiry in the two societies, it is necessary to take notice of an interesting development in American sociology, and the contrast it presents to the trends in the Soviet one. Over the past few years, probably in response to the developments in American society at large, American sociology is beginning to show some tendencies toward a growing politicization, a groping for ideological commitments and partisanship.[14] The ideals of scientific neutrality, detachment, and objectivity are being challenged by a vocal minority who wish to see a greater in-

---

three connotations. First, it is used as a euphemism for anything that serves the interests of a given group; it stands for "useful" or "approved of" or "desirable." Second, the term is being used synonymously with "meaningful," that which helps to make sense of contemporary life, or imparts new meaning to it. Third, it often seems to mean "familiar"—especially in the educational context.

[14] This phenomenon is not limited to sociology:

Today politics has the prestige and enchantment that religion had in Western thought until the end of the seventeenth century and that economics acquired after Marxism began to spread in the late nineteenth century. To go to the root of a thing today is to go to its politics. Everything . . . must be placed in the category of politics . . . it is a rare book indeed whose appeal to readers cannot be increased by adding, however irrelevantly, to the title the words "the politics of . . ." (Nisbet, 1968:163).

volvement on the part of sociology in the solution of the most pressing problems of the society (see Hoult, 1968; Gamson, 1968; and Neuwirth, 1968). Paradoxically, these demands are linked to the rejection of involvement with government agencies, foundations, industry, and business—of areas and institutions of society that the partisans of involvement devalue or dislike. What they favor is involvement with selected aspects of society, not involvement in general. Thus, they often reject applied research in the name of the ethical neutrality of the social sciences, that is, they disapprove of certain types of applied research and the institutions or organizations that would benefit from it.

There is, then, a renewal of the tradition in American sociology that wished to make sociology a tool of social change. As noted earlier, this orientation is supported by the merciless unearthing and ventilation of the defects of American society, a trend that is likely to continue. Consequently, the future historian will have at his disposal an ever-increasing volume of information of the failures of American society while inventories of its accomplishments are static or shrinking, relatively speaking.

While American sociology does show signs of becoming more ideological and politicized and turning away, or at least muting the emphasis on the virtues of detached scientific inquiry, Soviet sociology is slowly moving in the other direction. It is becoming less ideological, more concerned with method, techniques, and the attainment of scientific standards of precision and reliability (see Kharchev, 1966; Moscow University Publishing House, 1966). However, the balance between emphasis on accomplishments versus failures is also shifting, since the Soviet sociologist—as opposed to the American—is in a better position to reveal the weaknesses in Soviet social structure when this is legitimated by appeals to scientific detachment and objectivity and empirical fact-finding than if it were legitimated by political-ideological motives and values.

CONTRASTS IN CROSS-NATIONAL PERCEPTIONS

   . . . there is already clearly discernible a major process of convergence by which on the one hand the "social gains" of the Western democracies have already gone far to bring the older working class fully into the general social community, and, on the other hand, the Communist world, notably in Soviet Russia, has already begun to move away from the rigid patterns which were the source of the most serious conflict of institutional structure with the Western world (Parsons, 1964:389–399).

   In glorifying capitalism, which has supposedly changed radically . . . and has come "closer" to socialism, bourgeois ideologists are even prepared to recognize certain successes of socialism, for the purpose of giving their judgments a semblance of objectivity. Bourgeois propaganda widely advertises the theories of a "unified industrial society," the rapprochement of capitalism and socialism, the "convergence" of the two social systems. These theories serve a certain ideological purpose: to implant the illusion in the working people that capitalism has already ceased being capitalism ... (CDSP, 1968:9).

Finally we might ask: to what extent do the two sociologies reflect the mutual awareness of the two societies and of their similarities, which have preoccupied many social scientists in both countries in the late 1950s and the 1960s? In America there are four basic motives behind the belief in the growing similarity of the United States and the USSR (some of these motives are often combined). The first is simply congenital optimism, the desire for wish fulfillment, based on the conviction that if the structures of the two societies become sufficiently similar, then the political conflicts and tensions between them will decline. In particular, much hope is attached to the "erosion of ideology" seen as the propelling force of Soviet aggressiveness and expansionism (see, for example, Sorokin, 1964). Second, a pessimistic belief in the convergence of the two societies originates in the feeling that industrialization inexorably produces the same one-dimensional mass society, with the attendant regimentation and conformity (Moore, 1958; Marcuse, 1964). Third, those inclined to some form of economic determinism, optimists and pessimists alike, are persuaded that similar levels of economic development create similar, if not identical, institutional superstructures and values (Rostow, 1960; Galbraith, 1967; Inkeles, 1960). And fourth, some American social scientists are inclined to perceive a convergence because it supports the theory-building enterprise by affirming the existence of overarching uniformities between various societies. If all industrial societies are alike, eventually all societies will be alike (since unquestionably industrialization is proceeding apace), and if this is the case there is once more[15] room for explor-

---

[15] "Once more" because contemporary American sociologists by and large have moved away from the aspirations of their professional ancestors, the nineteenth-century theory-builders (such as Comte, Durkheim, Marx, Spencer) to settle down to the more humble efforts of developing "middle-range" theories, recognizing the fruitlessness of the more grandiose theoretical aspirations. Interestingly enough, although Soviet sociologists are, by birth, so to speak, the inheritors of the Marxist theoretical framework—by no means one that accepts a patchwork of limited generalizations about the social world—there has recently been a call for precisely middle-range theorizing:

> We have a reliable general sociological theory—historical materialism. The difficulty, however, is that between global sociological theory and the concrete social phenomena studied by empirical methods some transitional steps must be interposed in the form of special theories for the aspects under study: for example a sociological theory of man's labor activity or a theory of personality (Yadov, 1968:7).

ing or discovering the general laws of social existence. It must also be noted that the future historian scrutinizing American sociology of the 1960s will not find many actual comparative studies of selected aspects of American and Soviet society. Most of the statements on the subject are more theoretical and speculative than empirically comparative.

On the Soviet side more attention has been given to the problem, though again almost exclusively on the theoretical-ideological rather than empirical level. Soviet sociologists take, and are called upon to take, a totally different position on this subject. They reject categorically, unequivocally, and vehemently the notion of growing similarities between the two societies. Moreover, to the extent that they have to partake of the official, paranoid visions of a raging ideological struggle being waged by the United States against the Soviet Union, they treat the theme of convergence, or the "single-industrial-society" model, as yet another cunning device employed by the propagandists and propagators of American imperialism and the American way of life. More specifically, there are several reasons for the Soviet hostility to the notion of growing similarities between American and Soviet society. Most important, it undermines the Soviet claim of the historical uniqueness and superiority of Soviet society over the American (and all others, for that matter). For a very long time the entire Soviet political educational system, the schools and mass media included, has been geared to the intensive dissemination and inculcation of the proposition that American society is a particularly hideous form of the capitalist social order, characterized by innumerable contradictions, crises, exploitation, repression, and injustice.[16] To the extent that Soviet sociologists have turned their attention to the world out-

---

[16] By contrast, the views of American social scientists and especially sociologists have been far more favorable toward Soviet society. First of all, they draw a radical dividing line between the Stalin and post-Stalin period, reserving most of their criticism for the former. Second, they view Soviet society as being the process of slow, gradual improvement or evolution in a direction they approve of, toward less repression, greater diversity, less aggressive posture in foreign affairs, and a greater degree of material well-being. Many social scientists in America have also been willing to balance political deprivations against economic development, or blunt the edge of their critical sentiments by the argument that the harshness of the Soviet political-social environment is more or less inevitable given the historical traditions and overall backwardness of Russian society. In many cases there is an underlying, optimistic evolutionary belief that perceives of the coming of political pluralism as a necessary outcome of economic development in the Soviet Union as elsewhere. Such views contrast very sharply with the Soviet one, which is rooted in the traditional Marxist premises postulating the historically determined downfall and doom of all capitalist societies and in the light of which social-economic and political conditions in the United States can only deteriorate until the system is destroyed by its internal contradictions. These premises color every Soviet appraisal of the United States and of every institution, policy, and social phenomena in it.

side, this official vision of American society has found reflection in their work (see, for example, Zamoshkin, 1965). More recently Soviet sociologists have focused on the deep spiritual and moral crisis of American life, partially supplanting the earlier stress on the endemic economic malfunctioning of American society. America, far from being similar to the Soviet Union, has been presented as its polar opposite. Soviet spokesmen have also emphasized that the single industrial society model ignores the underlying differences between the two societies; the control and ownership of the means of production is in the hands of a small group of capitalists in the United States, whereas in the USSR it is vested in the public and society at large. The convergence hypothesis could also undermine its distinctiveness as a model of industrialization and nation-building that the Soviet Union strives to present to the developing nations. In view of these factors it is not surprising that we find no echoes of the American viewpoints in the writing of Soviet social scientists concerning any degree or kind of similarity—emerging, partial, or potential—between the two societies.

CONCLUSION

This brief survey provided at least some illustrations of the ways in which American and Soviet sociology hold a mirror to the society in which they are embedded. As a rule, and with some notable exceptions, sociologists cannot transcend the limitations placed upon them by their membership in their society. They are neither heroes nor intellectual supermen. They lash out in every direction when conditions permit, as they do in America (where ideas are not treated as dangerous weapons[17]), or they show prudent restraint in the questions raised when the broader environment is less hospitable to free inquiry, as is the case in the USSR. The best among them, even under such conditions, will focus on the significant rather than the trivial and will try to accumulate new knowledge the best he can. The dispute about the uses to which sociological findings are put do not trouble our Soviet colleagues. Many of them no doubt have no ideological-political objection to seeing their findings used in strengthening and improving the Soviet social order. Others, one

---

[17] Treating ideas as weapons or subversive substances is among the most tenacious traditions in Soviet social-political thought and practice. It explains not only censorship, the jailing of unorthodox writers, the place of political indoctrination in formal education and the immunity of certain subjects from sociological research, but also the entire range of deeply suspicious official attitudes toward free expression and dissent. In the pragmatic American tradition ideas are treated far less seriously, which might have some disadvantages but at the same time provides conditions for free expression and a multiplicity of viewpoints in the social sciences as in society at large.

may presume, feel that they cannot accept responsibility for the possible use or misuse of their findings even in patching up a social-political system that remains authoritarian and repressive in many ways. Probably more and more of them are motivated primarily by the desire to become scientists and aspire to the expertise and relative freedom in research such expertise confers, as it does on the more established and secure natural scientists.

In America, as we remarked before, holding a mirror to society is becoming a more complicated task subject to many strains and conflicting interpretations. The desire for rapid social change is becoming so urgent and intense for some that the social engineering impulse may overwhelm every other motive and perspective. But sociology must at least *try* to transcend the passions of its time if it is to aspire to tell more about the social world than everybody already knows, and if it wants to go beyond the level of "relevance," represented by the mass media. Sociology must continue to tread the narrow path between commitment and detachment, involvement and an open mind, strong convictions and double standards.[18] As a recent commentator put it, ". . . it is in the ethico-political arena that we are most prone to use our heads to justify our interest and to rationalize our personal discontent. . . . With the death of gods and the elevation of reasons, we seek to prove our values by facts" (Nettler, 1968:201, 202).

We may be slowly moving into an era in American sociology when the intellectual substance and quality of insight of our discipline is less threatened by the familiar pursuit of the safely trivial and narrowly empirical, or by the unreal phantoms of the abstract-theoretical. The new threat lies in the ideological engulfment of the significant issues of sociology and society.

Thus, paradoxically enough, the potential dangers to the fruitfulness of the sociological enterprise are in some ways greater in the United States than in the Soviet Union. In the former the pressures toward distortion and partisanship come from the self, from intense personal commitments, making the drive to prove values by facts stronger and more effective. In the Soviet Union the corresponding pressures come from the institutional environment and its prevailing doctrines. Such pressures, because they are external, easily discernible, and visibly imposed are easier to evade and combat than those that spring from the innermost core of a person. Let us conclude in the hope that the increasingly fashionable but

---

[18] It is a tribute to the occasional relevance of the past that, at least in my opinion, nobody has yet improved upon the observations and exhortations of Max Weber on this subject (see Weber, 1957).

230   Paul Hollander

narrow interpretations of "relevance" will not impair the value and validity of the work of the emerging and future generation of American sociologists, that what they have to say about American society will endure beyond the controversies and conflicts of our times. Sociology, to be successful—both in the scientific and humanistic sense—must emancipate itself not only from the more obvious and crude ideological orthodoxies and constraints of the dominant social institutions and doctrines, but also from the more subtle orthodoxies of one's personal value commitments and desires.

REFERENCES

Alexandrov, A.
    1968   "The Formation of the Individual." Current Digest of the Soviet Press (CDSP) (April 10).
Becker, Howard
    1966   Introduction in Howard Becker (ed.), Social Problems. New York: John Wiley & Sons.
Boorstin, Daniel J.
    1964   The Image. New York: Harper-Colophon.
CDSP
    1968   "The lofty responsibility of social scientists," All Union Conference of Department Heads (July 10).
DuBois, Cora
    1955   "The dominant value profile of American culture." American Anthropologist (December):1232–1239.
Frantsev, Yu., and Yu. Filonovich
    1965   "The philosopher's stone." CDSP (October 13).
Galbraith, John Kenneth
    1967   The New Industrial State. Boston: Houghton Mifflin.
Gamson, William
    1968   "Sociology's children of affluence." American Sociologist (November):286–289.
Gouldner, Alvin W.
    1968   "Disorder and social theory." Science (October 11):247–249.
Grushin, B.
    1967   Svobodnoye Vremya–Aktualniye Problemi (Free Time–Contemporary Problems). Moscow: "Thought" Publishing House, pp. 90–99.
Grushin, B. A., and V. V. Chikin
    1962   Ispoved Pokeleniya (Confessions of a Generation). Moscow: Young Communist League Publishing House.
Herberg, Will
    1955   Protestant, Catholic, Jew. Garden City, N.Y.; Doubleday.

Hollander, Paul
    1965   "The dilemmas of soviet sociology." Problems of Communism (November-December):1–9.

Hoult, Thomas Ford
    1968   ". . . Who shall prepare himself to the battle." American Sociologist (February):3–7.

Inkeles, Alex
    1960   "Industrial man." American Journal of Sociology (July):1–31.
    1964   What is Sociology? Englewood Cliffs, N.J.: Prentice-Hall.

Kantorovich, V.
    1966   "A science kindred to us." CDSP (July 20).
    1968   "Sociology and literature." Current Abstracts of the Soviet Press (May).

Kharchev, A. G.
    1964   "On some results of a study of the motives for marriage." Soviet Review (Summer):3–13.
    1966   Kolichestvenniye Metodi v Sotsiologii (Quantitative Methods in Sociology). Moscow: Science Publishing House.

Kuznetsova, L.
    1968   "The new face of the madonna." Current Abstracts of the Soviet Press (May).

Lipset, Seymour Martin
    1963   The First New Nation. New York: Basic Books.

Mannheim, Karl
    1963   "American sociology." First published in 1932, quoted from Maurice Stein and Arthur Vidich: Sociology on Trial. Englewood Cliffs, N.J.: Prentice-Hall.

Marcuse, Herbert
    1964   One Dimensional Man. Boston: Beacon Press.

Mead, Margaret
    1965   And Keep Your Powder Dry. New York: William Morrow.

Merton, Robert
    1957   "Social structure and anomie" in his Social Theory and Social Structure. Glencoe: Free Press.

Merton, Robert, and Robert Nisbet (eds.)
    1966   Contemporary Social Problems (rev. ed.). New York: Harcourt, Brace and World.

Mills, C. Wright
    1959   The Sociological Imagination. New York: Oxford University Press.

Minkovsky, G. M.
    1966   "Problems of criminology: some causes of juvenile delinquency in the USSR and measures to prevent it." CDSP (August 17):10–11.

Moore, Barrington Jr.
    1958   "Reflections on conformity in industrial society" in his Political

Power and Social Theory. Cambridge, Mass.: Harvard University Press.

Moscow University Publishing House
1966   Metodologicheskiye Voprosi Obshchestvennikh Nauk (The Methodological Questions of Social Sciences). Moscow: Moscow University Publishing House.

Nettler, Gwynn
1968   "Using our heads." The American Sociologist (August):200–207.

Neuwirth, Gertrude
1968   "The failure and reluctance of the dons of sociology." American Sociologist (May):153–154.

Nisbet, Robert
1968   Tradition and Revolt. New York: Random House.

Parsons, Talcott
1962   "Youth in the context of American society." Daedalus (Winter).
1964   "Communism and the west: the sociology of the conflict." Pp. 390–399 in Amitai and Eva Etzioni (eds.), Social Change. New York: Basic Books.
1968   "Introduction," in Talcott Parsons (ed.), American Sociology—Perspectives, Problems, Methods. New York: Basic Books.

Rostow, W. W.
1960   The Stages of Economic Growth. Cambridge, England: Cambridge University Press.

Rumyantsev, A.
1968   "Concrete social research: tasks and prospects." CDSP (July 3).

Shinakova, G., and A. Yanov
1966   "Sociological essay: anxieties of Smolensk Province." CDSP (September 7).

Simirenko, Alex
1968   "International contributions by soviet sociologists." Paper presented at the Annual Meetings of the American Sociological Association, Boston.

Sorokin, Pitirim
1964   "Mutual convergence of the U.S. and USSR . . ." from his Basic Trends of Our Times. New Haven, Conn.: College and University Press.

Strumilin, S.
1961   "Family and community in the society of the future." Soviet Review (February):3–29.

Tilly, Charles
1969   "Clio and Minerva." Pp. 433–466 in John C. McKinney and Edward A. Tiryakian (eds.), Theoretical Sociology: Perspectives and Developments. New York: Appleton-Century-Crofts.

Tumin, Melvin M.
1968   "Some social consequences of research on racial relations." The American Sociologist (May):117–124.

Weber, Max
  1957   "Science as a vocation." Pp. 138–156 in H. H. Gerth and C. W. Mills (eds.), Max Weber: Essays in Sociology. London: Routledge and Kegan Paul.
Yadov, V.
  1968   "Prestige in danger." CDSP (March 27).
Yevdokimov, V.
  1968   "Concrete social research and atheism." Current Abstracts of the Soviet Press (May).
Zamoshkin, Yu.
  1965   Krizis Burzhuaznovo Individualizma i Lichnosti (The Crisis of Bourgeois Individualism and Personality). Moscow: Science Publishing House.

Research and Policy: Images of the Future in Action

The four chapters in Part IV deal with research and policy, with images of the future in action. The first is by Robert Boguslaw, who discusses perceptions of social reality, values, decision-making, and social action in an evaluation of the limitations of conventional planning perspectives. It is difficult for social planners to break out of the present, he says, because they tend to be "reasonable" and thus a part of existing value and goal structures. Yet creative solutions for contemporary social difficulties may necessarily involve significant alterations in existing goals and perceptions of reality. Technical elites may not be able to transcend current goals and values, nurtured as they are "on a diet of weapons system development and a criterion framework of time and cost efficiency." Such groups as those represented by the hippies, however, who are to some degree outsiders, have been able to generate new sets of requirements beyond existing organizational forms through what Boguslaw calls "psychedelic planning."

All of us are victims of the people who specify, create, or limit our alternatives of choice. Such people may not be the planners at all, but are likely to be the persons who are the instruments of implementation, who engage in the actual behaviors that shape the future. The holders of technical expertise—from the TV repairman to the military staff officer—are in positions "to make decisions that shape the design of the future without any necessary reference to those who are most affected by the decisions." Although beliefs and values may shape decisions, some people may have a near monopoly on relevant information with respect to a particular set of actions, so that their own beliefs about the nature of social reality and their own values, perhaps representing special interests, come to dominate and control the emerging future. Thus, among other things, Boguslaw urges sociologists to adopt "a design perspective" rather than a conventionally "scientific" orientation to certain problems. He would have social scientists study the people who carry out the operations and the methods and technology they use, because such people have enormous consequences for the shape of the future.

What people, operations, methods, and technologies, for example, are responsible for the most massive failure of American society in the second half of the twentieth century? That failure is the shocking state of American cities, which have been a national disgrace for a decade and a matter of informed concern long before that. Scott Greer, in the second chapter in Part IV, analyzes images of the city and urban policy in the United States. The nation, clinging to no longer accurate beliefs about the nature of urban America and refusing to accept the emergent vision of a continental city-state, embarked on urban renewal and governmental reforms that, he says, were—and are—mere "sops to outraged conscience."

Greer says that his chapter "deals with the study of futures, not with ontrolling them," yet he notes the important fact that "accurate study is n some degree dependent on control—who leaves political change out of his forecast does so at his peril." And Greer calls for political change, a national urban policy, to handle the problems of location and transportation, and of homogeneity and heterogeneity of an "urban fabric without harply demarcated spatial boundaries" of "a vast, horizontal network of ettlement held together by rapid means of transportation" and communication.

His proposed urban government would be divided into viable subunits, related to each other, and to the larger whole on those issues that made a broad perspective and overall control necessary. He would "optimize a wide range of values," and lists some "aspects of urban structures which a national policy should consider and form or reform." Before his proposals have much chance for success in the political arena, however, planners and citizens alike must reject many of the beliefs they hold about the nature of the city and break out of the "tunnel vision" that has prevented them from seeing "the vast, interrelated network that is urban America."

In the third chapter, J. Victor Baldridge looks at images of the future in action in a case study of organizational change at New York University. He shows how both structural constraints and images of the future "dovetail in an adequate interpretation of organizational change."

An existing major educational mission of NYU as the "School of Opportunity" was threatened by the growth and changing character of the public colleges and universities after World War II. With more direct access to government treasuries, they could expand, seemingly indefinitely, to meet mass needs for higher education while maintaining low tuition costs. Thus, NYU's traditional roles of general service and opportunity were usurped. Perceiving their competitive disadvantages in relation to the public universities, decision-makers at NYU began a conscious search for a new image of the future that would define a new educational mission, distinctively setting NYU off from the public universities.

After more than a year of self-study, fact-finding, committee proposals, and debate, a new set of purposes was formulated, providing both a new distinctive identity vis-à-vis the New York public universities and a new image of the future. Among the important aspects of that future were upgrading of the quality of students admitted and of programs offered in a drive toward excellence, emphasizing graduate and professional education, and becoming an "urban university."

Several things should be noted about Baldridge's chapter: the fact that there are often favorable as well as unfavorable attitudes to both existing and emergent images of the future is well illustrated by the discussion of the sources of opposition to and support for the planned organizational changes; the struggle to control the future took on features that made a conflict or political model useful and involved redistributions of people, jobs, power, and prestige; and the utility of most of the concepts in the cybernetic-decisional model of social change is demonstrated: beliefs about the nature of social reality, goals (mission or purpose), values, decision-making, individual and collective action, population (in this case students and faculty), resources, the nature of the organizational setting (including constraints), and, of course, images of the future.

Ivar Oxaal was with us in the British Caribbean in the early 1960s during our studies there of nationalism, leadership, and the belief in progress, and he completed *Black Intellectuals Come to Power: The Rise of Creole Nationalism in Trinidad and Tobago*. As a co-participant in the West Indies Study Program, he shared with us many of the experiences that led to the concerns behind this book: how knowledge of man and society gets to be what it is, its relevance to the issues of the day, and its consequences for images of the future, decision-making, and social action. These shared experiences—typical for social researchers in developing nations—undoubtedly led him to return to the West Indies as head of a new department of sociology at the University of Guyana and to accept the challenge of chairing a commission of inquiry into social and industrial relations in an important segment of the Guyanese economy.

His "Methodology and the Quest for Utopia: A Case Study from El Dorado" is a personal account of his involvement in social research that was fully entwined with social policy, action, and political conflict involving different images of the future. Here is an account of some of the possibilities and problems involved in the pursuit of an activist sociology. At one point or another, Oxaal followed many of our directives regarding how to make social research relevant to the study of the emerging future. The result gives us pause: great personal costs were involved—enormous energy, frayed nerves, strained friendships, political attack; political polarization could not be avoided; acceptance of the existing system of power relations and the march of history seemed necessary—or acceptance of insurgency; public criticism and scorn had to be faced, public defense demanded, public condemnation from some quarters tolerated; his university base itself was threatened with politicization; no protection from risk was found; and the desire to change society, he concludes, may inevitably conflict with the effort to create a science of society. Although the cleavages and conflicts in Guyana were unusually extreme, the results of Oxaal's experiment should not be dismissed as idiosyncratic. Although it is true that the study of the future does not have to be con-

ucted as applied research in the midst of a confrontation situation, such
s that including workers, union, management, and a mélange of others
hat Oxaal faced, some of the issues of being "engaged" emerge sharply
rom Oxaal's account precisely because of the passions generated and
he clear-cut differences of attitudes and beliefs.

We value Oxaal's contribution to this volume as "a cautionary tale,"
especially for any of our readers who take what we have said as exhorta-
ion to rush into the breach of politics garbed in the robes of social
science. We aim to increase the bearing of social research on alternative
utures, not to transform social scientists into politicians.

The Design Perspective in Sociology

ROBERT BOGUSLAW

I should like to begin this chapter with what for sociologists is perhaps a truism that may not even be "true." I plan to examine the implications of this truism for the work that sociologists do, and try to trace its relevance and the relevance of some other matters to things that are happening in the contemporary world. I hope to be able to show why it is that the work many sociologists are doing is becoming increasingly less relevant to the contemporary world and to the world of the future, although sociology as an intellectual enterprise has possibly never had more potential relevance to the workaday world. I expect to conclude with some suggestions about how this state of affairs can be improved.

The truism is, "Perception is functionally selective." The experimental evidence for this truism is enormous. I shall make no effort to review it here. Suffice it to say that the hungry man examining a menu "sees" the food items; the thirsty man "sees" the drink items; some men see only the pretty girl on the cover. What does the sociologist see?

On a more general level, it seems appropriate to ask: What does the sociologist see when he looks at the world about him? The conventional answer in this age of science is, of course, that he sees "order." Why does he see order? Because he can do science with order and science is his business or avocation.

Thus to some sociologists, for example, George Homans (1961:398),

Portions of an early version of this paper under the title, "Social Planning and Social Action," were delivered at the annual meeting of the American Sociological Association held in San Francisco, California, August 1967. Portions of a later version under the title "The Design Perspective in Sociology," were delivered at the annual meeting of the American Psychological Association held in San Francisco, California, August 1968.

cience is the one peculiar institution that may just conceivably help men deal with the ancient problem of how to reconcile their institutions with their social nature. Homans is slightly embarrassed by the word "science." He finds calling what he does in sociology "science" almost as inappropriate as calling your wife "Mrs. Smith" in the bedroom; the name is too formal for the situation. His defense of conventional science is a familiar one: (1) it may ultimately be useful; (2) in the meantime, it is fun.

Now there is no quarreling with anyone's idea of what is fun. And there really should be no quarreling with what anyone does in his bedroom. Nevertheless, the word "science," as used by Mr. Homans, is not a very useful one for me. To avoid semantic battles, I propose to leave science in the bedroom to Mr. Homans and Mrs. Smith, and to use the term "social design" for the things I find interesting and important.

For the moment, I will ask you to think of social design as an activity directed toward the future, and having as its primary consequence the specification of a range of alternatives for channeling social behavior. I think of it in terms of present rather than future actions, although it consists of social behaviors that form new alternatives for subsequent actions. I would reserve the term "social planning" for social behaviors taken within the framework of existing alternatives.

Since I am quite conscious of looking at social phenomena selectively, I do not limit my vision to "order." I am quite prepared to see disorder, even if I am not yet prepared to account for all the elements that go into its construction. I am not alone in this view of the world. I find, as I look out there, that other people see the same things I see. Some of these people are not very happy with what they see and try to introduce order into what they initially perceive as chaos or uncertainty. For better or worse we can call these people "social designers" whether or not they think of themselves in these terms. Many, probably most of them, are not social scientists. They may be engineers, physicists, politicians, businessmen, labor leaders, or farmers. They introduce or try to impose order upon a variety of areas of social life. In this sense, they are men who exercise power. They do this not by directly coercing another person, or even by succeeding in achieving their purposes more frequently than others do. They operate by restricting the alternatives available to others. What are the mechanisms through which this is accomplished?

MECHANISMS OF SOCIAL DESIGN

Paradigm specification. Let us begin by examining the activity traditionally involved in efforts to *uncover* order: the conventional scientific enterprise. Here, if anywhere, we should expect to find an absence of re stricted alternatives, or conversely, complete freedom to follow one's ow: scientific intuitions. At the very heart of the scientific tradition is the be lief that it is essential for scientific investigations to proceed without con straint—to search for truth boldly and unfettered by existing doctrine received truths, or folk wisdom.

However, Thomas Kuhn (1964), in his remarkable book, *The Struc ture of Scientific Revolutions,* has shown that this is not at all the case Much of the success of the scientific enterprise, Kuhn points out, is base on the willingness of the scientific community to defend the assumptio that its members know what the world is like *before* they begin their in vestigations. Fundamental novelties that subvert this assumption tend t be suppressed.

Kuhn uses the term "paradigm" to describe those frames of refer ence that are not quite models or patterns but are more like accepted judi cial decisions under common law. These paradigms become generall accepted and respected when they are more successful than their compet itors in solving problems some groups of practitioners regard as acute "Closely examined, whether historically or in the contemporary labo ratory, that enterprise (normal science) seems an attempt to force natur into the preformed and relatively inflexible box that the paradigm sup plies. No part of the aim of normal science is to call forth new sorts o phenomena; indeed, those that will not fit the box are often not seen a all" (Kuhn, 1964:24).

All this is not meant to imply that science is a fraud. It is obviou that even "normal" science has and does "discover" facts about qualitie and relationships in our physical and social environments. The point i simply that the characteristics of admissible new facts and the context i which they have any meaning has been determined by the paradigm o accepted frame of reference within which the scientific community ha: agreed to work in that time and place. In our terms, the designer of scien tific discoveries is the person or persons most instrumental in defining th outlines of the paradigm within which subsequent scientific effort take: place.

Paradigm specification does not appear to be restricted to the domai of conventional scientific activity. New technologies and inventions o all kinds seem to have enormous paradigm-like effects upon subsequen social efforts to deal with the physical and social environment. Consider for example, the case of military radar systems.

Within the framework of these systems an equipment complex be comes accepted as a reliable means for detecting the existence of aircraf within a more or less definite range expressed in terms of height and dis tance from a given antenna. It is then possible to define a three-dimensional space in the heavens within which approaching enemy aircraft can be detected, identified, and, if necessary, destroyed. To accomplish this purpose the equipment must be supplemented with a set of procedures for keeping track of "friendly" aircraft, for maintaining current information about the availability of friendly interceptor planes, etc. The three-dimensional space can be indefinitely expanded by adding additional detection-identification-destruction units. Ultimately, however, the size of this space is circumscribed by the range and sensitivity of the radar equipment. Thus, there does not exist anything one might call "absolute" air defense.

For purposes of military operations a more or less definite band in the heavens is envisioned within which enemy aircraft move only with considerable risk to themselves. After this space has been defined in more or less exact terms, it is possible to make further improvements to the system only by increasing its internal efficiency, for example, by increasing the speed with which information is processed. Thus, the enormously expensive SAGE air defense system, established by the United States Air Defense Command some years ago, represented a highly significant forward step in the field of computer development and information-processing techniques; but the entire system retained essentially the same basic detection range as the older "manual" system. The size of the air space covered by this system was so limited that it proved to be virtually useless against missile attack. It is easy to see how a new paradigm could be developed (or promised) as an answer to this new threat of missile attack. You need only pay for a detection concept and equipment to cover a greater area of space. If you then succeed in further decreasing information-processing time, you may have an "antiballistic missile system."

But ultimately one must ask the question: how far is up? To what limits must one extend the capabilities of his system to ensure "acceptable" protection? And, of course, air space is only one small dimension of the problem. Radar systems and antiballistic missile systems do not begin to furnish protection against domestic insurrection, close-in submarine attack, or organized guerrilla activities. Here the point is a simple one: beginning with the paradigm of a defensive system, one can successively design new and more effective cocoons. Whose cocoon is larger? Whose more impenetrable? How does one deflate the enemy's cocoon?

One is tempted to ask the simple question: which came first—the radar or the cocoon? Was it the equipment paradigm that gave rise to the cocoon mode of resolving international problems, or did the development of radar occur because of the prior existence of a cocoon mentality?

One would guess that, in general, the cocoon mentality predated

radar by several thousands of years, and that the development of rada
was simply a tired response to habitual modes of problem solution in international affairs. If this is indeed the case, then the most powerfu
force in shaping new designs for a peaceful world is to be found, not ir
contemporary technological developments, but rather in the reformula
tion of ancient paradigms that continue to limit the scope of innovativ
efforts in the field of international relations.

Environmental access management. Future historians, searching fo
an appropriate phrase to describe the decades immediately after Work
War II, may well arrive at something like "The Age of Technologica
Theocracy." Nuclear energy, computer technology, jet propulsion, spac
travel, laser beams, and all the rest have served to make ordinary men no
merely humble, but reverent in the face of a new set of deities. And now
increasingly, we hear the pronouncements of men who have ascended tc
our latter-day Mount Olympus and announce the form of the new work
which is about to be created.

One of the most imaginative of these new prophets is Buckminste:
Fuller (1967:32) who tells us: "The ultimate revolution—now to be re
solved only by scientific inventing and engineering competence instead o
by now outmoded political initiatives—will swiftly bring about a higl
standard of survival for all."

Fuller is understandably impatient with political barriers to the goo
life. The notion that we have finally reached the point where technologi
cal solutions to the problems of war and poverty are feasible is, o
course, an eminently reasonable one. Other writers have stressed simila
themes, especially in the context of developments in computer technology. Thus, for years, Robert Theobald has been insisting upon the ne
cessity for re-examining the traditional assumption of the science of eco
nomics that material goods are scarce. If modern technology makes i
possible to discard this notion, then one can question the relevance o
conventional market analyses and insist upon something like the guaran
teed income as a solution to the poverty problem. The significant differ
ence between Fuller and Theobald seems to be that Theobald has quit
deliberately proposed a political and social solution to the dilemmas o
economics. Fuller has also proposed a political and social solution bu
presents it as asocial and apolitical. The larger the energy-wealth system
Fuller observes, the more efficiently it operates. Ultra High Voltage sys
tems now being designed will, within a few years, completely intercon
nect all electrical generation and transmission systems within the Unitec
States "bringing such important cost reductions and profit increases tha
both the public and private ownership sectors will be vastly advantaged'
(Fuller, 1967:63).

The extensions of these linkages to other hemispheres will bring additional economies and unheard-of capacities. And all this will rapidly erode ideological differences. "Every nation welcomed and employed the transistor. All will welcome technical-economic desalinization. All the world, properly informed of the design and invention revolution, will applaud it" (Fuller, 1967:63). A clue to the power mechanism at work here is to be found in Fuller's use of the singular noun in discussing "revolution." He has isolated a single enemy in what one is tempted to call the "political establishment," and he advocates that it be replaced by what one might call the "scientific," or "technological" or even "more efficient" establishment.

But, of course, he has not really shown us a "scientific," a "technological," nor even an "efficient" solution to the world's problems. He has traced the outlines of a revolution that is a simple, if not pure, shift in the focus of power. He makes the implicit assumption that freedom for individuals to define new alternatives for themselves is of less importance than the necessity to provide standardized services at reduced rates. And, one is tempted to question whether his contemplated shift in power is in any sense a real one. One suspects that existing political and economic forces would remain firmly in control throughout the Fullerian Transformation—with less opposition than was possible before the Transformation occurred.

Fuller is not, of course, a crude Orwellian. He recognizes the importance of geographical mobility for individuals, if he ignores problems of social mobility. For an initial investment of $7 billion, he assures us, we can (for $600 each) mass-produce an integrated chemical-energy regenerator to take care of all sanitary and energy-generating requirements of family living. With the assistance of this four-feet-in-diameter rocket-capsule energy-regenerating accessory, "men may deploy almost invisibly about the earth in air-delivered, geodesicly enclosed dwelling machines, and survive with only helicopter and television communication at luxuriously simplified high standards of living—operative at negligible land-anchorage costs similar to telephone service charges" (Fuller, 1967:32).

Fuller's "man" will have all the freedom of a bishop or even a queen on a chessboard. The bishop may choose (or be chosen) to alight on any square on the board provided he does so through successive diagonal moves. A red bishop is, however, forever destined to remain on red squares; and a black bishop is forever destined to remain on black squares. And, even the queen, with her enormous freedom of mobility and exalted social status, is forever doomed to move within the sixty-four squares of the chessboard. There is no possibility for her to define a sixty-fifth square to which she might wish to move. Her universe has been defined for her eternally and rigorously, although she may be completely unaware of the extent to which this is true. Ask a queen, "What constraints are there on your movements?" and she may well reply, "None whatsoever."

The power exerted by the Fullerian technologist consists in defining the mode of access to the physical environment. In a very real sense technology can serve as a filter that permits only limited elements of the physical environment to contact the shielded human being. In this sense the most primitive of men possesses maximum degrees of freedom: there exist only minimal filtering devices between him and his environment. Give stone age man an air-conditioned or heated hut, and you have protected him from the extremes of heat, cold, and humidity. You have protected him from the elements but you have denied him direct access to "fresh" air. And, more significantly, you have made his future survival dependent upon the continued good graces of the gas or electric company and its air-conditioning and furnace technicians.

Goal management. One of the more comforting aspects of dealing with a world of human beings as compared to, say, a world of robots, is our cherished belief that people can set goals for themselves. This is a very useful ability, since it helps us to believe that the world will continue to go around in the absence of central planning. This, of course, is the credo that if we need a carpenter, plumber, or baker, the necessary skills will be provided (for a price). It assures us that farmers will make some of their grain crop available to the baker, and that the baker will bake some bread, which ultimately will be available for our dinner table.

However, John Kenneth Galbraith, among others, tells us that the market economy has ceased to be reliable as a means of mutually adjusting the needs of consumers and producers. One important reason for this is the simple fact that the time requirements of contemporary technology demand that consumer needs be anticipated months and even years in advance. It is becoming impossible to depend upon the vagaries of an uncertain market to furnish labor, materials, equipment, and consumer demand. As a result, Galbraith points out, it has become necessary to replace the market with planning. But the more familiar, traditional planning that involves *prediction* of market trends, is no longer satisfactory. Increasingly it is becoming necessary for industrial firms to plan, in the sense of *control* the environment within which they must operate (Galbraith, 1967:60–61).

Industrial planning requires a great variety of information, specialized talent, and an ability to coordinate this talent and information. Planning decisions are not made by managers. The "effective power of decision," Galbraith (1967:71) reminds us, "is lodged deeply in the technical, planning, and other specialized staff." It is this somewhat less than manifest group personality and its decision-making organization that Galbraith calls the "Technostructure." Industrial planning requires a vantage point from which the planner decides to view the world. Having fixed this vantage point, the planner then finds it possible to state goals, develop alternatives, and do whatever else it is that the planner wishes to do. Social psychology has a long tradition addressed to the problem of understanding the motivational and goal structure of individuals and groups. Galbraith dips into this tradition in his efforts to define distinctive goals for the Technostructure. He finds it possesses a distinctive motivational pattern and reward system that calls into question some of the motivational assumptions used by conventional economists. In doing so, he comes close to substituting one rational and hedonistic economic man for another and then continuing in a conventional manner. He seems to maintain a temporal distinction between planning and action that is analytically comforting but probably not empirically justifiable. The accepted common sense of industrial decision-making holds that planning controls the future and that actions are taken in the present as a consequence of yesterday's plans. I am suggesting that the reverse is a more nearly accurate account of what actually occurs—that industrial planning is more characteristically a *consequence* of action, and characteristically becomes a post hoc justification of action. It is the operating units engaged in social behavior rather than the formally designated planners who tend to make the industrial decisions critical for shaping and designing industrial and related futures. Thus, the most effective way of understanding the empirically valid plans of a large industrial firm is carefully to examine the operations in which they are currently engaged rather than to interview their long-range planners. And, of course, what large firms are actually doing today has enormous implications not only for the firms themselves but for the larger society as well. There are many reasons: it is easier to obtain financial and other forms of support for activities that have a demonstrable success record either in this firm or in a similar one. It is also less expensive to engage in production with the skills, techniques, and machines that are currently operating or readily available. New equipment should be of a sort that has demonstrated its effectiveness elsewhere, if possible. The demand for products similar to those previously produced is more easily managed than the demand for esoteric or completely new lines. And this principle operates even in those areas such as space exploration and new weapons system development where it would seem that innovation is the name of the game. Perhaps the most cogent reason is to be found in the value and goal structure of planners, which must, to be "reasonable," be bound intimately to the value and

goal structure of existing operations. Thus structure exercises a compelling influence over the kinds of goals that individuals will establish for
themselves and the organizations (private or public) in which they find
themselves.

Secrecy. Max Weber observed many years ago that one of the most
powerful tools available to a bureaucracy is secrecy. To the extent that
members of a bureaucracy can keep their knowledge and intentions secret, they increase the importance of "professional know-how." Whether
they do this within the shelter of the law or simply at their own discretion
is in this connection not relevant. (Some writers reserve the term "secrecy" for the former, and use "privacy" for the latter; see Westin
1967:26). The use of privacy by organizations has been defended as a
"necessary element for the protection of organizational autonomy, gathering of information and advice, preparation of positions, internal decision making, interorganizational negotiations, and timing of disclosure.
Privacy is thus not a luxury for organizational life; it is a vital lubricant
for the organizational system in free societies" (Westin, 1967:51).

The validity of this assertion is not immediately relevant. What is
relevant is the fact that secrecy (privacy) within organizations can be and
is indeed defended as necessary and even vital for organizational life. The
same rationale can be used to justify the needs for privacy by subunits
within an organizational structure and, with some modification, to justify
the needs of individual members of organizations as well. In practice, of
course, organizations tend to insist that their subordinate or coordinate
units have only minimal rights of privacy with respect to the higher
echelons. But however much lip service subordinate units give to this
principle, they must, to survive, learn to resist these demands.

The contest for private information becomes a battle for scarce resources. The person, unit, or organization obtaining control over these
resources in a very real sense of the term has achieved power. And the
battle for private information is rapidly becoming one of the most critical forms of power conflict to be found in the contemporary industrial
as well as the political, world. A salesman who keeps the nature of his
"contacts" secret; a secretary who keeps the organization of her files secret; the television repairman or automobile mechanic who keeps his
diagnosis secret—all of these are exercising power in the sense of restricting alternatives available for future action. In each of these instances
and in countless others, to yield secrets is to yield power. It is possible for
the holders of secrets to enforce economic or other demands upon persons
who do not have access to the secrets. This is what allows the secretary,
salesman, or department chairman to become "indispensable" and the
auto mechanic and television repairman to obtain high prices for their

ervices. But more relevant, for our present purpose, is the power they re able to wield through the ability to make decisions that appear to be rivial. The decision of the repairman about replacement tubes; the decision of the salesman about which contacts should be pursued; the decision of the department chairman about how strenuously he will seek unds for any given purpose—all these decisions are made by the holders of secrets and shape the design of the future without any necessary refernce to those who are most affected by the decisions. The role of the techical expert, as I have discussed elsewhere (Boguslaw, 1965), is especially rucial as significant decisions about the design of contemporary compuerized systems increasingly become delegated to the holders of "technial" information—an increasingly more widely used euphemism for what Max Weber referred to simply as "secrets."

Military and diplomatic organizations have a special and widely acepted requirement for secrecy. The necessity for shielding one's own trength and intentions from potential enemies is one of the most hallowed doctrines of military tradition. The impact of this tradition upon ontemporary foreign policy and the course of international relations is ecoming increasingly more evident. The insistence of military "experts" hat a particular piece of territory is "vital for national defense" is a diffiult argument for "laymen," i.e., persons who do not have access to all he "facts," to refute. Thus an argument that a specific revolution in a pecific country has been instigated by "world communism" is especially lifficult to refute by persons who are denied access to the range of relevant information presumably in the possession of those who assert the ruth of the argument. One might well examine the course of midcentury American foreign policy from this perspective. How many "vital" naional decisions were taken at the behest of military men or diplomats vho described the state of the world in terms of their own value and speial interest orientations? These data are not normally available for inpection by "objective" social scientists until after the possibility for making significant alternate decisions has passed.

Emergent decision control. In the world of everyday affairs, the fuure often cannot be designed with precision because of uncertainties bout the state of future environments, uncertainties about the state of uture action systems, or simply because the analytic capability to calcuate optimal decisions for future action is not available. In short, it is ften necessary to make decisions in "emergent situations" (see Boguslaw, 1965).

How are design decisions made under these circumstances? One neans is to establish a set of working principles that can serve as a guide or specific actions as these become necessary. In the game of chess, a principle or heuristic, such as "Develop your pieces," may be used by the player who does not have any other specific guide for action in a particular situation. A government may use a heuristic such as "Try to maintain in power only friendly governments." A private corporation may use a heuristic like "Try to get business that will help insure long-run diversification for the firm," or, "Try to get business that will help maximize short-term profits."

In each of these cases, both the enunciation of the heuristic, and the opportunity to act upon it in a situation, constitute design decisions of enormous consequence for the shape of the future. The outcome of a chess match, or the future destiny of a business firm or country, can be shaped by the precise character of these heuristics and the precise way in which they are translated into action. When they are stated at an excessively high level of generality, a wide range of diverse decisions can be justified within their rubric. The designers of the future, under these circumstances, are not those who have enunciated the heuristics or even those who formally preside over their execution, but rather, those who implement the actions taken within their framework. In the case of a business firm, the dictum "Produce profits" is stated at this excessively high level of generality. Operating under this heuristic, the future of the firm may well be dependent upon the action steps taken by the sales force. In the case of a government, an illustration of a heuristic, stated at an excessively high level of generality, might be the following: "Red governments should be ousted from power; democratic governments should be supported." The definition of "red" or "democratic" is left to the discretion of the working diplomats and military planners.

Another mode of dealing with emergent situations is to invoke the use of "operating units" that make decisions whether or not these have been formulated in advance. Whether the operating unit is an antimissile system that will consider only the data its structure equips it to deal with or an ambassador or general who is given the prerogative to make "on-the-spot decisions," the design of the future properly begins with the selection of the equipment, or the ambassador, or the general, rather than with their actions or the broad operating directives that serve as their guides for action.

Another method for dealing with emergent situations is simply to determine that one will pay attention only to certain selected environments and make decisions in the future in terms of the readings made of these environments. Here, it is the determination about which environments or aspects of the environment are significant that constitutes the critical design decision.

TWO EXAMPLES

Having examined some of the characteristics of power mechanisms used in the imposition of order, I should now like to examine somewhat more closely two examples of these social design mechanisms in what may appear to be diametrically opposite areas of social concern. I shall call the first, "Program Budgeting Design," and the second, "Psychedelic Design."

Program budgeting design. This example is associated with a specific "planning technique" introduced by presidential fiat to the entire federal establishment of the United States in 1966—the technique of program budgeting.

The rationale for program budgeting is a relatively simple one. A modern government is concerned, we are told (Smithies, 1965), with the broad objectives of defense, law and order, health, education, and welfare, economic development, and with conducting certain business operations such as the Post Office. Since resources are always limited, each government must ultimately compromise among these objectives. The job of making the necessary compromises is the function of planning, programming, and budgeting. To make these compromises, it is necessary to express various government activities in terms of a common denominator; and the only one available is money. Although it may be difficult to compare the relative merits of an additional military division and an additional university, it is often feasible to compare the relative merits of spending an additional billion dollars in one direction or the other. To make this sort of comparison, it is first necessary to know how much an additional billion dollars will add to military strength and how much to university education (Smithies, 1965:25). In short, planning, programming, and budgeting involve the following:

1. Appraisals and comparisons of various government activities in terms of their contributions to national objectives.
2. Determination of how given objectives can be attained with minimum expenditure of resources.
3. Projection of government activities over an adequate time horizon.
4. Comparison of the relative contribution of private and public activities to national objectives.
5. Revisions of objectives, programs and budgets in the light of experience and changing circumstances (Smithies, 1965).

The analytic tradition from which all this is derived is, of course, cost-benefit analysis in economics, where attempts to obtain an efficient allocation of resources has become a familiar preoccupation. To conduct a

cost-benefit analysis of anything, it is important to keep in mind the van
tage point from which the analysis proceeds. Thus it might be possible tc
investigate motor vehicle accidents as if one were a rational governmen
decision-maker whose concern it is to maximize the net take in taxes ovei
some period of years. From this vantage point it would be possible tc
analyze the short-run or long-run tax costs of various measures designec
to reduce accidents. Within the framework of such an analysis, sooner oi
later it would become apparent that some accident prevention measure:
are not justified in terms of the tax benefits derivable from them. It woulc
be quite appropriate to place a monetary value on human life as civi
courts frequently do. Indeed, to exclude the fiscal value of human life
would be to make the analysis incomplete, given the vantage point from
which it was conducted.

Similarly, one could dramatically demonstrate the consequences oi
inadequate welfare and employment programs in our major cities by cal-
culating the total cost of urban riots in terms of insurance claims, loss oi
business, and property damage. It would be tempting to conduct such ar
analysis. One should, however, be prepared for the consideration of preventive measures such as shooting certain types of citizens on sight as the
most economical means for dealing with the problem. The burden oi
proof would then be placed upon those who did not wish to favor such
tactics to demonstrate its economic insufficiency. My personal objection
to such measures would rest on quite different grounds. And it is obvious
my concerns can be expressed in quantitative—but not necessarily in
economic—terms.

In a presumably pluralistic society one can postulate a plurality of
basic values among legislators and others, as well as a plurality of short-
range goals. Cost-benefit analysis can provide a useful service by displaying the implications of alternate programs so that they can be examined
from different value perspectives. From at least some of these, it is not
necessary (or desirable) to estimate such noneconomic factors as the
value of saving a human life. It is simply necessary to display the fact
that some programs result in more loss of life or degradation of the quality of life than others do.

The point I am trying to make is a simple one and not simply academic. Cost-benefit analyses and program budgeting are currently being
applied to the whole spectrum of federal government activities, including
welfare services, educational development, and urban planning—to say
nothing of defense. Economic data are available to serve as an impressive basis for program budgeting in the welfare field. Thus, it can be, and
has been, suggested that alternate welfare programs might be evaluated

by comparing the long-run benefits to "society" derivable from each of them. How does one compute "benefits to society"? By comparing earnings and tax returns of those individuals who are subjected to one welfare treatment with those subjected to another.

Conventional "planning" consists of behaviors taken within the framework of existing alternatives. A tool like program budgeting appears to be nothing more than a useful aid for conducting such planning. But the decision that specifies the range of alternatives to be considered is in fact a *design* decision. It is *not* a "scientific" decision.

In the practice of "science," problems for which adequate investigatory techniques are not available may be overlooked or quite deliberately ignored. A cardinal principle of conventional scientific investigation states that one must limit the size of one's problem to something that is manageable within the current inventory of scientific tools. One may address his efforts to the problem of enlarging this inventory, but even this investigation must finally be validated within the framework of currently acceptable instruments. If science chooses to provide no answer to a problem, one is provided by nonscientists or within the framework of nonscience. In social design efforts, it is equally true that some effects are more readily measured or estimated than others. In the program budgeting illustration, however, it is clear that benefits recommended for older recipients, or for those whose potential economic contribution to society is circumscribed because of racial discrimination or chronic illness, will be less than those recommended for others who are younger or have more prospects for financial success, given their skin color and other life circumstance.

If your value system includes a concern with people independent of their potential economic contribution to society, then it is necessary to begin with a completely different vantage point and develop a completely different set of measures. But unless a designer is found who wishes to represent this vantage point or who is required to conduct an analysis from this different perspective, it will not be done. And the analysis that is done will be completely defensible in its own terms. What is the "scientific" answer to this question? How many different vantage points must be represented in a social design process of this sort?

It is probably possible to demonstrate that there is an infinity of different vantage points from which an analysis *might* be conducted. The ones that *are* conducted are those representing sufficiently powerful interests so that the perspective from which they view the world cannot be ignored. But then, is it simply a political process? Do we resolve the problem by conducting a census of the various politically relevant interests in a given polity and prepare tentative designs from the view of each of them, letting the normal political process determine which of the various frameworks will be acceptable?

But it is not at all obvious that existing formally organized interest groups represent the range of de facto interests and value orientations that must or should be represented in a given society. Who will take the responsibility for defining the nonrepresented value orientations and conducting the necessary design from the perspective of these latent interests? Whose role is it to design social changes requiring fundamental modifications in basic social structures?

The guaranteed income proposed by Robert Theobald can be seen either as a simple substitute plan for existing welfare services or as a design involving fundamental alterations in the existing social structure. Theobald has described his proposal as an attempt to arrive at revolutionary change through evolutionary means. He sees it as culminating in a community where money doesn't matter very much. One can conceive of a cost-benefit analysis or program budgeting effort addressed to the problem of analyzing the guaranteed income proposal as an alternative to a range of war on poverty proposals or welfare programs that have burgeoned in recent years. The difficulty in carrying out such a planning effort would stem largely from the difficulty in ensuring that *all* relevant factors have been included within the framework of the analysis. As a design effort, however, the proposal begins from quite a different vantage point than do legislative programs of a more familiar variety. As a design effort, the guaranteed income proposal begins with fundamental changes in assumptions about the empirical manifestations of pleasure and pain. Money cannot provide pleasure because money is not a scarce commodity; absence of money cannot bring pain for the same reason. The guaranteed income proposal involves a view of people which sees them as sui generis, rather than as necessary adjuncts to a productive process. Within this different orientation, it is not at all obvious that certain forms of training or education would, in fact, constitute benefits and certain kinds of financial expenditures could reasonably be seen as costs. Under "normal" conditions, it is probable that no administration could afford the political risks involved in analyzing such a proposal from its own value perspective. Thus, Theobald's proposal is currently being widely discussed as the basis for a "negative income tax." In these terms it receives inside support from conservative economists and politicians concerned with reducing welfare expenditures. In these terms it remains a plan rather than a direct mechanism of social design. It can be seen as a social design effort only to the extent that, as a proposal, it opens up a new set of perspectives, creates a set of adherents, and culminates in the formation of an interest structure that will *do* something about its implementation, either on a public and political level or on a "bureaucratic," "secret," or "technical" level.

There is a growing (some commentators insist it is disappearing) interest structure in this country and other countries whose members apparently approach their own problems of living and acting in society from a vantage point very similar to that adopted by Theobald. They arrive, however, at quite different designs. I refer, of course, to the hippies. Their efforts constitute the second of the two examples in this section. Let us now briefly consider their mode of social design which we may call "Psychedelic Design."

Psychedelic design. It may well turn out that the hippies will prove to constitute the most significant change agents of our times. The professed values of the hippies include a formal disdain for most of the things that are valued very highly by the more conventional members of organized society. It is not only that money is not sought after (at least by authentic members of this interest structure), but conventional forms of status gratification and the physical concomitants of this gratification are rejected. The raison d'être for social participation is consciously proclaimed to be the living human being rather than the production of conventional goods and services. The rejection of dominant values includes not only the values of capitalistic society, but what appears to be the actual characteristics of many socialist societies as well. As Galbraith (1967:33–34) has put it, "The modern large corporation and the modern apparatus of socialist planning are variant accommodations to the same need. It is open to every free-born man to dislike this accommodation. But he must direct his attack to the cause. He must not ask that jet aircraft, nuclear power plants, or even the modern automobile in its modern volume be produced by firms that are subject to unfixed prices and unmanaged demand. He must ask instead that they not be produced."

A superficial reading of Galbraith would indicate he feels it is really asking too much to insist that these modern products not be produced in their present volume. Yet it should be observed that the hippie movement, in its implicit, if not always explicit, value orientation, addresses itself precisely to this problem. By consciously scaling down the level of their requirements for the products of modern industry and, indeed, generating new sets of requirements that cannot readily be provided by existing organizational forms, the hippies are rapidly constituting themselves as one of the most direct challenges to the "new industrial state."

But this challenge consists less in what the hippies themselves do or don't do than in the possible effects they may have upon the value orientations of the larger society. By explicitly calling into question some of the most cherished shibboleths of contemporary Western culture, the hippies may have an impact extending far beyond their wildest dreams. They are not planning a utopia; they are acting out and designing a utopia. And if the pitiful communitarian forms in which their social structures are couched depend ultimately upon a reciprocal benignancy, and even direct charity from the larger society, so much the better. They are not involved in a direct attack on institutions, but rather in a confrontation with alien value orientations. It is at this point that the most fundamental challenge to existing patterns of social design can occur.

I suppose I am saying simply that psychedelic planning is too important to be left to the hippies alone. Its major thrust, as I see it, involves alterations in sensory inputs so that new configurations of value, system states, and environmental content can be perceived. These new configurations can provide new vantage points from which social design can occur and new social forms brought into being. The use of drugs in this context is simply a less than completely satisfactory tool. It aids in the necessary restructuring but has a set of unfortunate side effects. Suppose one were to launch a research and development program to produce LSD with no undesirable effects. Or, suppose one could develop training and therapeutic techniques that would allow students or patients to see the world about them with completely new sets of lenses? The thought is not, of course, completely esoteric or even very new. Social psychologists for years have been experimenting with varieties of role playing, sociodramatic and psychodramatic techniques addressed more or less directly to this end (see the pioneering work of Moreno, 1946 and 1953). What new alternatives could middle-class America perceive and adopt as the basis for social design? Perhaps the most cogent criticism one can make of existing forms of social action and social planning carried out at the national, state, and community levels is that they are insufficiently psychedelic. Contemporary social planning does not involve sufficient alterations in existing perceptions of reality. It, therefore, does not lead to creative solutions for contemporary social difficulties.

PLANNING VERSUS ACTION

I began by asking you to think of social design as an activity directed toward the future and having as its primary consequence the specification of a range of alternatives for channeling social behavior. I asked you to think of social planning as something focused in the present consisting of social behaviors taken within the framework of existing alternatives.

Who are the more conventional specifiers of alternatives? They are the people who engage in social action. They are "doers." They are the "scientists," "engineers," and others who produced atomic bombs, high-speed computers, and missile systems. They are the architects who decided that uncovered heating pipes and incinerators on every other floor of a public housing project are "good enough" for the residents; the board of education that decided to build new public high schools to conform with existing patterns of segregation; the military staff officer who decided that military disaster would occur unless supplies were prevented from coming in from the north. They are also the commander-in-chief who decided there is no considerable risk in bombing targets on the border of mainland China. In each of these cases the action taken has the effect of broadly specifying ranges of future action alternatives. Subsequent social "planning" under these circumstances degenerates into little more than bureaucratic detail.

What can sociologists and deliberate social designers do about all this? They can adopt a "design" rather than a conventionally "scientific" orientation with respect to design problems. This inevitably involves social action on some level. Doing things and posing questions are both ingredients of effective social actions. Specifically:

1. They can identify significant perspectives for which no organized interest groups now exist. Biologists and chemists have helped identify problems resulting from such things as nuclear fallout, smog, and river pollution. Identification of the problem has resulted in interest group formation and more or less effective social action (the fact that this has been mostly less is another kind of problem). Demographers and others have pointed to the potential consequences of uncontrolled population growth. In other areas, economists have been active in attempting to demonstrate that the growth of automation does not constitute a severe economic threat to anyone if rate of increase in industrial productivity is used as a criterion. What about the social threats in the form of shifts in the distribution of power? Whose alternatives are being increased and whose decreased as a result of specific technological developments?

2. What are the dimensions of long-range social design implicit in contemporary social decisions? What slums are being designed through existing zoning codes or the current decisions and behavior of land developers? What military confrontations are implicitly being designed for today's students by products now on the drawing boards in computer, electronics, and aircraft industries? What implications do existing curricula in engineering schools have for the kinds of tasks to which future

generations of engineers and sociologists will address themselves? What impact will current financing practices in large corporations have for the kinds of entrepreneurial activities in which they will engage?

3. What technological breakthroughs *should* be made to help eliminate poverty and, slums, and to help ensure a peaceful world? What can mass-produced housing do? Or synthetic food products? Or transportation alternatives for the automobile and airplane? Is it technologically possible to eliminate poverty or are we really inevitably doomed to the necessity for political solutions that generate new classes of have-nots and require large-scale violence to ensure survival for the victors?

4. What are the technological as well as the political dimensions of social design? Can technical elites nurtured on a diet of weapons system development, a criterion framework of time and cost efficiency, and a "free enterprise" management ethos really address themselves to the technological tasks involved in providing human dignity and a peaceful planet? Can they and others really turn on and turn in?

Or must we all drop out?

REFERENCES

Boguslaw Robert
    1965   The New Utopians. Englewood Cliffs, N.J.: Prentice-Hall.
Fuller, Buckminster
    1967   "Report on the 'geosocial revolution.'" Saturday Review (September 16): 31–33, 63.
Galbraith, John Kenneth
    1967   The New Industrial State. Boston: Houghton Mifflin.
Homans, George Caspar
    1961   Social Behavior: Its Elementary Forms. New York: Harcourt, Brace & World.
Kuhn, Thomas S.
    1964   The Structure of Scientific Revolutions. Chicago & London: University of Chicago Press, first Phoenix edition.
Moreno, J. L.
    1946   Psychodrama. Vol. I. Beacon, N.Y.: Beacon House.
    1953   Who Shall Survive. Beacon, N.Y.: Beacon House.
Smithies, Arthur
    1965   "Conceptual framework for the program budget." Pp. 24–60 in David Novick (ed.), Program Budgeting, Program Analysis and the Federal Budget. Cambridge, Mass.: Harvard University Press.
Westin, Alan F.
    1967   Privacy and Freedom. New York: Atheneum.

Policy and the Urban Future

SCOTT GREER

It is my assumption that images of the future determine present actions. They may or may not determine the nature of the future—that depends upon a much more complex set of circumstances. But willy-nilly, much of our behavior is postulated upon images of a possible and/or desirable future. Furthermore, it seems useful to assume that certain assumptions about the immutable, the changeless and inescapable, limit and to a degree determine images of a possible and/or desirable future. Thus images of the future invasion and decline of a neighborhood influence the behavior of investor, dealer, and seller of real estate: the prophecy is fulfilled. But contrariwise, images of growth lead some to invest in worthless acres of Western desert: the prophecy was not fulfilled but the action was determined.

A very common image of cities in the United States is that of disorder, regression, decadence—in short, disorganization. There is neither space nor purpose for expanding this observation, nor for allocating responsibility for its currency. Suffice it to say that muckraking political scientists, welfare-oriented sociologists, and doomsday-identifying demagogues have tended to end with a similar image: "Things fall apart, the center cannot hold. Mere anarchy is loosed upon the world."

Of course, changes in organization will look like disorganization if one compares them only with a past state of affairs. Thus the processes of rapid urban settlement in the nineteenth and early twentieth centuries were widely regarded as a species of disorganization. The city was seen as intrinsically evil and evil in its results: some went so far as to organize the planned movement of urban youth back to the villages (while tens of thousands were sent back, however, other hundreds of thousands came forward).

Later the process of suburbanization was regarded as equally immoral. The growth of the horizontal neighborhoods on the peripheries (called slurbs), the proliferation of suburban municipalities (called a governmental crazy quilt), the declining dominance of the old downtown (called decay at the center) reflect a tacit comparison of current change with the real or imagined city of another age.

In similar fashion, changes in the ethnic mixture of the society were regarded as calamitous. Whether we read Thoreau's description of the Irish countryman who built his hut near Walden Pond or Henry Adams' reflections on the mongrelization of the United States, the comparison implied is the same. That ethnic mixture was richest in the cities, and there we find concern with Americanizing the immigrant, the decline of political standards with machine politics, the dominance of racial and religious differences in the urban polity. Moving, however, to a new state of the system, the release of ethnic votes from machine dominance and the release of social energy among the ethnic poor, black and white alike, provoke further alarm; some become nostalgic for the older situation where these energies were impounded by the bloc politics of the machines.

In short, our images of the urban future have been calamitous and catastrophic in their tonalities, for they have taken the past as norm and change as evil. Now changes *are* disorganizing, but only when they are partial and run contrary to fixed structures that predominate. But when a given change is congruent with other changes in the structure, it is possible that a *new* pattern will predominate. Universal literacy was seen as a potential disaster by those who felt it would be impossible to keep the lower orders in their place; as it turned out, literacy allowed for a transformation of the economy that radically improved the place of these orders. Of course, it is always a gamble as to just how change in one aspect will affect and be affected by other changes; my aim is to draw attention to it as a hazard, a gamble, and not an intrinsic evil. (We may note in passing that stability may also be disorganizing. When it is partial and contrary to a changing structure that predominates, it becomes as much a threat as partial change in a static structure. Racism in America is such a stability, destructive in its conflict with expanding economic and political scale.)

Thus I will reformulate the earlier proposition. While present policy is based upon images of futures and these are, in turn, limited by our notions of the immutable, these notions of the immutable are essentially ways of hedging our bets as to just what will prevail. Since what prevails is, to some degree, dependent upon what we do at present (as our efficacy depends upon the accuracy of our assessment), it is clear that we need the most rigorous standards for our images of the future city if our policy is to be more than sympathetic magic and public ritual.

IMAGES OF URBAN FORM

Our most prevalent image of the city is still one based upon the railroad centers of the *fin du siècle*. It is a clearly bounded, dense, centralized container for people, goods, and activities. Its boundaries—economic, political, and other—are congruent in space; the headquarters of each order is located near others at the center of the city. Center city is organizational hub and symbolic hearth of the metropolis as a whole; here power and wealth, style and grace, are on exhibit; here the urbanite communes with the meaningful symbols of his life.

The image rests upon a belief that centrality is an immutable necessity for an urban order. A single dominant area is thought to be required if a city is to persist (functionalism), if it is to maximize its wealth and numbers (boosterism), or if it is to optimize its contributions to social life (utopianism).

The policy directives of such an image are clear enough. One must try to effect a recentralization of those activities and structures that have got away from the center; one must maintain those that remain; to do these things one will most likely have to rebuild the core. One must also reincorporate activities outside the boundaries into the city, discouraging scatteration and sprawl.

The first set of policies, concerned with maintaining centrality, are clearly the inspiration for most of what is known as Urban Renewal. If central position has immutable value, then urban renewal efforts consist in making that value accessible for new investment. The second set of policies, aimed at reincorporation of the suburban areas, is clearly the base for the "metropolitan government" movements. Believing that clearly defined boundaries including all the relevant urban population are necessary for meaningful city government, backers of such movements aim at a redefinition of the city's political form.

But there is a second and competing image of the city. This image is of a vast, horizontal network of settlement held together by rapid means of transportation. In this image there is no single center; instead, there are many subcenters of activity and urbanites orient their activities to one or two of these, ignoring the others and ignoring the city as a whole. In this image of the city boundaries are vague; urban area, fringe, and hinterland merge; and growth at the peripheries is continuous. Such a view is sometimes called "conurbation"; I prefer to see it as an urban *texture* replacing the older urban *form*.

Underlying the image is the notion that the immutable process is that of decentralization. Decentralization is seen as an absolute requisite. For the city to persist as a functioning unit, decentralization is necessary, for a single center simply could not handle the transactions when population and activities pass a certain point. For the maximization of population one must maximize space; to maximize production one must also maximize space; thus the decentralized city is necessary to maximize profits. Finally, to optimize such amenities as private houselots, horizontal structures for industry and commerce, playgrounds and parking lots, decentralization is again necessary.

Should one accept decentralization as ineluctable and the horizontal urban texture as the accurate image of the city, certain policy directives follow. Ignoring the older core, once a center by historical and technological accident, one encourages decentralization by means of a developing, efficient transportation grid. One tries to guide the spreading texture of activity, to plan the subcenters so that they will provide the range of necessities and desirables, and to allow for adequate communication within and between the various subcenters. Policy is less interested in the incorporation of all the urban settlement within a single governmental unit—indeed, the boundaries of settlement may be so hazy that units are quite arbitrary. Instead, one looks for viable governmental subunits and ways of relating them to each other and to the larger whole, insofar as that is necessary.

CONCERNING IMMUTABLES

Of course, neither centrality nor decentralization is immutable and ineluctable. The first is not required, the second is not inescapable. A great deal of the dialogue between proponents of the two images simply rests upon generalizations from past views of one's favorite cities. But some of it rests upon major structural variables in the American political economy. They are givens, from the point of view of those concerned with any given city, but they are not inescapable for the nation as a whole.

Let us state these constraints in another form: *if* the national government allows local option in land use, and *if* it allows private option in location, *then* there can be no local urban policy. The free movement of the factors of production means that the economy, most basic in structuring the city, is beyond local control; that in-and-out migration, most basic in creating the city's human structure, is beyond local control; and finally, of course, that capital for new development and maintenance is also beyond local control. However, there cannot be a *national* policy for urban form either; local option in land use prevents it, and private option in mobility reinforces that prevention.

Given such limits, the most useful image of urban America is one based on the national playing field. The given urban settlement is a specialized part within a grid of locations ultimately determined by national markets in land, labor, and capital, and large-scale organizations (including governmental agencies) are the major players. For this "national city" there is no national policy; it is a collective output, the result of a great many aggregated and interacting decisions.

We may note a case parallel to that of urban form in the way civil rights have been handled. *If* we have local option in the definition of rights and their protection, and *if* we have private options in migration, hiring, lending and selling, *then* we have no possibility of local policy (because of private option) nor of a national policy (because of local options). But if we continue the analogy we note an important change: when political forces at the national level call civil rights a major problem for the national government, "immutables" are shifted around and changed. The result has been a decline in both local and private option, based upon increase in the national government's power.

When the shape and texture of our cities becomes a problem of major national interest, one would expect a similar development. The given dichotomies of control, between local and national, private and public, would be shifted in the direction of increasing national and public powers. For many purposes the corporation boundaries of the given city would become irrelevant, and even the metropolitan region would be subordinate to a larger image—that of the continental city-state. In an age of instantaneous communication and very rapid movement of men and materials, the national metropolitan network is as easy to move across as is any one of the great metropolitan complexes now emerging.

A NATIONAL URBAN POLICY

What would a national urban policy be like? First, remember that any policy has several dimensions; one we have discussed earlier—should we try to aim at a minimal order, at the simple persistence of a given state of things? (Most structural-functionalist theory really deals with no more than survival.) Or, should we aim at maximizing certain values—as the production and consumption of automobiles or the size of the Gross National Product? (Both require shoddy construction and rapid obsolescence to succeed.) A third alternative, more difficult intellectually and politically, would be to optimize a wide range of values for the cities, of which private profits and civic mercantilism would be only two. Let us look at some aspects of urban structures that a national policy should consider and form or reform.

Location and transportation. A national policy would certainly handle the question of the desirable size of population centers at given locations, in terms of a wide range of values. We get a notion of some of them through looking at the assorting process now going on. Population sometimes clusters around such natural resources as the factors of material production, but increasingly it is attracted by such resources as climate, landscape, foliage, and topography. Then too, accessibility of resources—whether it is the desert and beach, or clusters of universities, or the Broadway theater—has attraction. This leads us to ask: how would one so distribute the sites of action as to maximize choice and minimize the friction of space? Another perspective: How large should various cities be? How much concentration is required to provide a given range of opportunities? And, what ranges are desirable in terms of the present preferences of the population, as well as the preferences they *might* have if they were available?

The questions of efficiency of economic production and distribution remain. These, however, are not absolutes; our laissez-faire ideology has allowed them to become so. We must think in terms of opportunity costs, realizing that maximizing production of automobiles may vitiate esthetic and moral values. As a crude example, it is possible to minimize the death and disfigurement of human beings by automobile traffic through the use of engineering, layout, enforcement, and education programs. We can actually estimate the cost, in dollars spent (or average speed per mile traveled), of a human life. It can be programmed; but, when we do it, it becomes clear that we pay either way. How shall we decide how to optimize? What counts in the layout of urban America?

Thus far the marketplace, modified by temporary threats and bribes from state and local government, has been decisive. If we find we cannot afford this method of land allocation, then our only alternatives are overall control, either through administrative decree or piecemeal through the polity. Choices among values are finally amenable to neither science nor technology.

Science and technology do constitute dynamics in the process of policy formation: they increase our degrees of freedom. On the one hand, it is possible today, for the first time, to handle the enormous details of land-use data rapidly: with computers we can finally understand where we are without losing five years in gathering and processing data. On the other hand, we are increasingly free to engineer topography, climate, and amenities. Changes in transportation and communication shift the cost of separation in space, and the substitutability of materials makes the "resource base" city a candidate for extinction. Thus any policy for the location of urban sites and their integration must be sensitive to the changing limits of policy choice as well as the changing value hierarchies among the population.

Homogeneity and heterogeneity. A national urban policy would also deal with the problem of specialization versus given mixes of activity, economic and otherwise, for both the city as a whole and subareas within the city. Some specialization is already evident today, in university towns, resort towns, and various resource-based settlements. It could go much further; those who speak of the "Science City," or the "Educational Park" are proposing systematic and extreme forms of spatial concentration (and therefore segregation), of functions and of the populations that perform them.

One can argue for such concentration in terms of economies of scale. If it is necessary to have a special environment for a given activity, then the overhead declines per unit as we increase the action. At the same time, we would benefit from the multiplier effect. Thus if two physicists working together (or near one another) are more than twice as effective as when working alone, then concentration is the directive. Such activities as research, development, education and health, will undoubtedly absorb an increasing proportion of human time and energies; it is possible to build cities around such armatures, as we once built a Pittsburgh around iron and coal or, more to the point, a Las Vegas around sunshine and roulette wheels.

Within the city one can also argue for concentration and, therefore, segregation. To take an extreme case, one can argue for the utility of the ghetto for East European Jews; it provided a familiar shared environment, a protective community, and a specialized market for distinctively Jewish goods and services, including temple and school. Some argue for the utility of the present black ghettos; though there is an element of rationalization here, since most urban Negroes will probably live in black slums all their lives, there is also some validity. The argument for the Jewish ghetto holds in large part; in addition, it can be argued that there is more chance for a Negro child to grow up with self-respect and confidence when surrounded by his "peers" than when integrated with more affluent children of different pigmentation. And, at the same time, there is more possibility of political leverage, thus political education, in the bloc politics of the slum.

Both types of concentration, and the middle category, the planned suburbs (miscalled new towns) produce similar costs. They structure intergroup differences by using physical distance as barrier; they result in reinforcing the boundaries between the components of the society. They act to perpetuate existing differences and to generate new ones. The schism resulting may easily become parapolitical, political, or violently antipolitical. The latter result is, of course, most frightening to American sensibilities; it represents riot, rebellion, and revolution. However, we should not dismiss such alternatives out of hand; it may be argued that there is no way out of our impasse short of revolution.

Another objection offered to concentration and segregation is the sheer fact of separating the components of the world. Interdependence exists but is not perceived; and it gives the citizen a dangerously misleading map of his world. He knows, if he is white, that the black ghetto is strange, dangerous, and explosive; he does not know how important the black labor force and market are in the economy of the United States. In turn, the black man in the ghetto knows the white suburbs are exclusionist if not racist, snobbish, and wealthy and callous. They are exploiters. He does not know how critical to the working economy of the country are the droves of technicians, entrepreneurs, managers, and professionals who crowd the freeways in the rush hours.

And one may multiply such examples. Age and sex segregation are also well structured. How fares the middle-class male child who has never seen his father work? The women who have only the vaguest notion of where their money comes from? Businessmen, in their self-pitying moods, claim that nobody understands them; the toughest politician will occasionally say the same thing. Both are nearly correct and the same holds for many other specialties in our society. Increasing segregation, through Science City, might promote understanding within what is, after all, a narrow segment of the population, at the cost of increasing the superstitious popular view of the scientist as humanoid.

To summarize: if we concentrate, we segregate. The results may maximize the values of a specialized environment, may have a multiplier effect (for physicists or black politicians), or may be seedbeds for new cultural variations and inventions. They will certainly reinforce intergroup differences, actual and perceived, which has political dangers as well as dangers for the city as a teaching machine.

How shall we optimize? We experiment today with transportation as the binder, busing children out of their "neighborhood school" to others where the racial mix is different. We struggle for integration in an increasingly specialized and intellectually segregated world through experiments with "general education." But powerful knowledge, as Whitehead remarks, is specialized knowledge. How to avoid the ruts of social stereotype and intellectual narrowness—and the frightful dangers each represents for the human community? Would it help to mix activities on the same or adjacent sites, to bring work closer to the home? Would John Dewey's ideas, once tried for a while in the Gary schools, yet work? Could we, as the Soviets do, combine real work with study for youngsters, and systematically vary their work experiences? These questions are implicit in the major policy dilemma: how shall we relate a heterogeneous population so as to maximize, and thus optimize, both social creativity and social integration?

And again, we must accept the likelihood of major change. There will be, through public education and the mass media, a continuing acculturation to the broad normative and belief system of lumpen-middle-class America. This system will also be in motion with new inputs from a society increasingly college-educated. Technology, which already makes many locational decisions of the past obsolete, will continue its dance of Shiva, destroying as it creates. As the labor force continues to move from industry to the services and professions, the reasons for towns change. And, as the quinary industries—health, education, welfare, research and development, the arts and crafts—become increasingly important, we may forego the massive urban complex for a reticulated system of land use, with areas of high concentration in one activity shading off into areas where the activity is cognate but different. Thus, one could imagine an urban fabric without sharply demarcated spatial boundaries. As for social and cultural integration, we have hardly begun to put our minds to it; our policies have been hand-me-downs from an earlier era, strongly tinctured of Social Darwinism and minimal charity.

Local and national government. A national urban policy is contingent on a reordering of local government and would make such a reordering possible. The problem is still that of the relationships possible and desirable between the smaller community and the large, between part and whole. With our federal system we have maximized the freedom of the states and, through them, the municipalities to control their own destinies at the cost of stalemate, confusion, and inaction. We have tried to increase citizen participation and the adequacy of representation through using small communities as polities; we frequently achieve citizen indifference and do-nothing representation. One of the reasons is the trivial issues of local government, due to what Robert Wood calls the "segregation of needs from resources," and due also to the limited scope of the jurisdiction.

To be specific, this range of values is involved: (1) a working consensus, thus legitimacy, for local government; (2) democratic processes at the local level; (3) efficacy in resolving conflict and in directing collective enterprises; and (4) a scope of action adequate to the empirically problematic situation. The first is required of all government; the second is the American solution to the problem, "Whose ox shall be gored?"; the third is the difference between government and custom; the fourth is implied by the third. Thus we must find in local government answers to such questions as: Who should control the use of land? How shall we tax and whom and how much? Failing consensus on issues, whose norms shall be honored in such matters as civil rights, urban renewal, educational policy?

In optimizing values at the level of local government we shall have to recognize the increasing interpenetration of the nation and the city. Many of the major decisions, for any given city, are made far away; if the city is to have any say in its destiny, it must depend upon a *national* interest brokerage, a national policy, to guarantee it. Equity in taxing and spending must be national, for the notion of minimal standards (in housing, education, health) implies redistribution of income from rich regions to poor. Planning, as we have already noted, must in its broad outlines be national for the whole playing field is involved.

Yet the local community may still be viewed as a laboratory for the discovery and improvement of democracy. At the local level of government, as in more private enterprises, there is a potential of creativity and sensitivity that are worth nurturance. Thus within an increasingly national policy it would be possible to allow for the maximum freedom to vary congruent with national goals. The smaller communities are interrelated within the framework of the larger; this is an obvious fact, yet our eighteenth-century jealousy of central government has blinded us to it. But this is true only for government. Everyone knows his profession, his corporation, his union, to be deeply dependent upon a larger network within which his state and city are only parts—as each profession, corporation, or union is only one part of his city. The problem is, in short, to reform government in view of the organizational topography of the total society.

And this must be done within a context of change; thus we should not repeat the mistake of those who, believing history was over, wrote constitutions "once and for all." We can expect the space-time ratio to continue to shrink, accessibility among the parts of the country to increase. We can expect organizational and physical space to change in their relationships as a consequence. We once saw centralization as the dominant fact in our social organization; with today's technology one sees, in many enterprises, a centralization of control and a decentralization of activities. Publishing is centered in New York City, but printing is a much more decentralized activity. Television broadcasting is centered in Hollywood, but the consumption is as scattered as households are. In short, our use of physical space changes our social organization. Government must accept and, if possible, use this fact.

Decentralization of the routine functions of local government is beginning to appear in a number of cities. More important, there is considerable interest in decentralizing certain classes of decision-making; who after all should be concerned with the location and design of a neighborhood park, street lights, or traffic signals? There are certain broad limits, since the neighborhood is part of a larger matrix of activity, but within these limits probably the people who live there.

CODA: CAN WE GET THERE FROM HERE?

The basic problem is still the expansion of national public power, at the expense of local and private control. And a national policy, is, as noted, contingent on changing local-national relationships. How can it come about? This chapter deals with the study of futures, not with controlling them, yet it is important to note that accurate study is in some degree dependent on control—who leaves political change out of his forecast does so at his peril.

I see several trends moving us toward basic decisions on the proper state of the nation. First, the crescive changes, the massive trends that are not the result of policy but whose effects and side effects condition and trigger policy. Rising educational levels, instantaneous communication through electronic media, increasing prosperity, all point toward increased leisure for political learning and action among the masses. If it is true that responsibility is a luxury that only the powerful can afford, we are socializing the potential for power at a great rate. It may result in a demand for a national government.

This trend will be reinforced by the continuing harvest of our present policies. By default we have concentrated "outsiders"—poor, black, and volatile—at the vulnerable centers of our metropolitan complexes; besides them we have concentrated others, "semi-outsiders," poor, white and volatile. We have given over the function of policing to still others, barely insiders, who have bitter memories of racial competition and conflict. We have built self-perpetuating enclaves of people who are indifferent to, if not enemies of, the dominant moral order of middle-class white society, and they can be moved against the physical structure of that society.

The result is pressure for national urban policy. That policy may take into account the range of values I have been adumbrating in this paper; it may move through the expensive and difficult and unpredictable paths of innovation and amelioration. We have many signs of such a movement. It may, of course, result in the brutal logic of suppression with the troops who today patrol a large part of the non-American earth recalled to patrol the centers of our great cities. Much depends upon the efficacy of our education, formal and informal; what have Americans learned from their public school, mass media, and the community—their teaching machines?

We may have learned enough to demand or at least accept a national urban policy. It would allow us to break the stasis that has left us without the will or tools to shape the communities where most of us are at home; it would be frightening to many, for it would mean a final rejection of many myths of the agrarian past.

One such is the belief that urban government is general government rather than specialized and limited; another is the conviction that the inhabitants of a given area have some basic right to govern themselves; another is the continuing belief that the city is "hallowed ground," with a putative immortality. These are aesthetic yearnings at best, fraudulent claims at worst; in any event, they have resulted in tunnel vision. Focusing upon the given concrete sprawl of buildings and activity, we have been unable to see the vast, interrelated network that is urban America. Until we do so, our urban renewal and governmental reforms are, in Norton Long's words, "civic fig leaves," sops to outraged conscience.

REFERENCES

Long, Norton
    1962   The Polity. Chicago: Rand McNally.
Whitehead, Albert North
    1925   Science and the Modern World. New York: New American Library.
Wood, Robert C.
    1961   1400 Governments. Cambridge, Mass.: Harvard University Press.

Images of the Future and Organizational Change: The Case of New York University

J. VICTOR BALDRIDGE

Most studies on organizational change have focused on "rational planning" as it is implemented in business organizations. Although such studies often mention future-oriented goals that guide the development of rational plans, such future orientations themselves are seldom critical foci of research. One exception was Philip Selznick's (1948) work on the Tennessee Valley Authority, in which he devoted considerable attention to the image of the future that the TVA articulated, and the consequences of putting that image into practice. Also, Charles Perrow (1961), among others, has dealt with the problem of goal-setting in organizations, but the systematic analysis of future images was not an important feature of his work. All in all, organizational theorists have devoted little attention to orientations toward the future, beliefs, and values as they bear on organizational change.

This chapter reports the results of a study of organizational change that focused on images of the future and goal-directed behavior as they affect organizational policy and planning. The research, which is being funded by the "organizational context group" of the Stanford Research and Development Center on Teaching, grows out of an analysis of change in organizations. It is part of a long-term project that is attempting to develop some theoretical frameworks and empirical support for a theory of organizational change. In addition, this particular chapter depends heavily upon research on organizational change that I conducted a New York University (NYU) in 1967 and 1968 (Baldridge, 1971). Tha project was a field study in which interviews, participant observatior techniques, documentary analysis, and a questionnaire of the facult were used to assemble data about policy formulation procedures.

ORGANIZATIONAL CHANGE: CONSTRAINED NECESSITY OR IMAGES OF THE FUTURE?

It is necessary to touch briefly upon one of the most persistent argu ments cutting through the study of social change, because it is relevant tc the concerns of this research. There seem to be two dominant answers tc the question of how change is caused (see Etzioni, 1964: especially 6–9) On one hand, a school of social change, usually associated with Marx, ar gues that change is provoked by constraining factors that force some type of adaptation. This theory might be called "adaptation to con straints." Although Marx took somewhat different points of view in var ious writings, he is interpreted by most writers as saying that socia change was promoted by the material and economic features of society and that value positions and ideological statements were only an intellec tual superstructure for justifying and explaining that material base. Al though oversimplified as stated, this is a persistent theme in sociologica analyses of change: that change is promoted by external conditions, ma terial factors, or structural features. From this perspective, change is largely a question of adaptation to necessity or to chance, not of rationa planning or goal-oriented behavior. Most organizational change theo rists seem to fall more or less within this school, since they emphasize the importance of technological advances, the unintended consequences of bureaucratic structure, and the unplanned and unintended features of in formal group processes. For them change is not planned or goal-directed but is instead dictated by the necessity to adapt to some structural con dition, be it economic, organizational, or technological.

On the other hand, a second explanation for the causes of change grows out of the work of Max Weber. Rather than focusing upon Marx's "real factoren," Weber focused upon the "ideal factoren." Where Marx had focused upon the technological, economic, structural, and material istic base as the prime agents of social change, Weber stressed the role of future orientations, ideological components, and value positions. His classic study of *The Protestant Ethic and the Spirit of Capitalism* (Weber, 1958) attempts to show how value orientations promoted socia change in Puritan America. This strand of sociological analysis empha sizes the importance of planning and the critical role that—to use the erms of this book—"images of the future" play in promoting social change.

Thus, there has been a long-standing debate about social change. On one hand are the proponents of "hard" factors such as structural features of the organization, technological innovation, and economic necessity. On the other hand are the proponents of rational planning, values, and future orientations as causes of social change. Although the battle between the "realists" and the "idealists" continues, it is increasingly obvious that the two views are actually complementary.

This chapter stresses the role of ideal factors, ideological positions, and images of the future as they affect organizational change. It will be necessary throughout the chapter, however, to point out the interrelationships between structural and the ideal factors, since the latter are always framed and supported by structural features and the external environment. Thus, much of our discussion will be related to showing how "images of the future" and "constrained necessity" dovetail in an adequate interpretation of organizational change. This is one of the critical theoretical issues to which the research at New York University was addressed, and it is to that case study that we now turn.

The following are some of the critical questions that guided the study of change processes at NYU:

1. How do constraint factors and images of the future interact in the empirical situation as the organization changes? In other words, how can we weave together the insights derived from Marx and Weber?

2. What is the role of critical organizational elites and interest groups in change?

3. How do groups in the organization interact to set the content of the image of the future?

4. How do abstract images of the future become operationalized into concrete policy?

5. Once the image has been operationalized, what kinds of political debate and activity surround its implementation?

6. How are structural adjustments made to protect the new goals and images?

7. What kinds of consequences, intended and unintended, flow from the implementation of the image?

CHANGE AT NYU: IMAGES OF THE FUTURE IN ACTION

Pressures for changing NYU's traditional role. The role that a university plays in society is both planned and accidental, both deliberate and a whim of fate. The role that NYU plays as an institution of higher education, for example, is a strange mixture of historical events, deliberate planning, and pressure from many sources. For many years NYU had a consistent interpretation of its role in New York higher education. From its founding the university offered educational advantages to all types of people, including underprivileged minority groups. NYU accepted students of relatively low academic ability, giving them the opportunity to get an education if they applied themselves, this policy being part of a consistent philosophy about the university as a "School of Opportunity." In this sense NYU was in the best tradition of the great "American Dream."

This orientation was more than idle rhetoric, since in many ways it was an operating principle of the university, which permeated the campus and gave it a distinct "institutional character." Generations of NYU students and faculty testify to the importance of this philosophy to their lives, and many a Wall Street businessman and New York teacher will give credit to the chance that NYU afforded him. Large groups of the faculty were strongly dedicated to this ideal, and were willing to fight when that image of the university was threatened.

Times were changing, however, and this image of NYU came under attack. Not all the members of the university community were happy with a philosophy that accepted large numbers of relatively poor students and then failed many of them. As one professor said during my field work in 1967–1968:

> Sure, we were the great teacher of the masses in New York City. In a
> sense this was a good thing, and we undoubtedly helped thousands of stu-
> dents who otherwise would never have had a chance. But we were also
> very cruel. We had almost no admissions standards, and a live body with
> cash in hand was almost assured of admission. But we *did* have academic
> standards and we were brutal about failing people. There were many years
> in which no more than 25–30% of an entering class would graduate. Sure,
> we were the great "School of Opportunity" for New York, but the truth of
> the matter is that we were also the "Great Slop Bucket" that took every-
> body and later massacred them (Baldridge, 1971, Interview #11).

From the inside, then, there was mounting opposition to the "School of Opportunity" philosophy with its low admission standards and high failure rates. In particular, professors from liberal arts and graduate units objected to standards that lowered the university's student quality. Internal pressure was slowly building up for a different image for NYU.

External events were also pressing the university toward a re-evaluation of its mission and image. Organizations are seldom the sole masters of their fates, because external forces of various kinds impinge upon them, shaping, remaking, and molding them in many ways. NYU exists in an environment in which other universities are competing for resources, students, and social influence. For many years NYU was the major "service university" in New York that took the masses of students. Both the City University of New York and Columbia maintained extremely high standards, and did not serve the bulk of the student population.

In the late 1950s, however, the picture changed, and the state and city began to assume more responsibility for educating the masses. An extensive network of junior and senior colleges was opened and expanded, and the public university enrollments shot up dramatically. The public institutions charged very little tuition, while privately supported NYU was forced to charge extremely high fees—in fact, among the highest in the nation. In short, the competitive position of NYU with respect to the public colleges and universities was eroded as the public colleges and universities began usurping the role of educating the masses in New York City.

The effects of the expansion of the public colleges were rapid and dramatic. In 1956 NYU published the results of its *Self-Study*. This study was a major attempt at long-range planning and foreshadowed many of the changes that were to occur shortly. The authors of that farsighted document were at least aware of the threat that the public institutions held for NYU, but it is doubtful that they understood how close that threat was. In fact, they stated with some confidence,

> Even the enormous expansion of the tuition-free city college system with its excellent physical plan has not as yet substantially affected the character of NYU. . . . (New York University, 1956:11)

The *Self-Study* went on to predict increasing enrollments for NYU over the decade from 1955 to 1966. By the early 1960s, however, it was obvious that the expected growth was simply not materializing, and that thousands of students who previously would have come to NYU were going to public institutions. Figure 1 gives a comparison between the *Self-Study* projections and the actual enrollments for the period 1955–1966. By 1966 the actual figures were running a full 20 percent—over 9,000 students—behind the predictions. As one administrator viewed it, "We certainly anticipated pressure from the City. University, but frankly the pinch came ten years ahead of our expectations" (Baldridge, 1971, interview #16).

NYU was seriously threatened by the competition of the public universities; they were losing potential students and the financial stability of the institution was being undermined by the loss of vitally needed expected tuition. The question was how to meet the challenge, how to frame

Number of Students Enrolled

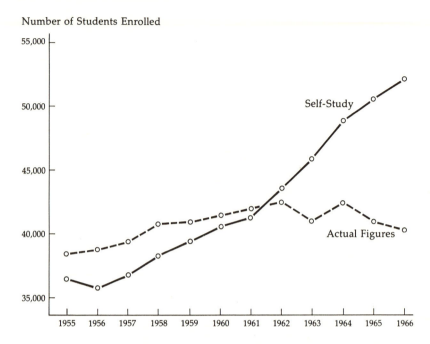

Source: *The Self-Study.* New York: New York University Press, 1956, p. 9.

Figure 1. Comparison of enrollment figures: *Self-Study* projections and actual figures, 1955–1966.

a new image of the university that would serve the educational needs of the people and the organizational needs of NYU.

The struggle for a new image of the future. From a sociological perspective it is critical to see that the resultant plans for the future were framed by a context of conflict, and that pressures were impinging on the decision-makers from different sides. Internally, there were the pressures for change from the liberal arts groups and from the graduate schools, and externally there were challenges from the public universities. Although the forces for change were great, there were also groups, inside and outside the university, that had strong vested interests in the status quo. At least two major units of the university, the School of Education and the School of Commerce, were strongly committed to the "School of Opportunity" image. Many influential alumni, moreover, were committed to this same approach, since they had benefited from it. It was, of course, exactly this philosophy that was being challenged as the university searched for its new educational role. Thus, a confrontation was virtually inevitable.

By the end of 1961 a debate about the future of the university was raging behind closed doors, the disagreements going far deeper than the mere question of how to recruit more students, since the essential issue was really about NYU's total educational mission. Could NYU continue with business-as-usual, or was this a critical turning point? Many of the top administrators felt that the time was ripe for a deep-rooted and sweeping evaluation of NYU's future destiny, particularly in light of the financial crisis that was facing the institution.

Relevant to the analysis of images of the future that we have been trying to carry out in this research, the debate at this point involved the *goals* and long-range commitments of the university. The assessment at this stage was *not* that the university should adopt some new type of management techniques to solve its financial crisis, but that it would have to develop new goals and new orientations to the future if it was to survive as a significant contributor to American higher education. Confronted with pressures from many sides, the leaders of the university deliberately started to "tinker with the future." NYU consciously sought to change its goals, and deliberately began the creation and projection of a new self-image, a new institutional character. In essence a paradox was developing. The "constraint" factors were forcing the university into an examination of its future goals and ideological commitments; in turn this would lead to new structures and organizational behavior and, of course, to new and different future constraints. Marx and Weber were joining hands.

Several events accelerated the changes. First, in 1962 James Hester, who had been the Executive Dean of the Liberal Arts units, was selected to be the new president. He was acutely aware of the problems facing the university and made it his first order of business to confront them. Second, the Ford Foundation invited NYU to make an application for a comprehensive development grant. This opportunity was seized as a critical element of financial support for the planned changes. Eventually Ford made one of the largest grants in its history, $25 million, to support NYU's planned changes.

In early 1962 several committees were appointed to formulate plans for the Ford request. At this time it became progressively clearer that many of NYU's critical problems had to be faced if the grant was to be educationally meaningful. Many questions about NYU's future educational role came under scrutiny. Numerous faculty bodies were invited to prepare plans that would be included in the Ford requests. How those discussions eventually reached the decision stage is debatable. Many faculty members claim that the critical decisions were really made by a small group of administrators without much consideration of the faculty, while some administrators claim that the faculty's contribution was limited because of the faculty's inability to look beyond the needs of their individual departments or schools to the needs of the entire university.

In any event, it is fascinating to note how deliberately and consciously the university community began to plan its future. The debates, fact-finding, and committee work for the Ford requests went on for more than a year. During this time the university's future was being debated on one of those rare occasions when an organization really maps out its destiny. Rather than responding impulsively to the pressures of the moment, the university was attempting to plot realistically its future course after a careful study of its needs, and then to engage in explicit decision-making.

By the fall of 1963 the Ford Report was completed and the implementation of future policies awaited the Foundation's decision. Ford responded generously, expressing strong confidence in the plans for the reshaping of NYU. NYU was challenged to raise $75 million from other sources to match Ford's $25 million. The financial resources for the changes were now at least possible, although securing the $75 million did not look easy.

There was no single plan that emerged from the Ford Report evaluation, but instead there was a complex, interconnected series of changes to promote NYU's new image of the future. They included:

1. Undergraduate admissions standards would be raised substantially.

2. The fragmented undergraduate program (with Education, Commerce, Washington Square College, Engineering and University College each having separate programs) would be unified.

3. An "urban university" orientation would be developed.

4. More full-time faculty and students would be recruited, and more on-campus residences would be provided.

5. More energy would be directed toward graduate and professional training, so that direct undergraduate competition with the state university would be avoided.

Although not all these decisions were implemented at the same time, over a period of months these moves began to gain momentum. It is important to note several things about these decisions. First, they represented basic, far-reaching changes concerning the very nature of NYU. In a sense, the old NYU was to be significantly transformed. Second, the relation to the external social context is particularly critical, for NYU was under serious attack from competing institutions that were undermining its traditional role. In large measure these decisions represented a "posture of defense" for NYU, since without them it is quite probable that the university would have been forced into severe retrenchment and

stagnation as the public institutions assumed its traditional role and cap-
tured its traditional student population. Third, however, the posture of
defense allowed a realistic confrontation with reality and the development of new images of the future which could well turn NYU from potential disaster toward a vital new educational role. Thus, the "constrained necessity" interpretation of organizational change interlocks
here with the "image of the future" approach.

The role of critical elites in shaping the new image. All studies of future images as causes of social change have to confront the question of
whose image is accepted, and this raises the question of elites and interest
groups. From the point of view of most people at NYU the new decisions "came down from the top." Without doubt, a small group of top administrators made the critical decisions. There were many strong complaints that the new policies were often arbitrarily made by top officials
with little faculty consultation.

To be sure, the University Senate was consulted about most of the
plans, but at that time the Senate was relatively weak and most people
believe that it merely rubber-stamped a series of decisions that had already been made. As one Senate member put it;

> We were "informed" about these matters, and we were asked to vote our
> approval, but I wouldn't say we were actually "consulted" in any meaning-
> ful way. It was a one-way street—they told us what they were going to do
> and we said "OK" (Baldridge, 1971, interview #23).

Of course, many faculty committees were working on the Ford Report,
but many people suggest that the critical decisions did not actually come
from these committees. The first time most of the faculty knew about
them was when they were publicly announced, as one rather bitter professor in the School of Commerce commented:

> The School of Commerce was about to have its throat cut and we didn't
> even know about it until after the blood was flowing! Sure, Hester came
> over and gave us a little pep talk about how much this was going to im-
> prove things, but he didn't really ask our advice on the issue. He didn't
> exactly say it was going to be his way "or else," but we got the point
> (Baldridge, 1971, interview #20).

On the other side of the issue, the administration clearly saw the
threats facing NYU from the public universities. From their perspective
it was clear that something radical had to be done—and quickly. Several
administrators expressed strong disappointment in the faculty's contribution to the Ford report, declaring that most of their ideas were conservative and bound by entrenched loyalties to departments and schools. In effect, many administrators thought—probably correctly—that they had a

broader perspective from which to view the problem than most of the faculty, and therefore that it was their duty to move into the situation as the key "change agents." It is also clear that they knew some of the moves would be violently opposed, and extensive consultation might arouse enough hostility to kill the whole matter. As President Hester explained it to me:

> The University was confronted with critical conditions. We had to undertake action that was radical from the standpoint of many people in the University. Some of these changes had to be undertaken over strong opposition and were implemented by administrative directives. In two of the undergraduate schools a number of faculty members had accepted the "school of opportunity" philosophy as a primary purpose of their school. This had been justifiable at one time, but no longer. Many faculty members simply did not recognize that circumstances had changed and did not accept the fact that the service they were accustomed to performing was now being assumed by public institutions at far less cost to the students.
>
> At this point the administration had to be the agent for change. It was incumbent upon us to exercise the initiative that is the key to administrative leadership. In the process, we did interfere with the traditional autonomy of the schools, but we believed this was necessary if they and the University were to continue to function (Baldridge, 1971, interview #24).

It might be helpful to examine some of the factors that enabled the administrators, as a critical elite, to execute this change so successfully. Strong opposition to the planned changes could reasonably be expected, since many people would be adversely affected. In additon, some people resented what they believed was arbitrary action from the top. How did the policy succeed despite this opposition? What factors were working in favor of the central administration as it moved to implement these transformations? Why was one elite successful in winning the battle over the new image of the future?

First, the power of the central administration had been greatly enhanced after nearly a decade of centralization in the university, starting with the strong leadership of President Henry Heald in the early 1950s. Before Heald's administration NYU had been a very loose collection of essentially autonomous schools. During his tenure, however, many changes were implemented that brought much power to the central administration. President Hester's success very much depended on President Heald's success several years earlier. If the same moves had been attempted a decade earlier, they might well have failed.

Second, Hester was a new, popular president who could still rely heavily on the "honeymoon effect" to win support without too much threat. The trustees were obviously going to back their new man, even if a substantial part of the faculty opposed the move—which they did not. As one Commerce professor noted, moreover, "He's as close to a popular president as any you'll find, and that makes him a hard man to beat on most issues." The general faculty appears to agree with this verdict. When they were asked to indicate their "General confidence in the central administration of the university" on a questionnaire, they indicated a high degree of confidence. We can show the increase by comparing this identical question with a 1959 Faculty Senate Survey.

Degree of Confidence in the Central Administration
(in percent)

	High	Medium	Low	Total	Number of Cases
1959 (Faculty Senate Survey)	40	18	42	100	(596)
1968 (Baldridge Survey)	47	32	21	100	(693)

The popularity of the central administration and Dr. Hester's newness to the presidency were major assets as the administration struggled to implement its decisions.

Third, large segments of the faculty offered considerable support for these changes. Cross-pressures from interest groups on either side of an issue often allow decision-makers more freedom, and allow them to press for changes that would have been impossible if most groups lined up in opposition. In this case, many liberal arts professors were strongly in favor of the rise in admissions standards, especially since the new standards hurt the nonliberal-arts units hardest. In addition, many graduate-level professors felt that raised standards in the undergraduate levels would indirectly improve the graduate programs and would certainly give them better undergraduates to teach. Thus, there were powerful interest groups supporting the change, as well as opposing it.

Fourth, the decisions were successful because of the obvious bureaucratic weapons that the central administration controls. The admissions office at NYU is centralized, and the central administration could achieve some of its new goals simply by instructing the admissions office to raise standards, thus effectively by-passing the opposition that centered in some schools. In addition, the twin powers of the budget and personnel appointment were brought to bear often in the struggles that followed the decisions.

Finally, one of the most important reasons that these dramatic changes could be introduced was the external threat that NYU faced from the public institutions. It is one of the most common findings of sociological research that groups threatened by outside forces will tolerate many internal changes that otherwise they would adamantly oppose. NYU was in truth threatened. The administration recognized the threat and was willing to fight to implement changes that would protect the university. The trustees, moreover, were convinced that these changes were imperative, and they stood solidly behind the administration in the struggles that erupted.

Translating an image of the future into action. The years 1962–1963 and 1963–1964 were clearly watershed years for NYU, for the decisions based on a new image of the future began to be carried out during that period. The effects were dramatic and had repercussions throughout the university. For one thing, admissions of undergraduates dropped sharply. In the period from 1962 to 1965, undergraduate admissions dropped by a stunning 20 percent. This dramatic change is illustrated in Figure 2, which compares new entering students (both freshmen and transfers) and the entire enrollment (both full-time and the full-time equivalent). The sharp dip is largely due to the increased admissions standards. It is extremely important to remember that the drop in enrollment cut off vitally needed tuition funds at the very moment when approximately $10 million above normal costs were desperately needed in order to carry out various aspects of the quality upgrading. By 1967, however, the new policy appears to have been successful, for enrollment was again rising as the university attracted large numbers of better students (see Figure 2).

A second indicator of the impact of the changes was the rise in the test scores of entering freshmen. Figure 3 shows the Scholastic Aptitude Test (S.A.T.) scores of entering NYU freshmen from 1961 to 1966. Arnold Goren, the Director of Admissions, is probably doing more than exercising his public relations duties when he calls this a "fantastic" increase for this short time.

A third indicator of the changes is related to student housing. As part of the new role for NYU, more emphasis was placed on obtaining more students from outside New York City, and upon drawing more full-time resident students. The university was forced to provide student housing on a large scale. The recruitment of a full-time faculty, moreover, also demanded more housing, and the university added faculty residences almost as rapidly as it did student housing. The increase in students who are housed directly by the university is shown in Figure 4.

A fourth change that accompanied the new image of the future was the change in the composition of the graduate student enrollment. There has been a major shift in emphasis toward more full-time graduate students, while the number of professional students has remained relatively constant. This change is very clearly shown in Figure 5. Changing the numbers to percentages, in 1960 only 23 percent of the graduate enrollment was full-time, while by 1967 the full-time percentage was 55. This means that the absolute number of full-time graduate students has *tripled* in only seven years. In fact, NYU's commitment to graduate and professional education is shown by the fact that of the total number of degrees granted in 1967 (6,908) nearly two-thirds were either graduate or professional (4,549).

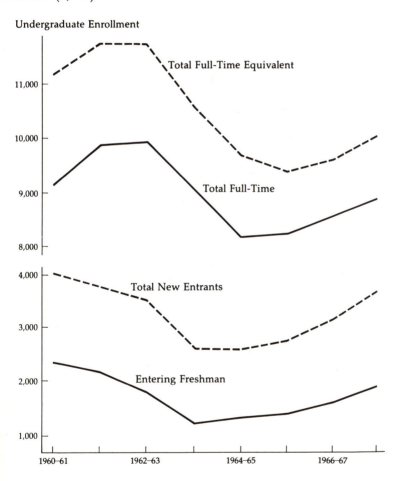

Undergraduate Enrollment

Total Full-Time Equivalent

11,000

10,000

9,000

Total Full-Time

8,000

4,000

Total New Entrants

3,000

2,000

Entering Freshman

1,000

1960–61   1962–63   1964–65   1966–67

Source: Chancellor Allan M. Cartter, "An Analysis of New York University." New York: New York University, mimeographed, 1968.

Figure 2. Undergraduate enrollment, New York University, fall 1960 through 1967–1968.

A fifth change was the development of the Coordinated Liberal Studies Program. NYU had undergraduate programs in Washington Square College, University College, School of Engineering, School of Commerce, and the School of Education. Many of these programs were almost exact duplications, and often courses even had the same titles. High administrative overhead, inefficient use of faculty, and the ineffective utilization of space were only a few of the problems caused by this duplication. In addition, segregation of the courses into schools meant that students were often isolated and could seldom have the intellectual stimulation that is encouraged by diversity in the classroom.

By the mid-1950s many people believed that the goals of the university could be best served by a consolidation of the undergraduate programs. From a purely rational or purely financial basis, there seemed to be little justification for the fragmentation of the undergraduate units, and the so-called "Gallatin College" concept was proposed by Chancellor George Stoddard. This college was to consolidate all the undergraduate units for the first two years, including the professional schools. The plan seemed reasonable, and would eliminate much duplication while

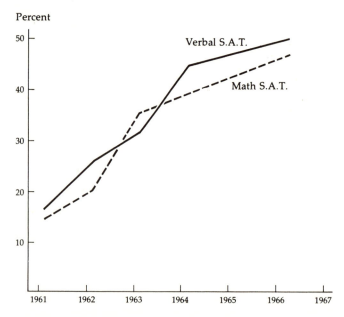

SOURCE: Chancellor Allan M. Cartter, "An Analysis of New York University." New York: New York University, mimeographed, 1968.

FIGURE 3. Percentage of freshmen with S.A.T. scores above 600, 1961–1966.

lowering educational costs and expanding the horizons of the students. At that time, however, the plan was politically premature and was quickly killed by the opposition of the various schools that had vested interests in the fragmented pattern. The only action was a committee set up to study the problem of duplication.

In 1960 James Hester became the Executive Dean of Arts and Science at NYU. Coming from outside the university, he was amazed at the administrative duplication in the undergraduate program. But he was unable to do anything from that vantage point in the university, especially since the Gallatin College idea was so strongly opposed. In 1962 when Hester became President of the university, he was in a position to renew the battle for coordination. In February 1963 a commission was set up to make new plans for some type of compromise coordination system. Eventually plans for the Coordinated Liberal Studies Program were included in the Ford Report. In September 1964 the program was officially launched, over the strong opposition of the same groups that had pre-

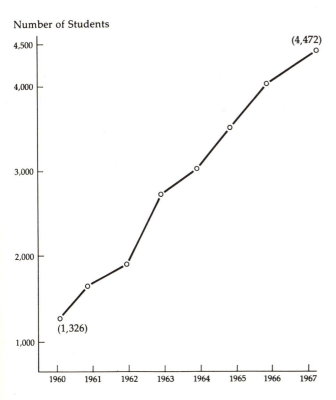

FIGURE 4. Number of students in university housing, 1960–1967.

Number of Students

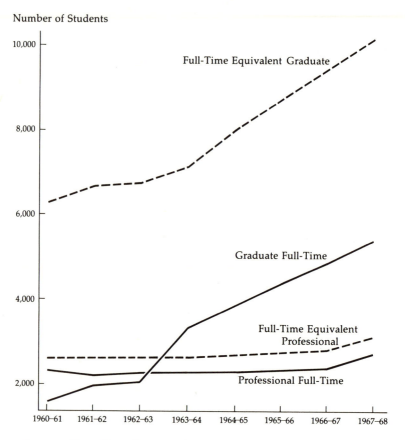

SOURCE: Chancellor Allan M. Cartter, "An Analysis of New York University."
New York: New York University, mimeographed, 1968.

FIGURE 5. Enrollment in graduate and advanced professional education,
1960–1967.

viously been opposed to the Gallatin College idea. This time, however,
the plan was much less radical, for it involved only the combination of
the first two years of study for Washington Square College, Education,
and Commerce. Thus, the battle was not completely lost by the oppo-
nents, and the strength of the resistance is obvious from the fact that it
took all the power of the president's office to ensure that it got even a
trial run. The plan has been in operation several years now and most of
the controversy has subsided.

**When images of the future clash: the impact on the School of Com-
merce.** Increasing admission standards, moving to full-time students and

faculty, and a general upgrading in quality changed the School of Commerce dramatically. Commerce was one of the schools most fully dedicated to the "School of Opportunity" image and it had a large core of professors who fought strongly for this value when it was threatened. The officials in the central administration had made the critical decisions, but vested interest groups in Commerce were determined to fight it all the way.

The situation is complicated, however, for not all the faculties of business education in the university were opposed to the changes. To be sure, there was one massive interest group in Commerce that opposed the changes fervently, but it is interesting to note that the Graduate School of Business (GSB), a separate unit for graduate and advanced professional degrees in business, took the opposite side. GSB wanted to establish itself as a major research center and as a nationally reputable business education unit. Its professors were much more oriented to scholarly research on industry and business, and they feared that the undergraduate School of Commerce was damaging the reputation of business studies at NYU. Thus, the professors of business education at NYU formed two distinct interest groups with two different emphases, each fighting for a different image of the future for NYU. The central administration had allies for its view in the GSB professors.

This division did not, however, make the battle any less difficult, since the Commerce professors believed they might be out of a job if all these changes were instituted. They feared reduced enrollments, a loss of the night school program, decreases in the size of the faculty, and a general weakening of their influence in the university. It is now clear that exactly the things they feared most were to happen in a short time!

Probably the majority of the Commerce faculty were opposed to major changes in their basic philosophy, or to changes in admissions policies. Moreover, the administration's chief representative on the scene, Dean John Prime, was not totally convinced that the changes were desirable. Dean Prime resisted many of the changes, and his faculty was strongly behind him. A real power struggle developed, but in this battle the administration had most of the weapons. As one professor put it:

> I guess now that it's all over these changes were good for us. But we fought it all the way; there was a fantastic battle. Actually, I'd say it was rammed down our throats. Several foundations made reports which suggested we were too "provincial," and we needed to upgrade standards and eliminate the duplication in our undergraduate programs. But remember, this was done by academic types, who really didn't understand a professional school and were prejudiced against us. This would not have happened a few years ago when the whole University lived off Commerce's

surplus money. It is only our growing weakness which made this change possible. The various schools are always competing and at this moment we are in a bad relative position (Baldridge, 1971, interview #20).

For many months the task of convincing the faculty to cooperate with the new changes went on against strong opposition. Finally, two major changes in Commerce leadership were announced. First, in April 1962, Commerce was placed under an "Executive Dean" who supervises both Commerce and the Graduate School of Business. Second, in September 1963, Dean Prime resigned, and Dean Abraham Gitlow was appointed as local dean at Commerce. To no one's great surprise both Executive Dean Joseph Taggart and Dean Gitlow favored the administration's plans for upgrading quality in the School of Commerce. About that time the major breakthrough came in faculty cooperation.

By almost any yardstick the School of Commerce is radically different from what it was a few years ago. The most dramatic example is what might be called the "X" effect. Figure 6 shows how S.A.T. scores went up and how enrollment figures went down!

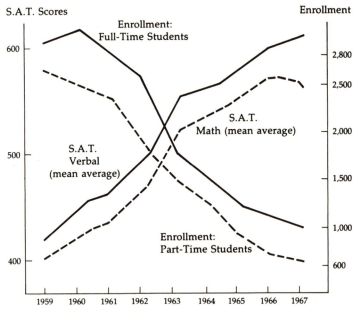

Source: Based on various statistics reported in "A Report from the School of Commerce." New York: New York University School of Commerce, internal house publication.

Figure 6. Changes in enrollment and S.A.T. scores of the School of Commerce, 1959–1967.

Many Commerce professors feared that they might lose their jobs if enrollments were drastically cut—and they were right. From a high of nearly 300 faculty members in the late 1950s the number dropped to 61 in 1967–1968. Although not all these were full-time faculty, it is no secret that not only were many part-timers dropped and many nontenured people never tenured, but that even a few senior men were "bought off" to retire early. Furthermore, very few new people were hired during that time, and many current faculty members left. The faculty often opposed the new changes for the simple reason that they might lose their jobs. Certainly NYU lived up to all its contractual obligations; nevertheless, the end result was that many people had to find jobs elsewhere.

The changes hit Commerce hard. A resisting faculty was cut to the bone; a resistant dean retired; the autonomous School of Commerce was placed under an "executive dean" who was also in charge of the Graduate School of Business; many courses were wrested away from Commerce and put in the Coordinated Liberal Studies program; and student enrollments were drastically cut. Yet the quality of the students, faculty, and program was vastly improved. Most people at NYU—even present members of the Commerce faculty—now believe that these changes were necessary. Nevertheless, in the struggle the old School of Commerce died, and one of the most powerful organizational interest groups on campus was hobbled. As one Commerce professor put it, "We lost the fight, and now we have less influence on the university than we have had in 50 years."

NYU's new image of the future: a summary. The chart on page 290 will serve as a summary of the changes at NYU. Of course, the chart is oversimplified, because many more factors went into these changes than the ones that have been discussed. The interest groups that supported or opposed the changes, moreover, were not monolithic masses and included many shades of opinion. The issues were complex, and the groups were often subdivided among themselves. Nonetheless, the main outlines of the process of change at NYU during the period discussed are accurately shown.

CONCLUSIONS

Let us turn now from the case study material on NYU and look at some of the uniformities we might expect to hold in other situations. A review of the questions asked at the beginning of the chapter will help accomplish this goal.

How does "necessity" interact with "future planning"? It is clear that organizations change both because of the force of circumstances and

DEVELOPING A NEW IMAGE OF THE FUTURE FOR NYU

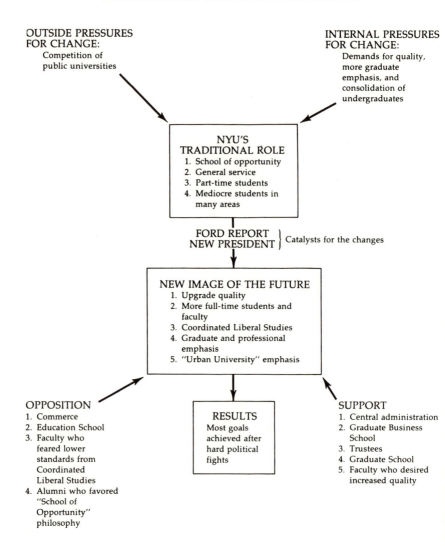

OUTSIDE PRESSURES
FOR CHANGE:
   Competition of
   public universities

INTERNAL PRESSURES
FOR CHANGE:
   Demands for quality,
   more graduate
   emphasis, and
   consolidation of
   undergraduates

NYU'S
TRADITIONAL ROLE
1. School of opportunity
2. General service
3. Part-time students
4. Mediocre students in
   many areas

FORD REPORT
NEW PRESIDENT } Catalysts for the changes

NEW IMAGE OF THE FUTURE
1. Upgrade quality
2. More full-time students and
   faculty
3. Coordinated Liberal Studies
4. Graduate and professional
   emphasis
5. "Urban University" emphasis

OPPOSITION
1. Commerce
2. Education School
3. Faculty who
   feared lower
   standards from
   Coordinated
   Liberal Studies
4. Alumni who favored
   "School of
   Opportunity"
   philosophy

RESULTS
Most goals
achieved after
hard political
fights

SUPPORT
1. Central administration
2. Graduate Business
   School
3. Trustees
4. Graduate School
5. Faculty who desired
   increased quality

because of the future-oriented plans that are made. In a real sense determining which approach causes change is a false question, and the more interesting issue is how planning and the constraint of circumstances interact. In this case NYU was faced with a whole set of external events that threatened its very existence, and this hard necessity set off a whole chain of events in which future-oriented planning became a critical feature of the institution's response. Of course, it is quite conceivable that the university might *not* have responded in this manner, but could have muddled through, making ad hoc adjustments rather than bold plans. Thus, necessity and the force of changing circumstances allow the *possibility* for creative planning but do not always generate that reaction. The Marxian and the Weberian insights contribute much to each other, for hard necessity and the future-oriented plans of men are almost always jointly involved in the change processes of the real world.

What is the role of critical elites and interest groups in organizational change? "Hard necessity" may well develop out of the impersonal forces that surround the organization, such as population growth or interorganization competition, but the ideas and dreams that form the new image of the future for the organization always come from men. It is always critical to examine the issue of *whose* goals and images of the future are being used as a basis of action. There are many groups of elites in a large organization that have divergent goals and images of the future. For example, at NYU the central administration was one critical elite that had a vision of the future radically different from that of the School of Commerce faculty. A delineation of the various interest groups and their values is a critical component for the analysis of change processes.

How do groups in the organization interact to set the content of the new image of the future? Identifying the various interest groups and their values is a first step, but the analysis must also determine how these groups interact, and how one set of organizational interest groups is able to impose *its* image of the future on the organization. This, of course, is the classic question of conflict and its resolution, and a political framework is extremely helpful for the organization theorist concerned with change processes. In fact, the larger report on the NYU study deals extensively with building a "political model" for studying organizational change (see Baldridge, 1971). A political analysis of elite interest groups must include a discussion of the differences in values held by the groups, the tactics they utilize, the nature of coalition formation between the groups, and the kind of decision-making mechanisms that are used to settle the dispute (see Thompson, 1967, Chapter 9). Setting the new image for the organization is essentially a political process by which "dominant coalitions" impose their values on the organization, and plans are articulated in light of the compromises which emerge from that political debate.

How do abstract images of the future become operationalized into concrete policy? The political goal-setting process emerges with a set of future-oriented plans, but these must always be translated from abstract images into concrete policy that guides the organization's action. In the

NYU situation the abstract concept of "quality" was translated into concrete policies about higher admissions standards, more full-time students, and more emphasis on urban education. In the process of translation from the abstract to the concrete, images of the future often undergo subtle and important changes, so the analyst must always be alert to the degree of overlap between abstract idea and concrete policy.

What kinds of political activity surround attempts to realize the image of the future once it is operationalized? Concrete policy articulates the abstract goal but is rarely enough to ensure that it is completely carried out. One of the pervasive features of political systems is that the very act of implementing a goal often results in changes of that goal. Even after policy has been stated the political battle goes on, for those elites and interest groups which lost the original round of battle over the image will struggle to recoup some advantages as the policy is being implemented. For example, the stated policies of the university were vigorously opposed by the School of Commerce faculty long after the original decisions and policies had been set. Thus, the analyst of change in organizations must be sensitive to the continued controversy over an image—it is not a static thing which once-and-for-all settles issues, but instead is a living encounter between the dreams and goals of conflicting interest groups and elites.

How are structural adjustments made to protect the goals and images? Organizational theorists, in particular, are sensitive to the issue of structural arrangements for carrying out human goals. Selznick (1957) has argued that values and goals are not self-sustaining, but instead require the protection of interested elites and structural frameworks. In fact, organizations are the ingenious technique of modern man for translating his images of the future and his values into stabilized structures which work to actualize them. At NYU, for example, many structural changes in the organization were designed to advance the new image, including the creation of a new Coordinated Liberal Studies Program and the restructuring of the relations between the School of Commerce and the Graduate School of Business. Values and images must be translated into protective structures if they are not to wither and die on the organizational vine.

What kinds of consequences, intended and unintended, flow from the implementation of the image? The best-laid plans of mice and men often go awry—but remarkably enough they also work out right sometimes. The image of the future defines a course of action, and often this is the outcome that actually occurs. NYU was taken out of direct competition with the state university, succeeded in attracting higher quality students, and began to build a much stronger image of quality in many areas.

But this is only part of the story, and it is only fair to mention the high cost of such an enterprise, both in financial commitment and in terms of the human cost that unavoidably accompanied such a major readjustment. One of the most pervasive outcomes of the implementation of any image is the continued political controversy and readjustment, which eventually builds up to the point that new images of the future are proposed and new battle-lines are drawn—and the process of image-building and image-articulation begins again. In this way dynamic organizations struggle to implement the images and goals of men.

REFERENCES

Baldridge, J. Victor
   1971   Power and Conflict in the University. New York: Wiley.
Etzioni, Amitai (ed.)
   1964   Social Change. New York: Basic Books.
New York University
   1956   The Self-Study. New York: New York University Press.
Perrow, Charles
   1961   "The analysis of goals in complex organizations." American Sociological Review 26:854–866.
Selznick, Philip
   1957   Leadership in Administration. Evanston, Ill.: Row, Peterson.
   1948   TVA and the Grass Roots. Los Angeles and Berkeley: University of California Press.
Thompson, James
   1967   Organizations in Action. New York: McGraw-Hill.
Weber, Max
   1958   The Protestant Ethic and the Spirit of Capitalism. Talcott Parsons (trans.). New York: Charles Scribner & Sons.

Methodology and the Quest for Utopia: A Case Study from El Dorado

IVAR OXAAL

This chapter is really a methodological appendix in search of a mono-graph. My purpose in writing it is not primarily to add another item to the confessional literature in sociology, although it probably fits that genre of professional writing closer than any other.[1] My main concern— which arises out of long-standing association with the spirit of the ideas expressed by the editors of this volume[2]—will be to explore, in a con-crete setting, the relevance and potential hazards of the research strate-gies and directives they outline in Part I. This will be done by briefly re-lating my personal experiences as a sociologist in the new nation of Guyana (formerly British Guiana), in South America, where I was priv-ileged—or presumed, rather—to fashion for myself the role of a direct agent of social change, consciously basing my activities on many of the precepts suggested by the editors. Neither my necessarily brief and epi-sodic analysis of Guyana, however, nor my present analysis of my role there is meant to be more than a cautionary tale open, I realize, to various

---

[1] The list grows longer each year. Recent examples of introspection include Hadley Cantril's *The Human Dimension: Experiences in Policy Research* (1967); Phil-lip E. Hammond's *Sociologists at Work* (1967); Paul F. Lazarsfeld, William H. Sewell, and Harold L. Wilensky's *The Uses of Sociology* (1967); and Gideon Sjoberg's *Ethics, Politics, and Social Research* (1967). Especially pertinent in the present context is Ir-ving L. Horowitz's *The Rise and Fall of Operation Camelot* (1967).

[2] In 1960 I joined the West Indies study program headed by Wendell Bell in the Department of Sociology at the University of California, Los Angeles. James A. Mau was also a member of that group. For an idea of the approach developed out of that study see Bell (1967).

denunciations—some of which I will supply myself while leaving ample room for additional critiques.

It has by now become a cliché, in the literature on modernization, to stress the impact of metropolitan institutions and levels of living on the aspirations of the newly independent countries. As Edward Shils (1960: 379) wrote in a classic essay: "The elites of the new states have lying before them not an image of a future in which no one has yet lived or of fragments of a still living and accepted past, but rather an image of their own future profoundly different from their own past, to be lived along the lines of the already existent modern states, which are their contemporaries." To the extent that this generalization holds true for individual cases and classes of countries, it has meant in practical terms that the new nations increasingly come to define economic and social development along many of the same indexes employed by industrial countries in evaluating their general well-being: GNP, levels of literacy, rates of employment, life expectancy, per capita income, etc. "The future," so far as politicians, social planners, and citizenry are concerned, tends to be reduced to the Gomperian demand for "more": more investment, more schools, more jobs, more hospitals, more personal income.

The pragmatic approach to development has been evident in the British Caribbean since the 1930s and was, almost from the outset, associated with nationalist parties, based largely on the model of the Labour Party, pledged to achieve progress by parliamentary means. Demands for more of the amenities of life and more democracy went hand in hand. The middle-class political leaders saw themselves in terms analagous to the position of American liberals. Their aspirations and tactics had much in common with American liberals; the Puerto Rican model was very influential and, with one major exception, West Indian nationalism was characterized by an "Operation Bootstrap" ideology. The single major exception was, and remains, British Guiana. Dr. Cheddi B. Jagan, alone among the leading West Indian nationalists, would see the Operation Bootstrap approach—with its heavy reliance on foreign private investment capital—as merely an expansion of imperialism. Why and how the nationalist movement in British Guiana developed along what by the general trends in the West Indies was a deviant course will be considered in a moment because it will be impossible to explain the context of my activities there without some appreciation of the colony's historical legacies and current conditions. As Wilbert E. Moore (1967:161) has observed: "Arising from both the particular historical legacies and from what we may term the trajectory of modernization, the characteristic tensions are likely to differ from one society (or closely related group of countries) to another, and the way those tensions are managed is also likely to be different." In the Guyanese case, conflicting interpretations of past, present, and future split the nationalist leadership and developed into chronic and dangerous divisions. In such a situation, the sociologist who holds a particular image of the future, and who pretends to affect the trajectory of change, may find himself pressed to declare whose side he is on; he may, indeed, find himself publicly accountable for his beliefs and actions.

THE LEGACY OF EL DORADO

By 1967 it was a matter for open speculation in Georgetown as to whether the General Elections, constitutionally due by March 1969, would—or even should—be held. When a Negro storeowner outside town told Wendell Bell, "We don't need elections too soon again" (the unspoken implication was: "if ever"), he was expressing a skepticism and weariness of the electoral process commonly found in the Negro middle class and among some leading businessmen as well. It was a self-interested skepticism, to be sure, because the "pro-Western," predominantly Negro party headed by L. Forbes Burnham was in office, thanks to a coalition with the members of a small party led by a Portuguese businessman, Peter D'Aguiar. In the opposition stood Dr. Cheddi Jagan, leader of the East Indian party, who, although repeatedly charging that the elections would not be held (or if held, rigged), was confident that his party could eventually regain office.

Jagan's confidence was based on both world politics and arithmetic. In his view, the ethnically unified Marxist nationalist movement, which had been split apart in the 1950s by the capitalist stooge Burnham, could be reconstituted once the imperialist pressures exerted by the United States were weakened in the struggle for national liberation throughout the world. The CIA had played a role in making it impossible for Jagan to govern while he had been in office a few years before, but that kind of interference would become untenable once the world balance of power began to shift more decisively in favor of the socialist camp. Of equal or greater importance was the apparently shifting balance of ethnic distribution in Guyana. As of the end of 1964, according to census data, the East Indians represented 50.2 percent of the total Guyana population of 638,030. "Africans" were only 31.3 percent of the population, "Mixed Races" (chiefly mixed with Africans) were 11.9 percent, Amerindians 4 percent and the remainder—Portuguese, Chinese, and European —2 percent.[3]

---

[3] Taken from statistical tables cited by Jagan (1966). However, I have not seen recent data on the relative proportions broken down by age of East Indians and Negroes.

Perhaps the title of this section should have been "The Curse of El Dorado," the mythical golden kingdom sought in the vicinity of the Guiana highlands by Sir Walter Raleigh and other early explorers. There was, and is, gold—and diamonds too—in those hills; not to mention bauxite and manganese, both of which have been mined in large commercial quantities for many years. Unlike the West Indian islands, British Guiana—80,000 square miles, larger in territory than England itself, as the locals like to boast—had a relatively vast and romantic interior. The "Porkknockers," an indigenous species of rugged prospectors akin to "the Mountain Men," who preceded the opening of the American interior, produced legends and songs of adventure, resourcefulness, violence, and easy riches that have appeal to this day. And significant strikes do still sometimes occur; small-scale prospecting, particularly in the streams and rivers, is carried on by both local and foreign entrepreneurs who generally seem to realize enough to at least cover their expenses. At least one well-publicized local "millionaire," a modest and hard-working Negro, has recently emerged from the obscurity of years of steady work on his claim.

The major mineral resource, however, is bauxite, which, as in Surinam and Jamaica, is a major source of government revenue. Although of high grade, Guyanese bauxite is hard to extract; it generally lies below hundreds of feet of white sand, which has to be laboriously scraped, dug, and hosed away by some of the most gargantuan earth-moving equipment in the world. The operations of the Demerara Bauxite Company (a subsidiary of Alcan), 65 miles up the Demerara River from Georgetown, are nothing short of spectacular. Here, towering over the jungle stands an advanced heavy industrial complex serviced by ore boats of such immense size that they dwarf the 25,000-member community of Mackenzie-Wismar when they are in port.

Thus, while Guyana may seem like a distant backwater, in some respects it has the size, facilities, resources, and legends that make it possible to seriously believe in the concept of a national economy—a concept that, in the smaller sugar-producing West Indian islands, has traditionally led a less plausible existence. Moreover, the mighty, muddy, rivers of Guyana (Amerindian for "land of many waters") ensure that the country will never develop a beach-centered tourist industry, which might, in the view of some nationalists, tend to trivialize discussion of economic development. Tourists from such organizations as the Sierra Club occasionally arrive by Pan Am jet at Atkinson airport, but their interest is in the interior, especially the great 600-foot Kaiteur Falls, which in full flow is indeed a magnificent spectacle and serves as a symbol of the natural beauty and unharnessed power in the interior.

Jagan and Guyanese politics. "Non-co-operation with evil is a sacred duty." The quotation is from Gandhi and it appears at the beginning of the first chapter of the 1966 autobiography by Cheddi Jagan entitled, *The West on Trial: My Fight for Guyana's Freedom*.

Few who meet Cheddi Jagan fail to be impressed by his vivacious charm, his flashing smile and good humor, his handsome looks, and his deep dedication to his native country. He's a Guyanese, after all, and these positive traits were formerly thought to be characteristic of Guyanese generally, according to the interisland stereotypes that flourish in the West Indies.

The second quotation that opens that first chapter of Jagan's autobiography is the familiar one from Eugene Debs: "While there is a lower class, I am in it; while there is a criminal element, I am of it; while there is a soul in prison, I am not free. . . ." Similar inspirational and radical homilies, including the opening lines of the United States Declaration of Independence, occur at the heads of succeeding chapters. Lincoln's Gettysburg Address is reproduced in toto in Chapter 3. Although they may seem trite to more jaded or sophisticated minds, they reflect the moral qualities of the man and the way he sees the world.

Because he is what we conventionally label a Communist, Cheddi Jagan is by West Indian standards a unique phenomenon: a Marxist politician determined to break not only the traditional colonial political control, but to diversify and possibly reorient the Guyanese economy toward more profitable trade with the Eastern bloc. As I was flying into Guyana for the first time in 1963, an experienced economist from India who was a consultant to the Jagan government told me emphatically: "This is the only place in the British Caribbean—the *only* place—where they understand what independence is supposed to be all about."

Like many of the world's nationalist politicians who emerged to inherit the dissolving colonial empires, Cheddi Jagan's concepts of social and political justice were formed by direct exposure to the crucible of competing metropolitan ideologies of the Left, particularly those variations that flowed out of the Bolshevik revolution and the Stalinist drive toward industrialization. Whether one reads of Ho Chi Minh's struggle in Paris to make sense of the debates between the Second and Third International—and finally opting firmly for the Third—or of Kwame Nkrumah's development as a student in Pennsylvania and London, one must be impressed by the degree to which they internalized the ideological conflicts engendered by disruptions in the advancing industrial economies themselves.[4]

---

[4] For a discussion of this process of political socialization elsewhere in the West Indies, see Oxaal (1967).

Jagan was essentially a product of the New Deal generation, a generation that believed in a postwar future radically different from the past. Born March 22, 1918, son of an East Indian sugar estate foreman employed at Port Mourant, 75 miles down the east coast from Georgetown, Cheddi attended secondary school in the capital before leaving for Howard University in September 1936, where he enrolled in the two-year predental course. In 1938 he moved on to Northwestern University where he completed a four-year dental course, received his DDS degree and returned to British Guiana in October 1943. Energetic and intellectually curious, he had, while pursuing his professional studies, acquired a white wife (Janet Rosenberg, herself a young radical, whose parents had vowed to shoot Cheddi on sight); read such classic Chicago sociological studies as *The Gold Coast and the Slum*, and had spent a summer peddling patent medicines in Harlem. His autobiography does not clearly indicate just how he came by his Communist leanings—not uncommon among the American intelligentsia during that period—but it is generally thought that Janet Rosenberg was an important influence at that time, as indeed she is still as General Secretary of the People's Progressive Party (PPP).

Space does not permit an extensive description of what happened to the Jagans and Guyanese politics during the years following the war. Leo A. Despres (1967:9–10) summarizes the situation in his book, *Cultural Pluralism and Nationalist Politics in British Guiana*, in this way: "First, in the late forties and early fifties, a comprehensive nationalist movement emerged. It represented a united front expressly organized to achieve national goals. Second, between 1953 and 1957, that front disintegrated almost completely. The sense of national identity it had so carefully nurtured evaporated. Third, between 1957 and 1961, disparate nationalist movements developed. . . . The ultimate result has been political instability and economic chaos." The key event triggering this dismal record was the 1953 suspension, by the Colonial Office, of the Guianese constitution after the united PPP had won the elections. The Colonial Office took fright at some of the declarations of the newly elected government, and Jagan was imprisoned with several of his colleagues. Two years later Forbes Burnham, a brilliant young British-trained Negro barrister and the leading Negro in the PPP, split with Jagan—the circumstances were extremely complex—and took with him the support of nearly all of the colony's Negroes. Although he identified himself as a "socialist," Burnham opposed Jagan's flirtations with the Eastern bloc countries and thus the ideology and power politics of the Cold War became superimposed on the ethnic divisions of the society. Jagan, however, managed to win two succeeding elections; and it was not until 1966, the year of independence, that Burnham managed to achieve control of the government. Meantime,

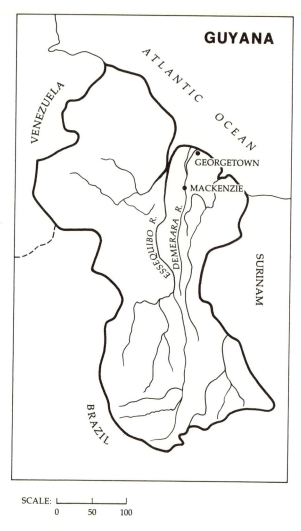

SCALE: |⎣____⎣____⎦|
     0   50   100

SOURCE: Cheddi Jagan, *The West on Trial*, London: Michael Joseph, 1966.

in 1963 and 1964 there had taken place widespread rioting, disorders, murders, and atrocities visited by Negro on East Indian and vice versa. When disorders broke out up in Mackenzie-Wismar, the Demerara Bauxite Company assisted in the evacuation of several thousand East Indians, thus leaving the area almost exclusively in the hands of Negroes. Similar racial resegregation took place along the coastal sugar belt. Negroes fled predominantly Indian villages and East Indians moved out of Negro villages. Georgetown, the stronghold of the Negro faction, was in a virtual state of siege as British troops patrolled the streets.

Who was responsible for this sorry state of affairs? Variously blamed have been: the government of the United States for failing to tolerate Jagan; Burnham for splitting the nationalist movement; the Colonial Office for suspending the constitution; and Jagan for failing to recognize the limitations on action and ideology possible in the Western Hemisphere. Jagan's downfall, perhaps, came because he was too much of a nationalist; too passionately committed to making the legend of El Dorado come true in modern Guyana.

"THE UP-RIVER PROBE"

I was in England, at Hull University, early in 1966 when a cable arrived from the Vice Chancellor at the newly formed University of Guyana inquiring whether I would be willing to come there to form a department of sociology. Because of previous research on Trinidad and a strong continuing interest in West Indian affairs (I had been married, with the fanfare reserved for mixed unions, to a Guyanese in Georgetown in 1963), I accepted this offer almost immediately. It appeared that this would afford me a chance to continue the research begun in Trinidad on its sociological brother, Guyana. In a follow-up letter the Vice Chancellor explained that my presence was desired as soon as possible because an inquiry was being planned into social and industrial relations in Mackenzie and my name had been mooted as a possible chairman of the inquiry. When we met in London some weeks later I learned that these plans were advancing; other members of the team had been selected and my presence was awaited in June.

The reason for what the Guyanese press later referred to as "the up-river probe" was the penchant of the bauxite workers for staging wildcat strikes. The precipitating incident that had produced a public outcry for an investigation of the area had been the dismissal of a Guyanese geologist a few months earlier. The circumstances surrounding his dismissal had been cloudy—indeed, it would never be fully clear—and racial discrimination had been charged. Workers had walked off the job for a day and feeling was running high that the government should look into the situation.

By the time I arrived on the scene, it was obvious that there were several peculiar features to this particular inquiry. First of all, it was not to be an official team appointed by the Burnham government. Rather, following informal discussions between the company and the government, it had been decided that the company itself would finance the undertaking and would have a direct voice in determining the composition of the team and the official terms of reference. Such was the power of the Demerara Bauxite Company (Demba); such, too, was its informal liaison, through a close advisor of the Prime Minister, in handling a very sticky issue affecting its vital interests. Why did the government not initiate the inquiry itself? In later months I was never satisfied that I really knew the answer to that. My guesses, however, were as follows: first, Burnham—who some months later negotiated plans in Canada for Alcan to establish a small aluminum smelter in Guyana—did not wish to alienate company goodwill by appearing overly aggressive in this matter; second, Macken-zie workers were solidly devoted to Burnham and his party—it was therefore not politically necessary for the government to embark on what would appear as an overdue punitive expedition against Demba; third, per-haps the government did not really feel itself able to immediately take on heavier responsibilities in this area. Instead, a peculiar compromise was reached: the government would monitor what was essentially an exercise in corporate self-criticism.

Having been critical of "managerial sociology" as a graduate stu-dent, I was naturally suspicious of this entire undertaking. Several fac-tors, however, convinced me to press ahead with it. The most important of these was that one of the members of the four-man team would be a young Guyanese sociologist who I knew to be a militant nationalist and sympathetic to the cause of rapid social change. He had already been up to Mackenzie and had analyzed the Demba top management as contain-ing representatives of both old-line management and younger, progres-sive elements interested in the modernization of the area. His feeling at that time (he would afterwards feel that it had been a mistake in judg-ment) was that by working together we would be able to provide lever-age for the progressives in the company and achieve some practical re-sults. Of equal importance, in my view, was the fact that the Guyana Mine Worker's Union had agreed to participate in drafting the terms of reference of the inquiry and would be privy to its findings along with the company and the government. Moreover, with the union in posses-sion of the final report we had good reason to suppose that selective leaks to the press would result in demands for publication despite the com-pany's desire to maintain control. So our role would not be simply that of company consultants: we would be working under the aegis of the gov-ernment and union as well.

Nonetheless, and I discussed this with my colleague at an early stage of the study, there was no blinking the fact that by lending our-selves to the inquiry we were intervening directly in a very sensitive political area. I fully recognized, as perhaps my colleague did not, that an nquiry of this kind was pre-eminently a political act; that to the extent ve were successful in initiating company reforms we were, in effect, triking a blow for Revisionism—such was the language that seemed apropriate to our discussion—supporting the Burnham interpretation of lobal political realities as opposed to Jagan's. To the extent that we conributed to a public image of Demba as a company willing to undertake to ectify the evil policies of the past—or even participated in a presumably bjective appraisal of the situation—we might help to repair the comany's image as an insensitive, recalcitrant exploiter of the national vealth. In a sharply polarized political climate such as existed in Guyana here was no way of ducking this issue; regardless of its substantive findngs the inquiry would in all likelihood serve to strengthen capitalism and he "neocolonial" position of Guyana. I was not happy about the fact hat we would be open to the charge of being "stooges of capitalism" but was prepared, for once, and as an experiment, to see to what extent a ociologist could function in a situation of some apparent influence. (In ny case, and that of my colleague, financial inducements did not figure n the matter. The arrangement was that the university would defer payng my salary until September, my fee from Demba being in the meanime roughly equivalent to three months' income on the university payoll.)

But my consideration of whether to participate went beyond immeliate calculations of possible effectiveness. I had already arrived, before even setting foot in Guyana, at a position that in Marxist parlance would be labeled "revolutionary defeatism." I had come to the conclusion despite Jagan's sincerity and my personal sympathy with much of his worldview—but were Burnham's social objectives all that different? I doubted it—that the internal social divisions and pressures from outside had made Jagan's Marxist politics, his continued primary identification with the Communist countries, anachronistic and self-destructive. I reckoned that if it came to a showdown again between Indian and African in Guyana, as well it might, the American Marines who might be summoned ashore in Georgetown would be garlanded by an overjoyed Negro populace as their saviors; that the PPP, if it persisted in its Marxist course, and threatened to take office again, would sooner or later be crushed. After the Bay of Pigs and Dominican interventions it seemed folly to underestimate the propensity of the United States to intervene unilaterally against "subversive" politicians like Jagan, particularly when a popular, democratic leader like Burnham was willing to play the role of anti-Communist bulwark. This skepticism over the prospects for radical change—possibly after the Cuban pattern—was not one I attempted to conceal. In free-spirited Guyana you can discuss these matters

with just about anyone. On one occasion I raised these doubts with D
Jagan during a conversation in my home but could not be persuaded b
his prognosis that American interventionism would wither away. Eve
after America withdrew from Vietnam, I felt there was no reason to sup
pose that little Caribbean countries would be exempted from our patrol
and influence. In the meantime, social change like politics had to be de
fined as the art of the possible. Reforms within the context of the inter
national capitalist economy seemed the only available strategy to Guy
anese nationalism.

In addition to these broad considerations of the political context
was quickly educated in the more intimate and direct cross-currents tha
would be part and parcel of the inquiry. During a luncheon with to
company officials at the once-exclusive Georgetown Club, my credential
and attitudes were informally examined, while I in turn attempted t
distinguish possible divisions of attitude among my hosts. At this firs
luncheon Jim Campbell, the managing director, and Keith Tisshaw, th
company public relations officer, suggested, over brandy and cigars, tha
the inquiry was really a private affair and that while some sections of th
report might be made public we wanted to avoid turning it into a "polit
ical football" by releasing the more strongly critical sections. In reply,
pointed out that this would correctly be viewed by the public as compan
control of the inquiry and therefore self-defeating, even from their ow
public relations standpoint. I emphasized that once the investigation ha
been launched the team had to proceed as an autonomous body; the fac
that the company had played a role in its selection and would pay fo
it had already made it suspect; so far as I was concerned, the com
pany could not expect to exercise any further control. In the ensuin
months this issue would recur with the public relations officer's impuls
being always, rather wistfully, and unsuccessfully—but understandabl
—to back away from a public definition of the investigation while I con
tinually stressed, in public and private, the operational independence o
the group. In actual practice, despite reservations and some apparen
anxiety, this fundamental ground-rule was scrupulously observed by th
company. However, as I began to understand that the government wa
not interested in using this particular inquiry as a wedge for promotin
change in the area, and that the trade union was largely impotent, I en
deavored not to alienate the top management on whose voluntary action
the success of our recommendations seemed very largely to depend.

The second major set of relationships in which the inquiry was en
meshed was, of course, the members of the "probe team" themselves.
had complete confidence in my Guyanese colleague, but the two othe
members were question marks. The first was Mr. James Ramphal, a for

ner East Indian school master and official in the Ministry of Labour, who ad been a member of the government at the time of constitutional sus- ension and was therefore cordially detested by the Jagans. "Jimmy" Ramphal was now well advanced in years and had been living in Toronto where he had recently suffered a stroke. He was the father of the Attor- ney General in Burnham's government, an official who was generally viewed as the number two man in the administration—and a friend of the Demba management. The other member of the team was Frank Wal- cott, a Negro, head of the Barbados Workers' Union and elected politician in the Barbados legislature with a reputation for "responsible" attitudes and close links with the American and British trade union movement. The composition of the team seemed to me to have been carefully stacked in a conservative direction; that the company could take comfort in the ex- pectation that, with Frank and Jimmy aboard, we unpredictable sociolo- gists would be operating under a fairly tight rein. As a sociologist I should not have been surprised that nothing of the kind developed. Because of Jimmy's illness and Frank's preoccupation with the upcoming Barbados elections, neither of them was able to spend much time in active investi- gation in Mackenzie. But more important, when we four were thrown to- gether in close quarters and eating at the same table for several weeks— in housing located in the working-class area of Mackenzie—there emerged a rather definite consensus of attitude toward conditions in the area. This consensus was by no means complete, but we came to share strong criticisms of the past and present social attitudes and performance of Demba, and we developed a strong sense of identification with the plight of the local work force.

A third reference group in the situation was the trade union. Soon after the initial luncheon meeting with the Demba management we went to Mackenzie to discuss terms of reference of the inquiry with the union leadership. Although the Guyana Mine Worker's President, Winston Verbeke—jet black, a man of slow but sincere and likable shrewdness —expressed reservations about our motives, my colleague and I satisfied him that we had no intention of setting out to whitewash the company; that although our terms of reference would focus on the relationship between community conditions and the causes of unofficial strikes, we would call the shots as we saw them regardless of how this might affect the image of the various interested parties whether company, union, or government. In truth, I believe that from our manner Winston imme- diately saw the inquiry as providing possible corroboration for his insis- tent attacks against the aloofness and arrogance of the Demba manage- ment. His repeated public defense of the inquiry, and of me personally, was indispensable to what success we did achieve in establishing rapport with the working-class community. I must add, however, that since lack of control over the rank-and-file by the union leaders was a major ingredient in the industrial instability of the area, the blessings of that leadership by no means alleviated all suspicion.

My colleague and I established our headquarters in two small, new houses of foreman grade in Mackenzie shortly thereafter. We had hardly unpacked our bags when news reached us that workers had just struck the alumina plant and were congregating at union headquarters in Mackenzie. This strike—management speculated, with rueful humor, that it had been spontaneously staged specifically for "the probe team's" benefit—would turn out to be the longest and costliest in several years with the entire operation closed down for over a week. Whatever role our presence may have played—if a reverse Hawthorne effect was present, ours was certainly one of the most expensive consultant fees on record—we did have a splendid opportunity to follow a Demba wildcat strike in intimate detail, attending all union-management bargaining sessions, meetings of the union, and behind-the-scenes discussions. It was an exhausting but exhilarating experience beginning with a challenge from fist-shaking workers to justify our presence at a turbulent strike meeting through days and nights of interviews with the participants until a talented East Indian Ministry of Labour conciliator arrived and managed to work out a tenuous truce. I say we were exhilarated and we were rarely are sociologists given the nearly total access to the working out of an explosive conflict situation such as we experienced; moreover, in the heat of battle we were able to observe and record many types of behavior and deepseated attitudes that were useful in interpreting the overall situation. An abbreviated account of that strike became a chapter in our final report.

Frank Walcott and Jimmy Ramphal arrived on the scene after the strike was settled and the four of us then had a chance to survey the broad outlines of the community structure together. The following summarizes my own viewpoint, as eventually expressed in the report, although the others were in substantial agreement.

Here was an enclave of 25,000 souls, many living under the most primitive conditions surrounded by the South American rain forest, in the shadow of a technologically sophisticated, foreign-owned, industrial plant; sharply divided along nationality, class, and racial lines, with the most rudimentary and powerless local government, isolated from the mainstream of coastal life but for an all-day trip by crowded river steamer or jeep. It was, moreover, a society not yet one generation out of the period of industrial feudalism, which characterized its development for many years as a company town. Older workers could well remember

1e paternalism and apartheid conditions that prevailed before—as they
1w it—the potential threat posed by the nationalist movement in the
950s had set the company on a slow and grudging road to reform. This
evere indictment of the past they passed along to younger workers as
rell, and these bitter memories were reinforced by the fact that the two
op managers at Demba—who now purported to be sponsoring an inde-
endent panel of inquiry to suggest reforms—had been with the comany in the bad old days. Moreover, from the worker's standpoint, the
cology of the apartheid regime remained intact, and many of them were
onvinced that the social attitudes of the past were still firmly entrenched.

The social and functional geography of the community was, it
eemed to me, of the utmost importance not only because of its symbolic
ssociation with the feudal past but because it continued to structure in-
erpersonal encounters. Picture the following: dominating the landscape
n the right bank of the Demerara River were two enormous industrial
nclosures. Downriver, at the extreme end of the residential section of
Mackenzie stood the alumina plant; a mile and a half upriver, connected
y rail to the more sophisticated operations needed for the production of
lumina, stood the bauxite plant. Sandwiched in between was the town
self. Arvida Road, the main street, was not much to look at: one gas sta-
ion, a handful of stores, three churches, a grassy public square with an
pen-air market and a cinema along the river, a ramshackle school, a
ank—and there you were at the entrance of the bauxite plant. The hous-
1g in Mackenzie was mainly a mixture of the old multifamily, wooden
arrack-like "ranges" with their communal toilets of ill renown (very
imilar to company housing on the sugar estates) and the newer, im-
orted, aluminum (naturally) prefabs. Although there were some com-
laints that the latter were hot during the day and noisy at night (as the
un-heated metal contracted and caused them to ping at 3:00 A.M.) they
ould be made quite livable by an enterprising homeowner. For several
ears the company had been attempting to totally divest itself of owner-
hip of this company town by means of a housing trust—the operations
f which, by virtue of its being a creature of the company, had created
nuch ill will.

If Mackenzie failed to inspire enthusiasm in "the probe team," con-
litions directly across the river in Wismar were far worse. Most of Mac-
enzie at least had graveled hard-surface streets, electricity, and a sup-
ly of pure water; but Wismar, which the company had never owned,
lad grown up as an orphan of the bauxite industry, yet it contained prob-
bly two-thirds of the Demba work force plus a small horde of penny-
apitalist shopkeepers operating out of riverside stores the size of large
acking-crates. There was also a large fringe of squatters. The only motor

vehicle capable of negotiating Wismar's "streets"—all neatly demarcate on a company map of the area—was a jeep. To venture up the shanty town slopes meant grinding in low-gear, axle-deep in sand. The commo and only means of crossing the river was by one of the fleet of privatel owned small skiffs driven by outboard motors.

Perhaps conditions in Mackenzie, or even Wismar, were not all tha much worse than elsewhere in the West Indies, but the contrast betwee these two major working-class areas and the housing provided by th company for staff members was extreme. Upriver, on the right bank, be yond the bauxite plant, past the main company offices, past the compan hospital, there stretched the tree-shrouded residential areas of "Wa tooka"—spacious, older bungalows situated between the river and th golf course—and "Richmond Hill"—attractive "contemporary" home dotted around a serpentine drive. To be a member of the managerial-tech nical staff at Demba entailed a claim not only to a subsidized home, bu likewise access to such company-furnished perquisites as the comforts o the exclusive staff club, the private primary school, the staff cinema, an other amenities. In addition, nearly all staff families had black Guyanes servants and drove automobiles. Outside the staff area about the onl place they could motor was down to the Mackenzie shopping distric The regular afternoon appearance there of company wives in pincurls an shorts engaged in spending relatively lavish sums of money on grocerie and liquor was one of the few, if not very endearing, occasions for extra curricular encounters between the working-class and staff families tucke away, as I later put it, without conscious double entendre, "in the tigh little world of Watooka." During the strike the workers had obligingl staged for us at the outset of the investigation we had occasion to ob serve the fear and apprehension felt by some staff members about ever venturing into Mackenzie. This was based as much on prudence as o paranoia. Soon after, we witnessed an incident—not the first of its kind— in which an expatriate staff wife struck a Negro boy with her auto on Ar vida Road, quickly found herself surrounded by a hostile black crowd a she attempted to minister to him, and then drove off in a panic back t Watooka where, we learned, she collapsed in hysterics. The bifurcatio of social classes could hardly have been more acute. There it was, th global dilemma in miniature: the Affluent Society locked eyeball-to-eye ball with the Culture of Poverty.

Although polarized between a largely expatriate technical elite an an Afro-Guyanese work force, the race-nationality-class correlation wa by no means complete. The official company policy of "Guyanization" had, by the time of our study, conferred staff status on some 40 Guyan ese out of a total staff complement of 160. Some of these were concer

ated in a "junior staff" housing scheme across the golf course from Wa-
ooka, but others were scattered, in accordance with some metaphysical
dispensation based on rank and preference, throughout Watooka and
Richmond Hill. Additionally, it was calculated that upwards to a third
of the pupils in the staff school were colored Guyanese children. To be
sure, with one possible exception, no Guyanese had yet acceded to what
we would consider a post of some policy-making importance. This was a
sore point with Guyanese staff members, and relations between them and
the expatriate management, while seemingly covered with a veneer of
cordiality, were marked by a degree of mistrust. Management, in turn,
was disappointed that the Guyanese staff had so far largely failed to
serve as a buffer, or bridge, to the working-class community. Guyanese
staff, it appeared, were in a really marginal position: their presence in
Watooka led to charges by workers that they had "sold out" or were engaged in carrying out the expatriates' "dirty tricks."

From these features and impressions of the community, I was well
on the way to conviction that a basic precipitant of wildcat strikes was
the apartheid legacies of the community, and the continuation of the
sharp separation of the staff and working-class worlds. These factors
stood in naked contradiction to the values and rhetoric of self-determination stressed by the nationalist movement. Workers sought avenues to
assert their newly won sense of pride and potency. Institutional channels
for asserting their sentiments and interests were, however, weak or nonexistent. While sincere, the trade union leadership—whose local offices
consisted of a two-room shack on Arvida Road—was usually absent in
Georgetown at their "national" headquarters although 75 percent of
their membership were at Demba. The effects of this absentee trade union
leadership was exacerbated by the fact that local government organs,
haltingly moving into the power vacuum created by Demba's depaternal-
izing exodus from Mackenzie, were also at a primitive stage of evolution.
In the planning stage, but yet to come, was a locally elected community
authority resting on a local tax base. As a consequence, the only direct
political action available to workers was through their intensive and
nearly unanimous identification with the Burnham government. This
commitment, associated as it was with a heightened sense of racial soli-
darity, did little to create a conciliatory mood toward the white expatriate
class. Indeed, I and other members of the panel tended to view the wildcat strike as the only means available by which workers could express
and demonstrate their grievances.

The model we began to develop then, was that the diffuse community strains had preconditioned, or created an attitudinal set, in
which the wildcat strike became both a conscious and unconscious "pre-

text" for expressing a broader range of frustrations and grievances. O
the basis of what we saw and heard during the first couple of weeks c
the inquiry this seemed to be the most plausible explanation. There wa
however, another major causal possibility; namely, that on-the-job fric
tion itself rather than community relations was at the heart of the matte
In fact, it was quite impossible to separate industrial from community re
lationships: the direct precipitant of the strikes was nearly always indus
trial; the language of the grievances in the strike we observed, howeve
quickly shifted from industrial specifics to a broader sense of grievanc
against the company. Nonetheless, it seemed important to look into th
question further under more controlled conditions.

With the assistance of other members of the team I assembled
questionnaire of 27 attitude items and 13 background variables. The att
tude items dealt mainly with the way workers viewed on-the-job rela
tionships, but also included items on their attitudes toward strikes, th
trade union, and other local conditions and agencies. This questionnair
was administered at our headquarters to 100 production workers selecte
by taking every thirty-fourth name from an alphabetized list of 3,400 em
ployees provided by Demba's accounting office. The union gave its bless
ing to this enterprise and workers were given time off by the company t
complete the questionnaire; we privately interviewed each of them imme
diately afterwards for 10 to 45 minutes. Cooperation and candor was, un
der the circumstances, surprisingly good. I cannot review our findings i
detail here but several major conclusions may be cited. The first dea
with a notion favored in company circles that most workers did not ac
tually support the stikes but were coerced into doing so by an irrespons
ble minority—the "agitator" hypothesis, which always seems attractiv
to conservative analysts of collective behavior. In our questionnaire an
interview sessions we asked workers what their reaction had been to tw
strikes, including the one we had just witnessed. Of the workers, 65 pe
cent said they had either "strongly supported" or "supported" the recer
strike; 19 percent said they "had no feelings about it one way or an
other"; 10 percent felt the strike "was probably not justified"; while
percent "strongly opposed" the strike. Responses to an earlier strike fo
lowed the same pattern: 58 percent said they had favored that actior
while only 16 percent said they had been opposed to walking off the job.

The numerous items bearing on routine job relationships and work
ing conditions did not yield a picture of majority and acute disconten
On only one question, dealing with whether or not company policies ar
clear, did more than 10 percent of the respondents choose the mos
strongly negative response category. They tended to rate the Demb
management as competent but as not really interested in the worker

onsistent with the findings showing support for wildcat strikes workers
ated other employees as on the whole agreeable to work with and, some-
hat to our surprise, foremen received high marks for being friendly and
elpful and being able to administer discipline. These findings did not,
f course, provide us with proof that community rather than industrial
onditions were decisive ones, but they did seem to suggest that in the
ale of grievances the former ranked higher than the latter. This inter-
retation was borne out by the fact that it was precisely on items dealing
ith living conditions that the highest levels of distress were registered.
o less than 67 percent regarded their housing as unsatisfactory—50 per-
ent said "most unsatisfactory"; 69 percent thought sanitation was badly
oked after; 47 percent stated that treatment at the company-run hospi-
al was poor. Based on these findings, and our own observations, we
oncluded in our report that: "It is clear that a substantial lessening of
issatisfactions with the community cannot come by improving 'human
elations' alone; the basic amenities of modern life—health, sanitation
nd housing must be tackled on a major scale immediately." Elementary,
erhaps, but in light of the antagonism, myth, defensiveness and frus-
ation that characterized the outlook of some company officials it
eemed essential to document and spell out the implications of this find-
ng.

The worker survey occupied my sociological colleague and myself
or over two weeks. Some personal tensions had arisen among all of us
n the compressed atmosphere of those weeks: Frank and Jimmy were un-
erstandably growing restive during this time and were eager to write
nis to the undertaking. Before departing, however, we had agreed to par-
icipate in a collective feedback session with the Demba top manage-
ent and two leading executives from Alcan, the parent company in
Montreal. This confrontation, held in a conference room at the Demba
ffices in Watooka, was interesting because Frank and Jimmy, who had
een relatively inactive during the investigation, actually stole the show.
hey told the corporation representatives that the mutinous attitudes of
he work force could be directly attributed to company attitudes and poli-
ies. Frank accused Demba executives of hiding behind a "bureaucratic
lockade"; Jimmy recounted past community grievances and, thumping
n the table, warned Demba to mend its ways. These criticisms, coming
s they did from the older, "conservative," "responsible" members of the
eam undoubtedly carried much greater weight—particularly with the
isiting brass from Montreal—than if they had come from the mouths
f us sociological babes. It was a pivotal session so far as I was concerned
ecause my senior colleagues' outspokenness at the meeting, as I later
aw, would arm me with *a critical collective point of view* that was the

outcome of the investigation of a panel of consultants the company ha
itself selected. Demba could scarcely dismiss us as hostile outsiders in
posed on them by the government. We were their hand-picked mer
After Frank and Jimmy's performance I thought that there was not onl
a gratifying irony in the way the investigation had turned out, but pe:
haps an object lesson for any zealous public relations officer as well: be
ware of the apparent tractability of men whose interests do not exactl
coincide with your own.

The probe team shortly thereafter disbanded, two months after it
inception, amidst the popping of champagne corks and an innocent org
of nostalgia and self-congratulation at our little headquarters. Now be
gan the really difficult part of the exercise, the writing of the report itsel
Each member of the team was to send me a memorandum and I would a
tempt to weave these together, along with other data and observation.
into a document to which all could affix their signatures. I thought it im
portant to draft a report that everyone would sign because if there wer
abstentions—particularly from our senior colleagues—this might ser:
ously weaken the report's impact on company policy. The problem wa
to strike a kind of line of best fit through attitudes and recommendation
of four quite different persons. This posed questions of tone and style a
well as content, and, since the government had shown no special interes
in the inquiry, I was constantly aware that our primary readers would b
the company hierarchy itself. This situation suggested a tone, which
while critical and pulling no punches in terms of our collective percep
tions, was not hostile to the firm but rather gave due credit to its willing
ness to change and indicated the responsibilities of other agencies—pa:
ticularly the government and union—in the area.

The memorandum Jimmy sent down from Toronto posed no partic
ular difficulties. One of his major suggestions, which was embodied i
the report, was that a Bauxite Worker's Welfare Fund be established i
order to aggregate capital for various development schemes, this fund t
be based on a prototype that had been successfully inaugurated in th
sugar belt some years before. Frank's memorandum on industrial condi
tions proposed that the trade union should be strengthened by union
izing company foremen. I was personally opposed to this recommenda
tion and, while attending the twenty-fifth anniversary of the Barbado
Worker's Union in Barbados some weeks later, I tried to persuade him to
drop it. My reasons were not based on an objection to unionizing fore
men in general; rather, my concern was that in this instance the placin;
of foremen under union discipline would undermine the role this stratun
might play as a mediating middle class. The company Community Rela
tions department had already begun to construct housing for foremen i

Watooka. After our feedback session with company officials a member of the community relations staff had remarked to me, nodding his head toward the dignitaries from Montreal: "You've just saved us six months in getting those houses built." Company officials asserted, and I agreed with them, that if the foremen ranks were to provide a basis for recruitment into management positions it seemed unlikely that this process would be accelerated by having them participate in, or possibly lead, strikes. Walcott, on the other hand, argued from a trade unionist standpoint that the unionizing of foremen would strengthen the union and thus contribute to industrial stability. I appreciated this argument, but we had to agree to disagree on this point. The report would ambiguously urge "further study" of this problem.

The discussion with Frank Walcott took place shortly after I had circulated my first draft of the report to team members. The company was anxious to know what was in store for them and, in keeping with my desire to maximize our influence with them, I agreed to meet privately with the top four or five executives at their offices in Georgetown. I was by now primarily involved in various difficulties that had arisen at the university. Among these was the resistance I had encountered from members of the university administration regarding an invitation I had extended to Dr. Jagan to deliver to my class in introductory sociology a lecture on the Marxist theory of stratification. I had been urged to withdraw this invitation, which Dr. Jagan had accepted, on the grounds that he represented "the enemy." This I declined to do, and the Board of Governors subsequently endorsed the lecture invitation, which was held without incident. Since Demba supported the idea of the university—partly as an ideological counterpoise to the Jagans—and the Vice Chancellor was a Canadian national, it will be understood that my position as corporation consultant was not without a certain degree of ambiguity at this point. However, I met with the company officials and went over the draft report in detail with them.

That they wanted changes did not surprise me. What did surprise me was the nature of the changes they suggested—a word here, a phrase there, a minor factual correction elsewhere. There was no suggestion of coercion and little attempt at persuasion. I yielded on some petty and inconsequential points, and corrected only one factual point of substance. The plant manager had assured me that a former Community Relations Director had in fact not been fired for living in the workers' quarter of Mackenzie—as was widely believed among older workers—but rather had resigned of his own volition for reasons of health. My judgment of the plant manager was that, whatever his faults in the area of human relations, he was a man of personal integrity, and I did not hesitate to incorporate his version of this incident into the report. Otherwise the concessions made were trivial ones; and I thought that, having insisted on the team's autonomy from the outset, it would now be politic to give the company a few crumbs of satisfaction by being personally responsive to their point of view. There was, in addition, one major change which I will describe in a moment, suggested by a company executive, in the wording of a recommendation.

During these weeks I also tried to stay in touch with the other interested parties to the report. Winston Verbeke's lieutenant in the mineworker's union came over to our house in Georgetown one evening, accompanied by his wife, and we argued at length, assisted by a considerable amount of Russian Bear rum, about the need for action in establishing a strong union headquarters in Mackenzie. Was it because they received a per diem allowance from the union treasury when living away from Mackenzie that he and Mr. Verbeke were so attached to life in the capital? These, and other issues were debated, and I outlined in some detail what criticisms and suggestions the report would contain. "Suppose" I said, "that I were to tell you that we have urged that, for a beginning, the company cut two holes off the golf course and arrange for the construction of workers' housing in Watooka?" He said: "Jack, my grandchildren won't live to see that." I continued: the report advocated the closing of the staff cinema, the integration of the staff school with an improved public school, and the demolition of present company offices to be rebuilt, with a public cafeteria, on the workers' side of the bauxite plant. The rum had obviously gone to my head, he scoffed. Furthermore, I said, we have urged that the company adopt a policy of Guyanization in which they affirm that it is not enough for them to be merely diligent, as in the recent past, in hiring Guyanese but that they must set up a timetable and a training program which ensure that the staff will be largely Guyanese and West Indian within a few years. This, I added, was essential because I had come to the conclusion that the aspirations and cultural differences between the expatriate staff and local people were too great; superimposed on top of the sharp class differences that existed they made for an insupportable situation. Rapid Guyanization within the context of a more integrated community setting, while undoubtedly generating problems of its own—how egalitarian were the middle-class Guyanese?—would lessen the traditional cultural strains and at least provide some new openings or crises for further democratization of the social order. To be sure, if such changes produced greater stability it would be in the interests of Demba—but also in the long-term interests of Guyanese socialism. If nationalization of the industry should be seriously placed on the agenda at some future date, the prior liquidation of the olonial social heritage would make the transition to public ownership much less difficult. I could not subscribe to the naive assumption of some of my Leninist friends in Georgetown that a perpetuation of reactionary ocial conditions was going to lead to revolutionary demands by a largely reorganizational, black Mackenzie proletariat committed to the gradual-st policies of Mr. Burnham. When published, the recommendations of our report could serve as the point of a wedge containing trade union and other community-organized demands for change in the area. This was my hope, as I expressed it on this and other occasions to the union leader-hip and to the public.[5]

Mr. Ramphal died in Canada while the report was being prepared and so was unable to comment on the final version. Frank Walcott had agreed to sign it; but in the weeks following the field work, my Guyanese sociological colleague underwent, I believe, a crisis of conscience regard-ng the moral and political implications of the report. He seemed to wish to disassociate himself from the exercise because, when all was said and done, the report did point toward a constructive future role for Demba and, in his view, underplayed—in a clause inserted at his request—"the continuing existence of racial discrimination which at this stage of devel-opment is still linked-up with class and national differences." After a heated discussion, in which I was forced to remind him of our friendship, he agreed to become a reluctant signatory to the report.

The manuscript was now turned over to the company for typing and mimeographing, a task that seemed to take an inordinate length of time—some weeks, in fact. I finally received a call from Keith Tisshaw, the com-pany's public relations officer, who said that it was ready for distribution. I went to his office and was given four numbered copies: one for the union; one for the Ministry of Labour, and two for myself. It was clear that Keith now sought to keep the circulation of the report to the bare minimum, reverting to the position that we were essentially a "panel of consultants." He must have known that this was a vain hope. The union's copy went, I believe, almost directly to the linotypists of two of the Georgetown newspapers, one of which printed much of the text, and all of the conclusions and recommendations, in a Sunday edition. I could not have wished for a more effective means of publication; Winston Ver-beke told me later that the clippings were being saved and avidly dis-cussed in Mackenzie. Perhaps.

But my main concern was that, although contrary to the initial cal-

---

[5] As this goes to press in 1971, the Burnham government, with Jagan's support, is moving to nationalize Demba. There has been talk of rapprochement between the two men, and a far more dynamic political situation exists in the West Indies today than when this chapter was written.

culations of some in the company, the report had now become public property; it might well suffer the fate of many another nine-day crusade whipped up by the West Indian press. The key to implementation of changes in Mackenzie still lay with Demba top management, and Demba, its *amour propre* wounded, might well respond to this unwanted publicity by raising the drawbridge and rejecting the counsel of some of the tentative crypto-liberals within its organization. I decided upon the following stratagem: I was scheduled to give a public lecture on social change in the West Indies, in a series sponsored by the university, the following Sunday morning. I telephoned Keith Tisshaw and told him: "You fellows are going to have to adopt some public position on the report. Why don't you take the bull by the horns and participate, along with the union and Ministry of Labour in a public lecture which I will hold next Sunday dealing with the situation in detail?" He thought it was worth considering. "Look," I said, "you know that I'm not out to administer a public horse-whipping to Demba. There are a lot of factual misunderstandings about the situation up there and where it is warranted, I'll defend you." This assurance may have tipped the scales. Consultations among top management took place the rest of that day; and, in the meantime, I obtained the assent of Mr. Verbeke and the Ministry of Labour who agreed to send a representative. I later learned that opinion among the Demba managers had been divided; Jim Campbell, the managing director, slept on it, and the next day agreed that Bob Rosane, his Harvard-trained personnel manager, would be the company representative. The meeting was announced in the newspapers as an "action seminar" and the stage was thus set for a public confrontation and accounting in which the corporation would itself participate.

The lecture rooms at the Government Technical Institute were filled to overflowering on Sunday morning as I began my lecture. Many members of official Georgetown were in attendance; Bob Rosane and Winston Verbeke were on the platform with me. As I began reading and interpolating the report I noticed that Bob was conspicuously fingering a pamphlet entitled "Fabian Publications in Print"—was he trying to tell me something? The lecture lasted nearly two hours. I had read most of the report and attempted, in summation, to state my personal views on what it contained, as I have described it in the preceding pages.

Then came question period. My assertion that Demba did not practice apartheid but rather class segregation produced numerous emotional and critical statements and questions from some of the Negroes present. One spoke of "exterminating the expatriates." Some of the Communists present dismissed the report as a whitewash and asked Bob Rosane to produce detailed figures on how much surplus value Alcan had taken from the country since it began mining operations. Winston Verbeke—one of the few Mackenzie people present—rose and called the report "an historic document." A heckler from the floor demanded to know if he had read it. Flustered, he answered "No—," and the house dissolved in laughter. On and on it went; a proper grilling. Finally, the chairman called a merciful halt.

Afterwards, there were congratulations and rum. "Unflappable!" my Vice Chancellor said, shaking my hand. A recently arrived British psychiatrist came up to the platform and inquired plaintively: "Does this sort of thing go on all the time?" Next day the Guyana *Graphic* featured the lecture on the front page along with a large photograph of a haggard-looking probe team chairman. The editorial response in the press was quite favorable, although skeptical of the proposals for social integration of worker and staff. The recommendation most applauded was the acceleration and deliberate planning of the Guyanization policy. The strong wording of that recommendation was lauded by several commentators. No one knew, nor would they be likely to believe, that it had been dictated to me verbatim by Bob Rosane during the private conference I had held with company officials in Georgetown.

Demba now wished me to give a repeat performance in Mackenzie, but this I declined to do. It seemed to me that, in staging a public discussion, I had probably miscalculated the degree to which Guyanese would readily be able to accept or act upon the analysis and image of the future presented under the circumstances of our investigation. The Marxists could not accept piecemeal social reforms—these were denounced in Jagan's newspaper—the Negroes were too angry over the past injustices of the company to accept the idea of cooperation and a new beginning from that quarter. I weighed the idea of going to Mackenzie under other auspices but was afraid that such a meeting might well produce unmanageable immediate demands, and quite possibly yet another wildcat strike. As a professional sociologist and as a foreigner, I had to draw the line somewhere. In addition, I learned that the government had, as a result of my lecture, ordered dozens of copies of the report for distribution to the Cabinet and other officials. So I contented myself with a couple of additional articles in the press in which I expressed the hope that Demba realized, if it needed any reminder, that rapid action was necessary. This did not, however, prevent Dr. Jagan, from speaking in public about "CIA professors at the university"—a charge that did not produce any particular animosity on my part, politics being politics. I last saw Cheddi looking jaunty and debonair on the street during the Independence Day celebration in 1967. He waved, smiled and said, "Hey, boy; better hurry up or you'll miss the parade."

CONCLUSION

The foregoing is the account of one sociologist's personal experiment in attempting to achieve *control* over a particular system of social relations by utilizing his professional skills and status to (1) *investigate* albeit superficially, that system of social relations; (2) *propagate* an image of a more humane, democratic future for that system; and (3) attempt to directly and indirectly *manipulate* the decision-making process so as to increase the likelihood of that future being attained. There was much more to it than I have been able to state here, but perhaps I have sketched in enough of the details of the experience to indicate that, although they were imperfectly realized in execution, my guidelines for behavior closely followed those enumerated by Bell and Mau in the opening section of this book. In their words, I attempted, implicitly following the directives of "value relevance," of "manipulative priority" and the rest, to participate "in the process of deciding what the future should be and finding the means for making it come about that way."

Before attempting to assess this experiment one fact should be recognized: whatever evaluation may be made of my conduct, a single case such as this serves neither to validate nor invalidate the general precepts advanced by Bell and Mau. In many ways the experience I have related is an extreme and atypical one. The sharpness of the ideological conflict the fact of my foreign nationality, the ambiguity of the sponsorship, the complications of the mixed "team" approach, and other variables make it difficult to treat this as a textbook case. Lawyers say that hard cases make bad law; nonetheless, if social scientists are to proceed in the general directions laid out in this volume, then candid self-criticism, uncomfortable disclosures, and the consideration of alternative strategies are indispensable.

The first observation I want to make is that "the up-river probe" took a hell of a lot out of me. In retrospect, writing a year later in New York, I am alternately amused and appalled at my *chutzpah*. To come into a society in which you are barely known and attempt to influence the calling of the shots at a fairly significant level takes a degree of nerve I do not really possess. But I was, and am, a victim of the passionate state of mind when it comes to the West Indies; I deeply care and worry about these societies and therefore I can be accused of falling prey to that bugbear of the anthropologist: "overidentification." In further extenuation it may be said that the dominant public rhetoric and raison d'être of the University of Guyana was that of "community service." My participation in the Mackenzie venture was touted by the administration as an indication of this commitment by the university. The trouble—and it was rouble to a degree I have not really begun to suggest—was that the uniersity itself was rent by the same ideological, racial, and locals-vs.-exatriates squabbles as obtained in Mackenzie. The radicals saw the uniersity as a creature of the Burnham government and the neocolonial ystem. This rather special circumstance meant that my immediate academic context was bereft of a critically supportive *peer system* (to borrow rom Howard E. Freeman's useful discussion [1963] on the strategy of olicy research), but rather was explicitly committed to the *policy system* s an institution. Thus my participation in the up-river probe was simply n extension rather than a contradiction of my academic role as locally lefined. But it will have been noticed that my identification with the soci·ty could not be an indiscriminate one. In order to play a role, however ninor, in the institutionalized decision-making process it was necessary o make some very difficult and problematic judgments about the politcal alignments of the society and about the probable uncontrollable facors—notably future development under American suzerainty and the ountry's pluralistic social system—in order to "plug myself in" at what ippeared to be a point of effectiveness. In so doing—and I believe this operation is indigenous in some form to most "policy-influencing" research, however innocuous—I committed myself to a standpoint which las been called, among other things, "historicism."

"Historicism" as discussed by Karl Popper (1961:50–51) in *The Poverty of Historicism*, covers a multitude of sins but the following quotation vill convey its saliency for the present discussion:

> Those who desire an increase in the influence of reason in social life can only be advised by historicism to study and interpret history in order to discover the laws of its development. If such interpretation reveals that changes answering to the desire are impending, then the desire is a reasonable one, for it agrees with scientific prediction. If the impending development happens to tend in another direction, then the wish to make the world more reasonable turns out to be entirely unreasonable; to historicists it is just a Utopian dream. *Activism can be justified only so long as it acquiesces in impending changes and helps them along* (emphasis added).

Please note two awkward facts about this quotation: First, Popper's polemic is directed primarily against Marxism and its prescriptions for "correct" social action, which flows from an acceptance of historical materialism. Second, to make things a bit more convoluted, this quotation had been contained in a critical footnote in a study I had made of Trinidad several years before going to Guyana. In Trinidad, indeed in the "neocolonial" world generally, as I saw it, nationalist leaders were caught in the grip of the historicist vise: regardless of their private political views the urgent exigencies of economic development required, as a fun damental postulate, acquiescence to the impending changes, which would be hopefully wrought by private, mainly American, foreign investmen and handouts. For the reasons described, in order to play an activist role and following the precept of "manipulative priority" my activities can rightly be described as a species of vulgar historicism—"vulgar" because not derived from a compelling theory of historical change (on the exist ence of which I am agnostic), but rather on an empirical projection of present-day political realities. To reiterate the general point: my commit ment was not unique among policy-oriented social scientists. The aim of influencing policy presumes the existence of policy-makers, within some institutionalized, on-going system of power, firmly ensconced or insur gent. If my reading of global trends had been the reverse of what it was and I had become involved in a study—e.g., the stratification system of a neocolonial society—that might be helpful to the Jaganites, my general position would have been in the abstract identical. (Indeed, for purposes of drawing up a roster of possible priorities for research at the University of Guyana and by visiting foreign scholars, I had made an appoint ment with Mrs. Jagan and the surprisingly muscular PPP Education Committee to obtain suggestions for types of studies they felt would illuminate local conditions. It proved unproductive. They were firm in the belief that "it's all economic," i.e., that when the Negroes finally awoke —as Burnham's bungling and the failure of American imperialism would inevitably awaken them—to the fact that they were basically an exploited class rather than an ethnic section, then the locomotive of change would be back on the rails. Research on the contemporary neocolonial social structure was therefore superfluous because it was a passing phase.)

Historicism—or, less politely, sociological opportunism—appears to be a dangerous assumption for the policy-oriented sociologists. If reg ularly practiced, given the present-day status of the Western university, it could lead to an undermining of public acceptance of the very foun dations of the legitimacy we claim as academics. *Given the present status of the Western university.* The problem is one of sailing under false colors; of taking advantage of one's lofty status as a university man to gain entrée into the tension-management activities of the society. It may be argued that academic economists regularly do this, but they generally attempt to manipulate variables at once more remote, impersonal, and esoteric than the sociologist who directly investigates and prescribes for a particular community or organization. If sociology is to move in the direction of a primary and overt concern with problem-solving, then its legitimacy can perhaps not rest on its status in the traditional university, or on an appeal to "science," but rather on institutions in which the primary commitment to *praxis* is acknowledged. In short, the first order of business for a sociology of the future would seem to be a programmatic sociology of the sociology of the future. However, in situations of acute conflict I doubt if we can have our cake and eat it: I do not think we will be able to claim sanctuary in the academy *and* direct participation *as sociologists* in the on-going struggle to shape the future. An activist role will probably have to be lived more dangerously and openly than the usual academic ambit. If this challenge were made, however, it can be anticipated that most sociologists would opt for the comforts of the present schizoid mode; preferring to rationalize the itch for influence by embracing the Weberian distinction between activities appropriate to their professional or academic role as scientists and their role as citizens. This is a neat formulation (does it partly account for Max Weber's longevity as an authoritative advisor?), but in practice these supposedly distinct "roles" often seem to interpenetrate, if not violate, each other.

My conscious acceptance of a historicist perspective vis-à-vis Guyanese society led me to a course of action, which, it now strikes me, must be inherent in the attempt to synthesize the production of knowledge and the exercise of control. It is manifest that in the quest for control the time, effort, and discretionary freedom that is devoted to *investigation* is under constant assault from the will to *propagate* models of the future and to *manipulate* conditions to bring them about. Indeed, it may be axiomatic that the greater the degree of power—control over sanctions and resources—the stronger the tendency of the investigative function to recede in importance, or to serve as a rationalizing tool of social change: to a search for the most economical handles of a social structure, to a technical and ideological servicing of the party of progress. This danger of reducing truth to ideology is manifestly inherent in a totalitarian regime, but it would seem to apply to situations in which the sociologist is operating within a democratic, pluralistic context as well. Any societal situation in which there exists, at some critical level, both the resources and the will to change to a new pattern—both of which, despite the apparent tensions, were sufficiently present in Mackenzie— is a situation in which the arts of advocacy and midwifery rather than diagnosis will be most crucial. In Mackenzie the company wanted change, the union wanted change, the government wanted change, the people wanted change—all in varying amounts, and with real conflicts down the road but heading in the same general direction, toward a more indigenous, stable, and democratic community. I may therefore be entitled to judge myself less harshly by a broader moral standard insofar as my activities probably did give this total process a nudge in the right direction.

But I am of a mixed mind about that. Is a unity of theory and practice attainable under the kind of segmented role relations into which the professional sociologist is usually thrust vis-à-vis the clients and subjects of his inquiry? Perhaps the role and methodology I adopted betrayed a fundamental lack of seriousness and commitment to my radical aspirations. Perhaps I confused and confounded an essentially revolutionary objective with a secure and rather petty style of operation. Perhaps, so I sometimes think in my more desperate moments, it will someday be necessary to stop being a sociologist and start being—what? In the meantime, the case for the sociologist as a direct agent of social change in democratic societies must rest, it seems to me, on a broader appeal to reason and tolerance on the part of the public; on the publicized premise that we are morally and intellectually fallible, but that like all men, we try to do our best according to our lights.

REFERENCES

Bell, Wendell (ed.)
    1967   The Democratic Revolution in the West Indies: Studies in Nationalism, Leadership, and the Belief in Progress. Cambridge, Mass.: Schenkman.
Cantril, Hadley
    1967   The Human Dimension: Experiences in Policy Research. New Brunswick, N.J.: Rutgers University Press.
Despres, Leo A.
    1967   Cultural Pluralism and Nationalist Politics in British Guiana. Chicago: Rand McNally.
Freeman, Howard E.
    1963   "The strategy of social policy research." The Social Welfare Forum, Brandeis University.
Hammond, Phillip E. (ed.)
    1967   Sociologists at Work. Garden City, N.Y.: Doubleday, Anchor Books.
Horowitz, Irving L. (ed.)
    1967   The Rise and Fall of Operation Camelot. Cambridge, Mass.: MIT Press.
Jagan, Cheddi
    1966   The West On Trial: My Fight for Guyana's Freedom. London: Michael Joseph.
Lazarsfeld, Paul F., William H. Sewell, and Harold L. Wilensky (eds.)
    1967   The Uses of Sociology. New York: Basic Books.

Moore, Wilbert E.
  1967   Order and Change: Essays in Comparative Sociology. New York:
             Wiley.
Oxaal, Ivar
  1967   "The intellectual background to the democratic revolution in
             Trinidad." Pp. 20–49 in Wendell Bell (ed.), The Democratic Revo-
             lution in the West Indies. Cambridge, Mass.: Schenkman.
Popper, Karl
  1961   The Poverty of Historicism. London: Routledge and Kegan Paul.
Shils, Edward
  1960   "Political development in the New States: II." Comparative Stud-
             ies in Society and History 2 (July): 4–26.
Sjoberg, Gideon
  1967   Ethics, Politics, and Social Research. Cambridge, Mass.: Schenk-
             man.

Epilogue

WENDELL BELL

In the foregoing pages, we have tried to show that the study of the future should have a place of priority on the sociological agenda and that a sociology of the future is emerging. We have given some theories, methods, and philosophies involved in it. We have adopted the viewpoint of the sociology of knowledge, both that experience shapes thought and that thought shapes experience, which is especially evident in the perceptive analyses of Bart, Burch, Boldt, and Hollander. Also, we have illustrated by specific case studies some of the results of conscious efforts to consider the implications of sociology for the future and some research designed to study images of the future in the context of decision-making and social action. Finally, in the annotated bibliography, which follows the epilogue, Bettina J. Huber has compiled a guide to some of the most important social science studies of the future that have been attempted to date. We have, thus, come to the end of our task, and we do not intend to repeat here what has already been said. Yet it remains to say a few final words in an effort to show how what we have tried to do in this volume relates to the current crisis in American sociology.

Indeed, there is a crisis in American sociology—perhaps in Western social science, maybe a more general crisis for rational intellectual thought everywhere. For example, in his presidential address before the American Sociological Association, August 31, 1970, Reinhard Bendix (1970:831) said: "We meet amidst upheaval directly affecting the academic community. The social sciences, and sociology in particular, are at the center of the storm." He spoke of "the ethic of social despair," "the distrust of reason," and "a crisis of legitimacy." And Alvin W. Gouldner (1970) has recently published *The Coming Crisis of Western Sociology*, into which title more than one of our colleagues in sociology has mentally inserted "[sic]" after "Coming." The crisis is here.

Of course, one may temper both his perceptions of the crisis and his reactions to it with a historical perspective and, thus, with a recognition that "crises" come and go. One may avoid the hysteria, the despair, and the rage that tends to surround it. One may comfort oneself that the sky has not yet fallen, that the world is not yet burning; that around the corner is a new generation of students who want to learn, not destroy; that the streets and the campuses will return to normal; that soon one crisp fall day even the chimes of the founder's tower will be drowned out by the sweet music of shuffling feet, of students dedicated to learning moving lightheartedly from one class to another. As sure as the pendulum swings, one may believe that it will come.

Yet in taking a long view, in thus being "reasonable" and "mature," in avoiding the panic of the moment, one touches a sensitive nerve that may intensify for some people the sense of crisis itself. For there is in the very lack of urgency thus expressed a complacency that is odious to those persons who have reached the conclusion that the present state of Western society and culture is threatening to destroy not only freedom but life itself. It is this basic difference in judgment that is part of the current crisis, the temporizing on the one hand and on the other hand the unwillingness—or the inability in the face of a presumedly intolerable future—to withhold anything of oneself or of one's sociology in the service of not just a good, but the only and the necessary and the "now," cause.

The manifestations of this confrontation around us in the larger society and on our university campuses are too numerous, too well-known, and, for some people, too painful to enumerate here. It is enough to say that they include smatterings of official repression and anonymous random violence, a growing anti-intellectualism among some national leaders and a prideful antirationality among some self-styled revolutionaries, the duplicity of some public officials and the deceitfulness of some radicals, and such repugnant sights as members of the Establishment wiping their feet on earnest mimeographed pleas for justice, and "crazies" shouting invective at college administrators who are willing to sit across the table and listen to them. Not all is so grim, of course, and there is evidence too of civility and constructive change, of understanding and rational dialogue, and even of hope. Nonetheless, uneasiness remains and, among persons of all ages and of different political colorations, the reckless urge to destroy seeks out its all-too-willing instruments.

Within sociology today, the question "How is society possible?" has taken on new meaning. How, indeed, can the conflicts around us be prevented from destroying our national community, our neighborhoods, our schools, and our community of sociologists? How can they be prevented from destroying our calling itself and that dream of a science of society to which sociologists have been dedicated? We have had our name-calling and shoving contests at the annual meetings of our professional society; our clashes between "true believers." There are the sociologists of the Sociology Liberation Movement, radical sociologists, activist sociologists, black separatist sociologists, feminist sociologists, and street sociologists. There are also the reactions to them, some open and constructive to be sure, but others ranging from sly cooptation to outright antagonism. There are cynics who promote female, radical, activist, and black nominees who otherwise have few qualifications for high office in our professional organizations; there are both radical and Establishment sociologists rushing into the "relevance" of research and action programs dealing with race, the inner city, and urban education where, let it be said, the sluices of wealth for the social scientists, if not for the "subjects" themselves, have run free and strong; there is the instant fame of callow youths who demand the right to speak before plenary sessions of thousands of sociologists, a right many sociologists never may get and for which others have waited and worked for decades; and there is the gutlessness of forty-year-olds who, buying peace, can say no more than "Yes, the kids are right." The sociological fraternity, too, may have its silent majority, watching, at best in bewilderment and at worst in bitterness, the destruction of the sociological order, destruction by direct attack, by counterattack, and perhaps most of all by cynical opportunism.

Although we oversimplify for the sake of brevity, part of the problem within sociology is similar to that within the society itself: a fundamental difference in perception of the seriousness and pervasiveness of present threats. If people are being killed, if civilization is in danger, how, some ask, can anyone continue daily life, much less sociology, as usual? But others who do not judge the situation as being so urgent believe it is reasonable to proceed on the basis of one's faith in the unhurried search for truth. One's professional work of creating and communicating sociological knowledge and one's actions as a part-time citizen may yet be validated. The latter also remember Samuel A. Stouffer's fondness for pointing out that Mendel was doing "pure research," studying peas, in the midst of a widespread wheat famine. What could appear more irrelevant yet be more relevant? Similarly, doesn't sociological knowledge contain the power to help solve social ills? The pat answer, of course, is, "Not necessarily. For while you're doing your trivial sociological thing, the world you are studying is going down the drain taking you and sociology with it, something Mendel never had to worry about with his peas."

The issue, as all sociologists know, is far more complex than this. In the same breath with the charges of triviality and irrelevance may come the charge of working for established interests, for the top dogs of the Pentagon; Department of State; Health, Education, and Welfare; Standard Oil; or General Motors, in sum—the Welfare-Warfare state. From a world view, the charge is that American sociologists serve the rich nations at the expense of the poor; or, more particularly, the special interests of the United States. Large-scale surveys, some contend, have lost their validity because some racial groups and social classes no longer have the trust, if they ever did, to give straight answers. Participant-observation among underdog populations, even—perhaps especially—when done with sympathy, has been viewed as immoral spying. The intrusion into sociology of a world view that sees the alleviation of human suffering as merely helping to preserve the existence of a rotten society that ought to be destroyed and replaced by something better gives pause to those decent souls who would point out, quite rightly, that American sociology during the last seven decades has certainly had its moments of relevance and, on more than one occasion, has clearly aimed to help humanity and sometimes actually has been utilized to do so. To those sociologists who still cling to the value-free stance and the notion of a clear differentiation between their professional and citizenship roles, many sociologists can only offer their sympathy.

There are at least three interrelated, but different, sets of crises that can be noted in the above account, and they reside in the consciousness of sociologists today regardless of their feelings about them. Two of them are quite clear: (I) *the crises of the larger society* and (II) *the crises of the interpenetration of the larger society and sociology.* The third is more difficult to discern partly because of understandable resistance to seeing it, although two important books have recently been published bearing on it, one by Gouldner, already cited, and another by Robert W. Friedrichs, the provocative *A Sociology of Sociology* (1970). It is (III) *the crisis of the scientific revolution within sociology itself.* The study of the future, we think, offers some acceptable alternatives to ease the sense of crisis through responsible action in each case.

By the crises of the larger society, we refer to such familiar conflicts as those over America's role abroad, especially the war in Vietnam; nuclear arms proliferation; racial inequality; unequal educational opportunity and quality; overpopulation; urban decay; the quality of life generally; the growing gap between the rich and poor nations; and the sense of despair or rebellion that pervades certain segments of the society. These are conflicts between some elites and other elites, between some vested interests and others, as well as between elites and masses of more or less unorganized people. Many of them reflect a more general conflict between the forces of the democratic revolution and those of reaction that are satisfied with a future little different from the present. The former push for a continuation of the trends that have seen the emergence of lower socioeconomic and racial groups and the rising minimums of civil, political, economic, social, and cultural rights. They include those persons working out new twentieth-century meanings and new applications for the concepts of progress and freedom, those persons constructing images of a more just and egalitarian future.

The crises of type II, those arising because of the interpenetration of the larger society and sociology, are largely synonymous with those of the universities and the intellectual establishment more generally. On the one hand, the universities are deeply involved in a range of important tasks that are manifestly supportive of the interests and goals of the Welfare-Warfare state. Any fair evaluation must point out, however, the freedom and the large amount of independently generated intellectual activity that by and large exist on our campuses and must also include the judgment that much of the work connected with government, from agricultural extension activities to training grants from the National Institute of Mental Health, has been beneficial. Yet, perhaps more than we realized, the universities have been partially mobilized to help perpetuate a world comfortable to established interests. The universities are now being asked to examine objectively the extent to which this is so.

On the other hand, they are being asked to mobilize for anti-Establishment causes by the new spokesmen for the unfinished revolution, a revolution that perhaps is destined to remain unfinished as long as the institutions to which it gives rise fail to adequately embody its underlying values and images of the future. The social sciences, particularly sociology, have been shaken because the challenges and problems are partly psychological and historical, largely political and economic, and especially sociological.

We propose the social scientific study of the future in the framework of the theory, value, and action that are specified in this volume as one reasonable response to the crises of types I and II. It represents both a scheme for organizing and analyzing the social realities that confront us and a way of orienting and directing our efforts as sociologists. The study of the possibilities for the future may offer a way out of the present deadly confrontations, a way that allows a happy marriage between the old and hallowed values of science and the older, perhaps more hallowed, values of social responsibility. For the scientific study of alternative futures by its very nature combines the search for knowledge with an action orientation. In our view, science without some mechanism for the translation of theory into practice is sterile, and social action without knowledge is irresponsible, often ineffective. Again, it is more complicated. There are times when one should know and there are times when one must act, whether one knows or not. But knowing gives comfort in the belief that someone, somewhere, sometime may find the knowledge useful; acting seems riskier, since the sins of commission may be greater than the sins of omission and the deed done can perhaps never be undone. What we have tried to show in this volume is that, in the scientific study of the possibilities for the future, moral conviction, a concern with human values, and an activist stance merge with the objective, disciplined, and systematic search for the truth. We have tried to show that the minute and particular problems of life may be understood as examples of general principles and that general principles have their meaning in the reality of particular men and situations as they move through time. We have tried to show that humanistic man and scientific man can become as one in the sociology of the future.

The study of alternative futures, of course, has its pitfalls. Although there may be no inevitable conflict, as Ivar Oxaal fears, between trying to shape the future and trying to build a science of society, there certainly may be disturbing tensions. We have argued that trying to build a science of society while maintaining a future orientation and a sensitivity to the values and interests being served inevitably thrusts one consciously into the struggle to control the future. Such consciousness and involvement may cause pain. Yet the tensions of such a struggle are preferable to those tensions we now face that arise from mindless action and mindful inaction, whether on the part of radical students or contract researchers for the Central Intelligence Agency.

The voices proclaiming revolution in the streets and calling for revolution in the role of the university, crises of types I and II, are joined by others who describe what they believe to be a scientific revolution in sociology, what we have designated a crisis of type III. It is a crisis because a new world view is involved, a new conception of the role of the sociologist, and, for that matter, a new sociology. If there is a new sociology emerging, it cannot help being deeply disturbing to those of us who still remain committed to the old.

Following Thomas S. Kuhn (1962), although greatly oversimplifying him, we present a series of stages of scientific development:

Stage I. Paradigmatic pluralism. This is a prescientific stage only in that there is no dominant paradigm that defines a field, its relevant community members, the definition of problems, or the direction of work.

Stage II. Emergence of a unified paradigm. A single paradigm begins to dominate; it defines the field and its boundaries more clearly; its scientific community becomes more distinct; there is a convergence of effort directed to similar problems.

Stage III. Normal science. The dominance of a single paradigm is complete; the core of the field, its boundaries, and its membership are distinct; efforts are focused on problems generated by the science; puzzles are defined and solved within the reigning paradigm; great progress occurs, largely a mopping-up operation.

Stage IV. The beginning of doubt. Inconsistencies and uncertainties no longer are easily resolved within the paradigm and grow into persistent anomalies; some members of the scientific community begin to formulate questions that can't be answered within the reigning paradigm, and begin to depict other scientists as "dopes" (see Blum, 1970) and some aspects of the paradigm as problematic.

Stage V. The scientific revolution. The emergence of a new and competing paradigm occurs that appears to be an acceptable alternative to the old paradigm; its early supporters and founders struggle to gain a core of adherents, especially the gatekeepers to the journals and the textbooks and, thus, to indoctrinate the young; the scientific community becomes divided, some members never convert to the new paradigm and continue their work in the frame of the old; the science itself is, therefore, less unified than before.

Stage VI. The new reigning paradigm—normal science again. The new paradigm now dominates the field; the core of the field, its boundaries, and its membership are again clearly defined; efforts are again focused on the problems generated by the science; puzzles are again defined and solved within a reigning paradigm, the new one; great progress again occurs, a mopping-up operation within the terms of the new paradigm. The unconverted have died, retired, become deans, returned to teaching, or simply been defined out of the discipline.

And, then, of course, doubt may begin again.

Our contention is that sociology today is in Stage V, the period of a scientific revolution. To show this one needs to demonstrate, at a minimum, first that there has been a dominant paradigm in sociology; second, that it has been made problematic; and third, that an acceptable alternative paradigm exists.

Here, we must refer the reader to the recent works by Friedrichs and Gouldner, because it is the burden of their ambitious efforts to make such demonstrations. Each author is willing to concede that sociology has not had a paradigm as completely dominant and all-pervasive as Kuhn describes in his model. Yet each makes a good case for an approximation to it in the dominance over sociology that has been held by the structural-functional theory of Talcott Parsons, especially the later Parsons of the Social System. It is a case well supported by the empirical results of footnote counting in sociological journals or textbooks. The height of consensus over the Parsonsian paradigm, however, may have been reached in the 1950s with the divisions of the 1960s moving more and more sociologists into the period of growing doubt.

Both authors, especially Gouldner in his detailed, point-by-point confrontation with Parsons' functionalism, make the Parsonsian paradigm problematic. And both go beyond Kuhn to show how the Parsonsian theory of social systems was born in the larger sociocultural context and how the revolution was prepared there, thereby showing the connections between the three types of crises we have identified. Gouldner makes Parsons' paradigm problematic in a number of ways, including (1) showing how Parsons came to shape his functionalism as a result of his own particular personal experiences; (2) showing how Parsons' paradigm was influenced by, maintained by, and flourished under the particular social and cultural conditions of the larger society; and (3) showing that the ideological character of Parsons' paradigm represents a conservative bias. With respect to the last point, for example, Gouldner (1970:332) says:

> Although Functionalism is adaptable to all *established* industrial systems, it is not equally responsive to *new* orders that are only coming into being, for these may be the foes of those already established. What makes a theory conservative (or radical) is its posture toward the institutions of its own surrounding society. A theory is conservative to the extent that it: treats these institutions as given and unchangeable in essentials; proposes remedies for them so that they may work better, rather than devising alternatives to them; foresees no future that can be essentially better than the present, the conditions that already exist; and, explicitly or implicitly, counsels acceptance of or resignation to what exists, rather than struggling against it.

Adopting a science model, as we do, we would stress still another feature of the Parsonsian paradigm that makes it problematic. Much of what Parsons says *in his high-level theorizing* is, strictly speaking, nonsense. That is, it is largely uninterpretable and untestable. It is, therefore, difficult to show that the Parsonsian paradigm is false or true, because it is difficult to find "out there" in social reality many of the things that Parsons is talking about. We are, of course, aware of the many attempted empirical applications of the functionalist paradigm, but we remain skeptical of its isomorphism with social reality and are led to ask: Where are the operational definitions of the key concepts? Where are the detailed inductive and deductive steps that link empirical social relations to the paradigm? What indeed would Parsonsians consider to be adequate empirical data to reject the paradigm or any part of it?

But we have had many critiques of Parsons' paradigm before, and still it lingers on. Even Gouldner's point-by-point critique will not achieve its demise, because, as Kuhn points out, criticism alone is not enough to produce a paradigmatic shift. More to the point, but still insufficient we would argue, is the extent of congruence between the theory and the containing social and cultural conditions, the structure of prevailing sentiments. Gouldner, for example, looks for the erosion, though not the total demise, of the Parsonsian paradigm in the culture of the young, both the New Left and the Psychedelic Culture (compare the chapter by Boguslaw in this volume), and in the rapid growth of the Welfare State following World War II. Friederichs looks to the "climate of the times," to "an era of unparalleled conformity and commitment to the *status quo*," to explain the rise of Parsons' "system" theory. For its fall he looks to a "thorough-going shift in perspective within the sociocultural setting" that includes the domestic civil rights revolution, Marxist-motivated social change in underdeveloped countries, the rediscovery of the young humanistic Marx, existentialism, black power, and antagonism to the Vietnam war on the part of the intellectual community. Although all these factors may help prepare the way, a crucial ingredient for the demise of a paradigm is still missing.

The functionalist paradigm has had its important uses for sociology itself, considered simply as a scientific discipline. It has had the virtues of high generality to the point of subsuming much of the entire discipline and, thus, has tended to unify the various subdisciplines within sociology. For without some focus for the concentrated efforts of sociologists, there could be little progress in sociology. It has underlying simplicity in the formal sense; that is, it is systematic and interconnected. And it is appropriate to the sociological level of abstraction. These virtues are not easily given up, even if the concepts of the theory have little empirical import, even if the theory is ideologically biased, and even if its personal and social origins are exposed.

What is missing, of course, is an adequate alternative. The construction of a new paradigm acceptable to some significant number of sociologists is essential for a paradigmatic shift. Thus, the crisis of the scientific revolution in sociology is only partly a consequence of crises I and II. It is also a crisis within sociology itself of growing dissatisfaction with the old paradigm and lack of consensus concerning a new one. We are being called upon to make a long hard ride into the future; shall we risk it with our sure but old and tired horse trained for a different course? Or shall we risk it with an untried but promising and fresh mount raised on the track? Is there, indeed, a fresh mount available?

Although he devotes most of his attention to his critique of the Parsonsian paradigm, Gouldner summarizes in a final chapter his conception of an alternative, which he aptly calls "Reflexive Sociology." It is, however, not so much a conceptual and theoretical framework as it is a specification of some of the features that the new sociology may have, the chief one being an increase in the *self-awareness* of the sociologist himself (compare our directives). Friedrichs does somewhat more in this regard than does Gouldner, at least insofar as he has more fully described some of the alternative paradigms that are prominent contenders for the Parsonsian throne. He discusses a series of paradigms from Marx and Sartre to Peter Berger and Harold Garfinkel, and ends with a preference for a dialectical—or as he prefers to call it "dialogical"—scheme that is similar in some respects to Gouldner's Reflexive Sociology. For example, he says (1970:301):

> As the realization grows that the substantive focus of sociology includes social research and the resultant *awareness* that the very precipitation and comprehension of past and present order will inevitably to some degree be fed back through social interaction to deny that order, a dialectical paradigm becomes increasingly tenable (italics added).

Friedrichs believes that the new sociology will increase man's responsibility through the revelation of the potential results of his behavior and will increase man's freedom by spelling out ". . . the substantively verifiable manner in which the very perception of order will contribute to freeing one from compulsive repetition" (321).

From Gouldner and Friedrichs, as well as from what has been said earlier in this volume, some of the parameters of the new sociology, compared to functionalism, can be ventured. The role of the sociologist will be different. The new sociologist will see himself as part of the social reality he studies and will take account of the effects of his actions. He will be a responsible agent of history. He will be more personally involved in his hypotheses, drawing in part on his own experiences explicitly for shaping his sociological construction of the world. Our directives, for example, of studying the future and our directives concerning the role of the sociologist as maker of the future should be seen as interrelated.

The new sociology will not simply accept existing systems and institutions as they are, but will be oriented toward devising alternatives. It will encompass conflict and dialectics. It will be dynamic and change-oriented. It will deal with the emergent as well as the extant. It will be transcendental.

It will be concerned with values and their achievement and will be sensitive to the consequences of both stability and change with respect to manifest goals and unanticipated consequences. Although the design of research will ideally include a variety of possibilities for the future rather than a mere extension of the existing structures, one possibility will always be the value consequences of a "no change" condition. Yet society will be basically viewed as processual, geared to the notion of transforming, and to some extent open-ended.

The new sociology, and here we part company from Gouldner, will propose remedies for existing systems so that they may work better, keeping in mind that a series of minor changes may eventually result, as Marx said, in qualitative changes.

The new sociology will take man into account, and give him priority over institutions. It will be less deterministic, more volitional and voluntaristic. The new sociological actors will have considerable creativity, freedom, responsibility, and spontaneity. Man will be autonomous to some degree. There will be options, choices, and decision-making.

The new sociology will be control- and intervention-minded, instrumental, and action-oriented. The new sociology will be more sophisticated and explicit about the interests it serves. Trends will be studied to see how they can be accelerated, maintained, or brought to a halt. There may be a bifurcation of the discipline with the development of social clinicians whose chief work would concern the application of sociological knowledge for the solution of practical problems.

The new sociology will be humanistically, as well as scientifically, oriented. It will be explicitly moral, not just in its commitment to procedure but also in its commitment to bettering the human condition.

Because technological progress in the tools of sociological method can be expected to continue, the new sociology will also be more rigorous and sound, and more objective. And because it will not divest itself of its scientific pretensions, it will be more solidly grounded empirically.

If there is to be a new sociology, what then of the old? Although Kuhn exaggerates the extent to which the old paradigm is wiped out by the new in his book, he does make the point that the "new paradigm must promise to preserve a relatively large part of the concrete problem-solving ability that has accrued to science through its predecessors. . . As a result, though new paradigms seldom or never possess all the capabilities of their predecessors, they usually preserve a great deal of the most concrete parts of past achievement and they always permit additional concrete problem-solutions besides" (168). But most of Parsonsian theory is not concrete. Thus, if a new paradigm does begin to take shape, most of the old *paradigm* may go.

Much of sociology as it is, however, would be incorporated in the new. This would be so (1) because the Parsonsian paradigm has never been so dominant as we—and Friedrichs and Gouldner—have made out for the sake of discussion; (2) because much good sociological work linked to it by theory-starved researchers doesn't basically rest on it and can stand alone; and (3) because the various subdisciplines have had their own traditions of middle-range theories with which to work. We cannot stress enough our belief that part of what the development of the new sociology needs is the organization of empirical generalizations in specific areas of sociology into, not grand theory, but relational statements of some higher order than the immediately empirical. The search for the structure behind our observations and the formulation of empirically grounded theory are what are needed. The sort of theory, for example, that Blalock (1967) has constructed for minority-group relations could be done for other fields. Already, we have middle-level theorizing in criminology, delinquency, the family, and the community. The accumulated work in other areas shows presumptive evidence of underlying structure. It should be shown to "add up" even if in a series of partially unified subfields. If the new sociology is to have its status as a science confirmed, this grounded theoretical work must be done.

Of course, empirical work won't usually add up unless it is in some sense carried out within the same terms of reference. If subfields of sociology need to be ordered, so does the field of sociology as a whole or it may fragment into a number of smaller disciplines. Sociologists, to some extent, have to work on a similar set of problems if sociology is to progress. Here is where a grand, overall guiding paradigm is so important. But the Parsonsian model appears wobbly and increasingly problematic. Some sociological effort should be expended on this level of theorizing too.

We do not believe that we have presented an adequate alternative paradigm in this book, yet we hope that we have cast a light in the direction one might be found.[1] The sociology of the future matches the possible parameters of the new sociology we have enumerated. It does make different assumptions than the Parsonsian model. It contains a theory of social change—all too sketchily formulated—and it puts both man and sociologist into the scheme of things as effective actors. It includes values and beliefs. Most of all, it is dynamic and, of course, future-oriented. The sociological study of the future itself is, however, not substantive or general theory, but a perspective, a point of view that can be brought to any subfield of sociology. It is linked to the three crises we have mentioned: (1) it bears on the problems of the larger society from a perspective of future possibilities, as well as past or present limitations; (2) it offers a way of doing scholarly work within the general traditions of

---

[1] For a recent formulation of a systematic "theory of macro-action" that is generally consistent with the views expressed in this volume, see Etzioni (1968).

science while being consciously aware of one's relation to the larger society, reflexive in posture and *engagé;* and (3) its assumptions are antagonistic to the presently dominant functionalist paradigm.

REFERENCES

Bendix, Reinhard
    1970   "Sociology and the distrust of reason." American Sociological Review 35 (October):831–843.
Blalock, H. M.
    1967   Toward a Theory of Minority-Group Relations. New York: Wiley.
Blum, Alan F.
    1970   "The Corpus of Knowledge as a normative order: intellectual critiques of the social order of knowledge and the commonsense features of bodies of knowledge." Pp. 319–336 in John C. McKinney and Edward A. Tiryakian (eds.), Theoretical Sociology: Perspectives and Developments. New York: Appleton-Century-Crofts.
Etzioni, Amitai
    1968   The Active Society: A Theory of Societal and Political Processes. New York: Free Press.
Friedrichs, Robert W.
    1970   A Sociology of Sociology. New York: Free Press.
Gouldner, Alvin W.
    1970   The Coming Crisis of Western Sociology. New York: Basic Books.
Kuhn, Thomas S.
    1962   The Structure of Scientific Revolutions. Chicago: University of Chicago Press.

APPENDIX

A selected and annotated bibliography of social research on the future concludes the book. It was compiled by Bettina J. Huber and used by some of the authors in the early stages of the preparation of this volume. It is offered as a tool and may be of use in several ways:

1. One of the major objectives of the bibliography is to provide a sketch of the amount and type of work being undertaken to study the future. This should be of value to scholars who wish to gain an overview of what has been done to anticipate the shape of tomorrow's society, especially to those social scientists who have not yet had either the opportunity or the interest to follow the social scientific work on the future.

2.ʹ Another objective is to bring together in summary form the various arguments that have been given for the need and importance of studying the future. The rationale for any enterprise strikes us as an obvious candidate for examination and reflection, especially for an emergent direction of endeavor that may be in the process of becoming a separate discipline—futurology, futuristics, mellontology, or whatever it may be called.

3. A third objective is to permit easy access to the various methodologies and techniques of analysis that have been used to study the future. Questions of reliability and validity are sure to come to the reader's mind as he considers the various constructions of images of the future. A rough evaluation of both methods and data can be made from the following annotations.

4. A fourth purpose is to provide sociologists and other social scientists involved in forecasting with a range of specific predictions of societal changes that might lie ahead. This should serve to make the work of those in the same or related fields more easily accessible, and thereby enable the social scientist to take other forecasts into account while making his own study of the future.

5. Finally, the bibliography is organized to help the scholar in search of a particular reference. Should the reader want to know about a specific publication, he can find out where it is summarized through the alphabetical list of authors at the end of the bibliography. Thus, he can learn whether its contents would be of use to him and he can locate annotations of books and articles related by similarity of contents to the reference in question.

Studies of the Future:
A Selected and
Annotated Bibliography

BETTINA J. HUBER

Since earliest recorded history, man has been interested in the future, and has usually located his dreams of perfection there. His belief that those dreams would become a reality has been a beacon of hope lighting his otherwise dismal existence (for a delineation of "images of the future" prevalent in history, see Polak, 1961, volume 1). It has only been in recent years (since about 1930), however, that man has begun to seriously regard the future as something he could *mold* to fit his desires. By the late 1950s the belief in man's ability to shape his future was so widespread that a large-scale movement to study the future began to emerge. This annotated bibliography focuses on the recent blossoming of future-oriented research and traces its major avenues of development.

One of the champions of the need for future study was Nathan Israeli. While his dreams of a "social psychology of futurism" (Israeli, 1930) never materialized, he was able to establish experimentally that predictions about everyday occurrences are usually rational statements based on past events, rather than mere wish-fulfillments with no basis in fact. Although Israeli's work received little attention, a few researchers (e.g., McGregor and Cantril) did follow his lead and began to investigate factors that might influence the type of predictions an individual makes. Aside from these investigations into the nature of prediction, the 1930s also gave rise to a good many specific forecasts that depicted possible future states. The most important series of forecasts appeared under the title of *Today and Tomorrow*. Between 1924 and 1932 nearly one hundred British intellectuals (including E. E. Fournier D'Albe, J. B. S. Haldane, Bertrand Russell, Dora Russell, and Rebecca West) gave their views on the future within the framework of this series.

This early twentieth-century interest in the future, and how one might study it systematically, was limited. When World War II began concern with the study of the social future died out almost completely, not to be rekindled until the late 1950s (with the exception of futuristic aspects of cold war and defense problems). The reasons for this lull in the social science interest in the future are not entirely clear. Perhaps the atrocities of World War II made man question his ability to "create" the future, as well as question his belief that the future would bring a better world. But as war memories faded, so did the general pessimism and doubt regarding the future (C. P. Snow, 1958:124).

Of course, other factors have also helped to spark interest in the future. One of the more important ones is the introduction of planning into nearly all aspects of government and business. Such things as development plans, business cycles, and long-term budgets necessitate a concern with the future. Also, technological advances, especially in the field of computer technology, enable the construction of ever-better developmental models and more accurate prediction of the future (Bell, 1965:119ff) Another factor contributing to the reawakening of a future-orientation is what may be called "the acceleration of the historical process." Society has begun changing so rapidly that man cannot hope to cope with constantly emerging new forms unless he is in a position to foresee their appearance (Massenet, 1963b).

The abovementioned factors, along with the adaptation of "operations analysis techniques" to the study of social problems (Helmer 1966a), have contributed, and are continuing to contribute, to a sudden surge of interest in the future. In the late 1940s several recently republished articles by Ossip Flechtheim (1966) anticipated this trend. He noted that "increased concern about the future combined with the ability of science to deal with an ever-widening range of materials create a condition generally favorable towards a scientific study of the future" (p. 71). Although a "science of the future," such as Flechtheim advocated, has not yet materialized in any real sense, social science interest in studying the future has been increasing since about 1960. Organizations that propagate, and finance, systematic attempts at forecasting have sprung up in a number of countries. The range and diversity of their endeavors emerges from the following listing of the more important organizations:

1. The "Futuribles" project under the direction of Bertrand de Jouvenel (1963a). Its primary aim is to refine forecasts through group discussion. Thes

orecasts used to appear in the supplement *Futuribles* and now appear in the magazine *Analyse et Prévision*.

2. The Centre d'Études Prospectives. This organization focuses on isolating those factors that might accelerate, or hinder, future evolution. Its conclusions appear in *Prospective*.

3. The Committee for the Next Thirty Years, which is under the auspices of the English Social Science Research Council, and is directed by Michael Young and Mark Abrams (Bell, 1967a:140).

4. The Institute fuer Zukunftsfragen. This is a Swiss organization and is directed by Robert Jungk (for reference to it, see Winthrop, 1968:140). It publishes *Prognosen—Plaene—Perspektiven*.

5. Commission on the Year 2000. It is directed by Daniel Bell and is under the auspices of the American Academy of Arts and Sciences. It was originally established in 1965 and has a variety of aims, the major ones being: (1) to sketch alternative futures and evaluate the problems that would emerge if each hypothesis became a reality; (2) to propose various policies and institutions to deal with hypothetical futures; and (3) to delineate undesirable developments and ways by which they can be avoided (for a brief discussion of the Commission's creation, see *The Futurist*, 1967:65–67).

6. The World Future Society. This organization is located in Washington, D.C. and tries to cultivate an interest in the future among a broad spectrum of Americans (for a summary of its history and objectives, see *The Futurist*, 1967:1). One of its major mechanisms for generating such interest is its bimonthly magazine, *The Futurist*.

7. The World Resources Inventory at Southern Illinois University (Carbondale Campus). With the aid of computer facilities this project collects and interprets data on diverse trends (for a summary of this group's work, see *The Futurist*, August, 1967:56).

8. Mankind 2000, a project of the International Confederation for Disarmament and Peace (ICDP). Its major aim is to encourage the invention of desirable futures on an international level, as well as the design of new institutions that will help man to survive (for a brief description of this group's work, see Jungk, 1968a).

9. Institute for the Future (Middletown, Conn.), a nonprofit national organization that is still in the early stages of development. Its major goal is to study the long-range future comprehensively and systematically, improving the methodology involved in forecasting in the process. The Institute also participates in the publication of the quarterly *Futures* (for a summary of the Institute's founding and goals, see Institute for the Future, 1968).

Thus, from its beginnings in the 1930s, the modern social science effort to study the future has grown to the point where it is possible to say that a new discipline is on the verge of being created, one that cuts across the older boundaries of the social sciences. This emergent discipline combines science, values, and policy, and is linked to the development of organizations, such as those cited above, that are concerned not just with the study of the future, but with its conscious and deliberate shaping as well.

SCOPE OF THE BIBLIOGRAPHY

The preceding historical sketch indicates that attempts to investigate the future have been quite varied and diverse. Therefore, it proved impossible to compile an annotated bibliography without delimiting the range of material to be included. This bibliography is intended to explore the extent to which the future has been a focus of study in the *social sciences*. Thus, only publications with a social orientation were included. "Social science" was defined rather broadly to include writings dealing with any aspect of future *societal* forms that had any reasonable scientific—sometimes simply scholarly—pretensions. Thus, the works of historians, sociologists, social psychologists, anthropologists, political scientists, and even of some mathematicians and physicists, were summarized. Fictional presentations were excluded because they fall outside the major methodological and theoretical purposes of this book, which focuses on social research and the future. Consequently, *Walden II* by the psychologist B. F. Skinner was not summarized; while the work of Dennis Gabor, who is a natural scientist, was included (i.e., *Inventing the Future*).

Additionally, arising from our effort to arouse the interest of a broad section of the social science community, we made a decision to exclude publications having only a specialized appeal with respect to geographical area and subject matter. Thus, to be included, a work had to deal with more than one country and more than one aspect of society. One exception was made, however: publications about the United States were summarized to provide an example of the general type of work being undertaken to investigate the future of an individual country. Much of the research of the American Commission on the Year 2000, for example, is similar to that being done by the Indian Council for the Future or the French project "Futuribles" (although the latter is not exclusively national in focus). The forecasts dealing exclusively with the United States, therefore, also typify the efforts being made in other countries to anticipate the shape of the national future.

Furthermore, we eliminated most economic, technological, and demographic forecasts because they are too specialized. These forecasts were also excluded because they tend to serve as the basis for predictions about the social future in publications of broad scope and are already available. Consequently, the excellent demographic forecasts put out by the United Nations were not included, while the work of Harrison

Brown (*The Challenge of Mankind's Future*) was, because, although he focuses on demographic forecasts, he uses them to build a wider societal forecast. By the same token, Donald Michael's *The Next Generation* was not summarized, since it deals only with the problems of youth; while H. D. Lasswell's exposition of "The Garrison State" was included, because he considers the broad economic and social consequences of a military dictatorship as well as the nature of the political system. Although we have tried not to be arbitrary in the application of this guideline, a publication's suitability was not always clear-cut.

In addition to refining the range of material included in the bibliography with the aid of the above guidelines, we tried to keep the annotations as short as possible. Each summary consists of a short sketch of the contents of a book or article. Sometimes, a work covered such a variety of topics that it could have been classified under several headings. In these cases the publication was put in whichever category, or subcategory, encompassed the greatest part of its contents. Then, at the end of any classificatory group, are listed those publications grouped elsewhere that contain material relevant to the category in question. Therefore, if an article or book deals primarily with methodology, but also contains a forecast, it is placed in category III. At the end of the annotations for category IV.A, however, the reader is informed of the specific publications in category III that contain material relevant to IV.A.

Even with these limitations on the scope of the bibliography, it has proved impossible to annotate all the relevant publications. Although this incompleteness results in part from the limited time available for the endeavor, more important, it is a result of the recent wave of published material emerging from the increased interest in the future. The best we could achieve, therefore, was a sampling of publications, which is, we hope, fairly representative of the major work that has been, and is being, done.

CLASSIFICATORY SCHEME

The literature on the future has been subdivided into five major groups. The first category (I) includes those articles delineating *reasons for studying the future* of society; some writers advocate this type of study, while others analyze the reasons for its emergence. The second category (II) contains publications that investigate *the nature of the predictive process*. The methodological aspects of forecasting the future are grouped in the third major category (III). They range from broad epistemological dicta about how to study the future to descriptions of specific methods, or techniques, for studying tomorrow's world. The fourth

category (IV) is devoted to *forecasts of the future of society*—some ar
based on sample surveys and some are elaborations of individual opin
ions. The fifth, and last, category (V) is reserved for *periodicals or anthol*
ogies dealing with the future. In addition to these major divisions, mos
of the categories are broken down into several subclasses.

In outline, the following classificatory scheme was used to order th
annotated bibliography (the number in parentheses showing the numbe
of the summary that begins each section):

 I. Reasons for the scientific study of the future (1).
 A. The necessity of studying the future (1).
 1. The need for delineating general developmental possibilities (1).
 2. The need for specifying long-range goals (15).
 B. Reasons for the emergence of the scientific study of the future (27).
 II. The nature of the predictive process (31).
III. Methodological considerations in the scientific study of the future (42).
 A. General guidelines for studying the future (42).
 1. Guidelines for *forecasting* the future (42).
 2. Guidelines for *creating* the future (59).
 B. Specific techniques for studying the future (76).
 1. Techniques of conjecture (76).
 2. Quantitative techniques (95).
 IV. Forecasts of the future (109).
 A. Forecasts based on sample surveys (109).
 B. Forecasts based on individual opinion (124).
 1. Forecasts of mankind's future (124).
 2. Forecasts of the future of Western man (152).
 a. Western civilization as a whole (152).
 b. Europe (175).
 c. The United States (180).
 3. Forecasts of the developing nations' future (198).
 V. Periodicals or anthologies dealing with the future (199).
 A. Periodicals dealing with the future (199).
 1. Journals dealing exclusively with the study of the future (199).
 2. Journals publishing issues on the future (209).
 B. Anthologies about the future (216).

Reasons for the scientific study of the future. Most publications i
this first category (I) deal with the necessity of studying the future
Those in I.A.1 generally argue that it is imperative for man to pay mor
attention to the future and what it may bring. Some authors substantiat
this thesis by discussing the consequences of past neglect of the future
while others show how catastrophic the future will be if man continue
to ignore it. Frederik Polak (1961), for example, devotes the bulk of hi
two-volume work on the future to documenting the thesis that the ris

and fall of idealistic images of the future preceded the rise and fall of cultures throughout history. In his analysis of present Western civilization, Polak shows that modern societies are not inspired by positive future images. Unless, therefore, Western man begins to turn his attention to the future, and once again creates positive pictures of it, his civilization may be doomed. Although most of the other selections in this first sub-grouping are not as wide-ranging, or exhaustive, as Polak's analysis, they do contain similar lines of reasoning.

The publications in I.A.2 take a somewhat different approach. Although they also advocate greater concern with the future, their primary plea is for defining long-range goals. These articles and books are generally of a later vintage than those in the first group, and therefore, often build their theses upon arguments advanced in the earlier writings. A publication representative of the others in this group is Kenneth Boulding's *The Meaning of the Twentieth Century* (1965). The bulk of this book discusses the various problems (e.g., possibility of war, overpopulation, lack of energy sources, etc.) that man must overcome if he is to enter the "postcivilized" era of his history. Boulding's main thesis is that these problems can only be resolved if man creates long-range goals for which he can strive. Robert Theobald uses a similar line of reasoning in *The Challenge of Abundance* (1961). He discusses the social, economic, and international problems facing the modern world, and concludes they can best be overcome by a change in present values and goals. Mankind must give up its nationalistic allegiances and work for such changes as will benefit the world as a whole. Both Theobald's and Boulding's discussions reflect the general tenor of the publications in this second subgroup. Most state that, though a greater concern with the future is necessary, this is not possible until man specifies the goals for which he wants to strive. For, how can one try to mold, or change the future, if one does not know what one wants it to be like? Some authors, like Theobald, also believe that man's former goals are no longer appropriate to the demands of the modern age, and therefore, new ones must be found.

In category I.B, analysis substitutes for explicit exhortation, but the conclusions presented are similar to those arrived at by authors in category I.A. The general theme emerging from the publications in this first category is that man should pay more attention to his future and that his change of time perspective ought to take place in two steps: (1) a definition of appropriate long-range goals; and (2) a delineation of those instrumentalities the future holds for realizing them.

The nature of the predictive process. The second major category (II) contains publications reporting on early attempts to study the future in a systematic manner. Among the earliest undertakings were experiments by Nathan Israeli. Most of his work stemmed from a brief paper he wrote in 1930 discussing the various aspects of what he called "the social psychology of futurism" (Israeli, 1930). A major part of his social psychology involved the creation of scientific and systematic utopias toward which man could strive. Another aspect of his futuristic psychology was an evaluation of possible future trends, so that those patterns of present behavior leading to the most desirable future could be identified. After writing his first article, Israeli carried out a series of experiments aimed at isolating the nature of the predictive process (1932a 1932b; 1933a; 1933b; 1933c). These experiments fell short of fulfilling the promise of his first article, and excited little attention among social scientists, Israeli apparently being ahead of his time. Nonetheless, Israeli did establish experimentally that predictions are statements based on past experience rather than pure fantasy. He also tried to isolate other factors influencing the nature of prediction. His line of work was extended by Cantril, McGregor, and Toch, who tried to isolate the characteristics of good predictions and predictors. Both Douglas McGregor (1938) and Hadley Cantril (1938) wanted to know what factors influence the type of predictions an individual makes. They investigated this problem by using questionnaires that asked respondents to make a series of predictions, as well as to describe their social backgrounds and attitudes on a variety of issues. Specific predictions could then be compared in terms of a subject's background and attitudes.

Hans Toch (1958) was also interested in the predictive process. He analyzed a series of predictions about the state of the world in 1952 that had been collected by Cantril a decade earlier. Toch summarized his own findings, and those of McGregor and Cantril, by making the following generalizations about the nature of prediction: (1) accurate prediction is related to the individual's ability to foresee novelty and change (2) caution and accuracy seem to be positively related in the predictive endeavor; (3) subjective factors influence prediction to a greater extent if the predictor considers the event in question vital to his own interests and (4) immediate experience has considerable impact on the nature of given predictions and the aspects of the future they emphasize. It should be noted that the abovementioned factors do not influence predictions independently. Rather, if the influence of one factor is particularly strong it may well weaken the impact of other factors.

Other publications in category II extend the findings outlined above by enumerating the factors that must be considered for accurate predictions. The basic idea of this work is that the best way to foresee the future is to isolate good predictions or predictors. On the basis of these one could establish a kind of Delphic Oracle that would inform one of basi societal contours emerging in the future. This approach was largely abandoned after World War II.

Methodological considerations in the scientific study of the future. The subdivisions of category III.A parallel those in I.A. That is, authors who advocate delineating general developmental possibilities usually also concern themselves with guidelines for forecasting the future, while authors who believe that the major priority lies in specifying long-range goals tend to advocate the "creation" of the future.

Part A of category III also continues the historical progression observed in the second category. As was outlined in the introduction, interest shifted from the nature of the predictive process to actual attempts at forecasting after World War II. The general assumption seems to have been that "practice makes perfect," and therefore, researchers began to produce forecasting guidelines based on their own experience. Wilbert Moore (1964a), for example, through his investigation of the social change process, came to the conclusion that simple extrapolation is inadequate for forecasting discontinuous change. Such change can best be foreseen through a study of the effects of innovation, which requires the use of dynamic societal models able to anticipate cataclysmic change. The construction of such models, according to Moore, is a pressing task to which future-oriented research should turn its attention. Bertrand de Jouvenel (1963b; 1967), whose experience, and consequently also his suggestions for research priorities, have differed from Moore's, has argued that a vital gap in knowledge about the future relates to discovering how one can forecast and control the career of social ideas. The basic aim of idea forecasts would be to establish the degree of acceptance of an idea, how it would change through time, and in what facets of social life it would, or could, be applied. Jouvenel believes it is especially important to forecast the career of moral ideas because they have a direct effect on the public's willingness to accept future national policies. The type of endeavor that Jouvenel and Moore exemplify has been the dominant one until recently. It focuses on delineating methods for foreseeing the problems of the future before they become overwhelming. In this way, policies aimed at coping with emerging problems can be formulated. In addition, such policies should be designed, according to many writers, so as to accelerate those trends that bode well for the future of mankind.

In the last few years a somewhat different approach has been advocated. Proponents of the new outlook argue that with man's present technological capabilities he is in a position to create any type of future he desires. Thus, it is not enough to avoid the worst pitfalls or simply to accelerate already existing beneficial trends, man must actively strive

to make the world of the future an ideal place for everyone. Jacques Freymond (1965) has pointed out that this type of approach requires a shift
in focus: no longer should futurists concentrate on the immediate future,
but rather on a desirable goal located in the distant future. Their primary
task would change from predicting probable trends to outlining modes
of action that would make the desired future a reality. Such a shift in
emphasis also requires a reformulation of the whole planning process,
the nature of which has been investigated in some detail by Hasan Ozebekhan (1968), who argues that any planning endeavor ought to focus
primarily on making basic societal values more of a reality. This would
require a multifaceted approach that includes determining general goals,
outlining methods of achieving the specified goals, and determining the
priorities of various strategies for action.

It should be noted that the two approaches described above—one
stressing forecasting and the other creation—are by no means mutually
exclusive; both aim at achieving the best possible future. The basic difference between them lies in the way they approach their goal: forecasters
start by trying to foretell the shape of the future and then altering present
policies so as to "accentuate the positive and eliminate the negative,"
while creators begin by outlining the characteristics of a desirable future
and then examining present trends and structures to see how they should
be altered if the desirable image of the future is to be realized. Although
forecasting is not discarded by the creators, it is made the secondary, not
the primary, step in the process of studying the future.

The publications in III.B. deal with specific forecasting techniques
rather than general guidelines. Those in III.B.1 are usually employed by
individual forecasters, and there are four predictive modes that seem
most useful to them. These forecasting techniques have been outlined by
a number of authors, including Daniel Bell (1964), Bertrand de Jouvenel
(1962), and Erich Jantsch (1967), whose book on technological forecasting describes over one hundred techniques in considerable detail. One
of the more widely used forecasting methods is that of extrapolation,
which involves extending the uniform course of present trends or processes into the future. The second method of prediction has been called
"the method of movement" by Massenet (1963c) and is especially appropriate for analyzing the impact of new inventions. Its primary purpose
is to construct models of possible futures by isolating those factors that
are just barely perceptible today, but that might radically change the
years to come. The third widely applicable method of forecasting is that
of the "conditional hypothesis" and is based on the premise that the future is pluralistic. When trying to predict, therefore, one should enumerate all possible paths of development and then attempt to determine

which are most likely to materialize in light of the limitations imposed by the exigencies of the present. The fourth forecasting mode, "normative forecasting" (Jantsch, 1967:29–38), is used by the "creators" of the future discussed earlier, and is just coming into its own. It involves specifying the needs that must be fulfilled at some future date and then determining what advances would be necessitated. This technique not only forecasts, but also reveals what present action must be taken if future goals are to be realized.

The forecasting techniques described in category III.B.2 involve the analysis of mass data. In most cases the data come from respondents who have stated their opinions about aspects of the future. By analyzing these data, the researcher looks for agreement about what the future might be like. Methods using this type of approach include: (1) the "Self-Anchoring Striving Scale" devised by Hadley Cantril (1963) and Lloyd Free to allow respondents to express their hopes and fears about the future in terms familiar to them, while eliciting responses amenable to cross-cultural comparison; (2) Jiri Nehnevajsa's (1961; 1962a; 1962b) "Project Outcomes," which is a technique for delineating the future aspirations of nations by questioning their leaders and potential leaders; and (3) the "Delphi Technique," which Theodore Gordon and Olaf Helmer (1966) developed to tap the opinions of expert panels with regard to future developmental possibilities. In addition to this type of technique the subgroup III.B.2 also includes several publications dealing with methodologies utilizing trends rather than opinions as data. The trends are analyzed to assess the likelihood that specific future possibilities will become realities. Gordon and Hayward (1968), for example, have developed the "Cross-Impact Matrix," which uses an equation to evaluate the potential interaction effects between a series of projected trends.

The examples enumerated above serve to indicate that the methods described in III.B.2 are quantitative, at least in a rudimentary way, and usually involve large enough amounts of data to invite the aid of a computer. Those techniques grouped in III.B.1, in contrast, require only such information as is at the disposal of an individual working alone.

Forecasts of the future of society. The major classificatory distinction in category IV is the number of people contributing to a given forecast. The publications in IV.A describe the results of asking a large number of people about their ideas for the future. In some cases the questions are quite vague and open-ended, in others quite specific. Many of the sample surveys summarized were carried out using techniques described in III.B.2.

The forecasts in category IV.B. are elaborations of individual opinions and are grouped according to their unit of analysis. The major conclusion emerging from the grouping itself is that little research has been done involving the future of the developing countries as a whole. Rather, such work has involved an individual country or a specific aspect of the future (e.g., economic development). If the broader future of Africa or Asia is discussed, it is usually within the context of general discussions of mankind's future. Thus, the study of the collective future or futures of the Third World—certainly of great social significance in the coming years—constitutes a research gap of some importance.

Another conclusion concerns an historical shift in the type of forecasts being made. Those predictions made before World War II tend to be fairly sweeping in scope and consider all aspects of mankind's future (for example, Birkenhead, 1930; Low, 1925; or Whyte, 1944). They were often made on the premise that the future can be foreseen because man's evolutionary progression follows more or less immutable laws. In retrospect, these "laws" hardly seem to be immutable, since most of these early predictions are not very accurate. In general, the ones made about societal improvements are far too optimistic, while those made about scientific developments are too conservative. In contrast, more modern forecasts—those made after World War II—tend to be quite specific and concentrate on one or two aspects of the future. An example of this kind of predictive essay is Abraham Moles' (1962) discussion of the "scientific city." He foresees the development of a subsociety of scientists who will be the nation's managers and its intellectual creators of the future. Because of their functions they will form a new elite and develop a way of life distinctive from the rest of society. The many forecasts similar to Moles' in terms of the breadth of their scope (Baade, 1962; Bell, 1965; Calder, 1967a; Galtung, 1969; Heilbroner, 1966; and Mead, 1965) are generally based on extrapolations of present trends rather than "immutable laws," and foresee unlimited technological progress but doubtful social progress.

Most of the individual forecasts, regardless of when they were made, have a similar form. They generally consider a number of specific problems or trends evident in the present and try to show how these might affect the future. A concluding chapter usually discusses how this foreseen world might be improved upon, provided the author believes this lies within man's capabilities. This type of approach is reflected by Harrison Brown (1954), who devotes the bulk of his book to discussing the future consequences of trends in population growth rates, agricultural yields, and the supply of energy sources. In a final chapter he outlines the various futures open to man in view of his present problems and concludes that the most probable one is a return to an agrarian world. This state of affairs will result, he says, from a thermonuclear war, after which the earth will no longer have the resources to reindustrialize. Brown does, however, admit that there is a remote possibility that man may be able to avoid all-out war and industrialize the whole earth instead.

Another book typical of many written about the future is one by Roderick Seidenberg (1950). He shows that the future course of history is predetermined by tracing the course of man's technological development. In Seidenberg's view, man is destined to be overpowered by his own technological advances and can do little to avoid it. He simply has to resign himself to becoming an unfeeling cog in a perfectly functioning societal machine.

If the trend toward *creating* the future described earlier (see III.A) continues to gain strength, the current form of predictive essays exemplified by Seidenberg and Brown will probably change. The form of presentation may be reversed so that the author may begin by outlining the type of future world he—or some group—considers desirable and then continue by discussing how this future could best be achieved. If this approach were generally adopted, it might overcome two dysfunctional characteristics of present predictions: (1) the author is usually so overwhelmed by what he foresees that he is unable to conceive of how the future could be made more tolerable, let alone desirable; and (2) predictors tend to be bound by the shackles of the past or present, and are consequently unable to formulate truly new ways of making a better tomorrow. There are a few writers who already use this new approach, perhaps the best example being Dennis Gabor (1964). He devotes the first part of his book *Inventing the Future* to discussing the reasons for his belief that man will overcome any technological problems that he might encounter. He sees as man's greatest challenge the adjustment of his work-oriented way of life to the new "Age of Leisure," where only a minority of the population will have full-time employment. Gabor's book concludes with a lengthy discussion of ways in which man might best cope with the leisure that the future will bring. It is to be hoped—perhaps even safely predicted—that the type of approach used by Gabor will become much more widespread in the years to come.

Periodicals or anthologies dealing with the future. Category V contains periodicals and anthologies focusing on the study of the future. Their number is growing rapidly; at least ten periodicals are devoted exclusively to the study of the future, seven of which have been founded since the beginning of 1965. Popular and lay magazines, ranging from the *Saturday Review* to *Kaiser Aluminum News*, have devoted whole issues to the future in an effort to inform the public about the many "marvels," technological and otherwise, tomorrow will bring. Unfortunately, the general themes discussed tend to be quite similar and repetitive.

Anthologies, like periodicals, are in abundant supply. Most contain the proceedings of conferences investigating the nature of the future, usually through a series of papers in which experts discuss future developments in their areas of specialty. Some anthologies are part of the ongoing work of groups such as the Commission on the Year 2000 (1967a) or the "Futuribles" Project (Jouvenel, 1963; 1965). Most essay collections, however, are simply the end product of a single conference (for example, Boyko, ed., 1961; Ewald, ed., 1968; and Foreign Policy Association, 1968). The end result is an array of separate pictures depicting certain aspects of the future. Unfortunately, when one tries to superimpose these pictures, to get a complete image of tomorrow's world, they sometimes cancel each other out or become chaotic. It would seem therefore, that most conference collections could benefit from greater coordination and control in their design, such as a more well-defined thematic focus, a concern with interrelated implications, and a stress on both the goals and means of creating the future.

FURTHER RELEVANT MATERIAL

Because of the vast and growing literature on the future, a number of additional sources to which the reader can turn for further relevant literature should be given. A few are:

1. Jantsch, Erich
    1967   Technological Forecasting in Perspective. Paris: OECD Publications.
    At the end of this book there is an annotated bibliography summarizing over 400 works. Although it overlaps somewhat with this bibliography, Jantsch concentrates primarily on publications dealing with diverse aspects of technological forecasting.
2. Harrison, Annette
    1967   Bibliography on Automation and Technological Change and Studies of the Future. Rand Publication No. P–3365–2 (March).
    Encompasses about 300 works dealing with various aspects of technological forecasting.
3. The Futurist
    1967–   The Futurist. A Newsletter for Tomorrow's World. Washington, D.C.: World Future Society.
    A bimonthly magazine dealing with the future. Each issue reviews one or more books about the future, some of which deal with fairly specialized material.
4. Futures
    1968–   Futures: The Journal of Forecasting and Planning. London: Unwin Brothers Limited.

A quarterly devoted to articles about studying the future. In addition, each issue usually contains a number of book reviews.

5. Winter, Ernst F. (ed.)

    1966   Dokumentation ueber Zukunftsfragen (Documentation of Future Questions). Vienna: Institut fuer Zukunftsfragen.

    An annotated bibliography summarizing 72 publications; in German.

6. Futuribles

    1961–65 Futuribles—Supplement to Bulletin Sedeis. Bertrand de Jouvenel, Editor. Paris: S.E.D.E.I.S.

From time to time this magazine published selections by François Hetman summarizing literature directly or indirectly related to the study of the future. Much of the work discussed in these articles, which are in French, is by European authors who have not been translated into English. The articles can be found in the following *Futuribles* issues: no. 30 (May 10, 1962); no. 35 (July 20, 1962); no. 42 (November 1, 1962); no. 48 (January 10, 1963); no. 51 (March 20, 1963); no. 61 (July 1, 1963); no. 67 (November 10, 1963); no. 77 (May 20, 1964); no. 83 (November 1, 1964); no. 104 (November 10, 1965); and no. 107 (December 20, 1965).

7. John McHale (State University of New York; Albany) and Stefan Dedijer (University of Lund; Sweden) are compiling large-scale bibliographies on the future, which will be available soon.

Annotations

I. REASONS FOR THE SCIENTIFIC STUDY OF THE FUTURE

The necessity of studying the future is the major theme of most of the publications in this category. Those in the first subsection argue that mankind should concern itself with the future, and what it may bring, in a more conscious manner. While those in the second subsection also advocate systematic future study, they suggest this study be done through the definition of long-range goals. This category also contains a small group of publications that outline the reasons for the contemporary rebirth of interest in the future.

I.A. The necessity of studying the future. *1. The need for delineating general developmental possibilities*

1. Bell, Wendell, and James A. Mau
   1970   "Images of the future: theory and research strategies." Pp. 205–234 in J. McKinney and E. Tiryakian (eds.), Theoretical Sociology: Perspectives and Developments. New York: Appleton-Century-Crofts.

This paper argues that social science should become more cognizant of the future and of the role man's expectations play in the social change process. In the main it sets forth a theory of social change revolving around the concept of an "image of the future." This is "an expectation about the state of things to come at some future time. We may think most usefully of such expectations as a range of differentially probable possibilities rather than a single point on a continuum" (p. 22). Images of the future are an integral part of the social change process, which can best be thought of as a feedback cycle. In this cycle present structures, beliefs and values, images of the future, decisions, social action, and the emerging future are constantly modifying, and being modified by one another. The authors conclude by enumerating a number of directives that the researcher interested in making his work relevant to the future should follow.

2. Bertaux, Pierre
   1968   "The future of man." Pp 13–20 in William R. Ewald (ed.), Environment and Change: The Next Fifty Years. Bloomington: Indiana University Press.

The author briefly discusses the concept of "man," as well as the evolution of two of the most basic human beliefs: freedom and determinism. The contradiction between these two concepts can be reconciled through ideas about the future. "The future—in the form of the psychological fact of the image of the future—is capable of becoming an element of determination in the causal chain. Through an image of the future, the time-to-come is already affecting the present" (p. 20). Man can become free, therefore, by recognizing that "what shall be" is predetermined and that he has a responsibility to plan for it.

3. Dror, Yehezkel
1968 "The role of futures in government." Futures 1 (September):40–45.
Research on the future should become an integral part of public policy-making to prevent current problems from becoming full-scale crises. Those changes in governmental structure, personnel, and decision-making patterns necessary to achieve an integrated public policy and a systematic study of the future are discussed.

4. Hacker, Frederick J.
1969 "Human implications." Pp. 233–241 in Robert Jungk and Johan Galtung (eds.), Mankind 2000. Oslo: Universitetsforlaget.
Modern man has enough control over his environment to shape the future to fit his desires. Yet he seems unable to take advantage of the means at his disposal, and feels powerless in the face of his grand new technology. Consequently, a new kind of human being should be created, one who is able to cope with a rapidly changing world. To do this, the discipline of psychology will have to change its orientation and concentrate on helping man tolerate the risks and ambiguities involved in creating a future radically different from the present.

5. Hopkins, Frank S.
1967 "The United States in the year 2000. A proposal for the study of the American future." American Sociologist 2 (August):149–150.
To dramatize the pressing need for systematic study of the long-range future, the author suggests an annual "Seminar for the Year 2000." ". . . it would focus [instead] on the kind of society which might exist in the United States in the year 2000, and on courses of action which might be undertaken in the intervening years to minimize the difficulties of this society and to maximize its benefits. . . ." (p. 149). The major topics such a seminar might cover and how its basic framework might be established are discussed in some detail.

6. Israeli, Nathan
1930 "Some aspects of the social psychology of futurism." Journal of Abnormal and Social Psychology 25 (July):121–132.
This article describes the major tenets of a "Social Psychology of Futurism." One of its most important aspects would involve extending present so-

cietal trends into the future through the use of prophecy to create scientific and systematic utopias. Another facet would be a critical evaluation of orientations to the future prevalent in the past and in the present. The new social psychology ought also to specify desirable future states, thereby making it possible to delineate those patterns of present behavior which might facilitate their realization. This would necessitate integrating "criteria of the future" into the society's normative system. In this way "Futurism" could serve as a social philosophy and "the future would be harnessed for the present" (p. 129).

7. Jouvenel, Bertrand de
     1965   "Utopia for practical purposes." Daedalus 94 (Spring):437–453.
     Contemporary society seems plagued by a feeling of vague anxiety about the future, despite today's material well-being. This anxiety can best be overcome by the creation of scientific future-oriented Utopias. "It is time that experts represented the many different outcomes which can be obtained by different uses of our many and increasing possibilities" (p. 444). Such Utopias would focus on improving the life of the ordinary man by beautifying his natural surroundings and providing meaningful work to replace his empty hours of leisure.

8. McHale, John
     1967a   "The future of the future." Architectural Design 37 (February):65–66.
     Present scientific and technical knowledge make it possible for modern man to create his own future, both in collective and individual terms. The future will increasingly become what man desires it to be. Consequently, one of his greatest challenges is to decide how he wishes to shape the years to come.

9. Moore, Wilbert E.
     1966   "The utility of utopias." American Sociological Review 31 (December):765–772.
     Sociology is the "generalizing science of man's social behavior," and therefore, sociologists should be vitally concerned with predicting the future. So far they have avoided doing so; and unless they start soon, the whole area will be usurped by others, especially politicians and government planners. The sociologist can use "utopias" to articulate solutions to mankind's future problems. This would be beneficial because, if utopias are believed in, present action will be oriented toward them, thereby making them self-fulfilling. In this sense, the future truly causes the present.

10. Platt, John R.
     1968   The Step to Man. New York: Wiley.
     "These essays . . . examine, from several points of view, how the nature of man and his intellectual and social organization is changing today, and what changes may be expected and hoped for and worked for in the next generation" (p. 3). The author begins his enterprise by discussing recent advances in the organization of thought and knowledge. He then notes that man's greatest problems lie in correctly anticipating consequences, and in applying his intellect

to concerted action that will effectively reduce his needs and tensions. A solution might lie in the analysis of social chains and social causation—a theme pursued in some detail. Specific ideas in the scientific disciplines have led to greatly increased knowledge through chain reactions. The same could occur in the social arena, provided man becomes more determined in his search for social solutions. It is imperative that this happen, since man, still in the process of rapid evolution, must take positive action if he wants to ensure his future existence. "Everywhere now we begin to see men and nations beginning the deliberate design of development with a growing confidence in the choice and creation of their own future. . . ." (p. 203).

11. Polak, Fred. L.

1961 The Image of the Future: Enlightening the Past, Orienting the Present, Forecasting the Future. New York: Oceana Publications (2 volumes).

In this two-volume work the author delineates the various "images of the future" that have dominated the different epochs of Western civilization. He defines an image of the future as: ". . . the idea of a *Future* which is drastically different from the *Present*. This is the idea of the Future . . . as a new dimension of this world, the perfected antipode of the imperfect here and now" (p. 56). Most of the first volume analyzes past cultures and their future-oriented images in an effort to prove the thesis that the rise and fall of civilizations is preceded by the rise and fall of dominant images of the future. The second volume focuses on the relationship between cultural change and negative images of the future. The author believes that modern Western civilization is dominated by such negative images, and devotes considerable space to pinpointing them. The greatest danger to Western culture, therefore, is its lack of an idealistic image of the future. What it needs is creators of positive future-oriented images, a role that social scientists ought to assume. Man is in a better position to fashion the kind of society he desires than ever before, but without new images of an ideal future to guide his striving, his civilization is doomed.

12. Toffler, Alvin

1965 "The future as a way of life." Horizon 7 (Summer):108–116.

". . . the period we are now living through represents nothing less than the second great divide in human history, comparable in magnitude only with . . . the shift from barbarism to civilization" (p. 110). The basic alterations taking place in such areas as population growth, genetics, machine technology, and human values will completely transform the world of the future. Unless man begins to prepare for this transformation, he will be crushed by "future shock" (analogous to culture shock). Three types of preparation are discussed: (1) general encouragement of systematic exploration of the future, as well as widespread discussion of possible futures; (2) training in the methodologies of prediction and science; and (3) creation of an international institute to integrate future-oriented research. To survive "future shock" man must have more accurate conceptions of the world of tomorrow.

358 Bettina J. Huber

13. Winthrop, Henry
    1968   "The sociologist and the study of the future." American Sociologist 2 (May):136–145.

Sociologists have been unwilling to construct utopias because of their strong commitment to a value-free discipline. It is, however, quite possible to be concerned with the future without sacrificing a value-free stance. This can be achieved by considering the social implications of technological advances. To make such predictions the social scientist should be aware of current and future possibilities, and therefore, the work that has been undertaken to anticipate the technological patterns of tomorrow is summarized. The article concludes with a discussion of the reasons for sociologists' lack of interest in social philosophy and why they are invalid. If man is to enjoy a desirable future he must have more than mere predictions of technological possibilities; he needs ". . . a social philosophy which relates the potentialities of modern science and technology to man's deepest and most widely held needs" (p. 140).

14. Young, Michael
    1968   "Forecasting and the social sciences." Pp 1–37 in Michael Young (ed.), Forecasting and the Social Sciences. London: Heineman.

While forecasting is of great value to public and private administrators or planners, its usefulness for social science is not quite so obvious. This article discusses how forecasting, and the methodology associated with it, could be employed to enhance the social sciences. It argues that attempts to foresee the future could serve to isolate the relationship of various types of change. This, in turn, might lead to new theoretical insights, and eventually, new predictions about the future.

For further material on the need for delineating general future developments, see: nos. **44, 58, 68, 88, 140,** and **205.**

I.A.2. The need for specifying long-range goals

15. Boulding, Kenneth E.
    1965   The Meaning of the Twentieth Century (The Great Transition). New York: Harper & Row.

Man is coming to the end of a long transition period, and is about to enter the "post-civilized" stage of his history. To reach his new stage of development he must avoid the following "traps": (1) large-scale nuclear war; (2) overpopulation; (3) exhaustion of energy or mineral resources; and (4) atrophy of creativity or human energy due to lack of existential challenge and danger. To overcome these problems man should use all the intellectual resources at his disposal to create an image of the future, or set of long-range goals, toward which he can strive. This image should emphasize the limitless developmental possibilities open to mankind.

16. Feinberg, Gerald
    1968   The Prometheus Project: Mankind's Search for Long Range Goals. Garden City, N.Y.: Doubleday.

The rapidly emerging unity of mankind makes it desirable to create long-range goals for the whole world, thereby providing man with a renewed life plan or purpose. The need for such goals arises from two modern trends: (1) the ever-increasing interdependence of the world's nations; and (2) the emergence of a technology that enables a limited number of people to make earth-shaking decisions whose effects they are unable to foresee. Long-range future planning might make it possible to mold the future more consciously, and in a manner more consistent with mankind's desires. Also, general agreement on long-range goals might serve as a bridge between opposing ideologies. As the goals of the past no longer seem sufficient for the modern world, new goals should be developed, based on the insights of science and through widespread discussion among all sectors of mankind. The author concludes by discussing philosophical objections to the undertaking he has proposed, none of which he finds convincing.

17. Fitch, Lyle C.

1968   "National development and national policy." Pp. 283–317 in William Ewald (ed.), Environment and Policy: The Next Fifty Years. Bloomington: Indiana University Press.

This article begins with a discussion of the planning process and how it must be adjusted to cope with conditions of uncertainty. The bulk of it, however, delineates specific goals for America within the next fifty years. The two most general goals discussed are elimination of poverty and improvement of the environment. The more specific goals advocated include: population limitation; increase in the GNP; better urban living conditions; and modernization of state and local government.

18. Frank, Lawrence K.

1967   "The need for a new political theory." Daedalus 96 (Summer): 809–816.

The United States needs a new political theory to guide the development of its rapidly changing economy and society. It would replace that formulated by the Founding Fathers in 1776 and be geared to a welfare society.

19. Heckscher, August

1968   "The individual—not the mass." Pp. 287–296 in William R. Ewald (ed.), Environment and Change: The Next Fifty Years. Bloomington: Indiana University Press.

The emergence of the New Left, the hippies, and city dwellers who demand the right to plan for themselves, all indicate a rebirth of individualism. If it is to be kept afloat in the sea of conformity, we must consciously plan for its preservation. This could be done by a commission that would delineate those values conducive to a new affirmation of individuality. The commission would consider how individualism might be affected by future developments in the realms of privacy, environmental design, leisure, and technology.

20. Jouvenel, Bertrand de

    1969   "Technology as a means." Pp. 217–232 in K. Baier and N. Rescher (eds.), Values and the Future. New York: Free Press.

A widespread conception prevalent in Western society is that the future will be largely determined by the nature of technological developments. This ignores the fact that there is such a wide range of potential technological innovations that they cannot all be exploited at once due to a scarcity of monetary funds. Modern societies must, therefore, give priority to those research projects they consider most important and this necessitates decisions based on values. At present the government is the major judge of research priorities, and thereby, its administrators are shaping the future in terms of their own values. If other sectors of the society also wish to influence the future, it is imperative that they begin articulating their own developmental preferences more clearly.

21. McHale, John

    1968a   "A global view." Pp. 195–216 in Robert Theobald (ed.), Social Policies for America in the Seventies. Garden City, N.Y.: Doubleday.

"We have now reached the point in human affairs at which the requirements for sustaining the world community may take precedence over, and be supererogative to, the more transient value systems and vested interests of any local society" (p. 195). The "cybernetic" revolution (whose history is traced in some detail) has destroyed the premises of our present social and economic system. We must, therefore, shed our past concepts of "nation states," "local economies," and "ideologies," and create a social system appropriate to the cybernetic era. The bulk of the article discusses some of the tenets of this new social system. Two of its major aims would be: to help the underdeveloped countries achieve economic well-being; and to give the individual human dignity, as well as the opportunity to develop by giving new meaning to work and leisure.

22. National Goals Research Staff

22a.   1969a   "The White House looks to the future." The Futurist 3 (August):99–100.

22b.   1969b   "Goals staff will work with Moynihan." The Futurist 3 (August):100.

22c.   1969c   "Statement by President Nixon on creating a national goals research staff." Futures 1 (September):458–459.

"It is time we addressed ourselves, consciously and systematically, to the question of what kind of a nation we want to be as we begin our third century. . . . Only by focusing our attention further into the future can we marshal our resources effectively in the service of those social aims to which we are committed" (p. 99). With these words President Nixon established the National Goals Research Staff in mid-1969. Its aim is to increase America's knowledge about its future by making better use of the wide variety of newly developed forecasting techniques. The Goals Staff will have a threefold function: coordination of all information pertaining to the future of the United States; synthesis of existing forecasts and specification of interrelationships between various types of future change; and the establishment of a link between the forecasting and decision-making processes. The articles also discuss the preliminary make-up, aims, and goals of the Research Staff.

23. Polak, Fred. L.
    1969   "Towards the goal of goals." Pp. 307–331 in Robert Jungk and Johan Galtung (eds.), Mankind 2000. Oslo: Universitetsforlaget.
    The first part of this article explains the social scientist's lack of concern with the future. The two primary reasons are: (1) his desire to become an objective scientist; and (2) his inability to come to grips with the nature of social change. This neglect of the future has meant that mankind has failed to specify social goals commensurate with its great technological advances. Rather, man is letting his most basic values be overrun by technology. It is, therefore, imperative that social science be reoriented and reorganized in a manner allowing it to study the future and devise goals appropriate to man's needs. The process by which this could be accomplished is outlined in some detail.

24. Teilhard de Chardin, Pierre
    1964   The Future of Man. London: Collins.
    The greatest challenge facing twentieth-century man is the creation of worthwhile long-range goals. In an effort to lay the groundwork for such goals, the author discusses man's social and intellectual history, as well as the responsibilities his position in today's world entails. If mankind is to survive, it must rekindle faith in the future by specifying goals that everyone can strive for.

25. Theobald, Robert
    1961   The Challenge of Abundance. New York: Clarkson N. Potter.
    This book discusses those contemporary problems that will significantly affect the shape of tomorrow and ways in which they might be solved. It is written in the belief that by grappling with these problems today, we may be able to create a future in which all men can find a meaningful place. The book is divided into three major parts: (1) "the economic challenge" discusses the implications of material abundance for government, industry and the worker; (2) "the social challenge" sketches the present state of education and politics, as well as what some of America's goals for the future ought to be; and (3) "the international challenge" outlines the needs of the third world and the relationship between rich and poor countries. The book concludes with a plea for a greater sense of world citizenship. "Mankind must cease to be loyal to its country 'right or wrong' and adopt a wider commitment. We must seek a policy that will be best for the world as a whole rather than for one particular country. . . ." (p. 18).

26. Wright, Christopher
    1969   "Some requirements for viable social goals." Pp. 194–197 in
            Robert Jungk and Johan Galtung (eds.), Mankind 2000. Oslo:
            Universitetsforlaget.

A discussion of three tasks facing modern man in connection with social
goals: (1) understanding the relationship between a goal and the means for
achieving it (this is a task for the sociology of science); (2) creating political institutions which serve to specify the range of choice among goals; and (3) specifying new long-range goals (highly trained generalists are best qualified for
this).

For further material on the need to specify goals, see: nos. **13, 66, 68, 71,
73, 87, 178, 183, 196, 212,** and **234.**

I.B. Reasons for the emergence of the scientific study of the future

27. Bell, Daniel
    1965   "The study of the future." The Public Interest 1 (Fall):119–130.

The recent renewal of interest in the future has not led to a resurgence of
utopianism. Rather it is linked with the attempt to create a welfare state. There
seem to be several reasons for the emergence of concern with the future: (1)
memories of the horrors of World War II are fading; (2) better communication
has created a set of national values; (3) increasing commitment to the concept
of economic growth; (4) planning has become an important feature of public
policy; (5) technological advances permit more accurate prediction; and (6) emphasis on science and research. While this turn to the future has also brought a
desire to predict more accurately, methods for doing so are still very primitive
and speculative. Present predictive capabilities are explored in some detail. The
second part of the article discusses the "Delphi Technique"; see no. **98** for the
article on which it is based.

28. Lewinsohn, Richard
    1961   Science, Prophecy and Prediction. New York: Bell.

This book is a brief historical account of mankind's endeavors to foresee
the future. It begins with the great Prophets of the past, and moves on to a discussion of astrology and prophetic dreams. After delineating the development of
public opinion polls, the role of forecasting and prediction in the following
fields is evaluated: meteorology, medicine, demography, gambling, economics,
and national planning. The book concludes by discussing how the predictive
enterprise might develop in the future.

29. Massenet, Michel
    1963b   "Introduction à une sociologie de la prévision [Introduction to
            a sociology of conjecture]." Futuribles (no. 60)—Supplement to
            Bulletin Sedeis (Part 2) 857 (June 20).

Modern societies are characterized by rapid social change, and consequently, also by conjecture about the future. Man must be able to anticipate
new developments so that he can alter present social structures in an appropriate manner. If he does not do this, he will be inundated by a rapid succession

of changes. Conjecture should, therefore, orient action in modern society in three ways: (1) by pointing out static elements; (2) by isolating regularities or trends; and (3) by discovering new future possibilities that can become guidelines for the present. Such orientation helps "cause" the future by making one strive for the realization of projected possibilities.

30. Rolbiecki, Waldemar
>   1969   "Prognostication and prognoseology." Pp. 278–285 in Robert Jungk and Johan Galtung (eds.), Mankind 2000. Oslo: Universitetsforlaget.

Prognostication is "the art of seeing into the future and of making forecasts about it" (p. 278). This article describes the recent growth of such activity and the reasons for it. Then it presents various types of forecasts and the methodology associated with them. It concludes by outlining the philosophical problems involved in prognostication.

For further information on the need for creating the future, see: nos. **239, 240, 241, 242,** and **253.**

II. THE NATURE OF THE PREDICTIVE PROCESS

This category is reserved for publications that report on preliminary attempts to study the future in a systematic manner. The earlier writings focus on factors influencing the nature of prediction. The later works go a step further in that they describe forces important in accurate prediction.

31. Israeli, Nathan
>   1932a   "The social psychology of time." Journal of Abnormal and Social Psychology 27 (July):209–213.

In September 1930, two short questionnaires were administered to students at the University of Maine. Their aim was to determine the relative importance of past, present, and future for the individual, as well as his emotional orientation to each of these time concepts. The results of these experiments indicated that the future was by far the most important of the three time dimensions. In terms of emotional orientation, the future was invested with the most affect. Generally, subjects were also optimistic about its content.

32. Israeli, Nathan
>   1933c   "Group predictions of future events." Journal of Social Psychology 4 (May):201–222.

In an effort to throw some light on "the origin and makeup of notions of the future," students at the University of Maine were asked to make a series of predictions about specific future events. The responses were divided into nine groups and the results compared. In general, there was little variability in the predictions, both within and between groups. Those predictions dealing with the distant future tended to be conservative, while those concerned with the immediate future were surprisingly accurate. Predictions dealing with the next fifty years were quite optimistic.

33. Israeli, Nathan
    1932b   "Wishes concerning improbable future events: reactions to the future." Journal of Applied Psychology 16 (no. 5):584–588.

In an effort to ascertain what kind of events were considered utopian, or highly improbable, the researcher asked students at the University of Maine to state a series of things they felt would never occur. In general, the supposedly "impossible" events had a high probability of being realized sometime in the future. The greatest degree of consensus about what specific events were impossible was in the area of international affairs. It seems, therefore, that the analysis of events people consider impossible will indicate the boundaries of their time perspectives—in the case of the students studied they were fairly narrow.

34. Israeli, Nathan
    1933b   "Group estimates of the divorce rate for the years 1935–1975." Journal of Social Psychology 4 (February):102–115.

It is rarely asked whether various groups tend to guess alike or whether their predictions are related to past and present situational factors. In an experiment investigating these possibilities, students were asked to estimate divorce rates for the years 1935–1975. The results showed a systematic relationship between the variability of predictions and the certainty with which they were made. That is, there was a greater range of estimates among the "certain" predictions than among the "uncertain" ones. The results also showed little difference between the predictions based on more detailed past rates (i.e., 1890–1929) and those based solely on the 1929 rate. This is probably because the larger society believes that the divorce rate will increase in the future.

35. Israeli, Nathan
    1933c   "Attitudes to the *Decline of the West.*" Journal of Social Psychology 4 (February):92–101.

In 1931 students at the University of Maine were asked whether they concurred with Spengler's thesis in *Decline of the West*. About two-thirds of them said a decline was "quite probable" or "most probable." Approximately 50 percent felt the demise would occur around 2130. Most students believed it would lead to a better civilization, however, rather than the absolute end. In addition, the sample was split along disciplinary lines with regard to the factor most important in precipitating the decline. This indicates that future predictions are influenced by "cultural background." They also seem to be influenced by how certain the predictor is that the event in question will come to pass. That is, the more hesitant a person is to date the occurrence of an event, the less certain he is it will actually come to pass.

36. Cantril, Hadley
    1938   "The prediction of social events." Journal of Abnormal and Social Psychology 33 (July):364–389.

In an effort to find out if predictive judgments are influenced by knowledge, occupation, or range of interest, questionnaires were sent to a large group of people in selected occupational spheres. It was found that the less structured the circumstances of a situation, the more difficult it is to predict, and the less similar are predictions within a single occupational group. If there is no external structure to guide prediction at all, the individual relies on his internal value structure. It would seem, therefore, that the type of prediction made is based on the interplay of two factors: the nature of the external situation; and the content, and specificity, of internal value structures.

37. McGregor, Douglas
   1938   "The major determinants of the prediction of social events." Journal of Abnormal and Social Psychology 38 (April):179–204.
   In an experiment in which 400 persons (mostly students) were asked how problematic situations might be resolved, it was revealed that the extent to which subjective factors influence prediction depends on two things: the ambiguity of the stimulus situation (i.e., surrounding social realities); and how committed an individual is to those attitudes or desires relevant to the forecast being made. That is, the influence of subjective factors increases as the situation becomes more ambiguous and as the individual becomes more ego-involved. Amount of knowledge about the situation in question seems to have little effect on a person's predictions, though the nature of his knowledge is influential.

38. Toch, Hans H.
   1958   "The perception of future events: case studies in social prediction." Public Opinion Quarterly 22 (Spring):57–66.
   In 1941–1942 twenty-six professional people and public figures were asked to write an open-ended essay about the shape of the world in 1952 and the trends leading up to it. By comparing these predictions with the actual state of affairs in 1952, the following conclusions about the nature of prediction emerged: (1) accurate prediction is related to an individual's ability to foresee novelty and change; (2) immediate experience has considerable influence on the content of a given prediction; (3) subjective factors influence a prediction most strongly if the event in question is of vital personal importance to the predictor; and (4) there is a fairly strong correlation between cautious statements and accurate prediction.

39. Kaplan, Abraham, A. L. Skogstad, and M. A. Girshick
   1950   "The prediction of social and technological events." Public Opinion Quarterly 14 (Spring):93–111.
   By its very nature, policy-making involves an assessment of future possibilities and the policy-maker generally asks experts to make such assessments. To find out how good experts are at prediction, therefore, twenty-six highly educated individuals were asked to make a series of predictions about events one or more months in the future. An analysis of the accuracy of their predictions generated three major conclusions: (1) the degree of confidence an individual has in a prediction is often not a good indicator of how correct it is; (2) predictions based on group consensus are more likely to be correct than individual

predictions; and (3) the type of justification given for a prediction can be used to assess its reliability (i.e., if a person can justify a forecast, it is more likely to be correct).

40. Ogburn, William F.
   1946   "On predicting the future." Pp. 32–57 in W. F. Ogburn, The Social Effects of Aviation. Boston: Houghton Mifflin.

This article reviews considerations that should be borne in mind when forecasting social developments. The author begins by noting that there is much prediction in daily life and that it should be an integral part of any planning endeavor. He then describes various methods of prediction, focusing on techniques of extrapolation, correlation, and intuition. He concludes with a discussion of some factors that can limit the accuracy of one's predictions. They include: failure to appreciate the complexity of social phenomena, personal bias, wishful thinking, current fashions, and an overly cautious or conservative approach. (NOTE: the book also contains a chapter on the methodology, and difficulties, of predicting the social effects of inventions.)

41. Hart, Hornell
   1957   "Predicting future trends." Pp. 455–474 in Allen, Hart et al., Technology and Social Change. New York: Appleton-Century-Crofts.

Drawing on past predictions in the fields of technology, economics, and demography, the author argues that reliable social prediction is possible. "It must be recognized that the prediction of social phenomena is a difficult and hazardous process. However, instances cited . . . show that a number of quite specific predictions have been fulfilled. . . . If sociology is to become a science worthy of the name, the energies of its practitioners might better be directed toward improving the techniques of prediction rather than toward demonstrations that prediction is impossible" (p. 472).

III.   METHODOLOGICAL CONSIDERATIONS IN THE SCIENTIFIC STUDY OF THE FUTURE

Part A.1 of this category is devoted to publications outlining guidelines for actual forecasting. Through such endeavors the authors hope it will be possible to anticipate future problems, thereby avoiding them. The work in Part A.2 is based on a different assumption; namely, that with his present technology man can create any type of future he desires. The authors in this subcategory, therefore, discuss methods for achieving desirable futures.

The publications in Part B deal with specific forecasting techniques. Those in the first subsection describe methodologies useful for individual forecasting endeavors, while those in the second subsection specify ways of analyzing large amounts of data.

III.A. General guidelines for studying the future. *1. Guidelines for forecasting the future*

42. Commission on the Year 2000
   1967b   "Working session I." Daedalus 96 (Summer):652–704.
   In this first working session the aims of the Commission were defined more specifically. In essence, it will try to do six things: (1) sketch alternative futures and evaluate the problems that realization of any given hypothesis would bring; (2) propose alternative policies and institutions to deal with various hypothetical futures; (3) set up standards of social performance by anticipating future possibilities; (4) delineate undesirable developments and ways in which they can be avoided; (5) formulate a new political theory to guide the emerging pluralistic economy and welfare society; and (6) improve present planning endeavors by delineating the components of the planning process. The Commission members decided these goals could best be achieved with an eclectic methodology and delineated a variety of specific procedures. They also discussed how to redefine certain key concepts presently used in the social sciences.

43. Cornish, Edward S.
   1969   "The professional futurist." Pp. 244–250 in Robert Jungk and Johan Galtung (eds.), Mankind 2000. Oslo: Universitetsforlaget.
   The futurist must play three major roles, and therefore, has three tasks facing him: (1) as an artist he must sketch the multiplicity of available futures; (2) as a scientist he must assess the probability that these futures will become realities; and (3) as a cost-benefit analyst he must specify the effects various lines of development might have on society as a whole. The article also discusses the problems of deciding on a name for the emerging discipline of future-oriented study, and how the futurist might function as part of a large organization.

44. Flechtheim, Ossip K.
   1966   History and Futurology. Meisenheim am Glan (Germany): Verlag Anton Hain.
   This book is a collection of essays, most of which had been published previously. In the first part the author's conception of the future emerges from a critique of the theodocian school of historical thought. He finds that history is "an endless odyssey" of unexpected adventures and difficulties, and that the future is a continuation of this odyssey with new and unanticipated challenges. The second part of the book discusses some of the important characteristics of the future and how it might be studied. Due to the great acceleration of the pace of change, the future has suddenly emerged as an entity that is completely different from the past. Therefore, the future and its impact on the past and present, become worthy of investigation. This study could be undertaken by the new discipline of "Futurology," the major aim of which would be to establish the statistical probability, as well as the more intuitive credibility, of various future developments. Though Futurology may not enable man to manipulate what is to come, it will at least let him anticipate it, and thereby make it more bearable.

45. Flechtheim, Ossip K.
    1969   "Is futurology the answer to the challenge of the future?" Pp.
        264–269 in Robert Jungk and Johan Galtung (eds.), Mankind
        2000. Oslo: Universitetsforlaget.
    This article discusses the relationship between futurology, utopia, coun-
terutopia, and ideology. It concludes: "Fully aware of the tragic limitations of
human existence, but also inspired by the hope of human progress, the futurologist acts more critically than the utopianist, more hopefully than the counter-
utopianist, and more dynamically than the ideologist" (p. 269).

46. Hayashi, Yujiro
    1969   "The direction and orientation of futurology as a science." Pp.
        270–277 in Robert Jungk and Johan Galtung (eds.), Mankind
        2000. Oslo: Universitetsforlaget.
    There are two ways in which one can view the future: as an object of
cognition (futuro-epistemology); and as an object of conception (futuro-concep-
tionology). The former involves asking how the future can be objectively recognized, while the latter necessitates outlining possibilities for future development. This article discusses the implications of adopting one or the other of
these two views of the future.

47. Iklé, Fred Charles
    1967   "Can social predictions be evaluated?" Daedalus 96 (Summer):
        733–758.
    There are three types of predictions: (1) those formulated to guide present
actions; (2) those made in an effort to choose between two equally desirable
courses of action; and (3) those made for the sake of entertainment. Accuracy
in forecasting can be greatly improved if one clearly distinguishes between
these types of prediction and their uses. It can be further enhanced by evaluating the correctness of predictions. At present evaluative techniques are rather
rudimentary, but the author is able to point to four aspects of "guiding" predictions (the first type mentioned above) that can be used to assess their accuracy. It seems clear that technological developments will improve the quality of
forecasts. Nonetheless, the future will probably never be completely foreseeable.

48. The Institute for the Future
    1968   The Institute for the Future (A Prospectus). Middletown, Conn.:
        Institute for the Future–Riverview Center.
    "The Institute for the Future (IFF) is an independent non-profit corpora-
tion, dedicated to research in the public interest. . . . The purpose of IFF is to
institutionalize systematic and comprehensive studies of the long-range future"
(1). Its major aims are fivefold: (1) to assess long-term implications of present
policy decisions; (2) to forecast major socioeconomic trends and delineate ways
of altering them; (3) to clarify the U.S.'s major problems and specify possible
solutions; (4) to improve planning and forecasting technology by developing
simulation, and analytic, models; and (5) to critically assess, and disseminate,

the results of future-oriented research. In addition to outlining these goals, the monograph describes how the Institute was established and what its organizational structure is like. The nature of its research program is also described in some detail.

49. Jouvenel, Bertrand de.
 1963b "La prévision des idées [The prediction of ideas]." Futuribles (no. 68)–Supplement to Bulletin Sedeis 870 (December 1).
  The author's major concern in this article is how one might predict the "social career," or future development, of ideas already in existence. In this kind of undertaking one would try to establish the extent to which an idea will be accepted by society, how it will change through time, and in what areas it will be applied. With the aid of various examples the author discusses how one might attempt to conjecture about these aspects of an idea's future. He believes this could best be done by conceiving of all the ideas present within a society as an "ecosystem" composed of idea populations. The population of a given idea consists of all the minds that are cognizant of it. One could delineate the various subordinate and concurrent relationships that exist between idea populations with such a conceptualization. The author believes that the social career of moral ideas may be especially important to forecast because of their widespread influence.

50. Jouvenel, Bertrand de
 1965b "Political science and prevision." American Political Science Review 59 (March): 29–38.
  It is the responsibility of the political scientist to serve as a guide for public policy—he must be the teacher of public men. To be effective he should be able to do the following: (1) foresee the future and the changes it will bring; (2) determine the priority various problems should receive; (3) anticipate the indirect ramifications of a policy and make the necessary adjustments; (4) recognize the signs of developing disturbances; (5) consider factors that have led to past political eruptions, as well as traits of individual leaders, in making forecasts; (6) accurately assess human emotions and reactions to future situations; (7) foresee alterations needed in societal institutions so that they can cope with future changes in the social fabric; and (8) structure the future so as to preserve liberty.

51. Jungk, Robert
 1967 "The future of future research." Science Journal 3 (October):3–40.
  The author reviews the present state of systematic research on the future. He concludes that for rapid development of the field three things must be done: (1) improvement and refinement of methodological techniques; (2) avoidance of unnecessary constraints that might emerge through conventional academic rigor and preconceptions; and (3) clarification of the existing relationship between future-oriented research and political power groups, as well as clarification of the desirable one.

52. Lasswell, Harold D.
>   1966   "The changing image of human nature: the socio-cultural aspect (future-oriented man)." American Journal of Psychoanalysis 26 (no. 2):157–166.

The characteristic most sharply distinguishing modern Western civilization from earlier eras is the significance it assigns to the future. Modern man believes himself increasingly able to regulate his future, and planners are rapidly developing programs to guide the progress of every aspect of society. "Future-oriented man" is adapting his mental processes to the future. After delineating the development and nature of the policy sciences, the author continues his discussion of problem-solving and the efforts that have been made to apply it to the future. He notes that future difficulties must be considered as part of a larger whole and the impact of the social process on them must be isolated. In conclusion the author speculates that, though man may have unconscious predispositions opposing continuous change, they will not be strong enough to halt the acceleration of the historical process.

53. Lompe, Klaus
>   1968   "Problems of futures research in the social sciences." Futures 1 (September):47–53.

This article discusses how forecasting methodology can be improved. It begins by presenting a number of presently useful methodologies and suggests possible refinements. It then discusses the merits of qualitative and quantitative forecasts, concluding that both methods should be combined to isolate possible futures. After a short discussion of the sources of error in forecasting, the article concludes by pointing to the urgent need for interdisciplinary work. Not only should academics in different fields cooperate in planning the future, but so should intellectuals, government planners, and the general public. Each can teach and learn from the other, thereby contributing to the emergence of a better future.

54. McHale, John
>   1969b   "Future research: some integrative and communicative aspects." Pp. 256–263 in Robert Jungk and Johan Galtung (eds.), Mankind 2000. Oslo: Universitetsforlaget.

A bias towards "professionalization" is rapidly developing in the field of future-oriented research. That is, forecasts based on scientific methodologies are rapidly outstripping those of a more intuitive nature. This is an unfortunate trend and ought to be reversed because of the need for diverse images of the future. It has already led to neglect of areas of research that ought to receive more attention. They include: (1) incorporating a concern with the future into the educational process; (2) facilitating communication and cooperation between futurists; (3) designing new social forms; and (4) making the public aware of the possibilities the future holds.

55. Massenet, Michel

    1963a   "Etudes méthodologiques sur les futuribles, après les discussions de Genève (juin, 1962) [Methodological studies on 'futuribles' after the Geneva discussions of June, 1962]." Futuribles (no. 52)–Supplement to Bulletin Sedeis 849 (April 1).

In the course of five chapters the author summarizes the main conclusions of the Geneva conference with regard to the methodology of conjecture. In Chapter I ("Legitimate Ethics of Conjecture") the author notes that at the present modest stage of development any conception that the future is determined by the past or present should be avoided. He also states that there need be no conflict between values and knowledge about the future. The major focus of the second chapter ("Legitimate Logic of Conjecture") is on two major types of conjecture: that based on past happenings; and that based on extrapolation of present trends in light of a general theory. Chapter Three ("Methods of Conjecture") outlines the various procedural principles that the conference agreed upon. In his fourth chapter the author discusses the "Limits of Conjecture" and notes that neither personal futures nor the future of humanity can be foreseen, because both are too complex. Also, conjecture cannot precisely describe or date an event. At best it can somewhat reduce ignorance about the future. The last chapter deals with "How to Improve Conjecture," and its primary suggestion is that one should attempt to isolate those factors that gave rise to incorrect predictions in the past.

56. Miller, Cecil

    1961   "The self-fulfilling prophecy: a reappraisal." Ethics 72 (October):46–51.

There seems little doubt that Merton's concept of the self-fulfilling prophecy is of great importance to social science. It has, however, become taboo in recent years due to its injudicious use. Social scientists should realize that if they condemn self-fulfilling prophecies on the part of the masses, they may not themselves make them in the guise of "scientific statements." They should recognize that the self-fulfilling prophecy is simply a type of hypothesis that occurs in all human discourse, most commonly, and appropriately, in the social sciences. Furthermore, while many social scientific predictions may be self-fulfilling, some are more desirable than others in terms of societal and human well-being. By recognizing this value element in hypotheses, social science can be strengthened formally.

57. Schon, Donald A.

    1967   "Forecasting and technological forecasting." Daedalus 96 (Summer): 759–771.

Technological forecasting is primarily concerned with anticipating the development of technological innovations. Its effectiveness is limited by lack of data and the poor quality of available data. In view of this, many argue that all attempts at forecasting should be abandoned. This would be foolhardy, however, since assumptions about the future have become an integral part of decision-making. Rather, one should continue to use forecasts as decision-making tools, while simultaneously trying to improve them. This can best be accomplished by improving the quality, and quantity, of available data, and by constructing better models of the change process.

58. Toffler, Alvin
    1969   "Value impact forecaster—a profession of the future." Pp. 1–30 in K. Baier and N. Rescher (eds.), Values and the Future. New York: Free Press.

The bulk of this article consists of a summary of the book to which it forms the introduction. The author concludes that the book he has outlined is one of the few endeavors dealing with the effect of technological change on value structures. This points to the dire need for "value-impact forecasters" to analyze the value implications of all decisions about technological innovations. These men should be part of every organization that is at all involved in technological development, be it public, private, or academic. Their presence would serve to make scientists, technicians, administrators, and businessmen more aware of how their work might affect the larger society. The task of such forecasters, therefore, would not consist of ". . . merely describing present and future states of the value system, but [of] actively intervening in the process of value change" (p. 30).

For further material on guidelines for forecasting the future, see: nos. **9, 114, 128, 140, 167, 194, 243, 244, 245, 246,** and **247.**

III.A.2. Guidelines for creating the future

59. Calder, Nigel
    1969   "Goals, foresight, and politics." Pp. 251–255 in Robert Jungk and Johan Galtung (eds.), Mankind 2000. Oslo: Universitetsforlaget.

Research on the future can be of value only if the political implications of forecasts are developed. This not to say that the experts studying the future should determine its shape. Rather, they should attempt to show politicians the great variety of possibilities that the future holds. Once this has happened, a meaningful political dialogue about the best future can begin.

60. Commission on the Year 2000
    1967c   "Working session II." Daedalus 96 (Summer):936–984.

Two major conclusions emerged from the Commission's second set of discussions. The first was that basing one's forecasts on trends alone is inadequate. Rather, models of social change should be constructed that take into account present trends, the interrelationships between variables in the system, and major initiating elements. The second conclusion was that the Commission would not concentrate on what the future *might* bring, but on what the future *should* bring. That is, the major emphasis would be on what kind of future the Commission members consider desirable. "The problem of the future consists in defining one's priorities and making the necessary commitments. This is the intention of the Commission on the Year 2000" (p. 646).

61. Duhl, Leonard J.
  1967   "Planning and predicting: or what to do when you don't know the names of the variables." Daedalus 96 (Summer): 779–788.
  The planner-forecaster should not serve as an objective seer of events to come, but should attempt to modify various segments of society so that they can cope with the problems of the future. "Instead of speculating on what the world might be like in the year 2000, we would do well to consider what mechanisms, what people, and what decisions must be attended to today in order to shape all the years to come" (p. 788). This latter should be the task of the planner-forecaster.

62. Freymond, Jacques
  1965   "Introduction—forecasting and Europe." Pp. xiii–xxx in Bertrand de Jouvenel (ed.), Futuribles: Studies in Conjecture (II). Geneva: Droz.
  The essays in the volume, which this essay introduces (the book deals with the future of Europe), still remain valid despite the rather unexpected events that have taken place since they were written. The authors focused on the distant rather than the near future; they were not concerned with immediate changes, but with the final objective of a united Europe. Their primary aim was "less to describe the lines of force which must be followed in a probable or possible future than to delineate the policy which must be followed if the wished-for future is to become tomorrow's reality" (p. xiv). The essay concludes with an enumeration of factors that will shape Europe's future, though, of course, its exact character cannot be foreseen.

63. Jouvenel, Bertrand de
  1967   The Art of Conjecture. New York: Basic Books.
  "My aim in this book is to describe the 'mores' that our minds conform to in forethinking" (p. 127). The author does this by dividing the book into six sections, each of which discusses one of the following aspects of the future: (1) the general nature of the future and of the art of forecasting; (2) how the individual goes about constructing likely futures; (3) the shortcomings of past predictions and the conditions under which forecasting is relatively safe and simple; (4) conditions essential to forecasting in the social sphere with special emphasis on the "process" aspects of human action; (5) the origins, development and applications of quantitative forecasting; and (6) the difficulties prediction encounters in the social realm and the need for a "surmising forum" to systematize societal forecasting.

64. Jouvenel, Bertrand de
  1968   "On attending to the future." Pp. 21–29 in William R. Ewald (ed.), Environment and Change: The Next Fifty Years. Bloomington: Indiana University Press.

". . . endowed as we are in technologies of Doing, we are miserably poor in techniques of Undoing, which the progress of Doing shall make ever more necessary" (p. 24). It is, therefore, the primary job of people concerned with the future to develop techniques of controlling and harnessing technology for the good of mankind. In so doing the "Forwardist" has two functions: (1) to point out the likely consequences of given decisions or events; and (2) to develop plans for realizing the most desirable future. To carry out these functions especially the second, he should gain a deeper understanding of human nature and its developmental possibilities.

65. Jungk, Robert
      1968a   "About 'Mankind 2000'." Pp. 79–85 in Stanford Anderson (ed.) Planning for Diversity and Choice. Cambridge, Mass.: MIT Press.
This article describes "Mankind 2000," a project initiated by ICDP (International Confederation for Disarmament and Peace). "It is an international interdisciplinary, and interideological venture dedicated to the invention of desirable future conditions of life and to the design of institutions likely to ensure the survival of the human race" (p. 79). Its major function at present is to sponsor "workshops of the future" where concerned individuals try to outline desirable futures through intensive discussion. The article concludes by discussing two factors preventing more intensive and widespread study of the future: (1) experts are unwilling to risk their status by making bold and creative forecasts; and (2) the passivity of the general public—the average man has very vague ideas about the future.

66. Jungk, Robert
      1968b   "Human futures." Futures 1 (September):34–39.
It is high time that futurists began to devote some time to "human forecasting"; that is, to portraying the most desirable futures in human terms, as well as specifying ways of achieving them. Two problems "human forecasting" would have to grapple with involve: providing the underprivileged with their share of the world's abundance; and, devising ways of making mass democratic participation possible through decentralized decision-making. Before "human forecasting" can be utilized on a large scale, however, mankind must know what it wants. This means determining what long-range goals and basic values man wants to build the world of the future on.

67. Jungk, Robert
      1969a   "Look-out institutions for shaping the environment." Futures 1 (March):227–232.
Most research on the future is presently being done by people concerned with economic growth and military preparedness, and, therefore, the emerging future is being shaped by their priorities. If the future is also to realize wider social goals it is imperative that civilian "look-out" institutions be established to investigate how this might be accomplished. Their primary tasks would be: (1) to foster a multifaceted approach to the future; (2) to anticipate

grave social problems; (3) to educate the public about future possibilities; (4) to support future planning and research; and (5) to delineate broad social goals and values. Look-out institutions could only be successful if they encouraged democratic participation from all societal levels at all times.

68. McHale, John
   1967b   "The people future." Architectural Design 37 (February):94–95.
   The future of man will primarily be determined by what he deems desirable and necessary. This requires that man rid himself of preconceptions about the limits of human nature and the infallibility of the expert. "All futures are conditional on a present which is conditioned by the past. To invent the future, we must exorcise the present from obsolete past 'realities' which now operate as constraining mythologies" (p. 94). In addition, man should define a set of values appropriate to modern realities which can serve to shape future goals and developmental priorities.

69. Nisbet, Robert A.
   1968   "The year 2000 and all that." Commentary 45 (June):60–66.
   Present future-oriented analysis is no different from that undertaken by nineteenth-century philosophers of history (e.g., Tocqueville, Comte, Marx, etc.), except perhaps that it is usually of lower quality. The only utility such contemporary work can have is to provide insights into the nature of the present. This is so because the seeds of the future do not lie in the present—a mere chronological relationship (such as the one existing between past, present, and future) does not imply causality. The world of tomorrow will be shaped by "the Random Event," "the Maniac," "the Prophet," and "the Genius." These, by their very nature, are unforeseeable, and thereby, make any prediction of the future impossible. (NOTE: This article is classified in this section because the argument could be extended to imply that since prediction is impossible, man ought to devote his energies to creating the future.)

70. Ozebekhan, Hasan
   1965   The Idea of a "Look-Out" Institution. Santa Monica, Calif.: System Development Corporation (March).
   The aims of "Look-Out" institutions would be threefold: (1) to create a wide variety of images of the future; (2) to develop yardsticks for comparing their relative merits; and (3) to devise ways of achieving the most desirable futures given present limitations on natural and social resources. After describing the nature of these institutions in some detail, the author also outlines some of the methods they could use to carry on their work.

71. Ozebekhan, Hasan
   1966   Technology and Man's Future. Santa Monica, Calif.: System Development Corporation. Report no. SP–2494 (May 27).
   This monograph attempts to locate technological forecasting in the broader context of social technology. The author outlines present weaknesses in the field of forecasting in addition to indicating what new developments are

needed. He also explores a variety of desirable, and possible, future developments. He notes that long-range social goals ought to guide future technological progress rather than vice versa. This, however, will require a clearer specification of just what type of goals ought to be striven for.

72. Ozebekhan, Hasan

1968   "The triumph of technology: 'can' implies 'ought.' " Pp. 204–219 in Stanford Anderson (ed.), Planning for Diversity and Choice. Cambridge, Mass.: MIT Press.

Present planning endeavors are primarily deterministic in that they develop the most feasible futures in terms of present possibilities. Modern technology, which makes almost anything possible, demands a different approach, however. Planning ought to consist of developing methods for realizing the basic values of a society. This would require a multidimensional approach or an integrative theory of planning. It would involve three phases: (1) the normative plan (delineates general goals); (2) the strategic plan (outlines what can be done to achieve the specified goals); and (3) the operational plan (outlines in what order the strategies will be carried out). "Thus a planning-relevant framework needs . . . to reveal what *ought* to be done, what *can* be done, and what actually *will* be done" (p. 213).

73. Theobald, Robert

1968b   "Planning *with* people." Pp. 182–185 in William R. Ewald (ed.), Environment and Change: The Next Fifty Years. Bloomington: Indiana University Press.

Through an analysis of the problems presently facing American society, the author comes to the conclusion that future planning can be effective only if participated in by the average citizen. "If he is to do any good in the city and in the ghetto . . ., the planner will do it as consultant to people who live in the communities he is trying to change. He must cease to tell them what they ought to value and instead, in consort with them, design environments which will provide them with the capacity to develop their humanness" (p. 185).

74. Theobald, Robert

1968c   "Policy formation for new goals." Pp. 149–169 in Robert Theobald (ed.), Social Policies for America in the Seventies. Garden City, N.Y.: Doubleday.

"It will be the object of this essay to show that our present central goals are no longer appropriate and that we must therefore find new ways to define goals and purposes for the coming cybernated era" (p. 151). America's major goals of the past—national power and economic growth—are no longer appropriate because modern transportation has made nationalism obsolete, and because social justice now takes precedence over economic growth. The country must, therefore, create a new set of goals and a new social system through a three-step process: (1) set up desirable and feasible goals; (2) learn to understand the socioeconomic system so that changes necessary to implement goals can be carried out; and (3) develop new policies that reflect desired goals and developmental avenues. One of the most basic new goals should be individual development and a first step in realizing it would be a universal guaranteed income.

75. Wilkinson, John
    1967   "Futuribles: innovation vs. stability." Center Diary no. 17 (March-April):16–24.

The bulk of this article is devoted to a review of the wide variety of work on the study of the future. It stresses the conceptions of "process" and "time" underlying the future-oriented endeavors discussed. Most futurologists seem to assume that man will continue technological innovation without any regard for possible consequences. Since most innovations lie in the past, however, even while they are still being referred to in the future tense, it might be more useful to develop a "futurology" that stresses ecological stability instead of ever more frenzied innovation. The prerequisites for such a stable condition could then guide the innovative process along a path leading to benefits for all mankind.

For further material on guidelines for creating the future see: nos. **1, 6, 17, 133, 141, 151, 165, 248,** and **249.**

III.B. Specific techniques for studying the future. *1. Techniques of conjecture*

76. Ayres, Robert U.
    1969   Technological Forecasting and Long-Range Planning. New York: McGraw-Hill.

The bulk of this book discusses various forecasting techniques. It begins with a short history of forecasting, and a discussion of general considerations relevant to all forecasting, in which the author notes that any attempt at prediction must take cognizance of the dimensions of technological change. The actual techniques outlined include: morphological analysis, a relatively unknown method (involves identifying all possible means to a specific end and their probabilities of realization); extrapolation of trends; heuristic forecasts (specifying the type of developments a specific model of the future gives rise to); and intuitive forecasts by experts. The book concludes with several chapters about the relationship of forecasting and planning. It is argued that the direction and rate of future technological progress depends upon adequate planning based on insightful forecasts.

77. Bell, Daniel
    1964   "Twelve modes of prediction—a preliminary sorting of approaches in the social sciences." Daedalus 93 (Summer):845–880; *or* pp. 96–127 in Julius Gould (ed.), Penguin Survey of the Social Sciences. Baltimore: Penguin Books (1965).

A conscious transformation of society requires the ability to predict in the sense of explanation. Though man can do this only imperfectly, he does have various types of explanative prediction at his disposal, of which the author describes the following twelve: social physics; trends and forecasts; structural certainties; operational codes; operational systems; structural requisites; the overriding problem; the prime mover; sequential development; accounting schemes; alternative futures; and decision theory. The article concludes with a brief discussion of three future-oriented studies that might yield especially fruitful results.

78. Friedlaender, Saul
   1965   "Forecasting in international relations." Pp. 1–112 in Bertrand de Jouvenel (ed.), Futuribles: Studies in Conjecture (II). Geneva: Droz.

The aim of this article is to delineate those conditions under which rational forecasting is appropriate and those conditions under which various forecasting methods are most reliable. The bulk of it outlines principles for short-range forecasting (predictions for a two-year time span, which assume constancy in the international power pattern), and for long-range forecasting (attempts to isolate ten- to fifteen-year trends in the changing interstate power pattern).

79. Jantsch, Erich
   1967   Technological Forecasting in Perspective. Paris: OECD Publications.

In 1965 the Organization for Economic Cooperation and Development (OECD) commissioned a study to enumerate and evaluate technological forecasting techniques. This book summarizes the author's findings in visits to thirteen nations. It begins with a synopsis of his major conclusions and recommendations. The bulk of the book outlines over one hundred forecasting techniques. They are divided into the following major categories: (1) intuitive techniques; (2) exploratory techniques (extrapolation of patterns); (3) normative techniques (delineating future needs and the technological advances necessary to meet them); and (4) feedback techniques (combination of 2 and 3 to determine best resource allocation). The last two techniques seem to be most useful. The book concludes by discussing the type of forecasting being done in the countries visited.

80. Jouvenel, Bertrand de
   1962   "De la conjecture [On conjecture]." Futuribles (no. 27)—Supplement to Bulletin Sedeis (Part 2) 815 (March 20).

In an effort to isolate elements of the prognostication process, the author outlines a variety of famous predictions and their shortcomings, as well as several cases of political succession. On the basis of this discussion he is able to delineate the following types of conjecture: (1) isolation of those facets of the future already known; (2) "accompanying conjecture" (projecting broad developmental trends into the future); (3) "critical conjecture" (isolating volatile and disruptive forces which might upset present trends); and (4) "constructive conjecture" (outlining a coherent future from a disorganized and irregular present). All these predictive forms should be employed in outlining the future of societies.

81. Massenet, Michel

    1963c   "Les méthodes de prévision en sciences sociales [The methods of conjecture in the social sciences]." Futuribles (no. 66)–Supplement to Bulletin Sedeis (Part 2) 867 (Nov. 1).

    This article discusses the nature of two types of conjecture. The first one is extrapolation, which consists of extending stable aspects of the present into the future. The predictions that emerge from this process can be enriched in several ways, as the author shows. The second type of conjecture discussed is the "method of movement," which is more uncertain and imaginative than the first. It tries to delineate future changes not manifest in the present, and involves the following steps: (1) isolation of those factors that could radically change the future and those that will keep it static; (2) pinpointing the factor most critical in causing future changes; (3) enumerating those areas that might be affected by the "beginning cause" isolated in (2); and (4) sketching how the "beginning cause" will affect present trends, either by dislocating them or bringing them into greater harmony.

82. Murphy, Gardner

    1961   Human Potentialities. New York: Basic Books.

    "This book is an effort to describe the sources available within human nature for the outgrowing of human nature, the constitution of new varieties of human thought, value, and aspiration" (p. 6). The present potentialities within human nature should be assessed in terms of "emergence." This approach attempts to define the process by which various factors interact to form a new whole. One of the most important interactions to be considered is that between organism and environment, and it can best be isolated through field theory. The first step in foreseeing the development of present potentialities involves delineating the three different aspects of human nature (i.e., the biological, the cultural, the "creative thrust") and their evolution. At present these "human natures" are only partially fulfilled and often in direct conflict. A social order should be established, therefore, that can fulfill all three. It would be characterized by: (1) a strong desire to discover new methods of harnessing the environment, and curiosity about man himself; (2) a flexible and well-trained elite capable of controlling technological and social innovations; and (3) effective communication between the social strata, enabling the common man to participate more effectively in his society. This kind of social order could be achieved if man's present potentialities were permitted to develop in the desired directions.

83. Dubos, René

    1967   "Evolving psyche." Center Diary no. 17 (March–April):38–44.

    Man should evolve an ecological model of human events on the basis of which he can solve the vast problems that future technological advances will bring. Such a model would allow isolation of those "cohesive forces that maintain man in an integrated state physically, psychologically and socially, and enable him to relate successfully to his environment" (p. 44). It would also aid him in developing those psychological and social mechanisms necessary to make life in a technological society desirable. Provided man realizes that his basic aim should be the development of all human potentialities, rather than immediate material comfort or improvement, he will succeed in this endeavor.

84. Moore, Wilbert E.
>   1964a   "Predicting discontinuities in social change." American Socio-logical Review 29 (June):331–338.

The type of change that proceeds at an orderly consistent rate is relatively easy to foresee, as one need only extrapolate present trends. This approach is quite inadequate, however, for predicting sharp changes in the rate, or direction, of a given developmental process. Such change can only be forecast by studying the societal effects of innovation. This, in turn, requires the development of dynamic societal models. These "dynamic systems" would also be useful in anticipating cataclysmic change (i.e., revolution). In conclusion, the author discusses a variety of factors that affect different types of change.

85. Jantsch, Erich
>   1969   "Integrative planning of society and technology." Futures 1 (March):185–190.

To assess and guide technological advances so that they improve the quality of daily life, planners and forecasters should use a systems approach. This means analyzing the consequences of a given technological advance for the social system as a whole before deciding to invest in or accelerate it. Such integrative planning would only be feasible, however, if the present orientation of science and technology were completely reformulated. The author believes universities are the key to such a change in philosophy. "They have a unique opportunity to transform their teaching and research facilities, to bring together the various disciplines, and to guide government and industry" (p. 185).

86. Jantsch, Erich
>   1969   "Planning and designing for the future: the breakthrough of the systems approach." Futures 1 (September):440–444.

The systems, or integrative, approach involves viewing man in the context of those complex, interrelated, dynamic, feedback systems that surround him. It implies studying the relationship between man, his society, and his environment in terms of nature, technology, and social developments. When applied to the study of the future, this type of approach enables one to consider how the structure of various systems will change or will have to be changed. Three books published in the recent past (e.g., *So Human an Animal* by Rene Dubos, *Urban Dynamics* by Jay Forrester, and *The Chasm Ahead* by Aurelio Peccei) employ systems analysis to isolate future problems; and the author hopes that this trend will continue because of the valuable results it yields.

87. Michaelis, Michael
>   1968   "Can we build the world we want?" Bulletin of the Atomic Scientists 24 (January):43–49.

It is not lack of technological know-how that is preventing us from solving our problems, but the individual's fear of change. This fear of the new and different often prevents the implementation of innovations whose eventual benefits cannot be clearly delineated. The use of new methods is hindered further by a tendency to analyze urban and social problems in a piecemeal fashion rather than as part of an integrated whole. What is needed, therefore, is the "systems approach," which analyzes whole problem areas and requires an interdisciplinary, or intersector approach. To promote such cooperation the author suggests establishing a "Council for American Progress." Its major aims would be: to define national goals more clearly; and to delineate ways of achieving them through greater collaboration between government, industry, and business.

88. Stulman, Julius
 1968 Evolving Mankind's Future: The World Institute: A Problem-Solving Methodology. Philadelphia: Lippincott.
  This book describes the purpose and functions of the "World Institute" (it now exists in embryo form at the United Nations Plaza in New York City). Its major goal will be to find practical solutions to the grave problems facing mankind. It will investigate long-term trends in an effort to foresee the difficulties and developmental opportunities of the future. But it will not use conventional methods to do this; rather, it will try to arrive at new insights by integrating the orientations of all disciplines and nations. Only by breaking down the conventional barriers between academic and national areas can solutions to mankind's present dilemmas be found. The results of the Institute's investigations or its blueprints for action will be made available to everyone, but no effort will be made to force their implementation.

89. Eulau, Heinz
 1958 "H. D. Lasswell's developmental analysis." Western Political Quarterly 11 (June):229–242.
  The author's main purpose is to outline Lasswell's developmental analysis. It is a basic component of political science theory because it analyzes statements about the expected future that are couched in terms of certain fundamental concepts. Developmental analysis involves delineating developmental constructs, which isolate a probable chain of events beginning at some point in the past and ending in the future. In essence they are "ideal-type" statements about the progression of a given social process through time. Developmental analysis has two major advantages as a policy tool: (1) it enables the decision-maker to clarify his ideas about the future; and (2) it overcomes the problem of the self-fulfilling prophecy.

90. Massenet, Michel
 1965 "The foreign policy of a united Europe." Pp. 271–360 in Bertrand de Jouvenel (ed.), Futuribles: Studies in Conjecture (II). Geneva: Droz.
  The "method of conditional hypothesis" is based on the premise that the

nature of the future is pluralistic, as it is still in the course of development. This means that three steps should be taken in studying the future: (1) enumerate all the hypothetical paths of development; (2) evaluate each hypothesis in terms of limitations imposed by the present; and (3) assess the "costs of change" entailed in the realization of a specific hypothesis and associate a probability of realization with it. This type of analysis gives a much broader view of future possibilities than does mere analysis of present trends.

The author devotes a good deal of his essay to applying his method to the future of Europe. He concludes that its course of development in the next decade depends on how well it can resolve a paradox: the desire to be more independent of the United States, while being totally dependent upon her militarily. The best resolution, the author believes, would be the development of a common European foreign policy.

91. Jouvenel, Bertrand de
     1963a   "Introduction." Pp. ix–xi in Bertrand de Jouvenel (ed.), Futuribles: Studies in Conjecture (I). Geneva: Droz.

The basic premise of the "Futuribles" project is that a profitable dialogue will emerge from the evaluation of various experts' predictions about the future progress of their field of competence. "In short what we conceive is speculation initiated on a large front, narrowed down by constraints of coherence between the various aspects of the future, weeded out by critical discussion, and generally disciplined by slowly developed standards of reasoned surmising" (p. x). As a first step in this procedure a variety of experts wrote articles about their fields of specialization in the French publication *Futuribles* (see no. **203**). Many of these original forecasts have since been evaluated and elaborated. Some of them are being translated into English in an effort to broaden the group of intellectuals engaged in the vitally necessary task of forecasting the future in a systematic way.

92. Helmer, Olaf
     1966a   Social Technology. New York: Basic Books.

Western society's ability to adjust to the radical changes it is undergoing depends largely upon whether the social sciences develop a workable social technology based on "operations-analysis" techniques. Such techniques enable a researcher to construct tentative developmental models without the aid of a well-established theory. The author discusses the nature of operations analysis in some detail, as well as a number of techniques that would be especially useful to the social scientist (i.e., the simulation model and the "scenario"). He also notes that it is imperative for the researcher to seek expert advice in constructing future-oriented models. The author illustrates how operations analysis techniques are applicable to the following fields: urban development, educational reform, political forecasting and planning, juvenile delinquency, and long-range economic forecasting. He concludes that the future of Western man could be investigated systematically and comprehensively through a three-step process: (1) constructing forecasts delineating obvious major changes; (2) constructing more imaginative projections of presently unanticipated trends; and (3) determining which forecasts are most compatible with dominant societal values and preferences. (NOTE: for a discussion of this book's two appendices on long-range forecasting, see nos. **98** and **99**.)

93. Kahn, Herman, and Anthony J. Weiner
   1967b   "The next thirty-three years: a framework for speculation." Daedalus 96 (Summer):705–732.
   This article illustrates how the Hudson Institute makes systematic predictions about the future. It uses a three-step approach: (1) delineating long-term trends that will continue into the future; (2) isolating clusters of significant events that have occurred since 1900 to determine which long-term trends develop together; and (3) specifying probable future demographic trends. Through this process it is possible to make predictions about a "Standard World" and its possible variations. This world has the following characteristics: a postindustrial society; high per-capita income; major emphasis on the "meaning and purpose" of life; unrest in the developing nations; new intermediate powers; continued development of Europe and China; and a relative demise of the United States and the USSR.

94. Kahn, Herman
   1968   "The alternative world futures approach." Pp. 83–137 in Morton A. Kaplan (ed.), New Approaches to International Relations. New York: St. Martin's Press.
   A "World Future" is a coherent picture of what the life of tomorrow might be like. It contains two major elements: (1) several basic themes delineating factors of key importance; and (2) an assessment of how other variables might affect them. (These variables range from climate or natural resources to political events or complex change processes.) By combining different basic themes and varying the impact of other variables upon them, a number of alternative Future Worlds emerge.
   The author discusses twenty-one themes basic to the world of the future and how they might be affected by several variables. As a result, he is able to delineate a variety of specific developmental possibilities.

For further material on Techniques of Conjecture, see: nos. **47, 49, 53, 55, 60, 70, 176,** and **231.**

III.B.2. Quantitative techniques

95. Cantril, Hadley
   1963   "A study of aspirations." Scientific American 208 (February):41–45.
   To study aspirations comparatively one should do two things: (1) let subjects express their hopes and fears in terms familiar to them, yet (2) in a manner amenable to interclass and intercountry comparisons. The "Self-Anchoring Striving Scale" tries to do both these things simultaneously. The scale is con-

structed from a series of questions that ask the respondent to describe the best possible future he can imagine as well as the worst. The "best" future forms the upper limit of the Self-Anchoring Striving Scale, while the "worst" future forms the lower limit. The respondent is then asked to rank himself on this scale in terms of his present position, his position five years ago, and his anticipated position five years hence. The scale is administered with reference to an individual's own future, as well as to that he foresees for his country. In this manner it is possible to let an individual express his aspirations without prestructuring his responses. At the same time, the various scale rankings can be compared, as can the content of the expressed hopes and fears (for a brief summary of the techniques used, see no. 96).

The second half of the article summarizes the results obtained when the scale was administered in the United States, West Germany, Brazil, Cuba, and the Philippines.

96. Cantril, Hadley, and Lloyd Free
    1962   "Hopes and fears for self and country." Supplement to American Behavioral Scientist 6 (October).

If a social system is to be viable through time it must, at least in part, meet the demands its members make upon it. To study the major forces that influence such demands, the authors focused on those individual aspirations, fears, and preoccupations that are related to expectations about socioeconomic and political systems. They developed the "Self-Anchoring Striving Scale" as a research tool (for a summary of its construction, see no. **95**). The answers individuals gave in defining the limits of their scale were compared through content analysis. The previously determined categories used for this purpose are described in some detail. The authors also compare the results their scale yielded in Brazil (an underdeveloped country) and the United States (a developed country).

97. Kilpatrick, F. P., and Hadley Cantril
    1960   "Self-anchoring scaling, a measure of individuals' unique reality worlds." Journal of Individual Psychology 16 (November):158–173.

This article discusses those aspects of transactional psychology relevant to the "Self-Anchoring Striving Scale," as well as how the scale is constructed (for a description of the scale, see no. **95**).

98. Gordon, Theodore, and Olaf Helmer
    1966   "Report on a long-range forecasting study." Pp. 44–97 (Appendix I) in Olaf Helmer, Social Technology. New York: Basic Books.

The "Delphi Technique" is a method of forecasting the distant future. It consists of asking panels of experts to make a series of predictions in the following four phases: (1) a list of all feasible and needed changes is compiled by asking the experts to list those they foresee for the future; (2) each expert is asked to state the date when each change will occur—on the basis of this a median date and interquartile range of each projected change can be calculated; (3) of those changes on which there was considerable disagreement in phase 2, the more important ones are reconsidered; and (4) the exact nature of the projected changes is defined and each expert is asked if he agrees with the majority opinion or not. Preliminary trials show that the Delphi Technique could be improved in two ways: by instituting more phases to allow for a better appraisal of minority opinions; and by developing a better method of evaluating an expert's suitability for answering a given type of question.

The article also discusses the results of using the Delphi Technique to elicit a variety of scientific and technological predictions from a group of eighty-two experts. The authors specify the changes foreseen for 1984, 2000, and 2100, as well as those that will occur through time. They found that there were four areas of importance in avoiding a major catastrophe: war prevention, equitable distribution of resources, societal reorganization, and eugenics.

99. Brown, Bernice, and Olaf Helmer

1966   "Improvements in the reliability of a concensus through the use of self-rating." Pp. 98–110 (Appendix II) in Olaf Helmer, Social Technology. New York: Basic Books.

In an effort to improve the "Delphi Technique" as a tool of long-range forecasting (for a brief description, see no. **98**), the authors used a modified version to ask twenty-three Rand employees a series of general knowledge questions. The major modification involved asking respondents to rate their competence in answering each question. The authors found that by establishing an "elite group" (those with the highest competence rating), it was possible to isolate a group whose median answer was much closer to the real answer than was the total sample's. Self-ratings of competence may, therefore, be a powerful tool for increasing the reliability of the group estimates elicited by the Delphi Technique.

100. Dalkey, N.

1969   "An experimental study of group opinion: the Delphi method." Futures 1 (September):408–426.

In 1968 the Rand Corporation used a group of UCLA students to evaluate various aspects of the "Delphi Technique" (for a brief description, see no. **98**). The major finding that emerged was that the "controlled feedback interaction" that Delphi allows yields more accurate group predictions than direct face-to-face discussion. In addition, the use of individual competence ratings enabled the researcher to attach accuracy ratings to given group predictions. The article also discusses how work with the Delphi Technique has led to insights, especially quantitative ones, concerning the process by which a group generates information.

101. Helmer, Olaf

101a. 1966b   A Use of Simulation for the Study of Future Values. Rand Publication No. P–3443 (September).

101b.   1969   "Simulating the values of the future." Pp. 193–213 in K. Baier and N. Rescher (eds.), Values and the Future. New York: Free Press.

These two articles describe a "simulation workshop" designed to delineate two scenarios, or future projections, of what the world might be like by the year 2000. The workshop employs about forty people divided into ten groups. Two of these groups act as planners and try to construct a future world by raising the probability of realization assigned to those technological developments that will facilitate the achievement of their major goal (probabilities are raised by postulating government intervention). The primary aim of the first group is to increase the GNP, while the second tries to improve the implementation of dominant societal values. After the two futures are delineated, social prediction groups evaluate the probability and desirability of the social consequences attached to them (these consequences, and the range of technological developments are described in the appendix to an article by T. Gordon; see no. **114**). Next, six evaluation committees, each representing the interests of a different sector of society, consider the comparative desirability of the two projected worlds and their social consequences. The overall desirability of each world is an average of the evaluation committees' opinions. After the workshop, participants are asked to comment on the final results, as well as the method employed. The author hopes such workshops will yield insights into the nature of the social values of the future.

102. Gordon, Theodore, and H. Hayward
      1968   "Initial experiments with the cross impact matrix method of forecasting." Futures 1 (December):100–116.

Many forecasting methods fail to take into account the possible interaction between predicted events. "The research reported here is an attempt to develop a method by which the probabilities of an item in a forecasted set can be adjusted in view of judgements relating to the potential interactions of the forecasted items" (p. 100). The Cross Impact Matrix Method is based on an equation that expresses the interrelationship of two future events. This equation, once programmed into the computer, can be used to set up matrices showing the interrelationship of a large number of events. The method was applied to the probability of deploying the Minuteman missile program (an historical event) and the impact of automation on transportation. In both cases probabilities of occurrence were considerably different from what they had been when a given event was considered in isolation.

103. Osgood, Charles E., and Stuart Umpleby
      1969   "A computer-based system for exploration of possible futures for mankind 2000." Pp. 346–359 in Robert Jungk and Johan Galtung (eds.), Mankind 2000. Oslo: Universitetsforlaget.

The aim of the computer program, DELPHI, being developed by the "Mankind 2000" project at the University of Illinois is twofold: (1) to inform people about future developmental possibilities; and (2) to gather data on the ideas people have about the future. At present only the first aim has been achieved. It involves asking an "explorer" to indicate the relationship between a series of future possibilities (i.e., how the occurrence of one event would affect the others), as well as their probable occurrence dates. The explorer then receives a score that indicates how close his predictions are to those made by a group of experts. To achieve the second aim data-retrieving properties will be built into the DELPHI program. Furthermore, the authors hope to make the program a more realistic simulation of the process by which present decisions interact with the limits of reality to shape mankind's future.

104. Umpleby, Stuart
    1969   The Delphi Exploration (A Computer-Based System for Obtaining Subjective Judgements on Alternative Futures). Social Implications of Science and Technology Report F–1. Urbana, Illinois: Computer-Based Education Research Laboratory, University of Illinois.

    This is the second progress report on the DELPHI computer program being developed at the University of Illinois. The program's basic make-up has remained the same (for a brief description, see no. **103**), though it has been modified in a number of ways. The major modification involves inclusion of a decision-making framework in the body of the program, which the author discusses in some detail. Through a discussion of various concepts and methods of prediction, he then delineates other, more minor, refinements in the original program. He also outlines alterations in the mathematical model specifying the interrelationships between various future possibilities. The author concludes by considering how the modifications have increased the program's utility, what difficulties still have to be ironed out, and future uses of the program.

105. Danziger, Kurt
    1963   "Ideology and utopia in South Africa: a methodological contribution to the sociology of knowledge." British Journal of Sociology 14 (March):59–76.

    The bulk of this article describes how the author attempted to assess cognitive styles by asking South African students to write "histories of the future." He had them outline their country's course of development, as they foresaw it, between 1960 and 2010. He was able to divide the resulting essays into five groups reflecting different historical orientations: Conservative, Technicist, Catastrophic, Liberal, and Revolutionary. An individual's orientation was assessed in terms of the attitudes he displayed towards the following: (1) interrelationship of present and future; (2) interrelationship of means and ends; (3) conception of social change; and (4) conception of social causality.

    The article begins and ends with discussions of the nature of the sociology of knowledge and of the South African context.

106. McHale, John
    1967c   "The world game." Architectural Design 37 (February):92.

    This article briefly describes the computer program Buckminster Fuller is developing at the "Centennial World Resources Center" at the Edwardsville campus of Southern Illinois University. It is called "Worldgame" and is based on game and general systems theory. Its purpose is to allow teams of experts to test out possible futures, thereby developing ways of foreseeing and solving emerging world problems. The experts, who will be recruited from all over the world, "win" at Worldgame if they succeed in redistributing the world's resources fairly and abolishing the evil of politics. Once this is achieved, everyone will be happy.

107. Nehnevajsa, Jiri

107a.   1960b   Elements of Project Theory: From Concepts to Design. Air Force Office of Scientific Research. Technical Note TN–60–6 (October 20).

107b.   1961   A Methodology for the Analysis of Political Futures. Air Force Office of Scientific Research. AFOSR–374 (May 1).
    The aim of "Project Outcomes" is to understand the dynamics behind anticipations about the shape of the future. These anticipations, or "future states of affairs," are constructs of some specifically dated future world. Project Outcomes investigates the future aspirations of two types of leaders: parliamentarians and university students (the leaders of tomorrow). Groups of leaders were chosen because the future aspirations of a whole country can best be isolated by questioning influential persons; and because the future anticipations of individuals who affect each other should be studied as an interacting whole. Each respondent is asked to do a variety of things: (1) state the likelihood of realization of specific future states at given time intervals, as well as indicate the three most, and least, desirable states for his own country, for the United States and for the USSR; (2) describe his own sense of efficacy and that of his country; and (3) indicate how major alterations in the world situation would affect his anticipations. Project Outcomes should make it possible to gain insight into the dynamics of future aspirations, as well as indicating the extent to which those of various countries are in conflict, thereby throwing light on future world tensions.

108. Prehoda, Robert W.
    1967   Designing the Future: The Role of Technological Forecasting. Philadelphia: Chilton Books.
    Technological forecasting involves "the description or prediction of a foreseeable invention, specific scientific refinement, or likely discovery that promises to serve some useful function" (p. 12). Its primary aim is not to pinpoint specific discoveries, but to determine when given capabilities will become available. This requires isolating "Hahn-Strassman points" in the scientific evolutionary process. They occur at the discovery stage, when a new interpretation of existing knowledge makes great new advances possible. Locating these points would enable policy-makers to know in which areas of development the great-

est progress can be made, thereby making advantageous use of limited funds possible.

The last two-thirds of the book describe scientific fields in which Hahn-Strassman points have probably been reached. They include: automation, economic growth, education, city planning, cybernetics and communication, nutrition, and the development of the human mind.

For further material generally relevant to quantitative techniques, see: nos. 79, 121, 122, and 250 (Cross-Impact Matrix Method).

For applications of the "Self-Anchoring Striving Scale," see: nos. 109, 110, 111, and 112.

For applications of the "Delphi Technique," see: nos. 113, 114, and 115.

For applications of "Project Outcomes," see: nos. 118, 119, and 120.

IV. FORECASTS OF THE FUTURE

This category's major subdivision is made in terms of the number of persons involved in a specific forecast. The publications in Part A describe the results of large-scale sample surveys of individuals' ideas about the future. The forecasts in Part B rest on the ideas of single researchers about the nature of tomorrow's world. Their theses are, of course, based on previous work done by others, so they are not forecasting in isolation. These latter publications are grouped according to their unit of analysis.

IV.A. Forecasts based on sample surveys

109. Cantril, Hadley
  1965   The Pattern of Human Concerns. New Brunswick, N.J.: Rutgers University Press.

This book discusses the results of administering "The Self-Anchoring Striving Scale" to population samples in the following thirteen countries: the United States, West Germany, Yugoslavia, Poland, Brazil, Nigeria, India, Israel, Egypt, Cuba, the Dominican Republic, Panama, and the Philippines. The book is divided into six sections, each of which focuses on the following material: (1) the precepts of transactional psychology, on which the scale is based, and the scale's construction (for a summary, see nos. 95 and 96); (2) specific findings for each nation; (3) cross-national comparisons; (4) the most "satisfied" countries and societal segments, as well as the aspirations of political leaders; (5) general conclusions; and (6) methodological appendices.

110. Free, Lloyd
  1959   Six Allies and a Neutral. Glencoe, Ill.: Free Press.

This book is an analysis of international relations between the United States, several European powers, and two Eastern countries. Part of it describes the Self-Anchoring Striving Scales (for a description of the scale, see no. 95) constructed by national legislators in the following countries: the United States, West Germany, England, France, Italy, Japan, and India.

111. Free, Lloyd

111a.   1960a   Attitudes of the Cuban People toward the Castro Regime. Princeton, N.J.: Institute for International Social Research.

111b.   1960b   The Dynamics of Philippine Politics. Princeton, N.J.: Institute for International Social Research.

111c.   1964a   The Attitudes, Hopes, and Fears of Nigerians. Princeton, N.J.: Institute for International Social Research.

111d.   1964b   Some International Implications of the Political Psychology of Brazilians. Princeton, N.J.: Institute for International Social Research.

These monographs report on the administration of the Self-Anchoring Striving Scale in a variety of countries (for a description of the scale, see no. **95**).

112. Janicki, Peter

1960   America Speaks Up. Princeton, N.J.: Institute for International Social Research.

This monograph discusses the results of administering the Self-Anchoring Striving Scale (for a description, see no. **95**) to a nationwide American sample.

113. Dalkey, N., and Olaf Helmer

1963   "An experimental application of the Delphi method to the use of experts." Management Science 9 (April):458–467.

This article describes the original use of the Delphi Technique in the early 1950s. It begins by describing the methodology of the technique itself (for a brief summary, see no. **98**), and then summarizes the results of its first application. It was used to assess the following: (1) what the Soviets would consider the optimal United States industrial target system; and (2) the number of atomic bombs that would have to be detonated to reduce munitions production by given amounts. A variety of military experts were asked for their opinions on these issues.

114. Gordon, Theodore J.

1969a   "The feedback between technology and values." Pp. 148–192 in K. Baier and N. Rescher (eds.), Values and the Future. New York: Free Press.

Rather than postulate a direct relationship between values and technology, it is more useful to conceive of both as part of a larger feedback loop, which also includes research, planning, and other economic and sociopolitical factors. A variety of relationships exists between all parts of the system, but only the following are discussed in detail: the social factors influencing research priorities; the effect of technological change on values; and the interrelationship of planning and values. The article has an appendix that delineates the possible political, social and economic consequences of twenty technological advances (e.g., personality control drugs; ocean farming; artificial life; genetic control;

man-machine symbiosis, etc.) NOTE: this article and its appendix formed part of Helmer's simulation workshop for the study of future values (see no. **101**).

115. Helmer, Olaf
> 1969 "An abbreviated Delphi experiment in forecasting." Pp. 361–367 in Robert Jungk and Johan Galtung (eds.) Mankind 2000, Oslo: Universitetsforlaget.

This article presents group consensus forecasts made by the delegates to the International Future Research Inaugural Conference. Through an abbreviated form of the Delphi Technique (for a brief summary, see no. **98**) the delegates to the 1967 Oslo meeting were asked to date specific events in the following areas: population size; air pollution; economical use of nuclear energy; per capita Gross World Product; reduction of starving population portion; and production of oceanic food supplies.

116. Martino, Joseph P.
> 1967 "An experiment with the Delphi procedure for long-range forecasting, Parts I and II." United States Air Force. Report numbers AFOSR 67–0175 and AFOSR 67–0176.

The Air Force's Office for Scientific Research has found that the Delphi Technique (for a brief description, see no. **98**) is an inexpensive way of obtaining expert opinions on future developments. These two reports discuss the use of the technique to obtain forecasts for the period 1966–2015 from ten foreign affairs experts. The actual predictions that emerged are outlined in some detail.

117. Sulc, Otto
> 1969 "Interactions between technological and social changes: a forecasting model." Futures 1 (September):402–407.

This article summarizes a two-part investigation of the implications of future advances in computer technology. The study solicited opinions from two groups of experts by use of the Delphi Technique (for a brief description, see no. **98**). The first group's opinions were used to delineate future developments in computer technology. The second group—managerial experts—then tried to specify measures enabling society to adjust to and control the projected advances. This study illustrates a way in which the degree of social preparedness for technological advances might be assessed. It revealed that for the next five to ten years society will have few tools for coping with new innovations in computer technology.

118. Nehnevajsa, Jiri
> 1960a "Anticipatory analysis of ideational conflict." Paper read at the meetings of the American Sociological Association (August).

This paper outlines the purpose of "Project Outcomes" and the method it employs (for a brief description, see no. **107**). In a pretest of the technique, a variety of university students from Italy, Iran, China, and Canada were questioned about the future of the Cold War. The results indicate that Project Outcomes can be used to assess ideational conflict between nations.

119. Nehnevajsa, Jiri

    1962b   An Application of Project Outcomes (The Dilemma of Viet-Nam). Air Force Office of Scientific Research (January).

This monograph begins with a discussion of the nature and method of "Project Outcomes" (for a brief description, see no. **107**). It then outlines how the project could hypothetically be used to form a picture of the future aspirations of the Vietnamese.

120. Nehnevajsa, Jiri

    1962a   "Anticipations of cold war outcomes." Paper read at the meetings of the World, and American, Associations of Public Opinion Research (May).

This paper reports on an application of "Project Outcomes" (for a brief description, see no. **107**). Parliamentarians from several countries were asked to assess developmental possibilities for the future of the Cold War. The respondents came from Brazil, Finland, France, Germany, India, Japan, and Spain.

121. Gillespie, James M., and Gordon W. Allport

    1955   Youth's Outlook on the Future. Garden City, N.Y.: Doubleday.

This book reports on a study designed to isolate the future orientations of college-age students. Between 1949 and 1951 approximately 200 students in each of ten countries were asked to fill out a two-part questionnaire. The first part asked respondents to write an autobiography of their future and the second part focused on more specific questions, such as social background and values. Analysis of the questionnaires revealed that: (1) the next ten years were viewed as having the most substance and as likely to yield the greatest happiness; (2) futures were planned around the family; (3) in all nations there was a marked similarity of occupational outlooks, cultural and intellectual goals, hopes for travel, and scientific interests; and (4) war was usually viewed as needless and preventable, and greater equality between the races was desired.

122. Milburn, T. W. and J. F.

    1966   "Predictions of threats and beliefs about how to meet them." American Behavioral Scientist 9 (March):3–7.

This article summarizes a series of predictions about the 1970s made by two groups of experts. One group was composed of social scientists, while the other was made up of physical scientists. On the basis of individual questionnaires group measures were constructed for the two collectivities. In general, both groups had very similar opinions about the major dangers of the 1970s. They believed that there was little chance for any kind of nuclear conflict, though more limited wars and nonviolent conflicts were certain to be widespread. The two types of scientists diverged significantly in two areas: the relationship between actual threat and effectiveness of deterrence, and the stability of the Communist bloc.

123. Rescher, Nicholas

    1969   "A questionnaire study of American values by 2000 A.D." Pp.

133–147 in K. Baier and N. Rescher (eds.), Values and the Future. New York: Free Press.

The author, along with Olaf Helmer, distributed a questionnaire to fifty-eight academics and intellectuals to get preliminary answers to two questions: (1) how might American values be altered as a result of the widespread change imminent in the near future; and (2) what might be the nature, desirability, and causal mechanisms of such value change. The respondents answered questions about the validity of present value folklore; the degree and desirability of change in a wide variety of values (e.g., economic security, self-respect, law and order, equality, peace, human dignity, etc.); and how scientific, technological, demographic, social, or economic changes might affect values. The questionnaire results revealed that American values will have changed markedly by the year 2000, but not as a direct result of technological change. Rather, technical innovations will lead to political and social alterations, which in turn will lead to positive value changes.

For information about the methodology used to make quantitative forecasts see: no. **98** (Delphi Technique); nos. **95** and **96** (Self-Anchoring Striving Scale); and no. **107** (Project Outcomes).

IV.B. Forecasts based on individual opinion. *1. Forecasts of mankind's future*

124. Gibbs, Philip
1928   The Day after Tomorrow: What Is Going to Happen to the World? London: Hutchinson.
Through a series of essays this book attempts to foresee how the coming half century will be affected by present scientific advances. The major topics considered are: (1) technological advances (e.g., air travel, harnessing of radioactive energy, television, new weapons, etc.); (2) extension of the average life span; (3) implications of high population growth rates; (4) extrasensory perception and the possibility of thought control; (5) religion and morals; and (6) relationships between nations—the prospects for war and peace.

125. Whyte, Lancelot L.
1944   The Next Development in Man. London: Cresset Press.
Through an analysis of major trends in European history and the ideas of a number of great Western thinkers (ranging from Heraclitus and Plato through Descartes to Goethe, Marx, and Freud), the author shows that man is about to enter a new phase in his development. He will give up his old divisive nationalism and self-interest, and forge a single human community. "Europe committed suicide mainly through its failure to control the disintegrating influence of money. . . . During the coming decades the West may repeat this act of self-destruction. . . . I suggest that it will not; that the threat of the East will compel the West to subdue finance; that the emergence of a practical sense of world unity will put power in the hands of those whose aim is to fulfill their

own development in a unitary development of mankind as a whole; and that within the unitary doctrine East and West can cooperate" (p. 262).

126. Asimov, Isaac

1968   "The next 100 years: science-based estimate of what the century ahead may bring." Pp. 39–41 in The World Almanac and Book of Facts.

This article briefly delineates what the world might look like in 2068. The major characteristics foreseen are as follows: limited population growth; population quality through gene analysis; a unified world run by computers; infinite energy supplies from nuclear fusion and ocean resources; artificial or oceanic food production; underground cities not exposed to climatic exigencies; lack of routine labor, only creative work; rudimentary family units; an abundance of leisure and comfort; a prolonged educational process based on highly sophisticated techniques; and widespread space exploration and colonization. Man's primary problems in 2068 will be related to: the production of artificial life; attempts to reach other galaxies; and contacts with other forms of life.

127. Baade, Fritz

1962   The Race to the Year 2000. Garden City, N.Y.: Doubleday.

A general discussion of possible world progress in the following areas: population growth; food production; availability of industrial manpower; harnessing of energy sources; East-West relations; education; and racial harmony.

128. Beckwith, Burnham P.

1967   The Next Five Hundred Years. Jericho, N.Y.: Exposition-University Book.

This book contains over 1,000 specific predictions about developments the next five hundred years might bring. Though it begins with a discussion of methods for forecasting social trends, the bulk of it is devoted to analyzing major trends and specifying the type of future they might lead to. The topics covered include: population; education and knowledge; religion; relationship of work and leisure; technological development; role of government; individual rights; income distribution; humanitarian values; etc. The book also describes what life in the year 2500 might be like.

129. Behrendt, Richard F.

1969   "Some structural prerequisites for a global society based on nonviolent conflict resolution." Pp. 66–68 in Robert Jungk and Johan Galtung (eds.), Mankind 2000. Oslo: Universitetsforlaget.

A global society would require an international democracy in which all citizens participated and with which they identified. Such a democracy could exist only in a peaceful, and consequently disarmed, world. The greatest task facing modern man, therefore, is achieving worldwide peace. Basic changes in present attitudes that would greatly enhance the prospects for peace are briefly outlined.

130. Brown, Harrison
    1954   The Challenge of Man's Future. New York: Viking Press.
    The book begins with a brief history of human development and a description of present vital rates, agricultural production, and degree of industrialization. It then discusses the major problems facing modern man: (1) rising population growth rates; (2) the necessity of increasing agricultural yields; (3) dwindling traditional energy sources; and (4) the limited supply of mineral and metallic resources. There seem to be three possible futures open to man, depending on how he solves his present dilemmas. The first, and most likely, is the re-emergence of an agrarian world in the aftermath of a major nuclear war. The second possibility is a "completely controlled, collectivized industrial society." The third possibility, which is the most desirable and least likely, is a fully industrialized world in which everyone leads a comfortable and satisfying existence.

131. Calder, Nigel
    1965   "Summing up." Pp. 191–197 in Nigel Calder (ed.), The World in 1984 (vol. 2). Baltimore: Penguin Books.
    This article sums up the major trends and developments foreseen by the experts submitting brief forecasts to *New Scientist* during 1964. It is primarily composed of three tables, each of which focuses on a different aspect of the future: (1) major technological revolutions in the fields of information processing, comprehension and control of biological processes, oceanography and energy sources; (2) continuing evolutionary processes such as the race between food and population, automation, orientations toward home and family, and education; (3) choices open to man in the areas of world development (will it be rapid enough to help the poor?), international relations (war or cooperation?), government (democratic and rational or the opposite?), ecology (will the environment be preserved?), cities (crowding or sprawl?), and individual happiness (limited or unlimited?).

132. Calder, Nigel
    1967a   The Environment Game. London: Secker and Warburg.
    Widespread cultivation of the soil is *not* the most appropriate method of producing the food needed by the modern world. Agriculture ought to be replaced by artificial methods of food production (the bulk of this book documents this thesis). Our whole future way of life could be restructured if the land now devoted to food production could be used for other purposes. Self-sufficient towns surrounded by areas of wilderness could be created everywhere. They would be physically isolated, but bound together by a modern communications system. Built from scratch, the towns could be planned in a manner avoiding present urban problems. Many other contemporary dilemmas would be eliminated by the fact that individual allegiances would be reduced to two: the town one lived in and the world as a whole.

133. Calder, Nigel

1967b   "Future research." New Statesman 74 (September 29):399–400.

This article is an impressionistic report of the International Future Research Inaugural Conference, which took place in September 1967 in Oslo. After briefly describing the recent spurt of interest in future-oriented research, the article delineates the tenor of the deliberations on the developed nations and on the underdeveloped countries where the bulk of modern problems lie. It concludes by noting that the general consensus at the conference was that the future is not so much to be foreseen as created or invented. (NOTE: for a collection of the papers presented at the conference, see no. **230.**)

134. Chase, Stuart

1968   The Most Probable World. New York: Harper & Row.

The author outlines the characteristics of tomorrow's world (i.e., the year 2000), isolating present trends and projecting them into the future. He focuses on the following areas: (1) technological advances; (2) uneven population growth trends; (3) diminution of individual "living space"; (4) the spread and growth of dense urban areas (megalopolis); (5) peaceful applications of atomic energy; (6) the increasing mix of public and private enterprise; (7) effects of automation on work-oriented man; (8) continuation of the arms race; (9) mixed trends in nationalistic orientations; and (10) development of a unitary international community. The author believes trends 5, 6, and 10 are desirable; trends 2, 3, 4, and 8 are undesirable; and trends 1, 7, and 9 are mixed. The key to overcoming undesirable aspects of the future lies in a rapid spread of mass education and systematic application of new and existing knowledge to problem areas.

135. Darwin, Charles G.

1953   The Next Million Years. Garden City, N.Y.: Doubleday.

This book describes the more routine aspects of man's way of life during the next million years and outlines the broad limits of his future achievements. More specifically, it discusses: (1) man's fundamental problem—the threat of overpopulation; (2) the highlights of man's past history; (3) man's basically animal nature, which limits his reactive capacities and his ability to control population size for any period of time; and (4) the unlikely prospect of greater human happiness existing in the future. In sum, the fundamental features of the future will be laid down by overpopulation. A segment of humanity will always be starving because of scarce food supplies. The present era will be viewed as a past "golden age" because the future will be typified by sporadic conventional wars between independent dictatorial provinces.

136. Farson, Richard E.

1969   "Bill of Rights for 1984." Pp. 186–193 in Robert Jungk and Johan Galtung (eds.), Mankind 2000. Oslo: Universitetsforlaget.

The world of the future will be so different from our own that it will require a new Bill of Rights. This article delineates some of the rights it might contain and in the process sketches a possible future. The rights discussed concern leisure, health, beauty, intimacy, truth, study, travel, sexual fulfillment, peace and uniqueness.

137. Fuller, R. Buckminster
    1967   "The year 2000." Architectural Design 37 (February):62–63.
    The author delineates what some aspects of life in the year 2000 might be like. His predictions are rather wide-ranging and cover technological developments, population trends, politics, and ethics.

138. Galtung, Johan
    1969   "On the future of the international system." Pp. 12–41 in Robert Jungk and Johan Galtung (eds.), Mankind 2000. Oslo: Universitetsforlaget.
    This analysis of the international system's developmental possibilities adopts a tripartite approach: (1) a discussion of emerging common values; (2) an analysis of developmental trends; and (3) an exploration of the relationship between trends and values. It shows that national boundaries between the developed nations will steadily decline in importance and identifications will become increasingly international. Among the developing nations, in contrast, nationalism will increase, as will small-scale wars. Between the two major blocs (developed and developing) relations will be strained—while an international class war is unlikely, the wealthy nations will engage in small-scale military operations to avoid it. In conclusion, a number of ways in which the projected developments might be avoided are discussed.

139. Gordon, Theodore J.
    1965   The Future. New York: St. Martin's Press.
    This book discusses general nature of various aspects of the future. A chapter is devoted to each problem, or societal sector, believed to be of crucial importance to the shape of the future. In each case the positive and negative aspects of the topic under discussion are delineated, as is the probability that various projected futures will materialize. The major problems discussed are as follows: (1) limitations on individual freedom; (2) future wars; (3) implications of automation; (4) the future of religion and morality; (5) convergence of the capitalist and communist systems; and (6) the challenge of space exploration.

140. Kahn, Herman, and Anthony J. Weiner
    1967a   The Year 2000: A Framework for Speculation on the Next Thirty-Three Years. New York: Macmillan.
    This wide-ranging book summarizes the great diversity of forecasts formulated by the Hudson Institute about the distant future. It begins by discussing the need for future-oriented research and how it might make a better tomorrow possible. Most of the rest of the book describes facets of the world in the year 2000. Basically there are three developmental possibilities: (1) a peaceful, prosperous world with a good deal of arms control and political coordination; (2) a peaceful prosperous world with no arms control or political coor-

dination; and (3) a violent, troubled world often on the brink of a major war. Each of these possibilities can vary considerably with respect to its individual characteristics as is illustrated in some detail.

141. McHale, John
    1969a   The Future of the Future. New York: George Braziller.
    When thinking about and planning for the future, it is imperative to throw off the mental constraints that past traditions or ideologies impose. This is especially true when trying to create the single world community that the future requires. It will mean eradicating the imbalance between the rich and poor nations, developing the slowly emerging strands of a single cultural milieu, and reshaping present cultural patterns and social institutions, especially in the field of education. To delineate the breadth of reorganization necessary for the world of tomorrow, the author devotes the bulk of his book to discussing the implications of developments in areas such as: computers and cybernetics, control of biological processes, robot technology, surveying of natural resources, availability of energy and industrial resources, telecommunications, population, environmental purification, space exploration, and oceanographic research.

142. Mead, Margaret
    1965   "The future as the basis for establishing a shared culture." Daedalus 94 (Winter):135–155.
    The aim of this article is to construct a model of a shared culture that can serve as a guide for future progress. The new culture should increase communication between all ranks and segments of society, and, therefore, it must be made comprehensible to all peoples by incorporating the traditions of all countries in equal measure. In its final form the new culture should resemble a natural language that is constantly developing and evolving. The best setting for it would be the future, because it is least limited by the inadequacies of present conceptions and the stagnating elements of tradition. A good basis for the new culture would be the existing body of knowledge, especially more recent discoveries. Once such a culture has been created, it must be consciously transmitted through the educational system.

143. Miller, George A.
    1967   "Some psychological perspectives on the year 2000." Daedalus 96 (Summer):883–896.
    There are two trends that will continue until the year 2000: population growth and technological advance. This article discusses some of the psychological implications of these trends. Of special concern are the effect of crowded living conditions and changes in the motivation to learn.

144. Seidenberg, Roderick
    1950   Posthistoric Man: An Inquiry. Chapel Hill. University of North Carolina Press.
    Underlying all history is the struggle for dominance between instinct and

intelligence. In the very lengthy prehistoric period instinct reigned supreme. When intelligence entered the scene, what we know as history began. History is a short transitional phase of man's total development in which instinct and intelligence vie with one another for dominance. There was never any doubt which force would triumph, and therefore, history has been characterized by the increasing role of intelligence in the life of man. Eventually intelligence will completely dominate instinct—when this occurs, man will enter the posthistoric period of his development. Since intelligence manifests itself on the social level in the form of organization, the posthistoric era will be characterized by perfect organization. At this point ". . . consciousness will have accomplished its task, leaving mankind sealed . . . within patterns of frigid and unalterable perfection" (p. 180).

145. Seidenberg, Roderick
    1961   Anatomy of the Future. Chapel Hill: University of North Caro-
            lina Press.
    In essence this book presents the same general argument as *Posthistoric Man* (see no. **144**). In addition, however, it considers the possibility that man might be able to overcome the inevitable trend toward complete organization by use of his creative energies. Man's basic dilemma is that while his traditional values are no longer appropriate to a society structured by the dictates of or-ganizational efficiency, he is unable to change his values because his spontane-ous creative impulses have been so severely limited by societal regimentation.

146. Seidenberg, Roderick
    1967   "Justice for all, freedom for none." Center Diary no. 17 (March-
            April):25–37.
    The society of the future will be completely dominated by the precepts of technology. Man is increasingly adopting a social structure based solely on the dictates of science and rationality. As a result everyone will soon be equally un-free—that is, there will be no discrimination or injustice, but also no individual freedom because everyone will have to fit into a societal slot.

147. Snow, C. P.
    1958   "The future of man." The Nation 187 (September 13):124–125.
    Despite the atrocities of World War II, man has been slowly advancing in the area of "moral kindness." The world is better today than it was yesterday, and this trend will continue tomorrow. Even for the Asians and Africans the world is a better place because they have a little more to eat. They will con-tinue to strive for, and eventually achieve, a higher standard of living. Should there be a nuclear war, Africa and Asia will not be much affected, even though the West will be wiped out. As the underdeveloped countries begin to approach the standard of living of the West, they will quickly begin to exhibit the same degree of "moral kindness" that characterizes Western nations to-day.

148. Sola Pool, Ithiel de
  1967   "The international system in the next half century." Daedalus
  96 (Summer):930–935.
  This article sets forth the major characteristics of the system of world order
between 1965 and 1970, 1970 and 2000, and 2000 and 2015. It focuses on the
relations between various nations and the character of the nation-state.

149. Time
  1966   "The futurists: looking toward A.D. 2000." Time 87 (February
  25):28–29.
  After briefly describing some of the organizations doing future research,
this Time Essay outlines what futurists foresee for the year 2000. The major
topics covered include: population control, transportation, oceanic food production, increased biological learning capacity, climate control, medical advances,
prolongation of life, and the nature of everyday affairs. The essay concludes
that social and political developments are more difficult to anticipate than technological ones. Nonetheless, most futurists are optimistic because they believe
that man is not limited to merely foresee a fixed destiny, but can shape the
future to fit his desires.

150. Time
  1967   "The future—1984 plus 16." Time 90 (July 21):58–59.
  This article briefly delineates a wide variety of future developmental
trends. It is based on the Summer 1967 issue of Daedalus entitled "Toward the
Year 2000: Work in Progress" (see no. **222**).

151. Waskow, Arthur I.
  1969   "Looking forward: 1999." Pp. 78–98 in Robert Jungk and Johan
      Galtung (eds.), Mankind 2000. Oslo: Universitetsforlaget.
  One of the major obligations of modern intellectuals is to make the general public aware of the diverse possibilities that the future holds, so that
tomorrow's world can be shaped in a democratic manner. In addition, intellectuals should try to build desirable futures into present-day institutions. The
bulk of this article illustrates how the latter can be done by describing the non-
violent, nonmilitaristic world that might exist in 1999, isolating those present
trends leading to such a world, and showing how they might be accelerated. An
important part of the world of 1999 would be a "World Forum" that would
develop humane futures.

  For further forecasts delineating the future of mankind, see: nos. **10, 21,
82, 93, 94, 108, 109, 114, 115, 120, 214, 215, 218, 219, 220, 221, 226, 230, 232,
237, 239,** and **251.**

  IV.B.2. Forecasts of the future of Western man. a. Western civilization as
a whole

152. Birkenhead, Earl of

1930   The World in 2030. London: Hooper & Stoughton.

In this series of speculative essays on the future, the author is generally optimistic in his predictions. They focus on the following areas: general disarmament; industry; daily life; transportation advances (especially in the field of aviation); the development of large-scale international cooperation; and the role of women. The book concludes with a discussion of the future problems that the men of 2030 will be anticipating with the aid of improved forecasting methods.

153. Furnas, Clifford C.

1936   The Next Hundred Years: The Unfinished Business of Science. New York: Reynal and Hitchcock.

A number of technological developments are required for continued human progress in the future. This book concentrates on discussing those in the fields of biology, chemistry, physics, and engineering (the last includes advances in power, light, transportation, communication, mineral resources, agriculture, food production, and weather forecasting). It also discusses the social consequences of these developments by: (1) outlining the impact of inventions, especially on the structure of society (i.e., unemployment, standard of living, etc.); (2) exploring the impact on society of increasing leisure; and (3) showing how general security and happiness will be feasible in the future. The latter will require a great deal of scientific research, foresighted leadership, and intelligent human striving.

154. Haldene, J. B. S.

1927   "Man's destiny." Pp. 300–305 in J. B. S. Haldene, Possible Worlds and Other Essays. London: Chatto and Windus.

The author briefly sketches a number of developmental paths open to man. They include: (1) total annihilation through a collision with a heavenly body; (2) an end to civilization through a general war; (3) scientific creation of a Golden Age of happiness and peace after which man will degenerate; and (4) control of evolution through scientific research—this would make unlimited human development (including space exploration) possible. The third possibility seems to be the most likely course of future development.

155. Keynes, John Maynard

1932   "The economic possibilities of our grandchildren." Pp. 358–373 in John Maynard Keynes, Essays in Persuasion. New York: Harcourt, Brace.

Written in 1930, this essay puts forward the thesis that the Great Depression is only a temporary setback in mankind's economic development. A rapid pace of development would soon reassert itself. The essay also discusses how new inventions and innovations will make the future radically different from the past. Contemporary problems of economic scarcity are only temporary and might well be overcome in a century or so.

156. Langdon-Davies, John
1936 A Short History of the Future. London: George Routledge & Sons.

Man is an animal and must obey the laws of the animal kingdom; his ability to reason cannot help him circumvent them. The bulk of the book consists of a series of predictions based on this premise. Some of the more interesting ones are as follows: (1) eventual war in Europe is inevitable and will begin as a holy war with Russia opposing Germany and Japan; (2) by 1950 democracy will be dead and America will have become Fascist; (3) by 2000 there will have been sharp population declines in Western countries and crime will be nonexistent; (4) in 1960 people will work only three hours a day; there will be universal education, cheap power, and general material abundance; (5) by 1975 parents will not raise their children, and sex and marriage will be completely separate; and (6) the government will eventually foster limited individuality after a lengthy period of conformity.

157. Low, A. M.
1925 The Future. New York: International Publishers.

" 'The Future' is not an idle dream. It is based upon the study of the curve along which relentless civilization is steadily carrying the human race and upon logical scientific conclusions" (p. vi). Elements of tomorrow's world can be foreseen by extending the road of unceasing progress along which man is traveling into the future. Some of the scientific and technological developments that lie ahead are artificial light, automobiles, radios, interplanetary communication, etc. The other aspects of the future discussed include: urban development, sex roles, medicine, the institution of marriage, warfare, politics, art, religion, and extrasensory perception.

158. Beus, J. G. de
1953 The Future of the West. New York: Harper.

The bulk of this book develops a theory of the rise and fall of civilizations and analyzes the present state of Western civilization in terms of it. The last part, however, speculates about the future. It postulates that the creative spirit of the West will produce a single world society. It could come into being through a major war (which the West would win) or through an extended period of peace. America is destined to spearhead this transformation of the future, while Europe will be its active ally.

159. Brown, Harrison, James Bonner, and John Weir
1957 The Next Hundred Years. New York: Viking Press.

This collective effort treats what the long-range future might be like in light of trends in the following three areas: (1) availability of material resources and skilled manpower for industrial development; (2) rates of population growth and food production; and (3) availability of creative human beings to solve technical problems. (NOTE: the book summarizes a series of conferences for corporate executives on the long-range implications of resource availability.)

160. Clarke, Arthur C.

1962   Profiles of the Future. New York: Harper & Row.

It is impossible to predict the actual future in any detail. The best one can hope to do is to delineate the general direction that developments might take. In addition, imagination is as necessary for good prediction as is scientific knowledge, a fact well illustrated by the wide variety of incorrect predictions that have been made by "experts." The bulk of this book outlines the author's own imaginative forecasts for the next 150 years (up to 2100). The following fields are discussed: transportation, communications, manufacturing, and biology. Especially interesting is the description of the inorganic bodies men might someday inhabit.

161. Drucker, Peter

1968   The Age of Discontinuity: Guidelines to Our Changing Society. New York: Harper & Row.

This book analyzes a number of facets of economic development and how they will affect the society emerging around the year 2000. The specific areas discussed are: (1) industrial growth and the emergence of new industries (connected with information processing, the ocean, synthetics, etc.); (2) the development of a world economy; (3) the impact of mammoth corporations on government and the individual; and (4) modern education. Two dominant trends will emerge and will help to shape the future society: that is, far-reaching changes in technology will cause continued concern with production and productivity; and organizations will become a central part of society, thereby serving man rather than enslaving him. It seems, therefore, that the major tasks of the future will involve making piecemeal improvements in the social fabric rather than creating it anew.

162. Ellul, Jacques

1963   "Western man in 1970." Pp. 27–64 in Bertrand de Jouvenel (ed.), Futuribles: Studies in Conjecture (I). Geneva: Droz.

The aim of this article is to outline those tenets that will be common to all men in 1970 and that will form the underlying basis for the wealth of diversity that is bound to manifest itself. The major factor influencing man's development until 1970 will be increasing uniformity among, and within, Western societies. In light of this, Western man in 1970 will exhibit the following characteristics: (1) his material needs will be adequately taken care of; (2) he will be a specialist and his work will be the most important part of his life; (3) due to collectivization, he will constantly be surrounded by informal group interaction; (4) he will have a strong sense of responsibility toward his work and most of his decisions will be made for him by society; and (5) he will be tense and anxious owing to a rapidly changing environment and an uncertain future.

163. Ellul, Jacques

1964   The Technological Society. New York: Knopf.

"The term *technique,* as I use it, does not mean machines, technology, or this or that procedure for attaining an end. In our technological society *technique* is the *totality of methods rationally arrived at and having absolute efficiency* (for a given stage of development) in *every* field of human endeavor" (p. xxv). By delineating the history of the technical orientation from the Stone Age to the present, the author is able to show why he believes the future will bring a dictatorship of technocrats more oppressive than any man has yet experienced. Various aspects of modern life, especially the economy and the government, are rapidly becoming dominated by the technical orientation. This trend will continue until man becomes completely lost in his technological society and totally subservient to its dictates of rationality and efficiency.

164. Frisch, Alfred

    1964   "L'avenir des technocrates [The future of the technocrats]." Futuribles (no. 84)—Supplement to Bulletin Sedeis 901 (November 10).

This four-part essay delineates the tendencies moving Western society toward technocratic domination. In the first part a "technocrat" is described. He is someone who holds a position that gives him access to a good deal of power, which he uses to influence developments in the interests of society as a whole. In part two the conditions favoring technocratic proliferation are outlined, while the third part describes the activities of present technocrats. The last part of the essay focuses on the future and argues that since conditions favoring the emergence of technocrats are rapidly becoming permanent features of society, their influence and power will increase.

165. Gabor, Dennis

    1964   Inventing the Future. New York: Knopf.

"Our civilization faces three great dangers. The first is destruction by nuclear war, the second is over-population, and the third is the Age of Leisure" (p. 3). If the first two dangers come to pass, man will know how to react. Should the Age of Leisure become a reality, however, which may well occur within a generation, man will be unprepared to deal with it because of its novelty. In the past half century man has made tremendous strides toward abolishing work, but he has done little to prepare himself psychologically for his new leisure. What is needed, therefore, is a rebirth of creative imagination on two levels: short-range social engineering and long-range visions of future societies. In this way the present fear of the Age of Leisure can be replaced by the hope for a worthwhile future.

166. Kalven, Harry

    1967   "The problems of privacy in the year 2000." Daedalus 96 (Summer):876–882.

The author delineates trends that are threatening individual privacy. He also considers how these trends could be counteracted, but is not too optimistic about the success of his proposed countermeasures.

167. Lundberg, Ferdinand
    1963   The Coming World Transformation. Garden City, N.Y.: Double-
            day.
    An analysis of a variety of past predictions shows that social predictions
are in many ways just as reliable as predictions made for scientific phenomena.
In view of this the author delineates a "general theory of social prediction" by
isolating those factors that make forecasts of sociocultural change possible. The
nature of social change, and theories trying to explain it, provide the background for this theory of prediction. Once formulated, the author uses it to develop a forecast of what the world will be like in 150 years. His major predictions focus on: population, economy, government, and education. In a series of
briefer predictions he also outlines his ideas about the future of such things as
religion, medicine, science, urban areas, etc. Throughout, his major focus is on
Western man.

168. Michael, Donald N.
    1968   The Unprepared Society: Planning for a Precarious Future. New
            York: Basic Books.
    Man is presently unable to do the type of long-range planning necessary
to cope with the unparalleled change of the future. Though he has an abundance of technology available, the time and creative skills needed to use it for
the benefit of mankind are scarce. Consequently, it is quite likely that two types
of culture will emerge in the future: one for those who can cope with change
and one for those who cannot. To prevent this kind of split people must be
better prepared for life in tomorrow's highly complex world. A whole new approach to education, described in some detail, will be required. Education
should involve teaching a whole new way of life, rather than just facts and figures. To initiate this new approach, adults must first change themselves and
their institutions, so that they are equipped to show today's youth how to cope
with the world of the future.

169. Moles, Abraham
    1962   "La cité scientifique en 1972 [The scientific city in 1972]." Fu-
            turibles (no. 41)—Supplement to Bulletin Sedeis (Part 2) 833
            (October 20).
    An "intellectual city" is beginning to develop within the United States and
Europe and may be a dominant societal feature by 1972. Two elements of the
intellectual or scientific city are already beginning to appear: (1) economic
class distinctions are rapidly vanishing and the new basis for membership in
the power elite is ability to manipulate complex organisms; and (2) an intellectual elite is emerging to deal with and develop more complex ideas and concepts
such as those involving the future. Both segments of the new elite—the managers and the intellectuals—form a "city" insofar as they have their own distinctive characteristics. The parallels between the "scientific city" and the "human city" are, of course, many, but the differences are steadily becoming more

pronounced. By 1972 the "scientific city" will have acquired a good many more distinctive traits.

170. Paloczi-Horvath, Gyorgy
    1964   The Facts Rebel: The Future of Russia and the West. London: Secker and Warburg.

This book is primarily a two-part analysis of Russia and the West. For both the communist and the democratic worlds the following three aspects are discussed: (1) past history; (2) present patterns of change; and (3) prospects for the future (until 1999). Both Russia and the United States are changing very rapidly as a result of new technological developments, especially in the fields of automation, computer technology, and cybernetics. As they change, they are growing closer together and their problems are becoming similar (i.e., how to cope with technology). Should they succeed in becoming less ideologically rigid in their politics, they might achieve a reconciliation and cooperate in facing the challenges of the future, thereby serving all mankind.

171. Postan, M. M.
    1963   "The economic and social system: the prospect for 1970–1975." Pp. 155–179 in Bertrand de Jouvenel (ed.), Futuribles: Studies in Conjecture (I). Geneva: Droz.

The capitalist system has undergone a variety of changes, some of which will shape the economic and social system of 1970. The major changes of importance are as follows: (1) separation of ownership and control leading to the emergence of a new class of managers destined to form a single ruling class; (2) differentiation of the proletariat into an agglomeration of specialists, some of whom are beginning to share the values and hopes of the new managerial class; and (3) diversification of monopolistic enterprise, a trend that will increase considerably in the future. These changes indicate that the economic systems of East and West are steadily becoming more alike. Their underlying principles and values, however, will continue to be irreconcilable.

172. Shubik, Martin
    1967   "Information, rationality, and free choice in a future democratic society." Daedalus 96 (Summer):771–778.

This article focuses on the economic and political values that a democratic society of the future will want to espouse and the type of institutions needed to preserve them. The major cause for concern is the increasing limitation of individual free choice.

173. Thomson, Sir George
    1960   The Foreseeable Future (rev. ed.). Cambridge, England: Cambridge University Press.

Isolating likely technological developments, and the impact they might have on daily life, enables the author to make a series of general forecasts. The following areas are discussed: sources of energy; natural resources; transportation and communication; meteorology; food production; and intellectual development. The social consequences of these technological advances are also delineated.

174. Wall Street Journal Staff

1967   Here Comes Tomorrow: Living and Working in the Year 2000. New York: Dow Jones.

The staff of the *Wall Street Journal* delineate possible future developments until the turn of the century. Their forecasts are based on extensive interviews with scientists and other experts. The major fields covered by their predictions are: population growth, food production, communications, transportation, computer technology, energy sources, space exploration, urban development, innovations in household appliances, changes in dwelling types, education, medicine, and weapons development.

For further forecasts delineating the future of Western man, see: nos. **109, 117, 120, 121, 217, 223, 227, 230, 236, 238, 252,** and **253.**

IV.B.2.B. Europe

175. Calleo, David P.

1965   Europe's Future: the Grand Alternatives. New York: Horizon Press.

The path of development that Europe will follow in the years to come will be shaped by the area's dominant ideals and the relative strength of nationalist and federalist orientations. The feasible developmental possibilities include: (1) a federation based on the Common Market; (2) an independent Europe of separate states with France as its leader; and (3) a Europe closely allied with the United States to form an Atlantic community. The probability that each of these types of European unity might become a reality is assessed, and the ways in which it might occur outlined.

176. Bertram, Christoph

1968   "Models of western Europe in the 1970's—the alternative choices." Futures 1 (December):142–152.

To illustrate the usefulness of developmental models in forecasting, the author delineates a number of paths that Europe might follow during the coming decade. He discusses the following models: "Evolutionary Europe" (maintenance of status quo); "Atlanticised Europe" (United States accepted as leader of European community); "Europe des Etats" (coordination of political objectives among separate states); "Fragmented Europe" (disintegration of existent threads of unity and cohesion): "Partnership Europe" (a united Western Europe in equal partnership with the United States); and "Independent Federal Europe." An inspection of these models indicates that none of them offer a complete solution to Europe's problems. Its developmental possibilities are limited by present structural realities (i.e., separation of East and West) and any unified political structure must operate within them to succeed.

177. Le Breton, Jean-Marie

1965   "Supranational power in European institutions." Pp. 247–269 in Bertrand de Jouvenel (ed.), Futuribles: Studies in Conjecture (II). Geneva: Droz.

Two hypotheses can be advanced about the form of the European community by 1971:(1) the "strong hypothesis" predicts increased European unity as a result of invasion of the political realm by supranational organizations; (2) the "weak hypothesis" forecasts a decided decline in the enthusiasm for and pace of European unity. The increased autonomy and influence of existing European communities seems to indicate that the "strong hypothesis" is the accurate one. The continuation of the present trend depends on six factors: (1) the composition of the European Community; (2) the internal situation in member countries; (3) the orientation of European leaders; (4) the success of democratic parties in launching reform programs; (5) the international political situation; and (6) the international economic situation.

178. Rougement, Denis·de

1965   "Pointers towards a federal Europe." Pp. 113–148 in Bertrand de Jouvenel (ed.), Futuribles: Studies in Conjecture (II). Geneva: Droz.

"European union can come about only if it is willed, but there can be no will without a goal, without some guiding utopia, seen in the mind's eye and grasped in a passionate anticipation" (p. 113). This essay, therefore, depicts the goal—a federal Europe. Like all federal unions it would be characterized by: supranational authority; equality among member nations; protection of minority rights and national diversity; and a realization that the federation is for the benefit of all members. Exactly what the governmental, economic, and social institutions of a federal Europe would be like is described in detail. The essay also discusses how the structure of Europe should be altered to achieve federal union and what factors seem to be pushing Europe towards a federal solution to its problems.

179. Sidjanski, Dusan

1965   "Federative aspects of the European community"; and "Will Europe be united on federal lines?" Pp. 149–245 in Bertrand de Jouvenel (ed.), Futuribles: Studies in Conjecture (II). Geneva: Droz.

In the first essay the author describes the actual functioning of present European communities (EEC, ESC, and Euratom), the Court of Justice, the European Parliament, and the Economic and Social Committee. He pays special attention to their federal aspects. In the second essay he discusses the political form a united Europe should adopt. There are three alternatives: (1) increased nationalism; (2) a type of compromise commercial unification; and (3) federalism. The author favors the third possibility and delineates how it might become a reality by: (1) specifying the elements of federalism; (2) delineating presently existing federal elements; (3) presenting European planning efforts as evidence of a federal trend; and (4) discussing how the slowly emerging network of cross-national ties might become the pattern of the future.

For further forecasts delineating the future of Europe, see: nos. **62, 90,** and **110.**

IV.B.2.c. The United States

180. Altshuler, Alan
1968   "New institutions to serve the individual." Pp. 423–444 in William Ewald (ed.), Environment and Policy: The Next Fifty Years. Bloomington: Indiana University Press.

New means should be found to allow greater individual participation (and sense of political efficacy) in a society that is rapidly becoming controlled by a plethora of planning directives. There are basically two ways in which the individual can be given the right to participate in societal planning and question the appropriateness of specific measures: through debureaucratization and through decentralization. Debureaucratization would eliminate obsolescent programs or red tape, and develop techniques of "probabilistic" planning. Decentralization would consist of two parallel changes: dispersing some of the federal government's immense power to regional or local governmental bodies; and giving neighborhoods the power to control their own affairs.

181. Barzelon, David T.
1968   "The new factor in American society." Pp. 264–286 in William R. Ewald (ed.), Environment and Change: The Next Fifty Years. Bloomington: Indiana University Press.

"If men are still individuals with power, then the men of the organizations possess the relevant power for shaping the future" (p. 272). This article outlines the type of future society that might emerge through the efforts of this "new class" of organizational managers and administrators. The developments discussed include: (1) the emergence of education as the basis for class distinctions; (2) attempts to humanize the character of work; (3) the demise of the family; and (4) rebirth of a true morality and humanity.

182. Bell, Daniel
1967a   "Notes on the post-industrial society (I and II)." The Public Interest 6 (Winter):25–35; 7 (Spring):102–118.

The United States is rapidly becoming a postindustrial society. This type of society will have three major characteristics: (1) the primary economic focus will switch from production of goods to production of services; (2) the major occupational group will consist of professional technocrats and managers; and (3) societal innovation will depend primarily on increasing theoretical knowledge. The consequences of the postindustrial society are as follows: (1) fundamental changes in the class structure; (2) as a single communal society emerges, the political arena will become the center of nation-wide planning;

and (3) intellectual institutions will become all-important elements of society. Since economic achievement will lose its prime importance, progress will be measured in terms of social improvements. The greatest need of American society, therefore, is to specify a set of broad social goals and priorities in terms of which it can measure its future progress.

183. Bell, Daniel
   1967b   "The year 2000—the trajectory of an idea." Daedalus 96 (Summer):639–651.

This article briefly outlines the genesis of the Committee on the Year 2000 and the major features of future American society. The latter will be much like the society of today because the major problems Americans are grappling with will remain unsolved until the end of the century. There will, however, be four major areas of change: (1) technology (increasing longevity and better computer techniques); (2) the economy (existing goods and privileges will diffuse to presently poor segments of society); (3) the polity (centralization), and (4) the international sphere. The methods by which future change can be shaped in a desirable manner are also delineated.

184. Brown, Claude
   1968   "The effective society." Pp. 167–175 in William R. Ewald (ed.), Environment and Change: The Next Fifty Years. Bloomington: Indiana University Press.

An "effective society" is one that meets the needs of all of its classes, regardless of how small they are. To make it a reality three things must be done: (1) everyone must have the opportunity to participate in a meaningful way in shaping the society; (2) all classes must become involved in the society by having a vital stake in its continued existence; and (3) oligarchies and prejudiced planning must not be dominant. The article discusses how these three phases in the creation of an effective society could be carried out, thereby bringing a better future into being.

185. Drucker, Peter
   1955   America's Next Twenty Years. Harper's (March-June).

This four-part forecast presents a picture of what the United States might be like twenty years hence. Part I discusses population trends as they relate to the size of the labor force and shows that there will be plentiful opportunities for the educated worker. Part II delineates the implications of automation for the society of the future. The third part of the forecast is about the new tycoons of our society—the organizational administrators and managers. Their tremendous potential power is discussed and how their use, or nonuse, of it could affect the future. In Part IV eleven political issues that will become important in the future are delineated. They range from water and the country's geographical division through inflation and money to the demand for equality and more education.

186. Francis, Roy G.

1965   "Problems of tomorrow. Kapow!!: an argument and a forecast." Social Problems 12 (Winter): 328–335.

In American society there is a "ritual of speed, force and violence." One sees it everywhere—in the mass media, in sports, even in modern art. In addition, American society values "success" as the prime and all-important goal. These two themes (violence and success) will be dominant in determining the shape of tomorrow. The society of the future will be characterized by a separation of the "haves" and "have-nots" since present housing patterns are rapidly leading to physical divisions based on economic success. Violence will be localized and sanctioned in the slum areas. Furthermore, individual worth will be minimal and politics will be polarized. "Of course, projections of this kind are not the consequence of logical necessity. They are 'possible' and concerned people can concertedly work to prevent their occurrence" (p. 335).

187. Fromm, Erich

1968   The Revolution of Hope: Toward a Humanized Technology. New York: Harper & Row.

". . . we are at the crossroads: one road leads to a completely mechanized society with man as a helpless cog in the machine—if not to destruction by thermonuclear war; the other to a renaissance of humanism and hope—to a society that puts technique in the service of man's well-being" (p. vii). To make the latter a reality, the following must be done: (1) develop "humanistic planning" which maximizes human fulfillment rather than economic output or technological advance; (2) channel the general discontent with present trends into grass-roots communal action and participatory democracy; (3) restructure consumption patterns so they encourage creativity and self-development rather than mere acquisition of goods; (4) develop a modern equivalent for traditional religious forms.

188. Heilbroner, Robert L.

1960   The Future as History. New York: Harper.

America's past orientation to the future has consisted primarily of blind optimism and trust in the goodness of tomorrow. This orientation will no longer suffice, as the trends presently shaping America's future indicate: (1) developments in military technology make it impossible to solve problems through violence; (2) the demands of the underdeveloped countries for their share of the world's bounty will become more urgent; (3) socialistic planning will remold traditional capitalism; (4) technological and scientific developments will create more complex bureaucratic institutions; (5) governmental economic involvement will increase; and (6) the rapid growth rate will make a proper response to change impossible. The challenges of tomorrow can be met only if a new philosophy is developed that recognizes and accepts the inevitable aspects of the future while trying to shape the other aspects in the most desirable fashion.

189. Heilbroner, Robert L.
    1963   "On the seriousness of the future." American Scholar 32 (Autumn):556–562.
    There have been two major trends in recent history: (1) "The Great Awakening" (the underdeveloped countries are beginning to achieve a higher standard of living, and resentfully view the United States as the chief representative of the white, democratic, capitalistic minority); and (2) "The Great Paralysis" (the United States is unable to cope with its problems at home). "Can a society that half-educates and constantly diverts its citizenry, that extols nearly all private and denigrates all public activity, that addresses itself to the problems of the future in a language of the past—can such a society find an adequate response to the challenge of the Great Awakening or the Great Paralysis? I find it hard to answer this question affirmatively" (p. 562).

190. Heilbroner, Robert L.
    1966   "The future of capitalism." Commentary 41 (April):23–35.
    The American capitalist system can at best partially equalize the distribution of wealth at home and cope with Communist forces abroad, since ideological limitations make the complete resolution of these problems impossible. The tremendous growth of science and technology may, however, alter the capitalist system beyond recognition in the distant future. With the great amount of leisure that automation will bring, the old concepts of a market economy will rapidly become obsolete. The fading of capitalism will not, however, bring a better world in and of itself. The technological revolution creates grave social problems of its own and to cope with them is the challenge of the future.

191. Kahn, Herman
    1960   On Thermonuclear War. Princeton, N.J.: Princeton University Press.
    The possibility of nuclear war has been with us for fifteen years, but the United States has still not come to terms with it. Many of the policies that were delineated early in the nuclear era are badly in need of revision, and the book's major purpose is to consider how these policies might best be updated. The first part of the book shows that thermonuclear war need not result in total annihilation and discusses how to avoid it. The second part delineates situations leading to war and how they can be defused. The third part of the book focuses on eight major wars, only two of which have occurred, and delineates how the consequences of the six future wars could best be dealt with. A lengthy appendix outlines concrete ways in which the United States might better prepare for nuclear war.

192. Lasswell, Harold D.
    1941   "The garrison state." American Journal of Sociology 46 (January):455–469.
    The future "Garrison State" will have the following characteristics: (1) the

military will dominate the society, since war will be the primary occupation; (2) the ruling elite of highly skilled managers will have most of the power; (3) domestic violence will be aimed at the unskilled lower classes and those who oppose the government; (4) income disparities will be reduced somewhat so that the masses will not be demoralized; and (5) rates of production will be closely regulated. Of course, the author does not desire the creation of such a police state. He presents his construct in the hope that it will spur his colleagues to do research aimed at determining how the Garrison State's emergence can be avoided.

193. Lasswell, Harold D.
   1962   "The garrison state hypothesis today." Pp. 51–71 in Samuel P. Huntington (ed.), Changing Patterns of Military Politics. Glencoe, Ill.: Free Press.

"The garrison-state hypothesis was first published about a quarter of a century ago. The object of the present exercise is to consider the significance of the hypothesis in the light of scholarship and of the flow of history" (p. 51). The author does this by: considering several methodological issues; analyzing present trends toward militarism; delineating the decision-making structure of a variety of countries for the years to come; and outlining the scientific and policy implications of his discussion. Despite the passage of time, the United States is still quite militaristic in character. Its tendency toward violence can, however, be kept in check, if not overcome, by concerted public action and wise governmental decision-making.

194. Moore, Wilbert E.
   1964b   "Forecasting the future: the United States in 1980." Educational Record 45 (Fall):341–354.

Though the future cannot be foreseen in detail, its outlines can be isolated by evaluation of three factors: (1) those trends of the past and present persisting into the future; (2) those present givens remaining fixed in the future; and (3) future changes instituted through planning. By analyzing these factors the author is able to make the following statements about the United States in 1980: (1) the population size will be between 260 and 273 million; (2) the GNP will be about a trillion dollars; (3) skill levels required for jobs will be much higher; (4) standards of living and consumption levels will generally be more uniform; (5) large-scale suburban migration will continue; (6) new types of governmental authority will evolve; and (7) the major responsibilities of universities (i.e., preservation, dissemination, and increase of knowledge) will be more difficult to fulfill.

195. Riesman, David
   1967   "Notes on meritocracy." Daedalus 96 (Summer):897–908.

It is possible that the United States might be a "Meritocracy" by the year 2000. Such a society allocates everything on the basis of merit and accomplishment. If a meritocratic orientation does exist at the turn of the century, its sway will only be partial.

196. Theobald, Robert
    1968a   An Alternative Future for America. Chicago: Swallow Press.
    This collection of essays and speeches sets forth the author's ideas on
how America can achieve a better future. First he discusses present trends and
what they imply for the future. Contemporary violence and civil disobedience
are protests against the powerlessness of the individual in modern American society and the danger they represent lies in the response of the Establishment.
By drastically repressing this violence, America is well on the way to becoming a police state. The second part of the book discusses a different future—
one in which the individual is free to develop his talents and is not oppressed
by the state. It also discusses how America could achieve a future of freedom
rather than the totalitarian one it is heading for now. It would necessitate redefining national goals and priorities in a more humane manner, thereby creating
an image of a positive future that all Americans can strive for.

197. U.S. News and World Report
    1964   "What the future holds for America." U.S. News and World Re-
        port 56 (June 22):40–67.
    This article delineates America's near future in a variety of areas. It is
based on interviews with sixteen of President Johnson's "idea men," including:
Margaret Mead, David Riesman, Roger Revelle, John Kenneth Galbraith, Eugene Rostow, Leonard Broom, and Robert E. L. Faris. Each interviewee was
asked about problems facing the United States in his area of competence and
how they might be solved. The major aspects of the future considered are: the
country's growth rate; poverty; defense; race relations; economic trends; farmers; youth; women; conservation; law; the aged; and education.

For further forecasts delineating the future of the United States, see: nos.
110, 112, 122, 123, 214, 216, 217, 222, 224, 225, 234, 235, and **254.**

IV.B.3. Forecasts of the developing nations' future

198. Servoise, René
    1963   "Whither black Africa?" Pp. 181–294 in Bertrand de Jouvenel
        (ed.), Futuribles: Studies in Conjecture (I). Geneva: Droz.
    Many newly independent African nations are attempting to reconcile their
traditional cultures with Western ideas. Though this will be a difficult task,
the result will be a new African personality. In the next decade Africans will
face problems in the economic sphere in one of two ways: (1) by totalitarian
methods; and (2) by more moderate attempts to combine traditional African
and foreign European systems. Regardless of which approach is adopted, the
majority of countries will make only moderate progress in solving their economic problems. In the political sphere a similar prognosis can be made: moderate progress. This conclusion emerges from a discussion of the three phases of
African political development: (1) internal progress; (2) arrangement of "political space"; and (3) international relations.

For further forecasts dealing with the future of the developing nations, see: nos. **25, 109, 111, 130, 133, 138, 147, and 220.**

V. PERIODICALS OR ANTHOLOGIES DEALING WITH THE FUTURE

This category contains those periodicals and anthologies that deal with the future. A.1 is the subsection for periodicals whose exclusive focus is the systematic study of the future. Section A.2, in contrast, contains journals of a more general orientation that have published a whole issue on the future. Anthologies containing descriptions of various facets of tomorrow's world are found in Part B of this category.

V.A. Periodicals dealing with the future. *1. Journals dealing exclusively with the study of the future*

199. Analyse et Prévision

1966–   Analyse et Prévision (Analysis and Forecasting). Bertrand de Jouvenel (ed.). Paris: SEDEIS.

At the end of 1965 the editorial board of *Bulletin Sedeis* decided that the "Futuribles" series (see no. **203** for a brief description) was important enough to be more than a periodic supplement. In 1966, therefore, it became a major part of a new monthly *Analyse et Prévision*. This magazine is divided into three major parts: the first contains articles on present political situations; the second, entitled "Futuribles," contains one or more articles on the future; and the third section reviews books relevant to international affairs and political science. The magazine's articles on the future are generally of moderate length and discuss some aspect of the future (such as advanced industrial civilization or public administration) or methods for studying it systematically (i.e., systems analysis).

200. Analysen und Prognosen

1968–   Analysen und Prognosen [Analyses and Forecasts]. Berlin: Zentrum fuer Zukunftsforschung.

This quarterly journal is published by the newly established Zentrum fuer Zukunftsforschung (Center for Future Research) in Berlin. It contains articles on all aspects of the study of the future and is aimed at decision-makers in both government and business.

201. Fields within Fields . . . within Fields

1968–   Fields Within Fields . . . Within Fields. Jules Stulman (ed.). New York: World Institute Council.

The first issues of this magazine outline the basic methodology of the World Institute, as well as the necessity of applying it to the world's major problems. The aim of the Institute is to develop a truly international and interdisciplinary approach to problem-solving. It is only by giving up his parochial interests and linear thinking that man can hope to overcome his difficulties. To show how major problems could be solved with a global approach, later issues of this magazine apply the World Institute methodology in such areas as oceanographic research or urban development. (NOTE: for a more detailed discussion of the World Institute, see no. **88.**)

202. Futures

> 1968–   Futures: The Journal of Forecasting and Planning. London: Unwin.

This quarterly journal is published under the auspices of Iliffe Science and Technology Publications Limited (British) and the Institute for the Future (Middletown, Conn.). Its major aim is to collect a series of forecasts about specific trends that will be of use to decision-makers. This will also require developing and applying forecasting techniques. The journal is international in orientation, and prints three types of articles: (1) those delineating long-term trends in science, technology, economics, politics, or social conditions; (2) those discussing the specification, or achievement, of long-term goals; and (3) those dealing with forecasting methodology. (NOTE: for samples of articles from this magazine, see: nos. **3, 53, 66, 67, 85, 86, 100, 102,** and **117.**)

203. Futuribles

> 1961–   Futuribles—Supplement to Bulletin Sedeis. Bertrand de Jou-
> 1965   venel (ed.). Paris: SEDEIS.

This French magazine served as a forum in which members of the "Futuribles" project (for a brief description, see no. **91**) could express their opinions. Most of the magazine's articles were quite lengthy (usually one to an issue) and discussed some aspect of the future in considerable detail. The articles generally covered one of three topics: (1) the methodology of studying the future (i.e., the planning process or decision-making); (2) the future of some broad sphere or geographical area (i.e., political institutions or Europe); and (3) the future of some specific unit or institution (i.e., Burma or revolution). (NOTE: for samples of "Futuribles," see: nos. **29, 55, 80, 81, 164, 169, 228,** and **229.**)

204. The Futurist

> 1967–   The Futurist. A Newsletter for Tomorrow's World. Washington,
>   D.C.: World Future Society.

The World Future Society was officially established in October 1966 as a nonprofit, nonpartisan, scientific, and educational organization. Its major aims are fivefold: (1) to create an awareness of the importance of studying the future; (2) to improve and develop methods of future study; (3) to create public understanding and sympathy for investigations dealing with the shape of the future; (4) to increase scientific study of the future; and (5) to promote cooperation and communication between individuals or groups concerned with the future. To help fulfill these aims, the World Future Society publishes this magazine on a bimonthly basis. It contains articles about various aspects of the future, as well as frequent book reviews.

205. Futurum

1968– Futurum: Zeitschrift fuer Zukunftsforschung [Futurum: Journal for Future Research], Ossip K. Flechtheim (ed.). Meisenheim am Glan (Germany): Verlag Anton Hain.

The general outlines of the future can be foreseen today. If man wishes to mold the future to fit his desires, therefore, he ought to begin to study the implications of emerging trends with all the tools at his disposal. The aim of this periodical is to establish a forum where persons of all disciplines and specialities can discuss what the future will, or ought, to be like. Since knowledge about the future cannot be encompassed by one publication, this quarterly primarily publishes articles analyzing major developmental problems or discussing basic trends. The articles are fairly general in orientation and usually outline research or action necessary for a more desirable future.

206. Perspectives

1965– Perspectives: Studies in Social and Political Forecasting—Supplement to the Indian Journal of Public Administration. L. P. Singh (ed.). New Delhi: Indian Institute of Public Administration.

In October 1963, at the suggestion of Bertrand de Jouvenel, the Indian Council for the Future was set up by the Indian Institute of Public Administration. The aim of the Council is to sponsor studies about the social, economic and political aspects of India's future. In 1965 this magazine was created so some of the studies could be published. Its articles have generally presented a picture of what India might look like in 1975—the end of the fifth Five-Year Plan. The basic purpose of each study is to investigate some aspect of Indian society and isolate the process of change that it is undergoing. Also, the implications of present trends for the future are outlined. It is hoped the studies will be useful to the leaders and decision-makers who influence and mold India's future.

207. Prognosen—Plaene—Perspektiven

1967– Prognosen—Plaene—Perspektiven   [Forecasts—Plans—Prospects]. Vienna: Institut fuer Zukunftsfragen.

This journal is published by the Institut fuer Zukunftsfragen (Institute for Future Questions), whose director is Robert Jungk. It contains articles on various aspects of future-oriented research. Each issue also has a number of book reviews. (The magazine's publication was suspended for a time.)

208. Prospective

1958– Prospective [Prospect]. Centre d'Etudes Prospectives (Association Gaston Berger). Paris: Presses Universitaires de France.

The Centre D'Etudes Prospectives was organized to study those technological, economic, scientific and social forces that might accelerate the evolution of the modern world. It also tries to foresee any undesirable situations that might arise. In 1958 the Centre began to publish some of its studies in this magazine. The articles usually deal with the implications of a present situation or some future trend. Often a whole issue is devoted to a single theme.

V.A.2. Journals publishing issues on the future

209. Center Diary

1967   "Possible futures." Center Diary #17 (March-April):15–54.

A major section of this issue is devoted to several papers dealing with the future. They were presented at the Center for the Study of Democratic Institutions in the previous months. In most cases the discussion that followed the formal presentation is also reproduced. The individual articles are as follows: John Wilkinson, "Futuribles: Innovation vs. Stability" (see no. **75**); Rodderick Seidenberg, "Justice for All, Freedom for None" (see no. **146**); René Dubos, "Evolving Psyche" (see no. **83**); Huston Smith, "Toward a World Civilization."

210. Fabun, Don (ed.)

1967   The Dynamics of Change. Englewood Cliffs, N.J.: Prentice-Hall.

To celebrate its twentieth anniversary, in 1966 Kaiser Aluminum devoted the year's issues of its newsletter (*Kaiser Aluminum News*) to discussions of what the next twenty years might bring. Each of the six richly illustrated issues explored a different aspect of the future. The basic themes of the issues are as follows: (1) "The Dynamics of Change"—a general discussion of the major elements of the change process; (2) "The Promised Land"—an exploration of land uses; (3) "Telemobility: When Far is Near"—a discussion of transportation and communication; (4) "Life with a Little Black Box"—a projection of advances in computer techniques; (5) "The Theory of the Leisure Masses"—an exploration of the problems that will emerge from increased physical abundance and leisure; (6) "Foreseeing the Unforseeable"—a discussion of possible innovations and discoveries.

211. McHale, John (ed.)

1967   "2000+." Architectural Design 37 (February).

This issue explores the nature of the world at the turn of the century. It is richly illustrated and was compiled by John McHale (Executive Director of World Resources Inventory; Southern Illinois University). He is also the author of much of the text, as the following list of articles indicates: R. Buckminster Fuller, "Profile of the Industrial Revolution"; R. Buckminster Fuller, "The Year 2000" (see no. **137**); John McHale, "2000+"; John McHale, "The Future of the Future" (see no. **8**): John McHale, "Outer Space"; John McHale, "Inner Space"; John McHale, "Man+"; John McHale, "New Symbiosis"; John McHale, "World Game" (see no. **106**); John McHale, "The People Future" (see no. **68**); Theodore J. Gordon, "The Effects of Technology"; R. Middleton, "Living"; and Neil P. Hurley, "Communications Revolution."

212. McHale, John

1968b   "Toward the future." Design Quarterly No. 72.

Man is presently able to choose the kind of future he wants because of his highly sophisticated technological and scientific knowhow. "The future of the future becomes, therefore, what we determine it to be both individually and collectively" (p. 3). While an advanced technology is beneficial, it also presents great dangers since it has severely upset the world's delicate ecological balance. Much of this article, which forms the basis of the whole *Design Quarterly* issue, discusses those technologies that can help man eliminate air, water, and other types of pollution. Developments in space exploration, oceanography, machine technology, and meteorology serve to illustrate how greater environmental control can be achieved. The article concludes by discussing the need for long-range goals to guide technological development and the reasons for man's inability to define them as yet.

213. The New York Times Magazine
  1964   The Future. Pp. 86–118 of New York Times, April 19: section 6 (part II).
  This series of six articles outlines various aspects of the future in broad strokes. The contributions, each of which covers a fairly specialized area, include: Arnold Toynbee, "At Least the Beginning of One World," (discusses the possibilities for world government); Henry Steele Commager, "A Visit to the Year 2000" (future problems the U.S. will have to cope with); C. Randall, "Industry: Incredible New Markets"; J. B. S. Haldane, "A Scientific Revolution? Yes"; Margaret Mead, "Human Nature Will Flower, If"; and H. L. Dryden, "No Tourists on the Moon."

214. Saturday Review
  1964   "The prospects for American civilization." Saturday Review 47 (Aug. 29).
  This fortieth anniversary issue contains a series of articles dealing with various aspects of the future. The articles are as follows: Arnold Toynbee, "Conditions for Survival"; Barbara Ward, "The Uses of Prosperity"; Robert L. Heilbroner, "New Horizons in Economics"; Walter Reuther, "Freedom's Time of Testing"; R. Buckminster Fuller, "The Prospect for Humanity"; John Mason Brown, "More than 1,001 First Nights"; Jerome Beatty, "What's Happening to Humor?"; Allan Nevins, "The Outlook for Greatness"; Malcolm Cowley, "Dr. Canby's Team"; Roscoe Drummond, "Is the Government Ready for the Future?"; Editorial, "Life Inside the Centrifuge"; Granville Hicks, "Signatures to the Significance of the Self"; Rochelle Girson, "Mutations in the Body Politic"; David Dempsey, "Mr. Jenkins Sees It Through"; Margaret R. Weiss, "Trends in Transition"; Richard L. Tobin, "The Man with the Pencil of Light"; John Ciardi, "Adam and Eve and the Third Son"; James F. Fixx, "The Personal Touch"; Katherine Kuh, "Art's Voyage of Discovery"; Paul Woodring, "The Schools Educate Themselves"; and John Lear, "The Future of God."

215. Science Journal
  1967   "Forecasting the future." Science Journal 3 (October).
  This issue of *Science Journal* explores various aspects of the world of tomorrow. The articles contained within it are as follows: Robert Jungk, "The Future of Future Research" (see no. **51**); Erich Jantsch, "Forecasting the Future"; Olaf Helmer, "Science"; Ali Bulent Cambell, "Energy", Hasan Ozbekhan, "Automation"; John R. Pierce, "Communication"; Robert C. Seamans,

"Space"; Gabriel Bouladan, "Transport"; Robert U. Ayres, "Food"; William L. Swager, "Materials"; Roger Revelle, "Population"; and Herman Kahn, "World Futures."

For additional periodical issues dealing with the future see no. 255.

V.B. Anthologies about the future

216. Anderson, Stanford (ed.)

1968   Planning for Diversity and Choice: Possible Futures and Their Relations to the Man-Controlled Environment. Cambridge, Mass.: MIT Press.

The MIT conference for architects was entitled "Inventing the Future Environment" and was held in Boston in October 1966. Its basic aim was to explore the study of the future to determine whether it would be possible to develop "... a critical utopianism that would involve the creative imagining of possible futures, their critical evaluation, and an open-ended and flexible implementation of those possibilities which are most resistant to criticism" (p. 7). The various papers presented at the conference are as follows: I. C. Jarvie, "Utopian Thinking and the Architect"; Bernard Cazes, "Long-Range Studies of the Future and Their Role in French Planning"; Leonard J. Duhl, "The Parameters of Urban Planning"; Robert Jungk, "About 'Mankind 2000'" (see no. 65); Herbert Moller, "The Population of the United States in the Last Third of the Twentieth Century"; Harold J. Barnett, "Natural Resources in the Changing U.S. Economy"; Pardon E. Tillinghast, "Leisure: Old Patterns and New Problems"; Bruce Mazlish, "Obsolescence and 'Obsolesibles' in Planning for the Future"; Paul Davidoff, "Normative Planning"; Leonard J. Fein, "Ideology and Architecture: Dilemmas of Pluralism in Planning"; Hasan Ozbekhan, "The Triumph of Technology: 'Can' Implies 'Ought'" (see no. 72); Raymond A. Bauer, "Social Indicators: Or Working in a Society Which has Better Social Statistics"; Marx Wartofsky, "Telos and Technique: Models as Modes of Action"; Paul K. Feyerabend, "Outline of a Pluralistic Theory of Knowledge and Action"; Stanford Anderson, "Summary: Planning for Fullness"; and Melvin Charney, "Environmental Conjecture: In the Jungle of the Grand Prediction."

217. Baier, Kurt, and Nicholas Rescher (eds.)

1969   Values and the Future. New York: Free Press.

The major tasks of this book are "... to improve the conceptual apparatus for talking about values and value change, to remove the confusions hampering progress in the domain of evaluation, and to offer methodological suggestions for forecasting value change" (pp. v–vi). Consequently, this series of essays considers the nature of values, their relationship to technology, and the role they play in determining technological progress. Not all of the essays deal with the future, but those that do are listed below: Alvin Toffler, "Value Impact Forecaster—A Profession of the Future" (see no. 58); Nicholas Rescher, "What is Value Change? A Framework for Research"; Nicholas Rescher, "A Questionnaire Study of American Values by 2000 A.D." (see no. 123); Theodore J. Gordon, "The Feedback between Technology and Values" (see no. **114**); Olaf Helmer, "Simulating the Values of the Future" (see no. **101**); Bertrand de Jouvenel, "Technology as a Means" (see no. **20**); David Lewis, "New Urban Structures"; Leland Hazard, "Challenges for Urban Policy"; Kenneth E. Boulding, "The Emerging Superculture"; John Kenneth Galbraith, "Technology, Planning and Organization"; Bela Gold, "The Framework of Decision for Major Technological Innovation"; and Martin Bronfenbrenner, "Economic Consequences of Technological Change."

218. Boyko, Hugo (ed.)
  1961   Science and the Future of Mankind. Den Haag, Holland: Uitgeverij Dr. W. Junk.
  "It is a matter of urgency that scientists and men of learning of all countries . . . get together in an International Council to consider the problems science has raised, and . . . suggest what political and economic changes might be made to insure that our civilization might evolve to a wonderful new era. . . ." (p. 1). Such an International Council became a reality in 1960 when the World Academy of Art and Science was established. The collection of essays in this volume is its first attempt to suggest possible solutions to societal problems that have arisen from scientific advances. Each article is by an eminent expert and considers trends in a specific area. The individual essays are as follows: A. Einstein, "Die Internationale der Wissenschaft (The International Science Organization)"; H. Boyko, "The Need of a World Academy of Art and Science"; R. Oppenheimer, "Thoughts on Art and Science"; W. F. G. Swann, "Science and our Future"; H. J. Muller, "The Prospects of Genetic Progress"; H. D. Lasswell, "Science, Scientists and World Policy"; S. W. Tromp, "The Significance of Border Sciences for the Future of Mankind"; R. M. Field, "The Human Significance of the Natural Resources"; P. Dansereau, "Resource Planning: A Problem in Communication"; M. J. Sirks, "Food Supply and Increase of Population"; P. Chouard, "Quelques Voies Probables de Developpement des Nouvelles Techniques en Agronomie (Several Likely Views of the Development of New Techniques in Agriculture)"; J. Phillips, "Science in the Service of Man in Africa South of the Sahara"; T. Monod, "La Science et L'Homme au Seuil du Desert (Science and Man at the Edge of the Desert)"; H. F. Infield, "Human Needs and the Need for Ultimate Orientation"; L. K. Bush, "Practical Notes on Politics and Poesy"; W. Taylor Thom, "Science and Engineering and the Future of Man"; Europaeus, "War or Peace—A Biological Problem"; I. Berenblum, "Science and Modern Civilization"; W. C. de Leeuw, "New Ways with Science as Leader"; and B. Russell, "Per Aspera ad Astra."

219. Brinton, Crane (ed.)
  1961   The Fate of Man. New York: George Braziller.
  This series of essays deals with the significance of man's place in the universe. Most articles deal with the present or past, but there is a section on "Inventing the Future." In it the following authors present their ideas about the nature of tomorrow's world and man's place in it: René J. Dubos, "Utopias and

Human Goals"; Marston Bates, "Man and the Balance of Nature"; Sir Charles G. Darwin, "The Next Million Years" (see no. 135); Roderick Seidenberg, "Another Distant View." (see nos. 144 and 145); and Dennis Gabor, "The New Golden Age" (see no. 165).

220. Brown, Harrison, et al.
1967   The Next Ninety Years. Pasadena: California Institute of Technology.

The Cal Tech conference held in March 1967 was sponsored by the Office for Industrial Associates and entitled "The Next Ninety Years." Most of the conference was devoted to reanalyzing the forecasts made in *The Next Hundred Years* (see no. 159) ten years previously. Each of the authors of that book delineate how they would revise the predictions they had made: Harrison Brown discusses changes in population trends and their effect on society; James Bonner's paper concentrates on the state of food production; and John Weir outlines future trends in education. In addition, papers dealing with a number of other pressing problems were presented: Norman Brooks discusses the rapid advance of environmental pollution and its future implications; Thayer Scudder outlines how the emerging nations might resolve their problems of economic development; and the future implications of constructing a city from scratch are discussed by Athelstan Spilhaus. After each paper was presented the participants discussed it and the major views aired at this time have also been included in this book. The general tenor of the discussion, like that of the papers, is rather pessimistic.

221. Calder, Nigel (ed.)
1965   The World in 1984. Baltimore: Penguin Books (2 vols.).

These two volumes contain a series of ninety-nine short forecasts published by the journal *New Scientist* during 1964. Each article deals with a fairly specialized area and tries to anticipate the most likely developments of the next twenty years. Most of the authors are well-known authorities in the natural or social sciences or in public affairs. They include: A. R. Todd, I. I. Rabi, J. D. Cockcroft, Norbert Weiner, J. Lederberg, Wernher von Braun, B. J. Sen, R. Revelle, Guilio Natta, C. S. Cockerell, H. R. Hoggart, E. C. Dodds, Michael Young, B. F. Skinner, Ruth Glass, T. Kristensen, G. P. Thomson, J. de Castro, and Frank Press. The first volume focuses on scientific and technical issues, and covers the following topics: science and human goals, fundamental science, astronomy and space exploration, natural resources, food and agriculture, fuel and power, materials and manufacture, oceans, weather and climate, chemicals, computers, telecommunications, aviation, surface transport, and applications of biology. The second volume has a more social orientation. Its major themes are: human mind, health, domestic life, government, education, cities, leisure and the arts, trade, international relations, Britain, North America, Latin America, Africa, Asia, and the world in 1984. (NOTE: for a summary of the major developments delineated in these two volumes, see no. 131.)

222. Commission on the Year 2000

1967a   "Toward the year 2000: work in progress." Daedalus 96 (Summer):639–994.
   This issue of *Daedalus* summarizes the early deliberations of the Commission on the Year 2000, which was created by the American Academy of Arts and Sciences in 1965. In the two "Working Sessions" the major objectives of the Commission are defined, while in a series of articles by Commission members specific aspects of the future are discussed. There are also several articles on methodology. The individual items in the issue are as follows: Daniel Bell, "The Year 2000: The Trajectory of an Idea" (see no. **183**); Commission, "Working Session I" (see no. **42**); Herman Kahn and Anthony J. Weiner, "The Next Thirty-Three Years: A Framework for Speculation" (see no. **93**); Fred Charles Iklé, "Can Social Predictions be Evaluated?" (see no. **47**); Donald A. Schon, "Forecasting and Technological Forecasting" (see no. **57**); Martin Shubik, "Information, Rationality, and Free Choice in a Future Democratic Society" (see no. **172**); Leonard J. Duhl, "Planning and Predicting: Or What to Do When You Don't Know the Names of the Variables" (see no. **61**); Harvey S. Perloff, "Modernizing Urban Development"; Daniel P. Moynihan, "The Relationship of Federal to Local Authorities"; Lawrence K. Frank, "The Need for a New Political Theory" (see no. **18**); Stephen R. Graubard, "University Cities in the Year 2000"; Harold Orlans, "Educational and Scientific Institutions"; Ernst Mayr, "Biological Man and the Year 2000"; Gardner C. Quarton, "Deliberate Efforts to Control Human Behavior and Modify Personality"; Krister Stendahl, "Religion, Mysticism, and the Institutional Church"; Erik H. Erikson, "Memorandum on Youth"; Margaret Mead, "The Life Cycle and its Variations: The Division of Roles"; Harry Kalven, "The Problems of Privacy in the Year 2000" (see no. **166**); George A. Miller, "Some Psychological Perspectives on the Year 2000" (see no. **143**); David Riesman, "Notes on Meritocracy" (see no. **195**); John R. Pierce, "Communication"; Eugene V. Rostow, "Thinking About the Future of International Society"; Samuel P. Huntington, "Political Development and the Decline of the American System of World Order"; Ithiel de Sola Pool, "The International System in the Next Half Century" (see no. **148**); Commission, "Working Session II" (see no. **60**); and Daniel Bell, "Coda: Work in Further Progress."

223. Elton et al.

1948   The Prospect before Us: Some Thoughts on the Future. London: Sampson, Low, Marston.
   These essays were written in the belief that man is at a crossroads and that his present decisions will have profound and far-reaching consequences. If the general outline of the future could be delineated, it might enable man to take more enlightened action with regard to contemporary dilemmas. The individual essays focus on specific aspects of the future and are as follows: Lord Elton, "Foreword" (on the general value of forecasts); Professor C. H. Waddington, "Science and the Future"; Philip Toynbee, "The Future of Literature"; James

Agate, "The Future of Drama"; John Frederick Wolfenden, "The Future of Education"; Eric Blom, "the Future of Music"; Michael Ayrton, "The Future of Art"; Lord Horder, "The Future of Medicine"; and Commander Stephen King-Hall, "The Future of Politics."

224. Ewald, William R. (ed.)

1968b   Environment and Policy: The Next Fifty Years. Bloomington: Indiana University Press.

In honor of its fiftieth anniversary, the American Institute of Planners decided to sponsor a two-year investigation of how the environment might evolve in the next fifty years. Part II of its program focused on a conference in Washington, D.C. in October 1967. This volume contains those conference papers that dealt with possible policy goals for the next five decades. Each paper considers: (1) the policies or programs needed by 1970, 1980, 2000, and 2020; (2) implications of these policies for all levels of society; and (3) the professional disciplines needed to implement the policies or programs. The individual contributions are as follows: Bayard Rustin, "Minority Groups: Development of the Individual"; Robert M. Hutchins, "Education for a Full Life"; Odin W. Anderson, "Health Services in a Land of Plenty"; William H. Stewart, "Health—The Next Fifty Years"; Sebastian de Grazia, "The Problems and Promise of Leisure"; Keven Lynch, "The Possible City"; Max L. Feldman, "Transportation: An Equal Opportunity for Access"; Charles Abrams, "Housing in the Year 2000"; Jack Meltzer, "Manpower Needs for Planning for the Next Fifty Years"; Lyle C. Fitch, "National Development and National Policy" (see no. **17**); Joseph L. Fischer, "Natural Resources—Wise Use of the World's Inheritance"; Herbert A. Simon, "Research for Choice"; Daniel R. Mandelker, "New Incentives and Controls"; and Alan Altshuler, "New Institutions to Serve the Individual" (see no. **180**).

225. Ewald, William R. (ed.)

1968a   Environment and Change: The Next Fifty Years. Bloomington: Indiana University Press.

This volume contains some of the papers presented at the 1967 American Institute of Planners Conference in Washington, D.C. It is part of a larger enterprise to foresee man's environment fifty years hence. "This book contains those essentially 'philosophic' papers. . . . It seeks to define the human scope of the term environment, the forces of change, the competence we have so far developed to cope with change, the role of the individual and society in the future, and a recognition of the true context of the future: youth, technology and the world" (pp. 3–4). The titles of the individual papers are as follows: Pierre Bertaux, "The Future of Man" (see no. **2**). Bertrand de Jouvenel, "On Attending to the Future" (see no. **64**); Harold Taylor, "The Arts in Modern Society"; Joseph Sittler, "The Role of the Spirit in Creating the Future Environment"; John R. Platt, "Life Where Science Flows"; Ralph G. H. Siu, "Role of Technology in Creating the Future Environment"; Herman Kahn and Anthony J. Weiner,

"Faustian Powers and Human Choices: Some Twenty-First Century Technological and Economic Issues"; Emmanuel G. Mesthene, "How Technology Will Shape the Future"; Carl Oglesby, "The Young Rebels"; Claude Brown, "The Effective Society" (see no. **184**); Max Lerner, "On Whose Behalf is the Dream Being Dreamt?"; Robert Theobald, "Planning *With* People" (see no. **73**); John Burchard, "The Culture of Urban America"; Carl Feiss, "Taking Stock: A Resume of Planning Accomplishments in the United States"; Robert C. Wood, "The Development of Administrative and Political Planning in America"; Gunnar Myrdal, "The Necessity and Difficulty of Planning the Future Society"; David T. Barzelon, "The New Factor in American Society" (see no. **181**); August Heckscher, "The Individual—Not the Mass" (see no. **19**); Sir Geoffrey Vickers, "Individuals in a Collective Society"; Renato Severino, "Technology and the Underdeveloped World"; Ann Schrand, "The Hope There is in People"; John F. C. Turner, "The People Build with Their Hands"; R. Buckminster Fuller, "An Operating Manual for Spaceship Earth"; and William L. C. Wheaton, "Epilogue: Mood for Development."

226. Foreign Policy Association (ed.)
1968   Toward the Year 2018. New York: Cowles Education Corporation.
These essays commemorate the fiftieth anniversary of the Foreign Policy Association. Their aim is "to set the technological context of social and international policy over the next fifty years" (p. vii). The individual essays, by experts in various fields, are as follows: D. G. Brennan, "Weaponry"; Gordon J. F. MacDonald, "Space"; Najeeb E. Halaby, "Transportation"; J. R. Pierce, "Communication"; Thomas F. Malone, "Weather"; Anthony G. Oettinger, "Educational Technology"; Ithiel de Sola Pool, "Behavioral Technology"; Charles R. DeCarlo, "Computer Technology"; Charles A. Scarlott, "Energy"; D. Gale Johnson, "Food"; Philip M. Hauser, "Population"; Herman Kahn and Anthony J. Weiner, "Economics"; and Roger Revelle, "Oceanography."

227. Ginzberg, Eli (ed.)
1964   Technology and Social Change. New York: Columbia University Press.
This book summarizes the first sessions of the Columbia University Seminar on Social and Technological Change. The aims of the seminar are threefold: (1) to outline the past, present, and future effects of technological development; (2) to isolate the nature of social and technological change; and (3) to delineate the type of social system that could cope with the technology of the future. Each chapter is devoted to a single seminar session and consists of the paper presented at it, as well as a summary of the main points raised in the ensuing discussion. The chapters contain papers by the following people: Aaron W. Warner, "Introduction" (a description of the seminar's creation); Charles R. DeCarlo, "Perspectives on Technology"; Daniel Bell, "The Post-Industrial Society"; Earl P. Johnson, "The Aerospace Industry"; William O.

Baker, "The Dynamism of Science and Technology"; Solomon Fabricant, "Productivity and Economic Growth"; and Eli Ginzberg, "Confrontations and Directives."

228. Jouvenel, Bertrand de (ed.)
1963   Futuribles: Studies in Conjecture (I). Geneva: Droz.
This series of essays originally appeared in the French magazine *Futuribles* (a supplement to *Bulletin Sedeis*). They have been translated into English to reach a wider audience interested in the scientific study of the future. The individual essays are as follows: Bertrand de Jouvenel, "Introduction" (see no. **91**); Max Beloff, "British Constitutional Evolution 1960–1970"; Jacques Ellul, "Western Man in 1970" (see no. **162**); Bertrand de Jouvenel, "On the Evolution of Forms of Government"; Edmund Leach, "The Political Future of Burma"; M. M. Postan, "The Economic and Social System: The Prospects for 1970–1975" (see no. **171**); René Servoise, "Whither Black Africa?" (see no. **198**); and Leicester Webb, "Pakistan's Political Future."

229. Jouvenel, Bertrand de (ed.)
1965   Futuribles: Studies in Conjecture (II). Geneva: Droz.
This collection of articles was originally published in the French magazine *Futuribles* (supplement to *Bulletin Sedeis*). It primarily discusses the progress Europe might make toward becoming a federal community by 1970. The individual articles are as follows: Jacques Freymond, "Introduction" (see no. **62**); Saul Friedlaender, "Forecasting in International Relations" (see no. **78**); Denis de Rougemont, "Pointers Towards a Federal Europe" (see no. **178**); Dusan Sidjanski, "Federative Aspects of the European Community" and "Will Europe Be United on Federal Lines?" (see no. **179**); and Michel Massenet, "The Foreign Policy of a United Europe." (see no. **90**)

230. Jungk, Robert, and Johan Galtung, (eds.)
1969   Mankind 2000. Oslo: Universitetsforlaget.
This book summarizes the proceedings of the first International Future Research Conference which took place in Oslo, Norway, in September 1967. At this meeting experts from a wide variety of fields presented papers on aspects of future research. The titles of the papers are as follows: Johan Galtung, "On the Future of the International System" (see no. **138**); Jan Tinbergen, "International Planning of Peaceful Economic Development"; Seymour Melman, "A Proposal for Curtailing Small Wars"; Charles E. Osgood, "Conservative Words and Radical Sentences in the Semantics of International Politics"; Richard F. Behrendt, "Some Structural Prerequisites for a Global Society Based on Non-Violent Conflict Resolution" (see no. **129**); Peter Menke-Glueckert, "Proposals for an International Programme of Joint Technological Endeavours for Peaceful Purposes"; Arthur I. Waskow, "Looking Forward: 1999" (see no. **151**); Richard L. Meier, "Material Resources"; Hasan Ozbekhan, "The Role of Goals and Planning in the Solution of the World Food Problem"; Fritz Baade, "Material Resources for the Nutrition of Mankind"; Dennis Gabor, "Material Develop-

ment"; Karl Steinbuch, "Communication in the Year 2000"; Anthony R. Michaelis, "Television from Space Satellite—A Solution to the Population Explosion"; G. S. Khromov, "Significance and Perspectives of Space Research"; Richard E. Farson, "Bill of Rights for 1984" (see no. **136**); Christopher Wright, "Some Requirements for Viable Social Goals" (see no. **26**); R. Richta et al., "The Perspective of the Scientific and Technological Revolution"; Silvio Ceccato, "Future Applications of Cybernetics"; Werner Z. Hirsch, "Education and the Future"; Stanley Lesse and William Wolf, "Medicine and our Future Society"; John G. Papaioannou, "Some Highlights for A.D. 2000"; Federick J. Hacker, "Human Implications" (see no. **4**); Edward S. Cornish, "The Professional Futurist" (see no. **43**); Nigel Calder, "Goals, Foresight, and Politics" (see no. **59**); John McHale, "Future Research: Some Integrative and Communicative Aspects" (see no. **54**); Ossip Flechtheim, "Is Futurology the Answer to the Challenge of the Future?" (see no. **45**); Yujiro Hayashi, "The Direction and Orientation of Futurology as a Science" (see no. **46**); Waldemar Rolbiecki, "Prognostication and Prognoseology" (see no. **30**); Yehezkel Dror, "Some Requisites of Organizations' Better Taking into Account the Future"; David C. Miller, "Comprehensive Long-Range Forecasting Systems for Management"; I. V. Bestuzhev-Lada, "Social Prognostics Research in the Soviet Union"; Fred. L. Polak, "Towards the Goal of Goals" (see no. **23**); Charles E. Osgood and Stuart Umpleby, "A Computer-based System for Exploration of Possible Futures for Mankind 2000" (see no. **103**); and Olaf Helmer, "An Abbreviated Delphi Experiment in Forecasting" (see no. **115**).

231. Kahn, Herman
1962   Thinking about the Unthinkable. New York: Horizon Press.
This collection of articles explores the possibility of thermonuclear war and the ramifications thereof. The basic theme of each essay is as follows: (1) "In Defense of Thinking" argues that though nuclear war may *seem* impossible, it is not, and therefore, the U.S. ought to learn as much as possible about the dangers and consequences of a large-scale war. (2) "Some Possible Sizes and Shapes of Thermonuclear War" delineates four basic ways in which a major war might begin and eight ways in which it might progress. (3) "Thinking About Civil Defense" reviews the controversy about the desirability of extensive civilian defense preparations. (4) "Thinking About Deterrence" discusses types of deterrence the U.S. has used in the past, uses at present, and might use in the future. (5) "Some Strange Aids to Thought" outlines devices that military strategists use to help them conceptualize novel situations (e.g., the abstract model; the scenario; war and peace games; and the historical example). (6) "Some Thoughts on International Bargaining and the Game of Chicken" delineates six bargaining positions and a number of escalation ladders leading to large-scale war. (7) "New Technology and the Old Order" discusses how future technological advances will make present international arrangements obsolete and inadequate. (8) "Thinking About the Future" outlines a series of national policies the U.S. might adopt and several research projects that would enhance assessments of the probability of thermonuclear war.

232. Modelle fuer eine Neue Welt

1964–   Modelle fuer eine Neue Welt [Models for a New World]. Robert Jungk and Hans Josef Mundt (eds.). Vienna: Verlag Kurt Desch.

The aim of this German series is to inform the public of possibilities for the future and thereby create a forum for discussion. Most of the books are collections of articles by a variety of authors, but a few are by individual authors. The books that have been published so far are as follows (the full series is to consist of twenty books):

I. Jungk, Robert, and Hans Josef Mundt (eds.)

1964   Der Griff nach der Zukunft: Planen und Freiheit [Reaching for the Future: Planning and Freedom].

A series of nineteen articles dealing with various theoretical aspects of planning. Contributors include Pierre Bertaux, Ossip Flechtheim, Robert Jungk, and others.

II. Jungk, Robert, and Hans Josef Mundt (eds.)

1964   Wege ins Neue Jahrtausend: Wettkampf der Planungen in Ost und West [Paths to the New Century: Planning Contest between East and West].

A series of eighteen articles discussing planning endeavors in various parts of the world. Contributors include N. Sombart, Fritz Baade, Alfred Frisch, Robert Jungk, and others.

III. Jungk, Robert, and Hans Josef Mundt (eds.)

1964   Deutschland Ohne Konzeption: Am Beginn einer Neuen Epoche [Germany without a Plan: On the Doorstep of a New Era].

A collection of twenty essays discussing various aspects of Germany's future.

IV. Calder, Nigel (ed.)

1965   Unsere Welt 1985 [Our World in 1985].

A translation of the *New Scientist* series, *The World in 1984* (see no. **221**).

V. Jungk, Robert, and Hans Josef Mundt (eds.)

1966   Das Umstrittene Experiment: Der Mensch [The Disputed Experiment: Man].

A series of articles dealing with future implications of advances in the control of human biological processes.

VI. Manstein, Bodo

1967   Liebe und Hunger: Die Urtriebe im Licht der Zukunft [Love and Hunger: The Original Instincts as Illuminated by the Future].

A discussion of how the future will be affected by trends in population growth, food production, and available living space.

VII. Calder, Nigel

1968   Vor uns das Paradies?: Entwurf eines Gelobten Landes [Before Us Paradise?: Plan for a Promised Land].

A translation of *The Environment Game* (see no. **132**).

VIII. Graubard, Stephen (ed.)
    1968   Der Weg ins Jahr 2000 [The Path to the Year 2000].
A translation of the progress report of the Commission on the Year 2000 published in the Summer 1967 issue of *Daedalus* under the title of "Toward the Year 2000: Work in Progress" (see no. **222**).

233. Moore, Wilbert E.
    1967   "Forecasting the future." Pp. 253–305 in Wilbert E. Moore, *Order and Change: Essays in Comparative Sociology*. New York: Wiley.
This section of a book otherwise devoted to the nature of social change deals with various aspects of future-oriented study. It consists of the following four articles (all of which had been published previously): "Predicting Discontinuities in Social Change" (see no. **84**); "Global Sociology: The World as a Singular System"; "Forecasting the Future: The United States in 1980" (see no. **194**); and "The Utility of Utopias" (see no. **9**).

234. President's Commission on National Goals
    1960   The Goals for Americans—Programs for Action in the Sixties. Englewood Cliffs, N.J.: Prentice-Hall.
This book contains the report of the Eisenhower-appointed President's Commission on National Goals. It begins with a fairly general, and comprehensive, statement of what the long-range goals of the United States should be, both at home and abroad. The individual chapters that follow contain essays that served as the Commission's background material, and they discuss goals and trends in specific areas. The essays are as follows: Henry M. Wristen, "The Individual"; Clinton Rossiter, "The Democratic Process"; John W. Gardner, "National Goals in Education"; Warren Weaver, "A Great Age for Science"; August Heckscher, "The Quality of American Culture"; Clark Kerr, "An Effective and Democratic Organization of the Economy"; Herbert Stein and Edward F. Denison, "High Employment and Growth in the American Economy"; Thomas J. Watson, "Technological Change"; Lauren K. Soth, "Farm Policy for the Sixties"; Catherine Bauer Wurster, "Framework for an Urban Society"; James P. Dixon, "Meeting Human Needs"; Morton Grodzins, "The Federal System"; Wallace S. Sayre, "The Public Service"; William L. Langer, "The United States' Role in the World"; John J. McCloy, "Foreign Economic Policy and Objectives"; and William P. Bundy, "A Further Look Ahead."

235. Theobald, Robert (ed.)
    1968   Social Policies for America in the Seventies: Nine Divergent Views. Garden City, N.Y.: Doubleday.
"This book is concerned with the possible alterations in our economic and social values and systems as we enter a world that is being fundamentally altered by the impact of science and technology" (p. ix). Until recently domestic policy in the United States has been primarily aimed at maximizing economic growth. This book questions the appropriateness of this approach by showing

that social and environmental needs are far more important than economic ones. It argues that economic growth ought, therefore, to be subservient to the social and environmental requirements of the future. The book consists of the following nine essays: Leon L. Keyserling, "The Problem of Problems: Economic Growth"; Garth L. Mangum, "Guaranteeing Employment Opportunities"; F. Helmut Weymar, "The Poor Should Be Paid Bonuses"; Arthur Pearl, "New Careers: One Solution to Poverty"; Lawrence L. Suhm, "Cumulative Earned Leave: New Tool for Economic Planning"; Louis O. Kelso and Patricia Hetter, "Equality of Economic Ownership Through Capital Ownership"; Robert Theobald, "Policy Formation for New Goals" (see no. **74**); John Holdt, "Education for the Future"; and John McHale, "A Global View" (see no. **21**).

236. Today and Tomorrow
1924–   Today and Tomorrow—a series of monographs. London: Kegan
1932   Paul, Trench, Trubner.
This series was published in the last half of the 1920s and contains the opinions of about one hundred British intellectuals on the shape of the future. While the actual monographs focus on a specific aspect of the future and are no longer of great relevance, the series as a whole is of historical interest. Unfortunately, the individual volumes are long out of print and difficult to obtain. Some of the monographs are listed below in an effort to give an indication of the series' scope and character: F. G. Crookshank, "Aesculapius, or Man and Disease" and "The Mongol in our Midst: A Study of Man and his Three Faces"; E. E. Fournier D'Albe, "Hephaestus, the Soul of the Machine" and "Quo Vadimus?: Glimpses of the Future"; Bonamy Dobree, "The Future of Drama"; J. B. S. Haldene, "Callinicus, a Defense of Chemical Warfare" and "Daedalus, or Science and the Future"; B. H. Liddell Hart, "The Future of War"; E. S. P. Haynes, "The Future of the Law"; Gerald Heard, "Narcissus: An Anatomy of Clothes"; H. S. Jennings, "Promethius, or Biology and the Future of Man"; C. E. M. Joad, "Thrasymachus, the Future of Morals"; Vernon Lee, "Proteus, or the Future of Intelligence"; A. M. Low, "Wireless Possibilities"; Anthony M. Ludovici, "Lysistrata, or Woman's Future and Future Woman"; C. J. Patten, "The Passing of the Phantoms: A Study of Evolutionary Psychology and Morals"; Alan Porter, "The Evocation of Genius"; John Rodker, "The Future of Futurism" (about art); Bertrand Russell, "Icarus, or the Future of Science" and "What I Believe" (the author's future hopes); Dora Russell, "Hypatia, or Woman and Knowledge"; F. C. S. Schiller, "Tantalus, or the Future of Man"; H. F. Scott Stokes, "Perseus: Of Dragons"; R. C. Trevelyan, "Thamyris, or the Future of Poetry"; Rebecca West, "The Future of Sex" (will women or men be more important in public life?); and H. W. S. Wright, "The Conquest of Cancer."

237. Wolstenholme, Gordon (ed.)
1963   Man and his Future (Ciba Foundation Volume). Boston: Little,
Brown.
This book is a report of the proceedings of a Ciba Foundation symposium

that explored the broader implications of present biological advances for the future. Twenty-seven medical and biological experts participated in the symposium and their individual papers are as follows: Sir Julian Huxley, "The Future of Man—Evolutionary Aspects"; Colin Clark, "Agricultural Productivity in Relation to Population"; John F. Brock, "Sophisticated Diets and Man's Health"; Discussion on World Resources; Gregory Pincus, "Control of Reproduction in Mammals"; Alan S. Parkes, "The Sex-Ratio in Human Populations"; Discussion on World Population; Carleton S. Coon, "Growth and Development of Social Groups"; Arthur Glikson, "Man's Relationship to his Environment"; Donald M. MacKay, "Machines and Society"; Discussion of Sociological Aspects; Albert Szent-Gyorgyi, "The Promise of Medical Science"; Hilary Koprowski, "Future of Infectious and Malignant Diseases"; Alex Comfort, "Longevity of Man and his Tissues"; Discussion of Health and Disease; Hermann J. Muller, "Genetic Progress by Voluntarily Conducted Germinal Choice"; Joshua Lederberg, "Biological Future of Man"; Discussion of Eugenics and Genetics; Hudson Hoagland, "Potentialities in the Control of Behavior"; Brock Chisholm, "Future of the Mind"; Discussion on Future of the Mind; J. B. S. Haldane, "Biological Possibilities for the Human Species in the Next Thousand Years"; and Discussion on Ethical Considerations.

238. Young, Michael (ed.)
  1968   Forecasting and the Social Sciences. London: Heineman.
  Part of the task of the Social Science Research Council's "Next Thirty Years Committee" (a British organization) is to isolate those problems whose impact will not be fully evident until sometime in the future. By investigating their nature at present the worst effects of given problems can be avoided by long-range planning. This book is a collection of essays describing various future needs and problem areas. The essays also consider possible solutions and have been presented to the committee over the last few years. The individual articles are as follows: Michael Young, "Forecasting and the Social Sciences" (see no. 14); Mark Abrams, "Consumption in the Year 2000"; Fred E. Emery, "Concepts, Methods and Anticipations"; Christopher Foster, "Future Needs of Transport Planners"; David Grove, "Physical Planning and Social Change"; Peter Hall, "London—The Spread of Towns into the Country"; Bertrand de Jouvenel, "Notes on Social Forecasting"; Tony Lynes, "Social Security Research"; and R. W. Orson, "Forecasting in the Electricity Supply Industry."
  For additional anthologies about the future see: nos. 256 and 257.

ADDENDA

239. Ferkiss, Victor C.
  1969   Technological Man: The Myth and the Reality. New York: George Braziller.

A world society focusing on ever-higher levels of human achievement can become a future reality, provided "technological man" (a wise and perceptive citizen of the world having a grasp of both science and technology and viewing the earth's environment as a system of interacting parts) becomes dominant by the end of the century. At present this new species is far outnumbered by "bourgeois man," who has no comprehension of the modern world's essential nature and uses its technology for limited and selfish ends. It is the continued predominance of this type that threatens man's future survival rather than his scientific advances per se. If technological man is to become dominant, our whole society must be reshaped to make the emergence of a new philosophy, based on three basic tenets, possible: (1) "new naturalism" (man as a part of nature must live in harmony with it); (2) "new holism" (everything in the universe is interconnected); and (3) "new immanentism" (the whole is created from within).

240. Hubbard, Earl
  1969   The Search Is On: A View of Man's Future from the New Perspective of Space. Los Angeles: Pace Publications.
  Once man solved the basic problem of survival, he began to aim at providing everyone with the opportunity to be physically secure and free to develop his potentialities. Now that this latter goal is feasible (though not yet a reality), it is time for man to set himself a new, more far-reaching, goal. This goal would involve trying to comprehend the creative intention of the universe by exploring the new worlds of outer space. Within the broad framework of this new challenge, man could once again formulate a set of priorities for his survival on this planet and find a new point of orientation for his intellectual endeavors. In so doing he would be fulfilling his obligation to unborn generations to do all he can to make this a healthier, happier world.

241. Picht, Georg
  1969   Mut zur Utopie: Die Grossen Zukunftsaufgaben [Courage for Utopia: The Great Tasks of the Future. Munich: R. Piper & Co. Verlag.
  The basic theme of this series of twelve lectures is that man must begin to think in realistically utopian terms if he is to solve the world's pressing economic and social problems. The basic limitation of modern society is that its technological institutions are far superior to its social and political ones. The major need, therefore, is for supranational organizations responsible for guiding worldwide social development. The book focuses on outlining the specific political measures necessary for such an innovation and on discussing the role that science and technology would play. Political leaders must create international organizations as a context in which scientists can rationally map out solutions to current global problems. This would enable scientists, now free of national entanglements, to determine a set of priorities for best satisfying the needs of the future.

242. Piganiol, Pierre

    1969   "Introduction: futurology and prospective study." International Social Science Journal 21 (no. 4): 515–525.

This article, which forms the introduction to a whole issue on the future, sketches the broad outlines of the rapidly emerging discipline of futurology. The main focus has so far been the prediction of technological developments and their possible applications. It is now generally recognized, however, that mere anticipation of all possible new developments is of minor importance. Of far greater relevance is finding ways of deciding which of the many new technologies are most desirable, and therefore, worthy of perfection. Two equivalent methods of making such choices are discussed (cost-benefit analysis and relevance tree investigation). Neither method can be used in isolation, however, for ultimately the desirability of a given development must be evaluated in light of a society's underlying values. Consequently, it is imperative that new values appropriate to the technological age be articulated.

243. Bestuzhev-Lada, Igor

    1969   "Forecasting—an approach to the problems of the future." International Social Science Journal 21 (no. 4): 526–534.

Forecasting truly comes into its own only when applied to planning. For then it is no longer the imperfect tool of prophets, but a method of anticipating future possibilities, thereby establishing guidelines for more effective planning. The sophistication of forecasting varies widely, however, in various areas of endeavor. It is most highly developed in the scientific and technological areas and least developed in sociological and geographical fields. This imbalance can best be corrected by making futurological techniques an integral part of all scientific endeavor, rather than the basis for a separate discipline.

244. Helmer, Olaf, and N. Rescher

    1959   "On the epistemology of the inexact sciences." Management Science 6 (October): 25–52.

A discussion of some methodological innovations that might be appropriate in the "inexact sciences" (both physical and social sciences, where explanation and prediction do not have the same logical structure). After distinguishing between the exact and inexact sciences, the authors discuss the methodology of the former and the limits of its applicability to the latter. They then outline two new avenues of approach that the inexact sciences might explore with benefit, especially if concerned with prediction: (1) techniques for tapping expert opinion (e.g., enhancing the predictive competence of individuals or predictive consensus formation among experts); and (2) pseudo-experimentation (e.g., simulation or game theory).

245. Hetman, François

    1970   Le Langage de la Prévision—The Language of Forecasting. Paris: SEDEIS.

A collection of terms and phrases frequently used in literature about the future. Definitions are derived from the fund of future-oriented studies published since 1950. The aims of the book are to make the language employed in forecasting more precise and exact and to establish generally accepted meanings for ambiguous terms. The book is primarily organized as a bilingual dictionary, definitions being given in both French and English. Also, the entries themselves are given in German. There are two types of entries: general terms such as "utopia" or "values," and more specific terms or phrases that have limited usage such as "university city" or "war game." A source for each definition is given.

246. Taviss, Irene
   1969   "Futurology and the problem of values." International Journal of Social Science 21 (no. 4): 574–583.

The first section of this article shows that there is a close interconnection between value change and social change. Consequently, investigation of the future is of little utility unless value forecasting becomes an integral part of the futurologist's methodology. A number of ways in which this can be done are discussed. The second section surveys a variety of futuristic studies and shows that the researchers involved seem to share a similar ethos with regard to the world of tomorrow (i.e., generally optimistic and desirous of extending the present social system). Insofar as futurologists become involved in decision-making, therefore, their plans for the future might ignore values different from their own. Consequently, it is necessary to develop pluralistic planning techniques which would allow all segments of a society to make their preferences for the future known.

247. Winthrop, Henry
   1969   "Social costs and studies of the future." Futures 1 (December): 488–499.

A brief review of recent future-oriented studies reveals that most fail to consider the social costs of various projections. Researchers writing about the future either ignore the possible impact of forecast developments on mankind, or gloss over their negative aspects. Such tendencies have been especially pronounced in work dealing with applications of nuclear energy. The author uses the nuclear field to illustrate how assessments of social costs could be more systematically integrated into future projections. Unless social cost considerations become an integral part of all futuristic research, forecasts and projections will be of little value to public policy makers.

248. Jungk, Robert
   1969b   "Imagination and the future." International Social Science Journal 21 (no. 4): 557–562.

Much contemporary research about the future consists primarily of projecting present trends. Such work is inadequate because it fails to make use of imagination, which should be a basic tool of anyone interested in the future. The relationship between logical and imaginative processes, therefore, is of fundamental concern to futurology. There are three kinds of imagination, all of which should be used by forecasters. Logical imagination (extrapolation of present trends) is accepted as useful by most scientists, while the critical variety (negation of major trends) is just beginning to be utilized. Creative imagination, which focuses on constructing systems totally unrelated to the present, is almost never employed. The author discusses a number of ways in which the refinement of this last type of imagination might be fostered.

249. Richta, Radovan, and Ota Šulc
1969 "Forecasting and the scientific and technological revolution." International Journal of Social Science 21 (no. 4): 563–573.
Two rather divergent approaches have been used to develop forecasts: the theoretical (used by generalists to specify the broad outlines of the long-range future), and the pragmatic (used by highly trained specialists to forecast specific trends). Both approaches have tended to ignore the "human factor," and, therefore, incomplete pictures of the future have emerged. Man's technological knowledge has reached the point where a concern with societal values and the quality of human life must underlie all forecasting. Consequently, there is a need to develop methods for viewing all aspects of the future as parts of a dynamic interacting whole. Such development should proceed in three simultaneously occurring phases: (1) the scientific phase (specifying alternative futures and their consequences for the quality of human life); (2) the planning phase (developing blueprints for the implementation of the most humanly advantageous technological innovations); and (3) the public opinion phase (enabling the general public to indicate its preferences and priorities).

250. Gordon, Theodore J.
1969b "Cross-impact matrices: an illustration of their use for policy analysis." Futures 1 (December): 527–531.
The "cross-impact matrix method of forecasting" serves to assess the interrelationships between a series of anticipated events (see no. 102 for a brief description). This article describes the application of this technique to a number of interacting elements that will influence the educational scene of the future (e.g., collective bargaining laws for schools, unionization of teachers, unionization of students, parent-teacher conflict, and ethnic programs).

251. Galtung, Johan
1970 "On the future of human society." Futures 2 (June): 132–142.
Four basic societal types are distinguished, and the relative strengths and weaknesses of each are given. The major types differ in terms of: (1) the predominant social unit (collective vs. individualist) and (2) the nature of the social stratification system (vertical vs. horizontal). A number of characteristics of each societal type are discussed: life goals, happiness of the people, adjustment to change, degree of economic development, amount of social justice and the nature of the life cycle. Special attention is given to type four society (individualist-horizontal), as the author believes it offers the most beneficial state of affairs for the future.

252. Buchholz, A.

> 1968   Die Grosse Transformation [The Great Transformation]. Stutt-
> gart (Germany): Deutsche Verlagsanstalt.

This book focuses on the ever-accelerating process of technological change and how it might be better controlled. It begins by discussing the development of the modern scientific and technological revolutions, as well as examining the prospects for the future. The author then turns to a wide-ranging discussion of how technological progress might be harnessed so as to benefit mankind in greater measure. He concludes that it is within man's grasp to transform the whole world radically, so that material well-being and peace prevail everywhere. To make such a world a reality, however, man must first learn to use his new technology in a more humane manner.

253. Toffler, Alvin

> 1970   Future Shock. New York: Random House.

An exploration of the nature of "future shock," why it may overwhelm us in the years to come, and how we can attempt to cope with it. The author begins by elaborating the nature of "future shock," which occurs when the society in which one lives alters its basic character so drastically that old behavior patterns are no longer valid or useful. Unless man becomes able to overcome this type of shock by learning to cope with rapid change, any effort to plan for the future will be ineffective. The author expands on this theme by discussing how the nature of tomorrow's world will be quite different from what is generally anticipated. Unlike others, he foresees, among other things: greater individual freedom, less bureaucracy, an economy geared to the production of experience, and transcience as the dominant pattern in all aspects of life. The author concludes by outlining a number of ways in which we can prevent the future from overwhelming us. These include: reorienting our educational system to the future; controlling the technological change process; and instituting "anticipatory democracy," which would enable every citizen to help create the future.

254. Udall, Stuart L.

> 1968   1976: Agenda for Tomorrow. New York: Harcourt Brace &
> World.

"Our own past tells us we will not attain radiant cities unless, beyond all their physical elements, our minds encompass the foundations of a radiant social order as well. . . . Our ideas for cities, for conservation, and for social justice must coalesce in a single, interrelated concept" (p. 155). The aim is to outline the integral connection between the problems facing American society and to show that they can only be surmounted if they are treated as parts of an interconnected whole. The author begins by tracing the development of the problems presently confronting the United States. He then explores the type of solutions needed to alleviate such major problem areas as: the cities, the environment, the rate of population growth and the quality of life. He concludes by discussing how these solutions can become realities through a revitalization of the political process and the positive involvement of the younger generation.

255. Unesco

1969   "Futurology." International Social Science Journal 21 (December). This whole issue explores the nature of future-oriented study. Some of the major dimensions of the discipline are dealt with in a series of separate articles: Pierre Piganiol, "Introduction: Futurology and Prospective Study" (see no. **242**); Igor Bestuzhev-Lada, "Forecasting—an Approach to the Problems of the Future" (see no. **243**); Agnes Heller, "On the Future Relations Between the Sexes"; Irving Louis Horowitz, "Engineering and Sociological Perspectives on Development: Interdisciplinary Constraints in Social Forecasting"; Robert Jungk, "Imagination and the Future" (see no. **248**); Radovan Richta and Ota Šulc, "Forecasting and the Scientific and Technological Revolution" (see no. **249**); and Irene Taviss, "Futurology and the Problem of Values" (see no. **246**).

256. Arnfield, R. V. (ed.)

1969   Technological Forecasting. Edinburgh: Edinburgh University Press.

In 1968 an International Technological Forecasting Conference was held at Strathclyde University (Scotland). This book, which is divided into three major sections, contains the papers presented. The first part focuses on past efforts at technological forecasting and planning. Some articles discuss such efforts in general, while others discuss planning endeavors in a number of specific countries (e.g., France, Sweden, and Poland). Part two of the book concerns specific methodological techniques (e.g., Delphi Technique, morphological analysis, etc.) and the success of their application. Part three describes future trends in a number of specific areas such as transportation, urban development, energy sources, and computer technology.

257. Jantsch, Erich (ed.)

1969   Perspectives of Planning: Proceedings of the OECD Working Symposium on Long-Range Forecasting and Planning. Paris: OECD.

The proceedings of a 1968 conference held in Bellagio, Italy, are given. The focus is on the possibility of using systematic planning to overcome the economic and social problems confronting the world. Most of the papers do not deal with specific short-range techniques or problems, but examine the more general relationship of economic and social systems to their larger environment. Some also deal with the moral and human implications of technological innovation. A number of the more provocative contributions concern the following topics: the application of industrial principles to urban development (Forrester); enhancing individual freedom through planning (Gabor); planning technological development so it benefits the social system (Jantsch); and developing plans that encompass and benefit all aspects of society (Ozbekhan).

Alphabetical References

Altshuler, Alan
180   1968   "New institutions to serve the individual." Pp. 423–444 in
               William Ewald (ed.), Environment and Policy: The Next Fifty
               Years. Bloomington: Indiana University Press.
Analyse et Prévision
199   1966   Analyse et Prévision [Analysis and Forecasting]. Bertrand de
               Jouvenel (ed.). Paris: SEDEIS.
Analysen und Prognosen
200   1968   Analysen und Prognosen [Analyses and Forecasts]. Berlin:
               Zentrum fuer Zukunftsforchung.
Anderson, Stanford (ed.)
216   1968   Planning for Diversity and Choice: Possible Futures and
               Their Relations to the Man-Controlled Environment. Cam-
               bridge, Mass.: MIT Press.
Arnfield, R. V. (ed.)
256   1969   Technological Forecasting. Edinburgh: Edinburgh University
               Press.
Asimov, Isaac
126   1968   "The next 100 years: science-based estimate of what the cen-
               tury ahead may bring." Pp. 39–41 in The World Almanac and
               Book of Facts.
Ayres, Robert U.
 76   1969   Technological Forecasting and Long-Range Planning. New
               York: McGraw-Hill.
Baade, Fritz
127   1962   The Race to the Year 2000. Garden City, N.Y.: Doubleday.
Baier, Kurt, and Nicholas Rescher (eds.)
217   1969   Values and the Future. New York: Free Press.
Barzelon, David T.
181   1968   "The new factor in American society." Pp. 264–286 in Wil-
               liam R. Ewald (ed.), Environment and Change: The Next
               Fifty Years. Bloomington: Indiana University Press.
Beckwith, Burnham P.
128   1967   The Next Five Hundred Years. Jericho, N.Y.: Exposition-
               University Book.

Behrendt, Richard F.
129   1969   "Some structural prerequisites for a global society based on non-violent conflict resolution." Pp. 66–68 in Robert Jungk and Johan Galtung (eds.), Mankind 2000. Oslo: Universitets-forlaget.

Bell, Daniel
77   1964   "Twelve modes of prediction—a preliminary sorting of approaches in the social sciences." Daedalus 93 (Summer): 845–880; *or* pp. 96–127 in Julius Gould (ed.), Penguin Survey of the Social Sciences. Baltimore: Penguin Books (1965).
27   1965   "The study of the future." The Public Interest 1 (Fall): 119–130.
182   1967a   "Notes on the post-industrial society (I & II)." The Public Interest 6 (Winter):25–35; 7 (Spring):102–118.
183   1967b   "The year 2000—the trajectory of an idea." Daedalus 96 (Summer):639–651.

Bell, Wendell, and James A. Mau
1   1970   "Images of the future: theory and research strategies." Pp. 205–234 in J. McKinney and E. Tiryakian (eds.), Theoretical Sociology: Perspectives and Developments. New York: Appleton-Century-Crofts.

Bertaux, Pierre
2   1968   "The future of man." Pp. 13–20 in William R. Ewald (ed.), Environment and Change: The Next Fifty Years. Bloomington: Indiana University Press.

Bertram, Christoph
176   1968   "Models of western Europe in the 1970's—the alternative choices." Futures 1 (December):142–152.

Bestuzhev-Lada, Igor
243   1969   "Forecasting—an approach to the problems of the future." International Social Science Journal 21 (no. 4):526–534.

Beus, J. G. de
158   1953   The Future of the West. New York: Harper.

Birkenhead, Earl of
152   1930   The World in 2030. London: Hooper & Stoughton.

Boulding, Kenneth E.
15   1965   The Meaning of the Twentieth Century (The Great Transition). New York: Harper & Row.

Boyko, Hugo (ed.)
218   1961   Science and the Future of Mankind. Den Haag, Holland: Uitgeverij Dr. W. Junk.

Brinton, Crane (ed.)
219   1961   The Fate of Man. New York: George Braziller.

Brown, Bernice, and Olaf Helmer
99   1966   "Improvements in the reliability of a consensus through the use of self-rating." Pp. 98–110 (Appendix II) in Olaf Helmer, Social Technology. New York: Basic Books.

Brown, Claude
184   1968   "The effective society." Pp. 167–175 in William R. Ewald (ed.), Environment and Change: The Next Fifty Years. Bloomington: Indiana University Press.

Brown, Harrison
130   1954   The Challenge of Man's Future. New York: Viking Press.

Brown, Harrison, James Bonner, and John Weir
159   1957   The Next Hundred Years. New York: Viking Press.

Brown, Harrison, et al.
220   1967   The Next Ninety Years. Pasadena: California Institute of Technology.

Buchholz, A.
252   1968   Die Grosse Transformation [The Great Transformation]. Stuttgart (Germany): Deutsche Verlagsanstalt.

Calder, Nigel
131   1965   "Summing up." Pp. 191–197 in Nigel Calder (ed.), The World in 1984 (Vol. 2). Baltimore: Penguin Books.
132   1967a   The Environment Game. London: Secker & Warburg.
133   1967b   "Future research." New Statesman 74 (September 29):399–400.
59   1969   "Goals, foresight, and politics." Pp. 251–255 in Robert Jungk and Johan Galtung (eds.), Mankind 2000. Oslo: Universitetsforlaget.

Calder, Nigel (ed.)
221   1965   The World in 1984. Baltimore: Penguin Books (2 vols.).

Calleo, David P.
175   1965   Europe's Future: The Grand Alternatives. New York: Horizon Press.

Cantril, Hadley
36   1938   "The prediction of social events." Journal of Abnormal and Social Psychology 33 (July):364–389.
95   1963   "A study of aspirations." Scientific American 208 (February): 41–45.
109   1965   The Pattern of Human Concerns. New Brunswick, N.J.: Rutgers University Press.

Cantril, Hadley, and Lloyd Free
96   1962   "Hopes and fears for self and country." Supplement to American Behavioral Scientist 6 (October).

Center Diary
209   1967   "Possible futures." Center Diary #17 (March-April):15–54.

Chase, Stuart
134   1968   The Most Probable World. New York: Harper & Row.

Clarke, Arthur C.
160   1962   Profiles of the Future. New York: Harper & Row.
Commission on the Year 2000
222   1967a   "Toward the year 2000: work in progress." Daedalus 96 (Summer):639–994.
42   1967b   "Working session I." Daedalus 96 (Summer):652–704.
60   1967c   "Working session II." Daedalus 96 (Summer):936–984.
Cornish, Edward S.
43   1969   "The professional futurist." Pp. 244–250 in Robert Jungk and Johan Galtung (eds.), Mankind 2000. Oslo: Universitetsforlaget.

Dalkey, N.
100   1969   "An experimental study of group opinion: the Delphi method." Futures 1 (September):408–426.

Dalkey, N., and Olaf Helmer
113   1963   "An experimental application of the Delphi method to the use of experts." Management Science 9 (April):458–467.

Danziger, Kurt
105   1963   "Ideology and Utopia in South Africa: a methodological contribution to the sociology of knowledge." British Journal of Sociology 14 (March):59–76.

Darwin, Charles G.
135   1953   The Next Million Years. Garden City, N.Y.: Doubleday.
Dror, Yehezkel
3   1968   "The role of futures in government." Futures 1 (September): 40–45.

Drucker, Peter
185   1955   America's Next Twenty Years. Harper's (March–June).
161   1968   The Age of Discontinuity: Guidelines to Our Changing Society. New York: Harper & Row.

Dubos, René
83   1967   "Evolving psyche." Center Diary #17 (March–April):38–44.
Duhl, Leonard J.
61   1967   "Planning and predicting: or what to do when you don't know the names of the variables." Daedalus 96 (Summer): 779–788.

Ellul, Jacques
162   1963   "Western man in 1970." Pp. 27–64 in Bertrand de Jouvenel (ed.), Futuribles: Studies in Conjecture (I). Geneva: Droz.
163   1964   The Technological Society. New York: Knopf.
Elton et al.
223   1948   The Prospect before Us: Some Thoughts on the Future. London: Sampson, Low, Marston.

Eulau, Heinz
89   1958   "H. D. Lasswell's developmental analysis." Western Political Quarterly 11(June):229–242.

Ewald, William R. (ed.)
225   1968a   Environment and Change: The Next Fifty Years. Bloomington: Indiana University Press.
224   1968b   Environment and Policy: The Next Fifty Years. Bloomington:
Indiana University Press.

Fabun, Don (ed.)
210   1967   The Dynamics of Change. Englewood Cliffs, N.J.: Prentice-
Hall.

Farson, Richard E.
136   1969   "Bill of rights for 1984." Pp. 186–193 in Robert Jungk and
Johan Galtung (eds.), Mankind 2000. Oslo: Universitetsforlaget.

Feinberg, Gerald
16   1968   The Prometheus Project: Mankind's Search for Long-Range
Goals. Garden City, N.Y.: Doubleday.

Ferkiss, Victor C.
239   1969   Technological Man: The Myth and the Reality. New York:
George Braziller.

Fields within Fields . . . within Fields
201   1968–   Fields within Fields . . . within Fields. Jules Stulman (ed.).
New York: World Institute Council.

Fitch, Lyle C.
17   1968   "National development and national policy." Pp. 283–317
in William Ewald (ed.), Environment and Policy: The Next
Fifty Years. Bloomington: Indiana University Press.

Flechtheim, Ossip K.
44   1966   History and Futurology. Meisenheim am Glan (Germany):
Verlag Anton Hain.
45   1969   "Is futurology the answer to the challenge of the future?"
Pp. 264–269 in Robert Jungk and Johan Galtung (eds.), Mankind 2000. Oslo: Universitetsforlaget.

Foreign Policy Association (ed.)
226   1968   Toward the Year 2018. New York: Cowles Education Corporation.

Francis, Roy G.
186   1965   "Problems of tomorrow. Kapow!!: an argument and a forecast." Social Problems 12 (Winter):328–335.

Frank, Lawrence K.
18   1967   "The need for a new political theory." Daedalus 96 (Summer):809–816.

Free, Lloyd
110   1959   Six Allies and a Neutral. Glencoe, Ill.: Free Press.
111a   1960a   Attitudes of the Cuban People toward the Castro Regime.
Princeton, N.J.: Institute for International Social Research.
111b   1960b   The Dynamics of Philippine Politics. Princeton, N.J.: Institute for International Social Research.

111c   1964a   The Attitudes, Hopes, and Fears of Nigerians. Princeton, N.J.: Institute for International Social Research.

111d   1964b   Some International Implications of the Political Psychology of Brazilians. Princeton, N.J.: Institute for International Social Research.

Freymond, Jacques
62   1965   "Introduction—forecasting and Europe." Pp. xiii–xxx in Bertrand de Jouvenel (ed.), Futuribles: Studies in Conjecture (II). Geneva: Droz.

Friedlaender, Saul
78   1965   "Forecasting in international relations." Pp. 1–112 in Bertrand de Jouvenel (ed.), Futuribles: Studies in Conjecture (II). Geneva: Droz.

Frisch, Alfred
164   1964   "L'avenir des technocrates [The future of the technocrats]." Futuribles (no. 84)—Supplement to Bulletin Sedeis 901 (November 10).

Fromm, Erich
187   1968   The Revolution of Hope: Toward a Humanized Technology. New York: Harper & Row.

Fuller, R. Buckminster
137   1967   "The year 2000." Architectural Design 37 (February):62–63.

Furnas, Clifford C.
153   1936   The Next Hundred Years: The Unfinished Business of Science. New York: Reynal and Hitchcock.

Futures
202   1968–   Futures: The Journal of Forecasting and Planning. London: Unwin.

Futuribles
203   1961–
      1965   Futuribles—Supplement to Bulletin Sedeis. Bertrand de Jouvenel (ed.). Paris: SEDEIS.

The Futurist
204   1967–   The Futurist. A Newsletter for Tomorrow's World. Washington, D.C.: World Future Society.

Futurum
205   1968–   Futurum: Zeitschrift fuer Zukunftsforschung [Futurum: Journal for Future Research], Ossip K. Flechtheim (ed.). Meisenheim am Glan (Germany): Verlag Anton Hain.

Gabor, Dennis
165   1964   Inventing the Future. New York: Knopf.

Galtung, Johan
138   1969   "On the future of the international system." Pp. 12–41 in Robert Jungk and Johan Galtung (eds.), Mankind 2000. Oslo: Universitetsforlaget.

251   1970   "On the future of human society." Futures 2 (June):132–142.

Gibbs, Philip
124   1928   The Day after Tomorrow: What Is Going to Happen to the World? London: Hutchinson.

Gillespie, James M., and Gordon W. Allport
121   1955   Youth's Outlook on the Future. Garden City, N.Y.: Doubleday.

Ginzberg, Eli (ed.)
227   1964   Technology and Social Change. New York: Columbia University Press.

Gordon, Theodore J.
139   1965   The Future. New York: St. Martin's Press.
114   1969a   "The feedback between technology and values." Pp. 148–192 in K. Baier and N. Rescher (eds.), Values and the Future. New York: Free Press.
250   1969b   "Cross-impact matrices: an illustration of their use for policy analysis." Futures 1 (December):527–531.

Gordon, Theodore, and H. Hayward
102   1968   "Initial experiments with the cross impact matrix method of forecasting." Futures 1 (December):100–116.

Gordon, Theodore, and Olaf Helmer
98   1966   "Report on a long-range forecasting study." Pp. 44–97 (Appendix I) in Olaf Helmer, Social Technology. New York: Basic Books.

Hacker, Frederick J.
4   1969   "Human implications." Pp. 233–241 in Robert Jungk and Johan Galtung (eds.), Mankind 2000. Oslo: Universitetsforlaget.

Haldene, J. B. S.
154   1927   "Man's destiny." Pp. 300–305 in J. B. S. Haldene, Possible Worlds and Other Essays. London: Chatto and Windus.

Hart, Hornell
41   1957   "Predicting future trends." Pp. 455–474 in Allen, Hart et al., Technology and Social Change. New York: Appleton-Century-Crofts.

Hayashi, Yujiro
46   1969   "The direction and orientation of futurology as a science." Pp. 270–277 in Robert Jungk and Johan Galtung (eds.), Mankind 2000. Oslo: Universitetsforlaget.

Heckscher, August
19   1968   "The individual—not the mass." Pp. 287–296 in William R. Ewald (ed.), Environment and Change: The Next Fifty Years. Bloomington: Indiana University Press.

Heilbroner, Robert L.
188   1960   The Future as History. New York: Harper.

189   1963   "On the seriousness of the future." American Scholar 32 (Autumn):556–562.

190   1966   "The future of capitalism." Commentary 41 (April):23–35.

Helmer, Olaf

92   1966a   Social Technology. New York: Basic Books.

101a   1966b   A Use of Simulation for the Study of Future Values. Rand Publication No. P–3443 (September).

101b   1969   "Simulating the values of the future." Pp. 193–213 in K. Baier and N. Rescher (eds.), Values and the Future. New York: The Free Press.

115   1969   "An abbreviated Delphi experiment in forecasting." Pp. 361–367 in Robert Jungk and Johan Galtung (eds.), Mankind 2000, Oslo: Universitetsforlaget.

Helmer, Olaf, and N. Rescher

244   1959   "On the epistemology of the inexact sciences." Management Science 6 (October):25–52.

Hetman, François

245   1970   Le Langage de la Prévision—The Language of Forecasting. Paris: SEDEIS.

Hopkins, Frank S.

5   1967   "The United States in the year 2000. A proposal for the study of the American future." American Sociologist 2 (August): 149–150.

Hubbard, Earl

240   1969   The Search Is On: A View of Man's Future from the New Perspective of Space. Los Angeles: Pace Publications.

Iklé, Fred Charles

47   1967   "Can social predictions be evaluated?" Daedalus 96 (Summer):733–758.

The Institute for the Future

48   1968   The Institute for the Future (A Prospectus). Middletown, Conn.: Institute for the Future–Riverview Center.

Israeli, Nathan

6   1930   "Some aspects of the social psychology of futurism." Journal of Abnormal and Social Psychology, 25 (July):121–132.

31   1932a   "The social psychology of time." Journal of Abnormal and Social Psychology 27 (July):209–213.

33   1932b   "Wishes concerning improbable future events: reactions to the future." Journal of Applied Psychology 16 (no. 5):584–588.

35   1933a   "Attitudes to the Decline of the West." Journal of Social Psychology 4 (February):92–101.

34   1933b   "Group estimates of the divorce rate for the years 1935–1975." Journal of Social Psychology 4 (February):102–115.

32   1933c   "Group predictions of future events." Journal of Social Psychology 4 (May):201–222.

Janicki, Peter
112   1960   America Speaks Up. Princeton, N.J.: Institute for International Social Research.

Jantsch, Erich
79   1967   Technological Forecasting in Perspective. Paris: OECD Publications.
85   1969   "Integrative planning of society and technology." Futures 1 (March):185–190.
86   1969   "Planning and designing for the future: the breakthrough of the systems approach." Futures 1 (September):440–444.

Jantsch, Erich (ed.)
257   1969   Perspectives of Planning: Proceedings of the OECD Working Symposium on Long-Range Forecasting and Planning. Paris: OECD.

Jouvenel, Bertrand de
80   1962   "De la conjecture [On conjecture]." Futuribles (no. 27)—Supplement to Bulletin Sedeis (Part 2) 815 (March 20).
91   1963a   "Introduction." Pp. ix–xi in Bertrand de Jouvenel (ed.), Futuribles: Studies in Conjecture (I). Geneva: Droz.
49   1963b   "La prévision des idées [The prediction of ideas]." Futuribles (no. 68)—Supplement to Bulletin Sedeis 870 (December 1).
7   1965a   "Utopia for practical purposes." Daedalus 94 (Spring): 437–453.
50   1965b   "Political science and prevision." American Political Science Review 59 (March):29–38.
63   1967   The Art of Conjecture. New York: Basic Books.
64   1968   "On attending to the future." Pp. 21–29 in William R. Ewald (ed.), Environment and Change: The Next Fifty Years. Bloomington: Indiana University Press.
20   1969   "Technology as a means." Pp. 217–232 in K. Baier and N. Rescher (eds.), Values and the Future. New York: Free Press.

Jouvenel, Bertrand de (ed.)
228   1963   Futuribles: Studies in Conjecture (I). Geneva: Droz.
229   1965   Futuribles: Studies in Conjecture (II). Geneva: Droz.

Jungk, Robert
51   1967   "The future of future research." Science Journal 3 (October): 3–40.
65   1968a   "About 'Mankind 2000'." Pp. 79–85 in Stanford Anderson (ed.), Planning for Diversity and Choice. Cambridge, Mass.: MIT Press.
66   1968b   "Human futures." Futures 1 (September):34–39.
67   1969a   "Look-out institutions for shaping the environment." Futures 1 (March):227–232.
248   1969b   "Imagination and the future." International Social Science Journal 21 (no. 4):557–562.

Jungk, Robert, and Johan Galtung (eds.)
230   1969   Mankind 2000. Oslo: Universitetsforlaget.

Kahn, Herman
191   1960   On Thermonuclear War. Princeton, N.J.: Princeton University Press.
231   1962   Thinking about the Unthinkable. New York: Horizon Press.
94   1968   "The alternative world futures approach." Pp. 83–137 in Morton A. Kaplan (ed.), New Approaches to International Relations. New York: St. Martin's Press.

Kahn, Herman, and Anthony J. Weiner
140   1967a   The Year 2000: A Framework for Speculation on the Next Thirty-Three Years. New York: Macmillan.
93   1967b   "The next thirty-three years: a framework for speculation." Daedalus 96 (Summer):705–732.

Kalven, Harry
166   1967   "The problems of privacy in the year 2000." Daedalus 96 (Summer):876–882.

Kaplan, Abraham, A. L. Skogstad, and M. A. Girshick
39   1950   "The prediction of social and technological events." Public Opinion Quarterly 14 (Spring):93–111.

Keynes, John Maynard
155   1932   "The economic possibilities of our grandchildren." Pp. 358–373 in John Maynard Keynes, Essays in Persuasion. New York: Harcourt, Brace.

Kilpatrick, F. P., and Hadley Cantril
97   1960   "Self-anchoring scaling, a measure of individuals' unique reality worlds." Journal of Individual Psychology 16 (November):158–173.

Langdon-Davies, John
156   1936   A Short History of the Future. London: George Routledge & Sons.

Lasswell, Harold D.
192   1941   "The garrison state." American Journal of Sociology 46 (January):455–469.
193   1962   "The garrison state hypothesis today." Pp. 51–71 in Samuel P. Huntington (ed.), Changing Patterns of Military Politics. Glencoe, Ill.: Free Press.
52   1966   "The changing image of human nature: the socio-cultural aspect (future-oriented man)." American Journal of Psychoanalysis 26 (no. 2):157–166.

Le Breton, Jean-Marie
177   1965   "Supranational power in European institutions." Pp. 247–269 in Bertrand de Jouvenel (ed.), Futuribles: Studies in Conjecture (II). Geneva: Droz.

Lewinsohn, Richard
28   1961   Science, Prophecy and Prediction. New York: Bell.

Lompe, Klaus
53   1968   "Problems of futures research in the social sciences." Futures 1 (September):47–53.

Low, A. M.
157   1925   The Future. New York: International Publishers.

Lundberg, Ferdinand
167   1963   The Coming World Transformation. Garden City, N.Y.: Doubleday.

McGregor, Douglas
37   1938   "The major determinants of the prediction of social events." Journal of Abnormal and Social Psychology 38 (April):179–204.

McHale, John
8   1967a   "The future of the future." Architectural Design 37 (February):65–66.
68   1967b   "The people future." Architectural Design 37 (February):94–95.
106   1967c   "The world game." Architectural Design 37 (February):92.
21   1968a   "A global view." Pp. 195–216 in Robert Theobald (ed.), Social Policies for America in the Seventies. Garden City, N.Y.: Doubleday.
212   1968b   "Toward the future." Design Quarterly No. 72.
141   1969a   The Future of the Future. New York: George Braziller.
54   1969b   "Future research: some integrative and communicative aspects." Pp. 256–263 in Robert Jungk and Johan Galtung (eds.), Mankind 2000. Oslo: Universitetsforlaget.

McHale, John (ed.)
211   1967   "2000 +." Architectural Design 37 (February).

Martino, Joseph P.
116   1967   "An experiment with the Delphi procedure for long-range forecasting, Parts I and II." United States Air Force. Report numbers AFOSR 67–0175 and AFOSR 67–0176.

Massenet, Michel
55   1963a   "Etudes méthodologiques sur les futuribles, après les discussions de Genève (juin, 1962) [Methodological studies on 'Futuribles' after the Geneva discussion of June, 1962]." Futuribles (no. 52)—Supplement to Bulletin Sedeis 849 (April 1).
29   1963b   "Introduction à une sociologie de la prévision [Introduction to a sociology of conjecture]." Futuribles (no. 60)—supplement to Bulletin Sedeis (Part 2) 857 (June 20).
81   1963c   "Les méthodes de prévision en sciences sociales [The methods of conjecture in the social sciences]." Futuribles (no. 66)—Supplement to Bulletin Sedeis (Part 2) 867 (Nov. 1).
90   1965   "The foreign policy of a united Europe." Pp. 271–360 in

Bertrand de Jouvenel (ed.), Futuribles: Studies in Conjecture (II). Geneva: Droz.

Mead, Margaret
142   1965   "The future as the basis for establishing a shared culture." Daedalus 94 (Winter):135–155.

Michael, Donald N.
168   1968   The Unprepared Society: Planning for a Precarious Future. New York: Basic Books.

Michaelis, Michael
87   1968   "Can we build the world we want?" Bulletin of the Atomic Scientists 24 (January):43–49.

Milburn, T. W. and J. F.
122   1966   "Predictions of threats and beliefs about how to meet them." American Behavioral Scientist 9 (March):3–7.

Miller, Cecil
56   1961   "The self-fulfilling prophecy: a reappraisal." Ethics 72 (October):46–51.

Miller, George A.
143   1967   "Some psychological perspectives on the year 2000." Daedalus 96 (Summer):883–896.

Modelle fuer eine Neue Welt
232   1964–   Modelle fuer eine Neue Welt [Models for a New World]. Robert Jungk and Hans Josef Mundt (eds.), Vienna: Verlag Kurt Desch.

Moles, Abraham
169   1962   "La cité scientifique en 1972 [The scientific city in 1972]." Futuribles (no. 41)—Supplement to Bulletin Sedeis (Part 2) 833 (October 20).

Moore, Wilbert E.
84   1964a   "Predicting discontinuities in social change." American Sociological Review 29 (June):331–338.

194   1964b   "Forecasting the future: the United States in 1980." Educational Record 45 (Fall):341–354.

9   1966   "The utility of utopias." American Sociological Review 31 (December):765–772.

233   1967   "Forecasting the future." Pp. 253–305 in Wilbert E. Moore, Order and Change: Essays in Comparative Sociology. New York: Wiley.

Murphy, Gardner
82   1961   Human Potentialities. New York: Basic Books.

National Goals Research Staff
22a   1969a   "The White House looks to the future." The Futurist 3 (August):99–100.

22b   1969b   "Goals staff will work with Moynihan." The Futurist 3 (August):100.

22c   1969c   "Statement by President Nixon on creating a national goals research staff." Futures 1 (September):458–459.

Nehnevajsa, Jiri

118   1960a   "Anticipatory analysis of ideational conflict." Paper read at the meetings of the American Sociological Association (August).

107a   1960b   Elements of Project Theory: From Concepts to Design. Air Force Office of Scientific Research. Technical Note TN–60–6 (October 20).

107b   1961   A Methodology for the Analysis of Political Futures. Air Force Office of Scientific Research. AFOSR–374 (May 1).

120   1962a   "Anticipations of cold war outcomes." Paper read at the meetings of the World, and American, Associations of Public Opinion Research (May).

119   1962b   An Application of Project Outcomes (The Dilemma of Viet-Nam). Air Force Office of Scientific Research (January).

The New York Times Magazine

213   1964   The Future. Pp. 86–118 in the New York Times, April 19: section 6 (part II).

Nisbet, Robert A.

69   1968   "The year 2000 and all that." Commentary 45 (June):60–66.

Ogburn, William F.

40   1946   "On predicting the future." Pp. 32–57 in W. F. Ogburn, The Social Effects of Aviation. Boston: Houghton Mifflin.

Osgood, Charles E., and Stuart Umpleby

103   1969   "A computer-based system for exploration of possible futures for mankind 2000." Pp. 346–359 in Robert Jungk and Johan Galtung (eds.), Mankind 2000. Oslo: Universitetsforlaget.

Ozebekhan, Hasan

70   1965   The Idea of a "Look-Out" Institution. Santa Monica, Calif.: System Development Corporation (March).

71   1966   Technology and Man's Future. Santa Monica, Calif.: System Development Corporation. Report no. SP–2494 (May 27).

72   1968   "The triumph of technology: 'can' implies 'ought.' " Pp. 204–219 in Stanford Anderson (ed.), Planning for Diversity and Choice. Cambridge, Mass.: MIT Press.

Paloczi-Horvath, Gyorgy

170   1964   The Facts Rebel: The Future of Russia and the West. London: Secker & Warburg.

Perspectives

206   1965–   Perspectives: Studies in Social and Political Forecasting— Supplement to the Indian Journal of Public Administration. L. P. Singh (ed.), New Delhi: Indian Institute of Public Administration.

Picht, Georg

241   1969   Mut zur Utopie: Die Grossen Zukunftsaufgaben [Courage for Utopia: The Great Tasks of the Future]. Munich: R. Piper & Co. Verlag.

Piganiol, Pierre
242   1969   "Introduction: futurology and prospective study." International Social Science Journal 21 (no. 4):515–525.

Platt, John R.
10   1968   The Step to Man. New York: Wiley.

Polak, Fred. L.
11   1961   The Image of the Future: Enlightening the Past, Orienting the Present, Forecasting the Future. New York: Oceana Publications (2 volumes).
23   1969   "Towards the goal of goals." Pp. 307–331 in Robert Jungk and Johan Galtung (eds.), Mankind 2000. Oslo: Universitetsforlaget.

Postan, M. M.
171   1963   "The economic and social system: the prospect for 1970–1975." Pp. 155–179 in Bertrand de Jouvenel (ed.), Futuribles: Studies in Conjecture (I). Geneva: Droz.

Prehoda, Robert W.
108   1967   Designing the Future: The Role of Technological Forecasting. Philadelphia: Chilton Books.

President's Commission on National Goals
234   1960   The Goals for Americans—Programs for Action in the Sixties. Englewood Cliffs, N.J.: Prentice-Hall.

Prognosen—Plaene—Perspektiven
207   1967–   Prognosen—Plaene—Perspektiven [Forecasts—Plans—Prospects]. Vienna: Institut fuer Zukunftsfragen.

Prospective
208   1958–   Prospective [Prospect]. Centre d'Etudes Prospectives (Association Gaston Berger). Paris: Presses Universitaires de France.

Rescher, Nicholas
123   1969   "A questionnaire study of American values by 2000 A.D." Pp. 133–147 in K. Baier and N. Rescher (eds.), Values and the Future. New York: Free Press.

Richta, Radovan, and Ota Šulc
249   1969   "Forecasting and the scientific and technological revolution." International Journal of Social Science 21 (no. 4):563–573.

Riesman, David
195   1967   "Notes on meritocracy." Daedalus 96 (Summer):897–908.

Rolbiecki, Waldemar
30   1969   "Prognostication and prognoseology." Pp. 278–285 in Robert Jungk and Johan Galtung (eds.), Mankind 2000. Oslo: Universitetsforlaget.

Rougement, Denis de
178   1965   "Pointers towards a federal Europe." Pp. 113–148 in Bertrand

de Jouvenel (ed.), Futuribles: Studies in Conjecture (II). Geneva: Droz.

Saturday Review
214   1964   "The prospects for American civilization." Saturday Review 47 (August 29).

Schon, Donald A.
57   1967   "Forecasting and technological forecasting." Daedalus 96 (Summer):759–771.

Science Journal
215   1967   "Forecasting the future." Science Journal 3 (October).

Seidenberg, Roderick
144   1950   Posthistoric Man: An Inquiry. Chapel Hill: University of North Carolina Press.

145   1961   Anatomy of the Future. Chapel Hill: University of North Carolina Press.

146   1967   "Justice for all, freedom for none." Center Diary #17 (March–April):25–37.

Servoise, René
198   1963   "Whither black Africa?" Pp. 181–294 in Bertrand de Jouvenel (ed.), Futuribles: Studies in Conjecture (I). Geneva: Droz.

Shubik, Martin
172   1967   "Information, rationality, and free choice in a future democratic society." Daedalus 96 (Summer):771–778.

Sidjanski, Dusan
179   1965   "Federative aspects of the European community"; and "Will Europe be United on federal lines?" Pp. 149–245 in Bertrand de Jouvenel (ed.), Futuribles: Studies in Conjecture (II). Geneva: Droz.

Snow, C. P.
147   1958   "The future of man." The Nation 187 (September 13):124–125.

Sola Pool, Ithiel de
148   1967   "The international system in the next half century." Daedalus 96 (Summer):930–935.

Stulman, Julius
88   1968   Evolving Mankind's Future: The World Institute: A Problem-Solving Methodology. Philadelphia: Lippincott.

Sulc, Otto
117   1969   "Interactions between technological and social changes: a forecasting model." Futures 1 (September):402–407.

Taviss, Irene
246   1969   "Futurology and the problem of values." International Journal of Social Science 21 (no. 4):574–583.

Teilhard de Chardin, Pierre
24   1964   The Future of Man. London: Collins.

Theobald, Robert

25   1961   The Challenge of Abundance. New York: Clarkson N. Potter.

196   1968a   An Alternative Future for America. Chicago: Swallow Press.

73   1968b   "Planning *with* people." Pp. 182–185 in William R. Ewald (ed.), Environment and Change: The Next Fifty Years. Bloomington: Indiana University Press.

74   1968c   "Policy formation for new goals." Pp. 149–169 in Robert Theobald (ed.), Social Policies for America in the Seventies. Garden City, N.Y.: Doubleday.

Theobald, Robert (ed.)

235   1968   Social Policies for America in the Seventies: Nine Divergent Views. Garden City, N.Y.: Doubleday.

Thomson, Sir George

173   1960   The Foreseeable Future (rev. ed.). Cambridge, England: Cambridge University Press.

Time

149   1966   "The futurists: looking toward A.D. 2000." Time 87 (February 25):28–29.

150   1967   "The future—1984 plus 16." Time 90 (July 21):58–59.

Toch, Hans H.

38   1958   "The perception of future events: case studies in social prediction." Public Opinion Quarterly 22 (Spring):57–66.

Today and Tomorrow

236   1924–
         1932   Today and Tomorrow—a series of monographs. London: Kegan Paul, Trench, Trubner.

Toffler, Alvin

12   1965   "The future as a way of life." Horizon 7 (Summer):108–116.

58   1969   "Value impact forecaster—a profession of the future." Pp. 1–30 in K. Baier and N. Rescher (eds.), Values and the Future. New York: Free Press.

253   1970   Future Shock. New York: Random House.

Udall, Stuart L.

254   1968   1976: Agenda for Tomorrow. New York: Harcourt Brace & World.

Umpleby, Stuart

104   1969   The Delphi Exploration (A Computer-Based System for Obtaining Subjective Judgements on Alternative Futures). Social Implications of Science and Technology Report F–1. Urbana, Illinois: Computer-Based Education Research Laboratory, University of Illinois.

Unesco

255   1969   "Futurology." International Social Science Journal 21 (December).

454   Bettina J. Huber

U.S. News and World Report
197   1964   "What the future holds for America." U.S. News and World
Report 56 (June 22):40–67.
Wall Street Journal Staff
174   1967   Here Comes Tomorrow: Living and Working in the Year
2000. New York: Dow Jones.
Waskow, Arthur I.
151   1969   "Looking forward: 1999." Pp. 78–98 in Robert Jungk and
Johan Galtung (eds.), Mankind 2000. Oslo: Universitetsforlaget.
Whyte, Lancelot L.
125   1944   The Next Development in Man. London: Cresset Press.
Wilkinson, John
75   1967   "Futuribles: innovation vs. stability." Center Diary #17
(March–April):16–24.
Winthrop, Henry
13   1968   "The sociologist and the study of the future." American
Sociologist 2 (May):136–145.
247   1969   "Social costs and studies of the future." Futures 1 (Decem-
ber):488–499.
Wolstenholme, Gordon (ed.)
237   1963   Man and his Future (Ciba Foundation Volume). Boston:
Little, Brown.
Wright, Christopher
26   1969   "Some requirements for viable social goals." Pp. 194–197 in
Robert Jungk and Johan Galtung (eds.), Mankind 2000. Oslo:
Universitetsforlaget.
Young, Michael
14   1968   "Forecasting and the social sciences." Pp. 1–37 in Michael
Young (ed.), Forecasting and the Social Sciences. London:
Heineman.
Young, Michael (ed.)
238   1968   Forecasting and the Social Sciences. London: Heineman.

Name Index

Subject Index